METHODS OF MACROECONOMIC DYNAMICS

Stephen J. Turnovsky

D1241227

The MIT Press
Cambridge, Massachusetts
London, England

This book was set in Times Roman by Asco Trade Typesetting Ltd., Hong Kong and was printed and bound in the United States of America.

Library of Congress Cataloging-in-Publication Data

Turnovsky, Stephen J.
  Methods of macroeconomic dynamics / Stephen J. Turnovsky.
    p.   cm.
  Includes bibliographical references and index.
  ISBN 0-262-20098-8 (hc : alk. paper)
  1. Macroeconomics. 2. Macroeconomics—Mathematical models.
3. Statics and dynamics (Social sciences) I. Title.
HB172.5.T785   1995
339—dc20   95-13032
                                                          CIP

Contents

Preface

Macroeconomics has undergone radical changes over the past fifty years. It seems that every decade or so, just as it appears that some kind of consensus may be emerging, the paradigm changes. Prior to the mid-1960s, the *IS-LM* model was the standard workhorse of macroeconomics. But as economists became more adept at the methods of macrodynamics, the limitations of the static *IS-LM* framework became evident, and models stressing the dynamics associated with asset accumulation gained prominence. During this period macroeconomists also began to recognize the importance of expectations—particularly inflationary expectations—which these asset accumulation models did not treat in an internally consistent way. Thus from the mid-1970s to the mid-1980s, macroeconomics was preoccupied with the intrinsic forward-looking nature of expectations, and the assumption that expectations are rational became the critical focus of these models. However, the rational expectations models of the 1970s were linear and usually otherwise arbitrarily specified, and they in turn became the target of criticism. The need to provide macro models with firm microeconomic foundations (meaning models derived from some form of intertemporal optimization) has become the dominant focus during the last decade. Many variants of such models exist, and while they continue to dominate current research in macroeconomic theory, they too receive their share of criticism. The usefulness of the representative agent framework has certainly come into question. Thus, as this chronology suggests, we may expect to be in for another paradigm change, though the precise direction that it will take is open to conjecture.

In 1977, I published a book with the Cambridge University Press entitled *Macroeconomic Analysis and Stabilization Policy*. The manuscript was completed just prior to the advent of the "rational expectations revolution" of the mid-1970s, but despite that it was remarkably successful, particularly in Europe, where the notion and methods of rational expectations were much slower to gain acceptance. The editors at CUP wanted me to revise the book by adding material on rational expectations, but it was evident to me that the rational expectations methodology represented a fundamental change in the methods of macrodynamic analysis and that a satisfactory treatment could not be introduced simply by means of a superficial revision. It would involve an entirely new book.

In the summer of 1986, I drafted several chapters discussing the methods of rational expectations. This formed the basis for what is Part II of this book, though the material was set aside for several years. This coincided with the development of the intertemporal optimizing representative agent model, and I did not feel inclined to produce a book that might quickly become outdated. Meanwhile, I continued with my own research on the representative agent model.

Two events motivated me to put the material together and complete this book. The first was the visit of Terry Vaughn, the economics acquisition editor of The MIT Press, to Seattle in the summer of 1992, when the University of Washington hosted the North American summer meetings of the Econometric Society. He showed great interest in the material I had previously prepared and encouraged me to pursue the project further, which I was initially reluctant to do. The other event was a chance meeting with a Japanese economist at a conference in Palm Cove, Australia, in August 1993; he recalled with obvious sincerity how he had pored over my 1977 Cambridge book, and how it had been the source of his background in macrodynamics. That brief remark convinced me that it was time to put this material together and finish the new book.

Macroeconomics has never reached a consensus and probably never will. The subject is too diverse and the approaches too varied for that to become likely. My objective in this book is to emphasize the methods of analysis, in part from a historical perspective, but also in a way that will make them applicable and attractive to macroeconomists having a diverse range of interests and points of view. As I have already indicated, much of the earlier material has been around for some time. Part I is what is left of my 1977 book, which was written while I was at the Australian National University. Part II evolved from the graduate course I gave at the University of Illinois in the mid-1980s. Part III has formed the basis for part of the course on macrodynamics I have given at the University of Washington for the past several years.

As will be evident, much of the material is drawn from my own research efforts. It therefore represents a somewhat idiosyncratic approach to the subject, which may not be a bad thing. But in all cases, where the exposition has been based upon previous material, it has been revised, adapted, updated, sometimes generalized, and modified in order to present a coherent approach to the subject. Chapter 2 is about what remains of my earlier book. The example in Section 6.1 is based on "Dynamic Macroeconomic Stability with or without Equilibrium in Money and Labor Markets," *Economica 48* (1981), coauthored with E. Burmeister and R. Flood, and the Appendix to the chapter is a revised version of an unpublished appendix to that paper. The example in Section 6.2 is adapted from a portion of "The Effects of Government Policy on the Term Structure of Interest Rates," *Journal of Money, Credit, and Banking* 16 (1984), coauthored with M. H. Miller. The example in 6.3 is drawn from the first part of "The Stability of Exchange Rate Dynamics under Perfect Myopic Foresight," *International Economic Review* 20 (1979), coauthored with M. R. Gray. Chapter 7 uses material from "Nonuniqueness and Instability under Rational Expectations: The Case of a Bond-Financed Government Deficit," in G. Gandolfo and F. Marzano (eds.), *Essays in Memory of Vittorio Guiffre* (Milano, 1987), coauthored with W. Scarth. The material on money-financed deficit was originally included in an expanded unpublished manuscript written with Scarth. Some of the material in Chapter 8 was adapted from "Optimal Monetary Policy and Wage Indexation under Alternative Disturbances and Information Structures," *Journal of Money, Credit, and Banking* 19 (1987).

Chapter 10 is drawn from "The Analysis of Macroeconomic Policies in Perfect Foresight Equilibrium," *International Economic Review* 22 (1981), coauthored with W. A. Brock, and the first part of Chapter 11 uses material from "The Effects of Taxes and Dividend Policy on Capital Accumulation and Macroeconomic Behavior," *Journal of Economic Dynamics and Control* 14 (1990). The basic model in Chapter 12 was first presented in "Fiscal Policy, Capital Accumulation, and Debt in an Open Economy," *Oxford Economic Papers* 43 (1991), coauthored with P. Sen. Finally, the material in Part IV is in part adapted from work with E. Grinols. Specifically, Section 14.5 is a simplified version of material contained in an unpublished manuscript, while the open economy model of Chapter 15 is adapted from our paper "Exchange Rate Determination and Asset Prices in a Stochastic Small Open Economy," *Journal of International Economics* 36 (1994).

I wish to reiterate, however, that because it is free of the constraints imposed by the limitations of journal space, the exposition here tends to be more leisurely, with more attention paid to ensuring that sufficient details and intuition are included, to make the discussion as comprehensible as possible. Also, in many cases, the analysis has been modified in substantive ways. The mastery of the methods of macrodynamics requires practice. Accordingly, a workbook containing problem sets designed to accompany the material in each chapter has been prepared in collaboration with Michael Hendrickson and is being published by MIT Press.

Much of my work has been conducted with colleagues and former students, and it is a pleasure to acknowledge their contribution, either as it appears directly in the joint work noted above, or indirectly, as it is discussed elsewhere in this volume. In this regard, I wish to express my gratitude to Arthur Benavie, Marcelo Bianconi, Philip Brock, William Brock, Edwin Burmeister, Walter Fisher, Robert Flood, Malcolm Gray, Earl Grinols, Richard Marston, Marcus Miller, Thomas Nguyen, William Scarth, Partha Sen, and Peter Stemp. Helpful comments were made by graduate students in macroeconomics at the University of Illinois and the University of Washington who were exposed to parts of the material in draft form. Also, while in the process of revising the manuscript, I had the opportunity to present a series of lectures based on the latter part of the book to advanced students at the University of Paris I. This too provided helpful feedback. I would also like to thank Marian Bolan for her typing of Parts I and II of the manuscript, Michael Hendrickson and Tina Sun for proofreading, and Christian Murray for preparing the index. I am grateful to Terry Vaughn, Melissa Vaughn, and Ann Sochi of The MIT Press for their efficient handling of this project and to the five anonymous reviewers for their thoughtful advice. Finally, the work underlying this book has occupied a large fraction of my working career, and I am grateful to my wife Michelle for her patience and support over a long period of time.

Stephen J. Turnovsky
Seattle, WA, May 1994

1   Introduction and Overview

1.1   The Evolution of Macrodynamics

The methods employed by economists to analyze macroeconomic systems and to address issues in macroeconomic policy have changed dramatically over the last fifty years or so. The beginnings of modern macroeconomic dynamics can be conveniently dated to the famous models of business cycles introduced by Samuelson (1939) and Hicks (1950). This was followed by a period of intensive research on economic growth models during the 1950s and 1960s, which was comprehensively reviewed by Burmeister and Dobell (1970).

The analysis of dynamic macroeconomic systems that evolved from this literature was all _backward looking_. That is, the dynamics were assumed to evolve from some given initial state. This was certainly true, for example, of my own book (Turnovsky 1977), which emphasized what I called the _intrinsic dynamics_ of the macroeconomic system. This term was used to describe the dynamics inherent in the process by which some groups in the economy create securities to finance their activities, while other groups absorb these securities in the course of saving and accumulating assets. These relationships necessarily impose a dynamic structure on the macroeconomic system, even if all the underlying behavioral relationships are static, because the accumulation of wealth affects consumption and other aspects of aggregate demand. In terms of the simplest textbook model, the accumulation of wealth causes the _IS_ and _LM_ curves to shift over time. Expectations in this kind of analysis were also assumed to be generated by looking at the past, and hypotheses such as adaptive expectations were standard at the time.

There are probably two main reasons for the backward-looking nature of the dynamics in this literature. First, the traditional theory of differential equations (or difference equations) that was being applied was largely borrowed from the applied physical sciences, in which the objects being studied can be viewed most naturally as evolving gradually from some given starting point. Initial positions and initial speeds in mechanics are usually what determine the arbitrary constants of integration that arise in the process of solving the differential equation describing their motion. A rocket is fired from the ground with some initial acceleration, and that determines its trajectory through time. But in addition, it natural to think of certain economic variables—such as the capital stock that was in fact the primary focus of economic growth theory—as changing gradually over time.

In the mid-1970s the methods of macroeconomic dynamics changed in a fundamental way with the impact of rational expectations theory, which had lain dormant for over a decade since Muth (1961) first introduced the concept in a different context. The key methodological innovation here was the observation that although certain economic variables were backward looking, others embodied expectations about the future and were therefore forward looking. The capital stock is a natural example of the former, whereas financial variables such as interest rates and the exchange rate are examples of the latter. This view fundamentally changed the way macroeconomic dynamics was carried out. Instead of starting from some given initial state, macrodynamics came to be determined by a combination of backward-looking dynamics and forward-looking dynamics, reflecting the fact that some economic variables are tied to the past, whereas others are looking to the future. This distinction was embodied into macrodynamics by the treatment of some variables as "jump variables" (meaning that they can respond instantaneously to new information), and other variables as "sluggish variables" (meaning that their evolution is constrained to continuous adjustments over time).

The rational expectations methodology was initially applied to linear models and in this form dominated macroeconomic dynamics for the decade between 1975 and 1985. One criticism leveled at this approach, however was that whereas these models assumed rational behavior in the sense of expectations not being systematically wrong, the rest of the model in which the expectations were embedded was typically arbitrarily specified. Critics argued that a good macro model should be based on sound microeconomic foundations, and that involved deriving the behavioral relationships of the macro model from the intertemporal optimization of micro agents. This has led to the so-called representative agent model, which in the past decade has become the dominant macro paradigm. It too has its critics, however, and some of the arguments will be noted below.

Most of the literature employing the representative agent framework is deterministic. Stochastic intertemporal optimization is difficult and often very formal. One approach that many researchers have found to be fruitful is the method of continuous time stochastic calculus. This approach has played a prominent role in the theory of finance but has been little used in macroeconomic dynamics. It suffers from the drawback that it is tractable only under restrictive conditions and for specific functional forms, but when it is tractable it offers tremendous insight and typically is much more transparent than the corresponding discrete time methods. Under the assumption that the underlying stochastic processes are Brownian motions, it naturally leads to an equilibrium in which the means and variances of the relevant variables are jointly determined. This has the advantage of being able to integrate issues in corporate finance, which are of relevance to macroeconomics, in a meaningful way. Issues such as the determinants of risk premia, the role of risk on key macroeconomic indicators of performance, such as growth and inflation, can now be addressed in a tractable and enlightening way.

1.2 Scope of the Book

The thrust of this book is to provide an overview of this evolution in the *methods* of macroeconomic dynamics as we have briefly outlined them. Setting out this kind of objective raises immediately the question of balance. How much of the old approaches should one discuss, even though they may have been superseded? This is a question of judgment and, presumably, taste. There are good reasons for including material based on what some would view as obsolete models. For one thing, economic theory is somewhat like the clothing industry in that it is subject to fads and fashions. It is commonplace for one particular topic to be an area of intense research activity for some period of time, then fall out of fashion for a period, only to engage the attention of researchers again at some future time. Growth theory is a good example: after being intensively studied during the period 1955–1970, it was essentially dropped from the research agenda during the next fifteen years while macroeconomists focused on issues of inflation and unemployment. Since the publication of Romer's (1986) paper, there has been a revival in the new growth theory, and economic growth now seems to be attracting the same kind of attention that it did thirty years ago.

A second important reason for not discarding old techniques and models entirely is that by keeping a historical perspective, one gains a better understanding of the current models and methods of analysis. Related to this is the fact that some of the equilibrium properties of state-of-the-art models turn out to be very similar to superseded models. For example, there are cases where adaptive expectations and rational expectations coincide. Being familiar with the former enhances our understanding of the latter.

One further reason for a longer-term perspective is that each of the various approaches has introduced some methodological aspect that is of more lasting interest. Although the backward-looking dynamics of the traditional macro model may be deemed inappropriate in a context where agents are forward looking, the model may still be of relevance for other issues where expectations are not relevant. The insights of linear rational expectations models are important, even though the systems in which they are embedded may no longer be at the frontier.

By being oriented toward methods of analysis, the book attempts to illustrate their application in a variety of areas. In particular, the evolution of macroeconomic models that we noted in Section 1.1 has proceeded in parallel in both closed and open economies. Thus rather than develop the macroeconomic models for a closed economy and then add a chapter or two at the end to cover the extension to the open economy—in the way that international aspects have traditionally been included in macroeconomics, at least until fairly recently—we attempt to incorporate international issues in a more integrated way as we proceed. Accordingly each of the three main parts includes some applications of the particular method to an international situation.

The book is not intended to be comprehensive in its coverage of topics. For example, it does not deal with New Keynesian economics, mainly because most of this literature has been static and abstracts from dynamics. It does not discuss the overlapping generations model either, however, which is truly dynamic. Nor does it discuss in any depth real business cycle models or recent developments in nonlinear dynamics. This is not to suggest that these topics are unimportant. They are clearly extremely important and are likely to become more so. But it is necessary to limit the scope of an individual book, and the restrictions that have been chosen have been determined in part by the application of comparative advantage. In addition, excellent treatments of these topics are available elsewhere. Readers wishing to study some overlapping generations models should consult the appropriate chapters of Blanchard and Fischer (1989) or Farmer (1993). If they want to pursue the subject further they might wish to study McCandless and Wallace (1993). An up-to-date collection of papers on nonlinear dynamics is provided by Benhabib (1992). Discrete-time dynamic programming methods are not discussed here, as they too are comprehensively treated elsewhere; see, for example, Sargent (1987). There are many aspects to macrodynamics, and many approaches to studying them; one book simply cannot cover them all. The treatment here is therefore somewhat idiosyncratic, and to some degree reflects the tastes of the author—but that may in fact be a good thing.

By the same token, this should not be viewed as a book of "mathematics for economists." It is certainly not that. Little space is devoted to developing formal mathematical techniques, except in one or two places where appendices are provided. There are two points of focus. The first is a comprehensive treatment of the methods and their application. But a careful exposition and illustration of these analytical tools inevitably requires a certain amount of formal detail, even if at times it seems a little tedious. The other focal point is strictly economics and the economic insights that emerge from the models that will be developed. In this respect an underlying theme of the book is the dynamics of economic policy-making and the impact of policy on the dynamic evolution of the economy. In short, the rigorous analysis of policy issues is the unifying thread running through the different models, with particular emphasis on the macroeconomic aspects of public finance.

The book focuses on methods of analysis in the hope that the tools being applied here may be of use in other contexts, or be applied to models professing a particular point of view. For example, although we do not devote much attention to real business cycle models, nevertheless the intertemporal optimizing models developed in Part III and in particular the stochastic versions in Part IV bear a strong resemblance to that approach. More structure is imposed, and the explicit analytical solutions obtained may help researchers in their study of real business cycles. In addition, these methods are entirely applicable to other models, such as the New Keynesian models or the overlapping generations model, which may reflect alternative views of the world.

One important methodological issue which arises in the modeling of dynamic economic systems is the choice of discrete versus continuous time. The merits of each have been long debated and are discussed in Turnovsky (1977). The preference in this book is toward continuous time formulation, mainly because I find it to be more tractable and often more transparent. But to some degree the choice is a matter of taste.

1.3   Outline of the Book

Part I, which consists of Chapter 2, outlines a standard dynamic portfolio balance macro model of 1970s' vintage, embeds this into a simple backward-looking dynamic model, and discusses stability issues in the traditional sense. The chapter is intended to provide background and historical context. The model also serves as a convenient vehicle for illustrating some of the points to be made at various stages in Part II.

Rational expectations models are discussed in Part II, which consists of Chapters 3 through 8. Chapter 3 introduces the concept of rational expectations. It begins by describing rational expectations in formal terms and covers some issues on specifying expectations in continuous time models. This chapter considers the simple Cagan (1956) monetary model as a vehicle for introducing rational expectations (perfect foresight) and for illustrating the difference between a backward-looking solution and a forward-looking solution to a dynamic problem. Several types of monetary shocks are introduced in order to illustrate the distinction between permanent and temporary shocks, on the one hand, and between unanticipated and anticipated shocks, on the other. Also, the solution is presented using both continuous time and discrete time, enabling us to lay out clearly the different solution procedures for solving linear rational expectations models. The next chapter embeds the assumption of rational expectations into a small complete macro model and discusses two issues, the Lucas Critique and policy neutrality, both of which were central to the rational expectations debate. It considers at some length the robustness of the policy neutrality proposition, the role of information, and various modifications to this basic model.

In general there are an infinite number of rational expectations equilibria. In many cases, all but one can be ruled out on the grounds of stability. That is, there is only one solution that has the property that it implies bounded behavior. However, in other cases this does not occur, and there may be many equilibria consistent with stability. This issue of nonuniqueness of rational expectations equilibria is discussed in Chapter 5. The fact that rational expectations models contained the potential for nonunique solutions was first noted by Black (1974) and Taylor (1977). Alternative procedures for dealing with this issue are discussed, and the nature of rational expectations solutions are characterized. We have already introduced the distinction between variables that evolve gradually over time—so-called sluggish variables—and variables that may respond instantaneously to new information as it becomes available—frequently referred to as jump variables. In general, a unique rational expectations equilibrium will obtain if the number of jump variables equals the number of unstable roots in the dynamic system. The further distinction is made between nonuniqueness issues that arise in linear models because of the configuration of eigenvalues ("too many" stable solutions) and those that arise because of the nonlinearity of the underlying macroeconomic models. These are distinct sources of multiplicity of equilibria, and examples of the latter are also provided.

Most rational expectations equilibria are characterized by what is known as saddlepoint behavior. This is characterized by a situation where the number of jump variables equals the number of unstable roots to the system. This topic is discussed in Chapter 6. The chapter begins by setting out the formal solution to a second-order differential equation system characterized by a saddlepoint. The next three sections then apply this procedure to three diverse examples. The first is the Cagan monetary model, modified to include sluggish wages. The second is a simple Blinder-Solow-type (1973) macro model incorporating a term structure of interest rates, which also can be shown in some cases to have the saddlepoint property. In the third example the procedure is applied to the famous

Dornbusch (1976a) model of exchange rate determination with sticky prices. Other examples of saddlepoint behavior will be presented in Part III.

Chapter 7 introduces deficit financing into the rational expectations macro model. It derives the rational expectations equilibrium under (a) money financing and (b) bond financing of the government deficit. It shows how the former yields a unique stable solution whereas the latter does not. One of the points of Chapter 7 is to apply the rational expectations solution methods to a more complex, yet tractable, stochastic dynamic system. Alternative procedures for choosing among a number of unstable paths are discussed. The role of growth as a stabilizing influence is also discussed, relating this discussion to the debate over the feasibility of bond financing in a growing economy. In many respects, this chapter is a rational expectations analogue to the literature analyzing the role of the government budget constraint in the traditional macrodynamic models of the 1970s summarized in Chapter 2.

Chapter 8 discusses macroeconomic stabilization policy under rational expectations. Two main issues are addressed, both of which have generated substantial literature. These involve wage indexation, on the one hand, and the choice of monetary policy rule on the other. These two literatures parallel one another closely and are in fact quite interrelated. The two approaches to stabilization are parallel in the sense that both require monitoring contemporaneous pieces of information, such as prices and financial variables. Wage indexation involves intervention on the supply side; monetary policy operates on the demand side. They are interdependent in that the choice of one form of policy has an impact on the efficacy of the other. Much of our discussion proceeds in terms of deriving an optimal integrated policy in a small open economy. There are at least three good reasons for this. First, the policy of wage indexation is typically prevalent among smaller economies. Second, the interdependence between wage indexation and monetary policy can be illustrated most simply in such economies. Third, this focus provides an opportunity to illustrate the rational expectations methods in the context of a stochastic small open economy, an area where they have been fruitfully applied. The latter part of Chapter 8 briefly discusses the merits of discretionary policy versus rules in a rational expectations context, introducing issues such as time consistency, which will be discussed again later in the context of the intertemporal optimizing model.

Part III, consisting of Chapters 9 through 13, presents a progression of models based on intertemporal optimization. Chapter 9 sets out the representative agent model, which underlies this approach. It begins with the Ramsey (1928) model of a central planner making allocation decisions based on the optimization of an intertemporal utility function, and then goes on to consider various extensions. The basic model is one in which population is stationary, labor is endogenously supplied, and capital accumulates gradually over time. Within this framework, a government issuing debt and financing its consumption expenditures using nondistortionary taxes is introduced. The role of terminal or transversality conditions and the implications for the intertemporal budget constraint of both the private sector and the government are discussed. The chapter briefly considers Ricardian equivalence and addresses the intertemporal aspects of consistent fiscal policy.

In order to study the dynamic adjustments to the economy it is necessary to subject the system to some kind of disturbance. In the present chapter, this role is served by government consumption expenditure, and the effects of both permanent and temporary disturbances in government expenditure on the dynamics of the economy will be analyzed. Other shocks, such as changes in technology and tastes, can be analyzed using these types of methods.

Traditionally, macroeconomics has focused on analyzing the effects of policy changes and other disturbances on various macroeconomic variables judged to be of interest. These have included output, unemployment, inflation, the capital stock, the balance of trade, among others. Most economic disturbances impact on the economy in a variety of conflicting ways, some desirable, some less so. Positive demand shocks, for example, may raise output, which is good, raise employment and reduce leisure, which may be bad, and raise the inflation rate, which is also likely bad. What is ultimately of interest is the impact on economic welfare, measured in some comprehensive and appropriate way. One of the attractive features of the representative agent model is that being grounded in intertemporal optimization, the welfare (utility) of the representative agent provides a natural framework for evaluating the overall benefits of a particular policy. This issue is pursued with respect to the effects of government expenditure. Specifically, the time path of instantaneous welfare of the representative agent, as well as his accumulated welfare over time (as measured by the integral of his utility function evaluated along the optimal path) is analyzed.

The latter part of this chapter introduces various modifications to this model. These include the introduction of government expenditure into the production function as a productive input, rather than as a consumption good as it has been traditionally treated. This alternative view is motivated by discussions on the importance of infrastructure. A second extension is the introduction of a term structure of interest rates to the basic model. The remaining two modifications include the introduction of money and of a growing population.

Chapter 10 develops a comprehensive decentralized macroeconomic equilibrium model, in which consumers hold private bonds and equities issued by firms to finance their investments together with government bonds and money issued by the government to finance its expenditures. The model includes various forms of personal and corporate distortionary taxes, as well as an endogenously determined inflation rate. It enables us to introduce notions from corporate finance into a macroeconomic setting, albeit in a restrictive way. For example, Modigliani and Miller (1958) type results are obtained pertaining to the capital financing decisions of firms, in which the presence of distortionary taxes play a key role. It is also shown how the chosen mode of corporate financing, in the face of given monetary policy and tax rates, in turn affects the macroeconomic consequences of changes in these policies themselves. Thus the introduction of a more complete corporate sector that responds rationally to the macroeconomic environment it faces is important in understanding the effectiveness of macroeconomic policy. This initial framework, based on the model of Brock and Turnovsky (1981) leads to a corner solution–type equilibrium in which firms employ either all debt or all equity financing, depending upon tax rates. A subsequent paper by Osterberg (1989) has extended this model by introducing increasing costs on issuing debt, leading to an interior solution. This model is discussed in the latter part of the chapter.

Chapter 11 extends the previous chapter in various directions. The model developed in Chapter 10 is quite detailed, and most of the chapter is taken up with spelling it out and deriving the equilibrium itself. There is little space for a detailed analysis of the dynamics and for considering important variations in the specification. Chapter 11 uses the model to focus more on the macrodynamic aspects of tax policy, which this framework is particularly well suited to analyze (see Lucas 1990). In particular, the following aspects are introduced. First, the analysis of Chapter 10 assumes that output can be transformed costlessly into investment goods. Chapter 11 assumes that investment is subject to convex costs of adjustment, as in Hayashi (1982), leading to the introduction of a Tobin-q into the system. Second, the chapter emphasizes the importance of alternative dividend policies in the presence of distortionary taxes and how they impact the cost of capital confronting the firm. Third, it spells out the dynamics of a three-dimensional system in (a) the shadow value of capital, (b) the stock of capital, and (c) the marginal utility of wealth, analyzing the dynamic adjustments in response to tax changes in some detail. Finally, the chapter discusses optimal tax policy and issues associated with it.

International macroeconomics has been a booming area of research since the 1970s. In particular, the representative agent model has become the standard approach, just as it has for the closed economy. Chapter 12 reviews some of the applications of the intertemporal optimizing approach to international macroeconomics. Detailed expositions are presented of a simple monetary model and of a basic one-sector real model incorporating the accumulation of real capital. The latter model, in particular, has been widely applied to the analysis of various real disturbances such as expenditure shocks, as well as changes in taxes, tariffs, and the terms of trade. Extensions to the model, which are the subject of current research activity, are also indicated.

As we have already noted, there has been a recent resurgence of interest in economic growth theory, beginning with the work by Romer (1986) and the current research on endogenous growth models. An introduction to some of this literature is presented in Chapter 13. It begins by discussing the Romer model, in which the endogenous growth arises through productive externalities generated by the aggregate capital stock. However, most of the attention is devoted to ongoing growth in models having a linear technology, and the chapter focuses on the role of fiscal policy in influencing the long-run growth rate. The ability of fiscal policy to influence the growth rate is an important dimension that distinguishes the current endogenous growth models from the more traditional neoclassical growth models, in which the long-run equilibrium growth is tied to population growth and productivity. This framework is very convenient for analyzing optimal tax and expenditure policies, and much of Chapter 13 is spent on these issues. We do not intend to provide a comprehensive treatment of the new growth theory; that is a huge subject in itself. Rather, by focusing on fiscal issues, the chapter serves as an extension of Chapter 11. At the same time, by dealing with a linear technology, it provides a transition to the discussion in Part IV of stochastic models that are based primarily on stochastic linear technologies.

The final part of the book, comprising Chapters 14 and 15, discusses intertemporal optimization using the continuous time stochastic calculus framework. These methods are generally less familiar to economists and are not usually included in basic graduate macroeconomic courses. But they are very attractive and, when tractable, provide much insight. Chapter 14 begins with a summary of the basic techniques associated with the use of continuous time stochastic calculus methods. These are then applied to several examples. Most of the attention is devoted to a linear technology with multiplicative stochastic disturbances, so that the absolute size of the shock is proportional to the size of the economy. This type of specification is a natural stochastic analogue to the linear endogenous growth models of Chapter 13. This model leads to a macroeconomic equilibrium in which the means and variances are simultaneously determined, and which can therefore be referred to as a *mean-variance* equilibrium. An important part of the model are the equilibrium relationships relating the tax-adjusted rates of return on the various assets. These can be written in terms of beta coefficients and expressed in terms of concepts familiar from finance. Thus, this approach enables us to integrate rudimentary corporate finance into a macroeconomic framework. Although Chapter 10 goes part of the way to doing this, it can only be undertaken satisfactorily in a stochastic framework. Once this macroeconomic equilibrium is derived, it is used to address issues pertaining to optimal fiscal policy, leading to results that are stochastic generalizations of those of previous chapters. While the focus of this chapter is somewhat different, it bears a close resemblance in some respects to the current real business cycle literature; that relationship is pursued to some extent.

The final chapter applies these techniques to develop a mean-variance equilibrium model for a small open economy. The model is used to examine the effects of means and variances of the policy shocks on the equilibrium and to analyze the determinants of the foreign exchange risk premium. Particular attention is devoted to analyzing the impact of risk on various aspects of the equilibrium growth rate. Much of the focus is on the structural effects of risk, but the chapter also discusses some of the implications for the correlations between contemporaneous shocks, a central aspect of the recent work on real business cycles.

I Traditional Macrodynamics

2 A Dynamic Portfolio Balance Macroeconomic Model

2.1 Some Preliminary Concepts

Macroeconomic theory is concerned with analyzing aggregate economic behavior. The key variables studied include: real variables such as the level of employment and measures of real income and its components, consumption and investment; financial variables such as the quantity of money, the rate of interest, and the rate of return on capital; nominal variables such as the level of prices and the rate of inflation; and, increasingly, international variables such as the balance of trade and the balance of payments. Invariably these aggregates are abstractions. There is no such thing as *the* rate of interest, or *the* level of prices, or *the* level of real output, etc. Rather, there are many rates of interest, and millions of different commodities, each with its own price. To formulate an economic model capable of studying each individual economic quantity is obviously impossible. Consequently a fundamental premise of macroeconomics is that the analysis of these aggregates provides useful insights into the workings of the economic system. Thus it should be clearly understood that macroeconomic analysis presupposes a considerable level of aggregation. The conventional intermediate textbook analysis of a closed economy typically aggregates the economy up to four markets, namely:

(i)   the output or product market,

(ii) the money market,

(iii) the bond market,

(iv) the labor market.

Because of Walras's law, only three of these markets are independent. Hence one of them can be eliminated, since its equilibrium is assured by the equilibrium of the other three. Traditionally, it is the bond market that is eliminated, and the analysis focuses on the other three. But there is really no reason why this should be so, and a well-defined macroeconomic theory could just as easily be developed in terms of, say, the money market, the bond market, and the labor market.

This chapter summarizes the elements of a dynamic macroeconomic model based on the portfolio balance framework of the 1970s. There are many good reasons for starting with this model, even though this approach to macroeconomic theory may already be largely superseded. First is the matter of historical context. In order to have a complete appreciation of current macroeconomic theory it is important to be aware of how it has evolved over time. Moreover, even though this framework may seem dated, it still often underlies the analyses of macroeconomic policy makers, particularly those using larger-scale econometric models. Of more immediate relevance, it provides a common starting point for the development of the more contemporary macrodynamic models to be developed later in this book. In this respect, elements of the basic model often serve as useful vehicles for illustrating more sophisticated and technical methods of macrodynamics. For example, many of the elements we are about to review play important roles in the rational expectations models to be discussed in Part II.

Because detailed treatments of the underlying relationships can be found in numerous textbooks, our discussion will necessarily be brief, focusing on those issues most relevant to subsequent discussion. The model is constructed by first developing the demand side of the system, described by the output and money markets. Next, one must consider the determination of supply, and this involves analyzing the labor market. The dynamics generated by the accumulation of assets and savings behavior, as well as inflationary expectations formation, are discussed. Finally, the latter sections of the chapter combine these various components into a dynamic macroeconomic model under a variety of assumptions with respect to the specification of monetary policy. The key characteristic of this dynamic system is that it is entirely *backward looking*; that is, its evolution is tied to the past.

The starting point for most macroeconomic models is the national income accounts. These can be looked at from different viewpoints, enabling one to break down gross domestic product (GDP) in several different ways. One basic way of considering GDP is from the point of view of expenditure on final output. In the case of the closed economy we shall be considering, this is described by the relationship

$$GDP = C + I + G \tag{2.1}$$

where

C = consumption expenditure by the private sector,

I = gross private domestic investment,

G = total government purchases of goods and services.

That is, output must either be consumed by the private sector, invested by the private sector, or purchased by the government. Throughout the book we shall assume that investment goods do not depreciate, so that there is no need to distinguish between gross and net investment.

In an open economy, the national income accounts must also take account of transactions involving foreign residents, so that (2.1) must be modified to:

$$GDP = C + I + G + X - M \tag{2.2}$$

where

X = exports,

M = imports.

Apart from the breakdown according to expenditure on final product, there are at least two other ways in which the flow of GDP can be divided. First, there is the relationship

$$GDP = C + S + T \tag{2.3}$$

where

S = total savings,

T = net tax payments.

This breakdown of GDP describes how the income earned by the sale of production of goods is disposed of. According to (2.3), it can be spent on consumption goods, it can be saved, or it can be used to pay taxes.

Second, income can be considered from the viewpoint of the type of income generated by the production process; that is, income may be earned in the form of wages and salaries, corporate profit, rental income, dividend income, interest income, etc. All of these ways of looking at income are important, and which form one chooses is dictated largely by the problem one is analyzing. In the main, the first two breakdowns are the most usual in conventional macro theory, although in analyzing distributional questions the income-component breakdown becomes particularly important.

Before turning to the analysis of the model, we should review the notion of nominal as opposed to real GDP. Conventional national income accounts are measured in current dollars, that is, in nominal terms. Thus an increase in the nominal GDP between two time periods may be due either to an increase in prices or to an increase in real output, or both. To get a measure of real activity, which is surely one of the key economic variables with which we are concerned, it is necessary to deflate the nominal GDP by an index of the price level. In practice the question of the deflator often poses a nasty statistical problem. In our case, because we shall be aggregating up to a single output, the index number problem implicit in the transition from nominal to real GDP largely disappears (or, more correctly, is avoided).

2.2   The Output Market

As just indicated, the basic assumption underlying our highly aggregated level of analysis is that the economy produces only one commodity. This can either be used for consumption or be invested. In this latter case it is accumulated as a capital good and combined with the other factor of production—labor—to produce more output. For a closed economy, equilibrium in the commodity market is described by the equation

$$Y = C + I + G \qquad (2.4)$$

where

Y = real output, or national income,

C = real private demand for consumption,

I = real private demand for investment,

G = real government expenditure.

Equation (2.4) must not be confused with the national income identity (2.1). It is an *equilibrium* condition and need not be satisfied; the national income identity, on the other hand, holds definitionally. The distinction between identities and equilibrium relationships has played a prominent role in the history of macroeconomic theory and has not always been clearly understood.

Equation (2.4) has been written in real terms. Given the assumption of a single output, it must apply whether written in real or in nominal terms. With more than one output, the conversion from nominal to real output would involve choosing a numeraire commodity in defining real income. The reason for focusing on real rather than nominal quantities, is the notion that individuals formulate their underlying demands in real terms. That is, they are concerned with *real* consumption or *real* investment, rather than with the corresponding nominal quantities. To what extent this is true is an empirical question, and some evidence, at least for consumption, suggests that individuals may be subject to some degree of "money illusion."[1] In any event, if people do formulate their plans in real terms, it is clearly more appropriate to postulate their behavior for C, I in real terms and hence to formulate our product market equilibrium in real terms as well.

It should be further noted that, as well as distinguishing between consumption and investment demand, we have also distinguished government expenditure from private expenditure. The reason for this is that government expenditure decisions are usually motivated by different considerations than are private expenditure plans. Consequently, different behavioral relationships are required to explain private and public demand for output. Nevertheless, it remains true that government expenditure must take the form of either consumption or investment. Some further discussion along these lines is presented in Chapter 9.

If we knew what determined the three components C, I, G, we would have a theory for Y. Thus the first task is to develop behavioral relationships for these demand aggregates. The simplest theory, taught in elementary books on the subject, postulates the consumption function[2]

$$C = C(Y) \qquad 0 < C' < 1 \tag{2.5}$$

with $I = \bar{I}$, $G = \bar{G}$. That is, consumption depends upon income, whereas investment and government expenditure are both exogenously determined. Substituting these relationships into (2.4) we obtain

$$Y = C(Y) + \bar{I} + \bar{G} \tag{2.6}$$

so that Y can be solved uniquely in terms of the exogenous values of investment and government expenditure. We thus have a theory of income, but not a very interesting one.

The next level of analysis involves postulating more reasonable and richer relationships for consumption and particularly for investment. As a first approximation, one might postulate consumption to be a function of real disposable income. That is,

$$C = C(Y^D) \qquad 0 < C' < 1 \tag{2.7}$$

where

$$Y^D = Y - T \tag{2.8}$$

and

Y^D denotes real disposable income,

T denotes real taxes.

Taxes themselves are typically endogenous, varying with the level of income. For the present purposes, however, T can be assumed to be constant without causing any difficulty.

Subsequently, more sophisticated studies of the consumption function have been based upon underlying utility maximization considerations.

This has a long history in macroeconomics, the rigor of which has increased over time as the methods of intertemporal optimization have evolved. The fundamental idea is that rather than being constrained by current income, as in (2.5) or (2.7), consumption is constrained by an intertemporal measure of income, reflecting the agent's lifetime expected earnings. This idea can be formulated in a variety of ways. One approach, originally due to Friedman (1957), is to convert the fluctuating lifetime income stream into a stable measure of "permanent income." The other, associated more with the "life cycle theory" developed by Modigliani and his associates, leads to proxying the agent's lifetime earnings by his current wealth as well as his current earnings, the latter also sometimes being interpreted as a proxy for expected future earnings. The upshot of these contributions is that consumption is typically hypothesized to depend upon wealth in some form, and possibly the interest rate, as well as disposable income.[3] Thus instead of (2.7), one would postulate

$$C = C(Y^D, r, A) \qquad 0 < C_1 < 1; C_3 > 0 \tag{2.9}$$

where

r = rate of interest,

A = real wealth of the private sector.

We do not attempt to justify (2.9) on more rigorous grounds here. This has been done in numerous textbooks, as well as in the original articles themselves.[4]

But without going through a formal derivation, several other matters are raised that require comment. First, there is the question of the appropriate definition of real disposable income. This issue was discussed at length by Turnovsky (1977). There it was shown that if the consistency of the model is to be preserved in real terms, the appropriate definition of disposable income is

$$Y^D = Y - T + \frac{rP_bB}{P} + X \tag{2.10}$$

where

B = nominal stock of government bonds,

P_b = price of government bonds,

P = price level of output,

X = rate of real capital gains (or losses) on wealth.

The definition of disposable income is adjusted to include interest earned on government bonds together with the expected capital gains or losses on real wealth. The precise specification of X depends upon the form in which assets are denominated (real or nominal) and upon how prices are expected to change; a specific example is given in Section 2.9. It was shown previously that defining Y^D in this way ensures the quality of savings and wealth accumulation in real terms. We should note, however, that although this definition is appropriate theoretically, this does not mean that it is incorrect to postulate a consumption function in terms of $(Y - T)$ alone. Rather, this specification would simply mean that the marginal propensity to consume out of interest income and capital gains income is zero. Whether or not this is true is an empirical question, just as is the validity of the specification (2.9) where the marginal propensities to consume out of all forms of income are assumed to be the same.

A second question is the form of the interest rate in (2.9). Early work on the consumption function typically excluded the interest rate, mainly on the grounds of statistical insignificance. Work by Weber (1970) suggested that this may have been due to misspecification of the way the interest rate enters the consumption function. Most early analysis included it linearly, finding it to be insignificant. Weber, on the other hand, introduced it nonlinearly, consistent with the underlying utility-maximizing theory and obtained significant results. In a follow-up study, Weber (1975) also tested for the effect of inflation, though he did not find it to be statistically significant. But despite these findings, intertemporal utility maximization of a consumption function, specified in terms of current and future real consumptions, indicates that the real interest rate, $r - \pi$, say, where π denotes the expected rate of inflation, is appropriate.

Finally, there is the question of the appropriate definition of real private wealth. A reasonably comprehensive definition for a small macroeconomic model is

$$A = \frac{M + P_b B + P_k K}{P} \qquad (2.11)$$

where

M = nominal stock of outside money, assumed to be the liability of the central bank,

K = real stock of physical capital,

P_k = price of capital goods.

Two issues are raised here. First, there is the nature of the government bonds, in this respect the literature usually adopts one of two polar assumptions:

(i) B are infinitesimally short bonds, with a fixed nominal price, so that, say, $P_b = 1$.

(ii) B are perpetuities, paying a fixed coupon (unity, say) per unit of time, with the price being inversely related to the nominal interest rate, $P_b = 1/r$.

Actually, the assumption of an efficient bond market, rational expectations, and risk neutrality leads to the following relationship between the nominal interest rate and the price of a bond with a unit coupon and a par value equal to $\bar{P}_b$, and due to mature at time T:

$$r(t) = \frac{1}{P_b(t)} + \frac{\dot{P}_b(t)}{P_b(t)} \qquad t \leq T; \qquad P_b(T) = \bar{P}_b. \tag{2.12}$$

Equation (2.12) asserts that, prior to the maturity date, risk-neutral arbitrage ensures that the short-term interest rate equals the rate of return earned on the coupon, $1/P_b$, plus the rate of capital gain, $\dot{P}_b/P_b$. At its maturity date, the bond is redeemed at its par, or face value, $\bar{P}_b$. This relationship has important implications for the "forward-looking" behavior of bond prices, which are analyzed in detail in Chapters 7 and 9, where a term structure of interest rates is introduced.

The other issue pertaining to wealth concerns the extent to which government bonds constitute real wealth. It has been argued that future tax liabilities on the interest earned on government bonds should be netted out. The present formulation treats government bonds fully as part of wealth, and makes no such adjustment at all. This relates to issues of Ricardian Equivalence, which are characteristic of the representative agent model to be discussed in Part III.

We now turn to private investment. The simplest version of the investment function postulates

$$I = I(r - \pi) \qquad I' < 0. \tag{2.13}$$

This can be justified in terms of the discounted present value criterion. Briefly, a profit-maximizing firm should invest in those projects yielding positive discounted present values. As the interest rate rises, the number of projects having this property will decline, so that the amount of investment undertaken by the firm will fall, implying the negative relationship (2.13). The opposite applies if the price level is expected to rise, making it clear that the relevant interest rate is the real rate, $r - \pi$.

While for many purposes (2.13) will suffice, more sophisticated versions of the investment function are frequently adopted. For example, many macro models postulate

$$I = I(r - \pi, Y, K) \qquad I_1 < 0, I_2 > 0, I_3 < 0 \tag{2.14}$$

where investment depends positively upon the level of income, and negatively upon the real interest rate and the level of existing capital stock.

While (2.14) is still fairly crude, it is nevertheless a significant theoretical improvement over (2.13). Under stringent conditions it can be justified within the framework of the "neoclassical" theory of investment as developed by Jorgenson.[5] For example, suppose that the desired capital stock K^*, is determined by

$$K^* = F(r - \pi, Y) \qquad F_1 < 0, F_2 > 0$$

and that the actual capital stock is adjusted toward K^* at a rate proportional to the gap $(K^* - K)$ (the conventional stock-adjustment relationship), so that

$$I = \dot{K} = \lambda(K^* - K).$$

One immediately derives an investment function having the properties of (2.14).

The basic macro model assumes that output can be transformed into investment costlessly. More recent developments in investment theory have introduced the cost of adjustment into this process, thereby explaining investment in terms of the "Tobin q".[6] This approach has not yet been incorporated into the intermediate model being reviewed here, and discussion of it will be postponed until Part III, where the more rigorously derived intertemporal macrodynamic model is developed.

Substituting for the consumption function and the investment function into the product market equilibrium relationship (2.4) yields the familiar IS-curve

$$Y = C\left(Y - T, r - \pi, \frac{M + B + P_k K}{P}\right) + I(r - \pi) + G. \tag{2.15}$$

In writing this equation, we have used the simplified measure of disposable income (2.8), and have set $P_b = 1$. Given the price of output P, the price of capital goods P_k, the expected rate of inflation π, and the stocks of assets M, B, and K, this curve gives the combinations of Y and r that will keep the product market in equilibrium. Differentiating both sides with respect to Y, we have

$$\left(\frac{dr}{dY}\right)_{IS} = \frac{1 - C_1}{I' + C_2},$$

which, provided $I' + C_2 < 0$, implies a downward-sloping curve as illustrated in Figure 2.1. The reason is clear. As income rises, consumption

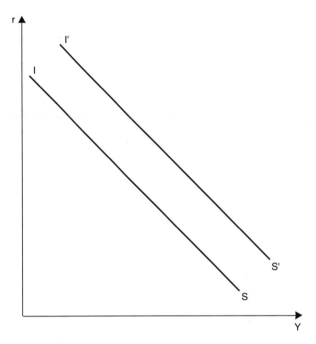

Figure 2.1
IS curve

rises, but by a lesser amount. The only way the excess output can be absorbed is by additional investment of consumption, and for this to be forthcoming, the interest rate must fall.

It is also apparent that the position of the *IS* curve depends upon the position of the investment function, the consumption function, and government expenditure. An increase in government expenditure, or equivalently an output shift in either the *C* or *I* functions, will push the *IS* curve outwards to *I'S'* in Figure 2.1. Such shifts can be brought about by either (i) an increase in the expected rate of inflation π, (ii) a fall in the price of output, (iii) a rise in the stock of assets, (iv) an increase in the price of capital, or (v) a reduction in the level of taxes.

2.3   The Financial Sector

It is clear that equilibrium in the product market alone is insufficient to determine the equilibrium of the system. The *IS* curve determines only pairs of Y, r, that are consistent in the output market. Even if the price level is held constant, another market is required to determine the unique

(Y, r) pair; this market is traditionally taken to be the money market. In extending the system in this direction, it is instructive to embed the money market within the more general monetary framework developed by Tobin (1969).[7]

A fundamental proposition from portfolio theory is that in determining their allocation of investable wealth, individuals balance off risk and return. The development of such a theory involves the derivation of asset demand functions, which include measures of risk—often measured by variances of returns—as well as the expected returns. A completely specified macroeconomic model requires these measures of risk to be endogenously determined, along with the other endogenous variables of the system. Such a task is a formidable one, and research in this direction is in its early stages. Part IV presents two relatively simple stochastic models that endogenize risk in this way.

In his seminal paper, Tobin captured the essential features of the portfolio allocation problem within a deterministic framework. His approach has provided a cornerstone for the specification of the financial sector in much of the subsequent work in macroeconomic theory, and its main features are reviewed here.

Suppose that the economy contains three outside assets: fiat money, government bonds, and physical capital. Tobin's system can be specified as follows:

$$\frac{M^d}{P} = L\left(Y, -\pi, r - \pi, r_k, \frac{M + B + P_k K}{P}\right)$$

$$L_1 > 0, L_2 > 0, L_3 < 0, L_4 < 0, 0 < L_5 < 1 \tag{2.16a}$$

$$\frac{B^d}{P} = J\left(Y, -\pi, r - \pi, r_k, \frac{M + B + P_k K}{P}\right)$$

$$J_1 \gtrless 0, J_2 < 0, J_3 > 0, J_4 < 0, 0 < J_5 < 1 \tag{2.16b}$$

$$\frac{P_k K^d}{P} = N\left(Y, -\pi, r - \pi, r_k, \frac{M + B + P_k K}{P}\right)$$

$$N_1 \gtrless 0, N_2 < 0, N_3 < 0, N_4 > 0, 0 < N_5 < 1 \tag{2.16c}$$

$$\frac{M^d + B^d + P_k K^d}{P} = \frac{M + B + P_k K}{P} = A \tag{2.16d}$$

$$r_k = \frac{PR\left(\frac{Y}{K}\right)}{P_k} \tag{2.16e}$$

where

the superscript ^{d} denotes demand,

r_k denotes the real rate of return on capital,

R denotes the marginal physical product of capital,

and all other symbols have been defined above. The demand functions for the assets are specified by equations (2.16a)–(2.16c). These depend upon (i) real output; (ii) real rates of return on the three assets, money, bond, and equities: $-\pi$, $r - \pi$, and r_k, respectively; and (iii) real wealth. Equation (2.16d) is the wealth constraint, which imposes a constraint on the underlying asset demand functions, only two of which are independent. A consequence of this is that if two of the asset markets are in equilibrium, then so, necessarily, must be the third.

In general, the constraint on the asset demand functions is derived from the underlying budget constraint facing individuals, and its exact specification depends upon whether the model is formulated in continuous or discrete time. The specification as a stock constraint in the Tobin model presumes that the model is viewed as being in continuous time. In this case, at each point in time, individuals must be prepared to hold the existing stock of assets. In discrete time, however, this is not necessarily so. The difference between the existing stock of assets and agents' desired holdings can be reconciled through savings over the period. The question of stock and flow constraints in discrete-time and continuous-time macro models is discussed at length in Turnovsky (1977, chapter 3) and is not pursued further here.

The presence of the stock constraint (2.16d) imposes the following "adding up" restrictions on the partial derivatives of the asset demand functions:

(i) $L_i + J_i + N_i = 0$ $i = 1, \ldots, 4$

$L_5 + J_5 + N_5 = 1$

These conditions assert that any increase in wealth must be allocated to some asset. On the other hand, any increase in the demand for a particular asset in response to a change in income or some real rate of return must be met by a compensating reduction in the demand for some other asset.

In addition to (i), it is usually assumed that

(ii)   the demand for each asset varies positively with its own real rate of return and nonpositively with the rates on other assets, that is, all assets are gross substitutes; and

(iii)   capital is not a transactions substitute for money, so that $N_1 = 0$, $L_1 = -J_1$.

In other words, any increase in the demand for money generated by a higher level of income and required for transactions purposes is met by instantaneously reducing bond holdings, not by adjusting holdings of capital.

Finally, it is often convenient to assume that

(iv)   The asset demand functions are homogeneous of degree one in income and wealth.

Equation (2.16e) relates the real rate of return on a unit of capital r_k and the underlying marginal physical product of capital R, generating the income stream. Under static expectations the rate of return equals the constant physical return divided by the unit price of the claim.

Eliminating the linearly dependent market, say, capital, and substituting for A and P_k, the financial sector can be reduced to the pair of equations:

$$\frac{M}{P} = L\left[Y, -\pi, r - \pi, r_k, \frac{M+B}{P} + \frac{RK}{r_k} \right] \tag{2.17a}$$

$$\frac{B}{P} = J\left[Y, -\pi, r - \pi, r_k, \frac{M+B}{P} + \frac{RK}{r_k} \right] \tag{2.17b}$$

Tobin treats Y, P, M, B, and K as given, in which case this pair of equations determines the rates of return r, r_k on the two assets.

The pair of equations (2.17a) and (2.17b) summarize the financial sector of the economy. Taken in conjunction with (2.15), these equations determine output in addition to the two rates of return r, r_k. This system can therefore be thought of as being an augmented *IS-LM* model. Under two assumptions, (2.17a) and (2.17b) reduce to the usual specification of the *LM* curve. First, suppose that bonds and capital are perfect substitutes, in which case the real rates of return on the two assets are the same:

$$r_k = r - \pi.$$

Independent asset demand functions $J(\cdot), N(\cdot)$ cease to exist; rather, there is a composite demand function $J(\cdot) + N(\cdot)$ for the single asset bonds-cum-capital. The stock constraint then implies the existence of only one independent asset market, which conventionally is taken to be the money market. Secondly, if asset demands depend upon differential rates of return, then $(r - \pi) - \pi = r$ and the independent money market equilibrium conditions reduces to

$$\frac{M}{P} = L(Y, r, A). \tag{2.18}$$

Various definitions of the nominal money supply exist, depending upon the liquidity of the assets included in the aggregate. But however M is defined, the conventional macroeconomic model usually considers it to be exogenous, determined directly by government control, so that the real money supply M/P varies inversely with the price level.

As a first approximation this may be adequate, but in fact the total nominal money supply is at best only an indirect policy instrument. The more direct variables of monetary control include the monetary base, which is essentially the unborrowed reserves of the commercial banking system, the discount rate, and the reserve requirement ratio. The monetary base tends to be the monetary instrument for short-run stabilization purposes and is controlled through open market operations, whereby the central bank enters the market for government securities. The other two instruments tend to be longer-run instruments of monetary control and tend to be adjusted infrequently.

The total money supply can be related to the money base by endogenizing the profit-maximizing behavior of the commercial banking sector. The upshot of this analysis is that the money supply is in fact endogenous, bearing a positive relationship to the market rate of interest r, as commercial banks expand their loans to take advantage of the higher earnings to be obtained from higher interest rates. However, the positive interest sensitivity of the money supply makes little difference to the conclusions of the conventional model, so that in fact little is lost by abstracting from the commercial banking system.

Thus treating M as exogenous, the money market equilibrium (2.18) defines the well-known LM curve. Given P, it determines the combinations of (Y, r) that will keep the money market in equilibrium. Differentiating (2.18) with respect to Y we obtain

$$\left(\frac{dr}{dY}\right)_{LM} = -\frac{L_1}{L_2} > 0,$$

implying an upward-sloping curve as indicated in Figure 2.2. The reason for this is that an increase in the interest rate leads to a fall in the demand for money as people switch to holding interest-bearing assets. With a fixed supply of money, equilibrium can be maintained only if people can be induced to hold more for transactions purposes, and this will be the case only if income is increased.

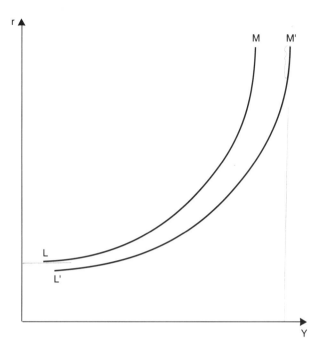

Figure 2.2
LM curve

As well as having a positive slope, the *LM* curve traditionally has the convex shape indicated in Figure 2.2. This reflects the notion that at high rates of interest speculative balances have been reduced to a minimum. Hence at that point any increase in the level of income must be accompanied by a relatively large increase in the rate of interest, in order to free the necessary money for the additional transactions needs. At the other extreme of a low interest rate, the *LM* curve is relatively flat. This is a consequence of the assumption that at low *r*, money and bonds become very close substitutes, making the demand for money much more interest elastic.

Note that if one were to replace the assumption of an exogenous money supply with an endogenous money supply function having a positive interest sensitivity, the *LM* curve would preserve its same upward-sloping shape. The only difference would be that the interest elasticity of the supply of money would give it a somewhat flatter slope.

Finally, we should note that the position of the *LM* curve depends upon the supply of money *M* and the price level *P*. An increase in *M* or a decrease in *P* will cause it to shift to the right as indicated to *L'M'*; a reduction in *M* or an increase in *P* will cause the reverse shift.

2.4   Equilibrium in Product and Money Markets

For given levels of predetermined and exogenous variables, the equilibrium level of income and interest rate is determined by combining the *IS* and *LM* curves. Considering the two equations

$$Y = C\left(Y - T, r - \pi, \frac{M + B}{P} + \frac{R(\cdot)K}{r - \pi}\right) + I(r - \pi) + G, \tag{2.19a}$$

$$\frac{M}{P} = L\left(Y, r, \frac{M + B}{P} + \frac{R(\cdot)K}{r - \pi}\right), \tag{2.19b}$$

it is clear that given our assumptions they can be solved uniquely for Y, r in terms of P, G, M, B, T, K, π. This can be seen graphically in Figure 2.3, where the equilibrium is obtained as the intersection of *IS* and *LM* curves.

In particular, the solution

$$Y = Y(P; M, B, K, \pi, G, T), \tag{2.20}$$

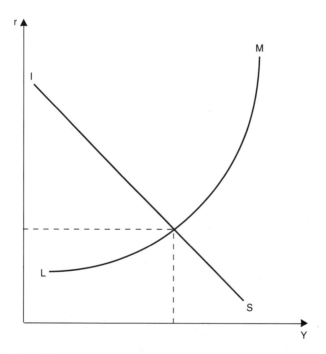

Figure 2.3
Determination of equilibrium

relating equilibrium income, as determined by demand, to price, can be viewed as an aggregate demand function. Differentiating the pair of equations (2.19) with respect to P, we obtain

$$
\begin{bmatrix}
1 - C_1 & -C_2 + C_3 \dfrac{RK}{(r - \pi)^2} - I' \\[4mm]
-L_1 & -L_2 + L_3 \dfrac{RK}{(r - \pi)^2}
\end{bmatrix}
\begin{pmatrix} dY \\[2mm] dr \end{pmatrix}
=
\begin{bmatrix}
-C_3 \left(\dfrac{M + B}{P^2} \right) \\[4mm]
\dfrac{M}{P^2} - L_3 \left(\dfrac{M + B}{P^2} \right)
\end{bmatrix}
dP
$$

$$(2.21)$$

Under quite mild conditions, (2.21) can be shown to imply

$$
\frac{\partial Y}{\partial P} < 0
\tag{2.20'}
$$

so that the aggregate demand curve is indeed downward sloping.

The pair of equilibrium equations can be used to analyze various policy changes such as increases in government expenditure, changes in taxes, and monetary policy. Such exercises for the *IS-LM* model are standard and are not pursued here.

2.5   The Supply Function

We have just seen how the output market and money market equilibrium conditions can be combined to yield an aggregate demand function for the economy. To determine the price level we must derive an aggregate supply curve. This is achieved by introducing the factors of production.

Aggregate output is assumed to be related to the labor input N and to the level of capital stock K by the aggregate production function

$$Y = F(N, K).$$

The time horizon considered by the traditional macro model is sufficiently short so that the capital stock is fixed at $\overline{K}$, say, leaving labor as the only variable factor of production. To highlight this we write nominal profit Π as

$$\Pi = Pf(N^D) - WN$$

where W denotes the money wage of labor and the demand for labor N^D is determined by

$$Pf'(N^D) = W. \tag{2.22}$$

This is the familiar first-order condition implying that the firm should employ labor up to the point where the value of its marginal product equals its wage rate. If the firm is a monopolist facing a downward-sloping demand curve for its product, it is easily shown that its demand for labor is determined by

$$P\left(1 + \frac{1}{e}\right)f'(N^D) = W \tag{2.22'}$$

where e = price elasticity of demand. Assuming the aggregate economy to be some average of competitive and monopolistic elements, this argument suggests an aggregate demand for labor depending on the real wage and of the form

$$\frac{W}{P} = \phi(N^D). \tag{2.23}$$

Moreover, the assumption of diminishing marginal product implies

$$\phi'(N^D) < 0$$

so that the demand for the labor curve is in fact downward sloping.

The supply of labor is traditionally determined within the context of an individual's work-leisure choice. Specifically, an individual is assumed to maximize a concave utility function that depends upon real income and leisure L subject to an income constraint.[8] Formally, the problem is

$$\text{Max } U(Y, L), \tag{2.24a}$$

subject to

$$\left.\begin{aligned} L &= T - N^S \\ Y &= \frac{W}{P}N^S \end{aligned}\right\} \tag{2.24b}$$

where T = fixed number of hours available to work. N^S thus measures the supply of labor in hours worked (man-hours when aggregated). Performing the maximization implies the optimality condition

$$U_1 \frac{W}{P} - U_2 = 0,$$

and this implies the labor supply function

$$\frac{W}{P} = \psi(N^S). \tag{2.25}$$

The assumption that individuals are interested in their real income results in a classical labor supply function in which labor supply depends upon the real wage. The restrictions imposed on the utility function U are not sufficient to rule out the possibility of a backward-bending portion of the labor supply curve. We do not consider this portion, however, and simply assume an upward-sloping supply curve

$$\psi' > 0$$

in the relevant range.

Equilibrium in the labor market is thus obtained where (2.22) and (2.25) hold, and in addition where

$$N^D = N^S = N. \tag{2.26}$$

We can thus write our equilibrium condition in the form

$$\frac{W}{P} = \phi(N) = \psi(N). \tag{2.27}$$

Solving (2.27) with the production function, the labor market implies an aggregate supply function, which is independent of P. Output remains fixed at its full-employment level. The properties of such a classical economy are well known and are reviewed in Turnovsky (1977).

2.6   The Phillips Curve

The *IS-LM* and Classical models represent polar extremes. In the former, the price level is fixed and can be interpreted as representing an infinitely elastic supply function. All adjustments in the economy are therefore borne by output and none by the price level. In the Classical economy, on the other hand, output is fixed at its full-employment level, in which case all adjustments are reflected in the price level and none in output.

The Phillips curve, which has played an important role in macroeconomic theory since the early 1960s, can be viewed as an intermediate form of supply function, in which prices are partially, but not fully, flexible so that both the level of output and the price level share in the adjustment to the various shocks impinging on the economy. In Turnovsky (1977, Chapter 5) we reviewed at some length the early theoretical and empirical work underlying the Phillips curve. Here we shall simply record the form in which it shall be employed in subsequent analysis, namely

$$P = \alpha(Y - \overline{Y}) + \pi \tag{2.28}$$

where

$p \equiv \dot{P}/P$ = rate of inflation,

$\overline{Y}$ = natural (full-employment) level of output.

In this equation, the rate of inflation depends of part upon the deviation of output from its full-employment level. It also adjusts fully for increases in the expected rate of inflation, reflecting the absence of money illusion in the adjustment of prices.

Equation (2.28) represents a standard specification of the Phillips curve in the literature. Its derivation as a reduced form for the wage-price sector and some of the policy implications are reviewed in our earlier work.

Equations (2.15), (2.18), and (2.28) make up what is frequently called an *IS-LM*-Phillips curve macroeconomic system, and jointly determine the short-run equilibrium value of output, the rate of interest, and the rate of inflation for given values of the price level, the expected rate of inflation, and stocks of financial assets. The effects of policy changes, as well as changes in inflationary expectations, are discussed at length in Turnovsky (1977, Chapter 6), and some of these are reviewed for the dynamic model developed in Section 2.9.

2.7   Dynamics of Asset Accumulation

The elements of the model so far discussed are essentially static. Yet any macroeconomic system is intrinsically dynamic. Some agents in the economy (firms and the government) create securities to finance their activities, while other groups (households) absorb these securities in the process of saving. These relationships necessarily impose a dynamic structure on the macroeconomic system.

We begin with the government budget constraint. Assuming for simplicity $P_b = 1$, this is expressed in nominal terms by

$$\dot{M} + \dot{B} = P[G - T] + rB. \tag{2.29}$$

The right-hand side of this equation defines the government deficit in nominal terms. This equals the nominal value of government expenditures on goods and services, plus the nominal value of interest payments on outstanding government bonds, less revenue raised by taxes. This deficit is financed either by issuing additional money, by selling more bonds, by some combination of the two.

The choice of financial mix (bond versus money financing) is a policy decision that has an important bearing on the dynamic evolution of the economy. Starting with early work by Ott and Ott (1965) and by Christ

(1967, 1968), this has been analyzed by many authors, including Blinder and Solow (1973) and subsequent writers. While the initial work in effect appended the government budget constraint (2.29) to the *IS-LM* fixed-price model, subsequent analysis was considerably more sophisticated. Much of this literature is summarized in Turnovsky (1977, Chapters 4, 7, 8).

The model to be analyzed in the latter sections of this chapter is characterized by having a steady rate of inflation, rather than a constant price level. For such a system it is convenient to specify the government budget constraint in real terms. To do this, define the real stocks of money and bonds

$$m \equiv \frac{M}{P}; \qquad b \equiv \frac{B}{P}.$$

Differentiating these quantities with respect to time yields

$$\dot{m} = \frac{\dot{M}}{P} - pm; \qquad \dot{b} = \frac{\dot{B}}{P} - pb,$$

and substituting into (2.29), the government budget constraint may be rewritten as

$$\dot{m} + \dot{b} = G - T + rb - p(m + b). \tag{2.30}$$

Writing it in this way, we see that $-p(m + b)$ serves as a source of real revenue to the government. It is the inflation tax on the forms of government debt that are denominated in nominal terms. The right-hand side of (2.30) therefore measures the real government deficit, and the left-hand side specifies the changes in the real stocks of money and bonds necessary to finance it.

The other key source of asset accumulation is investment. This is described by the relationship

$$\dot{K} = I. \tag{2.31}$$

However, most traditional short-run macro models do not incorporate the role of capital accumulation into their macrodynamic analysis, arguing that it involves a longer-run order of dynamics than does the financing of the deficit. They focus on the demand side of investment but do not take account of the effects of the investment on the stock of capital in the economy and its productive capacity. This aspect has traditionally been left to the study of growth theory, although over time the growth of capital has become an integral part of macrodynamics as well. It will be a cornerstone of the dynamic models to be developed in Parts III and IV.

To this point our specification does not distinguish between physical capital and the underlying financial claims on it. For many purposes this is not a serious issue. However, the distinction becomes more important when one specifies the corporate sector in greater detail as is done is Chapters 10 and 11.

2.8   Expectations

The final component of the macroeconomic model concerns the formation of expectations, and in particular, inflationary expectations. Traditionally in both macroeconomics and other branches of theory, expectations were typically hypothesized to be generated autoregressively; that is, they were postulated to depend upon past values of the variable being forecast. A variety of such schemes can be found in the literature, the most famous being the so-called adaptive expectations hypothesis; see Nerlove (1958). As applied to inflationary expectations, it can be specified using continuous time by

$$\dot{\pi} = \gamma(p - \pi) \qquad \gamma > 0. \tag{2.32}$$

That is, the rate at which the forecast is revised at any point in time is proportional to the forecast error currently being committed. If the agent's current or most recent forecast of the inflation rate underpredicts the corresponding actual inflation rate, the forecast is revised upward and vice versa. Solving (2.32), the current forecast can be expressed as an exponentially declining weighted average of the past rates of inflation. The key feature of this and other autoregressive forecasting procedures is that they are entirely backward looking; they are formed by looking at the past evolution of the relevant variable.

Since the mid-1970s, the rational expectations hypothesis (REH) has come to dominate macroeconomic theory. This theory, due originally to Muth (1961), is very simple and was developed at least in part in response to shortcomings that had been shown to be associated with autoregressive hypotheses. Most notable among these was that they involve systematic errors in forecasting the future. By contrast, the REH assumes that individuals do not make systematic errors in forecasting the future. Or, expressed in another way, it asserts that, on average, forecasters are correct. This is not to say that forecasters are always correct, for obviously they are not. Rather, the hypothesis means that the forecasting errors can be treated as purely random fluctuations, having no systematic component. As we will see, the implications of this seemingly innocuous assumption for macroeconomic theory and policy are of fundamental importance. The rational expectations methodology has had a profound effect on the development of macroeconomic theory and the analysis of macroeconomic policy.

There are many aspects to the rational expectations discussion, and these will be explored in Part II. By hypothesizing that expectations are, on average, correct, the REH ensures that expectations are formed consistently with the economist's modeling of the economy. As a consequence, they become simultaneously determined, along with the other endogenous variables, as part of the model, rather than being treated as a predetermined input, as in the traditional autoregressive approach.

Formally, in a nonstochastic macroeconomic model such as that described here, the rational forecast of the rate of inflation is

$$\pi = p.$$

It is sometimes thought that rational expectations can be obtained by simply letting $\gamma \to \infty$ in (2.32). While in a purely formal sense this may be true, this view misses the most crucial aspect of rational expectations models. Setting $\pi = p$ typically leads to dynamic models generating *unstable* dynamic behavior in the usual sense of having eigenvalues with positive real parts. The derivation of bounded solutions in these circumstances is achieved by solving such solutions forward, rather than backward as in traditional dynamic models, and allowing the price level to undergo an initial discrete jump. As a consequence, expectations become genuinely forward looking instead of being tied to the past as with adaptive expectations. The anticipation or announcement that some change will occur at some point in the future gives rise to immediate effects on the economy, before the anticipated event actually takes place. These anticipation effects can never arise in adaptive expectations models, given their undying assumption that the evolution of expectations is determined by the past. These issues will be explored in detail in subsequent chapters.

2.9   A Complete Dynamic Macro Model

We are now ready to combine the elements introduced in the previous sections to construct an initial dynamic macroeconomic model. The economy we shall consider is one in which the short-run equilibrium values of output, the interest rate, and the rate of inflation are determined jointly by the *IS-LM*-Phillips curve system. These solutions are obtained in terms of the expected rate of inflation and the stocks of financial assets, all of which evolve gradually over time. Inflationary expectations are assumed to be formed adaptively, whereas the accumulation of financial assets occurs as a result of the financing of the government budget deficit. We shall also abstract from the accumulation of capital, so that the dynamics is decidedly short run. The long run is characterized by a steady rate of inflation, so that steady-state equilibrium is one in which nominal quantities all grow at a constant (steady) rate, but real quantities are fixed. As a steady state, this is probably of greater practical relevance than the more familiar equilibrium where nominal as well as real quantities are assumed to be constant. This type of equilibrium was characteristic of much of the macrodynamic and monetary growth literature of the 1970s.[9]

The formal model is described by the following set of equations:

$$Y = D(Y^D, r - \pi, A) + G \qquad 0 < D_1 < 1, D_2 < 0, D_3 > 0 \tag{2.33a}$$

$$Y^D = Y - T + rb - \pi A \tag{2.33b}$$

$$A = m + b \qquad \text{Financial wealth} \tag{2.33c}$$

$$m = L(Y, r, A) \qquad L_1 > 0, L_2 < 0, 0 \le L_3 \le 1 \tag{2.33d}$$

$$p = \alpha(Y - \overline{Y}) + \pi \qquad \alpha > 0 \tag{2.33e}$$

$$\dot{\pi} = \gamma(p - \pi) \qquad \gamma > 0 \qquad \wedge \in \mathsf{H} \tag{2.34a}$$

$$\dot{A} = \dot{m} + \dot{b} = G - T + rb - p(m + b) \qquad \text{Gov't budget constraint} \tag{2.34b}$$

where all variables are as defined previously. (Note that r denotes the nominal rate of interest, and real taxes, T, are assumed to be exogenous.)

Since the model does not incorporate the process of capital accumulation, we do not distinguish between private consumption and investment. Rather, these are aggregated together into real private expenditure, denoted by D. Equation (2.33a) is the product market equilibrium condition, (2.15), in which private demand increases with real private disposable income and real wealth, and decreases with the real rate of interest. Equation (2.33b), the analogue to (2.10), defines real private disposable income to be real factor income, plus interest income on government bonds, less expected capital losses on financial wealth (the expected inflation tax on wealth) and exogenous real taxes. Our treatment of taxes as exogenous is purely for convenience; nothing of substance is added by allowing taxes to vary endogenously with income. This is in contrast to the basic Christ (1968) model where the endogenous adjustment of taxes is the crucial stabilizing element in the dynamic adjustment.[10] As we shall see below, in the present model this role is taken over by the inflation tax on wealth.

From (2.33b) and the definition of D it is seen that an increase in $r(\pi)$ will have both a positive (negative) income effect and a negative (positive) substitution effect. Assuming that the substitution effect dominates in each case, we impose the restrictions

$$D_r = D_1 b + D_2 < 0, \tag{2.35a}$$

$$D_\pi = -D_1 A - D_2 > 0. \tag{2.35b}$$

Likewise an increase in A will have an income effect and a wealth effect. The sign of the income effect will depend upon the form in which the additional wealth occurs. If it is in the form of real bonds (as in [2.36a]), and assuming that the real interest rate is positive,[11] the income effect will be $(r - \pi)D_1 > 0$, in which case the total effect of an increase in A is given by

$$D_A = D_3 + (r - \pi)D_1 > 0. \tag{2.35c}$$

If it is in the form of real money (as in [2.36c]), the income effect will be $-\pi D_1 < 0$ and will be offsetting. Assuming in this case that the positive wealth effect dominates, we impose the restriction

$$D_A' = D_3 - \pi D_1 > 0.$$

Financial wealth is defined by (2.33c) to consist of the stock of money plus government bonds outstanding and is the analogue to (2.16d). Because of the stock constraint, only one financial market need be considered, and as usual we focus our attention on the money market. Equilibrium in this market is described by (2.33d), where the demand for real money balances is as specified in (2.18). Equation (2.33e) is the expectations-augmented Phillips curve (2.28).

These five equations make up an instantaneous set of relationships, in which the five variables, Y, Y^D, r, p, and m or b (depending upon the government financing policy), are determined instantaneously in terms of the predetermined values of π, A, b or m, and other exogenous factors. It is just the conventional IS-LM model, augmented by the inclusion of the Phillips curve.

The dynamics of the system are described by equations (2.34). The first of these describes the evolution of inflationary expectations, which are assumed to follow a conventional adaptive process, precisely as in (2.32). The second is the government budget constraint (2.30), expressed in real terms with rb being the interest payments on the outstanding government debt and $-p(m + b)$ describing the "inflation tax" on government debt. By virtue of (2.33c) this relationship also describes the rate of wealth accumulation by the private sector.

To close the model, government policy must be specified, and its budget constraint imposes a restriction on the policy choices open to the government. Of the four policy instruments—debt, money, taxes, and government expenditure—only three can be chosen independently. We have chosen to set the fiscal instruments G and T exogenously, so the remaining decision concerns the mix between bond and money financing of the deficit.

In an inflationary environment such as that being considered in this model, it is necessary to choose an appropriate benchmark policy against which to measure some policy change. The traditional static macroeconomic model typically describes monetary policies in terms of the *nominal* money stock. A passive policy is defined (usually only implicitly) as one in which the nominal quantity remains fixed. An expansionary (contractionary) policy is then defined by an increase (decrease) in this nominal quantity.

But what is a reasonable notion of a passive policy in an inflationary environment? With rising prices, a policy of pegging the nominal money stock means that the real stock is being contracted, and this does not seem an appropriate benchmark policy. In fact, in an inflationary context, two alternative definitions of a passive monetary policy suggest themselves:

(i)   holding the *real* stock of money constant;

(ii) allowing the *nominal* stock of money to grow at a constant rate.

The corresponding expansionary monetary policies are then identified as an increase in the real stock of money, and an increase in the rate of nominal monetary growth, respectively.

Both of these definitions have been adopted throughout the literature. The first is perhaps the most direct inflationary analogue to the conventional definition and is used explicitly by Turnovsky (1977) as well as being implicit in some of Friedman's (1968) arguments. Despite the fact that this policy is specified in real terms, this is not to deny that the policy instruments available to the monetary authorities are nominal magnitudes. Indeed, underlying it is the notion of an "accommodating" monetary policy, in which the authorities increase the nominal money supply so as to meet the nominal transactions needs, which at each level of real income will be growing at the rate of inflation.[12] This policy is also adopted by Sargent and Wallace (1973a) and by Sargent (1977), who motivate it with the idea that in seeking to maintain its real expenditures, the government will respond to a decline in the real purchasing power of money by increasing the rate at which it is adding to the nominal stock.

The second specification is the prevalent one in the monetary growth literature (see, e.g., Sidrauski 1967a, 1967b; Tobin 1968; Dornbusch and Frenkel 1973). This approach yields an equilibrium in which the rate of inflation is equal to (determined by) the exogenously chosen rate of monetary expansion.[13] As we shall demonstrate in Sections 2.10 and 2.11, these two alternative specifications differ from one another both in terms of their dynamic properties and in terms of some of their implications for steady-state policy changes.

An active monetary policy conducted via an open market operation involves an exchange of money for bonds (or vice versa) by the monetary authorities. Hence a natural alternative definition of a passive monetary policy in the traditional fixed-price macroeconomic model is in terms of a constant nominal stock of government bonds. The analogous extension of this to an inflationary context is to define a passive monetary policy as one that holds the *real* stock of these bonds constant, and to specify an expansionary policy by a decrease in this real stock. This policy is also considered and shown to be generally more stable than either of the other two.

These three forms of monetary policy may be formally expressed as follows:

(i)   maintaining the real stock of money constant

$$m = \bar{m} \qquad \bar{m} \text{ constant};$$ (2.36a)

(ii)   maintaining a constant rate of nominal monetary growth

$$\dot{M} = \mu M \qquad \mu \text{ constant},$$ (2.36b)

which in terms of the *real* stock of money m can be expressed as

$$\dot{m} = (\mu - p)m;$$ (2.36b′)

(iii) maintaining a fixed real stock of government bonds

$$b = \bar{b} \qquad \bar{b} \text{ constant}.$$ (2.36c)

Observe that policy (i) can also be expressed in terms of the nominal money supply M by

$$M(t) = \bar{m}P(t)$$ (2.36a′)

so that the nominal money supply is proportional to the price level (which itself is endogenously determined by integrating the solution for $p = \dot{P}/P$). Similarly, policy (iii) can be expressed in terms of the nominal stock of bonds B by

$$B(t) = \bar{b}P(t).$$ (2.36c′)

Using the fact that for a given deficit, an increase in B must be accompanied by a reduction in M, it follows that an increase in $\bar{b}$ must result at least instantaneously in a reduction in M. Thus it is clear that an increase in $\bar{m}, \mu$, and a reduction in $\bar{b}$, all represent expansionary monetary policies in the sense of yielding a higher stock of nominal money balances at least in the very short run, although the precise changes in M will differ in the three cases.[14]

2.10   Fixed Real Stock of Money Policy

Consider the first form of passive monetary policy, specified by $m = \bar{m}$. In this case, by substitution the system reduces to

$$Y = D(Y - T + r(A - \bar{m}) - \pi A, r - \pi, A) + G \tag{2.37a}$$

$$\bar{m} = L(Y, r, A) \tag{2.37b}$$

$$p = \alpha(Y - \bar{Y}) + \pi \tag{2.37c}$$

$$\dot{\pi} = \gamma(p - \pi) \tag{2.38a}$$

$$\dot{A} = G - T + r(A - \bar{m}) - pA \tag{2.38b}$$

with the endogenous adjustment of bonds being determined residually from (2.33c). Since in this policy the real stock of money is held constant and the accumulation of real wealth takes the form of real bonds, it is natural to refer to the government deficit as *bond-financed*.

The three equations (2.37a), (2.37b), and (2.37c) determine the instantaneous equilibrium for Y, p, and r in terms of $G, \bar{m}, \pi$, and A. The impact effects of changes in these exogenous or predetermined variables on the instantaneous (short-run) equilibrium are given in Table 2.1A. First, we see that a bond-financed increase in government expenditure will instantaneously raise the level of income, the rate of inflation, and the nominal and real rates of interest. Second, an expansionary monetary policy will reduce the rate of interest (both nominal and real). As a consequence, its effect on the level of income and the rate of inflation becomes indeterminate. The conventional expansionary and inflationary impact is offset, at least in part, by a contractionary and deflationary effect arising from the reduction in interest payments stemming from the fall in r. Presumably, though, one would expect the conventional effects to dominate. Third, an instantaneous increase in the anticipated rate of inflation will also increase income, causing a more than proportionate increase in the actual rate of inflation. The nominal interest rate will rise, but less than proportionately, causing a fall in the real rate of interest. All of these effects

Table 2.1
Fixed real stock of money policy

A. Impact effects of changes

	G	$\bar{m}$	π	A
Output Y:	$-\dfrac{L_2}{J_2} > 0$	$\dfrac{(L_2 D_1 r - D_r)}{J_2}$	$-\dfrac{D_\pi L_2}{J_2} > 0$	$\dfrac{-L_2 D_A + D_r L_3}{J_2}$
Inflation rate p:	$\dfrac{\alpha L_2}{J_2} > 0$	$\dfrac{\alpha(L_2 D_1 r - D_r)}{J_2}$	$1 - \dfrac{\alpha D_\pi L_2}{J_2} > 1$	$\dfrac{\alpha(-L_2 D_A + D_r L_3)}{J_2}$
Nominal interest rate r:	$\dfrac{L_1}{J_2} > 0$	$\dfrac{-(1-D_1) - L_1 D_r}{J_2} < 0$	$\dfrac{D_\pi L_1}{J_2} > 0$	$\dfrac{L_3(1-D_1) + D_A L_1}{J_2} > 0$
Real interest rate $r_b \equiv r - p$:	$\dfrac{L_1}{J_2} > 0$	$\dfrac{-(1-D_1) - L_1 D_r}{J_2} < 0$	$\dfrac{L_2(1-D_1) - L_1 D_1 \bar{m}}{J_2} < 0$	$\dfrac{L_3(1-D_1) + D_A L_1}{J_2} > 0$

$$J_2 \equiv -L_2(1-D_1) - L_1 D_r > 0$$

B. Steady-state effects of changes

	G	$\bar{m}$
Nominal interest rate r:	$\dfrac{L_3[D_2 - (1-D_1)A]}{J_0} < 0$	$\dfrac{[D_2(r-p) - D_2 L_3 r - D_3 A]}{J_0}$
Inflation rate p:	$\dfrac{\{L_3[D_2 - (1-D_1)b] + L_2[(1-D_1)(r-p) - D_3]\}}{J_0}$	$\dfrac{[D_2(r-p) - D_2 L_3 r + D_3(L_2 r - b)]}{J_0}$
Real interest rate $r_b \equiv r - p$:	$\dfrac{\{-[L_3\bar{m} + L_2(r-p)](1-D_1) + L_2 D_3\}}{J_0}$	$-\dfrac{D_3 \bar{m}(1+e)}{J_0}$
Wealth A:	$\dfrac{L_2[(1-D_1)A - D_2]}{J_0} < 0$	$\dfrac{D_2 \bar{m}(1+e)}{J_0}$

$$J_0 = (r-p)L_2 D_2 + \bar{m} L_3 D_2 - L_2 D_3 A \quad (> 0 \text{ for stability})$$

$$e \equiv L_2 r/m$$

have been discussed at length elsewhere (see, e.g., Turnovsky 1977) and need not be dwelled upon further here. Finally, although an instantaneous increase in wealth leads to an unambiguous increase in the interest rate, its effect on income and the rate of inflation is indeterminate. This is because the wealth effect in private expenditure is expansionary, whereas the wealth effect in the demand for money is contractionary.

The linearized dynamics for this policy are described as follows:

$$\begin{pmatrix} \dot{\pi} \\ \dot{A} \end{pmatrix} = \begin{pmatrix} \gamma(\partial p/\partial \pi - 1)\frac{\partial \pi}{\partial m} & \gamma\,\partial p/\partial A \\ A(\partial r/\partial \pi - \partial p/\partial \pi) & (r - p) + A(\partial r/\partial A - \partial p/\partial A) \end{pmatrix} \begin{pmatrix} \pi - \tilde{\pi} \\ A - \tilde{A} \end{pmatrix}$$

$$(2.39)$$

where the partial derivatives appearing in (2.39) are obtained from the short-run effects summarized in Table 2.1A. The formal conditions for local stability are obtained by imposing the condition that the two eigenvalues of the matrix appearing in (2.39) have negative real parts.[15] By examining the characteristic equation to this equation, this policy can be seen to be potentially highly unstable. Indeed, the existence of a positive wealth effect in private expenditure becomes *necessary* for stability, while the existence of a positive wealth effect in the demand for money provides a destabilizing influence.

Rather than dwell on formal stability conditions, which are not so illuminating, our discussion of stability will be carried out at a more intuitive level. To facilitate this, we assume that the system is initially in a steady-state equilibrium where $\dot{A} = \dot{\pi} = 0$, which is disturbed by, say, an exogenous increase in government expenditure G. The immediate effect of this is to increase $Y, r,$ and p and to create a budget deficit. The financing of this deficit leads to an increase in real private wealth A, while the instantaneous increase in the rate of inflation will cause inflationary expectations to be revised upward. These induced increases in A and π will have further effects on the system. Because of the fact that a given increase in π leads to a more than proportionate increase in p (see Table 2.1A), there will be a tendency for π to increase further, thereby introducing an immediate destabilizing element into the adjustment process. At the same time, the simultaneous increases in A and π will lead to further increases in r, thereby further increasing the interest payments on government debt and creating a larger deficit. Furthermore, if $D_A = 0$, the effect of the increase in A is to reduce p, thereby reducing the inflation tax on wealth, which is the critical stabilizing influence. If this is so, the system is unambiguously unstable. On the other hand, if $D_A > 0$, it is possible that $\partial p/\partial A > 0$, in which case the inflation tax may be sufficiently strong to offset the other destabilizing influences in the system.

The potential instability of the present policy should not be surprising in the light of previous studies that have demontrated the likely instability of bond-financed government deficits; see, e.g., Blinder and Solow (1973), Scarth (1976), and Turnovsky (1977). As in these earlier works, one critical destabilizing element is the interest payments on government bonds, which continually must be financed. In addition, the present model assumes an expectations coefficient of unity in the Phillips curve, and this provides a second important source of instability. But provided α, D_A are sufficiently large, stability is certainly possible, and on the assumption that this is the case, we proceed to the steady state.

From the stationary solutions to (2.38a) and (2.38b), steady-state equilibrium requires that

$$p = \pi, \tag{2.40a}$$

$$G - T + r(A - \overline{m}) = pA. \tag{2.40b}$$

That is, inflationary expectations must be realized, and the inflation tax generated on financial wealth must be sufficient to finance the (exogenous) real current net expenditure $G - T$, plus the interest owing on the outstanding debt. Steady-state disposable income Y^D becomes simply $\overline{Y} - G$, that is, total output less government expenditure. Substituting these conditions into (2.37a), (2.37b), and (2.38b) yields the equilibrium set of relationships

$$\overline{Y} - D(\overline{Y} - G, r - p, A) - G = 0 \tag{2.41a}$$

$$\overline{m} - L(\overline{Y}, r, A) = 0 \tag{2.41b}$$

$$(G - T) + r(A - \overline{m}) - pA = 0. \tag{2.41c}$$

It will be observed that by virtue of the expectations coefficient of unity in the Phillips curve, real output Y is fixed exogenously at its capacity level $\overline{Y}$ and is therefore independent of any government policy variables. And this is true for all forms of neutral monetary policy. These three equations thus determine the solutions for r, p, and A in terms of the exogenously given variables G and $\overline{m}$.

The comparative statics of these steady-state equilibrium relationships are summarized in Table 2.1B. There it is seen that these include some perverse and counterintuitive responses. In effect, these are imposed by the strong restrictions required for stability to prevail.

In particular, an increase in G (bond-financed) will reduce the nominal rate of interest and the real level of private wealth. The economic reasoning behind this latter result can be seen most simply by assuming $L_3 = 0$, when it follows directly from (2.41b) that $\partial r / \partial G = 0$. Taking the differential of the product market equilibrium condition,

$$(1 - D_1)\,dG - D_2\,dp + D_3\,dA = 0 \tag{2.42}$$

it can be seen that an increase in G will result in an increase in total demand of $(1 - D_1)\,dG$. With steady-state output fixed at $\overline{Y}$, product market equilibrium can be maintained only if private demand is correspondingly reduced. This requires either a reduction in the steady-state rate of inflation (thereby raising the real rate of interest), or a reduction in wealth, or perhaps both. Suppose, however, that wealth were actually to increase. In this case a correspondingly larger reduction in inflation would be required. At the same time, government budget balance requires that the additional inflation tax revenue generated must just match the additional government expenditure plus the extra induced interest payments. From the differential of (2.41c), we require

$$dG + (r - p)\,dA - A\,dp = 0. \tag{2.43}$$

Thus, if in response to an increase in government expenditure wealth were to rise and inflation were to fall, we see from (2.43) that it would be impossible to generate sufficient additional tax revenues to restore budget balance. Hence real wealth must in fact *fall*. It then follows from the money market equilibrium condition that if $L_3 > 0$ (but is still sufficiently small for stability to obtain), then A and r must move in the same direction, implying a fall in r as well. Hence, while in the short run an increase in government expenditure will lead to a higher interest rate, this is only temporary; ultimately this movement must be reversed if long-run stability is to prevail.

One consequence of the fall in equilibrium real wealth is that the effect of an increase in government expenditure on the real interest rate, r_b, becomes ambiguous. The reason for this can be seen from (2.41a). On the one hand, an increase in government expenditure raises aggregate demand by $(1 - D_1)$ units. At the same time, by lowering private wealth, it reduces aggregate demand by an amount of $D_3\,\partial A / \partial G$ units. If the former effect dominates, overall aggregate demand is increased, in which case the real interest rate must rise in order for product market equilibrium to be maintained. But if the latter effect dominates, then the real interest rate must fall. The response of the equilibrium rate of inflation is similarly ambiguous, as can be seen from (2.41c). Although an increase in G obviously tends to raise the deficit, the resulting fall in r and A—the latter being equivalent, under bond financing, to a reduction in real bonds—reduces the interest payments component of the government deficit. The response of the inflation rate is then determined by which of these two effects dominates and whether a rise or fall in the inflation tax is required to balance the government budget (in real terms).

An expansionary monetary policy also leads to generally indeterminate effects. Provided the interest elasticity of the demand for money, $e = L_2 r/m$, is less than unity in magnitude, an increase in $\bar{m}$ will yield a reduction in both real wealth and the real rate of interest; in the less likely case where this elasticity exceeds unity, these variables will both increase. It is also seen that the Fisherian proposition—asserting the independence of the real rate of interest from the real money supply— holds if and only if either $D_3 = 0$, in which case the present policy becomes unstable, or $e = -1$. Abstracting again from wealth effects in the demand for money, an increase in $\bar{m}$ is seen to reduce both the nominal rate of interest and the rate of inflation. Although this latter result may seem counterintuitive, the economic reasoning for it can be easily understood by setting $L_3 = 0$ and tracing through the incremental effects of a change in $\bar{m}$ as we did above for G.

The immediate effect of the reduction in r following the expansion in the real money supply is to raise private expenditure demand. With output fixed, this necessitates either a reduction in p or a reduction in A in order for product market equilibrium to be maintained. If in fact p were to increase, a larger reduction in A would be required. In this case it can be shown from the government budget constraint that too much additional inflation tax would be generated to restore budget balance. Hence the equilibrium rate of inflation must fall.

2.11   Constant Rate of Nominal Monetary Growth Policy

Consider now the second passive monetary policy, where the authority allows the nominal money supply to increase at a constant rate. The system is now described by

$$Y = D(Y - T + r(A - m) - \pi A, r - \pi, A) + G \tag{2.44a}$$

$$m = L(Y, r, A) \tag{2.44b}$$

$$p = \alpha(Y - \bar{Y}) + \pi \tag{2.44c}$$

$$\dot{\pi} = \gamma(p - \pi). \tag{2.45a}$$

$$\dot{A} = G - T + r(A - m) - pA \tag{2.45b}$$

$$\dot{m} = (\mu - p)m. \tag{2.45c}$$

As before, the instantaneous equilibrium for Y, p, r is determined for given values of $G, \pi, A,$ and m. The time path of these variables, and hence of the entire system, is then determined by the evolution of inflationary expectations, the accumulation of wealth, and the money supply rule.

The instantaneous multipliers with respect to G, π, A, and m are precisely the same as in Table 2.1A. It therefore follows that the instantaneous impact effects of an increase in the rate of monetary growth μ on the *level* of income, rate of inflation, and nominal rate of interest are all zero. Instead, an increase in μ affects the *rate of change* of these variables. Writing

$$Y = Y(\pi, A, m, G),$$

it follows that for G fixed,

$$\dot{Y} = \frac{\partial Y}{\partial \pi} \dot{\pi} + \frac{\partial Y}{\partial A} \dot{A} + \frac{\partial Y}{\partial m} \dot{m}$$

so that

$$\frac{\partial \dot{Y}}{\partial \mu} = \frac{\partial Y}{\partial m} m, \tag{2.46}$$

which is qualitatively of the same sign as the expressions in Table 2.1A. And the same argument applies with respect to $\dot{p}$ and $\dot{r}$. In essence, these results are reflecting the fact that it takes a finite time for a change in the growth rate of money to affect the level of money and hence these variables.

The dynamics are now a third-order system. While it is straightforward to write down the characteristic equation to this dynamic system and examine its eigenvalues for local stability, the resulting expressions are too complex to enable us to make simple intuitive statements about whether specific influences are stabilizing or not. Many of them have both stabilizing and destabilizing effects. However, overall, it would seem that this policy is likely to be at least as unstable as setting $m = \bar{m}$. The reason is that with the money supply being generated by an exogenous rule, the deficit is essentially bond-financed, and the stability associated with that policy still remains. Likewise, the instability associated with the unit expectations coefficient in the Phillips curve, and noted in connection with the previous policy, is also still present. In addition, to the extent that an increase in the real money stock may cause the current inflation rate to fall, a further destabilizing element is introduced. This is because the rate of real monetary growth $(\mu - p)$ becomes an increasing function of the current real money stock. These conclusions are strongly supported by an exhaustive numerical simulation method investigating the dynamics of these three policies, conducted by Nguyen and Turnovsky (1979).

When stability does prevail, the steady state is characterized by[16]

$$p = \mu = \pi \tag{2.47}$$

so that both the actual and anticipated rates of inflation are tied to the rate of nominal monetary growth. Equilibrium is thus described by

$$\overline{Y} - D(\overline{Y} - G, r - \mu, A) - G = 0 \tag{2.48a}$$

$$m - L(\overline{Y}, r, A) = 0 \tag{2.48b}$$

$$G - T + r(A - m) - \mu A = 0 \tag{2.48c}$$

determining the solutions for r, A, and m in terms of G and μ. Note that in contrast to the short run, the rate of monetary growth *will* have an influence on the equilibrium level of the system.

The equilibrium comparative statics are given in Table 2.2B. With p determined solely by μ, an increase in government expenditure will have no effect on the equilibrium rate of inflation; it will have an indeterminate effect upon r and therefore upon the real interest rate. In contrast to the fixed $\overline{m}$ policy, it will lead to an unambiguous increase in real wealth. As we have seen, an increase in the rate of monetary growth will result in an equal increase in the rate of inflation. Its effects on r, r_b, and A are all ambiguous, but are qualitatively identical to the corresponding effects of an increase in $\overline{m}$. In the latter two cases, the critical element in determining the response is whether or not the interest elasticity of the demand for money exceeds unity.

Table 2.2
Constant rate of nominal monetary growth policy

A.   Impact effects of changes

The impact effects of changes in G, π, A, on Y, p, r, and r_b are as given in Table 2.1A. The instantaneous impacts of a change in the monetary growth rate μ on $\dot{Y}, \dot{p}, \dot{r}$, and $\dot{r}_b$ are the same as those of $\overline{m}$ on Y, p, r, r_b in Table 2.1A.

B.   Steady-state effects of changes

	G	μ
Nominal interest rate r:	$\dfrac{[-(1 - D_1)[r(1 - L_3) - \mu] + D_3]}{H_0}$	$\dfrac{[D_2(r - \mu) - D_2 L_3 r - D_3 A]}{H_0}$
Inflation rate p:	0	1
Real interest rate $r_b \equiv r - p$:	$\dfrac{[-(1 - D_1)[r(1 - L_3) - \mu] + D_3]}{H_0}$	$-\dfrac{D_3 m(1 + e)}{H_0}$
Wealth A:	$\dfrac{[(b - L_2 r)(1 - D_1) - D_2]}{H_0} > 0$	$\dfrac{D_2 m(1 + e)}{H_0}$
	$H_0 \equiv (r - \mu)D_2 + L_2 D_3 r - r D_2 L_3 - b D_3 \quad (> 0 \text{ for stability})$	$e \equiv L_2 r / m$

2.12   Fixed Real Stock of Government Bonds Policy

We turn now to the third form of passive monetary policy, where $b = \bar{b}$, which corresponds to the deficit being *money-financed* in real terms. The system now becomes

$$Y - D(Y - T + r\bar{b} - \pi A, r - \pi, A) + G \tag{2.49a}$$

$$A - \bar{b} = L(Y, r, A) \tag{2.49b}$$

$$p = \alpha(Y - \bar{Y}) + \pi \tag{2.49c}$$

$$\dot{\pi} = \gamma(p - \pi). \tag{2.50a}$$

$$\dot{A} = G - T + r\bar{b} - pA \tag{2.50b}$$

The instantaneous variables Y, p, and r can now be solved at each point in time in terms of G, π, A, and $\bar{b}$. The impact effects of these predetermined variables are given in Table 2.3A. The effects of an increase in G are identical to those given in Table 2.1A. Thus, instantaneously, the manner in which the budget is financed (all bonds or all money) is of no consequence, a point that has been made by Dornbusch (1976b). Likewise the impact effects of an increase in $\bar{b}$ are identical in magnitude, but opposite in sign, to those of an increase in $\bar{m}$. Thus, instantaneously at least, the effects of an expansionary monetary policy, as expressed as an increase in the real stock of money, are identical to those where the policy takes the form of a reduction (of equal magnitude) in the real stock of bonds. The impact effects of an increase in wealth are somewhat different from what they are when $m = \bar{m}$. An increase in A will raise Y and p but will have an ambiguous effect on the nominal rate of interest. The net wealth effect in the money market is now proportional to $(1 - L_3)$ and becomes *inflationary* rather than deflationary. The reason for this can be seen most clearly by considering the case $D_A' = 0$. In this case, an increase in A with b fixed at $\bar{b}$ will create an excess supply of money and will lower the nominal rate of interest. The only way equilibrium in the money market can be restored is if the transactions demand for money is forced up through an increase in income. This in turn means a higher rate of inflation.

This policy is much more stable than either of the two policies we have previously discussed. A large wealth effect in private expenditure and a low wealth effect in the demand for money provide generally, but not unambiguously, stabilizing effects. In any event, no strong restrictions are imposed on the magnitudes of D_3 and L_3, and stability is possible even in the absence of wealth effects.

Table 2.3
Fixed real stock of government bonds policy

A. Impact effects of changes

	G	$\bar{b}$	π	A
Output Y:	As Table 2.1A	$-\partial Y/\partial \bar{m}$ in 2.1A	As Table 2.1A	$\dfrac{[-L_2 D_A' - D_r(1-L_3)]}{J_2} > 0$
Inflation rate p:	As Table 2.1A	$-\partial p/\partial \bar{m}$ in 2.1A	As Table 2.1A	$\dfrac{\alpha[-L_2 D_A' - D_r(1-L_3)]}{J_2} > 0$
Nominal interest rate r:	As Table 2.1A	$-\partial r/\partial \bar{m}$ in 2.1A	As Table 2.1A	$\dfrac{[L_1 D_A - (1-D_1)(1-L_3)]}{J_2}$
Real interest rate $r_b \equiv r - p$:	As Table 2.1A	$-\partial r_b/\partial \bar{m}$ in 2.1A	As Table 2.1A	$\dfrac{[L_1 D_A - (1-D_1)(1-L_3)]}{J_2}$

B. Steady-state effects of changes

	G	$\bar{b}$
Nominal interest rate r:	$\dfrac{(1-L_3)[-D_2+(1-D_1)A]}{F_0} > 0$	$\dfrac{[-D_2(r-p)+D_2 L_3 r+D_3 A]}{F_0}$
Inflation rate p:	$\dfrac{\{(1-L_3)[(1-D_1)\bar{b}-D_2]-L_2[(1-D_1)p+D_3]\}}{F_0} > 0$	$\dfrac{[-D_2(r-p)+D_2 L_3 r-D_3(L_2 r-b)]}{F_0}$
Real interest rate $r_b \equiv r - p$:	$\dfrac{\{(1-D_1)[m(1-L_3)+pL_2)]+L_2 D_3\}}{F_0}$	$\dfrac{D_3 m(1+e)}{F_0}$
Wealth A:	$\dfrac{L_2[(1-D_1)A - D_2]}{F_0} < 0$	$\dfrac{-D_2 m(1+e)}{F_0}$

$$F_0 \equiv pL_2 D_2 - mD_2(1-L_3) - L_2 D_3 A \qquad (> 0 \text{ for stability})$$

$$e \equiv L_2 r/m$$

In order to provide some intuition to these stability conditions, it is again convenient to consider an initial steady-state equilibrium that is disturbed by an increase in G. The immediate effects of this are to raise Y, r, and p, and to create a budget deficit. The financing of this deficit leads to an increase in wealth, while the instantaneous increase in the rate of inflation will cause inflationary expectations to be revised upward. Moreover, the induced increase in π will lead to a more than proportionate increase in p, again introducing a destabilizing element into the dynamics. All this remains unchanged from before. However, the difference lies in the subsequent effects of the increased real wealth, which are now stabilizing. As is seen from Table 2.3A, the higher wealth will increase the rate of inflation, thereby increasing the inflation tax on wealth and providing the critical stabilizing force. Moreover, it is now quite possible for the nominal interest rate to fall, reducing the interest income component of the budget deficit and yielding an additional stabilizing effect. But at the same time stability is still not assured, and the possibility of instability cannot be dismissed.

Steady-state equilibrium is described by

$$\overline{Y} - D(\overline{Y} - G, r - p, A) - G = 0 \tag{2.51a}$$

$$A - \overline{b} - L(\overline{Y}, r, A) = 0 \tag{2.51b}$$

$$G - T + r\overline{b} - pA = 0 \tag{2.51c}$$

with the corresponding multipliers given in Table 2.3B. An increase in government expenditure will have its conventional inflationary effect and will raise the nominal interest rate; it will reduce wealth and have an ambiguous effect on the real rate of interest. The steady-state effects of an expansionary monetary policy, specified by a reduction in $\overline{b}$, are qualitatively identical to (although possibly different in magnitude from) those obtained when the monetary expansion is described by an increase in $\overline{m}$. The comments made previously thus apply here as well.

2.13   Conclusions: Some Methodological Remarks

This chapter has developed a dynamic portfolio balance model and used it to analyze three forms of government deficit financing in an inflationary environment: one in which the real stock of money is held fixed $(m = \overline{m})$; a second in which the rate of nominal monetary growth is held constant $(\dot{M} = \mu M)$; and a third in which the real stock of government bonds is held fixed $(b = \overline{b})$. The corresponding expansionary policies have been defined as increases in the fixed parameters, $\bar{m}$ and μ, and a decrease in $\bar{b}$, respectively. These policies are analyzed within the framework of a relatively simple macroeconomic model in which both the dynamics of wealth accumulation and the evolution of inflationary expectations play central roles.

For all policies, the issue of stability has been discussed, though somewhat informally. At least within the context of this particular model, all three forms of passive monetary policy we consider are potentially unstable. One source of instability is the specification of the Phillips curve. Following the "accelerationist" view, the expectations coefficient is assumed to be unity, and to the extent that an increase in inflationary expectations leads to a short-run increase in output, a destabilizing element is immediately introduced into the system. Stability can prevail only if the other stabilizing influences in the model—particularly the inflation tax on financial wealth—are sufficiently strong to offset this unstable, component of the complete system. Of the policies considered, $m = \bar{m}$ is highly unstable, and indeed a necessary condition for stability is that the wealth effect in private expenditure demand be positive. The policy is therefore definitely unstable in the absence of such wealth effects. The constant rate of nominal monetary growth policy is also highly unstable, and a positive wealth effect in the demand for money becomes necessary for stability. The third policy, the fixed real stock of bonds policy, is the most stable and does not require any wealth effects for stability to prevail. This is because it tends to be the most inflationary policy, generating the greatest inflation tax revenues and thereby providing the strongest stabilizing influence.

Some of the implications of expansionary monetary policies that correspond to the three forms of passive policies introduced can also be contrasted. First, the effects of a monetary expansion specified by an increase in the real stock of money $\bar{m}$ are qualitatively identical, both instantaneously and in the steady state, with those in which it is specified by a fall in the real stock of bonds $\bar{b}$. In the *short run*, an increase in the rates of nominal monetary expansion affects only the *rate of change* of the system, and not its levels. But these effects on the rate of change are also qualitatively identical to those of an increase in $\bar{m}$ (or a fall in $\bar{b}$) on the level. By contrast, the rate of monetary expansion does influence the *steady-state level* of the system. Indeed, an increase in μ has identical effects to the other two policies as far as the steady-state nominal and real rates of interest, and real wealth are concerned. The effects on the steady-state rate of inflation, on the other hand, can be rather different. Whereas an increase in the rate of monetary growth will always lead to an equal rise in the equilibrium rate of inflation, a monetary expansion taking the form of an increase in the real stock will almost certainly lead to a lower rate of inflation.

Finally, we wish to conclude with some general remarks on the methodology employed in this chapter. We have adopted the usual strategy of macroeconomic dynamics of considering an instantaneous (short-run) equilibrium and a steady-state (long-run) equilibrium and used conventional comparative static techniques to analyze the short-run and long-run effects of various policy changes. Also, stability conditions have been analyzed to determine whether or not a system disturbed from an initial equilibrium will in fact converge to a new steady state. Although these procedures have been and in many respects continue to be the standard analytical methods of macroeconomic dynamics, they do have their limitations. First, even in models that are only modestly complex, comparative static effects are often ambiguous, so that the implications of these models may be inconclusive even at a qualitative level. Moreover, even where the responses can be established qualitatively, the formal expressions may give little idea of the magnitudes involved. Second, as we have noted, stability analysis is almost inevitably an intractable exercise. Even when one can write down formal stability conditions, it is often difficult to give them simple intuitive interpretations. Third, unless the model has a particularly simple dynamic structure, these traditional methods may tell relatively little about the time profile of adjustment paths. Indeed, one might argue that the two extreme equilibria usually analyzed are themselves of limited economic interest. The instantaneous equilibrium is too short in that it allows insufficient time for relevant feedbacks to occur; the steady state is too long, in that it takes an infinite time to be reached. Yet it is precisely the nature of the intermediate transition that many people would consider to be of prime interest, and the traditional methods provide little insight into this aspect of the adjustment process.

In view of these considerations, Nguyen and Turnovsky (1979) have studied essentially the model of this chapter, using numerical simulation methods. This involves working with specific functional forms and parameters. By considering a range of values for each parameter, they generate about 120,000 combinations of parameter values. They find that pegging the rate of monetary growth is the least stable policy, yielding stability in only 0.06 percent of the cases. Given the important role this policy has played in monetarist discussions, this numerical finding is of some interest. The policy of pegging the real money supply is also highly unstable. Indeed it is stable for only about 10 percent of the sample set and only when the wealth effect in the demand for money is zero or very small. The policy of pegging the real stock of bonds is by far the most stable, being so for about 96 percent of the cases considered. These numerical results serve to reinforce the qualitative results discussed in this chapter. But at the same time further insight into the nature of the transitional path is provided. For example, their analysis illustrates how the policy of pegging the real money stock involves more oscillations and requires more time to achieve convergence than does the policy of pegging the real stock of bonds. Details such as this are very hard to obtain from a formal analysis of a model even as simple as this one.

Some economists would argue that the entire analysis of stability represented by the approach we have been discussing is misleading. This is because we have considered linearized systems and the associated notion of stability, namely convergence to some steady-state equilibrium point, which is unrealistic. They would argue that, instead, we should consider nonlinear systems and amend the notion of stability to require that the system remain within some bounded region of an equilibrium point, rather than converging to the point itself. This view has been expressed within respect to deterministic systems, such as that developed here, so the issue is not one of stochastic fluctuations. Results from chaos theory have suggested that it is possible to construct plausible deterministic macroeconomic systems that, when linearized, are unstable, but which have higher-order terms that are stable and prevail when the system strays too far from its equilibrium. The behavior of such systems can be shown to include nonlinear stable cyclical motion about steady-state equilibria and to exhibit what Samuelson (1947) called "stability of the second kind."[17] The formal analysis of nonlinear systems is difficult but will surely become more accessible in the future.

Notes

1. See Branson and Klevorick (1969) for some early evidence.

2. Throughout this book, where no ambiguity can arise we shall adopt the convention of letting primes denote total derivatives and denoting partial derivatives by appropriate subscripts. Time derivatives will be denoted by dots above the variable concerned. Thus we shall let

$$f'(x) \equiv \frac{df}{dx}; \quad f_i(x_i, \ldots, x_n) \equiv \frac{\partial f}{\partial x_i}; \quad i = 1, \ldots, n, \quad f_{ij}(x_1, \ldots, x_n) \equiv \frac{\partial^2 f}{\partial x_i \partial x_j} \text{ etc.}, \quad \dot{x} \equiv \frac{dx}{dt}.$$

The application of a bar to a letter is used to denote either a stationary equilibrium value to a dynamic system, or the fact that the variable to which it is applied is fixed exogenously. The intended meaning should be clear from the particular context.

3. The seminal works include Duesenberry (1948), Friedman (1957), and Ando and Modigliani (1963). The formulation (2.9) is closest to the Ando-Modigliani version of the consumption function, although the three approaches have many common elements.

4. The consumer optimality conditions derived in the process of determining the macro-economic equilibrium in the intertemporal optimizing models in Part III essentially define the agent's consumption function. These conditions form the basis for the current empirical research on the consumption function; see, e.g., Hall (1978, 1979).

5. See Jorgenson (1963, 1965).

6. Early models introducing costs of adjustment into investment include Lucas (1967), Gould (1968). Hayashi (1982) related it to the Tobin q.

7. This approach was pioneered by Patinkin (1965).

8. Specifically, the utility function has the property

$$U_1 > 0, \quad U_2 > 0, \quad U_{11} < 0, \quad U_{22} < 0, \quad U_{11}U_{22} - U_{12}^2 > 0.$$

9. See, e.g., Sidrauski (1967a, 1967b), Foley and Sidrauski (1971), Tobin (1968), Dornbusch and Frenkel (1973), Turnovsky (1977).

10. Closely related to this is the well-known Christ proposition, which asserts that, abstracting from interest payments, the steady-state government expenditure multiplier equals the inverse of the marginal tax rate. This stems from the fact that for the system to be in equilibrium, income must adjust so as to generate sufficient tax receipts to balance the budget. The endogeneity of income taxes is obviously a critical part of this process, and indeed with exogenous taxes no steady state would be possible in the Christ system. In the present model, it is inflation tax receipts that adjust endogenously to balance the budget.

11. Throughout this analysis we assume that the rate of inflation and the real rate of interest remain positive. Where necessary, the argument can be easily adapted to accommodate negative values of these variables.

12. See also Tobin (1970), who describes a similar kind of policy as responding to the "needs of trade." It is also similar to the "real bills" regime discussed by Sargent (1977).

13. The special case where this rate is chosen to be zero corresponds to the traditional static definition of a fixed nominal money stock.

14. Foley and Sidrauski (1971) define a passive policy in terms of maintaining a constant ratio of money to total government debt. This policy will be considered in Chapter 15 as the policy specification in a stochastic growth model.

15. We use the term (local) stability in its conventional sense. That is, the system is locally stable if, for sufficiently small displacements from equilibrium, the system will tend to return to equilibrium. This requires that the real parts of all eigenvalues be negative.

16. Note that the conventional specification of a passive monetary policy by a fixed nominal stock of money and obtained by setting $\mu = 0$, implies a zero equilibrium rate of inflation; i.e., a constant equilibrium price level.

17. Samuelson (1947) characterized stability of the second kind to be like that of a pendulum, which swings indefinitely in a bounded arc about some stationary equilibrium point.

II Rational Expectations

3 Rational Expectations: Some Basic Issues

This chapter introduces the rational expectations hypothesis and discusses some basic issues with respect to both its formulation and the solution of macroeconomic models in which it is embodied. The basic hypothesis was originally formulated by Muth (1961) within the context of a discrete-time stochastic model of a commodities market.[1] However, since many dynamic macroeconomic models are formulated using continuous time, the continuous-time analogue is also discussed. The basic solution procedures are illustrated using the familiar Cagan (1956) model of the monetary sector. The model has the advantage of simplicity and makes clear how the rational expectations solution is forward looking, in contrast with the adaptive hypothesis, upon which the original Cagan model was based.

3.1 The Rational Expectations Hypothesis

Formally, the rational expectations hypothesis may be stated as follows:

$$P^*_{t+s,t} = E_t(P_{t+s}) \tag{3.1}$$

where P is the variable being forecast (e.g., the price level),

$P^*_{t+s,t}$ = the prediction of the price level for time $t + s$, formed at time t,

E_t = the statistical expectation conditional on information available at time t, when the forecast is made.

The rational expectations hypothesis (REH) requires that the prediction made by the forecaster be consistent with the prediction generated by the model, conditional on information available at that time. Setting $s = 1$, equation (3.1) implies that

$$P_{t+1} = P^*_{t+1,t} + e_{t+1}. \tag{3.2}$$

This equation asserts that the price fluctuates about its forecast level with a purely random error e_{t+1} that has zero mean. This relationship between the price and its prediction is sometimes said to characterize an efficient market. It means that prices fully reflect available information, thus eliminating any systematic opportunities for making supernormal profits. As an empirical description, this assumption is an appealing one for asset and financial markets, in which information is generally readily available. But it is probably less appealing for forecasts of such quantities as the consumer price index, which are likely to be based on far inferior information. In the remainder of this section we consider some of the theoretical arguments for and against the hypothesis.

One of the most compelling arguments in favor of the REH is the weakness of the alternatives. As already noted, traditional expectations schemes, such as the adaptive hypotheses, involve systematic forecasting errors. This is not particularly desirable, since one would expect individuals to learn this eventually and to abandon such rules or to modify them in some way. By contrast, the REH generates expectations that are self-fulfilling to within a random error, which cannot be predicted on the basis of information available at the date when the expectations are formed. This surely is an appealing notion. But despite this appeal, the REH has been criticized by many authors over the years, although the criticism seems to have become more muted as the hypothesis has gained wider acceptance and understanding. The following objections are among those that have been raised from time to time and should be addressed.

The rational expectations solution of even a relatively simple economic model is usually very complicated to obtain, involving the expectations of the economy over all (an infinite number of) future time periods. A common objection is that the computation of such expectations is simply not feasible for the typical individual, whose expectations the model is attempting to capture. One response to this charge is that it is not necessary for all individuals to perform these calculations. Forecast research institutions using sophisticated models and having the resources to compute these expectations do exist, and their forecasts are disseminated widely to other individuals who lack the necessary resources. Alternatively, the elaborate computations can be viewed as a formalization of forecasting procedures that forecasters approach in a more intuitive way.

Another objection concerns the fact that the application of the REH requires the knowledge not only of the structure of the model but also of all relevant coefficients and parameters. Professional economists typically cannot agree on a model, but even if they do, they usually obtain varying estimates of relevant coefficients. How then can the public, which is presumably less sophisticated in economic theory, but whose expectations we are trying to model, have such information? There is no doubt some merit to this informational argument. The REH must be viewed as a polar case, a situation in which all individuals in the economy agree on the structure and on the relevant parameters. The theory as applied does permit different agents to have different degrees of information. But where information is commonly shared, it is held unanimously. One of the areas of recent and current research is the combination of the REH with a theory of the accumulation of information, so that agents acquire their knowledge of the structure of the economy through some learning process over time. This idea will be discussed briefly in Section 3.7.

The prevailing treatment of rational expectations in the macro literature, however, generally assumes that in effect this knowledge is complete, except for purely random disturbances that can never be learned in advance.[2]

A third limitation of the REH is that it requires all relationships to be linear because it makes extensive use of the application of expectations operators. In a sense this is a technical limitation, similar to the use of linear regression techniques in econometric modeling. The computation of rational expectations equilibria in nonlinear models is extremely difficult, if not impossible, although perhaps it will become more feasible as computing capabilities develop.

In summary, the REH is a polar assumption but one that, by virtue of its simplicity, yields sharp predictions that provide important insights into macroeconomic theory and policy.

3.2   Specification of Expectations in Continuous-Time Models

The relative merits of continuous-time versus discrete-time modeling have been debated over the years. Both approaches are approximations, and as a pragmatic procedure one should use the method that serves one's purpose most satisfactorily. In any event, many dynamic macroeconomic models are formulated using continuous-time modeling, one of whose main advantages is its analytical tractability. In setting up models in this way, it is important to specify precisely the expectations they incorporate and exactly what information they embody. The consistent formulation of expectations in continuous-time systems raises certain technical issues, which are important but nevertheless are of specialized interest. Readers not interested in these technical details can skip the present section without loss of continuity.

A continuous-time model is obtained as the limit of an underlying discrete-time model, as the unit time interval shrinks to zero. In order to derive the continuous time limit of expectations, therefore, we first consider a forecast horizon is of arbitrary, but strictly positive, length—h, say—and then let $h \to 0$. Thus let

$P(t)$ be the actual value of some economic variable, say the price level at time t,

$P^*(t + h, t)$ be the prediction of $P(t + h)$ formed at time t.

We assume initially that $P(t)$ is continuously differentiable with respect to t, thereby ruling out discrete jumps in this variable. We also assume that forecasters have instantaneous access to information on $P(t)$ so that at each point of time they know $P(t)$. Under this condition, any rational forecasting method must satisfy what Turnovsky and Burmeister (1977) called the *weak consistency condition*, that is,

$$(W) \quad P^*(t, t) = P(t) \tag{3.3}$$

That is, with instantaneous information, the expectations formed at time t for the same instant t must equal the actual value prevailing at that time. Without such information (W) need not hold.

Turnovsky and Burmeister (1977) also introduced what they called the *strong consistency axiom*, namely[3]

$$(S) \quad \lim_{h \to 0^+} \left[\frac{P^*(t + h, t) - P(t)}{h} \right] = \lim_{h \to 0^+} \left[\frac{P(t + h, t) - P(t)}{h} \right] = \dot{P}(t). \tag{3.4}$$

It should be noted that the limits appearing in (S) are right-hand or forward-looking limits, that is, they are the limits as $h \to 0$ through positive values. Letting $h \to 0$ and using (W) yields

$$P_1^*(t, t) = \dot{P}(t) \tag{3.5}$$

where $P_1^*(t, t)$ defines the expected rate of change of P at time t. Thus the strong consistency condition (S) asserts that the expected rate of change of P equals the actual rate of change of P. Turnovsky and Burmeister show how under their assumption (S) implies (W), but not the reverse.

The relationship contained in (3.5) is often referred to as *perfect myopic foresight*, in that current changes are predicted precisely and without error. It is distinct from the notion of *perfect foresight*, which is said to prevail when events occurring at finite times in the future are predicted without error. This latter concept is the deterministic analogue to rational expectations and may be formally described by

$$P^*(t + h, t) = P(t + h) \qquad \text{for } h > 0 \tag{3.2'}$$

Gray and Turnovsky (1979a) proceed by generalizing the notion of weak consistency to

$$(GW) \quad P^*(t - h, t) = P(t - h) \qquad \text{for } \bar{h} > h \geq 0. \tag{3.6}$$

This condition states that the economic agent's memory extends at least $\bar{h}$ periods into the past. Asked to recall the current or some previous value of P lying within his memory span, he replies correctly with the actual value for the time in question. The period $\bar{h}$ may be infinite, in which case his memory is infinitely long. But for our purposes any finite $\bar{h}$ will suffice, because we shall be concerned with considering limits as $h \to 0$. (GW) implies (W), but not vice versa. However, the only rationalization for the acceptance of (W) but the rejection of (GW) would appear to be that the agent, having accurately perceived the current value of $P(t)$, immediately forgets it. This seems a little far-fetched.

Another way of expressing the difference between (W) and (GW) is to say that the former merely equips the agent with the knowledge of $P(t)$ at some point t, whereas the latter tells him the shape of the function $P(\cdot)$ in some interval leading up to the point t. The importance of this is that for points lying within this interval, the agent can deduce the rate of change of P from the shape of the $P(\cdot)$ function. More formally,

$$P_1^*(t - h, t) \equiv \lim_{\zeta \to 0} \left[\frac{P^*(t - h + \zeta, t) - P^*(t - h, t)}{\zeta} \right]$$

defines the rate of change of P remembered as t as occurring at time $t - h$. Using (GW) we may write

$$P_1^*(t - h, t) = \lim_{\zeta \to 0} \left[\frac{P(t - h + \zeta, t) - P(t - h, t)}{\zeta} \right] \quad \text{for } \bar{h} > h > 0$$

$$= \dot{P}(t - h) \quad \text{for } \bar{h} > h > 0. \tag{3.7}$$

Since $P(t)$ is differentiable for all t, equation (3.7) immediately implies the existence of the partial derivative P_1^* at the point $(t - h, t)$ for $\bar{h} > h > 0$. But notice that we cannot immediately assert that (3.7) is true at the most recent point of the time interval, that is, for $h = 0$. This is because (GW) does not assert that $P^*(t + \zeta, t) = P(t + \zeta)$ for positive ζ, and this would be required in order to calculate the derivative at that point. However, adopting the usual definition of the left-hand or backward-looking derivative, that is,

$$P_{1-}^*(t - h, t) = \lim_{\zeta \to 0^-} \left[\frac{P^*(t - h + \zeta, t) - P^*(t - h, t)}{\zeta} \right],$$

(GW) does imply

$$P_{1-}^*(t, t) = \dot{P}_-(t)$$

with $\dot{P}_-(t)$ being known as time t, from previously collected information. Moreover, since $P(t)$ is differentiable, we have

$$\dot{P}_-(t) = \dot{P}_+(t) = \dot{P}(t) \tag{3.8}$$

where $\dot{P}_+(t)$ is the right-hand derivative of $P(t)$ and is defined by the limit in (3.4).

Now $P_{1+}^*(t, t)$ is given by

$$P_{1+}^*(t, t) \equiv \lim_{\zeta \to 0^+} \left[\frac{P^*(t + \zeta, t) - P^*(t, t)}{\zeta} \right]$$

and is the agent's prediction of $\dot{P}_+(t)$, the forward-looking rate of change at t. But the essence of the differentiability condition (3.8) is that this is *known* at time t (from $\dot{P}_-(t)$), and assuming that available information is used efficiently for forecasting, we require that

$$P_{1+}^*(t,t) = \dot{P}_+(t) = \dot{P}_-(t) = P(t), \tag{3.9a}$$

implying

$$P_{1+}^*(t,t) = P_{1-}^*(t,t) = P_1^*(t,t). \tag{3.9b}$$

That is, the differentiability of $P(t)$ implies the partial differentiability of $P^*(.,.)$ with respect to its first argument at the point (t,t); furthermore, this partial derivative is equal to the actual derivative of P at time t. Using the definition of $P_{1+}^*(t,t)$ we see that (3.9) contains (S), and hence we have shown that (GW) implies (S). In other words, the assumption of the *differentiability* of $P(t)$ enables the forecaster to transform backward-looking information over an infinitesimally short period to forward-looking information over an infinitesimally short period. Moreover, using (3.9) now enables one to extend (3.7) to include the endpoint $h = 0$,

$$P_1^*(t-h,t) = \dot{P}(t-h) \qquad \text{for } \bar{h} > h \geq 0. \tag{3.10}$$

If there are values of t for which $P(t)$ is nondifferentiable, then at those points (GW) will *not* imply (S). For example, if we allow this function to be continuous with kinks, then at the points where such kinks occur, the left-hand derivative and the right-hand derivative will not be equal. The link between the past and future contained in differentiability and described by (3.9a) breaks down, and the distinction between (W) and (S) stressed by Turnovsky and Burmeister (1977) reemerges. However, if $P(t)$ is the solution of an economic model formulated in terms of differential equations, we would expect $P(t)$ to be differentiable almost everywhere; hence the relationship between (GW) and (S) will hold almost everywhere.[4]

The equivalence of (W) and (S) under (GW) has important implications for the specification of expectations hypotheses in continuous time. Specifically, if one assumes as typically the case (if only implicitly) in specifying continuous-time models that

(i)   forecasters have instantaneous access to relevant information and some ability to store that information; and

(ii) the time path for the variable being forecast is differentiable;

then expectations satisfy perfect myopic foresight

$$P_1^*(t,t) = \dot{P}(t),$$

that is, the forecast formed over an infinitesimally short time horizon is always correct. Thus if, as is also typically the case in continuous-time macroeconomic models, the decision horizon is infinitesimally short and forecasts need be made for only the next instant of time; all forecasting errors are ruled out. This is true for both deterministic and stochastic systems. Moreover, all autoregressive forecasting procedures, such as the adaptive, are redundant; perfect forecasts for the next instant of time can be obtained simply by observing current behavior.

This conclusion can be interpreted as an argument for adopting the continuous-time analogue of rational expectations, namely perfect myopic foresight, when formulating expectations in continuous-time models. For some purposes this is undoubtedly appropriate. But in other circumstances there may be reasons for a different strategy in response to the issues raised. The evolution of expectations is a critical aspect in the modeling of disequilibrium dynamics, the distinguishing features of which are failure of plans to be realized, divergences of prices and other variables from their equilibrium values, and uncertainty about the future. In this situation, the prediction of the future becomes a hazardous exercise during which mistakes are bound to occur. Perfect myopic foresight is not a good characterization of decision makers' behavior here, implying as it does that mistakes are never made. One can abandon continuous-time modeling of disequilibrium situations, but this would be to dispense with the many analytical and other advantages of the model. The problem may be seen as follows. Simple autoregressive schemes may be seen as low-cost expectations formation schemes in situations where decision makers' information is severely limited or unreliable, and their inclusion in disequilibrium models is thus desirable. However, the conventional implementation of such schemes in continuous-time models produces the extreme characteristics we have just described. In order to avoid these difficulties, one must abandon either of the assumptions (i) and (ii) or assume that the forecast horizon remains strictly finite. Some attempts along these lines have been undertaken in the literature and are noted here.

One possibility is to drop the assumption of differentiability. Specifically, one might assume that the relevant variables are generated by nondifferentiable stochastic processes, the best known of which is the Brownian motion or Wiener process. This approach is pursued in the stochastic models developed in Part IV. However, this particular process is characterized by independent increments, so that the best predictor of $P(t + h)$ at time t is simply $P(t)$ adjusted by a possible drift factor. In this case any autoregressive procedure, such as the adaptive hypothesis, would be inappropriate. But there may be other more general nondifferentiable stochastic processes, such as the Ornstein-Uhlenbeck process, for which hypotheses of continuous-time stochastic models involve highly specialized techniques with which many economists are frequently unfamiliar. This may impede lucid exposition and may render the intuitive interpretation of the model very difficult. Moreover, although the introduction of nondifferentiable stochastic processes offers a technical solution to the problem, it may not always be easily motivated in terms of the underlying economic behavior. For example, although the Wiener process is typically justified as an approximation, it is not always clear what is being approximated and how the approximation has been derived.

Other approaches involve either dropping the assumption of the instantaneous availability of information or retaining the assumption of a finite forecast horizon. The effect of either of these is to introduce a delay into the system. As Gray and Turnovsky (1979a) demonstrate, such a delay can arise very naturally in the course of aggregating over individuals who are making decisions over nonsynchronized finite forecast horizons; or it may arise from an information lag reflecting the time taken in collecting such basis statistics as the consumer price index. In either case, a finite lag leading to a mixed differential-difference equation system is generated, raising several important issues for the modeling of continuous-time systems. First, it implies that in many circumstances it will become necessary to model expectations of both the levels and the rate of change of a given variable, and this must be done consistently. Second, where the levels variable being replaced by a predetermined expectation is a price, which previously had performed an equilibrating function in the corresponding market, it may become necessary to abandon the assumption of continuous-time market equilibrium and to introduce instead some appropriate disequilibrium adjustment process. Third, the possibility of forecast error is reintroduced, allowing also for the possible role of arbitrary but simple forecasting procedures.

These issues have been developed at some length by Gray and Turnovsky (1979a), using the Cagan (1956) model as an illustration. The solution methods for mixed differential-difference equations are not easy, and it would take us too far afield to discuss them in detail here. But that approach may see greater use in the future, particularly as computer capabilities increase.

3.3 The Cagan Monetary Model

As a starting point for our discussion of rational expectations, we consider the well-known Cagan model of hyperinflation. This is described by the pair of equations

$$m(t) - p(t) = -\alpha\pi(t) \qquad\qquad (3.11)$$

$$\dot{\pi}(t) = \gamma(\dot{p} - \pi) \qquad\qquad (3.12)$$

where[5]

$m = \ln M$, and M = nominal stock of money;

$p = \ln P$, and P = price level;

π = expected rate of inflation.

The model is a very simple one, in which output and the real interest rate are assumed to remain fixed and wealth effects are ignored. The demand for money is taken to be inversely related to the nominal interest rate, which with a fixed real rate is just the expected rate of inflation. Equation (3.11) describes continuous money market equilibrium, where the expected rate of inflation is specified by the usual form of the adaptive hypothesis.

The logarithmic specification of the model is characteristic of many of the formulations of rational expectations models. It means that changes of corresponding variables are percentage changes, so that $\dot{p}(t)$ in (3.12) represents the rate of inflation $\dot{P}(t)/P(t)$. Also, coefficients of logarithmic variables have simple interpretations as elasticities. Note, however, that since π is measured as a rate, the coefficient

$$\alpha = \frac{(dM/M)}{d\pi}$$

is a *semi*-elasticity of demand, that is, it measures the percentage change in the demand for money per percentage point change in the expected inflation rate.

The pair of equations can be interpreted as a subsystem of the more general model specified in Chapter 2, which allows for changes in income as well as in financial wealth. The critical question concerns the stability of the system described by (3.11) and (3.12).

Differentiating (3.11) with respect to t and assuming that, apart from a possible once-and-for-all increase, the nominal money stock remains constant, yields

$$\dot{p}(t) = \alpha\dot{\pi}(t). \qquad\qquad (3.13)$$

Eliminating $\pi, \dot{\pi}$ between (3.11), (3.12) and (3.13), we obtain the following differential equation in the logarithm of the price level:

$$\dot{p} = \frac{\gamma}{1 - \alpha\gamma}[m - p]. \qquad\qquad (3.14)$$

Suppose that there is now a once-and-for-all rise in the nominal quantity of money m. It is clear from (3.14) that the adjustment of prices will be stable if and only if

$$\alpha\gamma < 1. \tag{3.15}$$

This is the well-known Cagan stability condition. It emphasizes the trade-off between the semi-elasticity of the demand for money with respect to inflationary expectations on the one hand, and the rate of adaptation of inflationary expectations on the other, which is consistent with stability. A highly sensitive demand for money function is compatible with stability only if inflationary expectations adapt sufficiently slowly to past inflation rates.

Letting $\gamma \to \infty$ in (3.12) yields the continuous time limit of rational expectations,

$$\pi(t) = \dot{p}(t), \tag{3.16}$$

where inflationary expectations satisfy perfect myopic foresight. Substituting (3.16) into 3.11), the differential equation for the (logarithm of the) price level is now given by

$$m - p = -\alpha\dot{p}. \tag{3.17}$$

It is clear that the Cagan stability condition (3.15) is violated. The eigenvalue of (3.17) is $\lambda = 1/\alpha > 0$, so that this equation is unstable in the conventional dynamic sense of following an unbounded path from some given initial point.

The reason for this is easily seen if one follows the methods of traditional dynamics and treats the price level as being predetermined, with (3.17) determining the rate of inflation $\dot{p}(t)$. Suppose that the economy is initially in steady state and that there is a once-and-for-all increase in the money supply. With the price level predetermined at p_0, say, the monetary expansion increases the real money stock $m - p_0$. In order for money market equilibrium to be restored, the demand for money must increase, and for this to occur the expected (equal to the current) inflation rate must fall. But as the inflation rate falls, the price level starts to fall, so that with the nominal money stock now fixed, following the initial expansion, the real money stock starts to increase further. Money market equilibrium therefore requires a further increase in the demand for money, which in turn is brought about by a further reduction in the inflation rate. This means that the price level continues to decline (at an increasing rate) generating further increases in the real stock of money $m - p$. This process occurs continuously, and we find that the ever-increasing real stock of money is accompanied by an ever-declining price level. The upshot is that an initial once-and-for-all expansion in the nominal stock of money has generated an infinite deflationary process. This rather bizarre behavior in the economy is simply a manifestation of the instability (in the traditional sense) of the economy as described by (3.17).

3.4   Forward-Looking Solution to the Cagan Model

The key assumption of the solution to the Cagan model outlined in Section 3.3 is that the price level at all points is a continuous function of time. In particular, its initial value is predetermined, being inherited from the past. This represents the traditional approach to solving differential equations, borrowing solution techniques from the physical and engineering sciences. The rationalization here is clear; physical bodies are typically constrained to move continuously from any predetermined state. Although in many cases it is also appropriate to view certain dynamic economic variables as evolving from the past, this is not always the case. Indeed, in Chapter 5, we shall draw the distinction between those variables that are constrained to move continuously—so-called sluggish variables—and those that are free to move discontinuously at appropriate points—so-called jump variables. The classification of economic variables in this way may be somewhat arbitrary and determined by the specific context and market structure. The idea that the price level need not be a sluggish variable was first introduced by Sargent and Wallace (1973b) in a short but powerful paper. They showed that by relaxing the requirement that $P(t)$ be continuous everywhere, the anomalous behavior outlined in the previous section could be resolved.

Outline of General Solution

Consider equation (3.17), which we rewrite in the form

$$\dot{p}(t) - \frac{1}{\alpha}p(t) = -\frac{1}{\alpha}m(t). \tag{3.18}$$

The general solution to this equation is

$$p(t) = Ae^{t/\alpha} - \frac{1}{\alpha}\int_0^t m(s)e^{(t-s)/\alpha}\,ds \tag{3.19}$$

where A is an arbitrary constant. The critical aspect concerns the determination of A. The solution discussed in Section 3.3 assumes that initially $p(0) = p_0$, say, so that setting $t = 0$ in (3.19) implies $A = p_0$. Assuming m to be constant, $m = \bar{m}$, say, this solution is

$$p(t) = \bar{m} + (p_0 - \bar{m})e^{t/\alpha}.$$

So long as $p_0 \neq \bar{m}$, the solution for $p(t)$ given by this equation will diverge.

Sargent and Wallace, on the other hand, proposed instead to allow $p(0)$ to be endogenously determined. Rather than determining A by an initial condition, they determined it by a terminal condition. The terminal condition they imposed is that the price level remain bounded, as $t \to \infty$. There are at least two rationales that may be given for imposing this condition. First, at a somewhat pragmatic level, it seems reasonable to suppose that the kind of time paths for the money supply observed in practice are unlikely to lead to an exploding price level. At least, except in isolated episodes of hyperinflation, we do not observe wildly unstable behavior of prices. Even if we view the world as being characterized by secular inflation, inflation rates tend in the long run to be steady and moderate, not explosive as would be suggested by the solution outlined in Section 3.3.

Second, more formally, the boundedness of the price level can be imposed by appealing to the transversality conditions at infinity derived from optimizing models. Here the general argument runs as follows. Although the model specified in (3.18) is descriptive and is not derived from any underlying optimization, nevertheless we would like it to behave consistently with what would emerge from optimizing behavior. One important element of the intertemporal optimization approach consists of the transversality conditions, which impose conditions on the valuation of assets at the end of the planning horizon, which in turn may be either finite or infinite. In the latter case, this requires the discounted present values of stocks, appropriately valued, to be zero. Under certain conditions, which are usually met, this leads to a bounded price level.

Thus it is now standard procedure in solving rational expectations models such as this to impose boundedness on the solution. While this practice is typically justified in terms of appealing to the transversality conditions, we should also note that there are restrictions on the underlying utility functions, which are required in order to yield a bounded solution. Moreover, it is not necessarily the case that the Cagan model, which is so widely used, is in fact consistent with the required restrictions; see Brock (1977), Kingston (1982). We will discuss the transversality conditions in great detail in Part III, when we develop the intertemporal optimizing model. Here we shall simply impose the condition that the solution for $p(t)$ remains bounded.

Writing (3.19) as

$$p(t) = e^{t/\alpha} \left[A - \frac{1}{\alpha} \int_0^t m(s) e^{-s/\alpha} \, ds \right] \tag{3.20}$$

we see that in order for $p(t)$ to remain bounded as $t \to \infty$, we require

$$A = \frac{1}{\alpha} \lim_{t \to \infty} \int_0^t m(s) e^{-s/\alpha} \, ds = \frac{1}{\alpha} \int_0^\infty m(s) e^{-s/\alpha} \, ds,$$

and substituting this value for A into (3.20) yields the solution

$$p(t) = \frac{1}{\alpha} e^{t/\alpha} \int_t^\infty m(s) e^{-s/\alpha} \, ds \qquad \text{for all} \quad t. \tag{3.21}$$

The crucial thing to observe is that this solution for the current price level is entirely *forward looking*. The price level at any time t depends upon the discounted future values of the money supply from that time on. Implicit in the solution (3.21) is the assumption that economic agents know the time path for the future money supply. The case where this is not necessarily so, but where they have only expectations of the future, will be dealt with in our discrete-time discussion in Section 3.5. However, it is clear by analogy, and in fact can be shown more formally, that in that case the solution would be of the form

$$p(t) = \frac{1}{\alpha} e^{t/\alpha} \int_0^\infty m^*(s, t) e^{-s/\alpha} \, ds \tag{3.21'}$$

where $m^*(s, t)$ is the expectation of the money supply for time s, held at time t. Actual future money supplies are simply replaced by their expectations held at time t.

Returning to (3.21), in order for $p(t)$ to remain bounded, we require

$$\lim_{s \to \infty} m(s) e^{(t-s)\alpha} = 0. \tag{3.22}$$

This imposes an upper bound upon the rate of monetary growth. The condition is obviously met if m is fixed at $m = \bar{m}$, say. If m grows exponentially, so that $m(s) = \bar{m} e^{\mu s}$, then the limit will be met provided $\mu < 1/\alpha$. Note that the constraint translates into a much faster growth rate in the levels of the money supply. But note also that (3.22) is only a necessary, but not a sufficient, condition for $p(t)$ to remain bounded. An example where (3.22) is met but $p(t)$ is ultimately unbounded is given below.

Some Examples of Monetary Disturbances

The solution (3.21) enables us to analyze the effects of a variety of monetary disturbances on the behavior of the price level. Four examples will be discussed.

Unanticipated Permanent Increase in the Money Supply

Consider first the response of the price level following an initially unannounced once-and-for-all increase in the money supply at time 0. By
choice of units the initial and final money stocks are 0 and $\bar{m}$, say, respectively.

Solving (3.21), we obtain

$$p(t) = \frac{1}{\alpha} e^{t/\alpha} \bar{m} \int_t^\infty e^{-s/\alpha} \, ds = \bar{m},$$

and recalling that m and p are measured in logarithms, we see that an
initial once-and-for-all increase in the money supply leads to an immediate proportionate increase in the price level. In other words, the price
level jumps instantaneously to its new steady-state equilibrium level and
there are no transitional dynamics. This is illustrated by a jump from the
point O to P in Figure 3.1. This solution is far more appealing from an
economic viewpoint than the one outlined in the previous section. If
people have rational expectations and know that the initial monetary
expansion will continue indefinitely, then it seems reasonable, in the
absence of any impediments, for the price level to respond fully instantaneously. The key feature of the solution for the price level given in (3.21)
is that it is *forward looking* and therefore embodies knowledge (expectations) of the future path of the money supply.

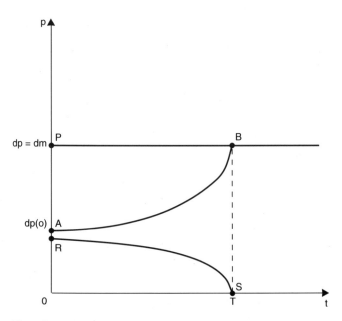

Figure 3.1
Response of price level to alternative monetary expansions

Anticipated Future Permanent Monetary Expansion

As a second example, suppose that at time 0 the monetary authorities announce that the once-and-for-all expansion in the money supply $\bar{m}$ is to take place at time T in the future, so that

$$m(s) = 0 \qquad 0 \le t \le T$$
$$m(s) = \bar{m} \qquad t \ge T. \tag{3.23}$$

Note that because the money supply is assumed to remain unchanged until time $T, m(s)$ is equal to its initial level of zero before then.

Substituting (3.23) into (3.21) and evaluating the integral, we obtain

$$p(t) = \bar{m}e^{(t-T)/\alpha} \qquad 0 \le t \le T$$
$$p(t) = \bar{m} \qquad t \ge T. \tag{3.24}$$

The time path for price movements is also illustrated in Figure 3.1. The adjustment has two phases. First, the announcement of the *future* expansion in the money supply has an immediate effect on the *current* price level. At time 0 it increases by an amount $\bar{m}e^{-T/\alpha}$, which is a dampening down of the ultimate proportionate response by a factor proportional to the lead time T. The farther into the future is the announcement expansion, the smaller is the current response in the price level. This is represented by an initial jump from O to A in Figure 3.1. With the nominal money supply remaining fixed at time 0, the initial increase in the price level represents an initial contraction in the real money supply. In order for money market equilibrium to be maintained, the real demand for money must be reduced, and for this to occur the rate of inflation must rise. This means that prices will continue to rise, thereby further contracting the real money supply. The economy moves along the locus AB until the point B is reached at time T. At that time, the announced monetary expansion eventually takes place, the real money supply is restored to its original level, and the price level ceases to rise. All price adjustment will have been completed by the time the anticipated expansion actually occurs.

Unanticipated Temporary Monetary Expansion

As a third example, suppose that at time 0 the money supply is unexpectedly increased, but once this has occurred, it is known to be only temporary and will cease at time $T > 0$. The time profile for the money supply is now

$$m(s) = \bar{m} \qquad 0 \le t \le T$$
$$m(s) = 0 \qquad t \ge T, \tag{3.25}$$

tion, however, is fixed. But with a steadily increasing nominal stock this is exactly what should obtain.

Two Further Issues

The Sargent and Wallace forward-looking solution is both stable and intuitively attractive. One of its key features is that the solution involves a jump in the price level. In commenting on the paper, Calvo (1977) pointed out the nonuniqueness of the Sargent and Wallace solution in that it does not specify when the jump takes place. Thus, following Calvo's argument, one can show that whereas

$$p(t) = \overline{m} \qquad t \geq 0$$

is one perfect foresight solution for the price level, following an initially unanticipated monetary expansion, the path

$$p(t) = \overline{m} + (p_0 - \overline{m})e^{t/\alpha} \qquad 0 \leq t \leq t_0$$

$$p(t) = \overline{m} \qquad t > t_0,$$

where p_0 is the predetermined price level, is another. In the latter, the price level begins by following the continuous unstable path passing through the predetermined price level, until time t_0, when it undergoes a discrete upward jump to the new equilibrium level $\overline{m}$. Because the world is one of no stochastic shocks and because agents know the future, they foresee perfectly the upward jump in the price level at time t_0. At that time, the rate of return on holding money instantaneously becomes infinitely negative. Agents, knowing this, generate an infinitely negative demand for money, which with a finite money supply is obviously incompatible with money market equilibrium.

The solution that resolves this difficulty is to allow the jumps to occur only at points where new information hits the economy. Jumps in the price level in response to such "news" are not foreseen, so that agents are unable to plan their portfolios in response to them. In the present examples, the new information occurs at time 0, when either a previously unanticipated monetary expansion occurs or it is announced that one will take place at some time in the future. At the time when some previously announced monetary expansion actually takes place, it is not new information, and any jump in the price level at that time would lead to the difficulties just noted. Thus the solution proposed by Sargent and Wallace of allowing the price level to jump at time zero, but requiring it to evolve continuously thereafter, is the natural one.

One final point concerns the instability of the market (3.18) in the sense of its eigenvalue being positive. While rational expectations and

tion, however, is fixed. But with a steadily increasing nominal stock this is exactly what should obtain.

Two Further Issues

The Sargent and Wallace forward-looking solution is both stable and intuitively attractive. One of its key features is that the solution involves a jump in the price level. In commenting on the paper, Calvo (1977) pointed out the nonuniqueness of the Sargent and Wallace solution in that it does not specify when the jump takes place. Thus, following Calvo's argument, one can show that whereas

$$p(t) = \overline{m} \qquad t \geq 0$$

is one perfect foresight solution for the price level, following an initially unanticipated monetary expansion, the path

$$p(t) = \overline{m} + (p_0 - \overline{m})e^{t/\alpha} \qquad 0 \leq t \leq t_0$$

$$p(t) = \overline{m} \qquad t > t_0,$$

where p_0 is the predetermined price level, is another. In the latter, the price level begins by following the continuous unstable path passing through the predetermined price level, until time t_0, when it undergoes a discrete upward jump to the new equilibrium level $\overline{m}$. Because the world is one of no stochastic shocks and because agents know the future, they foresee perfectly the upward jump in the price level at time t_0. At that time, the rate of return on holding money instantaneously becomes infinitely negative. Agents, knowing this, generate an infinitely negative demand for money, which with a finite money supply is obviously incompatible with money market equilibrium.

The solution that resolves this difficulty is to allow the jumps to occur only at points where new information hits the economy. Jumps in the price level in response to such "news" are not foreseen, so that agents are unable to plan their portfolios in response to them. In the present examples, the new information occurs at time 0, when either a previously unanticipated monetary expansion occurs or it is announced that one will take place at some time in the future. At the time when some previously announced monetary expansion actually takes place, it is not new information, and any jump in the price level at that time would lead to the difficulties just noted. Thus the solution proposed by Sargent and Wallace of allowing the price level to jump at time zero, but requiring it to evolve continuously thereafter, is the natural one.

One final point concerns the instability of the market (3.18) in the sense of its eigenvalue being positive. While rational expectations and perfect-foresight models are typically associated with dynamic systems having unstable roots, this need not necessarily be so. Rather, it is the combination of rational expectations *and* continuous market clearance that gives rise to this phenomenon. It is possible to restore stability (in this traditional sense) by coupling the assumption of rational expectations with sluggish adjustment in the money market.

Specifically, let us replace (3.17) with

$$m^d(t) = p(t) - \alpha \dot{p}(t) \tag{3.29a}$$

$$\dot{p}(t) = \theta[m - m^d(t)] \qquad \theta > 0. \tag{3.29b}$$

That is, we postulate a money market equilibrium of the Cagan type, but instead of assuming a continuously clearing money market, we hypothesize gradual adjustment with prices adjusting in response to excess supply. Combining (3.29a) with (3.29b) yields

$$\dot{p}(t) = \frac{\theta}{1 - \theta\alpha}[m - p(t)], \tag{3.29}$$

and this is stable, in the sense of having a negative eigenvalue, if and only if

$$\theta\alpha < 1. \tag{3.30}$$

Thus we see that with gradual adjustment in the money market, a positive eigenvalue is not inevitable. Rather, we get a kind of trade-off between the semi-elasticity of the demand for money α and the rate of price adjustment θ, directly analogous to the Cagan condition (3.15). Finally, we observe that if (3.30) is met, so that the eigenvalue of (3.29') is negative, the rationale for jumps in the price level—which otherwise are required to bring about stability but which nonetheless embody forward-looking behavior—lose some of their force.

3.5   Discrete-Time Cagan Model

We turn now to the discrete-time formulation of the Cagan model, specified by

$$m_t - p_t = -\alpha(p^*_{t+1,t} - p_t). \tag{3.31}$$

where $p^*_{t+1,t} \equiv E_t(p_{t+1})$. In defining the expected rate of inflation over the period $(t, t + 1)$ as in (3.31), we are assuming that the current price level, p_t, is observed at time t. The discrete-time formulation is more convenient than the continuous-time model for incorporating stochastic shocks and for distinguishing between expectations and actual outcomes on the one hand, and permanent and transitory disturbances on the other. The Cagan model, with its simple structure, serves as a useful starting point for illustrating the methods for solving stochastic rational expectations models. Two widely used methods of solution are described. These are referred to as (i) the method of iterated expectations, and (ii) the method of undetermined coefficients.

Method of Iterated Expectations

The essence of the method of iterated expressions is first to solve for the expected price level, $p_{t+1,t}^*$, and then to substitute this solution into (3.31) and solve for the actual price level p_t. To determine $p_{t+1,t}^*$, we begin by taking conditional expectations of (3.31) at time t, for time $t + i$, say. This yields the equation

$$m_{t+i,t}^* - p_{t+i,t}^* = -\alpha(p_{t+i+1,t}^* - p_{t+i,t}^*) \qquad i = 1, 2, \ldots \tag{3.32}$$

where $m_{t+i,t}^*$ is the expected supply of money for time $t + i$, formed at time t. In writing (3.32) we have used the following result on conditional expectations:

$$E_t[E_{t+s}(p_{t+s+1})] = E_t(p_{t+s+1}).$$

Equation (3.32) is a difference equation in price expectations $p_{t+i,t}^*$. Writing it in the form

$$\alpha p_{t+i+1,t}^* - (1 + \alpha)p_{t+i,t}^* = -m_{t+i,t}^*,$$

the general solution for $p_{t+i,t}^*$ is

$$p_{t+i,t}^* = A_t\left(\frac{1+\alpha}{\alpha}\right)^i + \frac{1}{1+\alpha}\sum_{j=0}^{\infty} m_{t+i+j,t}^*\left(\frac{\alpha}{1+\alpha}\right)^j \tag{3.33}$$

where A_t is a constant that may depend upon the time when forecasts are made, t, but which is independent of the forecast horizon, i. Since $(1 + \alpha)/\alpha > 1$, the first term on the right-hand side of (3.33) will diverge unless $A_t = 0$, in which case the solution for price expectations is

$$p_{t+i,t}^* = \frac{1}{1+\alpha}\sum_{j=0}^{\infty} m_{t+i+j,t}^*\left(\frac{\alpha}{1+\alpha}\right)^j. \tag{3.34}$$

Equation (3.34) asserts that the expected price for time $t + i$, formed at time t, equals the discounted sum of all expected future money stocks, starting at time $t + i$ and extending for all periods beyond. This equation is the stochastic analogue to (3.21), given previously for the deterministic continuous-time version. From (3.34) we see that an expected unit increase in the money supply starting at time $t + i + n$ and lasting for k periods beyond will raise the expected price for time $t + i$ by an amount

$$\left(\frac{\alpha}{1+\alpha}\right)^n \left[1 - \left(\frac{\alpha}{1+\alpha}\right)^{k+1}\right].$$

Two special cases are worth noting.

(i)   An expected transitory unit increase in the money supply for time $t + i + n$, say $(k = 0)$, will raise the expected price for time $t + i$ by an amount $\alpha^n/(1 + \alpha)^{n+1}$.

(ii) An expected permanent unit increase in the money supply starting at time $t + i + n$, say $(k \to \infty)$, will raise the expected price for time $t + i$ by an amount $\alpha^n/(1 + \alpha)^n$. If, further, the monetary expansion is expected to begin at time $t + i$ $(j = 0)$, then the expected price at that time is expected to rise proportionately.

Other possible time profiles for expected monetary disturbances can be considered using (3.34), but are not pursued here.

Setting $i = 1$ in (3.34), the solution for the expected price one period ahead is

$$p^*_{t+1,t} = \frac{1}{1+\alpha} \sum_{j=0}^{\infty} m^*_{t+1+j,t} \left(\frac{\alpha}{1+\alpha}\right)^j, \qquad (3.35)$$

and, substituting for $p^*_{t+1,t}$ from (3.35) into (3.31), the solution for the current price level is

$$p_t = \frac{1}{1+\alpha} \left[m_t + \sum_{j=1}^{\infty} m^*_{t+j,t} \left(\frac{\alpha}{1+\alpha}\right)^j\right]. \qquad (3.36)$$

The current price is therefore a weighted average of the current money stock and all expected future money stocks. A number of observations can be made.

(i)   A transitory unit increase in the current money stock (which is not expected to continue) raises the current price level by $1/(1 + \alpha)$.

(ii) An expected unit increase in the money supply starting at time $t + n$ and expected to last k periods raises the current price level by an amount

$$\left(\frac{\alpha}{1+\alpha}\right)^n \left[1 - \left(\frac{\alpha}{1+\alpha}\right)^k\right].$$

(iii) A unit increase in the current money supply that is expected to be permanent raises the current price level proportionately.

Method of Undetermined Coefficients

We now discuss an alternative, more direct procedure for solving (3.31). This involves postulating a form of solution and then determining coefficients to ensure that the hypothesized solution satisfies the equation. This procedure is a standard one in solving differential equations. However, in applying it, care must be taken to ensure that the correct form of solution is proposed. If not, the wrong solution will be obtained! In some cases, the correct form of solution is not always obvious. It is safe practice, when in doubt about the solution, to hypothesize as a general form that one feels is feasibly relevant. Any extraneous elements will drop out of the solution.

To illustrate, suppose that one does not have the benefit of the solution (3.36) and postulates

$$p_t = \sum_{i=0}^{\infty} \mu_i m_{t-i} + \sum_{j=1}^{\infty} \lambda_j m^*_{t+j,t}. \tag{3.37}$$

That is, the current price is assumed to be a linear function of all past money stocks and all expected future money stocks. Writing (3.37) at time $t + 1$,

$$p_{t+1} = \sum_{i=0}^{\infty} \mu_i m_{t+1-i} + \sum_{j=1}^{\infty} \lambda_j m^*_{t+1+j,t+1},$$

and taking conditional expectations of this expression at time t, yields

$$p^*_{t+1,t} = \mu_0 m^*_{t+1,t} + \sum_{i=1}^{\infty} \mu_i m_{t+1-i} + \sum_{j=1}^{\infty} \lambda_j m^*_{t+1+j,t}. \tag{3.38}$$

In forming the conditional expectation in (3.38) we are assuming that the current money stock m_t is observed instantaneously at time t, and all past money stocks are known (or recalled) at time t, so that $m^*_{t,t} = m_t$, $m^*_{t-i,t} = m_{t-i}$. This is just the assumption of a memory, discussed earlier. Writing (3.31) as

$$\alpha p^*_{t+1,t} - (1 + \alpha)p_t + m_t = 0 \tag{3.31'}$$

and substituting for (3.37), (3.38) we obtain

$$\alpha \mu_0 m^*_{t+1,t} + \alpha \sum_{i=1}^{\infty} \mu_i m_{t+1-i} + \alpha \sum_{j=1}^{\infty} \lambda_j m^*_{t+1+j,t}$$

$$- (1 + \alpha) \sum_{i=0}^{\infty} \mu_i m_{t-i} - (1 + \alpha) \sum_{j=1}^{\infty} \lambda_j m^*_{t+j,t} + m_t = 0.$$

In order for (3.37) to be a solution, this must be an identity in m_t, m_{t-i}, $m^*_{t+j,t}$ and the corresponding coefficients must be zero. Setting the coefficient of m_t to zero yields

$$\alpha\mu_1 - (1 + \alpha)\mu_0 + 1 = 0, \tag{3.39a}$$

and setting coefficients of lagged money stocks m_{t-i} to zero yields the set of relationships

$$\mu_i = \left(\frac{1 + \alpha}{\alpha}\right)^{i-1} \mu_1 \qquad i = 2, 3, \dots . \tag{3.39b}$$

Likewise setting the coefficients $m^*_{t+i,t}$ to zero, we obtain

$$\alpha\mu_0 - (1 + \alpha)\lambda_1 = 0, \tag{3.40a}$$

$$\lambda_j = \left(\frac{\alpha}{1 + \alpha}\right)^{j-1} \lambda_1 \qquad j = 2, 3, \dots . \tag{3.40b}$$

Thus from (3.39) and (3.40), the solution for p_t may be written as

$$p_t = \mu_0 m_t + \mu_1 \sum_{i=1}^{\infty} m_{t-i}\left(\frac{1 + \alpha}{\alpha}\right)^{i-1} + \lambda_1 \sum_{j=1}^{\infty} m^*_{t+j,t}\left(\frac{\alpha}{1 + \alpha}\right)^{j-1}$$

where μ_0, μ_1, λ_1 satisfy (3.39a), (3.40a). Since $(1 + \alpha)/\alpha > 1$, p_t is a geometrically increasing function of past money stocks m_{t-i}. This implies that unless $\mu_1 = 0$, the current price level is ultimately unbounded. Thus imposing boundedness and setting $\mu_1 = 0$, we find further from (3.39a), (3.40a) that

$$\mu_0 = \frac{1}{1 + \alpha}; \qquad \lambda_1 = \frac{\alpha}{(1 + \alpha)^2}$$

so that

$$p_t = \frac{1}{1 + \alpha}\left[m_t + \sum_{j=1}^{\infty} m^*_{t+j,t}\left(\frac{\alpha}{1 + \alpha}\right)^j\right]. \tag{3.36}$$

Thus the previous solution for p_t, given by (3.36), is again obtained. The two solution procedures are therefore completely consistent.

3.6 Bubbles

The stochastic difference equation (3.31) describing the discrete-time Cagan model is of the generic form

$$y_t = aE_t(y_{t+1}) + bx_t \equiv ay^*_{t+1,t} + bx_t \tag{3.41}$$

with $a = \alpha/(1 + \alpha)$, $b = 1/(1 + \alpha)$. This type of equation arises in other contexts as well, such as in asset pricing. This section briefly discusses this equation further. A more comprehensive treatment of this and of the topic of bubbles in general is provided by Blanchard and Fischer (1989, chapter 5). Suppose initially $|a| < 1$ as in the Cagan model. Solving this equation recursively up until time T leads to the solution

$$y_t = b \sum_{i=0}^{T} a^i x^*_{t+i,t} + a^{T+1} y^*_{t+T+1,t}.$$

Provided $\lim_{t \to \infty} a^{T+1} y^*_{t+T+1,t} = 0$, then the solution to (3.41) is

$$y_t = b \sum_{i=0}^{\infty} a^i x^*_{t+i,t}. \tag{3.42}$$

Setting $a = \alpha/(1 + \alpha)$, $b = 1/(1 + \alpha)$, and assuming that $x^*_{t,t} = x_t$ (the weak consistency axiom), this is indeed identical to the solution (3.36) for the Cagan model. Being based on the underlying economic factor x, it is referred to as the "fundamental" solution and will be stable as long as x^*_t does not grow too fast; compare to (3.22).

Now consider the expression $y_t + z_t$. With y_t satisfying (3.42), this will be a solution to (3.41) for any z_t that satisfies the relationship

$$z_t = aE_t(z_{t+1}) \equiv az^*_{t+1,t}. \tag{3.43}$$

The Cagan example corresponds to assuming $z_t = A_t$, where $A_{t+1} = A_t((1 + \alpha)/\alpha)$. This relationship therefore satisfies (3.43) so that adding $A_t = A_0((1 + \alpha)/\alpha)^t$ to (3.36) is still a solution to the Cagan model. With $a < 1$, the solution to (3.43) explodes, as it does in the Cagan example, and for this reason this component is referred to as the "bubble" solution. In fact this bubble solution can be generalized by modifying z_t to $z_t = A_t + e_t$ where e_t is a stochastic term having the property $E_t(e_{t+1}) = 0$.

As long as $|a| < 1$, as in the Cagan model, the bubble solution can be ruled out by appealing to stability, and that, in fact, was the procedure we followed by setting $A_t = 0$. That leaves the fundamental solution as the unique stable solution. Many, but not all, rational expectations models share this characteristic. But it is possible for $|a| > 1$, in which case the fundamental solution may not converge and there will be an infinite number of stable bubble solutions. Examples where this occurs, and procedures to resolve these difficulties, will be discussed in Chapter 6.

3.7   Learning

Thus far we have been assuming that the agent has complete knowledge of the entire system except for the purely stochastic disturbances. The stringency of this assumption is self-evident and is one of the bases on which the rational expectations hypothesis has been criticized. Over the past several years, a number of economists have introduced processes describing how the agents learn the underlying economic structure over time. The interaction of the dynamics of this learning process with that of the system itself is important, and not all learning processes need be stable.

One tractable approach, due to Evans (1985, 1986) and Evans and Honkapohja (1992), is the method of expectational stability, which can be illustrated by the following scalar example. Suppose

$$y_t = a + b y^*_{t,t-1} + c x_t, \tag{3.44a}$$

$$x_t = \rho x_{t-1} + v_t \tag{3.44b}$$

where v_t is an independently distributed random variable, having mean zero and finite variance. This pair of equations asserts that the variable y_t depends upon its own expectations plus a stochastic term generated by a first-order autoregressive process. It does not correspond to the Cagan formulation. Rather, we can interpret it as describing an expectations-augmented Phillips curve where the inflation rate (denoted by y_t) depends upon the previous prediction and employment, say, denoted by x_t, which evolves gradually over time. Using either of the procedures discussed in Section 3.5, the rational expectations solution to this system is

$$y_t = \frac{a}{1-b} + \frac{c\rho}{1-b} x_{t-1} + c v_t. \tag{3.45}$$

Suppose that the agent knows that y_t is driven by a linear function of x_{t-1} and v_t. He also knows the autoregressive parameter ρ, though not the primary structural parameters, a, b, c, and instead perceives output as being generated by

$$y_t = \alpha_n + \beta_n x_{t-1} + \gamma_n v_t. \tag{3.46}$$

The subscript n here indexes the period over which expectations are revised. Believing this to be the structure, the agent forms his expectations at time $t - 1$ from

$$y^*_{t,t-1} = \alpha_n + \beta_n x_{t-1}.$$

But the way expectations are formed will influence the actual evolution of y_t, and substituting this expression, together with (3.44b), into (3.44a), y_t will be generated by

$$y_t = (a + b\alpha_n) + (b\beta_n + c\rho)x_{t+1} + cv_t. \tag{3.47}$$

After another time unit of observing the system he eventually learns (3.47), and at time $n + 1$ revises his perception of the economy to

$$y_t = \alpha_{n+1} + \beta_{n+1}x_{t-1} + \gamma_{n+1}v_t. \tag{3.48}$$

Relating the coefficients in (3.47) and (3.48) implies

$$\alpha_{n+1} = a + b\alpha_n; \qquad \beta_{n+1} = c\rho + b\beta_n \qquad \gamma_{n+1} = c. \tag{3.49}$$

These three equations yield processes whereby estimates of the structural parameters are updated and the system is learned. The combination of the system and learning dynamics is described by (3.48) and (3.49).

As long as $|b| < 1$, the learning processes for α_n, β_n will eventually converge to the true parameter values $a/(1 - b)$, $c\rho/(1 - b)$, respectively, while from the third relationship the agent learns c in just one learning period. In this case, the agent will ultimately learn the true economic structure. However, if $|b| > 1$, the first two learning processes will diverge, and this will cause the dynamics of the overall system to diverge.

Frequently, the learning process gives rise to nonlinear updating equations. This would be the case in the above example if the agent also had to learn the true value of the autoregressive parameter ρ. A simple example illustrating this, originally due to Evans (1985) and discussed by Blanchard and Fischer (1989, chapter 5), is the following. Suppose (3.44a) is modified to

$$y_t = a + by^*_{t+1,t} + v_t \tag{3.50}$$

where, as before v_t is white noise. We also assume $|b| < 1$. Suppose the agent knows the true model and has rational expectations. Suppose also that at time t, when expectations are formed, the agent knows past values of y_{t-i}, v_{t-i}, but not the present values. Within the class of such solutions, using the method of undetermined coefficients, one can show that the solution is of the form

$$y_t = \phi_0 + \phi_1 y_{t-1} + v_t + \phi_2 v_{t-1} \tag{3.51}$$

where the coefficients ϕ_i satisfy either

$$\phi_0 = a/(1 - b); \qquad \phi_1 = \phi_2 = 0, \tag{3.52a}$$

or

$$\phi_0 = -a/b; \qquad \phi_1 = 1/b; \qquad \phi_2 \text{ undertermined.} \tag{3.52b}$$

The solution presented in (3.52a) is the fundamental solution, whereas (3.52b) includes a bubble.

Suppose now that the agent does not know the model. But, analogous to (3.46), he believes that it is described by a linear equation of the form (3.51), namely:

$$y_t = \alpha_n + \beta_n y_{t-1} + \gamma_n v_t + \delta_n v_{t-1} \tag{3.53}$$

where n denotes the learning period. Assuming that the agent believes (3.53), the rational forecast of y_{t+1}, formed on the basis of information available at time t, is

$$y_{t+1,t}^* = \alpha_n(1 + \beta_n) + \beta_n^2 y_{t-1} + \beta_n \delta_n v_{t-1}. \tag{3.54}$$

Substituting this expression for expectations into (3.51), it follows that y_t is generated by

$$y_t = [a + b\alpha_n(1 + \beta_n)] + b\beta_n^2 y_{t-1} + v_t + b\beta_n \delta_n v_{t-1}. \tag{3.55}$$

After the completion of a learning period, the agent revises his view of the economy to

$$y_t = \alpha_{n+1} + \beta_{n+1} y_{t-1} + \gamma_{n+1} v_t + \delta_{n+1} v_{t-1}. \tag{3.56}$$

Thus, relating the coefficients in (3.55) and (3.56) implies the relationships

$$\alpha_{n+1} = a + b\alpha_n(1 + \beta_n); \qquad \beta_{n+1} = b\beta_n^2; \qquad \gamma_{n+1} = 1; \qquad \delta_{n+1} = b\beta_n \delta_n.$$

The important feature of these recursive relationships is that they are now nonlinear. The equation $\beta_{n+1} = b\beta_n^2$ has two stationary solutions: $\tilde{\beta}_1 = 0$, which is stable, and $\tilde{\beta}_2 = 1/b$, which is unstable. If β_n starts out sufficiently small so that $\beta_n \to 0$ (the stable solution), then provided $|b < 1|$, $\alpha_n \to a/(1 - b)$, while $\delta_n \to 0$. Note that $\gamma_{n+1} = 1$ within one learning period. Thus in this case, the economy converges to the fundamental solution (3.52a). Blanchard and Fischer (1989, chapter 5) also discuss the case where $|b| > 1$.

These two examples are simple but illuminating and capture the essence of the updating of information associated with learning. The imposition of expectational consistency, in these examples the requirement that $|b| < 1$, is often of assistance in resolving nonuniqueness problems. An example of this will be presented in Chapter 6.

Two other approaches have been used and should be noted. The first is a Bayesian updating procedure used by Bray and Savin (1986). The second is more formal least-squares learning, whereby the parameters appearing in (3.46) are estimated each period using least squares; see, for example, Marcet and Sargent (1989a, 1989b). Under certain conditions both of these procedures can reduce to adaptive expectations, which in some circumstances can be viewed as a learning process that converges to rational expectations.[6]

Notes

1. We should note that at about the same time as Muth introduced the concept of rational expectations, Mills (1962) introduced the term *implicit expectations*. This procedure involves proxying an expectation of some unknown variable by its observation and is clearly closely related to Muth's definition. Unfortunately, Mills's contribution is unrecognized by most economists.

2. There is a limited macroeconomic literature that considers differential information; see, e.g., Canzoneri, Henderson, and Rogoff (1983). Several of the authors in Frydman and Phelps (1983) also discuss the consequences of differential information.

3. $\lim_{h \to 0^+}$ means that $h \to 0$ through positive values and is standard; likewise for $\lim_{h \to 0^-}$.

4. By "almost everywhere" we mean at all but possibly a finite number of points. It would be possible to generate $P(t)$ having an infinite number of nondifferentiabilities by specifying a sufficiently exotic forcing function. But providing an economic rationale would be more difficult.

5. In this chapter lowercase letters denote logarithms rather than real quantities as in Chapter 2.

6. Turnovsky (1969) showed in another context how under certain conditions a Bayesian learning process may lead to adaptive expectations. Friedman (1979) demonstrated the same type of result for a least-squares learning process.

4 Rational Expectations and Policy Neutrality

The Cagan model is a pure monetary model; output is assumed to remain fixed at the full-employment level. Yet much of the controversy generated by the rational expectations hypothesis has concerned its implications for the ability (or lack of ability) of macroeconomic policy to influence the *real* performance of the economy. To address this issue, we therefore need to extend the Cagan model to allow for the endogenous determination of real output. A critical component in the debate surrounding the policy implications of the rational expectations hypothesis concerns the form of the aggregate supply function. This is developed in detail in Section 4.1. A complete macroeconomic model embodying rational expectations and the Lucas supply function is then outlined in Section 4.2.

Before considering the issue of policy neutrality, Section 4.3 begins by discussing the "Lucas Critique." This proposition is the observation that the economic structure is not invariant with respect to the policy regime. A change in the regime will typically change the parameters of the reduced form of the model, and this has important implications for both policy analysis and the empirical estimation of reduced-form relationships.

As will become evident below, the policy neutrality proposition is a very strong one, and its robustness is examined in some detail in Sections 4.4–4.6. Section 4.4 introduces alternative assumptions regarding the information set of policymakers, the numbers of commodities, stickiness of prices, and so on. Section 4.5 considers an alternative benchmark level of output and shows how in some cases policy neutrality, which previously could break down, is in fact restored if this alternative—and possibly more appropriate—benchmark equilibrium level of output is used. Section 4.6 introduces an alternative information set and shows how neutrality ceases to hold under this alternative but perfectly reasonable assumption. Finally, Section 4.7 discusses the question of "persistence" of output movements in response to shocks and briefly discusses some recent work on stochastic business cycles.

4.1 The Lucas Supply Function

A standard specification of the aggregate supply function in descriptive rational expectations macroeconomic models is some version of what is known as the "Lucas supply function." In simple form, this can be specified by the equation

$$y_t = \bar{y} + \gamma(p_t + p_{t,t-1}^*) + v_t \tag{4.1}$$

where

y_t denotes the level of output, measured in logarithms,

$\bar{y}$ denotes the natural level of output, measured in logarithms,

p_t denotes the price level at time t, measured in logarithms,

$p^*_{t,t-1}$ denotes the prediction of p for time t, formed at time $t-1$,

v_t is a random supply disturbance, assumed to have zero mean and to be independently distributed over time.

Equation (4.1) asserts that the deviation in output for time t from its natural rate level (say, the full employment level) depends upon (i) the error in predicting the current price level, and (ii) the current supply shock. Several justifications for (4.1) can be given and shall be considered in turn. These reflect very different views concerning the structure of the economy.

Lucas Supply Function as a Phillips Curve

First, one can view (4.1) as an inverse form of the Phillips curve. To see this, consider the usual expectations-augmented Phillips curve as initially introduced in equation (2.28). In log-linear form this can be expressed as

$$p_t - p_{t-1} = \rho(y_t - \bar{y}) + (p^*_{t,t-1} - p_{t-1}) + \varsigma_t \qquad (4.2)$$

where $(p_t - p_{t-1})$ is the actual rate of inflation over the period $(t-1, t)$, $(p^*_{t,t-1} - p_{t-1})$, is the anticipated rate of inflation over the period $(t-1, t)$, and ς_t is a stochastic disturbance. (The model is expressed in logarithms so that $p_t - p_{t-1}$ is an approximation to the rate of inflation.) Adding p_{t-1} to both sides of (4.2) yields

$$p_t - p^*_{t,t-1} = \rho(y_t - \bar{y}) + \varsigma_t,$$

from which (4.1) is readily derived.

Lucas Island Model

The theoretical underpinnings of the Phillips curve have long been criticized. Lucas himself provided an entirely different rationale from the above for (4.1), in terms of what has become known as the Lucas island model; see Lucas (1972, 1973, 1975). The most convenient version for our purposes is Lucas (1973), which we shall follow closely in our exposition.

  The key feature of the model is that there are a large number of suppliers located in a large number of scattered competitive markets. Decisions depend upon relative prices. Demand for goods in each period is distributed unevenly over markets, leading to relative, as well as general, price movements. However, because of imperfect information, agents are unable to distinguish these relative price movements from absolute price changes. Hence the situation as perceived by individual suppliers is quite different from the aggregate situation as it would be seen by some outside observer.

We begin by considering first the situation faced by an individual producer. The quantity supplied in each market is assumed to be the product of a normal component, common to all markets, and a cyclical component that varies between markets. Expressed in logarithms, this relationship is described by

$$y_t(n) = \bar{y} + y_t^c(n) \tag{4.3}$$

where

n indexes the market,

$\bar{y}$ is the normal component of output,

y_t^c is the cyclical component of output.

For simplicity, we take $\bar{y}$ to be constant, although Lucas allows it to follow a time trend. The cyclical component of output is hypothesized to vary with the perceived relative price

$$y_t^c(n) = \gamma[p_t(n) - E(p_t|I_t(n))] \tag{4.4}$$

where

$p_t(n)$ is the actual price in market n at time t, measured in logarithms,

$E[p_t|I_t(n)]$ is the perceived mean general price level, given the information available in market n at time t, namely $I_t(n)$.

Lucas also allows for a lagged adjustment in y_t^c, but for simplicity this too is omitted.

The information available to suppliers in market n at time t comes from two sources. First, we assume that agents have a common prior distribution on the price level p_t, acquired from past information. This is assumed to be a normal distribution with mean $\bar{p}_t$ and a constant variance σ^2. Second, the actual price in market n deviates from the mean general price level p_t by an amount that is distributed independently of p_t. This can be written as

$$p_t(n) = p_t + n \tag{4.5}$$

where n is normally distributed, independent of p_t, with mean 0 and variance ω^2. The information set $I_t(n)$ relevant for estimating the general price level p_t consists of (i) the information contained in the prior distribution and (ii) the observed value $p_t(n)$.

To determine the perceived mean general price level is a straightforward problem in Bayesian statistics. From these two pieces of information and the assumption of normality, suppliers can update their prior estimates of the mean $\bar{p}_t$, as follows:

$$E[p_t|I_t(n)] = \frac{\frac{1}{\sigma^2}}{\frac{1}{\sigma^2} + \frac{1}{\omega^2}}\bar{p}_t + \frac{\frac{1}{\omega^2}}{\frac{1}{\sigma^2} + \frac{1}{\omega^2}}p_t(n). \tag{4.6}$$

The quantities $1/\sigma^2, 1/\omega^2$, which are the inverses of the variances, are referred to as the "precisions" of the distributions and measure the confidence with which the forecasters view the respective pieces of information. Thus (4.6) says that the two pieces of information—the prior mean and the observed price in market n—should be weighted by their respective precisions. Letting

$$\theta \equiv \frac{\omega^2}{\sigma^2 + \omega^2}$$

yields

$$E(p_t|I_t(n)) = \theta\bar{p}_t + (1 - \theta)p_t(n), \tag{4.7}$$

which makes it clear how the updated (posterior) distribution is a weighted average of the two pieces of information. Combining (4.3), (4.4), and (4.7) yields

$$y_t(n) = \bar{y} + \gamma\theta(p_t(n) - \bar{p}_t),$$

and averaging over the n markets gives the aggregate supply function

$$y_t = \bar{y} + \gamma\theta(p_t - \bar{p}_t). \tag{4.8}$$

The slope of the aggregate supply function depends upon θ, the fraction of total individual price variances, $\sigma^2 + \omega^2$, that is due to *relative* price variation. In cases where ω^2 is relatively small, so that individual price changes almost certainly reflect general price changes, $y_t \cong \bar{y}$, in which case output is virtually fixed. On the other hand, the more variation is specific to a firm, the steeper is the supply curve, the slope in the limit being γ. Apart from the additive shock v_t, which we have not introduced, equation (4.8) is equivalent to (4.1). Finally, allowing for a linear trend in $\bar{y}$ and a lagged adjustment in y_t^c, (4.8) is modified to

$$y_t = \bar{y}_t + \gamma\theta(p_t - \bar{p}_t) + \lambda[y_{t-1} - \bar{y}_{t-1}]. \tag{4.8'}$$

The modification of the supply function to include lagged adjustment is relevant for our discussion in Section 4.7 of persistence of shocks and stochastic business cycles.

The Wage Contract Model

A third rationale for the Lucas supply function is in terms of the one-period wage contract model of Gray (1976) and Fischer (1977a). In this framework, wages are set one period in advance, before the stochastic disturbances in that period are known. This contract wage is chosen so as to clear the market at the price expected on the basis of previous information.

To obtain the form of supply function (4.1), we consider an economy consisting of K firms, each of which produces output by means of a Cobb-Douglas production function of the form

$$Y_t^i = (L_t^i)^{1-\theta} e^{\varepsilon_t^i} \qquad i = 1, \ldots, K \tag{4.9}$$

where

Y_t^i denotes the level of output of firm i, in natural units,

L_t^i denotes the employment of labor by firm i, measured in natural units,

ε_t^i denotes the productivity shock of firm i, assumed to have zero mean and finite variance and to be independently distributed over time.

Profit of the ith firm is therefore given by the expression

$$\Pi_t^i = P_t (L_t^i)^{1-\theta} e^{\varepsilon_t^i} - W_t^c L_t^i \tag{4.10}$$

where

P_t denotes the price of output, measured in natural units,

W_t^c denotes the contract wage, measured in natural units.

Expected profit of firm i, conditional on information at time $t - 1$, is therefore equal to

$$E_{t-1}[\Pi_t^i] = (L_t^i)^{1-\theta} E_{t-1}[P_t e^{\varepsilon_t^i}] - W_t^c L_t^i \tag{4.11}$$

where E_{t-1} denotes the conditional expectation.

The ex ante demand for labor, based on the maximization of (4.11), is determined by the first-order condition

$$(1 - \theta)(L_t^i)^{-\theta} E_{t-1}[P_t e^{\varepsilon_t^i}] = W_t^c. \tag{4.12}$$

Taking logarithms of this equation and denoting logarithms by lower-case letters, the demand for labor by the ith firm, $(l_t^i)^d$, is given by

$$(l_t^i)^d = \frac{1}{\theta}[\ln(1 - \theta) + \ln E_{t-1}[P_t e^{\varepsilon_t^i}] - w_t^c]$$ (4.13)

Consider now the term $E_{t-1}(P_t e^{\varepsilon_t^i})$. Expanding $P_t e^{\varepsilon_t^i}$ in a second-order Taylor series about the point $(P_{t,t-1}^*, 0)$ yields the approximation

$$P_t e^{\varepsilon_t^i} \simeq P_{t,t}^*{}_1 + (P_t - P_{t,t-1}^*) + P_{t,t-1}^* \varepsilon_t^i + \frac{1}{2} P_{t,t-1}^* (\varepsilon_t^i)^2 + (P_t - P_{t,t-1}^*)\varepsilon_t^i.$$

Next, take expected values of this at time $t - 1$ to obtain

$$E_{t-1}[P_t e^{\varepsilon_t^i}] \cong P_{t,t-1}^* \left[1 + \frac{1}{2}\sigma_\varepsilon^2 + \frac{\text{cov}_{t-1}[P_t, \varepsilon_t^i]}{P_{t,t-1}^*}\right]$$ (4.14)

where σ_ε^2 denotes the variance ε_t^i assumed to be common to all firms, and cov_{t-1} denotes the conditional covariance. The logarithm of (4.14) is then given by

$$\ln E_{t-1}[P_t e^{\varepsilon_t^i}] \cong p_{t,t-1}^* + \ln\left[1 + \frac{1}{2}\sigma_\varepsilon^2 + \frac{\text{cov}_{t-1}[P_t, \varepsilon_t^i]}{P_{t,t-1}^*}\right].$$ (4.15)

If we now write the term

$$\frac{\text{cov}_{t-1}[P_t, \varepsilon_t^i]}{P_{t,t-1}^*} = \rho_{P,\varepsilon_i} \gamma_P \sigma_{\varepsilon_i}$$

where ρ_{P,ε_i} denotes the correlation coefficient between p and ε_i, and γ_P is the coefficient of variation of P_t, and assume that these quantities are constant, we may write (4.15) in the form

$$\ln E_{t-1}(P_t e^{\varepsilon_t^i}) \cong p_{t,t-1}^* + \chi$$

where χ is a constant that is a function of the second moments of the distributions of prices and productivity disturbances. Hence the demand for labor by the representative firm is

$$l_t^d = \frac{1}{K} \sum_{i=1}^K (l_t^i)^d = \frac{1}{\theta}[\ln(1 - \theta) + \chi + p_{t,t-1}^* - w_t^c].$$ (4.16)

The aggregate supply of labor, l_t^s, is hypothesized to be an increasing function of the expected real wage, namely

$$l_t^s = n(w_t^c - p_{t,t-1}^*)$$ (4.17)

where $n > 0$ denotes the elasticity of labor supply. The contract wage w_t^c is then determined by equating the demand for labor from (4.16) with the supply of labor from (4.17), resulting in

$$w_t^c = p_{t,t-1}^* + \frac{\ln(1-\theta) + \chi}{1 + \theta n}. \tag{4.18}$$

The contract nominal wage therefore varies proportionately with the expected price level, so that the ex ante expected real wage is constant.

Having determined the contract wage, the model assumes that actual employment is derived from the short-run marginal productivity condition for firms, obtained after the stochastic variables p_t and ε_t are known. For the representative firm this involves choosing employment to maximize (4.10). The amount of labor actually employed by the representative firm is given by

$$l_t^i = \frac{1}{\theta}[\ln(1-\theta) + p_t - w_t^c + \varepsilon_t^i],$$

and summing over all firms, aggregate employment is

$$l_t = \frac{1}{\theta}[\ln(1-\theta) + p_t - w_t^c + \varepsilon_t] \tag{4.19}$$

where ε_t is the aggregate productivity disturbance.

To derive the aggregate supply function, first substitute the contract wage (4.18) into (4.19) to yield

$$l_t = \frac{n\ln(1-\theta) - \chi}{1 + n\theta} + \frac{1}{\theta}(p_t - p_{t,t-1}^*) + \frac{\varepsilon_t}{\theta}. \tag{4.20}$$

Next take logarithms of the production function

$$y_t = (1 - \theta)l_t + \varepsilon_t \tag{4.21}$$

so that combining (4.20) and (4.21) yields

$$y_t = \frac{(1-\theta)[n\ln(1-\theta) - \chi]}{1 + n\theta} + \left(\frac{1-\theta}{\theta}\right)(p_t - p_{t,t-1}^*) + \frac{\varepsilon_t}{\theta}. \tag{4.22}$$

This is of the basic form of the Lucas supply function (4.1).

4.2   A Complete Rational Expectations Macro Model

As noted in Chapter 3, most rational expectations models are specified log linearly. In this section we outline a basic model that we take to consist of an *IS* curve, an *LM* curve, and a Lucas supply function. The specific model we consider is described by the following:

$$\left\{\begin{array}{l} y_t = d_1 y_t - d_2[r_t - (p^*_{t+1,t-1} - p^*_{t,t-1})] + g_t + u_{1t} \qquad 0 < d_1 < 1, d_2 > 0 \\ \qquad\qquad\qquad\qquad\qquad\qquad\qquad\qquad\qquad\qquad\qquad (4.23\text{a}) \\[4pt] m_t - p_t = \alpha_1 y_t - \alpha_2 r_t + u_{2t} \qquad \alpha_1 > 0, \quad \alpha_2 > 0 \qquad (4.23\text{b}) \\[4pt] y_t = \bar{y} + \gamma(p_t - p^*_{t,t-1}) + v_t \qquad \gamma > 0 \qquad\qquad\qquad (4.23\text{c}) \end{array}\right.$$

where $y_t, \bar{y}_t, p_t$, and v_t have all been defined previously, and in addition

g_t is a logarithmic measure of government expenditure, defined more explicitly below;

$p^*_{t+i,t}$ is the prediction of p for time $t + i$, formed at time t;

r_t is the nominal interest rate at time t;

u_{1t} is a stochastic disturbance in the demand for output, assumed to have zero mean, finite variance, and to be independently distributed over time;

u_{2t} is a stochastic disturbance in the demand for money, assumed to have zero mean, finite variance, and to be independently distributed over time.

Equation (4.23a) is a logarithmic version of the product market equilibrium condition. Since aggregate demand is the sum of expenditures measured in natural units (not logarithms), the logarithmic specification (4.23a) requires further explanation. Specifically, let

Z_t = real private expenditures in natural units,

G_t = real government expenditures in natural units.

Then, as usual, product market equilibrium is described by

$$Y_t = Z_t + G_t. \qquad (4.24)$$

Suppose real private expenditures are of the exponential form

$$Z_t = Y^{d_1} e^{-d_2[r_t - (p^*_{t+1,t-1} - p^*_{t,t-1})]}$$

and we define the ratio of real government expenditure to real private expenditure by

$$G_t = \lambda_t Z_t.$$

Then substituting for Z_t and G_t into the product market equilibrium relationship (4.24),

$$Y_t = (1 + \lambda_t) Y^{d_1} e^{-d_2[r_t - (p^*_{t+1,t-1} - p^*_{t,t-1})]} + u_{1t},$$

and taking logarithms yields

$$y_t = d_1 y_t - d_2[r_t - (p^*_{t+1,t-1} - p^*_{t,t-1})] + g_t + u_{1t},$$

where

$$g_t = \ln(1 + \lambda_t).$$

Thus in a logarithmic model, the government expenditure variable is essentially a relative measure of the ratio of government to private expenditures.

With d_1 (which now measures an elasticity rather than a marginal propensity to consume) being less than one, the logarithmic *IS* curve, considered as a relationship between real expenditure and the real interest rate, is downward sloping. The expected rate of inflation incorporated in the real interest rate is taken to be over the period t to $t + 1$ and, being measured by $(p^*_{t+1,t-1} - p^*_{t,t-1})$, is conditional on information available up until time $t - 1$. That is, the price level at time t is assumed to be unknown and must be predicted. As will become apparent in due course, this choice of definition of the expected inflation rate turns out to be very important for the solution and the policy implications that stem from it.

Equation (4.23b) is a typical logarithmic version of an *LM* curve. It is an immediate consequence of postulating an exponential money demand function, with money market equilibrium

$$\frac{M}{P} = Y^{\alpha_1} e^{-\alpha_2 r_t + u_t}.$$

Finally, (4.23c) is the Lucas supply function discussed at length in Section 1.

4.3   The Lucas Critique and Policy Neutrality

The simple macro model outlined in equations (4.23a)–(4.23c), together with the hypothesis that expectations are rational, namely

$$p^*_{t+s,t} = E_t(p_{t+s}), \tag{4.25}$$

suffices to establish the policy neutrality proposition. We begin by taking conditional expectations of the supply function (4.23c) at time $t - 1$. Using the rational expectations condition (4.25), this yields

$$y^*_{t+s,t-1} = E_{t-1}(y_{t+s}) = \bar{y}. \tag{4.26}$$

That is, with rational expectations, output is always expected to equal its natural level $\bar{y}$. In other words, on average, output will equal its natural level and will be independent of government policy, except insofar as this may influence $\bar{y}$. This can be viewed as a type of policy neutrality proposition, but one that is much weaker than the one to be developed below.

Next, take conditional expectations of (4.23a), (4.23b) at time $t - 1$ to obtain

$$y_{t,t-1}^* = d_1 y_{t,t-1}^* - d_2[r_{t,t-1}^* - (p_{t+1,t-1}^* - p_{t,t-1}^*)] + g_{t,t-1}^*, \qquad (4.27a)$$

$$m_{t,t-1}^* - p_{t,t-1}^* = \alpha_1 y_{t,t-1}^* - \alpha_2 r_{t,t-1}^*. \qquad (4.27b)$$

Now subtracting (4.27a) and (4.27b) from (4.23a) and (4.23b) respectively and noting (4.26), we obtain the pair of equations

$$(1 - d_1)(y_t - \bar{y}) + d_2(r_t - r_{t,t-1}^*) = (g_t - g_{t,t-1}^*) + u_{1t}, \qquad (4.28a)$$

$$(m_t - m_{t,t-1}^*) - (p_t - p_{t,t-1}^*) = \alpha_1(y_t - \bar{y}) - \alpha_2(r_t - r_{t,t-1}^*) + u_{2t}. \qquad (4.28b)$$

The quantities of the form $(x_t - x_{t,t-1}^*)$ measure the differences between the actual variable x_t and the anticipated variable $x_{t,t-1}^*$; they are therefore unanticipated movements in these variables. Combining these last two equations with the Lucas supply function (4.23c), we may solve for the deviation in output $(y_t - \bar{y})$ in the form

$$y_t = \bar{y} = \frac{1}{D}[\gamma d_2(m_t - m_{t,t-1}^*) + \gamma\alpha_2(g_t - g_{t,t-1}^*) + \gamma\alpha_2 u_{1t} - \gamma d_2 u_{2t} + d_2 v_t], \qquad (4.29)$$

where

$$D \equiv \gamma[(1 - d_1)\alpha_2 + d_2\alpha_1] + d_2 > 0.$$

Equation (4.29) contains the essence of the results. It asserts that output deviates from its natural level $\bar{y}$ by an amount that depends upon the unanticipated components of the nominal money stock $(m_t - m_{t,t-1}^*)$ and real government expenditure $(g_t - g_{t,t-1}^*)$, together with the additive disturbances in demand (u_{1t}, u_{2t}) and supply (v_t).

Lucas Critique

To demonstrate the Lucas Critique, it suffices to abstract from fiscal policy by setting $g_t = g_{t,t-1}^* = 0$ and to focus on monetary policy alone. Suppose that the monetary authorities adjust the nominal money supply in accordance with a rule of the form

$$m_t = \phi_0 + \phi_1 y_{t-1} + \phi_2 m_{t-1} + w_{mt}. \qquad \text{Feedback rule} \qquad (4.30)$$

This particular rule asserts that the money stock is adjusted on the basis of the previous period's money stock, the previous period's income, and a random term w_{mt} that represents the stochastic element in the monetary authority's behavior. The coefficients ϕ_0, ϕ_1, ϕ_2 represent the policy parameters and describe the systematic part of the money supply. Based (apart from the random component) on the past state of the economy, a policy of this form is referred to as a "feedback rule." Assuming that y_{t-1} and m_{t-1} are known at time $t - 1$, the conditional expectation of the current money supply formed at time $t - 1$, $m^*_{t,t-1}$, is

$$m^*_{t,t-1} = \phi_0 + \phi_1 y_{t-1} + \phi_2 m_{t-1}. \tag{4.31}$$

Substituting (4.31) into (4.29) (with $g_t = g^*_{t,t-1} = 0$), the solution for output is given by

$$y_t = \bar{y} + \delta_0 + \delta_1 m_t + \delta_2 y_{t-1} + \delta_3 m_{t-1} + \zeta_t, \tag{4.32}$$

where

$$\delta_0 = -\frac{\gamma d_2 \phi_0}{D}; \qquad \delta_1 = \frac{\gamma d_2}{D}; \qquad \delta_2 = -\frac{\gamma d_2 \phi_1}{D},$$

$$\delta_3 = -\frac{\gamma d_2 \phi_2}{D}; \qquad \zeta_t = \frac{\gamma \alpha_2 u_{1t} - \gamma d_2 u_{2t} + d_2 v_t}{D}.$$

The important insight due to Lucas is the following observation. Suppose that the policymaker wishes to influence the time path of output by altering the policy parameters ϕ_0, ϕ_1, ϕ_2. For the authority to do so, under the assumption that coefficients describing the evolution of output remain fixed and invariant with respect to its chosen policy, would be nonrational. Clearly, changes in parameters appearing in the policy rule (4.30) lead to changes in the parameters appearing in the reduced-form equation (4.32). In other words, the reduced-form dynamics are not invariant with respect to changes in regime, as represented by changes in these policy parameters.

This observation has important implications for much of the work on what is often called the theory of policy. Beginning with Tinbergen (1952), the focus of this literature has been on analyzing the effects of changes in policy variables such as m, as well as on the determination of optimal policy, based on the assumption that the structural parameters of the system, the δ's, remain fixed. While the Lucas Critique casts serious doubt on the adequacy of this procedure, it must also be conceded that this earlier literature generally does not adopt the assumption of rational expectations. Or, put another way, the Lucas Critique can be interpreted as pointing out how the introduction of rational expectations leads to serious modifications of the theory of policy.

Second, the Lucas Critique calls into question the practice of econometrically estimating the parameters of a reduced-form equation such as (4.32). This is because as m_t varies, so do the structural parameters, and consequently the assumption that they remain fixed over the sample is not appropriate.

Finally, we should emphasize that the Lucas Critique is not restricted to the class of linear rational expectations models being developed in this chapter. It also applies to the type of model we shall discuss in Part III in which representative agents optimize intertemporally and current and future behavior depends upon announced policy. Changes in these announcements will change the environment of the private agent, thereby inducing changes in his behavior and that of the private sector in general. Examples of such changes in behavior in response to fiscal policy will be presented throughout Part III.

Policy Neutrality

To demonstrate the policy neutrality proposition, we simply subtract equation (4.31) from (4.30) to obtain

$$m_t - m_{t,t-1}^* = w_{mt}. \tag{4.33}$$

Likewise, if an analogous type of feedback rule were proposed for government expenditure, g_t, we would find

$$g_t - g_{t,t-1}^* = w_{gt} \tag{4.34}$$

where w_{gt} is the stochastic component of the rule. Substituting (4.33) and (4.34) into (4.29), the solution for output deviations is given by

$$y_t - \bar{y} = \frac{1}{D}[\gamma d_2 w_{mt} + \gamma \alpha_2 w_{gt} + \gamma \alpha_2 u_{1t} - \gamma d_2 u_{2t} + d_2 v_t]. \tag{4.35}$$

Equation (4.35) describes the policy neutrality proposition. After substituting for the policy rule(s), the level of output is *independent* of all the monetary policy parameters ϕ_0, ϕ_1, ϕ_2, as well as the analogous policy parameters for the fiscal rule. Indeed, output deviations depend only upon the exogenous additive disturbances $u_{1t}, u_{2t}, v_t, w_{mt}, w_{gt}$, as well as the coefficients of the underlying model, all of which are given to the stabilization authority and are beyond its control. Note, furthermore, that the random elements w_{mt}, w_{gt} are induced by the policymakers and, in general, will add to the variability of output. This provides an argument against any form of policy intervention; not only is it ineffective, it is actually destabilizing.

We now give an intuitive explanation for the policy neutrality proposition, focusing again on monetary policy. Consider an anticipated increase in the money supply resulting from an increase in the parameter ϕ_1. Since output is expected to remain fixed, the real interest rate is also expected to remain fixed. At the same time, the anticipated increase in the money supply leads to a proportional increase in the expected price level. This in turn raises the contract wage and lowers output. However, when the correctly anticipated monetary expansion takes place, demand is stimulated, thereby creating excess product demand. This will induce the actual price level to rise proportionately to the anticipated level (which in turn equals the anticipated monetary expansion), at which point output is restored to its initial natural rate level. There is therefore no effect on output.

On the other hand, an unanticipated monetary expansion, represented by the stochastic term w_{mt} in equation (4.30), will have no effect on the expected price level. It will, however, raise the actual price level, thereby stimulating output in accordance with the supply function (4.23c). The same applies to fiscal policy.

The policy neutrality proposition has fundamental implications for macroeconomic policy-making. Since only unanticipated policy changes have real effects, demand management policies are useless. The power of this proposition has generated an extensive debate among economists, directed at establishing its degree of robustness.

4.4   Robustness of the Policy Neutrality Proposition

The essential feature of the Lucas Critique, namely the sensitivity of the economic structure to changes in government policy parameters, is a general characteristic of rational expectations models and is now widely accepted by the economics profession. On the other hand, although the policy neutrality proposition is shown to hold under certain sets of assumptions, its validity turns out to be dependent upon the specification of the model. Consequently, the proposition has generated much controversy among economists. In this section we examine its robustness by considering variations to the basic model.

Instantaneous Information

The policy rule (4.30) is based solely on past information. Suppose in addition it includes some contemporaneous information such as, for example, the current interest rate. This is entirely plausible because data on financial variables typically are available virtually instantaneously. In this case the policy rule is modified to

$$m_t = \phi_0 + \phi_1 y_{t-1} + \phi_2 m_{t-1} + \phi_3 r_t \tag{4.30'}$$

so that

$$m_t - m^*_{t,t-1} = \phi_3(r_t - r^*_{t,t-1}) + w_{mt}. \tag{4.35}$$

The unanticipated change in the money stock therefore responds to the unanticipated movement in the interest rate as well as to the additive shock w_{mt}. Solving (4.28a), (4.28b), and (4.23c) together with (4.35), and for simplicity setting $g_t - g^*_{t,t-1} = 0$, we find

$$y_t - \bar{y} = \frac{\gamma d_2 w_{mt} + \gamma(\alpha_2 + \phi_3)u_{1t} - \gamma d_2 u_{2t} + d_2 v_t}{\gamma[(1 - d_1)(\alpha_2 + \phi_3) + d_2\alpha_1] + d_2}. \tag{4.36}$$

In this case we find that the deviation in output does depend upon the policy coefficient ϕ_3. This raises the question of the optimal choice of ϕ_3, an issue to which we shall return in Chapter 8.

In effect, the instantaneous observability of r_t implies the observability of a linear combination of the underlying disturbances. To see this, eliminate y_t and p_t from the three basic equations of the model, (4.23a)–(4.23c). The result is the linear relationship

$$Dr_t = -\gamma(1 - d_1)(m_t - u_{2t}) + (1 + \alpha_1\gamma)[d_2(p^*_{t+1,t-1} - p^*_{t,t-1}) + g_t + u_{1t}]$$

$$- (1 - d_1)[\bar{y} - \gamma p^*_{t,t-1} + v_t].$$

The observability of r_t, m_t, and g_t as well as the expectational variables $p^*_{t+1,t-1}, p^*_{t,t-1}$ means that, by observing the terms in this equation, the monetary authorities can in effect infer the composite disturbance

$$(1 + \alpha_1\gamma)u_{1t} + \gamma(1 - d_1)u_{2t} - (1 - d_1)v_t.$$

Or in other words, the observability of r_t provides some information on current disturbances, and this is what enables perfectly anticipated policy changes to influence the behavior of output. This possibility was recognized by Sargent and Wallace (1975) and characterized as a situation in which the stabilization authority has an informational advantage over the private sector; see also Woglom (1979).

Another example, considered by McCallum and Whitaker (1979) is where taxes are adjusted to current income by a rule of the form

$$T = t_0 + t_1 y.$$

Such a rule assigns an automatic stabilizer role to taxes, and it is easy to show that the deviation in output $(y_t - \bar{y})$ depends upon the chosen marginal tax rate t_1.

Optimizing Behavior

Fair (1978) criticized the rational expectations models on the following grounds. He argued that although such models posit rational behavior in the sense that agents know the model and use all available information in forming their forecasts, agents are at the same time irrational in the sense that their decisions are based largely on arbitrary behavior and are not derived from the assumption of optimization. His criticism focuses on the supply function, which is a key part of the model. He argues that if one derives this relationship from underlying optimization, it would include the interest rate as an additional variable because the output supply function depends on labor supply, which in turn depends upon the interest rate through the intertemporal substitution effects in the workers' utility-measuring decisions. The introduction of the interest rate in the supply function (4.23c) leads to an immediate breakdown of the policy neutrality proposition. Modifying (4.23c) to

$$y_t = \bar{y} + \gamma_1(p_t - p_{t,t-1}^*) + \gamma_2 r_t + v_t \qquad (4.37)$$

makes it clear that any anticipated monetary (or fiscal) expansion that affects the interest rate r_t, will thereby influence real output. The Fair criticism is an important one that underscores the need to derive macroeconomic models from underlying optimization. This issue is pursued further in Parts III and IV.

Existence of Multiple Commodities

The typical aggregate macroeconomic model assumes the existence of a single composite community. In reality, of course, there are countless goods, and these influence the decisions of firms and workers asymmetrically. To illustrate the point, suppose that there are just two goods in the economy, one produced domestically, the other imported from abroad. In terms of the contract model developed in Section 4.1, firms, in making their production decisions, determine their demand for labor based on the real wage, defined in terms of the price of the commodity they produce (the domestic good). Workers, on the other hand, in choosing their labor supply, base their decision on the real wage defined in terms of the domestic cost of living, which is some weighted average of domestic and foreign goods.

Repeating the analysis of Section 4.1, we can show that aggregate labor demand is, as before,

$$l_t^d = \frac{1}{\theta}[\ln(1 - \theta) + \chi + p_{t,t-1}^* - w_t^c],$$

while the labor supply is now

$$l_t^s = n(w_t^c - c_{t,t-1}^*)$$

where the domestic cost of living, given by

$$c_t = \delta p_t + (1 - \delta)q_t,$$

is a fixed geometric weighted average of the price of the domestic good p_t and the domestic price of the imported good q_t. Thus the contract wage, w_t^c, determined at a level that, given expectations, the market is expected to clear, is

$$w_t^c = \frac{\ln(1 - \theta) + \chi + p_{t,t-1}^* + \theta n c_{t,t-1}^*}{1 + \theta n}. \tag{4.38}$$

In particular, it will be observed that the contract wage is now a weighted average of the expected price of the domestic good and the expected cost of living. Substituting (4.38) into (4.22), the supply function is of the form

$$y_t = \bar{y} + \left(\frac{1 - \theta}{\theta}\right)\left[\frac{(p_t - p_{t,t-1}^*) + \theta n(p_t - c_{t,t-1}^*)}{1 + \theta n}\right] + v_t,$$

which may also be written as

$$y_t = \bar{y} + \left(\frac{1 - \theta}{\theta}\right)\left[p_t - p_{t,t-1}^* + \frac{\theta n(1 - \delta)}{1 + \theta n}(p_{t,t-1}^* - q_{t,t-1}^*)\right] + v_t. \tag{4.39}$$

In this two-commodity world, output now depends upon unanticipated movement in the price of domestic output and in the expected relative price. Anticipated domestic policy is able to influence the latter, and through it, the level of current real output. Policy neutrality therefore breaks down.

Sticky Prices

It has often been argued that the policy neutrality result depends upon complete price flexibility and that it will cease to hold if prices are sticky. The validity of this statement depends upon how the sticky prices are assumed to be set. For example, if we take the simple classical monetary equilibrium relationship

$$m_t = y_t + p_t$$

and assume that the price level p_t is fixed, then any change in m_t, anticipated or unanticipated, will necessarily have an effect on real output.

On the other hand, McCallum (1980) considers the following form of pricing equation, which replaces the Lucas supply function:

$$p_t - p_{t-1} = \gamma(y_{t-1} - \bar{y}_{t-1}) + E_{t-1}(\bar{p}_t - \bar{p}_{t-1}) \tag{4.40}$$

where $\bar{p}$ denotes the price level that would equate aggregate demand to capacity output $\bar{y}$. In this formulation, prices are temporarily sticky, in the sense that they are unaffected by current demand and supply conditions, yet they have been set through the expectational term to reflect previously formed expectations about monetary policy. McCallum shows how, despite the temporary rigidity of p_t, the policy neutrality proposition still applies.

To see why this is so, suppose that output in period $t - 1$ is low so that $y_{t-1} < \bar{y}_{t-1}$. Then, assuming $\phi_1 < 0$ in the policy rule (4.30), m_t is raised relative to what it would have been if $y_{t-1} = \bar{y}_{t-1}$. But this is anticipated, and so it will increase $m_{t,t-1}^*$ and therefore $\bar{p}_t$. The increase in $\bar{p}_t$ will lead to a corresponding increase in the current price level p_t, which in turn offsets the effect of expansion on aggregate demand.

Multiperiod Wage Contracts

The model summarized in equations (4.23a)–(4.23b) can be motivated in terms of a one-period wage contract that is negotiated every period. Fischer (1977a, 1977b) and Taylor (1979, 1980) formally developed the implications of overlapping wage contracts. Specifically, suppose that there are two groups of workers and firms, such that the first group negotiates nominal wage contracts each January and the second group does so each July. A nominal contract for either group is in force for two periods, so that they overlap. The fact that part of the private sector is locked into its wage for a given period on the basis of a previously signed contract, whereas the government is able to determine its policy anew each period, gives the government an informational advantage over the private sector. Because of this, it is able to influence real output in a systematic way.

4.5   Full Information Level of Output

The criterion implicit in the discussion of policy neutrality thus far is the stabilization of output about the natural rate level, which is assumed to be fixed. This can be stated more formally in terms of the minimization of the quadratic loss function $E(y - \bar{y})^2$. However, the welfare significance of the natural rate level, $\bar{y}$, and therefore the loss $(y - \bar{y})^2$ has never been made very clear, although loss functions of this type have a long tradition in linear-quadratic stabilization theory (see Turnovsky 1977).

Barro (1976) was the first to argue that the appropriate benchmark level of output is not $\bar{y}$ but rather what he called the "full information" level of output, y_t^f, say, defined to be the level of output that would be forthcoming in the absence of forecasting errors. For the basic Lucas supply function (4.23c) this is defined by setting $p_{t,t-1}^* = p_t$, in which case

$$y_t^f = \bar{y} + v_t. \tag{4.41}$$

Thus, the deviation in output about this full information level,

$$y_t - y_t^f = \gamma(p_t - p_{t,t-1}^*), \tag{4.42}$$

is proportional to the unanticipated change in the price level. Thus, minimizing a quadratic loss function $E(y_t - y_t^f)^2$ is equivalent to minimizing the effects of price surprises. The motivation given by Barro for this form of quadratic loss function is in terms of its being an approximation to the expected loss of consumer's surplus, the welfare properties of which are well understood.

For the basic Lucas supply function, (4.23a), the policy neutrality proposition holds for both deviations, $y_t - \bar{y}$ and $y_t - y_t^f$. However, the nonneutralities obtained with respect to the modified forms of supply functions (4.37) or (4.39) do not hold, when the objective is to stabilize about the full information level of output.

Specifically, for the supply function (4.37), the full information level of output is

$$y_t^f = \bar{y} + \gamma_2 r_t + v_t$$

so that subtracting from (4.35) yields

$$y_t - y_t^f = \gamma_1(p_t - p_{t,t-1}^*).$$

Deviation in output about y_t^f depends only upon price surprises, which therefore implies that policy neutrality must prevail.

Second, the full information level of output for the two-commodity economy is obtained by setting $p_{t,t-1}^* = p_t$, $q_{t,t-1}^* = q_t$ in (4.39), namely

$$y_t^f = \bar{y} + \frac{(1-\theta)n(1-\delta)}{1+\theta n}(p_t - q_t) + v_t.$$

In this case the deviation in output is

$$y_t - y_t^f = \left(\frac{1-\theta}{\theta}\right)\left[(p_t - p_{t,t-1}^*) - \frac{\theta n(1-\delta)}{1+\theta n}[(p_t - p_{t,t-1}^*) - (q_t - q_{t,t-1}^*)]\right]$$

$$= \left(\frac{1-\theta}{\theta}\right)\left[\frac{1+\theta n\delta}{1+\theta n}(p_t - p_{t,t-1}^*) + \frac{\theta n(1-\delta)}{1+\theta n}(q_t - q_{t,t-1}^*)\right],$$

which is a weighted average of domestic and foreign price surprises. But being a function of only unanticipated price movements, the deviation in output is again invariant with respect to anticipated policy changes.

The benchmark of the full information level of output is similar, but not identical to, the notion of the frictionless level of output used as the benchmark in the indexation literature. This will be discussed further in Chapter 8.

4.6   Alternative Information Set

The macroeconomic model analyzed thus far has assumed that the prediction of the rate of inflation over the period $(t, t + 1)$ is formed using information up to and including time $t - 1$. This means that the price level at time t is not observed, at least by those agents forming the predictions of the real rate of interest that are necessary for real expenditure decisions. On the other hand, the current price level is known by those agents in determining their nominal demand for money in (4.23b). It therefore does not seem unreasonable to assume that the current price level p_t is also observed by those individuals forming predictions of the inflation rate over the period $(t, t + 1)$. In this case, the basic macroeconomic model is modified to

$$y_t = d_1 y_t - d_2 [r_t - (p^*_{t+1,t} - p_t)] + g_t + u_{1t} \tag{4.23a'}$$

$$m_t - p_t = \alpha_1 y_t - \alpha_2 r_t + u_{2t} \tag{4.23b}$$

$$y_t = \bar{y} + \gamma(p_t + p^*_{t,t-1}) + v_t. \tag{4.23c}$$

The only amendment to the model is that under this alternative informational assumption the expected rate of inflation in the IS curve is defined by $(p^*_{t+1,t} - p_t)$. As we will now demonstrate, this seemingly modest change in the dating of expectations has devastating effects on the policy neutrality proposition; see Turnovsky (1980) and Weiss (1980). Moreover, in contrast to the situation discussed at the beginning of Section 4.4, the breakdown of neutrality in this case is not the result of the stabilization authority having an informational advantage. On the contrary, both private agents and the stabilization authority have access to the same information set.

Indeed, the choice of information set embodied in these two alternative definitions of the expected inflation rate is largely arbitrary and certainly either specification is logically consistent. As noted, both formulations can be found in the literature, and in fact, early work on the rational expectations hypothesis by Sargent (1973) adopted the definition based on current information. It is amusing to speculate that the debate about policy neutrality might never have occurred if Sargent and Wallace (1976) had chosen this specification, rather than using the nominal interest rate alone, in the *IS* curve.

Solution of Modified Model

We shall solve the system using the recursive solution procedure introduced in Section 3.5. We begin by taking the conditional expectations $j + 1$ periods ahead of (4.23a'), (4.23b), and (4.23c) at time $t - 1$:

$$(1 - d_1)y^*_{t+j,t-1} = -d_2[r^*_{t+j,t-1} - (p^*_{t+j+1,t-1} - p^*_{t+j,t-1})] + g^*_{t+j,t-1} \quad (4.43a)$$

$$m^*_{t+j,t-1} - p^*_{t+j,t-1} = \alpha_1 y^*_{t+j,t-1} - \alpha_2 r^*_{t+j,t-1} \quad (4.43b)$$

$$y^*_{t+j,t-1} = \bar{y}. \quad (4.43c)$$

Substituting for $y^*_{t+j,t-1}$ and eliminating $r^*_{t+j,t-1}$ leads to the following difference equation in price expectations:

$$\alpha_2 d_2 p^*_{t+j+1,t-1} - (1 + \alpha_2)d_2 p^*_{t+j,t-1} = -\alpha_2 g^*_{t+1,t-1} - d_2 m^*_{t+j,t-1}$$

$$+ [\alpha_2(1 - d_1) + \alpha_1 d_2]\bar{y}. \quad (4.44)$$

For notation convenience let

$$z_t \equiv m_t + \frac{\alpha_2}{d_2}g_t. \quad (4.45)$$

This represents a composite policy variable, reflecting the aggregate effects of monetary and fiscal policy. The conditional expectations of $z^*_{t+j,t-1}$ are

$$z^*_{t+j,t-1} = m^*_{t+j,t-1} + \frac{\alpha_2}{d_2}g^*_{t+j,t-1}, \quad (4.46)$$

so that (4.44) may be written as

$$\alpha_2 p^*_{t+j+1,t-1} - (1 + \alpha_2)p^*_{t+j,t-1} = z^*_{t+j,t-1} + \left[\frac{\alpha_2(1 - d_1) + \alpha_1 d_2}{d_2}\right]\bar{y}. \quad (4.47)$$

The stable solution to this equation is

$$p^*_{t+j,t-1} = \frac{1}{1 + \alpha_2}\sum_{i=0}^{\infty}z^*_{t+j+i,t-1}\left(\frac{\alpha_2}{1 + \alpha_2}\right)^i - \left[\frac{\alpha_2(1 - d_1) + \alpha_1 d_2}{d_2}\right]\bar{y}. \quad (4.48)$$

That is, price expectations are a discounted sum of all future expected values of the composite policy variable.

The next step is to take the conditional expectations of (4.23a'), (4.23b), and (4.23c) at time $t - 1$ for time t and subtract from the original system. This yields the matrix equation

$$\begin{bmatrix} 1 - d_1 & d_2 & d_2 \\ \alpha_1 & -\alpha_2 & 1 \\ 1 & 0 & -\gamma \end{bmatrix} \begin{bmatrix} y_t - \bar{y} \\ r_t - r^*_{t,t-1} \\ p_t - p^*_{t,t-1} \end{bmatrix}$$

$$= \begin{bmatrix} d_2(p^*_{t+1,t} - p^*_{t+1,t-1}) + (g_t - g^*_{t,t-1}) + u_{1t} \\ (m_t - m^*_{t,t-1}) - u_{2t} \\ v_t \end{bmatrix}.$$

Solving for the deviation in output from its natural level $\bar{y}$, we obtain

$$y_t - \bar{y} = \frac{1}{J}[\gamma\alpha_2 d_2(p^*_{t+1,t} - p^*_{t+1,t-1}) + \gamma\alpha_2(g_t - g^*_{t,t-1})$$

$$+ \gamma d_2(m_t - m^*_{t,t-1}) + u_t^y] \tag{4.49}$$

where

$$u_t^y \equiv \gamma\alpha_2 u_{1t} - \gamma d_2 u_{2t} + d_2(1 + \alpha_2)v_t,$$

$$J \equiv \gamma[\alpha_2(1 - d_1) + \alpha_1 d_2] + d_2(1 + \alpha_2).$$

Thus we see that the deviation in output about its mean depends upon (i) the unanticipated change in the current money supply $m_t - m^*_{t,t-1}$; (ii) the unanticipated change in the current government expenditure $g_t - g^*_{t,t-1}$; and (iii) the composite additive disturbance u_t^y. These elements all appear in the initial solution (4.29). But in addition, and most importantly, the deviation in output also depends upon $(p^*_{t+1,t} - p^*_{t+1,t-1})$, which measures the revisions to the forecasts of prices for time $t + 1$, updated between time $t - 1$ and time t, on the basis of new information forthcoming at that time. The expressions for the price expectations $p^*_{t+1,t} - p^*_{t+1,t-1}$ are obtained from (4.48). Substituting for these expressions yields

$$\alpha_2(p^*_{t+1,t} - p^*_{t+1,t-1}) = \sum_{i=1}^{\infty} (z^*_{t+i,t} - z^*_{t+i,t-1})\left(\frac{\alpha_2}{1 + \alpha_2}\right)^i,$$

which, using the definition of z_t, enables (4.49) to be rewritten as

$$y_t - \bar{y} = \frac{\gamma}{J}\Bigg[d_2(m_t - m^*_{t,t-1}) + \alpha_2(g_t - g^*_{t,t-1})$$

$$+ \sum_{i=1}^{\infty} \{d_2(m^*_{t+i,t} - m^*_{t+i,t-1}) + \alpha_2(g^*_{t+i,t} - g^*_{t+i,t-1})\}\left(\frac{\alpha_2}{1 + \alpha_2}\right)^i\Bigg]$$

$$+ \frac{u_t^y}{J}. \tag{4.50}$$

It is clear that the deviations in current output depend upon the revisions of forecasts of all future money supplies and government expenditures updated between $t - 1$ and t, since these are what drive the revisions to price expectations that occur at that time.

Nonneutrality of Policy

We shall now show how policy is nonneutral. We shall focus on monetary policy, abstracting from fiscal policy. But the same analysis applies to rules on government expenditure.

Suppose that monetary policy is governed by a simple feedback policy rule of the form

$$m_t = \phi u_{t-1}^y. \tag{4.51}$$

That is, the monetary authorities' decision is determined by the movement in the target variable, output, during the previous period, which we assumed to be observed by time t.

We assume further that all predictions made at time $t - 1$ are made after u_{t-1}^y is observed. Hence, since u_t^y is independently and identically distributed over time, taking conditional expectations of (4.51) yields the following:

$$m_{t,t-1}^* = \phi u_{t-1}^y = m_t \tag{4.52a}$$

$$m_{t+k,t-1}^* = 0 \qquad k = 1, 2, \ldots \tag{4.52b}$$

$$m_{t+1,t}^* = \phi u_t^y \tag{4.52c}$$

$$m_{t+k,t}^* = 0 \qquad k = 2, 3, \ldots. \tag{4.52d}$$

Now substituting (4.51), (4.52) into the solution (4.50), we find that current output is given by

$$y_t - \bar{y} = \frac{1}{J} \left[\gamma \frac{d_2 \phi \alpha_2}{1 + \alpha_2} + 1 \right] u_t^y. \tag{4.53}$$

The variance of output is minimized and indeed eliminated entirely by simply setting

$$\phi = -\frac{1}{\gamma d_2} \left(\frac{1 + \alpha_2}{\alpha_2} \right), \tag{4.54}$$

that is, by following the money supply rule

$$m_t = -\frac{1}{\gamma d_2} \left(\frac{1 + \alpha_2}{\alpha_2} \right) u_{t-1}^y. \tag{4.55}$$

Thus the optimal money supply rule is to contract the money supply in response to a positive disturbance in previous output and to expand it if output was low. The critical parameters determining the optimal response are: (i) semi-elasticity of the demand for money with respect to the nominal interest rate; (ii) the semi-elasticity of the demand for output with respect to the real interest rate; and (iii) the price elasticity of output.

To see how the money supply rule (4.51) is able to eliminate all the fluctuations in output, we embed the rule, together with its effects on expectations, into the complete system (4.23a′), (4.23b), (4.23c). First, substitute (4.51), (4.52), and the optimal policy (4.55) into (4.48) to obtain

$$p^*_{t+1,t} = \frac{m^*_{t+1,t}}{1 + \alpha_2} - \psi\bar{y} = \frac{m_{t+1}}{1 + \alpha_2} - \psi\bar{y} = -\frac{u^y_t}{\gamma\alpha_2 d_2} - \psi\bar{y} \qquad (4.56)$$

where, for notational convenience,

$$\psi \equiv \frac{(1 - d_1)\alpha_2 + d_2\alpha_1}{d_2}.$$

Thus the knowledge that the monetary authorities will contract the money supply in response to a positive disturbance in the previous period's output causes domestic agents to expect that a positive disturbance in the previous period's output will lead to a reduction in the price level. These expectational effects are less than proportional to the anticipated (and actual) change in the money supply.

Next, eliminating r_t from the IS and LM curves, the aggregate demand side can be written in the form

$$\psi\frac{d_2}{\alpha_2}y_t = -d_2\left(\frac{1 + \alpha_2}{\alpha_2}\right)p_t + \frac{d_2}{\alpha_2}m_t + d_2 p^*_{t+1,t} + u_{1t} - \frac{d_2}{\alpha_2}u_{2t}. \qquad (4.57)$$

Using (4.56) to eliminate m_t and $p^*_{t+1,t}$, we obtain

$$\psi\frac{d_2}{\alpha_2}(y_t - \bar{y}) + d_2\left(\frac{1 + \alpha_2}{\alpha_2}\right)(p_t - p^*_{t,t-1}) = -\frac{u^y_t}{\gamma\alpha_2} + u_{1t} - \frac{d_2}{\alpha_2}u_{2t}. \qquad (4.58)$$

Consider now the composite disturbance

$$-\frac{u^y_t}{\gamma\alpha_2} + u_{1t} - \frac{d_2}{\alpha_2}u_{2t}$$

appearing in (4.58). In particular, observe that the effect of the expected price level on aggregate demand is given by the term $-u^y_t/\gamma\alpha_2 = -u_{1t} + (d_2/\alpha_2)u_{2t} - d_2((1 + \alpha_2)/\alpha_2)(v_t/\gamma)$. Note that it incorporates the fluctuations in the demand for output u_{1t} and in the demand for money u_{2t} and precisely neutralizes the independent additive effects these two variables have on aggregate demand. Netting these effects out, (4.58) can be written as

$$\psi \frac{d_2}{\alpha_2}(y_t - \bar{y}) = -d_2 \left(\frac{1 + \alpha_2}{\alpha_2} \right) \left[p_t - p_{t,t-1}^* + \frac{v_t}{\gamma} \right]$$ (4.59)

and can be interpreted as an aggregate demand function (in deviation form) that incorporates the actual and anticipated effects of monetary policy. Combining this equation with the aggregate supply function (4.23c) makes it clear that these describe a pair of equations in output deviations $(y_t - \bar{y})$ and in unanticipated price change $(p_t - p_{t,t-1}^*)$. It is evident from considering these two equations that aggregate demand and aggregate supply will be in equilibrium if and only if

$$y_t = \bar{y},$$ (4.60a)

$$p_t = p_{t,t-1}^* - \frac{v_t}{\gamma} = -\frac{u_{t-1}^y}{\gamma \alpha_2 d_2} - \psi \bar{y} - \frac{v_t}{\gamma}.$$ (4.60b)

In short, current supply shocks are fully absorbed by the current price level, and the current demand shocks u_{1t} and u_{2t} are fully incorporated in the expected price level. These forms of adjustment permit the current output level to be stabilized perfectly each period at its natural rate level; see also Turnovsky (1980).

We have demonstrated that the optimal money supply rule (4.55) is capable of eliminating all of the variance in y_t, thereby stabilizing it perfectly. We now show that this rule is just one of an infinite number of policies capable of achieving the same result. Any rule of the form

$$m_t = \phi_i u_{t-i}^y \qquad i = 1, 2, \ldots,$$ (4.61)

so that the monetary authorities respond to disturbances in output i periods in the past, will do equally well. For this rule, the conditional expectations of (4.61) imply the following relationships:

$$m_{t+k,t-1}^* = \phi_i u_{t+k-i}^y \qquad k = 1, \ldots, i-1$$ (4.62a)

$$m_{t+k,t-1}^* = 0 \qquad k = i, \ldots$$ (4.62b)

$$m_{t+k,t}^* = \phi_i u_{t+k-i}^y \qquad k = 1, \ldots, i$$ (4.63a)

$$m_{t+k,t}^* = 0 \qquad k = i+1, \ldots.$$ (4.63b)

The solution for output is therefore

$$y_t - \bar{y} = \frac{1}{J} \left[\gamma d_2 \left(\frac{\alpha_2}{1 + \alpha_2} \right)^i \phi_i + 1 \right] u_t^y,$$ (4.64)

and the variance of output is reduced to zero by setting

$$\phi_i = -\frac{1}{\gamma d_2}\left(\frac{1+\alpha_2}{\alpha_2}\right)^i. \tag{4.65}$$

In other words, output can be stabilized fully if the monetary authorities follow a rule relating the money supply to disturbances in output pertaining to an arbitrary number of periods in the past, namely

$$m_t = -\frac{1}{\gamma d_2}\left(\frac{1+\alpha_2}{\alpha_2}\right)^i u^y_{t-i} \qquad i = 1, 2, \ldots. \tag{4.66}$$

All that is now required is that the response to a disturbance of a given magnitude must now be intensified by a factor $((1+\alpha_2)/\alpha_2)$ for each period in the past.

The explanation for this result is basically the same as for the one-period lag already discussed. To see this, we first substitute the expressions for the expectations of the future money supplies into (4.48) for $j = 1$, and at time t:

$$p^*_{t+1,t} = -\frac{1}{\gamma\alpha_2 d_2}\left[u^y_t + \left(\frac{1+\alpha_2}{\alpha_2}\right)u^y_{t-1} + \cdots + \left(\frac{1+\alpha_2}{\alpha_2}\right)^{i-1} u^y_{t-i+1}\right] - \psi\bar{y}. \tag{4.67}$$

It is seen that with the monetary rule based on shocks occurring with an i-period lag, the expectations of the price level one period ahead becomes a function of these shocks distributed over the previous i periods. Considering (4.67) at the previous period $t-1$ and noting (4.66), we can easily show that

$$p^*_{t+1,t} - \left(\frac{1+\alpha_2}{\alpha_2}\right)p^*_{t,t-1} = -\frac{u^y_t}{\gamma\alpha_2 d_2} - \frac{m_t}{\alpha_2} + \frac{\psi\bar{y}}{\alpha_2}. \tag{4.68}$$

Substituting (4.68) into the aggregate demand relationship (4.57) and recalling the definition of u^y_t, this reduces to (4.59). Thus, as before, (4.59) and the supply function (4.23c) determine the solutions for output and prices, given by (4.60a) and (4.60b) respectively. The only difference is that the expectations for $p^*_{t,t-1}$ are now functions of past disturbance u^y_{t-k} extending over i periods:

$$p^*_{t,t-1} = -\frac{1}{\gamma\alpha_2 d_2} \sum_{k=0}^{i-1}\left(\frac{1+\alpha_2}{\alpha_2}\right)^k u^y_{t-1-k} - \psi\bar{y}.$$

Two final points merit consideration. First, although we have shown that output can be stabilized perfectly about the natural rate level, $\bar{y}$, the analysis applies with minor modification to stabilization about the full information level of output, y^f_t. Rules of the type we have been considering will provide perfect stability of output about this level, as well. The economy can therefore be stabilized perfectly against price surprises. On the other hand, these rules are unable to provide perfect stability of the absolute price level. It is clear that the longer the lag embodied in the policy rule, the more past disturbances get built into price expectations and the larger the variance of the price level. Thus, among those policies that treat the elimination of fluctuations in output as the primary objective, the policy rule that uses information with only a one-period lag is optimal from the viewpoint of maximizing price stability.

4.7   Persistence of Shocks and Business Cycles

In the two formulations of the macroeconomic model presented in the foregoing sections, output at time t is a function of the new information forthcoming at that time. In the formulation considered in Sections 4.3–4.5 this is immediately apparent from the solution (4.29). In the modified model of Section 4.6, y_t depends upon revisions to forecasts made at time t, and this too depends upon the new information acquired at that time. Thus in either case we can view output as being described by a stochastic process of the form

$$y_t = \bar{y} + \zeta_t \tag{4.69}$$

where ζ_t is a composite function of the innovations to the random disturbances impinging on the economy at time t and is independently and identically distributed over time.

This means that fluctuations in output are purely random events. This implication, however, contradicts the empirical fact that fluctuations in output tend to have systematic components. A positive shock to output in period t, say, is likely to increase output not only during that period but also in subsequent periods, giving rise to possible cyclical behavior.

The theory of business cycles dominated the early work on macroeconomic dynamics that was developed during the 1930s through the 1950s (see, e.g., Samuelson 1939; Hicks 1950; Metzler 1941). The essential feature of this literature was to show how the interaction between the multiplier and the accelerator could generate a cyclical time path for output. However, for a variety of reasons, interest in business cycle theory seemed to wane in the 1960s. First, the multiplier-accelerator model is simplistic, abstracting from the financial sector of the economy. Second, the parameter values required to generate cycles were often implausible. Third, and most important, the models were linear and therefore could generate only linear cyclical behavior. That is, the cycles they yielded had to either die down or explode. They were unable to regenerate themselves. To achieve this, some form of nonlinearity was required. Hicks accomplished this by introducing a floor and a ceiling to the capacity of the economy. Other authors such as Goodwin (1951) and Kalecki (1935) achieved the necessary nonlinearity in other ways. Recent work such as that included in the recent edited volume by Benhabib (1992) on chaotic systems should prove to be important in studying business cycles.

Attempts to model the phenomenon of persistence of shocks within a rational expectations framework has given rise to stochastic models of the business cycle and contributed to a revival of interest in business cycle theory. Several approaches can be found in the literature; they are briefly described here.

Lagged Lucas Supply Function

First, as noted in Section 4.1, the original Lucas supply function included a lag in output, postulating it to be of the form

$$y_t - \bar{y} = \lambda(p_t - p^*_{t,t-1}) + \lambda(y_{t-1} - \bar{y}) + v_t.$$

In this case, with unanticipated price movements $p_t - p^*_{t,t-1}$ being white noise, output is generated by a first-order stochastic difference equation of the form

$$y_t - \bar{y} = \lambda(y_{t-1} - \bar{y}) + \zeta_t \tag{4.70}$$

where ζ_t is identically and independently distributed over time. A positive shock in ζ_t leads to an increase in output in time t and in all subsequent periods, giving rise to a persistence effect, which eventually dampens down to zero.

Capital in Supply Function

A related approach is to introduce capital into the supply function. This was done in a paper by Fischer (1979a). Specifically, he considered a model of the form

$$y_t = \alpha_0 + \alpha_1 k_t \qquad 0 < \alpha_1 < 1 \tag{4.71a}$$

$$\omega_t = \alpha_0 + \ln\alpha_1 - (1 - \alpha_1)k_t \tag{4.71b}$$

$$k_{t+1} = \beta_0 + \beta_1 \omega^*_{t+1,t} + \beta_2(p^*_{t+1,t} - p_t) + y_t \qquad \beta_1 \geq 0, \beta_2 \geq 0 \tag{4.71c}$$

$$m_t - p_t = \gamma_0 - \gamma_1 \omega^*_{t+1,t} - \gamma_2(p^*_{t+1,t} - p_t) + y_t \qquad \gamma_1 \geq 0, \gamma_2 \geq 0 \tag{4.71d}$$

where k_t denotes the logarithm of the capital stock, ω_t denotes the logarithm of the return to capital, and all other variables are as defined previously.

In this model, employment is fixed, so that (4.71a) denotes the production function, expressed logarithmically. Equation (4.71b) denotes the relationship between the real return to capital and capital, obtained by optimizing the firm's profit function. The final two equations denote the demand for capital and the demand for money, respectively. This represents a Tobin-type specification of asset markets, in which Fischer shows that provided $\beta_2 \neq 0$, so that the demand for capital is responsive to the expected rate of inflation, the capital stock and output is generated by an equation of the form

$$[1 + \beta_1(1 - \alpha_1)]k_{t+1} = [\alpha_0 + \beta_0 + (\alpha_0 + \ln\alpha_1)\beta_1]$$
$$+ \beta_2(p^*_{t+1,t} - p_t) + \alpha_1 k_t. \tag{4.72}$$

A monetary shock at time t, by altering the expected rate of inflation, will therefore generate real dynamic effects on capital and output. If $\beta_2 = 0$, on the other hand, k_t evolves along a path that is independent of the expected inflation rate and therefore of monetary policy.

Thus with $\beta_2 = 0$, monetary policy is nonneutral in Fischer's model. McCallum (1980) shows how policy neutrality is restored in this model if, instead of considering y_t (or k_t), one considers the path of output relative to capacity output, $\bar{y}_t$. In this case he shows how the deviation in output about its capacity level, $y_t - \bar{y}_t$, follows a path of the form

$$y_t - \bar{y}_t = \gamma_1(p_t - p^*_{t,t-1}) + \gamma_2(y_{t-1} - \bar{y}_{t-1}), \tag{4.73}$$

which is independent of monetary policy.

Inventories

The role of inventories has tended to be neglected in macroeconomic theory. Blinder and Fischer (1981) have introduced inventories into a rational expectations framework, demonstrating how for their specification the aggregate supply function (with output measured in levels) is modified to

$$y_t = \bar{y} + \gamma(p_t - p_{t,t-1}) + \lambda(N^*_t - N_t) + v_{1t} \tag{4.74}$$

where

N_t denotes the stock of inventories in levels,

N^*_t denotes the desired stock of inventories.

Thus, in addition to responding to price surprises, output responds to the difference between the desired and actual inventory stock. In addition, Blinder and Fischer postulate desired stock of inventories to depend upon the real interest rate,

$$N_t^* = N^* - \delta\omega_t, \tag{4.75}$$

and a stock adjustment of inventories of the form

$$N_{t+1} - N_t = \theta_1(N_t^* - N_t) - \theta_2(p_t - p_{t,t-1}^*) + v_{2t}. \tag{4.76}$$

Combining these relationships with the demand side, the end product is a stochastic difference equation for output, in which output is a distributed lag function of all past disturbances. Two principal conclusions are established in their analysis. First, an unanticipated change in the stock of money will generate a persistent change in output. Second, as long as desired inventories are sensitive to the real interest rate $\delta \neq 0$ in (4.75), then even a fully anticipated change in the stock of money will have real effects. Monetary policy is nonneutral.

Long-Plosser Model

A sectoral model of the stochastic business cycle has been developed by Long and Plosser (1983). The framework is an extension of the single-sector representative agent model we shall develop in Part III; it is a framework in which consumers optimize the expected value of an intertemporal utility function, specified in terms of a vector of consumptions of different goods and leisure. Each sector is subject to its own productivity shock and uses labor and the outputs of other sectors as inputs. Assuming a logarithmic utility function and Cobb-Douglas production functions, the equilibrium of the economy is reduced to a stochastic difference equation of the form

$$y_t = \bar{y} + A y_{t-1} + \eta_t \tag{4.77}$$

where y_t denotes a vector of outputs and η_t is a vector of stochastic disturbances. This vector equation clearly can yield complex dynamic time paths for outputs, and forms the basis for a detailed sectoral analysis. The Long-Plosser paper with its explicit optimization of stochastic systems, and the calibration of their model to real-world data, form the foundation for much of the current work on real business cycles. Some of this literature will be briefly discussed in Chapter 14.

Other Sources of Output Persistence

Most of the above analyses emphasize the role of capital in some form as being a source of output persistence. Kydland and Prescott (1982) introduce the fact that capital takes time to build, deriving a model that can also give rise to persistence. Using calibration methods, they suggest that the model replicates the covariance patterns characterizing aggregate U.S. data more satisfactorily than does the closely related cost of adjustment model, which we shall introduce in Part III. Other authors show how the gradual diffusion of information brings about gradual adjustments in output (see, e.g., Lucas 1975). Finally, long-term nominal staggered wage contracts provide yet another way for introducing lagged adjustment of output (see Taylor 1980).

4.8   Conclusions

The rational expectations hypothesis is often identified with policy neutrality. That is, it has often been said that under rational expectations, anticipated policies are ineffective; only unanticipated policy changes can have real effects. It should be clear from this chapter that this is not necessarily the case. It is possible for anticipated policies to have real effects on output under rational expectations, and much of our concern has been with determining the circumstances under which policy neutrality may or may not hold.

One of the key points emphasized in Section 4.6 concerns the dating of information. In fact, for the information set considered in that section, we have shown that a policy feedback rule based on past information will not only influence current output but, if chosen optimally, may actually reduce its variance to zero, thereby stabilizing it perfectly about some chosen target value. This is surely as strong an antineutrality proposition as one could possibly wish for.

The fact that the effectiveness or ineffectiveness of policy depends so critically on the dating of information is important. No macro model can be so precise with respect to such details. Furthermore, one of the most important and active areas of research employing the rational expectations hypothesis is its application to foreign exchange markets, where rational expectations are formed on exchange rates. Information on exchange rates is available virtually instantaneously, so that it makes sense to assume that exchange rate expectations for the future are conditioned on the observation of the current rate—or, in other words, to adopt the information structure of Section 4.6. Consequently, in this entire literature, policy neutrality breaks down for precisely the reasons discussed in that section.

Chapters 3 and 4 have discussed the standard procedures for solving linear rational expectations macroeconomic models. We have seen how the solution always involves an arbitrary constant (or constants). This has been determined so as to rule out explosive behavior in the economy. For many macroeconomic models, this imposition of stability suffices to determine unique values for the arbitrary constants, thereby determining the time path for the economy uniquely. But in other cases, stability alone may not suffice to determine a unique solution; an infinite number of rational expectations solutions, each consistent with a stable path, may exist. Such equilibria are based on extraneous sources of uncertainty and for this reason are traditionally referred to as "sunspot equilibria." Among this set of solutions, stronger conditions must be imposed in order to determine a particular rational expectations equilibrium solution.

In this chapter we will identify and discuss two distinct sources of nonuniqueness associated with rational expectations models. The first is of the sunspot variety where the essential issue concerns the determination of the arbitrary constants of integration. The first author to draw attention to the problem of nonuniqueness (or multiplicity) of solutions in such linear rational expectations models was Black (1974). Three years later, Taylor (1977) presented a procedure for resolving the nonuniqueness issue. His model and solution method is discussed in Section 5.1. In the Taylor model, the nonuniqueness arises through the introduction of real money balances in the production function. By contrast, in the Black model it arises through the specification of government stabilization policy; this issue is discussed in Section 5.2 using the Cagan model as the vehicle.

Although Taylor provides one way to resolve nonuniqueness, it is arbitrary and subject to certain criticisms, noted in Section 5.3. More recently, McCallum (1983) has proposed an alternative (also arbitrary) procedure for dealing with nonuniqueness; this is discussed in Sections 5.4 and 5.5. A formal characterization of the conditions for existence and uniqueness of solutions to dynamic rational expectations models was developed by Blanchard and Kahn (1980) and is considered in Section 5.6. For given coefficients, rational expectations models are invariably linear in the endogenous variables. And indeed, as we have seen, the solution methods rely heavily on the linearity of the system.

The second type of nonuniqueness is associated with the nonlinearity of the macroeconomic model itself. Even a simple ad hoc macro model, such as that discussed and analyzed in Chapter 2, is intrinsically nonlinear. Even if all underlying functions are linear, nonlinearities arise through terms such as rb, which represents the interest payments on government bonds, and pb, the inflation tax on government bonds. The multiplicity of equilibria in such models, and their associated stability characteristics, are considered in Section 5.7. A second potential source of nonlinearity arises when one derives the rational expectations structural models from underlying optimizing behavior. In the process, coefficients that are taken as given in the linear model themselves become endogenously determined, thereby making the complete system inherently nonlinear. This important observation was first made by McCafferty and Driskill (1980). They showed how this process raises questions of both nonexistence and nonuniqueness of equilibrium. But the reasons are very different from those discussed by Taylor and Black, having to do with solutions to nonlinear systems rather than with the determination of arbitrary constants to linear systems. This issue will be discussed further in Section 5.8.

5.1   The Taylor Model

We begin our discussion of nonuniqueness of rational expectations models by considering the model due to Taylor (1977), which consists of the following four equations:

$$y_t = -d_1[r_t - (p^*_{t+1,t-1} - p^*_{t,t-1})] + d_2(m_t - p_t) + u_{1t} \tag{5.1a}$$

$$m_t - p_t = y_t - \alpha_1 r_t + \alpha_2(m_t - p_t) + u_{2t} \tag{5.1b}$$

$$y_t = \gamma_0 + \gamma_1(m_t - p_t) + u_{3t} \tag{5.1c}$$

$$m_t = m \tag{5.1d}$$

where

y_t = real output, measured in logarithms, at time t,

r_t = nominal interest rate at time t,

p_t = price of output, measured in logarithms, at time t,

$p^*_{t+i,t-1}$ = prediction of p formed at time $t - 1$ for time $t + i$,

m_t = nominal stock of money balances, measured in logarithms, at time t,

u_{it} = $i = 1, 2, 3$ are random disturbances, with zero means, finite variance-covariance matrix, and independently distributed over time.

With the differences noted below, the model is generally similar in structure to that of Chapter 4. Equation (5.1a) is the *IS* curve, with aggregate demand depending negatively upon the real interest rate and positively upon real money balances. Observe that the expected rate of inflation is conditioned on information available at time $t - 1$. But this choice of timing is inessential to the present analysis. Equation (5.1b) is the *LM* curve, with the demand for money depending positively upon real income and real money balances but negatively upon the nominal interest rate. Again this is fairly standard. Aggregate supply is specified in (5.1c) to depend positively upon real money balances. This represents a significant departure from the Lucas-type supply functions we have utilized previously. The rationale for this specification was originally given by Levhari and Patinkin (1968) in terms of real money balances serving as an input in the production function. The rationale for this is that higher money balances mean a larger working capital, enabling the firm to purchase more inputs and thereby produce a greater output. Although the supporting evidence is inconclusive, this aspect of real money balances is crucial for generating the nonuniqueness in the Taylor model. Finally, equation (5.1d) simply asserts that real money balances remain fixed.

Eliminating r_t and y_t from equations (5.1a) through (5.1c) and using (5.1d) leads to the following stochastic difference equation in prices:

$$p^*_{t+1,t-1} = p^*_{t,t-1} + \delta_1 p_t + \delta_0 + u_t \tag{5.2}$$

where

$$\delta_1 \equiv (1 - \alpha_2)/\alpha_1 + d_2/d_1 - \gamma_1(1/\alpha_1 + 1/d_1)$$

$$\delta_0 \equiv \gamma_0(1/\alpha_1 + 1/d_1) - \delta_1 m$$

$$u_t \equiv -(1/d_1)u_{1t} + (1/\alpha_1)u_{2t} + (1/\alpha_1 + 1/d_1)u_{3t}.$$

Taylor solves this equation by using the method of undetermined coefficients. Postulating a solution of the form

$$p_t = \bar{p} + \sum_{i=0}^{\infty} \pi_i u_{t-i}, \tag{5.3}$$

we immediately obtain

$$p^*_{t,t-1} = \bar{p} + \sum_{i=1}^{\infty} \pi_i u_{t-i} \tag{5.4a}$$

$$p^*_{t+1,t-1} = \bar{p} + \sum_{i=2}^{\infty} \pi_i u_{t+1-i}. \tag{5.4b}$$

Substituting for (5.3) and (5.4) into (5.2) and equating coefficients yields the identities

$$\bar{p} = -\frac{\delta_0}{\delta_1}$$

$$\pi_0 = -\frac{1}{\delta_1}$$

$$\pi_{i+1} = (1 + \delta_1)\pi_i \qquad i = 1, 2, \dots. \tag{5.5}$$

The solution for p_t is therefore

$$p_t = -\frac{\delta_0}{\delta_1} - \left(\frac{1}{\delta_1}\right)u_t + \pi_1 \sum_{i=0}^{\infty} (1 + \delta_1)^i u_{t-i-1} \tag{5.6}$$

where π_1 remains undetermined. Squaring (5.6) and taking expected values, the unconditioned variance of p_t is

$$\text{var}(p_t) = \left[\left(\frac{1}{\delta_1}\right)^2 + \pi_1^2 \sum_{i=0}^{\infty} (1 + \delta_1)^{2i}\right]\sigma_u^2 \tag{5.7}$$

where σ_u^2 is the variance of the composite disturbance u_t.

If $\delta_1 > 0$, the only value of π_1 that yields a finite variance for p_t is $\pi_1 = 0$. Hence, when $\delta_1 > 0$, the finite variance criterion gives a unique solution for p_t, namely

$$p_t = \frac{-[\delta_0 + u_t]}{\delta_1}. \tag{5.8}$$

It is clear that one case in which $\delta_1 > 0$ is if $\gamma_1 = 0$, so that real balances do not affect aggregate supply. In this case, a unique stable (finite variance) solution will obtain even if real balances appear in the aggregate demand or money demand functions.

For any value of δ_1 lying in the range $-2 < \delta_1 < 0$, we have $|1 + \delta_1| < 1$, so that $\text{var}(p_t)$ is finite for any arbitrary value of π_1. In this case a multiplicity of stable rational expectations equilibria exist. It is clear from examining δ_1 that for γ_1 sufficiently large it is possible to generate values of δ_1 lying in the range $-2 < \delta_1 < 0$, thereby giving rise to multiple solutions.

The solutions to (5.6) that correspond to arbitrary values of π_1 are examples of *sunspot* equilibria. That is, they are equilibria that depend upon extraneous shocks, simply because agents form their expectations using this information. The bubbles solutions discussed in Section 3.6 are also examples of sunspot equilibria, but in most cases they are associated with unstable solutions. Here the multiplicity of arbitrary solutions are all stable.

This immediately raises the question of which solution to choose. Taylor resolves this matter by proposing to strengthen the criterion that var(p_t) be *finite* to, instead, that var(p_t) be *minimized*. In the present example π_1 is determined to minimize (5.7). This implies $\pi_1 = 0$, so that the solution for p_t again reduces to (5.8). In other words, imposing the condition that var(p_t) be minimized implies the unique solution for p_t (5.8) for *all* values of δ_1.

5.2   Nonuniqueness Due to Policy

We return to the discrete-time Cagan monetary model of Chapter 3:

$$m_t - p_t = -\alpha[p_{t+1,t}^* - p_t] + u_t \tag{5.9}$$

where all symbols are as defined previously and, for convenience, are interpreted as being in deviation form about some fixed equilibrium. Suppose now that the monetary authorities engage in active stabilization in accordance with the rule

$$m_t = -\lambda p_t. \tag{5.10}$$

That is, the money stock is adjusted in response to movements in the current price level, with λ being a policy parameter describing the direction and degree of intervention. In principle, λ can be of either sign. A value of $\lambda < 0$ means that the authorities are accommodating to current price movements, trying to maintain real money balances. A value of $\lambda > 0$ means that they seek to offset the higher inflationary pressures by engaging in monetary contraction. Which of these policies may be appropriate depends upon the policymaker's objective, and this question will be addressed to some extent in Chapter 8.

Substituting (5.10) into (5.9) leads to the following equation in p_t:

$$\alpha p_{t+1,t}^* - (1 + \alpha + \lambda)p_t = u_t. \tag{5.11}$$

Postulating a solution of the form

$$p_t = \sum_{i=0}^{\infty} \pi_i u_{t-i} \tag{5.12}$$

and applying the method of undetermined coefficients leads to the identities

$$\pi_0 = \frac{\alpha\pi_1 - 1}{1 + \alpha + \lambda}, \tag{5.13a}$$

$$\pi_{i+1} = \left[\frac{1 + \alpha + \lambda}{\alpha}\right]\pi_i \qquad i = 1, 2, \ldots \tag{5.13b}$$

so that the solution for p_t is

$$p_r = \left(\frac{\alpha \pi_1 - 1}{1 + \alpha + \lambda} \right) u_t + \pi_1 \left[u_{t-1} + \left(\frac{1 + \alpha + \lambda}{\alpha} \right) u_{t-2} + \cdots \right] \qquad (5.14)$$

where π_1 is undetermined.

In the absence of any active policy, $\lambda = 0$, in which case the only solution having a finite variance is $\pi_1 = 0$, implying

$$p_t = -\frac{u_t}{1 + \alpha}. \qquad (5.15)$$

This of course is precisely the solution obtained in Chapter 3; that is, it is what the solution (3.36) obtained there would reduce to if the monetary disturbances were white noise, as they are assumed to be here. Likewise for any value of the policy parameter λ for which

$$\left| \frac{1 + \alpha + \lambda}{\alpha} \right| > 1, \qquad (5.16a)$$

the same instability occurs, again necessitating the choice of $n_1 = 0$ for a finite variance. Notice that this includes all degrees of anti-inflationary monetary policies where $\lambda \geq 0$.

On the other hand, if $-(1 + 2\alpha) < \lambda < -1$, then

$$\left| \frac{1 + \alpha + \lambda}{\alpha} \right| < 1, \qquad (5.16b)$$

in which case var(p_t), given by the expression

$$\text{var}(p_t) = \left[\left(\frac{\alpha \pi_1 - 1}{1 + \alpha + \lambda} \right)^2 + \frac{\pi_1^2}{1 - \left(\frac{1 + \alpha + \lambda}{\alpha} \right)^2} \right] \sigma_u^2, \qquad (5.17)$$

is finite for all values of π_1. The minimum variance criterion, proposed by Taylor, involves choosing π_1 to minimize (5.17). Performing the minimization yields

$$\frac{\alpha(\alpha \pi_1 - 1)}{(1 + \alpha + \lambda)^2} + \frac{\pi_1}{1 - \left(\frac{1 + \alpha + \lambda}{\alpha} \right)^2} = 0,$$

which yields the following solution for π_1:

$$\pi_1 = \frac{\alpha^2 - (1 + \alpha + \lambda)^2}{\alpha^3} > 0. \qquad (5.18)$$

Thus for λ satisfying (5.16b), the minimum variance criterion implies that p_t is given by (5.14), where π_1 is given by (5.18).

5.3   Critique of the Minimum Variance Criterion

Although the minimum variance criterion may seem to be a very natural extension of the finite variance criterion, it is subject to several criticisms. First, it is by no means clear what mechanism is bringing about this minimization. Who is performing the minimization? Taylor argues that the minimum variance criterion is no less arbitrary than the finite variance criterion, but this seems dubious. The latter, which is equivalent to imposing stability, can often be justified in terms of transversality conditions, reflecting optimizing behavior; no analogous argument can be applied to justify a minimum variance. But there are other issues. For example, what variance is being minimized?

In the example given in Section 5.2 we have assumed that π_1 is chosen to minimize the asymptotic (unconditioned) variance of p_t. This implies the value of π_1 given in equation (5.18). But what if, instead, π_1 is chosen to minimize the one-period variance of p_t, namely

$$\sigma_p^2(1) \equiv E_{t-1}[p_t - E_{t-1}(p_t)]^2?$$

In this case, returning to (5.14), we see that

$$p_t - p_{t,t-1}^* = \left(\frac{\alpha\pi_1 - 1}{1 + \alpha + \lambda}\right)u_t$$

so that the one-period variance is

$$\sigma_p^2(1) = \left(\frac{\alpha\pi_1 - 1}{1 + \alpha + \lambda}\right)^2 \sigma_u^2. \tag{5.19}$$

To minimize this, set $\pi_1 = 1/\alpha$, yielding the equilibrium solution for p_t

$$p_t = \frac{1}{\alpha}\left[u_{t-1} + \left(\frac{1 + \alpha + \lambda}{\alpha}\right)u_{t-2} + \cdots\right]. \tag{5.20}$$

For this value of π_t, p_t is a function only of *past* disturbances, so that the minimized one-period variance is in fact zero. In any event, the stochastic process for p_t described by (5.20) is very different from the solution for (5.14) and (5.18) given in the previous section, where the asymptotic variance was being minimized. And nothing in any arbitrary macroeconomic model tells us which of these two variances—or, for that matter, of any other n-period variances—is the appropriate one to minimize.

A further problem with this procedure is that the solution as presented by Taylor, and followed in our exposition here, is in terms of solving a difference equation in the price level. This choice is frequently dictated by convenience. But we could equally well have chosen to eliminate output and the prices level and instead of (5.2) derived a difference equation expressed in terms of the nominal interest rate and its expectations. The problem is that the stochastic process that minimizes the (unconditional) variance of the interest rate is not in general the same as that which will minimize the variance of the price level, so that a further degree of arbitrariness exists. Are people seeking to minimize the variance of the price level, the interest rate, or some other variable? Again an arbitrary macro model such as this does not address this issue.

Finally, and perhaps most importantly, the minimum variance criterion can give rise to a rather bizarre discontinuity in the solution as the policy parameter λ varies. Specifically, if either $\lambda > -1$ or $\lambda < -(1 + 2\alpha)$ we have seen that the finite variance criterion implies $\pi_1 = 0$, so that the equilibrium solution for p_t is given by

$$p_t = -\frac{1}{1 + \alpha + \lambda} u_t. \tag{5.21}$$

The important point is that the current price level depends only upon the *current* disturbances, u_t. This is true for, say, any $\lambda > -1$. Now as λ passes through the value -1 and eventually becomes smaller, we move into the "stable" range where π_1 is arbitrary. The imposition of the minimum variance criterion leads to the solution for p_t given by the infinite distributed lag (5.14), with π_1 being determined by (5.18). In other words, as the policy parameter λ changes from, say, $\lambda = -.99$ to $\lambda = -1.01$, the nature of the rational expectations equilibrium solution for p_t changes dramatically, from an extremely simple stochastic process depending upon only current shocks, to a much more complicated one depending upon all past disturbances. This discontinuity in the nature of the process as the policy parameter crosses such boundary values seems, on reflection, to be unsatisfactory and arbitrary.

5.4   The Minimum State Representation Solution

The reactions of authors to the multiplicity of solutions in linear rational expectations models have been varied. Some writers have suggested that this calls into question the usefulness of the rational expectations hypothesis. Others take the position that the problem of the choice among the equilibria will be resolved as our theoretical understanding of the relevant markets progresses. In this respect, the minimum variance criterion must be viewed as being entirely arbitrary, since no compelling theoretical principles have been invoked to justify the minimization of one variance over another.

While the multiplicity of solutions has often been identified with rational expectations equilibria, it is in fact a generic property of dynamic models in general. The backward-looking adaptive expectations hypothesis also has an arbitrary constant. If expectations are generated according to

$$p^*_{t,t-1} - p^*_{t-1,t-2} = \gamma[p_{t-1} - p^*_{t-1,t-2}] \qquad 0 \le \gamma \le 1,$$

the solution for the forecast formed at time $t - 1$ is

$$p^*_{t,t-1} = A(1 - \gamma)^t + \gamma \sum_{j=0}^{\infty} (1 - \gamma)^j p_{t-j-1} \qquad (5.22)$$

where the constant A is arbitrary. There are therefore an infinite number of solutions, one for each chosen value of A. In fact, the multiplicity is likely to be much more serious than under rational expectations; the reason is that, because $(1 - \gamma) < 1$, there is no compelling stability argument to suggest setting $A = 0$, as is typically the case in rational expectations models. Furthermore, the arbitrariness of the solution (5.22) will carry over to any larger dynamic macro model embodying the adaptive hypothesis.

The upshot of the discussion to this point is that, in the absence of any "deep theorizing," any rational expectations solution is to some degree arbitrary. The issue is to select those equilibria that are of economic interest. In this connection, McCallum (1983) suggests a criterion based on the *minimal* set of state variables being employed in forming forecasting rules. This criterion, although also arbitrary, has some intuitive appeal. It recognizes the fact that information is scarce and costly, so that agents, in forming their forecasts, may seek to economize on its use.

We now apply this criterion to the examples from sections 5.1 and 5.2. In the case of the Taylor model, it will be recalled that the basic difference equation determining the rational expectations equilibrium is given by

$$p^*_{t+1,t-1} = p^*_{t,t-1} + \delta_1 p_t + \delta_0 + u_t. \qquad (5.2)$$

Instead of postulating a solution as general as (5.3), McCallum proposes the simplest solution that can be consistent with (5.2). In this case, the minimal form of the solution is

$$p_t = \bar{p} + \pi_0 u_t, \qquad (5.3')$$

in which the current price level depends upon the current disturbance u_t rather than all past disturbances as in (5.3). Taking conditional expectations of (5.3') immediately yields

$$p^*_{t,t-1} = p^*_{t+1,t-1} = \bar{p},\qquad(5.4')$$

and substituting (5.3') and (5.4') into (5.2) we find

$$\bar{p} = -\frac{\delta_0}{\delta_1},$$

$$\pi_0 = -\frac{1}{\delta_1},$$

implying the solution for p_t

$$p_t = -\frac{[\delta_0 + u_t]}{\delta_1}.\qquad(5.23)$$

Under the McCallum procedure, (5.23) is the solution for *all* values of δ_1. We have seen that under the finite variance criterion, (5.23) is the solution as long as $\delta_1 > 0$. For $\delta_1 < 0$, we have also seen that invoking the minimum variance criterion implies $\pi_1 = 0$ in (5.6), in which case the solution also reduces to (5.23). Hence in this example the McCallum minimal representation criterion and the Taylor minimum variance criterion yield identical equilibrium solutions. But this need not always be so.

To see how the equilibria may diverge, consider the example of Section 5.2. In this case, the minimal solution to (5.11) is of the form

$$p_t = \pi_0 u_t.\qquad(5.12')$$

This again implies

$$p^*_{t+1,t} = 0,$$

and the method of undetermined coefficients yields the solution

$$p_t = -\frac{u_t}{1 + \alpha + \lambda}.\qquad(5.24)$$

Again, this holds for all values of the policy parameter λ.

We have seen that this same solution is obtained using the minimum variance criterion, as long as λ lies in the range $\lambda > -1$ or $\lambda < -(2\alpha + 1)$. On the other hand, for λ lying outside this range, we have also seen that the minimum variance criterion yields the solution (5.14), with π_1 given by (5.18), which no longer coincides with the McCallum solution.

In some applications of the McCallum procedure, the application of the method of undetermined coefficients involves the solution of a non-linear equation, thereby creating a further possible source of nonuniqueness. In the Cagan model, for example, this occurs when the money supply is assumed to be adjusted to the past rather than the current price level. Specifically, consider the model consisting of

$$m_t - p_t = -\alpha(p_{t+1,t}^* - p_t) + w_t \tag{5.9}$$

together with the policy rule

$$m_t = -\lambda p_{t-1}. \tag{5.10'}$$

Combining these two equations yields the difference equation

$$\alpha p_{t+1,t}^* - (1 + \alpha)p_t - \lambda p_{t-1} = u_t. \tag{5.11'}$$

Observe that it differs from (5.11) by the inclusion of a term in p_{t-1}. As a consequence, the minimal solution is of the form

$$p_t = \pi_0 u_t + \pi_1 p_{t-1}, \tag{5.25}$$

from which we calculate the conditional expectation

$$p_{t+1,t}^* = \pi_1 p_t = \pi_1 [\pi_0 u_t + \pi_1 p_{t-1}]. \tag{5.26}$$

Substituting for (5.25) and (5.26) into (5.11') yields

$$\alpha \pi_1 [\pi_0 u_t + \pi_1 p_{t-1}] - (1 + \alpha)[\pi_0 u_t + \pi_1 p_{t-1}] - \lambda p_{t-1} = u_t,$$

and, equating coefficients of u_t, p_{t-1} in this equation, we obtain the identities

$$1 + (1 + \alpha)\pi_0 - \alpha\pi_0\pi_1 = 0, \tag{5.27a}$$

$$\alpha\pi_1^2 - (1 + \alpha)\pi_1 - \lambda = 0. \tag{5.27b}$$

The solution to the second of these equations is

$$\pi_1 = \frac{(1 + \alpha) \pm \sqrt{(1 + \alpha)^2 + 4\alpha\lambda}}{2\alpha}. \tag{5.28}$$

There are therefore two possible values for π_1, each of which implies a corresponding value for π_0.

To choose between them, consider the special case $\lambda = 0$. In this case p_{t-1} would disappear from (5.11') and would therefore not appear in the minimal set of state variables. In this case the solution for π_1 would be zero; this will be obtained only if the negative root is taken in (5.28). Continuity then suggests that the negative root is appropriate for all values of the policy parameter λ. McCallum justifies this procedure by arguing that the reduced-form coefficients must be continuous functions of the structural coefficients. By introducing this stipulation, the type of discontinuity noted in connection with the minimum variance criterion in Section 5.2 does not arise.

5.5   Some Objections to the Minimum State Representation Solution

Several objections have been raised in connection with the McCallum minimal state set criterion. First, Scarth (1985) notes that in applying McCallum's procedure to identify roots of nonlinear equations, one must be careful to consider all relevant extreme parameter values. He argues that it may be hard to narrow down the taxonomy of solutions because adequate evidence may not exist to decide which range of parameter values is relevant. Scarth shows further how ruling out unappealing dynamic paths may also assist in narrowing the range of parameter possibilities, in much the same way as the correspondence principle has traditionally been used in macroeconomic dynamics.

A second objection, noted by Evans (1986), is that in some cases the solution of the nonlinear equation analogous to (5.28) may yield only complex solutions even though real-valued solutions to the underlying model exist. In this case, the criterion will mislead one into believing that there is no economically feasible rational expectations solution, whereas in fact a perfectly well defined, but higher-order solution (i.e., one involving a larger number of state variables) in fact exists. An example of this is given by Evans and Honkapohja (1986).

Third, as pointed out by Evans (1986) and by Pesaran (1987), in some cases the criterion may lead to a solution that does not appear to be economically feasible. As an example of this, consider the following:

$$y_t = \alpha E_t y_{t+1} + w_t, \tag{5.29a}$$

$$w_t = \rho_0 + \rho_1 w_{t-1} + u_t \tag{5.29b}$$

where y_t is an endogenous variable, w_t is generated by the first-order process (5.29b), and u_t is white noise. The minimal state set solution is given by

$$y_t = \frac{\rho_0 \alpha}{(1 - \alpha)(1 - \alpha \rho_1)} + \frac{1}{(1 - \alpha \rho_1)} w_t, \tag{5.30}$$

provided $\alpha \neq 1$, $\rho_1 \neq 1$. Under the usual conditions $|\alpha| < 1$, $|\rho_1| < 1$, this provides a plausible solution. However, if $\alpha > 0$, $\rho_1 > 0$, and $\alpha \rho_1 > 1$, the solution appears to be less sensible, in that positive shocks in w_t drive y_t

below its mean. This observation was noted by McCallum, whose resolution of the issue was simply to include the condition $\alpha\rho_1 < 1$ as part of the model.

By contrast, Evans (1985, 1986) resolves these difficulties by imposing what he calls the condition of expectational stability, initially introduced in Section 3.7. Specifically, a rational expectations solution is said to be stable if, when it is subjected to a small disequilibrium deviation, the system returns to that equilibrium under a natural revision rule. To illustrate this, we consider the example described by equations (5.29a) and (5.29b), due to Evans (1986).

Taking conditional expectations of the solution (5.30) to this system yields the following expectations function:

$$E_t y_{t+1} = \frac{\rho_0}{(1-\alpha)(1-\alpha\rho_1)} + \frac{\rho_1}{1-\alpha\rho_1} w_t.$$

Consider now a deviation of the coefficients of this function; that is, expectations are generated by

$$\tilde{y}_{t+1}^N = c_N + a_N w_t \tag{5.31}$$

where

$$c_N \neq \frac{\rho_0}{(1-\alpha)(1-\alpha\rho_1)}, \qquad \alpha_N \neq \frac{\rho_1}{1-\alpha\rho_1}.$$

With expectations described by (5.31), the solution for y_t is

$$y_t = \alpha\tilde{y}_{t+1}^N + w_t;$$

that is,

$$y_t = \alpha c_N + (1 + \alpha a_N) w_t. \tag{5.32}$$

But if y_t is generated by (5.32), the unbiased forecast for y_{t+1} using this information is given by $\alpha c_N + (1 + \alpha a_N)E_t w_{t+1}$. Taking account of (5.29b) suggests that the forecast (5.31) should be revised to

$$\tilde{y}_{t+1}^{N+1} = \alpha c_N + (1 + \alpha a_N)(\rho_0 + \rho_1 w_t). \tag{5.33}$$

Comparing (5.33) with (5.31) we obtain the following recursive relationships for updating the coefficients c_N, and a_N:

$$c_{N+1} = \alpha c_N + \rho_0(1 + \alpha a_N), \tag{5.34a}$$

$$a_{N+1} = \rho_1(1 + \alpha a_N). \tag{5.34b}$$

From these two equations it can be shown that the coefficients c_N and a_N converge to

$$c = \frac{\rho_0}{(1 - \alpha)(1 - \alpha\rho_1)}, \qquad a = \frac{\rho_1}{1 - \alpha\rho_1}$$

if and only if

$$|\alpha\rho_1| < 1 \qquad \text{and} \qquad |\alpha| < 1. \tag{5.35}$$

In other words, the solution is expectationally stable if and only if (5.35) holds. This condition imposes restrictions on the underlying parameters of the model, thereby helping to resolve the nonuniqueness issue. The requirement of expectational stability is, in effect, a supplement to the McCallum procedure.

5.6   Characterization of Solutions of General Rational Expectations Systems

In any general dynamic system it is important to draw the distinction between (i) variables whose evolution is tied to the past—so-called pre-determined or "sluggish variables; and (ii) variables which are not so constrained—"jump" variables. The relation numbers of these two sets of variables are extremely important in determining the uniqueness or nonuniqueness of rational expectations equilibria.

In the examples considered thus far in our discussion of rational expectations, the dynamic structure has been exceedingly simple. We have basically considered only one dynamic variable, the price level, which we have treated as a jump variable. The dynamic model of Chapter 3 contained just one unstable root. The arbitrary constant in the solution was uniquely determined so as to eliminate the effects of the unstable root from the system. In the Taylor model, there is no unstable root. All solutions are consistent with stability, and that is the cause of the multiplicity of solutions.

The characterization of dynamic variables as sluggish or jump variables is generally dictated by the economic structure. Variables such as the capital stock, which take time to accumulate, clearly belong in the former category. On the other hand, financial variables such as exchange rates and interest rates, which typically incorporate new information as it becomes available, are most naturally viewed as jump variables. The treatment of the price of output is less clear-cut. In situations where the price is determined by contracts, it may be more appropriately treated as a sluggish variable, as in the Phillips curve, rather than as a jump variable, as we have been treating it here.

Blanchard and Kahn (1980) have sought to characterize the uniqueness of solution issue for a relatively general dynamic discrete-time rational expectations model. The structure they consider is described by the system

$$\begin{pmatrix} X_{t+1} \\ P^*_{t+1,t} \end{pmatrix} = A \begin{pmatrix} X_t \\ P_t \end{pmatrix} + BZ_t \tag{5.36}$$

where

X is a $(n \times 1)$ vector of variables predetermined at time t,

P is a $(m \times 1)$ vector of variables, nonpredetermined at time t,

Z is a $(k \times 1)$ vector of exogenous variables at time t,

$P^*_{t+1,t}$ is the expectation of P_{t+1} held at time t,

A is an $(n + m) \times (n + m)$ matrix,

B is an $(n + m) \times k$ matrix.

Expectations are rational so that

$$P^*_{t+1,t} = E_t(P_{t+1})$$

where $E_t(\cdot)$ is the statistical expectation, conditional on information available at time t. Finally, restrictions are imposed on the growth rate of the exogenous variables. These restrictions are analogous to those introduced in Chapter 3.

Blanchard and Kahn show how the formulation (5.36) embodies a large variety of, but certainly not all, linear economic structures. Examples are given that cannot be put in this form. As written, (5.36) is a dynamic system of order $(n + m)$, of which $\bar{m}$ roots lie outside the unit circle, with the remainder lying on or within the unit circle. The key to the solution to (5.36) involves the relationship between the number of unstable roots, $\bar{m}$, and the number of jump variables, m. Blanchard and Kahn establish the following propositions:

Proposition 5.1 If the number of unstable roots $\bar{m}$ equals the number of jump variables, m, then there exists a unique stable (nonexplosive) solution to (5.36).

Proposition 5.2 If the number of unstable roots $\bar{m}$ is less than the number of jump variables, m, there are an infinite number of stable solutions to (5.36).

Proposition 5.3 If the number of unstable roots, $\bar{m}$, exceeds the number of jump variables, m, there is no solution to (5.36) that is nonexplosive.

The unique solutions obtained in Chapters 3 and 4 are in effect examples of Proposition 1, and the multiplicity of solutions obtained in Sections

5.1 and 5.2 of this chapter are examples of Proposition 2. In Chapter 7 we will give an example of a dynamic system having "too many" unstable roots, so that no bounded solution exists, thereby illustrating Proposition 3. An analogous characterization of solutions in a continuous-time rational expectations model is provided by Buiter (1984).

5.7   A Nonlinear Macrodynamic Model

Consider the following macrodynamic model, specified in continuous time and similar to that introduced in Chapter 2:

$$Y = D(Y^D, r - \pi, A) + G \qquad 0 < D_1 < 1, D_2 < 0, D_3 > 0 \tag{5.37a}$$

$$Y^D = Y - T + rb - \pi A \tag{5.37b}$$

$$A = m + b \tag{5.37c}$$

$$m = L(Y, r, A) \qquad L_1 > 0, L_2 < 0, 0 \le L_3 \le 1 \tag{5.37d}$$

$$\left\{ \begin{array}{l} p = \alpha(Y - \overline{Y}) + \pi \qquad \alpha > 0 \tag{5.37e} \\[6pt] \pi = p \quad \text{perfect myopic foresight} \tag{5.37f} \end{array} \right.$$

$$\dot{m} = \theta(G - T + rb) - pm \qquad 0 \le \theta \le 1 \tag{5.37g}$$

$$\dot{b} = (1 - \theta)(G - T + rb) - pb \tag{5.37h}$$

where all the symbols remain as defined in Chapter 2. The first five equations are identical to (2.33a) through (2.33e), whereas (5.37f) describes the assumption of perfect myopic foresight. The new aspects are contained in equations (5.37g) and (5.37h), according to which a fraction θ of the real deficit $G - T + rB/P$ is financed by money, and the remaining proportion is financed by issuing bonds. Combining (5.37e) and (5.37f), it is seen that output is pegged at its full employment level $\overline{Y}$, and the model simplifies to

$$\overline{Y} = D(\overline{Y} - T + (r - p)b - pm, r - p, m + b) + G \tag{5.38a}$$

$$m = L(\overline{Y}, r, m + b) \tag{5.38b}$$

$$\dot{m} = \theta(G - T + rb) - pm \tag{5.38c}$$

$$\dot{b} = (1 - \theta)(G - T + rb) - pb \tag{5.38d}$$

where r and p are determined by (5.38a) and (5.38b), and m and b evolve in accordance with (5.38c) and (5.38d).

The steady-state equilibrium of this economy (denoted by tildes), obtained by setting $\dot{m} = \dot{b} = 0$, is described by the set of equations

$$\overline{Y} = D(\overline{Y} - G, \tilde{r} - \tilde{p}, \tilde{m} + \tilde{b}) + G \tag{5.39a}$$

$$\tilde{m} = L(\overline{Y}, \tilde{r}, \tilde{m} + \tilde{b}) \tag{5.39b}$$

$$\theta(G - T + \tilde{r}\tilde{b}) = \tilde{p}\tilde{m} \tag{5.39c}$$

$$(1 - \theta)(G - T + \tilde{r}\tilde{b}) = \tilde{p}\tilde{b} \tag{5.39d}$$

We shall treat $G - T$ and θ as exogenous government policy variables, and for each choice there are two classes of steady state. This possibility arises because of the nonlinearities stemming from the inflation taxes on money and bonds (pm, pb) together with the interest payments on government bonds (rb). One of the classes of steady state that may arise is described by equations (5.39a)–(5.39d), with $\theta \neq 0$, which in general is characterized by a nonzero steady-state rate of inflation (i.e., $\tilde{p} \neq 0$) and is dependent upon both government policy parameters, $G - T$ and θ. We shall refer to this as the *inflationary* steady state.

Alternatively, (5.39a)–(5.39d) will also be met if

$$\overline{Y} = D(\overline{Y} - G, \tilde{r} - \tilde{p}, \tilde{m} + \tilde{b}) + G \tag{5.39a}$$

$$\tilde{m} = L(\overline{Y}, \tilde{r}, \tilde{m} + \tilde{b}) \tag{5.39b}$$

$$G - T + \tilde{r}\tilde{b} = 0 \tag{5.39c$'$}$$

$$\tilde{p} = 0. \tag{5.39d$'$}$$

In this case the steady state involves government budget balance at zero inflation; it will be referred to as the *stable-price* steady state. Note that although it depends upon the fiscal policy parameter $G - T$, it is independent of the financial policy parameter θ.

By examining the two classes of steady states, we can see that each is associated with the possibility of zero, one, or multiple steady-state equilibria. The possibility of zero equilibria arises because, due to the nonlinearity, there is no presumption that the solution to either the inflationary or the stable-price equilibrium will yield solutions that are economically feasible in the sense that certain variables satisfy nonnegativity conditions. For example, (5.39c$'$) will yield a solution in which both the nominal interest rate and the stock of outstanding government debt are nonnegative if and only if the government runs a current surplus (i.e., if $G - T < 0$). Otherwise, one of these two variables will be negative. The potential multiplicity of solutions is again apparent from (5.39c$'$), which defines a rectangular hyperbola in r and b space. Depending upon the relationship between r and b determined by the demand side, equations (5.39a) and (5.39b) may yield one or two (or more) equilibrium values for these two variables. A similar range of possibilities applies in connection with the inflationary equilibrium.

The dynamics of the model are also sensitive to the steady state about which it is being linearized. This aspect has been studied in some detail for this model by Stemp and Turnovsky (1984). In the case of the inflationary equilibrium, it is possible for the eigenvalues to the linearized sytem, λ_1, λ_2, to have the following characteristics, depending upon the choice of the two policy parameters $G - T$ and θ:

i. $\lambda_1 < 0, \lambda_2 < 0$, in which case the dynamics is stable without any initial jump in the price level;

ii. $\lambda_1 < 0, \lambda_2 > 0$, in which case the system exhibits saddlepoint dynamics (to be discussed in Chapter 6). In this case stable adjustment is brought about by an initial jump in the price level.

iii. $\lambda_1 > 0, \lambda_2 > 0$, in which case the system is totally unstable. An initial jump in the price level is insufficient to ensure a stable adjustment. Some other discrete policy change is required as well.

In the neighborhood of the stable-price equilibrium, only the latter two alternatives are possible.

5.8   Endogeneity of Coefficients

Most ad hoc macroeconomic models take the coefficients as given. But when one derives the behavioral relationships from underlying optimization, these coefficients become endogenous, thereby rendering the model intrinsically nonlinear. This observation was first made by McCafferty and Driskill (1980) in the context of a rational expectations model of speculation. The particular model they considered is the original Muth model of speculation in inventories. They showed that the demand for inventories, I_t, is of the form

$$I_t = \frac{1}{R\sigma_p^2}(P^*_{t+1,t} - P_t) \equiv \eta(P^*_{t+1,t} - P_t) \tag{5.40}$$

where

P_t is the price of output,

σ_p^2 is the one-period variance of the price of output,

R is the coefficient of risk aversion, assumed to be exogenously given.

The demand for inventories is proportional to the expected change in the price of output. But the coefficient η, which measures the sensitivity to the expected price change, depends upon the one-period variance of the price level and is therefore endogenous. The determination of the rational expectations solutions involves determining P_t simultaneously with η, and this relationship is obviously highly nonlinear. McCafferty and Driskill show that in this particular example three possibilities exist:

i. there may be a unique rational expectations equilibrium;

ii. there may be no rational expectations equilibrium;

iii. there may be multiple rational expectations equilibria.

The fact that the coefficient η is endogenous also provides an extra channel by which government policy can have an influence. Government intervention in the market will typically influence the variance of the price of output. This will influence private speculative behavior, which in turn will have further effects on the equilibrium of the system.

The issue raised by McCafferty and Driskill is an extremely important one. Here, as in Section 5.7, the possibilities of nonuniqueness or nonexistence of solutions are associated not with the presence of arbitrary constants in the solution but rather with solving nonlinear systems. They are thus very different from the sources of nonuniqueness discussed earlier in the present chapter in connection with the Taylor model. But unfortunately, to incorporate the endogeneity of structural parameters is very difficult analytically and has been carried out only to a very limited degree. In typical cases, we are unable to study the resulting equilibrium analytically, and instead must resort to numerical simulations. But McCafferty and Driskill's contribution serves to highlight the importance of deriving rational expectations models from underlying optimizing behavior, a subject that is taken up again in Parts III and IV.

The examples we have been discussing in these last two sections obviously just scratch the surface with respect to the issue of the multiplicity of equilibria in nonlinear models. This is an important issue, and it frequently arises in the context of overlapping generations models, which are not discussed in this book. Important contributions to the relevant literature include Azariadis (1981), Grandmont (1985), and Kehoe and Levine (1985). An excellent introduction to the issues is provided by Blanchard and Fischer (1989, chapter 5). More detailed expositions are available in Azariadis (1993) and Farmer (1993).

6 Rational Expectations and Saddlepoint Behavior

Traditionally, most rational expectations models have been associated with saddlepoint behavior. That is, the dynamic system in which they are embedded involves both unstable and stable roots. As discussed in Chapter 5, the solution in such circumstances depends upon the relationship between the number of jump variables and the number of unstable roots. In many applications, the dynamics are described by a second-order system. The typical system includes one stable and one unstable root, with a corresponding single jump variable. This is an example of a pure saddlepoint. In the models we have been considering, it arises when the forward-looking dynamics associated with rational expectations is combined with backward-looking dynamics arising from some sluggish variable such as output, capital stock, or the accumulation of financial wealth. In the intertemporal optimization context to be discussed in Part III, saddlepoint dynamics are frequently associated with the sluggish dynamics of the capital stock and the forward-looking dynamics of its shadow value.

This chapter presents a range of examples of second-order systems having the saddlepoint property. We consider a model specified in continuous time, so that it is described by a second-order differential equation. The formal review of the dynamics of such a system is presented in the Appendix to the chapter. The formal mathematical solutions to such systems are available in appropriate mathematical textbooks; our presentation is in a form more suitable to economic applications. Section 6.1 presents the solution for the special case of saddlepoint dynamics and shows how it can incorporate "announcement effects" in a convenient way. The next three sections discuss three diverse applications. The first is an adaptation of the Cagan monetary model, extended to incorporate sluggish adjustment of wages. The second is an extension of the familiar Blinder-Solow (1973) dynamic model to include both short-term and long-term government bonds. The third is the determination of exchange rate expectations in a world of sluggish prices.

6.1 Saddlepoint Behavior

Any second-order scalar differential equation can be represented by a pair of first-order differential equations, and vice versa. The Appendix provides a general treatment of the dynamics and solutions for such a pair of first-order linear differential equations. It represents the dynamic evolution of a pair of variables $x(t)$ and $y(t)$, which are driven by arbitrary forcing functions $f_1(t), f_2(t)$. Given an arbitrary time profile for the forcing functions $f_1(t), f_2(t)$, one can derive the corresponding solutions for $x(t)$ and $y(t)$. In general, the solutions may turn out to be quite cumbersome, depending upon the nature of the functions $f_i(t)$.

In many economic applications, the forcing functions $f_i(t)$ take the form of once-and-for-all shifts from one constant level to the other. This is the case, for example, with respect to the expansion in the money supply, discussed in Chapter 3. These shifts may either occur at some initial time 0, in which case they are unannounced; or they may be announced (at time 0, say) to take place at some time T in the future. The response of the system to such one-time shifts is relatively easy to establish, and we now demonstrate this in the case where the dynamics are described by a saddlepoint.

Consider a linear system represented by the pair of dynamic equations

$$\dot{x}(t) = a_{11}x(t) + a_{12}y(t) + \bar{f}_1, \tag{6.1a}$$

$$\dot{y}(t) = a_{21}x(t) + a_{22}y(t) + \bar{f}_2 \tag{6.1b}$$

where $\bar{f}_1, \bar{f}_2$ represent constant values of some forcing function. The specific economic context is irrelevant at this point. The corresponding initial steady-state equilibrium solutions for x, y, denoted by $\bar{x}_1, \bar{y}_1$, say, are obtained by solving the pair of equations

$$a_{11}\bar{x}_1 + a_{12}\bar{y} + \bar{f}_1 = 0, \tag{6.2a}$$

$$a_{21}\bar{x}_1 + a_{22}\bar{y} + \bar{f}_2 = 0. \tag{6.2b}$$

Subtracting (6.2) from (6.1), the dynamics can be written in the form

$$\begin{bmatrix} \dot{x} \\ \dot{y} \end{bmatrix} = \begin{bmatrix} a_{11} & a_{12} \\ a_{21} & a_{22} \end{bmatrix} \begin{bmatrix} x - \bar{x}_1 \\ y - \bar{y}_1 \end{bmatrix}. \tag{6.3}$$

Suppose that at time 0 it is announced that $\bar{f}_1, \bar{f}_2$ are to increase, at time $T \geq 0$, to $\bar{\bar{f}}_1, \bar{\bar{f}}_2$, respectively. The new steady states after the shifts have occurred are obtained from

$$a_{11}\bar{x}_2 + a_{12}\bar{y}_2 + \bar{\bar{f}}_1 = 0, \tag{6.4a}$$

$$a_{21}\bar{x}_2 + a_{22}\bar{y}_2 + \bar{\bar{f}}_2 = 0, \tag{6.4b}$$

and the dynamics after the shift are specified by

$$\begin{bmatrix} \dot{x} \\ \dot{y} \end{bmatrix} = \begin{bmatrix} a_{11} & a_{12} \\ a_{21} & a_{22} \end{bmatrix} \begin{bmatrix} x - \bar{x}_2 \\ y - \bar{y}_2 \end{bmatrix}. \tag{6.5}$$

Comparing (6.3) with (6.5), we see that the equilibrium of the system shifts at time T, when the shifts in the forcing functions $\bar{f}_i$ occur. The solutions for $x(t), y(t)$ are obtained by solving the differential equations (6.3) and (6.5) and linking them up appropriately at time T. The arbitrary constants in the solutions are determined by imposing a combination of (i) initial conditions, (ii) terminal conditions, and (iii) continuity at time T.

As long as the shifts are *additive*, so that the coefficients a_{ij} remain unchanged between the two regimes, the eigenvalues λ_1, λ_2, say, of (6.3) and (6.5) are identical. For simplicity, and without loss of generality, we shall assume that they are real. The fact that the dynamics are described by a saddlepoint means that the product

$$\lambda_1 \lambda_2 = a_{11} a_{22} - a_{12} a_{21} < 0.$$

We shall assume $\lambda_1 < 0, \lambda_2 > 0$. In order to ensure stability, one of the variables, say $y(t)$, must be a jump variable, while the other, $x(t)$, is assumed to evolve continuously at all times.

Over the period $0 < t \leq T$, before the shifts in $\bar{f}_i$ occur, the solutions for $x(t), y(t)$ are of the form

$$x = \bar{x}_1 + A_1 e^{\lambda_1 t} + A_2 e^{\lambda_2 t}, \tag{6.6a}$$

$$y = \bar{y}_1 + \left(\frac{\lambda_1 - a_{11}}{a_{12}}\right) A_1 e^{\lambda_1 t} + \left(\frac{\lambda_2 - a_{11}}{a_{12}}\right) A_2 e^{\lambda_2 t}. \tag{6.6b}$$

Note that because λ_i are eigenvalues,

$$\frac{\lambda_i - a_{11}}{a_{12}} = \frac{a_{21}}{\lambda_i - a_{22}} \qquad i = 1, 2,$$

in which case (6.6b) can be rewritten equivalently as

$$y = \bar{y}_1 + \left(\frac{a_{21}}{\lambda_1 - a_{22}}\right) A_1 e^{\lambda_1 t} + \left(\frac{a_{21}}{\lambda_2 - a_{22}}\right) A_2 e^{\lambda_2 t}. \tag{6.6b$'$}$$

Likewise, for the period $t \geq T$, after the shifts have occurred, the solutions for $x(t), y(t)$ are

$$x = \bar{x}_2 = A_1' e^{\lambda_1 t} + A_2' e^{\lambda_2 t}, \tag{6.7a}$$

$$y = \bar{y}_2 + \left(\frac{\lambda_1 - a_{11}}{a_{12}}\right) A_1' e^{\lambda_1 t} + \left(\frac{\lambda_2 - a_{11}}{a_{12}}\right) A_2' e^{\lambda_2 t}. \tag{6.7b}$$

The key difference is in the shift in the steady-state equilibria. Completing the solutions involves the determination of the arbitrary constants A_1, A_2, A_1', A_2'.

We begin by imposing the condition that the solution be bounded. In order for $x(t)$ and $y(t)$ not to diverge as $t \to \infty$, it is clear that $A_2' = 0$, so that

$$x = \bar{x}_2 + A_1' e^{\lambda_1 t}, \tag{6.7a$'$}$$

$$y = \bar{y}_2 + \left(\frac{\lambda_1 - a_{11}}{a_{12}}\right) A_1' e^{\lambda_1 t}. \tag{6.7b$'$}$$

That is, after time $T, x(t), y(t)$ must follow the stable paths described by (6.7a') and (6.7b'). Eliminating $A_1' e^{\lambda_1 t}$ from these equations yields

$$(y - \bar{y}_2) = \left(\frac{\lambda_1 - a_{11}}{a_{12}}\right)(x - \bar{x}_2). \tag{6.8}$$

This is a locus in $y - x$ space that describes the stable arm of the saddle-point. Its slope depends upon the signs and magnitudes of the coefficients a_{ij}, and examples will be given below. Using the fact that λ_1 is an eigenvalue, (6.8) may be written equivalently as

$$(y - \bar{y}_2) = \left(\frac{a_{21}}{\lambda_1 - a_{12}}\right)(x - \bar{x}_2). \tag{6.8'}$$

The reason for noting these alternative ways of describing the stable path is that depending upon the signs of the coefficients a_{ij}, either (6.8) or (6.8') may prove to be more convenient in terms of indicating the slope of the locus they describe.

The remaining constants are obtained by imposing an initial condition on the sluggish variable $x(t)$ and continuity at time T. This latter condition precludes jumps that are foreseen. Thus, assuming $x(0) = \bar{x}_1$, say, (6.6a) implies

$$A_1 + A_2 = 0. \tag{6.9a}$$

The condition that the solutions be continuous at time T means that the solutions for $x(t), y(t)$ obtained from (6.3) and (6.5) should coincide at that time. Hence

$$(A_1 - A_1')e^{\lambda_1 T} + A_2 e^{\lambda_2 T} = d\bar{x}, \tag{6.9b}$$

$$\left(\frac{\lambda_1 - a_{11}}{a_{12}}\right)(A_1 - A_1')e^{\lambda_1 T} + \left(\frac{\lambda_2 - a_{11}}{a_{12}}\right)A_2 e^{\lambda_2 T} = d\bar{y} \tag{6.9c}$$

where $d\bar{x}, d\bar{y}$ represent the shifts in the steady states obtained from (6.2) and (6.4). Given these shifts, the constants A_1, A_2, A_1' can be determined. Substituting these into (6.7) and (6.7') yields the solutions before and after time T.

The essential feature of these solutions is that the dynamics involve three phases. The announcement at time 0, say, of a shift to occur at time T in the future generates an immediate response in the jump variable. Setting $t = 0$ in (6.6b) and using (6.9a), the initial response is given by

$$y(0) - \bar{y}_1 = \left(\frac{\lambda_2 - \lambda_1}{a_{12}}\right)A_2$$

where A_2 is obtained from (6.9b) and (6.9c). It can be shown that the size of the initial jump is inversely proportional to the lead time T. Following the initial jump, the system follows the unstable locus (6.6) until time T, when the announced policy is implemented. At that time, the system reaches the stable locus (6.8), which it then follows into the new equilibrium. In the case where $T = 0$, and the shift is unannounced, the system jumps instantaneously to the new stable locus (6.8).

6.2   Example 1: Cagan Model with Sluggish Wages

As a first example of a saddlepoint, we consider an extension of the Cagan model discussed in Chapter 3. The modification includes the gradual adjustment of money wages, with the corresponding variable employment of labor and output. The amended model is specified by the following relationships:

$$M - P = \alpha_1 Y - \alpha_2 \dot{P} \qquad \alpha_1 > 0, \alpha_2 > 0 \tag{6.10a}$$

$$Y = c + (1 - \theta)N \qquad 0 < \theta < 1 \tag{6.10b}$$

$$W - P = a - \theta N \tag{6.10c}$$

$$\dot{W} = \gamma(N - \bar{N}) \qquad \gamma > 0 \tag{6.10d}$$

where

Y is output,

N is employment,

$\bar{N}$ is full employment,

P is the price level,

$\bar{M}$ is the nominal money stock, assumed to be constant,

W is the wage rate,

and all variables are expressed in logarithms.

Equation (6.10a) describes money market equilibrium under conditions of perfect foresight, so that the anticipated rate of inflation equals the actual rate of inflation $\dot{P}$. The only difference from the Cagan model discussed previously is that output is now assumed to be variable and is therefore introduced explicitly into the demand for money function. Equation (6.10b) specifies output in terms of a Cobb-Douglas production function. The demand for labor (employment) is described by the corresponding marginal product condition (6.10c). Finally, money wages are assumed to evolve in accordance with the Phillips curve (6.10d).

Equations (6.10a)–(6.10d) may be reduced to the following pair of differential equations in W and P:

$$\begin{pmatrix} \dot{W} \\ \dot{P} \end{pmatrix} = \begin{pmatrix} a_{11} & a_{12} \\ a_{21} & a_{22} \end{pmatrix} \begin{pmatrix} W \\ P \end{pmatrix} + \begin{pmatrix} b_1 \\ b_2 \end{pmatrix} \tag{6.11}$$

where

$$a_{11} = -\frac{\gamma}{\theta} < 0; \qquad a_{12} = \frac{\gamma}{\theta} > 0;$$

$$a_{21} = -\frac{\alpha_1}{\alpha_2}\left(\frac{1-\theta}{\theta}\right) < 0; \qquad a_{22} = \frac{1}{\alpha_2} + \frac{\alpha_1}{\alpha_2}\left(\frac{1-\theta}{\theta}\right) > 0;$$

$$b_1 = \gamma\left[\frac{a}{\theta} - \overline{N}\right]; \qquad b_2 = \frac{\alpha_1}{\alpha_2}\left[c + a\left(\frac{1-\theta}{\theta}\right)\right] - \frac{\overline{M}}{\alpha_2}.$$

This is of the general form of equations (6.1) introduced above. We assume that the money supply remains constant, except for a once-and-for-all expansion from, say, $\overline{M}_1$ to $\overline{M}_2$, which is announced at time 0, to take effect at time $T \geq 0$. Our objective is to consider the effects of such an expansion—both its announcement and its implementation—on the time path of wages and prices in the economy.

From the above definitions of the elements a_{ij}, we find $a_{11}a_{22} - a_{12}a_{21} = -\gamma/\theta\alpha_2 < 0$, implying that the determinant of the matrix of coefficients in (6.11) is negative. The eigenvalues λ_1, λ_2, are of opposite signs; we have a saddlepoint with, say, $\lambda_1 < 0, \lambda_2 > 0$. We also assume that, as in the Sargent and Wallace (1973b) analysis, the price level is free to jump instantaneously whereas wages are constrained to move continuously. This is a reasonable characterization of the relative flexibilities of wages and prices in the real world and of the fact that wages, being determined by contracts, are constrained in their ability to adjust.

Our starting point is the initial steady state, corresponding to the initial level of money balances $\overline{M}$. The corresponding levels of money wages and prices are obtained by solving the pair of equations

$$-\frac{\gamma}{\theta}\overline{W} + \frac{\gamma}{\theta}\overline{P} + \gamma\left[\frac{a}{\theta} - \overline{N}\right] = 0,$$

$$-\frac{\alpha_1}{\alpha_2}\left(\frac{1-\theta}{\theta}\right)\overline{W} + \left[\frac{1}{\alpha_2} + \frac{\alpha_1}{\alpha_2}\left(\frac{1-\theta}{\theta}\right)\right]\overline{P} + \frac{\alpha_1}{\alpha_2}\left[c + a\left(\frac{1-\theta}{\theta}\right)\right] - \frac{\overline{M}}{\alpha_2} = 0.$$

The effect of the monetary expansion on the steady-state levels of wages and prices is simply

$$d\overline{P} = d\overline{W} = d\overline{M}.$$

That is, a 1 percent increase in the money supply leads to a 1 percent increase in both the price level and the nominal wage. The real wage remains unchanged, as does the long-run level of employment and output.

Applying the procedure discussed in Section 6.1, the solutions for wages and prices are of the form:

Period $0 \leq t \leq T$:

$$W(t) = \overline{W}_1 + A_1 e^{\lambda_1 t} + A_2 e^{\lambda_2 t}, \tag{6.12a}$$

$$P(t) = \overline{P}_1 + \left(\frac{\lambda_1 - a_{11}}{a_{12}}\right) A_1 e^{\lambda_1 t} + \left(\frac{\lambda_2 - a_{11}}{a_{12}}\right) A_2 e^{\lambda_2 t}. \tag{6.12b}$$

Period $t \geq T$:

$$W(t) = \overline{W}_1 + d\overline{M} + A_1' e^{\lambda_1 t}, \tag{6.13a}$$

$$P(t) = \overline{P}_1 + d\overline{M} + \left(\frac{\lambda_1 - a_{11}}{a_{12}}\right) A_1' e^{\lambda_1 t} \tag{6.13b}$$

where the constants A_1, A_2, A_1' are obtained by solving the equations

$$A_1 + A_2 = 0, \tag{6.14a}$$

$$(A_1 - A_1') e^{\lambda_1 T} + A_2 e^{\lambda_2 T} = d\overline{M}, \tag{6.14b}$$

$$\left(\frac{\lambda_1 - a_{11}}{a_{12}}\right)(A_1 - A_1') e^{\lambda_1 T} + \left(\frac{\lambda_2 - a_{11}}{a_{12}}\right) A_2 e^{\lambda_2 T} = d\overline{M}. \tag{6.14c}$$

Of particular interest is the initial jump in the price level. This is obtained by setting $t = 0$ in (6.12b), and using (6.14a) to write $A_1 = -A_2$:

$$P(0) = \overline{P}_1 + \left(\frac{\lambda_2 - \lambda_1}{a_{12}}\right) A_2.$$

Solving the pair of equations (6.14b), (6.14c) for A_2,

$$A_2 = \frac{\left[1 - \left(\frac{\lambda_1 - a_{11}}{a_{12}}\right)\right]}{\left(\frac{\lambda_2 - \lambda_1}{a_{12}}\right)} d\overline{M} e^{-\lambda_2 T},$$

so that

$$P(0) = \overline{P}_1 + \left[1 - \left(\frac{\lambda_1 - a_{11}}{a_{12}}\right)\right] e^{-\lambda_2 T} d\overline{M}.$$

Now

$$\bar{P}_2 = \bar{P}_1 + d\bar{M},$$

enabling us to write

$$P(0) = \bar{P}_2 + \left\{ \left[1 - \frac{a_{21}}{\lambda_1 - a_{22}} \right] e^{-\lambda_2 T} - 1 \right\} d\bar{M}. \qquad (6.1.5)$$

From this question we see that the announcement of the future monetary expansion generates an initial partial jump in the price level toward its new equilibrium level. The magnitude of the jump varies inversely with the lead time T.

The two sets of equations (6.12), (6.13) provide the formal solutions describing the behavior of wages and prices. However, further insight can be gained by a consideration of the phase diagram. This is illustrated in Figure 6.1 and may be constructed as follows.

First, the locus AA denotes the combination of the wage rate and price level that will maintain full employment so that $\dot{W} = 0$. From the system of equations (6.11), this has the unitary slope

$$\left(\frac{dP}{dW} \right)_{\dot{W}=0} = -\frac{a_{11}}{a_{12}} = 1. \qquad (6.16a)$$

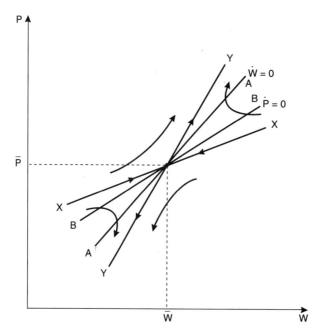

Figure 6.1
Phase diagram for Cagan example

Intuitively, an increase in W will lower the demand for labor. In order to maintain employment at its full employment level, the real wage will need to be restored to the full employment level and this will need to be accompanied by a proportionate increase in the price level. Likewise, BB is the combination of W and P that will maintain a stable price level, and from (6.11), this has the slope

$$\left(\frac{dP}{dW}\right)_{\dot{P}=0} = -\frac{a_{21}}{a_{22}}, \tag{6.16b}$$

This slope is also positive, although less so than that of AA. In this case, an increase in W reduces employment and therefore the real demand for money. Now a smaller increase in P is required to maintain money market equilibrium at a stable price level. This is because the higher price level also reduces the real stock of money.

The locus XX, described by

$$P - \bar{P} = \left(\frac{\lambda_1 - a_{11}}{a_{12}}\right)(W - \bar{W}) = \left(\frac{a_{21}}{\lambda_1 - a_{22}}\right)(W - \bar{W}), \tag{6.17a}$$

is the stable arm of the saddlepoint passing through the equilibrium point $(\bar{W}, \bar{P})$. Along this line, both W and P follow adjustment paths:

$$\dot{P} = \lambda_1(P - \bar{P}); \qquad \dot{W} = \lambda_1(W - \bar{W}),$$

which imply a stable adjustment of the system to its equilibrium. From the definitions of the a_{ij} the locus XX is seen to have a positive slope, but also less than unity.

Likewise, the locus YY, specified by

$$P - \bar{P} = \left(\frac{\lambda_2 - a_{11}}{a_{12}}\right)(W - \bar{W}) = \left(\frac{a_{21}}{\lambda_2 - a_{22}}\right)(W - \bar{W}), \tag{6.17b}$$

is the unstable arm of the saddlepoint passing through the equilibrium point $(\bar{W}, \bar{P})$. Along this path W and P follow adjustment paths

$$\dot{P} = \lambda_2(P - \bar{P}), \qquad \dot{W} = \lambda_2(W - \bar{W}),$$

which describe unstable adjustment of the system away from equilibrium. The slope of YY is also positive, but greater than unity, so that it is steeper than the XX curve.

Comparing the slopes reported in (6.16)–(6.17), we see that

$$\left(\frac{dP}{dW}\right)_{YY} > 1 = \left(\frac{dP}{dW}\right)_{\dot{W}=0} > \left(\frac{dP}{dW}\right)_{\dot{P}=0} > \left(\frac{dP}{dW}\right)_{XX} > 0.$$

Everywhere above the line AA is associated with a declining nominal wage (i.e., $\dot{W} < 0$) and everywhere below it with an increasing nominal wage. Likewise, everywhere above *BB* implies an increasing price level whereas everywhere below it the price level is declining. This implies the directions of motion as indicated by the arrows. All these loci have the characteristic of initially approaching the equilibrium before ultimately veering away. Note that when they cross the *AA* locus the direction of motion is vertical (there is no motion in the *W* direction) and when they cross the *BB* locus, the dynamics must be horizontal because at that point the price level is stationary.

The case of the once-and-for-all monetary expansion is illustrated in Figure 6.2. By choice of units the initial equilibrium is set at the origin, with the new steady state at *Q*, where $d\overline{W} = d\overline{P} = d\overline{M}$. This point therefore lies on a 45-degree line passing through the origin. Because the stable locus *XX* has a slope of less than unity, the stable arm passing through the new equilibrium *Q*, the locus *X'X'*, must lie above the corresponding line passing through the original point, namely *XX* (not drawn); that is, the monetary expansion leads to an upward shift in the stable locus.

Suppose that the monetary expansion is unannounced, that is, *T* = 0. Then at time 0, the price level jumps immediately to the point *B* lying on the new stable arm *X'X'*, passing through *Q*. Since wages are assumed to be sluggish, *W* does not change immediately, and the immediate adjust-

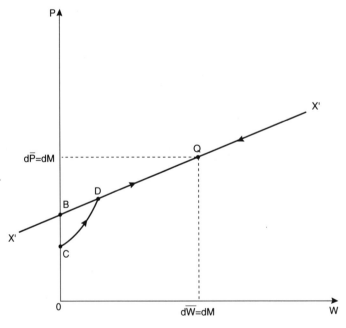

Figure 6.2
Once-and-for-all monetary expansion in Cagan example

ment is solely in the price dimension, as illustrated. The initial increase in the price level means that the real wage rate falls. This stimulates the demand for labor, so that employment and output immediately rise. The increase in labor demand generates an excess demand for labor, and the money wage rate begins to rise. The rise in output increases the demand for money. To some extent this is offset by an increase in the real money supply, due to the fact that the initial jump in the price level is less than the expansion in the money supply. But on balance, the initial increase in the price level generates an excess demand for money. To restore money market equilibrium, the nominal interest rate must rise, which means that with the real interest constant (as the Cagan model assumes), the price level must continue to rise. The initial stimulus to employment and output is gradually eroded by the adjustment in the real wage. As wages begin to catch up to prices, the demand for labor, and therefore output, will begin to fall. The nominal wage rate will continue to rise as long as N exceeds its full employment level, $\bar{N}$. Similarly, the price level will continue to rise as long as there is an excess demand for money. The economy follows the stable locus BQ to the new equilibrium Q. At that point, the adjustments in prices and wages will be complete. Real wages, employment, and output will all be restored to their original levels.

If the monetary expansion is announced at time 0 to take place at time T in the future, the initial jump in the price level is dampened down to the point C, say. For the period prior to time T, the economy follows the path CD, which, if pursued indefinitely, would be unstable. Because at this time the monetary expansion has not yet occurred, the initial jump in the price level generates an unambiguous excess demand for money. On the one hand, the reduction in the real wage stimulates employment and output, thereby increasing the transactions demand for money. At the same time, with the nominal stock of money remaining fixed prior to time T, the rise in the price level means a real monetary contraction. Both factors therefore contribute to a substantial excess demand for money, as a result of which a large increase in the rate of inflation is required in order to reduce the excess demand for money and maintain equilibrium. As before, the initial increase in employment means that the money wage begins to rise. Moreover, the rapid increase in inflation that is now generated means that as long as the monetary expansion has not occurred, the real money supply is continuing to be contracted, thereby putting additional upward pressure on the inflation rate. The continuing rising price level will stimulate the demand for labor, thereby putting upward pressure on the rate of wage inflation. This is the essence of the instability along the path CD. At time T, when the anticipated monetary expansion occurs, the economy reaches the point D. At that time, the monetary expansion relieves the upward pressure on the interest rate and the rate of inflation drops. From then on, the economy follows the stable path to the new equilibrium Q.

6.3   Example 2: Term Structure of Interest Rates

As a second example of a macroeconomic model generating saddlepoint behavior, we consider a model embodying the term structure of interest rates. Most formal macroeconomic models treat all assets as being of common maturity. Typically, time to maturity is assumed to be either extremely (infinitesimally) short (a short-term bill) or infinitely long (a perpetuity). In reality, of course, there exists a whole spectrum of assets having varying times to maturity. Moreover, different agents in the markets are concerned with rates of return extending over different time horizons. Participants in financial asset markets can typically adjust their portfolios virtually instantaneously, so that some short-run rate of return is appropriate as an argument of the relevant asset demand functions. On the other hand, investors in physical equipment are typically locked into some long-term financial arrangement, in which case it is some long-term rate that is the appropriate argument of the investment function. Provided that the financial markets operate efficiently, arbitrage by participants in the asset markets will bring the instantaneous rates of return on assets of varying maturities into equality.[1]

Our present objective is to introduce both a short rate and a long rate into a simple dynamic macroeconomic model. The framework we employ is the familiar Blinder-Solow (1973) model. It is shown how, through arbitrage, the current long rate at any point of time is an average of current and future short rates. The *forward-looking* information thereby contained in the long rate has important implications for the effects of monetary and fiscal policy in a dynamic macro model, as Blanchard (1981) and Turnovsky and Miller (1984) have shown.

In this respect, two related issues are worth highlighting. First, through such forward-looking behavior, policy changes announced to take effect at some future date impinge on the present state of the economy. Considerations of this sort may well have been relevant in explaining the high U.S. real interest rates and depressed real activity that occurred during the early 1980s. For example, the announcement at that time of a program of future tax cuts and continued monetary restraint would, in an efficient market, be expected to raise current long-term and medium-term interest rates, in advance of the actual implementation of the fiscal expansion, thereby reducing current output. In this section we explore the current impact of expected future increases in government expenditure; and the analysis translates directly to tax cuts in obvious ways. Second, the distinction between rates of different maturity involves explicit consideration of the term structure of interest rates in a macroeconomic framework. A principal purpose of the present analysis is to contrast the dynamic responses of the short and long rates to both expected and unexpected fiscal expansions.

The Modified Blinder-Solow Model

The framework we will use is a variant of the Blinder-Solow model used by Turnovsky and Miller (1984) and is described by the following five equations:

$$Y = C(Y^D, M + PB) + I(P) + G \quad 0 < C_1 < 1, C_2 > 0, I' > 0 \tag{6.18a}$$

$$Y^D = (Y + B + \dot{P}B)(1 - \tau) \tag{6.18b}$$

$$L(Y, s(1 - \tau), M + PB) = M \qquad L_1 > 0, L_2 < 0, 0 < L_3 < 1 \tag{6.18c}$$

$$s = \frac{1}{P} + \frac{\dot{P}}{P} \tag{6.18d}$$

$$P\dot{B} + \dot{M} = G + B - \tau(Y + B + \dot{P}B) \tag{6.18e}$$

where

Y = output,

Y^D = disposable income,

M = stock of money,

B = stock of government bonds, taken to be perpetuities paying \$1 coupon per unit of time, indefinitely,

G = government expenditure,

τ = rate of income tax,

P = current market price of a perpetuity,

s = instantaneous rate of return.

The following general features of the model should be noted. Each is introduced for purposes of simplification and can be relaxed in various ways without altering the substance of the analysis. First, the only outside interest-bearing assets are government bonds, B, which we take to be perpetuities. Any short-run (instantaneous) assets that exist are assumed to be inside assets and therefore net out in the definitions of wealth and disposable income. It is straightforward to introduce both short and long

government bonds. However, because we are assuming that long bonds
are priced efficiently, it turns out that the effects of the two types of
bonds are similar, so that there is no gain from introducing both separately. Second, as in the Blinder-Solow model, we assume that the price
of output remains fixed. This is done in order to emphasize the interaction between the dynamics associated with bond arbitrage and that
involving asset accumulation. Third, we assume that all forms of income
are taxed at the same rate, τ. The analysis remains unchanged if, for
example, we allow for a different (lower) rate of taxation on capital gains,
along the lines of Chapter 10.

Equation (6.18a) describes the *IS* curve, in which the consumption function is conventional. The investment function depends positively upon
the price of long bonds (which of course varies inversely with the long
rate), thereby reflecting the longer-run financial commitments associated
with real investment decisions. Disposable income consists of factor income plus interest income, plus the rate of capital gain on the holdings of
long bonds, all taxed at the rate τ.

Money market equilibrium is described by (6.18c), with the relevant
rate of return variable in the demand for money being the after-tax
instantaneous rate of interest. This return exactly matches that available on longer-dated financial assets under the assumption of perfect
arbitrage.

The behavior of bond prices is given in (6.18d). Efficient and risk-
neutral arbitrage ensures that in the absence of "news," the after-tax rate
of return on short bonds equals the after-tax rate of return on long
bonds. The latter consists of the rate of return earned on the coupon $1/P$,
and the rate of capital gain $\dot{P}/P$, both of which are taxed at the same rate
τ, so that the factor $(1 - \tau)$ cancels from both sides of this equation. It is
this relationship that introduces the forward-looking behavior into the
system. This equation may be integrated to yield the following solution
for $P(t)$, which remains bounded as $\tau \to \infty$:[2]

$$P(t) = \int_t^\infty e^{-\int_t^x s(t')\,dt'}\,dx. \tag{6.19}$$

Equation (6.19) expresses the price of long bonds at time t in terms of the
future short rates, assumed to be correctly forecast.[3] Furthermore, defining the long rate (i.e., the rate on perpetuities) to be

$$l(t) \equiv \frac{1}{P(t)},$$

we may rewrite (6.19) as

$$l(t) = \frac{1}{\int_t^\infty e^{-\int_t^x s(t')\,dt'}\,dx}.$$ (6.19′)

This relationship shows explicitly how the current long rate embodies information about the future (expected) short rates.

The final equation describes the government budget constraint. Tax receipts include taxes levied on factor income and interest income, together with the capital gains, all taxed at the rate τ.

Substituting (6.18d) into (6.18b) and (6.18e), the system reduces to the following equations:

$$Y = C[(1 - \tau)(Y + sBP), M + BP] + I(P) + G$$ (6.20a)

$$L(Y, s(1 - \tau), M + PB) = M$$ (6.20b)

$$\dot{P} = (sP - 1)$$ (6.20c)

$$P\dot{B} + \dot{M} = G + B - \tau(Y + sPB).$$ (6.20d)

The Blinder-Solow version is obtained by imposing the equality between the short and long rates (i.e., $s = l = 1/P$), in which case (6.20c) becomes redundant. In effect, Blinder and Solow require the steady-state bond pricing relationship (6.20c′) to hold throughout. Bonds are therefore priced as if the short rate will continue forever, an assumption that is inconsistent with the asset dynamics of the model itself.[4]

The evolution of the system proceeds as follows. Except at points where the price of bonds undergoes discrete jumps in response to "news" of some exogenous disturbance, P is continuous. The IS and LM curves thus determine instantaneous equilibrium solutions for output Y and the short rate s in terms of P, M, and B, the dynamics of which are described by the arbitrage condition together with the government budget constraint. To complete the specification, we must formulate government financial policy, and we shall restrict ourselves to the regime of a purely money-financed deficit; that is, $B = \bar{B}$.[5]

Short-Run Equilibrium

The solutions for Y and s derived from (6.20a) and (6.20b) are of the form

$$Y = Y(M, B, P; G)$$ (6.21a)

$$s = s(M, B, P; G)),$$ (6.21b)

and in order to derive the dynamics of the economy we must first solve for the short-run multipliers. Omitting details, these are given by the following expressions:

$$\frac{\partial Y}{\partial M} = \frac{-(1-\tau)[L_2 C_2 + (1-L_3)C_1 BP]}{\Delta}(>0) \tag{6.22a}$$

$$\frac{\partial Y}{\partial B} = \frac{-L_2(1-\tau)[C_1(1-\tau)s + C_2] + C_1(1-\tau)BP^2 L_3}{\Delta} > 0 \tag{6.22b}$$

$$\frac{\partial Y}{\partial P} = \frac{-L_2 I'(1-\tau)}{\Delta} + \frac{B}{P}\frac{\partial Y}{\partial B} > 0 \tag{6.22c}$$

$$\frac{\partial Y}{\partial G} = \frac{-L_2(1-\tau)}{\Delta} > 0 \tag{6.22d}$$

$$\frac{\partial s}{\partial M} = \frac{-(1-L_3)[1 - C_1(1-\tau)] + L_1 C_2}{\Delta}(<0) \tag{6.23a}$$

$$\frac{\partial s}{\partial B} = \frac{PL_3[1 - C_1(1-\tau)] + PL_1[C_1(1-\tau)s + C_2]}{\Delta} > 0 \tag{6.23b}$$

$$\frac{\partial s}{\partial P} = \frac{B}{P}\frac{\partial s}{\partial B} + \frac{L_1 I'}{\Delta} > 0 \tag{6.23c}$$

$$\frac{\partial s}{\partial G} = \frac{L_1}{\Delta} > 0 \tag{6.23d}$$

where $\Delta \equiv -(1-\tau)[L_2(1 - C_1(1-\tau)) + L_1 C_1 BP](>0)$.

The indeterminacies that appear in the above expressions are due to the presence of interest income in disposable income (in [6.22a]) and of wealth effects in consumption (in [6.23a]). These indeterminacies are a familiar aspect of the Blinder-Solow model and require no further discussion here. Provided that these effects are sufficiently small, the various instantaneous responses will have the signs indicated in parentheses and which henceforth we assume to apply.

The comparative static responses summarized by these expressions are generally standard. The only new aspect is the impact effect of a given increase in the price of bonds P, which raises both income and the short interest rate. The reason for this is that an increase in P will raise both private investment and wealth, thereby increasing aggregate demand and hence output. This increase in output and wealth also increases the demand for money, and given a constant money stock, the short interest rate must rise in order for money market equilibrium to be maintained.

The total impact effects of changes in the policy variables M, B, and G on the short-run variables s and Y are obtained by taking the total derivatives of (6.21a) and (6.21b). Thus, for example, the complete short-run effects of an increase in government expenditure are described by

$$\frac{dY}{dG} = \frac{\partial Y}{\partial G} + \frac{\partial Y}{\partial P}\frac{\partial P}{\partial G}, \tag{6.24a}$$

$$\frac{ds}{dG} = \frac{\partial s}{\partial G} + \frac{\partial s}{\partial P}\frac{\partial P}{\partial G}, \tag{6.24b}$$

each of which contains two components.

The first of these components, $\partial Y/\partial G, \partial s/\partial G$, described by (6.22d) and (6.23d), respectively, consists of the direct effects of the policy change, which occur when the policy is actually put into effect; we term these the *implementation effects*. They do not embody the induced jump in P, which must accompany such changes when they are unanticipated and which exerts further indirect effects. These are described by the second terms $(\partial Y/\partial P)(\partial P/\partial G), (\partial s/\partial P)(\partial P/\partial G)$, and are referred to as *news effects*. They incorporate the forward-looking behavior of bond prices and are considered in more detail when the transitional dynamics are discussed.

One further point should be noted. First, the two effects we have identified may occur independently. A fully anticipated policy change will not cause any discontinuous change in the bond price; it will therefore have only implementation effects. On the other hand, credible statements concerning future policies will generate news effects (or announcement effects) at the time they are announced. These news effects decrease in significance, however, the farther in the future the promised policy action lies.

Money-Financed Deficit

Under the policy of an all-money-financed deficit, the stock of government bonds remains pegged at $B = \bar{B}$, so that the dynamics (6.20c) and (6.20d) become

$$\dot{P} = (sP - 1) \tag{6.20c}$$

$$\dot{M} = G + \bar{B} - \tau(Y + sP\bar{B}). \tag{6.20d'}$$

The steady state of the system is defined by equations (6.20a) and (6.20b), together with the stationary solutions to (6.20c) and (6.20d'), namely,

$$sP = 1 \tag{6.20c'}$$

$$G - \tau Y + \bar{B}(1 - \tau) = 0. \tag{6.20d''}$$

The first of these two equations implies the long-run equilibrium equality between the short and long rates, namely,

$$l = \frac{1}{P} = s,$$

and the latter equation is the familiar long-run condition for government budget balance. These four equations determine the steady-state values of Y, s, P, and M. Denoting these equilibrium values by tildes, the following steady-state government expenditure multipliers can be calculated:

$$\frac{d\tilde{Y}}{dG} = \frac{1}{\tau} > 0 \tag{6.25a}$$

$$\frac{d\tilde{P}}{dG} = -\frac{P}{K}[C_2 L_1 - (1 - C_1)(1 - \tau)(1 - L_3)](> 0) \tag{6.25b}$$

$$\frac{d\tilde{s}}{dG} = \frac{-s}{P}\frac{d\tilde{P}}{dG}(< 0) \tag{6.25c}$$

$$\frac{d\tilde{M}}{dG} = \frac{-(1 - \tau)(1 - C_1)}{K}[L_2(1 - \tau)s - L_3\bar{B}P] + \frac{(C_2\bar{B} + I')L_1 P}{K} > 0 \tag{6.25d}$$

where $K \equiv \tau[(C_2 B + I')(1 - L_3)P - C_2 L_2(1 - \tau)s + C_2 L_3 BP] > 0$ and a sign in parentheses indicates a "probable" sign. Since the short rates and long rates coincide in equilibrium, these responses are identical to those of the Blinder-Solow model and therefore require little comment. With a money-financed deficit, the long-run government expenditure multiplier equals the inverse of the marginal tax rate.

Our main objective is to analyze the dynamic adjustment of the economy to a fiscal or monetary disturbance from some initial equilibrium. To consider this it is necessary to linearize the dynamics about the steady state. Thus from (6.20c), (6.20d′) we derive

$$\begin{bmatrix} \dot{P} \\ \dot{M} \end{bmatrix} = \begin{bmatrix} a_{11} & a_{12} \\ a_{21} & a_{22} \end{bmatrix} \begin{bmatrix} P - \tilde{P} \\ M - \tilde{M} \end{bmatrix} \tag{6.26}$$

where

$$a_{11} \equiv \left\{ s + P\frac{\partial s}{\partial P} \right\} > 0 \qquad a_{12} \equiv P\frac{\partial s}{\partial M} < 0$$

$$a_{21} \equiv \tau\left[\frac{\partial Y}{\partial P} + \bar{B}\left(s + P\frac{\partial s}{\partial P} \right) \right] \qquad a_{22} \equiv -\tau\left[\frac{\partial Y}{\partial M} + \bar{B}P\frac{\partial s}{\partial M} \right].$$

The partial derivatives $\partial s/\partial P$, $\partial s/\partial M$, $\partial Y/\partial M$ are reported in (6.22)–(6.23) above, while the a_{ij} are evaluated at the steady state when (6.20c′) and (6.20d″) hold.

Inspection of the roots of this differential equation indicate that it is a saddlepoint, with roots $\lambda_1 < 0$, $\lambda_2 > 0$, say.[6] Following the procedure of

Section 6.1, we focus on the stable solution to this equation, which is given by

$$P(t) = \tilde{P} + D_1 e^{\lambda_1 t}, \tag{6.27a}$$

$$M(t) = \tilde{M} + D_1 \left(\frac{\lambda_1 - a_{11}}{a_{12}}\right) e^{\lambda_1 t}. \tag{6.27b}$$

Eliminating $D_1 e^{\lambda_1 t}$ between these two equations yields

$$P - \tilde{P} = \left(\frac{a_{12}}{\lambda_1 - a_{11}}\right)(M - \tilde{M}). \tag{6.28}$$

This locus between M and P defines the stable arm of the saddlepoint passing through the steady state $(\tilde{M}, \tilde{P})$. Since $a_{12} < 0$, $\lambda_1 < 0$, and $a_{11} > 0$, this locus is positively sloped.

Increase in Government Expenditure with Money-Financed Deficit

The transitional behavior of the system in response to an unanticipated increase in government expenditure is illustrated in Figure 6.3. Initially,

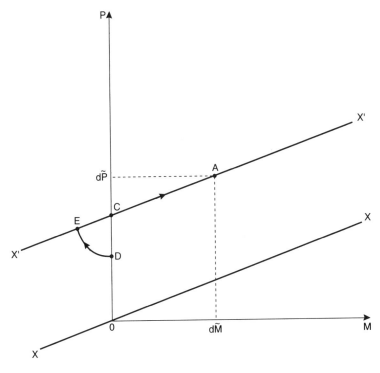

Figure 6.3
Increase in government expenditure with money-financed deficit

the system is assumed to be in steady state at the origin, say, which lies on the stable arm of the saddlepoint XX. If an increase in G, dG say, occurs, it follows from (6.25) that in the new steady state, $d\tilde{P} > 0$, $d\tilde{M} > 0$. It can also be shown that

$$\frac{d\tilde{P}/dG}{d\tilde{M}/dG} > \frac{-a_{12}}{a_{11}} > \frac{-a_{12}}{\lambda_1 - a_{11}} = \left(\frac{dP}{dM}\right)_{XX}. \tag{6.29}$$

As a consequence of this, the new steady state, corresponding to the higher level of government expenditure, is denoted by a point such as A that lies above the original stable arm. In other words, the increase in G leads to an upward shift in the stable arm to $X'X'$.

In order for the system to remain stable in the absence of future exogenous displacements, P and M must always lie on a stable arm. Thus any increase in G that leads to a shift in the stable arm $X'X'$ must give rise to a jump in the system, thereby enabling it to move instantaneously from the stable arm appropriate to the original equilibrium (the origin) to the unique path that ensures convergent adjustment to the new steady state (at A). In the absence of open-market operations, the money supply is constrained to adjust continuously; the jump in the system is therefore brought about by a jump in the price of bonds. In terms of Figure 6.3, as soon as the unanticipated increase in G occurs, the price of bonds jumps instantaneously from 0 on XX to C on the new stable arm $X'X'$. Thereafter, both the price of bonds and the money supply increase continuously as the system moves along the stable arm toward its new equilibrium A.

The following intuitive explanation for this adjustment may be given. The *implementation effect* of the increase in government expenditure is to push the IS curve out, thereby raising income and the short rate s and creating a budget deficit. The knowledge (which we attribute to bond holders) that this deficit will be financed by money creation, and that such money financing will in the long run lower interest rates below their original level, means that despite the initial rise in the short rate, the long bond rate, which embodies such forward-looking information, falls. The rise in the bond price P in turn exerts a *news effect*, which also raises income and the short rate for the reasons discussed previously and noted in equations (6.24a) and (6.24b).

Because short rates have increased but long rates have fallen, the price of bonds must continue to rise (i.e., $\dot{P} > 0$) in order for the arbitrage condition (6.1d) to be satisfied. At the same time, while the increase in income and the existence of positive capital gains ($\dot{P} > 0$) will generate additional tax revenues, these are insufficient to match the increase in G, so that the money supply must immediately begin to increase ($\dot{M} > 0$).

It is also instructive to focus on the comparative dynamic time paths followed by the short and long rates, s and l, respectively. These are illustrated in Figure 6.4A. We have seen that in steady state these two rates are identical, so that in steady-state equilibrium they must respond identically to any given exogenous shock; in particular, $d\tilde{l}/dG = d\tilde{s}/dG < 0$.[7] Along the transitional path, however, the two rates diverge. From the basic arbitrage condition, which we shall write as

$$s = l + \frac{\dot{P}}{P},\tag{6.30}$$

we see that with $\dot{P} > 0$ along the transitional path (i.e., the stable locus $X'X'$) the short rate must always lie above the long rate.

Even more striking is the contrast in the comparative *impact* effects of the increase in G on the short and long rates implied by the response in P. The positive jump in the price of bonds from 0 to C in Figure 6.3 means that on impact, the long rate falls. The effect on the short rate is described by (6.24); as noted, both the implementation effect and the news effect cause it to rise.

Although this contrast between the short-run responses of the short and long rates may at first appear surprising, it is in fact perfectly intuitive. Whereas in the short run the positive effect resulting from the (discrete) outward shift in the *IS* curve dominates, in the long run the negative effect resulting from the accumulated shifts in the *LM* curve prevails. Since the short rate is myopic, it is natural that this is influenced primarily by the *short-run positive* effect. On the other hand, the long rate is entirely forward looking. It is therefore equally natural that its short-run behavior should anticipate the *long-run negative* response.

The analysis thus far has dealt with an unanticipated increase in government expenditure. It is easy to extend the analysis to consider an increase in government expenditure that is announced at some date, say $t = 0$, to take place at some time in the future, say $t = T$. In this case, the transitional dynamic path can be shown to consist of three phases. At the announcement date $t = 0$, the price of bonds jumps to, say, D in Figure 6.3. It then follows the unstable path DE until it reaches the stable arm of the saddlepoint at E, which it does at time T, when the increase in government expenditure actually takes place. Thereafter, it follows the stable path toward the new steady-state equilibrium A. Note that the discontinuity in the price of bonds occurs at the time of announcement, and not when the promised fiscal expansion is actually implemented.

The paths followed by the short and long interest rates are illustrated in Figure 6.4B. In contrast to the long rate, the short rate exhibits two discontinuities, the first at the time of announcement, the second at the

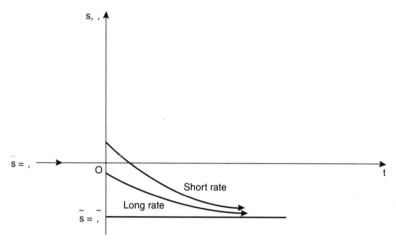

A. Unanticipated Increase in Government Expenditure

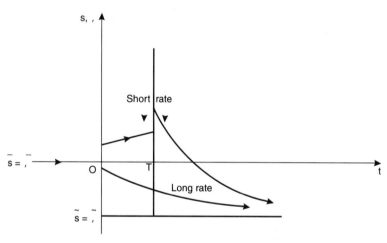

B. Announced Increase in Government Expenditure

Figure 6.4
Dynamic adjustments of short and long rates with money-financed deficit

time of implementation. The increase in the bond price at time zero stimulates the economy and so increases both output and the short-term interest rate. But such an increase in output, without any increase in government expenditure, leads to a government surplus and so to a gradual contraction in the money stock. This, together with the steady increase in bond prices, imposes gradual upward pressure on the short rates during the preimplementation period 0 to T. The actual implementation of the fiscal expansion leads to the second discontinuous adjustment in output and the short rate and converts the surplus to a deficit. The money supply begins to expand from time T onward, and the system proceeds down the stable branch of the saddlepoint with the short and long rates converging exponentially toward their new equilibrium values. As is apparent from Figure 6.4B, the short rate reaches a higher peak when the fiscal policy is preannounced than when it is unanticipated. This is because the initial period of contraction of the money supply puts the system further away from equilibrium when it reaches the stable branch at time T than is the case when it jumps immediately to the stable branch at time 0 (see Figure 6.3). It can also be shown that the longer the lead time T, the smaller the initial jump in the long rate.

6.4   Example 3: Exchange Rate Dynamics

As a third example of saddlepoint dynamics we present the celebrated model of exchange rate "overshooting" due to Dornbusch (1976a). This is a model of exchange rate determination in a small open economy under the assumption of perfect international capital mobility. The key feature of the model is that the exchange rate is determined in asset markets, which adjust quickly so as to clear at all times, whereas the price level evolves gradually to clear the goods market. Thus in terms of our previous characterization of variables, the exchange rate is the "jump" variable, and the price level is now the "sluggish" variable. This is in partial contrast with the Cagan example of Section 6.2 where the price level was allowed to respond instantaneously. The question of whether the price level should be treated as a jump variable or as a sluggish variable is sometimes characterized in terms of whether we view prices as being determined in "auction" markets, where prices react quickly, or in "contract" markets, where they adjust slowly. There is no uniformly correct treatment, and the appropriate formulation is dictated by the specific context and by one's view of the world. In the context of the Dornbusch model, few would argue with the proposition that exchange rates are much more volatile and responsive to changes in financial conditions than is the price of output, which may plausibly be treated as adjusting gradually to clear the goods market.

The Dornbusch model itself can be formulated by the following equations:

$$R = R^* + \dot{E} \tag{6.31a}$$

$$M - P = \alpha_1 Y - \alpha_2 R \qquad \alpha_1 > 0, \alpha_2 > 0 \tag{6.31b}$$

$$\dot{P} = \rho\{\beta_0 + (\beta_1 - 1)Y - \beta_2 R + \beta_3(E - P)\}$$
$$0 < \beta_1 < 1, \beta_2 > 0, \beta_3 > 0, \rho > 0 \tag{6.31c}$$

where R^* is the foreign nominal interest rate, taken to be exogenous; R is the domestic interest rate; E is logarithm of the current exchange rate, measured in terms of units of the domestic currency per unit of foreign currency; $\dot{E}$ is the expected percentage rate of change of the exchange rate, equal to the actual percentage rate of change of the exchange rate; M is the logarithm of the domestic money supply, taken to be exogenous; P is the logarithm of the domestic price level; and Y is the logarithm of the domestic output level, taken to be fixed.

Equation (6.31a) is a statement of uncovered interest parity. It asserts that, through arbitrage, the domestic interest rate equals the world interest rate plus the expected rate of change of the domestic currency price of foreign exchange. It is a restrictive condition, one that does not have much empirical support, but it is an assumption that is made in much of the international macroeconomic literature, including the Dornbusch model itself. The second equation describes continuous equilibrium in the domestic money market, with the demand for money being of the standard type. Equation (6.31c) is a price adjustment equation according to which the rate of domestic price adjustment is proportional to excess demand. This is given by the term in parentheses and is seen to vary negatively with domestic output and the domestic interest rate and positively with the relative price of the domestic goods, which with a logarithmic formulation is given by the difference $E - P$.

The model itself is based on all kinds of restrictive assumptions. For example, although output is fixed, the price level is sluggish, a formulation that runs counter to the classical model in which appropriate jumps in the price level provide the mechanism that enables output to remain fixed. Second, it does not differentiate between real and nominal interest rates, and, as we have noted, the assumption of uncovered interest parity does not receive much empirical support. Nevertheless, the model is a very attractive one, giving rise to a strong proposition regarding the impact of domestic monetary policy on the exchange rate. Specifically, it implies that, on impact, the exchange rate overreacts to a permanent monetary expansion, suggesting that undesired fluctuations in the exchange rate could be outcomes of domestic monetary policy. This so-called over-shooting of the exchange rate generated a good deal of interest, and for the decade or so following the appearance of the original model, a volu-minous literature evolved investigating both the theoretical robustness and the empirical relevance of this proposition. Our objective here is not to provide a critique of the Dornbusch model; there is a huge literature devoted to that. Rather, it is to show how the above formulation leads to a saddlepoint solution.

Consider the system (6.31) about some initial fixed equilibrium level of the money supply; we shall define lowercase letters to be the deviations about that equilibrium. Using (6.31a) to eliminate the domestic interest rate, the dynamics of the system about its initial equilibrium can be expressed in deviation form as

$$\begin{pmatrix} \dot{e} \\ \dot{p} \end{pmatrix} = \begin{pmatrix} 0 & 1/\alpha_2 \\ \rho\beta_3 & -\rho(\beta_3 + \beta_2/\alpha_2) \end{pmatrix} \begin{pmatrix} e \\ p \end{pmatrix} + \begin{pmatrix} -1/\alpha_2 \\ \rho\beta_2/\alpha_2 \end{pmatrix} m(t) \tag{6.32}$$

where lowercase letters measure deviations about the initial equilibrium. The characteristic equation for this system can be shown to have real roots of opposite sign, which we shall denote by $\lambda_1 < 0, \lambda_2 > 0$. The system as specified by (6.32) allows the money supply to follow an arbitrary, time-varying path.

Gray and Turnovsky (1979b) present a formal solution to this equa-tion, which is general enough to permit us to determine the bounded solution for the exchange rate and the price level in the presence of an arbitrary time profile for $m(t)$. The graphical solutions in response to one-time changes in the money supply, either now or anticipated in the future, can be found using the method introduced in Section 6.1. The stable and unstable saddlepaths are given by

$$E - \bar{E} = \frac{1}{\alpha_2 \lambda_1} (P - \bar{P}) \tag{6.33a}$$

$$E - \bar{E} = \frac{1}{\alpha_2 \lambda_2} (P - \bar{P}) \tag{6.33b}$$

where $\bar{P}$ and $\bar{E}$ are the associated equilibrium levels of the domestic price level and exchange rate, which correspond to some initial base level of the domestic money supply $\bar{M}$. These relationships are illustrated by the lines XX and YY in Figure 6.5 and are negatively and positively sloped, respectively.

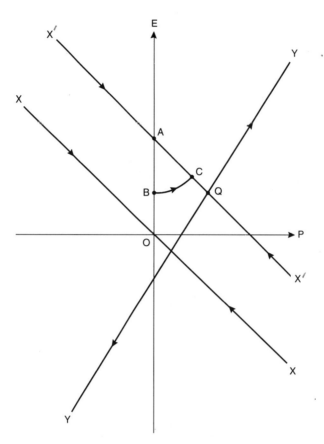

Figure 6.5
Response of exchange rate and price level to monetary expansion

By the usual saddlepoint argument we know that if no future shock is anticipated the system must lie on the stable locus XX. This observation, together with the long-run neutrality of money (also true in the Cagan model) immediately yields the celebrated short-run exchange rate "overshooting" associated with the Dornbusch model. To see this, consider the steady state associated with (6.31). In the long run, the domestic interest rate is tied to the world interest rate. A 1-percent increase in the domestic money supply leads to a 1-percent increase in the domestic price level, which in turn leads to a 1-percent depreciation of the domestic currency, in order for real-goods market equilibrium to prevail. That is $d\overline{E} = d\overline{P} = d\overline{M}$. With the price level moving sluggishly, P_0 is predetermined, and it follows that the initial response of the nominal exchange to an unanticipated permanent monetary expansion is given by

$$dE(0) = [1 - 1/\alpha_2\lambda_1]\,d\overline{M} > d\overline{M}. \tag{6.34}$$

That is, on impact, a 1-percent increase in the domestic money supply leads to more than a 1-percent depreciation of the exchange rate, and this is precisely the overshooting result.

The dynamics in response to both an unanticipated permanent and an announced (anticipated) future monetary expansion are illustrated in Figure 6.5. The initial equilibrium is at the origin, which lies on the stable arm XX. A 1-percent monetary expansion will shift the stable arm up to $X'X'$, with the new equilibrium being at the point Q, which lies on the 45-degree line through the origin.

Consider first a 1-percent unanticipated permanent monetary expansion. On impact, the price level remains unchanged and the exchange rate depreciates by the amount given in (6.34), taking it to the point A on the stable locus $X'X'$. This depreciation exceeds the long-run depreciation, so that exchange rate overshooting occurs. The predetermined price level implies an equivalent real monetary expansion, and in order for money market equilibrium to prevail, the domestic interest rate must fall below the world rate. By uncovered interest parity, this requires that agents expect the domestic currency to appreciate over time, and for this to occur it must depreciate excessively upon impact. A further consequence of the sluggish adjustment of prices is that the nominal depreciation of the exchange rate translates to an equivalent real depreciation. This raises the demand for domestic output, causing the domestic price level to begin to rise. As this occurs, the real domestic money supply declines, the downward pressure on the domestic interest rate diminishes, and the price level and exchange rate gradually follow the stable path AQ to the new equilibrium at Q.

Now suppose that a monetary expansion for time T is announced at time 0. The eventual long-run response of the system is as before. At time 0, the exchange rate will jump, though not by the full amount, taking it to a point such as B. In effect, since the monetary expansion will take place only in the future, it is discounted—more so, the farther it is in the future. Formally one can derive an expression analogous to (6.15), namely

$$dE(0) = \left(1 - \frac{1}{\alpha_2 \lambda_1}\right) e^{-\lambda_2 T} d\overline{M}, \tag{6.35}$$

from which it can be seen that the announcement moderates the initial jump in the exchange rate. Indeed, the exchange rate may or may not overshoot on impact.

Since the money supply is unchanged at time 0 and the price level is fixed instantaneously, the real money supply remains unchanged. There is therefore no short-run effect on the domestic interest rate, so that immediately following the jump $\dot{E} = 0$. At the same time, the nominal depreciation implies a real depreciation of the exchange rate, causing the price level to begin to rise, which, with the fixed nominal money supply, causes the real money supply to begin to rise. There is therefore a gradual domestic real monetary contraction. This puts a gradual upward pressure on the domestic interest rate, causing the domestic exchange rate to continue to depreciate, though now gradually. The path BC is thus followed until time T, when the anticipated monetary expansion actually occurs. At that time, there is a real monetary expansion, and with the price level not having fully expanded, there is exchange rate overshooting. Thereafter, the exchange rate appreciates and the economy approaches the new equilibrium at Q, as before.

These three examples complete our discussion of saddlepoint behavior in the context of linear rational expectations models. Other examples will occur in models based on intertemporal optimization, to be discussed in Part III.

Appendix: Dynamics of Second-Order System

We consider the following representation of a continuous-time economic system[8]

$$\dot{x}(t) = \alpha_{11}x(t) + \alpha_{12}y(t) + f_1(t) \tag{A.6.1a}$$

$$\dot{y}(t) = \alpha_{21}x(t) + \alpha_{22}y(t) + f_2(t) \tag{A.6.1b}$$

where $x(t)$, $y(t)$ are dynamically evolving variables and $f_1(t)$, $f_2(t)$ are forcing functions, which drive the underlying dynamics. Equations (A.6.1) may be viewed as a pair of reduced forms of structural equations in which expectations have been eliminated by the introduction of perfect foresight, as was done in Section 3.3. For present purposes, the specific interpretation of these equations is unimportant. The homogeneous part of (A.6.1) has the characteristic equation:

$$\lambda^2 - (\alpha_{11} + \alpha_{22})\lambda + (\alpha_{11}\alpha_{22} - \alpha_{12}\alpha_{21}) = 0$$

with roots λ_1, λ_2, whose magnitudes relative to zero are determined by the specific model. For simplicity, we shall assume these two roots are real, as they are in most economic applications. However, the case where the roots are complex can be analyzed in a similar way.

The solutions to the homogeneous system are

$$x_1(t) = q_1 e^{\lambda_1 t},$$

$$y_1(t) = e^{\lambda_1 t}$$

and

$$x_2(t) = q_2 e^{\lambda_2 t},$$

$$y_2(t) = e^{\lambda_2 t},$$

giving full homogeneous solutions as follows:

$$x^H(t) = c_1 q_1 e^{\lambda_1 t} + c_2 q_2 e^{\lambda_2 t}$$

$$y^H(t) = c_1 e^{\lambda_1 t} + c_2 e^{\lambda_2 t}$$

(A.6.2)

where c_1 and c_2 are arbitrary constants and q_1 and q_2 come from the normalized eigenvectors associated with λ_1 and λ_2, namely $\begin{pmatrix} q_1 \\ 1 \end{pmatrix}$ and $\begin{pmatrix} q_2 \\ 1 \end{pmatrix}$, respectively.

We next need to find a particular solution. The solution

$$x^P(t) = v_1(t)x_1(t) + v_2(t)x_2(t)$$

$$y^P(t) = v_1(t)y_1(t) + v_2(t)y_2(t)$$

is a particular solution if and only if

$$\dot{v}_1(t)x_1(t) + \dot{v}_2(t)x_2(t) = f_1(t)$$

and

$$\dot{v}_1(t)y_1(t) + \dot{v}_2(t)y_2(t) = f_2(t),$$

implying

$$\dot{v}_1(t) = \left(\frac{f_1(t) - q_2 f_2(t)}{q_1 - q_2} \right) e^{-\lambda_1 t}$$

$$\dot{v}_2(t) = \left(\frac{q_1 f_2(t) - f_1(t)}{q_1 - q_2} \right) e^{-\lambda_2 t}.$$

Upon integration,

$$v_1(t) = \int_a^t \left(\frac{f_1(\theta) - q_2 f_2(\theta)}{q_1 - q_2} \right) e^{-\lambda_1 \theta} \, d\theta$$

(A.6.3a)

$$v_2(t) = \int_b^t \left(\frac{q_1 f_2(\theta) - f_1(\theta)}{q_1 - q_2} \right) e^{-\lambda_2 \theta} \, d\theta.$$

(A.6.3b)

The limits of integration, a and b, in (A.6.3a), (A.6.3b) are to be determined in the context of the problem. In effect, they determine whether the solution is forward looking or backward looking, and their choice is dictated by the requirement that the system be stable.

The general solution of (A.6.1) is

$$x(t) = c_1 q_1 e^{\lambda_1 t} + c_2 q_2 e^{\lambda_2 t} + q_1 v_1(t) e^{\lambda_1 t} + q_2 v_2(t) e^{\lambda_2 t} \tag{A.6.4a}$$

$$y(t) = c_1 e^{\lambda_1 t} + c_2 e^{\lambda_2 t} + v_1(t) e^{\lambda_1 t} + v_2(t) e^{\lambda_2 t} \tag{A.6.4b}$$

with c_1, c_2 and bounds of integration in v_1, v_2 to be determined by the problem. With the roots being real, we have four cases to consider:

I. $\lambda_1 < 0, \quad \lambda_2 < 0$

II. $\lambda_1 > 0, \quad \lambda_2 < 0$

III. $\lambda_1 < 0, \quad \lambda_2 > 0$

IV. $\lambda_1 > 0, \quad \lambda_2 > 0$

Three pieces of information allow us to solve for the arbitrary constants c_1, c_2, a, and b in each of the four cases. These are (i) initial conditions; (ii) the assumption that $x(t), y(t)$ remain bounded; and (iii) the requirement that all integrals in the solution converge.

Case I $(\lambda_1 < 0, \lambda_2 < 0)$

One must check that

$$v_1(t) = \int_a^t F_1(\theta) e^{-\lambda_1 \theta} \, d\theta \qquad v_2(t) = \int_b^t F_2(\theta) e^{-\lambda_2 \theta} \, d\theta$$

where

$$F_1(\theta) \equiv \frac{f_1(\theta) - q_2 f_2(\theta)}{q_1 - q_2}, \qquad F_2(\theta) \equiv \frac{q_1 f_2(\theta) - f_1(\theta)}{q_1 - q_2}$$

converge for the chosen values of a and b. In order for the solutions to be general we will require a and b to assume values of either $+\infty$ or $-\infty$. However, we also adopt the convention that time $t = 0$ is the "start of the world" and define $F_1(\theta) = F_2(\theta) = 0$ for $\theta < 0$. Hence, when a or $b = -\infty$ is investigated we need only look at a or $b = 0$. We assume that $F_1(\theta)$ and $F_2(\theta)$ are bounded, that is,[9]

$$s \le F_1(\theta) \le S, \qquad s \le F_2(\theta) \le S.$$

For bounded $F_1(\theta), F_2(\theta)$,

$$s \int_a^t e^{-\lambda_1 \theta} \, d\theta \le \int_a^t F_1(\theta) e^{-\lambda_1 \theta} \, d\theta \le S \int_a^t e^{-\lambda_1 \theta} \, d\theta,$$

$$s \int_b^t e^{-\lambda_2 \theta} \, d\theta \le \int_b^t F_2(\theta) e^{-\lambda_2 \theta} \, d\theta \le S \int_b^t e^{-\lambda_2 \theta} \, d\theta.$$

Because both $\lambda_1, \lambda_2 < 0$, we need check only v_1 or v_2.

We will check v_1. Upon integration we obtain

$$-\frac{s}{\lambda_1}[e^{-\lambda_1\theta}]_a^t \leq \int_a^t F_1(\theta)e^{-\lambda_1\theta}\,d\theta \leq -\frac{S}{\lambda_1}[e^{-\lambda_1\theta}]_a^t.$$

Because $[e^{-\lambda_1\theta}]_a^t = e^{-\lambda_2 t} - e^{-\lambda_2 a}$, we find that both integrals converge for $a = b = 0$, and both diverge if $a = b = \infty$. Hence $a = b = 0$ are the appropriate bounds of integration.

Next we need to check stability. Once again, with both roots negative we need only check $v_1(t)$. This involves

$$\lim_{t\to\infty} q_1 e^{\lambda_1 t} \int_0^t F_1(\theta)e^{-\lambda_1\theta}\,d\theta,$$

but

$$-q_1 e^{\lambda_1 t}\frac{s}{\lambda_1}[e^{-\lambda_1\theta}]_0^t \leq q_1 e^{\lambda_1 t}\int_0^t F_1(\theta)e^{-\lambda_1\theta}\,d\theta \leq -q_1 e^{\lambda_1 t}\frac{S}{\lambda_1}[e^{-\lambda_1\theta}]_0^t.$$

Because

$$e^{\lambda_2 t}[e^{-\lambda_2\theta}]_0^t = 1 - e^{\lambda_2 t},$$

the limits $\lim_{t\to\infty} v_1(t)$ and $\lim_{t\to\infty} v_2(t)$ are bounded. Hence the model fulfills the requirement of stability.

Finally, initial conditions require

$$x(0) = \bar{x},$$

$$y(0) = \bar{y},$$

implying

$$\bar{x} = c_1 q_1 + c_2 q_2,$$

$$\bar{y} = c_1 + c_2.$$

The complete solution may be obtained from (A.6.4a) and (A.6.4b):

$$c_1 = \frac{(\bar{x} - q_2\bar{y})}{(q_1 - q_2)} \qquad c_2 = \frac{(q_1\bar{y} - \bar{x})}{(q_1 - q_2)}$$

$$v_1(t) = \int_0^t F_1(\theta)e^{-\lambda_1\theta}\,d\theta \qquad v_2(t) = \int_0^t F_2(\theta)e^{-\lambda_2\theta}\,d\theta.$$

Case II $(\lambda_1 > 0, \lambda_2 < 0)$

This is the case of a saddlepoint. Because λ_2 is still negative we need investigate only the portions of the solutions involving λ_1. Thus, from (A.6.4a) and (A.6.4b) we need consider only

$$\psi = c_1 e^{\lambda_1 t} + v_1(t) e^{\lambda_1 t}. \tag{A.6.5}$$

We retain the assumption that $F_1(\theta)$ is bounded. Thus

$$-\frac{S}{\lambda_1} [e^{-\lambda_1 \theta}]_a^t \leq \int_a^t F_1(\theta) e^{-\lambda_1 \theta} \, d\theta \leq -\frac{S}{\lambda_1} [e^{-\lambda_2 \theta}]_a^t.$$

It is obvious that v_1 converges for both $a = 0$ and $a = \infty$. However, only $a = \infty$ is consistent with the assumption of stability. To see this, note that the solution involves

$$-\frac{S}{\lambda_1} e^{\lambda_1 t} [e^{-\lambda_1 \theta}]_a^t \leq e^{\lambda_1 t} \int_a^t F_1(\theta) e^{-\lambda_1 \theta} \, d\theta \leq -\frac{S}{\lambda_1} e^{\lambda_1 t} [e^{-\lambda_1 \theta}]_a^t.$$

By setting $a = 0$ we obtain

$$-\frac{S}{\lambda_1} e^{\lambda_1 t} [e^{-\lambda_1 t} - 1] \leq e^{\lambda_1 t} v_1(t) \leq -\frac{S}{\lambda_1} e^{\lambda_1 t} [e^{-\lambda_1 t} - 1].$$

But $\lim_{t \to \infty} -[1 - e^{\lambda_1 t}] = +\infty$. Thus $\lim_{t \to \infty} e^{\lambda_1 t} v_1(t) = +\infty$ with $a = 0$. Now consider $a = \infty$:

$$-\frac{S}{\lambda_1} e^{\lambda_1 t} [e^{-\lambda_1 \theta}]_\infty^t \leq e^{\lambda_1 t} \int_\infty^t F_1(\theta) e^{-\lambda_1 \theta} \, d\theta \leq -\frac{S}{\lambda_1} e^{\lambda_1 t} [e^{-\lambda_1 \theta}]_\infty^t$$

that is

$$-\frac{S}{\lambda_1} e^{\lambda_1 t} [e^{-\lambda_1 t}] \leq e^{\lambda_1 t} v_1(t) \leq -\frac{S}{\lambda_1} e^{\lambda_1 t} [e^{-\lambda_1 t}].$$

Thus

$$-\frac{S}{\lambda_1} \leq e^{\lambda_1 t} v_1(t) \leq -\frac{S}{\lambda_1} \qquad \text{for all } t.$$

Hence the assumption of stability requires that we choose $a = \infty$. Further, the stability of the first term in $\psi, c_1 e^{\lambda_1 t}$, is satisfied only for $c_1 = 0$. Thus the solution is

$$x(t) = c_2 q_2 e^{\lambda_2 t} + q_1 v_1(t) e^{\lambda_1 t} + q_2 v_2(t) e^{\lambda_2 t},$$

$$y(t) = c_2 e^{\lambda_2 t} + v_1(t) e^{\lambda_1 t} + v_2(t) e^{\lambda_2 t}$$

with $v_2(t)$ defined as in Case I and $v_1(t)$ from the present discussion.

In order to find c_2 we require an initial condition on *either* $x(0)$ or $y(0)$. That is, one variable must be a "jump" variable. Which it is to be depends upon the economic context. Suppose it is $y(t)$, in which case the initial condition can be specified by, say, $y(0) = \bar{y}$. Then

$$\bar{y} = c_2 - \int_0^\infty F_1(\theta)e^{-\lambda_1\theta}\,d\theta$$

and $c_2 = \bar{y} + \int_0^\infty F_1(\theta)e^{-\lambda_1\theta}\,d\theta$. Next, the initial x, $x(0)$ is

$$x(0) = q_2\bar{y} + (q_2 - q_1)\int_0^\infty F_1(\theta)e^{-\lambda_1\theta}\,d\theta.$$

Hence, the complete Case II solution is obtained from (A.6.4a) and (A.6.4b) with

$$c_1 = 0 \qquad c_2 = \bar{y} + \int_0^\infty F_1(\theta)e^{-\lambda_1\theta}\,d\theta,$$

$$v_1(t) = \int_0^t F_1(\theta)e^{-\lambda_1\theta}\,d\theta \qquad v_2(t) = \int_\infty^t F_2(\theta)e^{-\lambda_1\theta}\,d\theta.$$

Case III $(\lambda_1 < 0, \lambda_2 > 0)$

This situation is essentially the same as Case II and need not be treated in detail. We note only that the solution involves

$$x(t) = c_1 q_1 e^{\lambda_1 t} + q_1 v_1(t)e^{\lambda_1 t} + q_2 v_2(t)e^{\lambda_2 t},$$

$$y(t) = c_1 e^{\lambda_1 t} + v_1(t)e^{\lambda_1 t} + v_2(t)e^{\lambda_2 t}$$

with $v_1(t)$ determined as in Case I and

$$v_2(t) = -\int_t^\infty F_2(\theta)e^{-\lambda_2\theta}\,d\theta.$$

Further, the initial condition on y, $y(0) = \bar{y}$ determines c_1:

$$c_1 = \bar{y} + \int_0^\infty F_2(\theta)e^{-\lambda_2\theta}\,d\theta.$$

Case IV $(\lambda_1 > 0, \lambda_2 > 0)$

For this case, stability of expectations requires

$$c_1 = c_2 = 0,$$

$$v_1(t) = \int_\infty^t F_1(\theta)e^{-\lambda_1\theta}\,d\theta,$$

$$v_2(t) = \int_\infty^t F_2(\theta)e^{-\lambda_2\theta}\,d\theta.$$

Both $x(t)$ and $y(t)$ must be jump variables, with $x(0)$ and $y(0)$ initially set at

$$x(0) = q_1 v_1(\theta) + q_2 v_2(0),$$

$$y(0) = v_1(0) + v_2(0).$$

Note: For concreteness, we have restricted our discussion to the case of two linear differential equations. The argument can easily be extended to an arbitrary number of linear differential equations.

Notes

1. This proposition is based on the assumption of risk neutrality. To take account adequately of risk-averse agents would require a full stochastic model, such as that developed in Part IV.

2. This forward-looking solution is obtained by involving a terminal (transversality) condition.

3. More generally, in the case where the future short rates are not necessarily correctly predicted, $s(t')$ would be replaced by $s^*(t', t)$, the prediction of the future short rate for time t', formed at time t.

4. Another (but much less important) difference in the present specification from that of Blinder and Solow is that the rate of return introduced into the money demand function is after-tax, rather than gross.

5. The case of a purely bond-financed deficit is discussed by Turnovsky and Miller (1984). It does not give rise to a saddlepoint, but instead has the usual instability associated with bond financing. For a clarification of this aspect of their analysis see Clark (1985).

6. This can be established by substituting for the short-run partial derivatives (6.22), (6.23) into a_{ij} and showing $a_{11}a_{22} - a_{12}a_{21} < 0$.

7. In Figure 6.4 we assume that by appropriate choice of units the initial steady-state levels of both the short and long rates are $\bar{s} = \bar{l} = 0$.

8. This section is a slight adaptation of an unpublished appendix to Burmeister, Flood, and Turnovsky (1981).

9. The assumption of finite bounds is stronger than is required for our argument. However, this assumption simplifies without materially altering the argument and will be retained. All of the discussion in this section can be duplicated for growth rates of $F_1(\theta)$ and $F_2(\theta)$ of less than exponential order. It also can be generalized to include the case of complex roots with $\lambda_1 = \alpha + \beta i, \lambda_2 = \alpha - \beta i, \beta \neq 0$.

The Stability of Government Deficit Financing under Rational Expectations

7.1 Introduction

Much of the work in macroeconomic dynamics between the late 1960s and the early 1980s stressed the role of the government budget constraint. Beginning with Ott and Ott (1965) and Christ (1967, 1968), several economists showed how this constraint forms an integral part of the dynamic structure of the system and examined the stability properties of alternative government financial policies. The proposition that money financing of the government deficit is generally stable whereas bond financing may plausibly generate instability has become a familiar one; see, for example, Blinder and Solow (1973), Tobin and Buiter (1976), Infante and Stein (1976), and Turnovsky (1977). On the one hand, money financing, being expansionary, raises the tax base and therefore tax receipts, thereby reducing the deficit and the quantity of additional money that must be created. Bond financing, on the other hand, is associated with accumulating interest payments, and it is the need to finance these payments that is the critical destabilizing element. Unless bond financing generates sufficient additional tax receipts to finance these mounting interest payments, the dynamics will be unstable. Furthermore, since bond financing tends to be less expansionary than money financing, due to the fact that it is associated with a rising rather than a falling interest rate, this possibility can by no means be ruled out. This literature is reviewed at length by Turnovsky (1977), as well as briefly in Chapter 2.

These analyses typically assume fixed prices or, alternatively, allow prices to be determined by some sluggish process, with inflationary expectations being formed adaptively, as in Chapter 2. The dynamics evolves continuously from some given initial condition and is therefore entirely backward looking. By contrast, most of the rational expectations literature makes assumptions about the forms of the relevant demand functions (namely, that they are independent of wealth and interest payments) and the financing of the deficit (namely, that it is bond-financed), which enable the government budget constraint to be ignored. Under these conditions, the stock of government bonds accumulated in the process of financing the deficit plays no role in the determination of income, or any other variable of interest.[1]

In this chapter we reintroduce assumptions into the rational expectations model so as to assign once again a central role to the government budget constraint as part of the dynamics of the system. Our concern is to determine in what sense, if any, the propositions regarding the relative stability of the alternative modes of deficit financing carry over to the rational expectations context. We shall establish the following key result. If the equilibrium stock of government bonds is assumed to be strictly positive, then money financing of the deficit is stable in the sense that there is a unique stochastic process consistent with all real and nominal variables having finite asymptotic variances. However, if the equilibrium stock of government bonds is zero—as it will be if the government sets expenditure to just match long-run tax revenue from current income—then money financing will be stable in the sense that all real magnitudes have finite variance; however, the price level and the nominal money supply have asymptotically infinite variances.[2] By contrast, if the deficit is bond-financed, the asymptotic variances of all variables, with the exception of current income, will in general be infinite; apart from two special cases there is no stochastic process that will generate a finite variance for these variables.

This last result is significant for the old debate concerning the desirability of adopting a fixed monetary growth rule. Previous dynamic models of the conventional "backward-looking" type, which do not assume rational expectations, typically find such rules to be associated with instability, in the sense of an ultimately diverging time path. The present analysis implies that, with rational expectations, such a rule is generally unstable in the sense that relevant variables have infinite asymptotic variances.

These stability properties of money and bond financing are examples of the propositions established by Blanchard and Kahn (1980) regarding the existence and uniqueness of rational expectations equilibria. Specifically, as we note in Propositions 5.1 and 5.3 of Chapter 5, they show that if the number of unstable roots in the underlying dynamic system $(\bar{n})$ equals the number of jump variables (m), then a unique solution having a finite variances exists; if $\bar{n}$ exceeds m, no solution exists, and if m exceeds $\bar{m}$, there are an infinite number of such solutions. Money financing generates a dynamic system having the property $\bar{m} = m$, whereas for bond financing $\bar{m} > m$.[3]

A paper by Sargent and Wallace (1981) generated some interest in the issue of deficit financing within a rational expectations framework. Specifically, they addressed the issue of the feasibility of bond financing in the context of a growing economy. Using a simple model, they demonstrated that bond financing is infeasible as long as the after-tax real rate of interest exceeds the growth rate. This has led to some debate, both theoretical and empirical, concerning the relative size of the growth rate and the after-tax real interest rate. Darby (1984) and McCallum (1981a) argued that deficits are feasible if the growth rate exceeds the after-tax interest rate. Moreover, Darby argued that this requirement has in fact been met in the United States over a long period. In reply, Miller and Sargent (1984) take issue with some of the assumptions made by Darby.

First, the Sargent-Wallace model, which takes the interest rate as fixed, should not be taken too literally. They argue that in fact the interest rate will be endogenous and is likely to rise with bond financing, eventually exceeding the growth rate in the economy. Finally, McCallum (1984) considered the issue within the context of the intertemporal utility maximizing model and drew the conclusion that the feasibility of bond financing depends upon whether the deficit is defined inclusive of interest payments. The intertemporal approach will be discussed further in Chapter 9.

But, as Darby notes, this discussion can be viewed as a generalization of the Blinder and Solow (1973) results on the instability of bond financing. It is straightforward to extend the analysis of the first part of the present chapter to focus on this issue within a growth context.

The remainder of the chapter proceeds as follows. Section 7.2 outlines the model underlying the analysis. Sections 7.3 and 7.4 then derive the solutions under the two modes of financing. The problem of nonexistence of a solution having a finite asymptotic variance raises certain methodological issues, which are considered in Section 7.5. The next section introduces growth and addresses the issue of the stability of bond financing in a growing economy. Some concluding remarks are contained in the final section.

We should point out that the introduction of the government budget constraint increases the dimensionality of the system, and this complicates the determination of the rational expectations solution. This complication is not only inevitable, but also a closer indication of the reality of using rational expectations models. The sad fact is that the derivation of rational expectations equilibria typically involves heavy computations for all but the simplest systems.

7.2   A Simple Macro Model

Consider the following macro model:

$$Y_t = d_1 Y_t^d - d_2 \left[R_t - \frac{(P_{t+1,t}^* - P_t)}{P_t} \right] + d_3 W_t + G + u_{1t}$$

$$0 < d_1 < 1, d_2 > 0, 0 < d_3 < 1 \tag{7.1a}$$

$$\frac{M_t}{P_t} = \alpha_1 Y_t - \alpha_2 R_t + \alpha_3 W_t + u_{2t} \qquad \alpha_1 > 0, \alpha_2 > 0, 0 < \alpha_3 < 1 \tag{7.1b}$$

$$Y_t^d = \left(Y_t + \frac{B_t}{P_t} \right)(1 - k) \qquad 0 < k < 1 \tag{7.1c}$$

$$W_t = \frac{M_t}{P_t} + \frac{B_t}{R_t P_t} \tag{7.1d}$$

$$Y_t - \bar{Y} = \gamma(P_t - P^*_{t,t-1}) + u_{3t} \qquad \gamma > 0 \tag{7.1e}$$

$$\frac{M_{t+1} - M_t}{P_t} + \frac{B_{t+1} - B_t}{R_t P_t} = G + \frac{B_t}{P_t} - k\left(Y_t + \frac{B_t}{P_t}\right) \tag{7.1f}$$

$$P^*_{t+s,t} \equiv E_t(P_{t+s}) \tag{7.1g}$$

where

Y_t = real output (income) at time t,

$\bar{Y}$ = full employment ("natural") level of real output,

Y^d_t = real disposable income,

R_t = nominal interest rate,

P_t = price level,

$P^*_{t+s,t}$ = expectation of price for time $t + s$, formed at time t,

$E(\cdot)$ = conditional expectations operator formed at time t,

W_t = real wealth,

G = real government expenditure, taken to be fixed,

M_t = nominal stock of money,

B_t = number of government bonds outstanding,

k = rate of income tax, assumed to be constant,

u_{it} = random disturbances, having zero means and finite variances.

The model defined by equations (7.1a)–(7.1g) is standard and requires little comment at this point. However, three aspects are worth noting. First, it turns out to be more convenient to assume that bonds are perpetuities, having a coupon rate of unity and a price $1/R_t$. Second, the equilibrium in the financial market is taken to be beginning-of-period equilibrium; that is, the interest rate adjusts to clear the money market at the initial real stock. Both of these assumptions could be amended without much effort. Third, it will be noted that we have abandoned the usual rational expectations specification of log-linearity. The reason is that the government budget constraint is a relationship expressed in natural units, and a model specified log linearly would require a log-linear approximation to this relationship. Although this too is a feasible way to proceed, its advantage over the approach adopted here is not obvious.

Turning to the equations, (7.1a) and (7.1b) are the *IS* and *LM* curves respectively, and disposable income and real private wealth are defined in (7.1c) and (7.1d). Supply is described by the Lucas supply function

(7.1e), and (7.1f) specifies the government budget constraint. Note that because M_t and B_t appear in the *IS* and *LM* curves, it is necessary to take account of (7.1f) in the determination of income. The conventional rational expectations models, such as those discussed in previous chapters, are justified in ignoring (7.1f) by virtue of (i) the assumption that $d_3 = \alpha_3 = 0$; (ii) the neglect of interest payments from disposable income; (iii) the assumption of all bond financing. The final equation, (7.1g), specifies that the expectations $P^*_{t+1,t}, P^*_{t,t-1}$ are assumed to be formed rationally; that is, they are expectations from the model, conditional on all information available at the time they are formed.

We define a mean steady state (denoted by bars) by

$$\bar{Y} = d_1 \bar{Y}^d - d_2 \bar{R} + d_3 \bar{W} + G \tag{7.2a}$$

$$\frac{\bar{M}}{\bar{P}} = \alpha_1 \bar{Y} - \alpha_2 \bar{R} + \alpha_3 \bar{W} \tag{7.2b}$$

$$\bar{Y}^d = \left(\bar{Y} + \frac{\bar{B}}{\bar{P}}\right)(1 - k) \tag{7.2c}$$

$$\bar{W} = \frac{\bar{M}}{\bar{P}} + \frac{\bar{B}}{\bar{R}\bar{P}} \tag{7.2d}$$

$$G + \frac{\bar{B}}{\bar{P}} - k\left(\bar{Y} + \frac{\bar{B}}{\bar{P}}\right) = 0. \tag{7.2e}$$

The level of output $\bar{Y}$ is given exogenously, so that these five equations, together with the policy specification, determine $\bar{R}, \bar{W}, \bar{Y}^d, \bar{P}, \bar{M}$, and $\bar{B}$.

To solve the model involves solving for the expectations, and to do this it is necessary to linearize (7.1a)–(7.1f) about the steady state (7.2a)–(7.2e). This yields the following approximate relationships:

$$\frac{M_t}{P_t} \cong \frac{\bar{M}}{\bar{P}} + \frac{1}{\bar{P}}(M_t - \bar{M}) - \frac{\bar{M}}{\bar{P}^2}(P_t - \bar{P}) \tag{7.3a}$$

$$\frac{P^*_{t+1,t} - P_t}{P_t} \cong \frac{P^*_{t+1,t} - P_t}{\bar{P}} \tag{7.3b}$$

$$W_t - \bar{W} \cong \frac{M_t - \bar{M}}{\bar{P}} + \frac{1}{\bar{R}\bar{P}}(B_t - \bar{B}) - \frac{\bar{W}}{\bar{P}}(P_t - \bar{P}) - \frac{\bar{B}}{\bar{R}^2\bar{P}}(R_t - \bar{R}) \tag{7.3c}$$

$$\frac{B_t}{P_t} \cong \frac{\bar{B}}{\bar{P}} + \frac{1}{\bar{P}}(B_t - \bar{B}) - \frac{\bar{B}}{\bar{P}^2}(P_t - \bar{P}) \tag{7.3d}$$

$$\frac{M_{t+1} - M_t}{P_t} + \frac{B_{t+1} - B_t}{R_t P_t} \cong \frac{M_{t+1} - M_t}{\bar{P}} + \frac{B_{t+1} - B_t}{\bar{R}\bar{P}}. \tag{7.3e}$$

Next, choosing units such that $\bar{P} = 1$ and letting lowercase letters denote deviations (i.e., $y_t \equiv Y_t - \bar{Y}$ etc.), we may write the linearized system in the form

$$[1 - d_1(1 - k)]y_t = -d_4 r_t + d_2 p^*_{t+1,t} - d_5 p_t + d_3 m_t + d_6 b_t + u_{1t} \tag{7.4a}$$

$$(1 - \alpha_3)m_t = \alpha_1 y_t - \alpha_4 r_t + \alpha_5 p_t + \frac{\alpha_3}{\bar{R}} b_t + u_{2t} \tag{7.4b}$$

$$y_t = \gamma(p_t - p^*_{t,t-1}) + u_{3t} \tag{7.4c}$$

$$m_{t+1} - m_t + \frac{b_{t+1} - b_t}{\bar{R}} = (b_t - \bar{B}p_t)(1 - k) - ky_t \tag{7.4d}$$

where

$$d_4 \equiv d_2 + d_3 \frac{\bar{B}}{\bar{R}^2} > 0, \qquad d_5 \equiv d_2 + d_1(1 - k)\bar{B} + d_3 \bar{W} > 0,$$

$$d_6 \equiv d_1(1 - k) + \frac{d_3}{\bar{R}} > 0,$$

$$\alpha_4 \equiv \alpha_2 + \alpha_3 \frac{\bar{B}}{\bar{R}^2} > 0, \qquad \alpha_5 \equiv \bar{M} - \alpha_3 \bar{W}.$$

This system forms the basis for our subsequent analysis.

7.3 Money-Financed Deficit

The case where the deficit is financed by money creation is obtained by setting $b_t = b_{t+1} = 0$ in equations (7.4a)–(7.4d), which thus become a system of four equations in y_t, m_t, r_t, p_t and price expectations, together with the random disturbances. To solve the system it is convenient to solve (7.4a)–(7.4c) for y_t and m_t in terms of $p_t, p^*_{t+1,t}, p^*_{t,t-1}$, and the random disturbances, and then to substitute these expressions into the government budget constraint, now modified to

$$m_{t+1} - m_t = -\bar{B}p_t(1 - k) - ky_t. \tag{7.4d'}$$

The expression for y_t is simply given by (7.4c), and the solution for m_t can be written as

$$m_t = h_1 p_t - h_2 p^*_{t+1,t} + h_3(p_t - p^*_{t,t-1}) + u_{mt} \tag{7.5}$$

where

$$h_1 \equiv \frac{d_4 \alpha_5 + d_5 \alpha_4}{\Delta} > 0, \qquad h_2 \equiv \frac{d_2 \alpha_4}{\Delta} > 0,$$

$$h_3 \equiv \frac{\gamma[\alpha_4[1 - d_1(1 - k)] + \alpha_1 d_4]}{\Delta} > 0,$$

$$\Delta \equiv (1 - \alpha_3)d_4 \, \alpha_4 d_3 > 0,$$

and the composite random disturbance

$$u_{mt} \equiv \frac{-\alpha_4 u_{1t} + d_4 u_{2t} + [\alpha_4[1 - d_1(1 - k)] + \alpha_1 d_4]u_{3t}}{\Delta}.$$

Substituting (7.5) into (7.4d′) yields the following stochastic difference equation in p_t and its expectations:

$$h_1 p_{t+1} - h_2 p_{t+2,t+1}^* + h_3(p_{t+1} - p_{t+1,t}^*) + [\bar{B}(1 - k) - h_1]p_t$$
$$+ h_2 p_{t+1,t}^* + (k\gamma - h_3)(p_t - p_{t,t-1}^*) = -u_{m,t+1} + u_{m,t} - ku_{3t}. \tag{7.6}$$

To solve the stochastic difference equation (7.6) it is convenient to postulate a solution of the form

$$p_t = \sum_{i=0}^{\infty} \lambda_i u_{m,t-i} + \sum_{i=0}^{\infty} \mu_i u_{3,t-i} \tag{7.7}$$

and to adopt the method of undetermined coefficients, discussed in Chapter 3. Calculating $p_{t+1}, p_{t+2,t+1}^*, p_{t+1,t}^*, p_t, p_{t,t-1}^*$ from this equation, inserting the resulting expressions back into (7.6), and equating coefficients $u_{m,t-i}, u_{3,t-i}$ yields the following relationships among the coefficients:

$$(h_1 + h_3)\lambda_0 - h_2 \lambda_1 + 1 = 0 \tag{7.8a}$$

$$[\bar{B}(1 - k) + k\gamma]\lambda_0 + h_1 \lambda_1 - h_2 \lambda_2 = 0 \tag{7.8b}$$

$$h_2 \lambda_{i+2} - (h_1 + h_2)\lambda_{i+1} + [h_1 - \bar{B}(1 - k)]\lambda_i = 0 \qquad i = 1, 2, \ldots \tag{7.8c}$$

$$(h_1 + h_3)\mu_0 - h_2 \mu_1 = 0 \tag{7.9a}$$

$$[\bar{B}(1 - k) + k\gamma]\mu_0 + h_1 \mu_1 - h_2 \mu_2 = -k \tag{7.9b}$$

$$h_2 \mu_{i+2} - (h_1 + h_2)\mu_{i+1} + [h_1 - \bar{B}(1 - k)]\mu_i = 0 \qquad i = 1, 2, \ldots . \tag{7.9c}$$

The general solution for p_t is therefore

$$p_t = \sum_{i=0}^{\infty} \lambda_i u_{m,t-i} + \sum_{i=0}^{\infty} \mu_i u_{3,t-i} \tag{7.7}$$

where $\lambda_0, \lambda_1, \lambda_2$, satisfy (7.8a), (7.8b); μ_0, μ_1, μ_2 satisfy (7.9a), (7.9b);

$$\lambda_i = A_1 v_1^i + A_2 v_2^i \qquad i = 1, 2, \ldots \tag{7.8c'}$$

$$\mu_i = C_1 v_1^i + C_2 v_2^i \qquad i = 1, 2, \ldots . \tag{7.9c'}$$

A_1, A_2, C_1, and C_2 are arbitrary constants and v_1, v_2 are the solutions to the quadratic equation

$$h_2 v^2 - (h_1 - h_2)v + h_1 - \bar{B}(1 - k) = 0. \tag{7.10}$$

Recalling the definitions of h_1, h_2, one can show that the roots v_1, v_2 to equation (7.10) are both real. However, until the arbitrary constants A_1, A_2, C_1, and C_2 are chosen, the solution is not determined. In effect, equations (7.8a) and (7.8b) impose two constraints on the three arbitrary parameters λ_0, A_1, and A_2, and the same applies to (7.9a), (7.9b). The appropriate additional constraint on these parameters, required to determine the system fully, depends upon the magnitudes of the roots v_1, v_2, which therefore require further investigation. For this purpose it is convenient to consider the two cases, (I) $\bar{B} > 0$ and (II) $\bar{B} = 0$, in turn.

Case I $\bar{B} > 0$

Further inspection of the characteristic equation (7.10) and observation of the definitions of h_1, h_2 reveal that the larger root, say v_2, satisfies $v_2 > 1$. The location of the other root, v_1, can be characterized as follows:

$$h_1 > \bar{B}(1 - k) \qquad 0 < v_1 < 1 \tag{7.11a}$$

$$h_1 < \bar{B}(1 - k) < 2(h_1 + h_2) \qquad -1 < v_1 < 0 \tag{7.11b}$$

$$2(h_1 + h_2) < \bar{B}(1 - k) \qquad v_1 < -1. \tag{7.11c}$$

In theory, none of these three possibilities can be eliminated. While case (7.11c) might arise if the given stock of bonds $\bar{B}$ is sufficiently large, by considering the underlying components of h_1 and h_2 (defined above), one can verify that it is the least likely of the three cases to occur. A simple and sufficient, but certainly not necessary, condition for $0 < v_1 < 1$ is that

$$\frac{\bar{M}}{(\bar{B}/\bar{R})} > \frac{\alpha_3}{1 - \alpha_3} + (1 - k)\bar{R}. \tag{7.12}$$

The wealth elasticity of the demand for money is defined by the expression $\alpha_3 \bar{W}/\bar{M}$. Given that there are only two tradable assets involved in agents' portfolios in this model, the wealth elasticity of the demand for bonds is $(1 - \alpha_3)\bar{W}\bar{R}/\bar{B}$. It is common practice to restrict the form of asset demand functions to ensure well-behaved steady-state properties, and the most common restriction in this regard is that each function be homogeneous of degree one in the wealth and income arguments. Because the demand for money depends positively on both income and wealth, the wealth elasticity $\alpha_3 \overline{W}/\overline{M} < 1$. Also, it follows from the stock constraint (applicable in a beginning-of-period equilibrium model) that the demand for bonds varies inversely with income. This, together with the homogeneity of the bond demand function, implies that the wealth elasticity of the demand for bonds $(1 - \alpha_3)\overline{W}\overline{R}/\overline{B} > 1$. Combining these two inequalities immediately yields the first part of the constraint, namely that $\overline{M}\overline{R}/\overline{B} > \alpha_3/(1 - \alpha_3)$. Taking $\alpha_3 = 0.2$, $k = 0.3$, $\overline{R} = 0.05$ as being representative values, inequality (7.12) involves only the mildest strengthening of this condition. We therefore assume (7.12) holds.[4] Furthermore, it must be remembered that inequality (7.12) is only sufficient, and not necessary, for stability. Even it can be relaxed somewhat if one merely wishes to ensure that v_1 is stable, an assumption that seems plausible and that henceforth we shall invoke.[5]

It is clear that in order for the asymptotic variance σ_p^2 to remain finite, it is necessary to eliminate the unstable root v_2 from the solution, that is, to set $A_2 = C_2 = 0$. Thus we get

$$\lambda_i = A_1 v_1^i, \qquad \mu_i = C_1 v_1^i. \tag{7.13}$$

Letting L denote the lag operator defined by $L^i x_t \equiv x_{t-i}$, the solution for p_t may be written in the form[6]

$$p_t = \left(\lambda_0 + \frac{A_1 v_1 L}{1 - v_1 L}\right) u_{mt} + \left(\mu_0 + \frac{C_1 v_1 L}{1 - v_1 L}\right) u_{3t} \tag{7.14a}$$

where

$$\left.\begin{array}{l} (h_1 + h_3)\lambda_0 - h_2 A_1 v_1 = -1 \\[2mm] [\overline{B}(1 - k) + k\gamma]\lambda_0 + (h_1 - h_2 v_1)A_1 v_1 = 0 \end{array}\right\} \tag{7.14b}$$

$$\left.\begin{array}{l} (h_1 + h_3)\mu_0 - h_2 C_1 v_1 = -1 \\[2mm] [\overline{B}(1 - k) + k\gamma]\mu_0 + (h_1 - h_2 v_1)A_1 v_1 = -k \end{array}\right\} \tag{7.14c}$$

and v_1 is the stable root $(0 < v_1 < 1)$ to

$$h_2 v^2 - (h_1 + h_2)v + h_1 - \overline{B}(1 - k) = 0. \tag{7.14d}$$

The solution for the stochastic process determining p_t, described by (7.14a)–(7.14d), is obtained as follows. The characteristic equation (7.14d) determines the stable root v_1. Given v_1, (7.14b) and (7.14c) then determine the initial constants λ_0, A_1 and v_0, C_1 respectively. Thus it is evident from (7.14a) that the solution for p_t is unique and the asymptotic variance σ_p^2 is finite. The solution is therefore stable in this sense.

From (7.14), the stochastic processes governing the other relevant variables can be derived. Thus current output, y_t, is given by

$$y_t = \gamma(p_t - p^*_{t,t-1}) + u_{3t}$$
$$= \gamma\lambda_0 u_{mt} + (1 + \gamma\mu_0)u_{3t} \tag{7.15}$$

and is a function of *current* disturbances only. Its asymptotic variance (also equal to the one-period variance) is therefore obviously finite.

To consider the money supply we substitute (7.14) and (7.15) into the government budget constraint (7.4d'), writing the expression as

$$(1 - L)m_{t+1} = -\left[[\bar{B}(1 - k) + k\gamma]\lambda_0 + \frac{\bar{B}(1 - k)\lambda_1 L}{1 - v_1 L}\right]u_{mt}$$
$$- \left[[\bar{B}(1 - k) + k\gamma]\mu_0 + k + \frac{\bar{B}(1 - k)\mu_1 L}{1 - v_1 L}\right]u_{3t}.$$

Using (7.13), (7.14b), (7.14c) and noting that v_1 is a root of the characteristic equation (7.14d), we obtain the following solution for m_{t+1}:

$$m_{t+1} = \frac{v_1(h_1 - h_2 v_1)(A_1 u_{mt} + C_1 u_{3t})}{1 - v_1 L}, \tag{7.16}$$

the asymptotic variance σ_m^2 of which is finite.

Given $\sigma_p^2, \sigma_y^2, \sigma_m^2$, expressions for the asymptotic variances of real wealth and the real and nominal interest rates, denoted by $\sigma_w^2, \sigma_{r_e}^2, \sigma_r^2$, respectively, can be derived from the *IS* and *LM* curves. These are obviously also finite, so that all relevant variables in the economy are stochastically stable in the sense of having finite asymptotic variances.

Case II $\bar{B} = 0$

This case arises if the government sets its level of expenditure G such that it just matches tax receipts at the full employment level of output; see equation (7.2e). The same case arises if the government bonds are assumed to be fully indexed, for in that case the real interest payments B_t/P_t are just constant. Thus, when converted to deviation form, the government budget constraint (7.4d') is simply

$$m_{t+1} - m_t = -ky_t \tag{7.4d''}$$

and is independent of the stock of bonds. Setting $\bar{B} = 0$, the solution to the characteristic equation (7.10) is

$$v_1 = 1, \quad v_2 = \frac{h_1}{h_2} > 1. \tag{7.17}$$

Thus the general solution for p_t is now described by (7.7), where $\lambda_0, \lambda_1,$ $\lambda_2,$ satisfy (7.8a), (7.8b); μ_0, μ_1, μ_2 satisfy (7.9a), (7.9b); in all cases $\bar{B} = 0$; and

$$\lambda_1 = A_1 + A_2 \left(\frac{h_1}{h_2}\right)^i \qquad i = 1, 2, \ldots \tag{7.8c''}$$

$$\mu_1 = C_1 + C_2 \left(\frac{h_1}{h_2}\right)^i \qquad i = 1, 2, \ldots . \tag{7.9c''}$$

It is evident that with the weights λ_i, μ_i, being generated by (7.8c''), (7.9c'') it is in general impossible for the asymptotic variance σ_p^2 to be finite. For this to be the case, the weights must either decline over time or must all be identically zero after some finite time. For λ_1, μ_i given by (7.8c''), (7.9c'') this requires $A_1 = A_2 = C_1 = C_2 = 0$, implying $\lambda_i = \mu_i = 0$, $i = 1,$ $2, \ldots .$ Imposing these conditions on (7.8a,b), (7.9a,b) yields the following pairs of equations for the remaining parameters λ_0, μ_0:

$$(h_1 + h_3)\lambda_0 + 1 = 0 \tag{7.18a}$$

$$k\gamma\lambda_0 = 0 \tag{7.18b}$$

$$(h_1 + h_3)\mu_0 = 0 \tag{7.19a}$$

$$k\gamma\mu_0 + k = 0, \tag{7.19b}$$

which in general are inconsistent. The one exception is if the income tax rate $k = 0$, in which case it follows from (7.2e) that $G = 0$ as well. In this one special case, $\mu_0 = 0$, $\lambda_0 = -1/(h_1 + h_3)$, the solution for p_t is simply

$$p_t = \frac{-u_{mt}}{h_1 + h_3},$$

the variance of which is finite.

In general, to determine fully the solution for p_t it is necessary to impose additional constraints on the constants $A_1, A_2, C_1,$ and C_2. With the exception just noted, whichever way this is done, the asymptotic variance σ_p^2 will be infinite. Further comments on the appropriate determination of the stochastic process will be made in Section 7.5 below. For the present, we shall consider the case in which $A_2 = C_2 = 0$, so that the clearly unstable root v_2 is eliminated. In this case the solution for p_t becomes

$$p_t = \left(\lambda_0 + \frac{A_1 L}{1 - L}\right)u_{mt} + \left(\mu_0 + \frac{C_1 L}{1 - L}\right)u_{3t} \tag{7.14a'}$$

where $\lambda_0, \mu_0, A_1, C_1,$ are solutions to (7.14b), (7.14c) as before, with $\bar{B}$ set equal to 0 in both cases. It is clear that σ_p^2 is infinite, while current output

$$y_t = \gamma \lambda_0 u_{mt} + (1 + \gamma \mu_0) u_{3t} \tag{7.15}$$

still has a finite variance. Setting $\bar{B} = 0$ in the government budget constraint (7.4d''), we obtain

$$m_{t+1} - m_t = -k y_t. \tag{7.4d''}$$

Substituting for y_t and solving for m_{t+1} yields

$$m_{t+1} = \frac{-k\gamma \lambda_0 u_{mt} + k(1 + \gamma \mu_0) u_{3t}}{1 - L}, \tag{7.16'}$$

the variance of which is also infinite. Intuitively, with current output being a function of current disturbances via the Lucas supply function, the nominal money stock follows a random walk process, the variance of which is infinite and is the source of the infinite asymptotic variance of the price level.

By contrast, the real stock of money, linearly approximated by $m_t - \bar{M} p_t$ (see (7.3a)), is given from (7.14a'), (7.16') together with (7.8b) and (7.9b) (setting $\bar{B} = 0$, $v_1 = 1$) by the expression

$$m_t - \bar{M} p_t = -(\lambda_0 u_{mt} + \mu_0 u_{3t}).$$

With $\bar{B} = 0$, this quantity also equals real wealth, and because they are dependent only upon current disturbances, the variances of both these variables, $\sigma_{m_r}^2$ and σ_w^2, are finite. From this, together with the fact that σ_y^2 is finite, we then deduce from the IS and LM curves that the asymptotic variances of the real and nominal interest rates, $\sigma_{r_e}^2, \sigma_r^2$, are also finite. Finally, it is an immediate consequence of the unit root in (7.14a') that the rate of inflation is asymptotically stable.

In summary, it is seen that the fixed stock of government bonds outstanding, $\bar{B}$, plays a critical role in stabilizing certain nominal variables for a money-financed deficit. With $\bar{B} > 0$, all variables have finite asymptotic variances; if $\bar{B} = 0$, on the other hand, it is possible to find a stochastic process for which only the price level and the nominal stock of money have infinite variances and for which all other variables are stochastically stable in the sense of having finite asymptotic variances.

7.4 Bond-Financed Deficit

The other polar case, in which the deficit is entirely bond-financed, is obtained by setting $m_{t+1} = m_t = 0$ in equations (7.4a)–(7.4d), which now involve the four endogenous variables y_t, b_t, r_t and p_t. The solution procedure is as before. We first solve equations (7.4a)–(7.4c) for y_t and b_t in terms of p_t, and so forth, and then substitute these expressions into the government budget constraint, now modified to

$$b_{t+1} = [1 + \bar{R}(1 - k)]b_t - \bar{B}\bar{R}(1 - k)p_t - k\bar{R}y_t. \tag{7.4d''}$$

The solution for b_t is of the same form as (7.5), namely

$$b_t = n_1 p_t - n_2 p^*_{t+1,t} + n_3(p_t - p^*_{t,t-1}) + u_{bt} \tag{7.20}$$

where

$$n_1 \equiv \frac{d_4\alpha_5 + d_5\alpha_4}{\Delta'}, \qquad n_2 \equiv \frac{d_2\alpha_4}{\Delta'},$$

$$n_3 \equiv \frac{\gamma[\alpha_4[1 - d_1(1 - k)] + \alpha_1 d_4]}{\Delta'}, \qquad \Delta' \equiv \alpha_4 d_6 - d_4\frac{\alpha_3}{R},$$

and the composite disturbance is now

$$u_{bt} \equiv \frac{-\alpha_4 u_{1t} + d_4 u_{2t} + [\alpha_4[1 - d_1(1 - k)] + \alpha_4 d_4]u_{3t}}{\Delta'}.$$

It will be observed that these expressions are identical to those obtained under money financing, with the exception that Δ is replaced by Δ'. Note that although Δ' is ambiguous in sign, we shall treat

$$\Delta' \equiv \alpha_2\left[d_1(1 - k) + \frac{d_3}{R}\right] + \alpha_3 d_1(1 - k)\frac{\bar{B}}{R^2} - \frac{\alpha_3 d_2}{R} > 0$$

as being the normal case. This inequality will be met provided that neither the interest elasticity of the demand for real output nor the wealth coefficient in the demand for money is not too large.[7] Analogous to (7.6), we derive the following difference equation in p_t:

$$n_1 p_{t+1} - n_2 p^*_{t+2,t+1} + n_3(p_{t+1} - p^*_{t+1,t}) + [\bar{B}\bar{R}(1 - k) - zn_1]p_t$$
$$+ zn_2 p^*_{t+1,t} + (\bar{R}k\gamma - zn_3)(p_t - p^*_{t,t-1}) = -u_{b,t+1} + zu_{bt} - k\bar{R}u_{3t} \tag{7.21}$$

where $z = 1 + \bar{R}(1 - k) > 1$. Again proposing a solution of the form

$$p_t = \sum_{i=0}^{\infty} \lambda_i u_{b,t-i} + \sum_{i=0}^{\infty} \mu_i u_{3,t-i}, \tag{7.22}$$

we obtain the following relationships among the coefficients:

$$(n_1 + n_3)\lambda_0 - n_2\lambda_1 + 1 = 0 \tag{7.23a}$$

$$[\bar{B}(1 - k) + k\gamma]\bar{R}\lambda_0 + n_1\lambda_1 - n_2\lambda_2 = 0 \tag{7.23b}$$

$$n_2\lambda_{i+2} - (n_1 + zn_2)\lambda_{i+1} + [zn_1 - \bar{B}\bar{R}(1 - k)]\lambda_i = 0 \qquad i = 1, 2, \ldots \tag{7.23c}$$

$$(n_1 + n_3)\mu_0 - n_2\mu_1 = 0 \tag{7.24a}$$

$$[\bar{B}(1-k) + k\gamma]\bar{R}\bar{\mu}_0 + n_1\mu_1 - n_2\mu_2 = -k\bar{R} \tag{7.24b}$$

$$n_2\mu_{i+2} - (n_1 + zn_2)\mu_{i+1} + [zn_1 - \bar{B}\bar{R}(1-k)]\mu_i = 0 \qquad i = 1, 2, \ldots . \tag{7.24c}$$

The general solution for p_t is therefore

$$p_t = \sum_{i=0}^{\infty} \lambda_i u_{b,t-i} + \sum_{i=0}^{\infty} \mu_i u_{3,t-i} \tag{7.22}$$

where $\lambda_0, \lambda_1, \lambda_2$, satisfy (7.23a), (7.23b); μ_0, μ_1, μ_2 satisfy (7.24a), (7.24b);

$$\lambda_i = A_1\omega_1^i + A_2\omega_2^i \qquad i = 1, 2, \ldots \tag{7.23c'}$$

$$\mu_i = C_1\omega_1^i + C_2\omega_2^i \qquad i = 1, 2, \ldots; \tag{7.24c'}$$

A_1, A_2, C_1, and C_2 are arbitrary constants; and ω_1 and ω_2 are the solutions to the quadratic equation

$$f(\omega) \equiv n_2\omega^2 - (n_1 + zn_2)\omega + zn_1 - \bar{B}\bar{R}(1-k) = 0, \tag{7.25}$$

both of which are real. In general, there are an infinite number of solutions for p_t, depending upon the choice of the arbitrary constants. Moreover, two sets of conditions are necessary and sufficient to ensure that both roots, ω_1 and ω_2, exceed unity, so that all solutions are unstable. These conditions are

i. $f(1) > 0$, together with $f'(1) < 0$;

ii. $f(1) < 0$, together with $f'(1) > 0$.

Using the definitions of the n_i's, d_i's, and α_i's to evaluate these expressions, we have

$$f(1) = \frac{\bar{B}\bar{R}(1-k)}{\Delta}[\alpha_4 d_3 + (1-\alpha_3)d_4],$$

$$f'(1) = -\frac{1}{\Delta}[\alpha_5 d_4 + \alpha_4[d_1(1-k)\bar{B} + d_2\bar{R}(1-k) + d_3W]],$$

and we see that condition (i) or (ii) obtains according to whether $\Delta \lessgtr 0$. Thus, in general, all solutions for p_t are both *nonunique* and *unstable*, in the sense of having infinite asymptotic variances.[8]

There are, however, two special cases in which the asymptotic variance σ_p^2 does turn out to be finite. For this to be so, we require $A_1 = A_2 = C_1 = C_2 = 0$, implying $\lambda_i = \mu_i = 0$ for $i = 1, 2, \ldots$. Thus equation (7.23a,b), (7.24a,b) reduce to

$$(n_1 + n_3)\lambda_0 + 1 = 0 \tag{7.26a}$$

$$[\bar{B}(1 - k) + k\gamma]\bar{R}\lambda_0 = 0 \tag{7.26b}$$

$$(n_1 + n_3)\mu_0 = 0 \tag{7.27a}$$

$$[\bar{B}(1 - k) + k\gamma]\bar{R}\mu_0 + k\bar{R} = 0. \tag{7.27b}$$

With two exceptions, these pairs of equations yield inconsistent solutions for the remaining undetermined coefficients λ_0, μ_0. The first exception is the case where the monetary authority chooses to peg the fixed stock of money $\bar{M}$ at the level where $\bar{R} = 0$. The second is if the tax rate $k = 0$, in which case these equations, together with (7.2e), imply that $\bar{B} = G = 0$ as well. In either case, we obtain

$$\mu_0 = 0, \qquad \lambda_0 = -\frac{1}{(n_1 + n_3)},$$

so that the solution for p_t reduces to

$$p_t = \frac{-u_{bt}}{n_1 + n_3},$$

the variance of which is finite.

But these two cases are very special.[9] In all other cases, there is *no* solution for p_t having a finite asymptotic variance. By contrast, because current output is a function of the unanticipated component of the current price, it depends only upon current disturbances, which are now given by

$$y_t = \gamma\lambda_0 u_{bt} + (1 + \gamma\mu_0)u_{3t}, \tag{7.28}$$

the variance of which is finite, irrespective of the choice of λ_0, μ_0. On the other hand, the fact that the nominal money supply remains fixed means that the stochastic process generating the real money supply is essentially identical to that determining the price level, so that its asymptotic variance also becomes infinite, as does that of real wealth. It can then be established from the *LM* and *IS* curves that the asymptotic variances of the nominal and real interest rates, σ_r^2 and $\sigma_{r_e}^2$ respectively, are also both infinite. All of these results make good intuitive sense and can be verified more formally through analysis of the underlying system (7.4a)–(7.4d).

In summary, bond financing of the deficit will lead to instability in the sense that the asymptotic variances of the price level, the real stock of money, real wealth, the nominal interest rate, the real interest rate, and the inflation rate are all infinite; only current output has a finite asymptotic variance.[10] This suggests that any rule of pegging the nominal money supply, by generating infinite asymptotic variances in important *real* variables, will be associated with serious forms of instability. This should cause some concern for proponents of a fixed monetary growth rule combined with exogenous government expenditure and tax policy.

7.5   Some Methodological Issues

In this section we shall discuss some of the methodological issues raised by the nonexistence of a solution having a finite asymptotic variance. We shall assume that the case of a money-financed deficit is, for all practical purposes, stable. As we have seen, the only instance of instability is if $\bar{B} = 0$, in which case the only variables that are unstable are the *nominal* money stock and the price level. However, we regard instability in these variables as being of little significance; it is simply an immediate consequence of the fact that with $\bar{B} = 0$ we are postulating the nominal money supply to follow a random walk, and any such process, which is commonly assumed in the macro literature, has this property. We shall therefore focus our attention on the case of bond financing, where the instabilities are associated with *real* magnitudes such as the real money supply and the real interest rate, which clearly are of greater significance.

The fact that rational expectations solutions are nonunique has been discussed at length in Chapter 5. In the case where there is only one stochastic process yielding a finite variance, the indeterminacy is immediately resolved by choosing that solution. Likewise, in the case discussed by Taylor (1977) where there are an infinite number of solutions yielding finite variances, the nonuniqueness is typically resolved by choosing the stochastic process that minimizes this variance. While this procedure is widely adopted, as we have noted in our previous discussion, it must still be viewed as somewhat arbitrary. There is no obvious market mechanism that ensures that the variance will be minimized in this way. In addition, the choice of variable whose variance is being minimized is arbitrary. For each choice of such a variable there will, in general, be a different stochastic process that will minimize its variance.

The instability encountered with bond financing in the present analysis gives rise to nonuniqueness that is in a sense opposite to that associated with Taylor. In his case it arises through there being *too many* stable roots to the system; in the present analysis there are *too few* stable roots. In a sense, the problems of indeterminacy so caused are more problematical than in the Taylor case. If the system is unstable in certain variables for all stochastic processes, the criterion for determining which of these (unstable) stochastic processes is relevant is even less clear-cut than in the Taylor case, where the choice is among a set of stable processes. We now consider a number of possible ways of resolving the indeterminacy problem.

Nonexistence of Equilibrium

One possibility is simply to interpret the nonexistence of a finite asymptotic variance as meaning the nonexistence of a rational expectations equilibrium. This, however, does not seem entirely satisfactory because not all variables are subject to this problem. In particular, in the present context, one of the key variables—output—has a finite variance for *all* stochastic processes.

Minimizing the One-Period Variance

Since the asymptotic variance is infinite, an alternative might be to choose the stochastic process to minimize the variance of the price level, say, over some finite time horizon, over which it will be finite. Taking the one-period variance, $E_{t-1}(p_t - E_{t-1}p_t)^2$, from (7.22) we obtain

$$p_t - E_{t-1}p_t = \lambda_0 u_{bt} + \mu_0 u_{3t},$$

the variance of which is minimized by setting $\lambda_0 = \mu_0 = 0$. Thus from (7.23) and (7.24) we find

$$\lambda_1 = \frac{1}{n_2}, \quad \lambda_2 = \frac{n_1}{n_2^2}, \quad \mu_1 = 0, \quad \mu_2 = \frac{k\bar{R}}{n_2},$$

and substituting these values into (7.23c'), (7.24c') enables us to calculate A_1, A_2, C_1, and C_2, yielding the following expressions for the weights:

$$\lambda_i = \frac{(\omega_2 n_2 - n_1)\omega_i^{i-1} + (n_1 - \omega_1 n_2)\omega_2^{i-1}}{n_2^2(\omega_2 - \omega_1)}, \quad \mu_i = \frac{k\bar{R}[\omega_2^{i-1} - \omega_1^{i-1}]}{n_2(\omega_2 - \omega_1)}$$

$$i = 1, 2, \dots.$$

The solution for p_t is thus uniquely determined. The minimized one-period variance is in fact zero, although the variances over lengthening time horizons diverge rapidly.[11] This approach suffers from the indeterminacy of the Taylor criterion; minimizing the one-period variance of the price level leads to a different stochastic process than does minimizing the one-period variance of, say, the nominal interest rate or income.[12]

Choosing the Slowest Rate of Divergence

One criterion, a direct extension of the usual procedure of obtaining uniqueness by eliminating unstable roots, is simply to eliminate as many unstable roots as necessary to obtain uniqueness (in this case, one) and to assume that the system diverges at the slowest rate. This procedure is analogous to the "overtaking criterion" familiar from the optimal growth literature when an undiscounted divergent utility index is used as a welfare criterion (see, e.g., von Weissäcker 1965).

In this case we eliminate the larger unstable root (ω_2, say) by setting $A_2 = C_2 = 0$. The (unique) solution for p_t now becomes

$$p_t + \lambda_0 u_{bt} + A_1 \sum_{i=1}^{\infty} u_{b,t-i} + \mu_0 u_{3t} + C_1 \sum_{i=0}^{\infty} \omega_1^i u_{3,t-i} \tag{7.29a}$$

where

$$(n_1 + n_3)\lambda_0 - n_2 A_1 \omega_1 = -1$$
$$[\bar{B}(1 - k) + k\gamma]\bar{R}\lambda_0 + A_1(n_1 - n_2\omega_1)\omega_1 = 0 \tag{7.29b}$$

$$(n_1 + n_3)\mu_0 - n_2 C_1 \omega_1 = -1$$
$$[\bar{B}(1 - k) + k\gamma]\bar{R}\mu_0 + (n_1 - n_2\omega_1)C_1\omega_1 = -k \tag{7.29b}$$

and ω_1 is the smaller (unstable) root of (7.25). The formal structure to this equation is parallel to (7.14) obtained for money financing, although with $\omega_1 > 1$, it is now unstable.

To find the magnitude of the smaller unstable root, it is convenient to consider first the case $B = 0$. The characteristic equation (7.25) then reduces to

$$n_2\omega^2 - (n_1 + zn_2)\omega + zn_1 = 0, \tag{7.25'}$$

the solutions to which are

$$\omega = z, \qquad \omega = \frac{n_1}{n_2}.$$

Under plausible conditions on the parameters, the smaller root will be $z = 1 + (1 - k)\bar{R}$; a sufficient condition for this to be so is

$$v < \frac{1 - \alpha_3}{1 - k} \tag{7.30}$$

where $v =$ interest elasticity of the demand for money. For example, taking $\alpha_3 = 0.2$, $k = 0.3$, (7.30) reduces to $v < 1.1$, a condition that will almost certainly be met. Thus we can identify $\omega_1 = z$, $\omega_2 = n_1/n_2$. Note that for $\bar{B} > 0$, the smaller root to (7.25) declines, while the larger root increases, so that, in particular, $\omega_1 < z$. Thus the procedure of choosing the smaller unstable root ensures that the system grows sufficiently slowly that the present value of wealth, discounted at the after-tax rate of return z, converges to zero. This of course is consistent with the transversality conditions that are appropriate to related optimization models and that frequently are used to provide justification for eliminating the unstable roots in rational expectations models. This justification applies here as well.

Minimum State Solution

As a further alternative, we consider the McCallum (1983) procedure for resolving the nonuniqueness problem, by postulating that the solution be represented by a minimal state representation. In this case, the solution for p_t is specified to be of the form

$$p_t = \phi_1 p_{t-1} + \phi_2 u_{bt} + \phi_3 u_{b,t-1} + \phi_4 u_{3t} + \phi_5 u_{3,t-1} \qquad (7.31)$$

where the coefficients ϕ_1 are solved for by the method of undetermined coefficients. Writing (7.31) in the form

$$p_t = \sum_{i=0}^{\infty} [\phi_2 u_{b,t-i} + \phi_3 u_{b,t-i-1} + \phi_4 u_{3,t-i} + \phi_5 u_{b,t-i-1}] \phi_1^i, \qquad (7.31')$$

we see that this minimal representation imposes restrictions on the co-efficients λ_i, μ_i, of our general solution, thereby reducing drastically the number of solutions. By direct application of this procedure, we establish that the solutions for ϕ_i are given by

$$n_2 \phi_1^2 - [n_1 + n_2 z]\phi_1 + z n_1 - \bar{B}\bar{R}(1 - k) = 0 \qquad (7.32a)$$

$$(n_1 + n_3)\phi_2 - n_2[\phi_1 \phi_2 + \phi_3] = -1 \qquad (7.32b)$$

$$(n_1 + n_2 z)\phi_3 - n_2 \phi_1 \phi_3 + (\bar{R}k - z n_3)\phi_2 = z \qquad (7.32c)$$

$$(n_1 + n_3)\phi_4 - n_2[\phi_1 \phi_4 + \phi_5] = 0 \qquad (7.32d)$$

$$(n_1 + z n_2)\phi_5 - n_2 \phi_1 \phi_5 + (2\bar{R}k - z n_3) = 0. \qquad (7.32e)$$

The key relationship is (7.32a), obtained by equating the coefficients of p_{t-1}. This equation is quadratic in ϕ_1 and is identical to (7.25) of the general solution. Given ϕ_1, the remaining equations (7.32b)–(7.32e) are linear in $\phi_2, \ldots, \phi_5$, and therefore each of the two values of ϕ_1 implies corresponding unique values for the remaining ϕ_1.

The minimal state representation procedure therefore reduces the infinity of solutions down to just two. McCallum proposes to resolve the remaining nonuniqueness associated with the quadratic by requiring that the relationship between the reduced-form coefficient (ϕ_1) and each structural parameter be a continuous function, even when special values for structural parameters are considered. For example, suppose $n_2 \to \infty$, in which case (7.32a) reduces to

$$\phi_1(\phi_1 - z) = 0. \tag{7.32a'}$$

This requires that the negative square root be chosen in general (i.e., when n_2 does not approach infinity). McCallum's method therefore requires that the *smaller* root be chosen for all parameter values, namely

$$\phi_1 = \frac{(n_1 + zn_2) - \{(n_1 + zn_2)^2 - 4n_2[zn_1 - \bar{B}\bar{R}(1-k)]\}^{1/2}}{2n_2}.$$

It is interesting to note that this solution coincides with the one proposed in the previous subsection. In this example, McCallum's solution is to choose the slowest-growing root, which, as we have seen, is less than z (but greater than 1), thereby implying that wealth discounted at the after-tax rate of return converges to zero, consistent with conventional transversality conditions.

Modification of the Dynamic System

None of these solution procedures, directed at resolving the nonuniqueness problem, eliminates the instability. The analytical reason for the asymptotic instability of bond financing is that the number of unstable roots (two) in the dynamic system exceeds the number of jump variables (one). Since this instability is encountered for all parameter values, the only way to eliminate it is to change the dynamic structure of the model in some way. In effect, to restore stability to bond financing one must introduce an additional jump variable, which itself must be generated by a sufficiently stable process to maintain the number of unstable roots equal to two. For example, one possibility is that, in response to the instability that we have shown will occur, a futures market in output evolves, with the current futures price being the additional jump variable. Work on futures prices in other contexts suggests that with risk-neutral speculators, futures prices often contribute unstable roots to the dynamic structure. However, with a sufficient degree of risk aversion, these roots become sufficiently damped so as to ensure stability. But these remarks are only conjectural, and it seems that this issue requires separate detailed analysis.

Another modification that may restore the possibility of convergence is growth. If exogenous growth in the natural rate of output is assumed, and if the asset and expenditure variables are redefined as ratios of $\bar{Y}$, then it is no longer necessary for the bond-issuing process to involve an unstable root; see McCallum (1981a). We now modify the model to consider this possibility in more detail.

7.6   Bond Financing and Stability in a Growing Economy

We now adapt the model to address the issue considered by Sargent and Wallace (1981) of the extent to which bond financing is feasible in a growing economy. We assume that the population, denoted by N_t, is growing at an exogenously given constant rate θ. Let us also assume that the basic IS and LM curves are homogeneous of degree one in income and wealth, while the supply function is homogeneous of degree zero in output at its full-employment level. In this case, the basic macro model (7.1a)–(7.1g) (considered as an approximation to one having the required homogeneity properties) can be written in per capita form:

$$\frac{Y_t}{N_t} = d_1\left[\frac{Y_t}{N_t} + \frac{B_t}{N_t P_t}\right](1-k) - d_2\left[R_t - \frac{(P^*_{t+1,t} - P_t)}{P_t}\right] + d_3\frac{W_t}{N_t} + \frac{G_t}{N_t} + u_{1t}$$

(7.33a)

$$\frac{M_t}{N_t P_t} = \alpha_1\frac{Y_t}{N_t} - \alpha_2 R_t + \alpha_3\frac{W_t}{N_t} + u_{2t}$$

(7.33b)

$$W_t = \frac{M_t}{P_t} + \frac{B_t}{R_t P_t}$$

(7.33c)

$$\frac{Y_t}{N_t} - \frac{\overline{Y}_t}{N_t} = \gamma[P_t - P^*_{t,t-1}] + u_{3t}$$

(7.33d)

$$\frac{M_{t+1} - M_t}{N_t} + \frac{B_{t+1} - B_t}{R_t N_t P_t} = \frac{G_t}{N_t} + \frac{B_t}{N_t P_t} - k\left[\frac{Y_t}{N_t} + \frac{B_t}{N_t P_t}\right]$$

(7.33e)

$$P^*_{t+s,t} \equiv E_t(P_{t+s})$$

(7.33f)

$$N_{t+1} = (1 + \theta)N_t$$

(7.33g)

with expectations again being rational. These relationships remain as before, the only change being that the growing population is specified by (7.33g).

We now define the per capita variables by

$$M'_t \equiv \frac{M_t}{N_t}; \quad B'_t \equiv \frac{B_t}{N_t}; \quad \text{etc.}$$

Assuming bond financing, $M_{t+1} = M_t$, and

$$\frac{B_{t+1} - B_t}{R_t N_t P_t} = \frac{B'_{t+1}(1 + \theta) - B'_t}{R_t P_t}.$$

Thus the system may be written in per capita form as

$$Y_t' = d_1[Y_t' + B_t'](1 - k) - d_2\left[R_t - \frac{(P_{t+1,t}^* - P_t)}{P_t}\right] + d_3 W_t' + G' + u_{1t}$$

$$(7.34a)$$

$$M_t' = \alpha_1 Y_t' - \alpha_2 R_t + \alpha_3 W_t' + u_{2t} \tag{7.34b}$$

$$W_t' = \frac{M_t'}{P_t} + \frac{B_t'}{R_t P_t} \tag{7.34c}$$

$$Y_t' - \bar{Y}_t' = \gamma(P_t - P_{t,t-1}^*) + u_{3t} \tag{7.34d}$$

$$\frac{B_{t+1}'(1 + \theta) - B_t'}{R_t P_t} = G' + B_t' - k[Y_t' + B_t']. \tag{7.34e}$$

Linearizing and letting lowercase letters denote deviations about the stationary equilibrium, (7.34) may be expressed as

$$[1 - d_1(1 - k)]y_t = -d_4 r_t + d_2 p_{t+1,t}^* - d_5 p_t + d_3 m_t + d_6 b_t + u_{1t}$$

$$(7.35a)$$

$$(1 - \alpha_3)m_t = \alpha_1 y_t - \alpha_4 r_t + \alpha_5 p_t + \frac{\alpha_3}{R} b_t + u_{2t} \tag{7.35b}$$

$$y_t = \gamma(p_t - p_{t,t-1}^*) + u_{3t} \tag{7.35c}$$

$$b_{t+1} = \frac{1}{1 + \theta}[[1 + \bar{R}(1 - k)]b_t - \bar{B}\bar{R}(1 - k)p_t - k\bar{R}y_t] \tag{7.35d}$$

where the coefficients remain as defined previously.

This modified system is virtually identical to the basic system (7.4a)–(7.4d), the only difference being that the bond accumulation equation is modified by the factor $1/(1 + \theta)$, which reflects the growth in the economy. The solution to (7.35) is obtained identically to that in Section 7.4. First, we can solve (7.35a)–(7.35c) for b_t; the solution is again given by (7.20) with the coefficients n_1, n_2, n_3, and the disturbance u_{bt} being as defined previously. Secondly, we substitute b_t into the government budget constraint (7.35d) to obtain the following equation in p_t:

$$n_1 p_{t+1} - n_2 p_{t+2,t+1}^* + n_3(p_{t+1} - p_{t+1,t}^*) + \frac{1}{1 + \theta}[\bar{B}\bar{R}(1 - k) - zn_1]p_t$$

$$+ \frac{zn_2}{1 + \theta}p_{t+1,t}^* + \frac{1}{1 + \theta}[\bar{R}k\gamma - zn_3](p_t - p_{t,t-1}^*) \tag{7.36}$$

$$= -u_{b,t+1} + \frac{zu_{bt}}{1 + \theta} - \frac{k\bar{R}}{1 + \theta}u_{3t}.$$

The only difference between (7.36) and (7.21) is due to the presence of the growth factor.

Proposing a solution of the form

$$p_t = \sum_{i=0}^{\infty} \lambda_i u_{b,y-i} + \sum_{i=0}^{\infty} \mu_i u_{3,t-i}, \tag{7.37}$$

we obtain the following relationships among the coefficients:

$$(n_1 + n_3)\lambda_0 - n_2\lambda_1 + 1 = 0 \tag{7.38a}$$

$$[\bar{B}(1 - k) + b\gamma]\frac{\bar{R}}{1 + \theta}\lambda_0 + n_1\lambda_1 - n_2\lambda_2 = 0 \tag{7.38b}$$

$$n_2\lambda_{i+2} - \left[n_1 + \frac{zn_2}{1 + \theta}\right]\lambda_{i+1} + \left[\frac{zn_1 - \bar{B}\bar{R}(1 - k)}{1 + \theta}\right]\lambda_i = 0 \tag{7.38c}$$

$$(n_1 + n_3)\mu_0 - n_2\mu_1 = 0 \tag{7.39a}$$

$$[\bar{B}(1 - k) + k\gamma]\frac{\bar{R}}{1 + \theta}\mu_0 + n_1\mu_1 - n_2\mu_2 = -\frac{k\bar{R}}{1 + \theta} \tag{7.39b}$$

$$n_2\mu_{i+2} - \left[n_1 + \frac{zn_2}{1 + \theta}\right]\mu_{i+1} + \left[\frac{zn_1 - \bar{B}\bar{R}(1 - k)}{1 + \theta}\right]\mu_i = 0. \tag{7.39c}$$

The general solution for p_t is therefore

$$p_t = \sum_{i=0}^{\infty} \lambda_i u_{b,t-i} + \sum_{i=0}^{\infty} \mu_i u_{3,t-i} \tag{7.37}$$

where $\lambda_0, \lambda_1, \lambda_2,$ satisfy (7.38a), (7.38b); μ_0, μ_1, μ_2 satisfy (7.39a), (7.39b);

$$\lambda_i = A_1\omega_1^i + A_2\omega_2^i \qquad i = 1, 2, \ldots; \tag{7.38c'}$$

$$\mu_i = C_1\omega_1^i + C_2\omega_2^i \qquad i = 1, 2, \ldots; \tag{7.39c'}$$

$A_1, A_2, C_1,$ and C_2 are arbitrary constants; and ω_1, ω_2 are now the solutions to the quadratic equation

$$f(\omega) \equiv n_2\omega^2 - \left[n_1 + \frac{zn_2}{1 + \theta}\right]\omega + \frac{zn_1 - \bar{B}\bar{R}(1 - k)}{1 + \theta} = 0. \tag{7.40}$$

Again, this equation differs from (7.25) only by the inclusion of the growth term $(1 + \theta)$. The feasibility of bond financing now hinges around whether or not either of the roots ω_1, ω_2, to (7.40) lies within the unit circle. As before, both roots can easily be shown to be real, and we also have

$$\omega_1 \omega_2 = \frac{z n_1 - \bar{B}\bar{R}(1 - k)}{n_2(1 + \theta)},$$

$$\omega_1 + \omega_2 = \frac{1}{n_2}\left[n_1 + \frac{z n_2}{1 + \theta}\right] > 0,$$

implying that both $\omega_1 > 0$ and $\omega_2 > 0$. The issue therefore reduces to whether $\omega_1 \lessgtr 1$ and whether $\omega_2 \lessgtr 1$.

In general, the necessary and sufficient conditions for the roots to (7.40) to lie within the unit circle are

i. $1 - \dfrac{z n_1 - \bar{B}\bar{R}(1 - k)}{n_2(1 - \theta)} > 0;$

ii. $1 + \dfrac{1}{n_2}\left[n_1 + \dfrac{z n_2}{1 + \theta}\right] + \dfrac{z n_1 - \bar{B}\bar{R}(1 - k)}{n_2(1 + \theta)} > 0;$

iii. $1 - \dfrac{1}{n_2}\left[n_1 + \dfrac{z n_2}{1 + \theta}\right] + \dfrac{z n_1 - \bar{B}\bar{R}(1 - k)}{n_2(1 + \theta)} > 0.$

Condition (ii) is automatically met, and (i) and (iii) can be combined to yield the pair of inequalities

$$\frac{z n_1 - n_2 - \bar{B}\bar{R}(1 - k)}{n_2} < \theta < \frac{(n_1 - n_2)(z - 1) - \bar{B}\bar{R}(1 - k)}{n_1 - n_2}. \tag{7.41}$$

By direct evaluation, we can show $[z n_1 - n_2 - \bar{B}\bar{R}(1 - k)]/n_2 > 0$, which implies that (7.41) cannot hold in the absence of growth when $\theta = 0$. This simply confirms the instability of bond financing demonstrated in Section 7.4. But in fact the pair of equalities is unlikely to be met for *any* value of θ. The reason is that for (7.41) to hold would require

$$\frac{z n_1 - n_2 - \bar{B}\bar{R}(1 - k)}{n_2} < \frac{(n_1 - n_2)(z - 1) - \bar{B}\bar{R}(1 - k)}{n_1 - n_2},$$

which in turn is equivalent to

$$(n_1 - n_2)^2 + \bar{R}(1 - k)[(n_1 - n_2)(n_1 - n_2 - \bar{B}) + \bar{B}n_2] < 0.$$

In the more likely case where $\Delta' > 0$, we know $n_1 > 0$, $n_2 > 0$, and we can also establish that $(n_1 - n_2) > 0$, $n_1 - n_2 - \bar{B} > 0$. In this case all terms on the left-hand side of (7.42) are positive, thereby violating the inequality. In the less likely case where $\Delta' < 0$, $n_1 < 0$, $n_2 < 0$, $n_1 - n_2 - \bar{B} < 0$, although (7.41) is not necessarily violated, it nevertheless is unlikely to hold.

Thus we can essentially rule out the possibility that both roots ω_1, ω_2 are stable; the larger root, ω_2, say, is greater than one. The remaining issue is whether or not the presence of growth creates reasonable conditions for the smaller root ω_1 to be less than one, in which case the solution is a saddlepoint, similar to that obtained under money financing.

To minimize detail, we consider the more likely case where $\Delta' > 0$, so that $n_1 > 0$, $n_2 > 0$. In this case, solving the quadratic equation (7.40), the smaller root is

$$\omega_1 = \frac{1}{2n_2}\left[\left(n_1 + \frac{zn_2}{1+\theta}\right) - \left\{\left(n_1 + \frac{zn_2}{1+\theta}\right)^2 - 4n_2\left[\frac{zn_1 - \bar{B}\bar{R}(1-k)}{1+\theta}\right]\right\}^{1/2}\right] < 1.$$

It therefore follows that the condition for $\omega_1 < 1$ is equivalent to

$$n_1 + \frac{zn_2}{1+\theta} - 2n_2 < \left[\left(n_1 + \frac{zn_2}{1+\theta}\right)^2 - 4n_2\left(\frac{zn_1 - \bar{B}\bar{R}(1-k)}{1+\theta}\right)\right]^{1/2} \equiv \phi.$$

(7.43)

Two possibilities exist and need to be considered:

i. if

$$-\phi < n_1 + \frac{zn_2}{1+\theta} - 2n_2,$$

then (7.43) is equivalent to

$$\left(n_1 + \frac{zn_1}{1+\theta} - 2n_2\right)^2 < \left(n_1 + \frac{zn_2}{1+\theta}\right)^2 - 4n_2\left(\frac{zn_1 - \bar{B}\bar{R}(1-k)}{1+\theta}\right)$$

(7.44a)

ii. if

$$n_1 + \frac{zn_2}{1+\theta} - 2n_2 < -\phi,$$

then (7.43) is equivalent to

$$\left(n_1 + \frac{zn_2}{1+\theta} - 2n_2\right)^2 > \left(n_1 + \frac{zn_2}{1+\theta}\right)^2 - 4n_2\left(\frac{zn_1 - \bar{B}\bar{R}(1-k)}{1+\theta}\right).$$

(7.44b)

The latter, however, can be ruled out, since it implies

$$\frac{1}{2n_2}\left[n_1 + \frac{zn_1}{1+\theta} + \phi\right] < 1.$$

But the left-hand side of this inequality is precisely the larger root ω_2, and this violates the fact that $\omega_2 > 1$. Thus, considering case (i), we can simplify (7.44a) to show that the smaller root $\omega_1 < 1$ if and only if

$$\theta > \theta^* \equiv \left(\frac{n_1 - n_2 - \bar{B}}{n_2 - n_2} \right) \bar{R}(1 - k). \tag{7.45}$$

Thus, a sufficient condition for $\omega_1 < 1$ is that

$$\theta > \bar{R}(1 - k). \tag{7.46}$$

The right-hand side of (7.46) is the equilibrium after-tax rate of interest. Consequently, any growth rate that exceeds this rate ensures that $\omega_1 < 1$. But it is also apparent from (7.45) that $\omega_1 < 1$ may still obtain for a positive but smaller growth rate.

Henceforth assume that (7.45) is met, so that $0 < \omega_1 < 1$. It is now possible to obtain a stable solution for p_t. To do so, we set $A_2 = C_2 = 0$, thereby eliminating the unstable root and yielding

$$\lambda_i = A_1 \omega_1^i, \qquad \mu_i = C_1 \omega_1^i. \tag{7.47}$$

The solution for p_t is now given by

$$p_t = \left(\lambda_0 + \frac{A_1 \omega_1 L}{1 - \omega_1 L} \right) u_{bt} + \left(\mu_0 + \frac{C_1 \omega_1 L}{1 - \omega_1 L} \right) u_{3t} \tag{7.48a}$$

where

$$\left. \begin{array}{l} (n_1 + n_3)\lambda_0 - n_2 A_1 \omega_1 = -1 \\[2mm] [\bar{B}(1 - k) + k\gamma] \dfrac{\bar{R}}{1 + \theta} \lambda_0 + (n_1 - n_2 \omega_1) A_1 \omega_1 = 0 \end{array} \right\} \tag{7.48b}$$

$$\left. \begin{array}{l} (n_1 + n_3)\mu_0 - n_2 C_1 \omega_1 = 0 \\[2mm] [\bar{B}(1 - k) + k\gamma] \dfrac{\bar{R}}{1 + \theta} \mu_0 + (n_1 - n_2 \omega_1) C_1 \omega_1 = \dfrac{-k\bar{R}}{1 + \theta} \end{array} \right\} \tag{7.48c}$$

and ω_1 is the stable root ($0 < \omega_1 < 1$) to

$$n_2 \omega^2 - \left[n_1 + \frac{zn_2}{1 + \theta} \right] \omega + \frac{zn_1 - \bar{B}\bar{R}(1 - k)}{1 + \theta} = 0. \tag{7.48d}$$

The solution for p_t is now obtained as for money financing. The stable root ω_1 is obtained from (7.48d). Given ω_1, equations (7.48b) and (7.48c) then jointly determine the constants λ_0, μ_0, A_1, and C_1. The solution for p_t is unique and its asymptotic variance is finite.

Current output, y_t, is given by

$$y_t = \gamma\lambda_0 u_{bt} + (1 + \gamma\mu_0)u_{3t},$$ (7.49)

which is also of the same general form as before. Its variance is also obviously finite.

To consider what happens to the stock of bonds, substitute for p_t and y_t into the government budget constraint (7.35d), writing it in the form

$$\left(1 - \frac{zL}{1+\theta}\right)b_{t+1}$$

$$= -\left[(\bar{B}(1-k) + k\gamma)\frac{\bar{R}\lambda_0}{1+\theta} + \frac{\bar{B}\bar{R}(1-k)(A_1\omega_1 L)}{(1+\theta)(1-\omega_1 L)}\right]u_{bt}$$ (7.50)

$$- \left[(\bar{B}(1-k) + k\gamma)\frac{\bar{R}\mu_0}{1+\theta} + \frac{k\bar{R}}{1+\theta} + \frac{\bar{B}\bar{R}(1-k)C_1\omega_1 L}{(1+\theta)(1-\omega_1 L)}\right]u_{3t}.$$

Using (7.47) and (7.48b), (7.48c), (7.48d) leads, with some manipulation, to the following equation:

$$\left(1 - \frac{zL}{1+\theta}\right)b_{t+1} = \frac{\omega_1(n_1 - n_2\omega_1)\left(1 - \frac{zL}{1+\theta}\right)(A_1 u_{bt} + C_1 u_{3t})}{(1 - \omega_1 L)}.$$ (7.51)

The asymptotic variance of b_t is therefore finite if and only if $z/(1+\theta) < 1$, that is, if and only if

$$\theta > \bar{R}(1 - k).$$

That is to say a growth rate that exceeds the after-tax interest rate is necessary and sufficient for the accumulation of bonds to be stable. But this case implies dynamic inefficiency; see Chapter 9.

To summarize, bond financing leads to long-run price stability, in the sense of the asymptotic variance σ_b^2 being finite, if and only if the growth rate satisfies equation (7.45). A sufficient, but not necessary, condition for this is that the growth rate exceed the equilibrium after-tax interest rate. The latter condition is both necessary and sufficient for the asymptotic variance of bonds, σ_b^2, to be finite. Therefore it is also necessary and sufficient for the asymptotic variances of the other key variables, such as the real and nominal interest rate and the real and nominal wealth, to be finite. Consequently, (7.45) can be viewed as a necessary and sufficient condition for bond financing to be a long-run feasible mode of deficit financing.

7.7 Conclusions

This chapter has analyzed the stability of money financing and bond financing of the government budget deficit under rational expectations. The main conclusions to be drawn include the following.

If the equilibrium stock of government bonds is strictly positive, then money financing is stable in the sense that there exists a unique stochastic process that ensures that all variables have finite asymptotic variances. If the equilibrium stock of government bonds is zero, then, apart from the nominal stock of money and the price level, which follow random walk processes, all variables continue to have finite asymptotic variances.

On the other hand, if the deficit is bond-financed, then, apart from certain very special polar cases, the asymptotic variances of all variables —with the exception of current output—will be infinite. There is no stochastic process for which these variables will be stable. This instability of financing is an example of proposition 3 of Blanchard and Kahn (1980), in which the number of unstable roots in the system exceeds the number of jump variables.

In fact, the problem of instability associated with bond financing in the present model is more acute than it is in the original Blinder-Solow model. This is due to the specification of the Lucas-type supply function, which is a standard component of rational expectations macro models. The analogous deterministic Blinder-Solow model would be one with continuous full employment. For such a variant of their model, one of the important stabilizing influences—namely, the expansion of income—is lost. In this case it can be shown that bond financing will be stable if and only if the elasticity of the price level with respect to an increase in the stock of bonds exceeds unity, a condition which almost certainly not be met.[13]

The fact that bond financing is associated with serious instability in real variables is important for macroeconomic policy. It raises serious doubts concerning the desirability of adopting a fixed monetary growth rule. While the instability of such a rule has been discussed previously, and also in Chapter 3, most analyses are based on models employing ad hoc expectational schemes. The present analysis suggests that even with rational expectations such a policy rule will lead to serious instability.

But these conditions are based on a stationary economy. We have also seen how the introduction of growth can stabilize the economy, thereby enabling bond financing to be a viable long-run model of deficit financing. Specifically, we have demonstrated that the economy will be stable, in the sense of all variables having finite asymptotic variances, if and only if the growth rate exceeds the equilibrium after-tax rate of interest.

Notes

1. Although this is certainly one interpretation of the model, others can also be given. For example, one can interpret the model as being one in which the government budget is always balanced (through the appropriate adjustment of some tax or transfer variable). In this case it is sensible for the private sector to fully discount bond interest payments (given the tax liability to service them), and disposable income is properly defined as output less government expenditure. Similarly, the wealth coefficients need not necessarily be zero, but rather bonds may simply be fully discounted as a component of wealth.

2. The bonds considered in this chapter are assumed to be denominated in nominal terms. These last propositions, which apply if the stock of such nonindexed bonds is zero, continue to hold for any arbitrarily given stock of fully indexed bonds, provided that the tax system is fully indexed (as we assume). These propositions are therefore of somewhat greater general interest than it may at first appear.

3. As noted by Blanchard and Kahn (1980), the case $\bar{a} = a$ is the most familiar one, arising in the case of the strict saddlepoint encountered in various optimal control models. They also cite cases, associated most recently with Taylor (1977), of $a > \bar{a}$, when an infinite number of solutions exists; they do not mention any cases of nonexistence of a finite variance, one of the cases encountered here. This probably reflects the general impression among economists that stability is no longer an issue with forward-looking expectations. Thus, our analysis for bond financing represents a counterexample that should be of general interest. In a subsequent note, Scarth (1980) also discusses the instability of bond financing in a rational expectations framework.

4. Interpreting M, B in terms of appropriate monetary magnitudes in the United States also suggests that (7.12) will be met in practice if B is taken to represent total U.S. government marketable securities outstanding; in 1980 the ratio $\overline{M}/(\overline{B}/\overline{R})$ ranged from around 0.5 for the narrow aggregate M1 A to around 3 for the broad aggregate M3. We should note, however, that the model fails to draw the distinction between base money and deposits. If this is introduced, the inequality (7.12) is modified to

$$\frac{\overline{M}}{\overline{B}/\overline{R}} > \frac{\alpha_3}{1 - \alpha_3/g} + (1 - k)\overline{R}$$

where $g \geq 1$ denotes the money multiplier. This revised inequality is actually weaker than (7.12), so that it too will quite plausibly be met.

5. An alternative pair of sufficient conditions to ensure $0 < v_1 < 1$ is

$$\alpha_3 d_1 > d_3 \qquad \alpha_3 > \frac{(1 - k)\overline{R}^2}{(1 - k)\overline{R}^2 + 1 - \overline{R}},$$

which again for plausible parameter values will be met.

6. The lag operator L can be manipulated like any algebraic quantity.

7. Using the notation of Blinder and Solow (1973), our $\Delta' > 0$ condition holds as long as their $F_B > 0$. Scarth (1976) has corrected Blinder and Solow's expression for F_B and considered plausible parameter values. This exercise supports the assumption that F_B and Δ' are positive.

8. In terms of the Blanchard-Kahn classification, the instability arises from the fact that with bond financing $\bar{a} = 2$ exceeds $a = 1$.

9. Given that the bonds in the model are assumed to be perpetuities, pegging the mean nominal interest rate at zero is equivalent to driving the price of bonds to infinity, and this presumably raises problems of feasibility.

10. Scarth (1980) also discusses the instability of bond financing in a rational expectations framework.

11. There is an analogy here to the phenomenon of "instrument instability," which may arise in optimal stabilization problems.

12. It is worth noting that the minimization of the one-period variance $E_{t-1}(p_t - E_{t-1}p_t)^2$ has been suggested as the appropriate indicator of welfare for models of this type; see Barro (1976) and the discussion in Section 4.5.

13. In the full employment, flexible price version of the Blinder-Solow model, the government budget constraint becomes (using continuous time)

$$\frac{\dot{B}}{PR} = G - \bar{Y}(1 - k) + \frac{B}{P}.$$

In the neighborhood of equilibrium,

$$\frac{\partial \dot{B}}{\partial B} = \bar{R}\left[(G - \bar{Y}(1 - k))\frac{\partial P}{\partial B} + 1\right] = \bar{R}\left[1 - \frac{\partial P}{\partial B}\frac{P}{B}\right].$$

For stability we require

$$\frac{\partial \dot{B}}{\partial B} < 0, \qquad \text{i.e.,} \qquad \frac{\partial P}{\partial B}\frac{P}{B} > 1.$$

This chapter addresses three issues pertaining to macroeconomic stabilization policy with rational expectations. The first concerns the question of wage indexation, and the second involves the choice of monetary instrument. These two subjects have generated extensive literatures in the context of both closed and open economies, but particularly with respect to the latter. We begin by setting out the basic model of indexation and then turn to the issue of the monetary policy instrument. Parallels exist between these two forms of policies, and they are in fact closely interrelated. Both involve monitoring pieces of contemporaneous information, assumed to be available to the policymaker. Wage indexation is a form of supply-side intervention, in which the policymaker adjusts the nominal wage to current price movements, thereby influencing the real wage faced by firms. Monetary policy operates on the demand side with the monetary authorities using contemporaneous information on financial variables to help determine their policy. In a closed economy, the monetary instrument problem has been cast in terms of choosing between the nominal interest rate and the money supply as the instrument of monetary control. In an open economy, this translates into the choice of fixed versus flexible exchange rates, which is another debate with a long history.

Authors such as Marston (1982), Flood and Marion (1982), and others have emphasized the interdependence between monetary policy and wage indexation policy.[1] They have shown how the choice between fixed and flexible exchange rates depends upon the degree of wage indexation, whereas the optimal degree of wage indexation depends upon the exchange rate regime. In Section 8.3, we therefore present an integrated analysis of optimal monetary and wage indexation policies within the context of a small open economy. There are several good reasons for choosing such an economy rather than presenting such an analysis within a closed economy. First, wage indexation has been particularly prevalent among small economies as a key component of an overall macroeconomic stabilization policy. Second, such an economy leads to a simplification of the demand side of the model, thereby simplifying the analytical details, while preserving the essential features of the trade-offs involved. Finally, it provides an opportunity to illustrate the use of rational expectations methods in open economies, where, because of the efficiency of exchange markets, they are particularly applicable and in fact have been widely adopted.

The third issue, introduced briefly in Section 8.7, concerns the merits of discretionary policy versus rules in a rational expectations context, and the incentives to renege. This question was introduced by Barro and Gordon (1983a, 1983b) and, like the other areas discussed, has generated significant research activity.

8.1   Wage Indexation

Many economies have employed wage indexation at some time. In some cases, such as Australia for example, it represents the outcome of a wage determination process carried out by a centralized authority. In other cases it might represent the outcome of a bilateral negotiation between employers and workers. We do not differentiate between these institutional arrangements in our description. In the 1970s it was thought that tying wages to prices (perhaps adjusted for productivity) was an appropriate policy for dealing with inflationary pressures. Gray (1976) and Fischer (1977a) were the first economists to introduce wage indexation into a formal macroeconomic model, and we shall begin with an exposition of their approach.

Equilibrium Output under Indexation

The basic model we shall construct is essentially that of Section 4.2. The demand side of the economy is unchanged from before and is specified by the two equations:

$$y_t = d_1 y_t - d_2 [r_t - (p^*_{t+1,t-1} - p^*_{t,t-1})] + u_{1t} \qquad 0 < d_1 < 1, d_2 > 0$$

$$\tag{8.1a}$$

$$m_t - p_t = \alpha_1 y_t - \alpha_2 r_t + u_{2t} \qquad\qquad \alpha_1 > 0, \alpha_2 > 0 \qquad (8.1b)$$

where y_t denotes aggregate output, p_t denotes the price level, and m_t denotes the money supply, all measured in logarithms; $p^*_{t+i,t}$ is the prediction of p_t for time $t + i$ formed at time t, and u_{it}, $i = 1, 2$ are random variables, assumed to have zero means and finite variances and to be independently distributed over time. For simplicity, we abstract from government consumption expenditure, which can be thought of as being incorporated in the stochastic term u_{1t}.

Indexation is a supply-side policy, and it is this aspect of the model that needs to be modified. Output is basically determined by a Lucas supply function, which, as we noted in Section 4.1, can be viewed as reflecting a one-period wage contract. Recall that the production function specified in (4.9) was of the Cobb-Douglas form, which, aggregated over all firms and expressed in logarithms, implies (4.21), repeated here for convenience:

$$y_t = (1 - \theta)l_t + \varepsilon_t \tag{8.2a}$$

where l_t denotes aggregate employment (measured in logarithms), $(1 - \theta)$ is the elasticity of labor in the production function, and ε_t is the aggregate productivity disturbance at time t, assumed to have zero mean and finite variance and to be independently distributed over time. The actual aggregate employment of labor, obtained by maximizing profit, is given, as in (4.19), by

$$l_t = \frac{1}{\theta}[\ln(1 - \theta) + p_t - w_t + \varepsilon_t] \tag{8.2b}$$

where w_t is the current wage rate measured in logarithms. In Section 4.1 this was equal to the contract wage w_t^c, the latter being determined by equating the expected demand for and supply of labor. The resulting expression was specified in (4.18) by

$$w_t^c = p_{t,t-1}^* + \frac{\ln(1 - \theta) + \chi}{1 + \theta n} \tag{8.2c}$$

where n is the elasticity of labor supply and χ is a constant embodying the second moments of the distributions of prices and productivity shocks. This latter term can be dropped henceforth without loss of generality. Substituting (8.2b) into (8.2a), aggregate output y_t may be expressed as

$$y_t = \frac{(1 - \theta)}{\theta}[\ln(1 - \theta) + p_t - w_t] + \frac{\varepsilon_t}{\theta}. \tag{8.2d}$$

The process of wage indexation allows for within-period adjustments of the actual wage from the contract wage and in the Gray-Fischer model is described by the relationship

$$w_t = w_t^c + \tau(p_t - p_{t,t-1}^*); \qquad 0 \le \tau \le 1. \tag{8.2e}$$

The degree of wage indexation is reflected in the parameter τ and describes the extent to which the nominal wage is adjusted in percentage terms to unexpected changes in the price level, which occur after the contract wage is determined. If $\tau = 0$, the nominal wage remains fixed at its contract level so that any unexpected increase in the price level leads to an unexpected reduction in (the logarithm of) the real wage $w_t - p_t$. The other extreme, $\tau = 1$, corresponds to full indexation of the nominal wage to the nominal price, so that the real wage is maintained equal to the expected level upon which the contract is based, that is, $w_t - p_t = w_t^c - p_{t,t-1}^*$. Substituting (8.2c) and (8.2e) into (8.2d) leads to the aggregate supply function

$$y_t = \frac{(1 - \theta)n\ln(1 - \theta)}{1 + n\theta} + \left(\frac{1 - \theta}{\theta}\right)(1 - \tau)(p_t - p_{t,t-1}^*) + \frac{\varepsilon_t}{\theta}. \tag{8.2f}$$

This equation is the supply function in the presence of wage indexation. Its resemblance to the supply function (4.22) is apparent; the key difference is that the impact of unexpected price disturbances on current output is inversely related to the degree of wage indexation. The complete model describing the movement of output, the price level, and the interest rate in an indexed economy consists of equations (8.1a), (8.1b), and (8.2f).

A Frictionless Economy

Wage contracts introduce rigidities into the economy, leading to welfare losses in comparison to a frictionless economy in which all prices, including wages, are fully flexible. Accordingly, the purpose of indexation policy is to attempt to "undo" these rigidities and to replicate as closely as possible the output of a frictionless economy, thereby minimizing the resulting welfare losses.[2] Returning to the model of Section 4.1, the profit of a typical firm operating in such an economy is

$$\Pi_t^i = P_i(L_t^i)^{1-\theta} e^{\varepsilon_t^i} - W_t L_t^i. \tag{8.3a}$$

Optimizing with respect to labor leads to the first-order condition, expressed in logarithms as

$$(l_t^i) = \frac{1}{\theta}[\ln(1-\theta) + p_t - w_t + \varepsilon_t^i],$$

which summed over all firms leads to the aggregate demand for labor

$$l_t^d = \frac{1}{\theta}[\ln(1-\theta) + p_t - w_t + \varepsilon_t] \tag{8.3b}$$

and is a decreasing function of the actual real wage. Aggregate supply of labor in this frictionless world is given by

$$l_t^s = n(w_t - p_t) \qquad n > 0, \tag{8.3c}$$

and with perfectly flexible real wages, the market-clearing real wage is determined by equating (8.3b) and (8.3c):

$$w_t - p_t = \frac{\ln(1-\theta)}{1+n\theta} + \frac{\varepsilon_t}{1+n\theta}. \tag{8.3d}$$

Finally, substituting (8.3d) into (8.3c), and thence into the aggregate production function (8.2a), leads to the output level of the frictionless economy:

$$\tilde{y}_t = \frac{(1-\theta)n\ln(1-\theta)}{1+n\theta} + \left(\frac{1+n}{1+n\theta}\right)\varepsilon_t. \tag{8.3e}$$

The output of the frictionless economy fluctuates about some fixed "natural" level in response to the productivity shocks. As long as the supply of labor is less than infinitely elastic, $\tilde{y}_t$ will overadjust to the short-run shocks in productivity ε_t.

The analogy between this frictionless level of output and the full information level of output, introduced in Section 4.5, should be apparent. Both move independently of unanticipated price movements $(p_t - p^*_{t,t-1})$, although their responses to productivity shocks are somewhat different, in that the response of $\tilde{y}_t$ reflects the labor supply conditions as measured by the elasticity n.

Optimal Degree of Indexation

Since the behavior of $\tilde{y}_t$ represents the Pareto optimal behavior of the unimpeded economy, the stated stabilization objective is to replicate the time path of $\tilde{y}_t$ as closely as possible. Subtracting $\tilde{y}_t$ from the output of the contract economy (8.2f) yields

$$y_t - \tilde{y}_t = \left(\frac{1-\theta}{\theta}\right)\left[(1-\tau)(p_t - p^*_{t,t-1}) + \frac{\varepsilon_t}{1+n\theta}\right], \tag{8.4a}$$

and the formal objective is to minimize the variance of y_t about $\tilde{y}_t$, $E(y_t - \tilde{y}_t)^2$. Taking conditional expectations of equations (8.1a), (8.1b), and (8.2f) at time $t-1$ and subtracting from the respective equations, the following expression for the unanticipated price change is obtained (cf. equations [4.27a], [4.27b]):

$$p_t - p^*_{t,t-1} = \frac{\alpha_2 u_{1t} - d_2 u_{2t} - [\alpha_2(1-d_1) + \alpha_1 d_2](\varepsilon_t/\theta)}{d_2 + ((1-\theta)/\theta)(1-\tau)[\alpha_2(1-d_1) + \alpha_1 d_2]}. \tag{8.4b}$$

From (8.4a) and (8.4b), the following can be inferred.

i. Increased wage indexation (i.e., a larger τ), will stabilize output relative to that of the frictionless economy in the face of the aggregate demand disturbances u_{1t}, u_{2t}. Since these disturbances impact on output entirely through unanticipated price movements, in the absence of productivity shocks the optimal degree of indexation from the viewpoint of relative output stability is to index wages fully, that is, to set $\tau = 1$. In this case, the demand disturbances will be fully absorbed by price movements, with no impact on output, which will therefore replicate perfectly the (fixed) frictionless output.

ii. Increased wage indexation will destabilize output relative to that of the frictionless economy in the face of supply disturbances ε_t. In this case, indexation will reduce the extent to which these disturbances will be absorbed in price movements, thereby increasing their impact on output. Thus, if the only disturbances impacting on the economy are productivity shocks, the optimal wage policy is not to index wages at all, that is, to set $\hat{\tau} = 0$. In this case, although the variance of (8.4a) will be minimized, frictionless output will not be replicated.

iii. There is an optimal degree of wage indexation $0 < \hat{\tau} < 1$, which is obtained when both demand and supply disturbances are present simultaneously and which provides the optimal trade-off between price stability and output stability. Explicit solutions for this optimal degree of indexation will be postponed until Section 8.5, where the more general model is discussed.

Some Extensions

This completes the description of the basic indexation model. It has formed the basis for an extensive literature that extends it in various directions. We have assumed that the wage is indexed to the current price level. In fact, many countries that have adopted wage indexation schemes have linked wage adjustments to past price movements, say over the previous quarter or two. This type of scheme would suggest modifying (8.2e) to something like

$$w_t - w_{t-1} = \tau(p_{t-1} - p_{t-2}) \tag{8.2e$'$}$$

and is considered by Fischer (1977b).

Most models of wage indexation assume that the wage rate is adjusted in response to price changes alone. That is in fact the economic variable to which most wage indexation schemes are tied. Other authors, for example, Karni (1983), have considered wage indexation schemes tied to stochastic movements in current output. This seems to be a less realistic schemes in that reliable data on output are typically available with less frequency than data on other variables, such as prices. Moreover, if output shocks can in fact be observed, then output can be stabilized perfectly and directly through some appropriate compensating expenditure policy, rather than indirectly through some form of wage indexation.

In the model as developed there is only one price, whereas in the real world there are, of course, many prices. This raises not only the question of to what extent to index (i.e., the choice of τ), but also the question of which price to index to, and, further, the possibility of differential rates of indexation to different prices. This problem is of particular significance for small open economies, many of which (e.g., Australia and Israel) have employed wage indexation schemes at various times. For such economies the question is, should one index against the CPI, which includes the price of imports, or against the GDP deflator, or against some other price index? This issue has been addressed by Marston (1984), and Marston and Turnovsky (1985).

8.2 Monetary Instrument Problem

In an important paper, Poole (1970) formally addressed the so-called monetary instrument problem, which concerns the following issue. Suppose that the monetary authorities wish to choose some monetary instrument to serve as an intermediate target of monetary policy: which should they choose? The two most natural such intermediate targets are the nominal interest rate and the nominal money supply. If the authorities choose the former, they must be willing to allow the money supply to accommodate as necessary so as to permit the interest rate to achieve its objective. If they choose the latter, the nominal interest rate will adjust endogenously in response to the stochastic disturbances impacting on the economy. The question is, which is better from the viewpoint of providing greater stability to the economy?

In the absence of any stochastic shocks, the choice is irrelevant. Targeting either the nominal interest rate or the money supply will work equally well in terms of enabling the level of income to achieve some target (full-employment) level. This is the old Tinbergen target-instrument problem, which asserts that in a linear economy and in the absence of risk, desired values for certain specified target variables can always be attained as long as the number of linearly independent policy instruments is not less than the number of targets (in this case, one). In order for the problem to become substantive, risk must be introduced in a significant way. Using a simple stochastic *IS-LM* model, Poole showed that the choice between pegging the nominal interest rate and pegging the nominal money supply, from the standpoint of providing greater output stability, depends upon the sources of risk impinging on the economy. If the shocks hitting the economy are primarily real demand shocks (i.e., shocks to the *IS* curve), then pegging the money supply is better. This will allow the interest rate to bear some of the shocks and thereby insulate output from the full brunt of the disturbances. On the other hand, if the shocks are primarily monetary shocks (i.e., shocks to the *LM* curve), then the preferred policy is to peg the interest rate, allowing the monetary shocks to be absorbed by an accommodating money supply, and insulating output. Neither of these is optimal, however, and Poole's "combination" policy, in which the money supply is accomodated partially to movements in the interest rate, is superior to both these extremes.

The same kind of issue can be addressed within a rational expectations framework. Setting $m_t = m_{t,t-1}^*, g_t = g_{t,t-1}^*$ in (4.29), Section 4.3 essentially yields the solution for output when the monetary authorities choose to peg the money supply. The corresponding variance of output can then be calculated from this expression in a routine manner.

Indeterminacy of Pegging Nominal Interest Rate

However, seemingly alarming things occur under rational expectations, when instead the monetary authorities choose to peg the nominal interest rate. As Sargent and Wallace (1975) first showed, this leads to an *indeterminate* price level.

To see this, we need focus only on the *IS* curve (4.23a) and the Lucas supply function (4.23c):

$$y_t = d_1 y_t - d_2 [\bar{r} - (p^*_{t+1,t-1} - p^*_{t,t-1})] + u_{1t} \tag{8.5a}$$

$$y_t = \bar{y} + \gamma(p_t - p^*_{t,t-1}) + v_t \quad (v_t \equiv \varepsilon_t/\theta) \tag{8.5b}$$

where $\bar{r}$ denotes the pegged value of the nominal interest rate. We begin by eliminating y_t from these two equations to yield the following relationship between the price level p_t and its expectations:

$$\gamma(1 - d_1)(p_t - p^*_{t,t-1}) - d_2(p^*_{t+1,t-1} - p^*_{t,t-1}) + \eta = z_t \tag{8.6}$$

where $\eta \equiv (1 - d_1)\bar{y} + d_2\bar{r}$ and $z_t \equiv u_{1t} - (1 - d_1)v_t$. Now, we propose a solution for p_t of the form

$$p_t = \bar{p} + \lambda t + \sum_{i=0}^{\infty} \delta_i z_{t-i} \tag{8.7}$$

where $\bar{p}, \lambda, \delta_i$ are parameters to be determined. Taking conditional expectations of (8.7) implies

$$p^*_{t,t-1} = \bar{p} + \lambda t + \sum_{i=1}^{\infty} \delta_i z_{t-i}$$

$$\tag{8.8}$$

$$p^*_{t+1,t-1} = \bar{p} + \lambda(t + 1) + \sum_{i=2}^{\infty} \delta_i z_{z+1-i},$$

and substituting for (8.7) and (8.8) into (8.6) leads to

$$\gamma(1 - d_1)\delta_o z_t - d_2 \sum_{i=0}^{\infty} (\delta_i - \delta_{i+1})z_{t-i} - d_2\lambda + \eta = z_t.$$

Equating coefficients of z_{t-i} and the constant implies the following:

$$\delta_o = \frac{1}{\gamma(1 - d_1)}; \qquad \delta_i = \bar{\delta}, i = 1,\ldots; \lambda = \eta/d_2$$

where $\bar{\delta}$ is a constant yet to be determined. Substituting these expressions into (8.7), the solution for the price level p_t is

$$p_t = \bar{p} + \frac{\eta}{d_2}t + \frac{1}{\gamma(1 - d_1)}z_t + \bar{\delta} \sum_{i=1}^{\infty} z_{t-i}$$

where $\bar{p}$ is also still undetermined. It is immediately apparent from this expression that if $\bar{\delta} \neq 0$, the asymptotic variance of p_t, σ_p^2 is infinite. If we now impose the requirement that σ_p^2 remain finite, it follows that $\bar{\delta} = 0$, so that the solution for p_t becomes

$$p_t = \bar{p} + \frac{\eta}{d_2} t + \frac{1}{\gamma(1 - d_1)} z_t. \tag{8.9}$$

Equation (8.9) highlights how a policy of pegging the nominal interest rate results in an indeterminate mean price level. Furthermore, unless the interest rate is pegged so that $\eta = 0$, the price level will fluctuate around a constant determinate deflationary or inflationary trend. But despite the indeterminacy of the mean price level and the presence of the trend, the asymptotic variance of p_t remains finite and determinate. Furthermore, taking conditional expectations of (8.9) and combining with (8.5b), the solution for output is

$$y_t = \bar{y} + \frac{u_{1t}}{1 - d_1}, \tag{8.10}$$

which is determinate and has a well-defined variance.

Thus we see that although the policy of pegging the nominal interest rate leads to an indeterminate mean price level, possibly with a steady (known) inflationary or deflationary trend, it does yield finite and determinate asymptotic variances for both income and prices. Accordingly, if the criterion used to assess the performance of alternative policies is defined in terms of such variances, the policy of pegging the nominal interest rate yields a perfectly well defined performance, which may be compared to other alternatives. Indeed, comparing the variance of (8.10) with the variance of (4.29), one finds that the Poole conclusion generally holds in the present context as well.

The indeterminacy of the mean price level is a consequence of the fact that equations (8.5a), (8.5b) are both real equations and provide no nominal anchor for determining the scale of the price level. However, this can be easily accomplished in either of two ways. The first, suggested by Parkin (1978), is for the monetary authorities to set the nominal interest rate $\bar{r}$ so as to achieve some exogenously announced monetary target, say, $\overline{M}$. The second is by modifying the aggregate demand function to depend upon the real money stock as in (5.1) (see, e.g., McCallum 1981b). Either of these respecifications of the model will restore determinacy to the price level, suggesting that the indeterminacy identified with pegging the nominal interest rate is more of a curiosum than an issue of substantive policy concern.

Fixed versus Flexible Exchange Rates

In an open economy, the most important aspect of monetary policy is the choice of exchange rate regime. The relative merits of fixed versus flexible exchange rate regimes have been debated since the 1950s; this question is the open-economy analogue to the monetary instrument problem we have been discussing.[3]

To see this, consider a small open economy operating in a world of perfect capital markets. We shall assume investors are risk neutral, so that the domestic nominal interest rate, r_t, is related to the world nominal interest rate, ω_t, by the uncovered interest rate parity (UIP) condition:

$$r_t = \omega_t + e^*_{t+1,t} - e_t \tag{8.11}$$

where e_t is the nominal exchange rate, measured in units of domestic currency per unit of foreign currency and expressed in logarithms, and $e^*_{t+1,t}$ is the forecast of e for time $t + 1$ formed at time t. The expected rate of return to a domestic resident on investing a dollar abroad over the period $(t, t + 1)$ equals the foreign interest rate plus the expected rate of depreciation of the domestic currency $(e^*_{t+1,t} - e_t)$ over that period. With a perfect world capital market and risk neutrality, the rate of return on such an investment must equal the rate of return on purchasing a domestic bond, thereby giving rise to the equality in (8.11).

If the domestic monetary authority chooses to peg the nominal exchange rate, so that $e^*_{t+1,t} = e_t = \bar{e}$, say, then (8.11) implies that, in effect, the small economy must tie its own domestic interest rate to the world rate. In this case, it must be willing to allow the domestic money supply to accommodate so as to sustain the exchange rate at its target level, just as the interest rate policy requires in the closed economy. Similarly, pegging the nominal money supply permits the exchange rate and domestic interest rate to adjust in response to the stochastic influences impinging on the economy.

8.3   Generalized Disturbances and the Role of Information

As noted earlier, contributions by Marston (1982) and Flood and Marion (1982) emphasized the interdependence between wage indexation and monetary policy, in the form of the choice of exchange rate regime, in an open economy. Extending this view, Turnovsky (1983, 1987b) and Aizenman and Frenkel (1985, 1986) took a more integrated approach to the stabilization of an open economy by analyzing general rules for wage indexation and monetary policy. These authors focused on the trade-offs between the two as stabilization instruments, and their approach was directed at the design of overall, integrated, stabilization policy packages. The degree of accommodation of the money supply to exchange rate movements impinges on the effectiveness of wage indexation and vice versa. Some degrees of wage indexation render monetary policy ineffective, and the reverse applies as well.

The next several sections pursue this interdependence further, extending the analyses of Sections 8.1 and 8.2 in several directions. First, these initial models, and in fact much of the literature, deal almost exclusively with *white noise* disturbances; that is, the stochastic shocks impacting on the economy are assumed to be unanticipated and transitory and to be independently distributed over time. But in practice, the distinction between permanent and transitory disturbances, on the one hand, and anticipated and unanticipated disturbances, on the other, are important, as we have discussed in previous chapters. Different types of disturbances impact on the economy differently and require different policy responses. Thus the exogenous disturbances we shall consider in the next sections may be of general types, in terms of how they are perceived by the agents in the economy.

Availability of Information

An important element in the analysis concerns the availability of information with respect to the stochastic disturbances impinging on the economy. We shall assume that there are two types of such random shocks. First, there are financial and price variables, information about which is assumed to be available to all agents instantaneously. Second, there are real and monetary shocks (stochastic shifts in the *IS* and *LM* curves and aggregate supply functions), which may or may not be observed contemporaneously. Indeed, we shall show how both the form of the optimal rules and, in some cases, their ability to replicate the frictionless economy depends critically upon the availability of information to agents in the economy. Our characterization of this is illustrated in Figure 8.1, considered from the viewpoint of time t, which we partition it into the infinitesimally short subperiod $(t, t+)$.

As we have already discussed, one motivation for the supply function is that the wage at time t is determined by a contract signed at time $t - 1$ on the basis of information available at time $t - 1$. Prices and financial variables are assumed to be observed instantaneously by all agents, so that everyone has complete current information on these variables when they make their respective decisions. More specifically, these instantaneously observed variables include

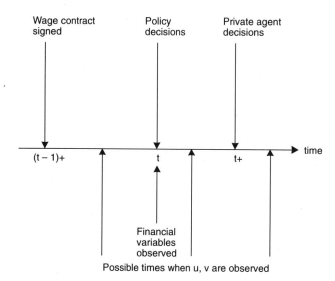

Figure 8.1
Timing of information and decisions

i. the domestic and foreign interest rates,

ii. the exchange rate,

iii. the domestic price level.

The model we shall develop includes just a single traded good. Thus in the absence of impediments to international trade, the domestic price of that good P must be related to the given foreign price Q and the exchange rate E, (where all prices are measured in natural units) by $P = QE$, which is referred to as purchasing power parity (PPP). Given this relationship, (ii) and (iii) imply the observability of the foreign price level as well.

At time t, two sets of decisions are made. First, there is the policy decision, that is, the implementation of the monetary intervention rule. Second, there are the decisions of the private agents in the economy, which include the production, portfolio, and consumption decisions, as well as the formation of forecasts for the next period. We assume that the two sets of decisions are made in the above order, at instances we denote by $t, t+$, respectively. This means that monetary policy, which is determined at time t, is known by the time the production decision is made at the next instant of time, $t+$.

This distinction in effect differentiates the information set available to the public and private agents in the economy. It is possible to make further distinctions among the various private agents along the lines of

Canzoneri, Henderson, and Rogoff (1983). For example, one can allow investors, who form predictions of the future exchange rate, to have different information from individuals concerned with predicting prices in the determination of the wage contract. And their information may differ from that of producers.

The key informational issue concerns the observability of the domestic monetary disturbance, which we shall now denote by u_t, and the domestic productivity disturbance, ε_t. Under the above assumptions, three different informational situations exist:

i. u_t and ε_t are observed instantaneously at time t by both public and private agents. This full-information assumption turns out to be, in effect, the information structure considered by Karni (1983) in his discussion of wage indexation policy.

ii. u_t and ε_t are observed in the time interval $(t, t+)$. They are therefore unobserved by the stabilization authority but known to private agents. This asymmetric information assumption is made throughout much of the literature and is implicit in the above analysis of wage indexation. It is also implicit in much of the analysis dealing with exchange rate intervention; see Canzoneri (1982) and several of the papers in Bhandari (1985).

iii. u_t and ε_t are observed after time $t+$. They are therefore unknown to both public and private agents at the time decisions for time t are made. In this case, agents form estimates of the two stochastic variables at time t, as required for forecasting decisions, by utilizing information on the observed financial variables. This information is again symmetric between public and private agents and is the assumption adopted by Aizenman and Frenkel (1985).

The informational issue we have been discussing pertains to the timing of the available information. The question of the role of this type of information in the conduct of optimal monetary policy is discussed at length by Turnovsky (1987b). Other authors have extended the role of differential information underlying the Lucas (1972, 1973) "islands" model to an open economy context. The essential informational asymmetry here arises from the notion that agents are trading in different local markets and thus observe different prices. Most of this literature does not address optimal policy, but rather focuses on the comparison of fixed versus flexible rates. For example, Kimbrough (1984) shows that the degree to which an unanticipated change in the money supply is perceived by agents, and therefore its impact on output, depends upon the exchange rate regime. Under flexible exchange rates, systematic monetary policy can have an effect on real output by altering the information content of the exchange rate. This is not the case under fixed exchange rates, because under that regime the exchange rate fails to provide useful information.

8.4   A Rational Expectations Model of a Small Open Economy

The assumptions of uncovered interest parity and purchasing power parity enable the demand side of the economy to be simplified to

$$r_t = \omega_t + e^*_{t+1,t} - e_t \tag{8.11}$$

$$p_t = q_t + e_t \tag{8.12}$$

$$m_t - p_t = \alpha_1 y_t - \alpha_2 r_t + u_t. \tag{8.1b'}$$

The supply side is again represented by the one-period wage contract model, with the contract wage for time t being determined at time $t - 1$, based on information available at that time. There are however, two differences from before. First, unlike the previous analysis, the productivity shock ε_t is not a temporally independently distributed random variable. Instead, firms may form predictions at time $t - 1$, denoted by $\varepsilon^*_{t,t-1}$. Following the previous argument, this modifies the contract wage to

$$w^c_t = p^*_{t,t-1} + \frac{\ln(1 - \theta)}{1 + \theta n} + \frac{\varepsilon^*_{t,t-1}}{1 + \theta n}. \tag{8.2c'}$$

An expected positive productivity disturbance will raise the expected marginal physical product of labor and therefore result in a higher contract wage.

Actual employment is determined by the short-run marginal product condition after the actual wage and price are known. However, the second difference is that the firm may or may not observe the actual productivity shock ε_t instantaneously. This leads to the following modification to the marginal productivity condition:

$$l_t = \frac{1}{\theta}[\ln(1 - \theta) + p_t - w_t + E_t(\varepsilon_t)], \tag{8.2b'}$$

where we have replaced ε_t by its instantaneous forecast, denoted by $E_t(\varepsilon_t)$, into this optimality condition. If ε_t is observed instantaneously, then $E_t(\varepsilon_t) = \varepsilon_t$ and (8.2b') reduces to (8.2b). Otherwise, the firm must infer it from available information on current observable variables using a linear forecasting technique, to be discussed below. Combining (8.2b') with (8.2a), current output is given by

$$y_t = \frac{(1-\theta)}{\theta}[\ln(1-\theta) + p_t - w_t + E_t(\varepsilon)] + \varepsilon_t, \tag{8.2d$'$}$$

which depends both on the firm's estimate of ε_t and on ε_t itself. In the event that ε_t is observed instantaneously, then (8.2d$'$) reduces to (8.2d).

In the situation where the productivity disturbance is observed instantaneously, the optimal form of wage indexation will emerge from the equilibrium; this condition will be discussed later. Otherwise, we assume that wages remain indexed in accordance with equation (8.2e), which, combined with (8.2c$'$) and (8.2d$'$), yields the following form of aggregate supply function:

$$y_t = \frac{(1-\theta)n\ln(1-\theta)}{1+n\theta} + \left(\frac{1-\theta}{\theta}\right)(1-\tau)(p_t - p_{t,t-1}^*)$$

$$+ \left(\frac{1-\theta}{\theta}\right)\left[E_t(\varepsilon_t) - \frac{\varepsilon_{t,t-1}^*}{1+n\theta}\right] + \varepsilon_t. \tag{8.13}$$

If the productivity disturbance is observable instantaneously, then (8.13) is modified by substituting $E_t(\varepsilon_t) = \varepsilon_t$ into this equation.

In the case that the monetary authority observes all disturbances instantaneously, the optimal rule will become self-evident; see (8.29) below. Otherwise, we assume that the money supply is adjusted in accordance with observed movements in the financial and price variables:

$$m_t = v_1 e_t + v_2 r_t + v_3 \omega_t + v_4 p_t. \tag{8.14}$$

Using the UIP condition (8.11), and the PPP condition (8.12), this equation can be expressed as

$$m_t = \mu_1 e_t + \mu_2 \varepsilon_{t+1,t}^* + \mu_3 \omega_t + \mu_4 q_t. \tag{8.14$'$}$$

The money supply is assumed to be adjusted to a wider range of pieces of information than are wages. This reflects the prevailing practice of restricting wage indexation to price movements. If, in addition, wages are assumed to be indexed to the foreign price level, nothing additional is gained as long as the money supply is adjusted to the foreign price level as well. There is a trade-off between μ_4 and the corresponding coefficient in the wage indexation rule.

With monetary policy being determined by a broad-based rule such as (8.14$'$), wage indexation turns out to be inessential. The optimum we achieve can always be attained by monetary policy alone. In some cases, it can also be achieved by a comprehensively based wage indexation scheme. But this is not always so, and in one important case, monetary policy is always required to achieve the optimal degree of stability; see Turnovsky (1987b).

As in Section 8.1, the target is to minimize the variance of output around the output of the frictionless economy. When productivity shocks are not necessarily observed instantaneously, the supply of output in such an economy becomes

$$\tilde{y}_t = \frac{(1 - \theta)n \ln(1 - \theta)}{1 + n\theta} + \frac{n(1 - \theta)}{1 + n\theta} \cdot E_t(\varepsilon_t) + \varepsilon_t. \tag{8.15}$$

This completes the description of the economy incorporating both wage indexation and monetary policy. The model consists of (8.11), (8.12), (8.1b'), (8.13), and (8.14'), which jointly determine e_t, p_t, r_t, m_t, y_t, and (8.15), which in turn determines the benchmark level of output, $\tilde{y}_t$. In the case where ε_t is observed instantaneously by private agents, $E_t(\varepsilon_t) = \varepsilon_t$, and (8.13) and (8.15) are amended accordingly. One point that should be clarified is that the notation $(t, t+)$ introduced previously is to parameterize the information sets available to the agents in the economy. All variables in the infinitesimal time interval $(t, t+)$ are determined simultaneously.

8.5   General Solution

We now solve this system under general assumptions regarding the forms of the exogenous shocks impacting on the economy. Purely for notational convenience we shall drop the observed constant quantity $((1 - \theta)n \ln(1 - \theta))/(1 + n\theta)$, which appears in the two equations (8.13) and (8.15), so that all variables should now be reinterpreted as being in deviation form about some initial equilibrium. The first thing to note is that the observability of the financial and price variables implies the observability of some linear combination of the unobserved stochastic disturbances. With m_t being adjusted in accordance with a known rule in response to observed variables, the real money supply $m_t - p_t$ is observed at time t. Substituting for output from (8.13) into (8.1b') leads to

$$m_t - p_t = \alpha_1 \left(\frac{1 - \theta}{\theta}\right) \left\{ (1 - \tau)[(e_t - e^*_{t,t-1}) + (q_t - q^*_{t,t-1})] \right.$$

$$\left. + E_t(\varepsilon_t) - \frac{\varepsilon^*_{t,t-1}}{1 + n\theta} \right\} - \alpha_2 r_t + (u_t + \alpha_1 \varepsilon_t). \tag{8.16}$$

The quantities $e_t, e^*_{t,t-1}, q_t, q^*_{t,t-1}, E_t(\varepsilon_t), \varepsilon^*_{t,t-1}, r_t$ are all observed at time t, enabling one to infer the value of the composite disturbance $(u_t + \alpha_1 \varepsilon_t)$. If we assume for simplicity that u_t, ε_t, are uncorrelated, the optimal estimates of each can be obtained from the observed composite disturbance by the least-squares projections

$$E_t(u_t) = \frac{\sigma_u^2}{\sigma_u^2 + \alpha_1^2 \sigma_\varepsilon^2} (u_t + \alpha_1 \varepsilon_t) \tag{8.17a}$$

$$E_t(v_t) = \frac{\alpha \sigma_\varepsilon^2}{\sigma_u^2 + \alpha_1^2 \sigma_\varepsilon^2} (u_t + \alpha_1 \varepsilon_t) \tag{8.17b}$$

where $\sigma_u^2, \sigma_\varepsilon^2$ are the variances of u_t, ε_t, respectively.

For notational convenience define

$$z_t \equiv u_t + \frac{\alpha_1(1 + n)}{1 + n\theta} \varepsilon_t + (1 - \mu_4)q_t - (\alpha_2 + \mu_3)\omega_t \tag{8.18}$$

so that the conditional expectations for time $t + j$, formed at time t, are

$$z_{t+j,t}^* \equiv u_{t+j,t}^* + \frac{\alpha_1(1 + n)}{1 + n\theta} \varepsilon_{t+j,t}^* + (1 - \mu_4)q_{t+j,t}^* - (\alpha_2 + \mu_3)\omega_{t+j,t}^*$$

$$j = 0, 1, 2, \ldots . \tag{8.19}$$

The instantaneous forecast, $z_{t,t}^*$ depends upon the observability of u_t, ε_t. In general, we have

$$E_t(z_t) \equiv z_{t,t}^* = E_t(u_t) + \frac{\alpha_1(1 + n)}{1 + n\theta} E_t(\varepsilon_t) + (1 - \mu_4)q_t - (\alpha_2 + \mu_3)\omega_t$$

$$= z_t + \frac{\alpha_1(1 - \theta)n}{1 + n\theta} [E_t(\varepsilon_t) - \varepsilon_t], \tag{8.19'}$$

with $z_{t,t}^* = z_t$, when ε_t is observed instantaneously.

Substituting (8.11), (8.12), (8.13), and (8.14') into (8.1b') and taking conditional expectations yields the following difference equation in exchange rate expectations:

$$(\alpha_2 + \mu_2)e_{t+i+1,t}^* - (1 + \alpha_2 - \mu_1)e_{t+i,t}^* = z_{t+i,t}^*; \qquad i = 1, 2, \ldots . \tag{8.20}$$

Using this notation, we can show that the deviation of output from its frictionless level, $y_t - \tilde{y}_t$, is

$$y_t - \tilde{y}_t = \frac{1}{\Delta}\left(\frac{1 - \theta}{\theta}\right)\Bigg\{(1 + \alpha_2 - \mu_1)\bigg[(1 - \tau)[-e_{t,t-1}^* + (q_t - q_{t,t-1}^*)]$$

$$+ \frac{E_t(\varepsilon_t) - \varepsilon_{t,t-1}^*}{1 + n\theta}\bigg] + (1 - \tau)\bigg[-z_t + (\alpha_2 + \mu_2)e_{t+1,t}^*$$

$$+ \frac{\alpha_1(1 - \theta)n}{1 + n\theta}[\varepsilon_t - E_t(\varepsilon_t)]\bigg]\Bigg\} \tag{8.21}$$

where $\Delta \equiv 1 + \alpha_2 - \mu_1 + \alpha_1(1 - \tau)((1 - \theta)/\theta)$. The exchange rate expectations $e^*_{t+1,t}$ and $e^*_{t,t-1}$ are obtained by solving (8.20) and are given by

$$e^*_{t+1,t} = -\frac{1}{1 + \alpha_2 - \mu_1}\left[\sum_{j=0}^{\infty} z^*_{t+1+j,t}\left(\frac{\alpha_2 + \mu_2}{1 + \alpha_2 - \mu_1}\right)^j\right] \text{ if } \left|\frac{1 + \alpha_2 - \mu_1}{\alpha_2 + \mu_2}\right| > 1$$

(8.22a)

$$= \frac{1}{\alpha_2 + \mu_2}\left[\sum_{j=0}^{\infty} z^*_{t-j,t}\left(\frac{1 + \alpha_2 - \mu_1}{\alpha_2 + \mu_1}\right)^j\right] \text{ if } \left|\frac{1 + \alpha_2 - \mu_1}{\alpha_2 + \mu_2}\right| > 1 \quad (8.22b)$$

where $z^*_{t+j,t}$ is defined in (8.19), (8.19').

In addition, the general solutions for expectations also contain a bubbles component, which has been eliminated, leaving us with these solutions expressed in terms of the "fundamentals." In the case of (8.22a) this is the only stable solution, though this is not the case in (8.22b). One rationale for the elimination of the bubbles term is the minimal state representation criterion, discussed in Chapter 5. Note further in (8.22b) that $z^*_{t-j,t} = z_{t-j}$ for $j \geq 1$, meaning that past values of z_t are known at time t. The case where expectations are backward looking, while consistent with rational expectations, is of less economic interest. In the main cases we shall discuss, expectations are always forward looking, with (8.22a) being the relevant case.

Setting $i = 1$ in (8.20) at time $t - 1$, using (8.19') and substituting into (8.21), the deviation in output from the frictionless level can be written equivalently as

$$y_t - \tilde{y}_t = \frac{1}{\Delta}\left(\frac{1-\theta}{\theta}\right)\left\{(1 - \tau)[(\alpha_2 + \mu_2)(e^*_{t+1,t} - e^*_{t+1,t-1}) - (E_t(z_t) - z^*_{t,t-1})]\right.$$

$$\left. + (1 + \alpha_2 - \mu_1)\left[(1 - \tau)(q_t - q^*_{t,t-1}) + \frac{E_t(\varepsilon_t) - \varepsilon^*_{t,t-1}}{1 + n\theta}\right]\right\}.$$

(8.21')

This equation indicates that the deviation in output from the frictionless level depends upon revisions to forecasts made between time $t - 1$ and time t in response to new information. In the case of observed variables such as q_t, this is the unanticipated change in that variable. In the case of exchange rate expectations, it is the update in the forecast for time $t + 1$, between time $t - 1$ and time t.

The analysis of optimal policy will focus on two important cases. The first is where all disturbances are unanticipated and transitory (the assumption made in Section 8.1 and 8.2), so that

$$e^*_{t+1,t} = 0 \qquad \text{for all } t. \qquad (8.23)$$

The second is where the expectations of the composite variable z formed at time t are uniform throughout all future periods. Formally, this is described by

$$z^*_{t+i,t} = z^*_t \quad \text{say} \quad i = 1, 2, \ldots, \qquad \text{for all } t. \tag{8.24}$$

In particular, we consider the important case where the current disturbance in z_t is expected to be permanent, so that $z^*_t = E_t(z_t)$. In this case, the stable solution for exchange rate expectations becomes

$$e^*_{t+1,t} = -\frac{E_t(z_t)}{1 - \mu_1 - \mu_2} \quad i = 1, 2, \ldots, \qquad \text{for all } t. \tag{8.25}$$

8.6 Jointly Optimal Wage Indexation and Monetary Policies

We now derive the optimal monetary policy and wage indexation rules under alternative sets of assumptions.

Full Information

Stabilization when both private agents and the stabilization authority have complete information on all random disturbances, including u_t, ε_t, is straightforward, either by means of wage indexation or monetary policy. We begin with the former.

Subtracting (8.2d') from (8.15), setting $E_t(\varepsilon_t) = \varepsilon_t$, and using (8.2c') leads to the expression

$$y_t - \tilde{y}_t = \left(\frac{1-\theta}{\theta}\right)\left[(p_t - p^*_{t,t-1}) - (w_t - w^c_t) + \frac{(\varepsilon_t - \varepsilon^*_{t,t-1})}{1 + n\theta}\right], \tag{8.26}$$

so that $y_t = \tilde{y}_t$, the frictionless level, provided wages are indexed in accordance with

$$w_t = w^c_t + (p_t - p^*_{t,t-1}) + \frac{1}{1 + n\theta}(\varepsilon_t - \varepsilon^*_{t,t-1}). \tag{8.27}$$

That is, the wage should be fully indexed to the unanticipated change in the price level and partially indexed to the unanticipated component of the productivity shock. Full indexation to the price change alone yields perfect stabilization if and only if the productivity disturbance is fully anticipated (i.e., $\varepsilon^*_{t,t-1} = \varepsilon_t$), or if the supply of labor is infinitely elastic (i.e., $n \to \infty$). Equation (8.27) may be written as

$$w_t = w^c_t + (p_t - p^*_{t,t-1}) + \frac{1}{1 + n}(y_t - y^*_{t,t-1}) \tag{8.28}$$

with the rule now being expressed in terms of the unanticipated movement in output. This rule is equivalent to the Karni (1983) stabilization rule, which dealt with unanticipated disturbances.

But output can be stabilized another way. Subtracting (8.2d′) (with $E_t(\varepsilon_t) = \varepsilon_t$ and omitting the constant) from the money market equilibrium condition, (8.1b′), we obtain

$$y_t - \tilde{y}_t - \frac{1}{\alpha_1}\left[m_t - p_t + \alpha_2 r_t - u_t - \alpha_1\left(\frac{1+n}{1+n\theta}\right)\varepsilon_t\right],$$

so that for perfect stabilization, we require

$$m_t = p_t - \alpha_2 r_t + u_t + \alpha_1\left(\frac{1+n}{1+n\theta}\right)\varepsilon_t. \tag{8.29}$$

Equations (8.28) and (8.29) provide alternative methods for replicating the output of the frictionless economy. Each of these approaches offers advantages for the policymaker. The wage indexation scheme involves monitoring fewer pieces of information, although it does involve forming forecasts of the current productivity disturbance. On the other hand, the monetary rule uses more information, but requires observations only on current disturbances. Moreover, the authority need not attempt to determine whether a disturbance is permanent or transitory. Its nature will be reflected by movements in the (observed) interest rate. Finally, eliminating p_t between (8.27) and (8.29) yields a trade-off between the adjustment in the money supply and the wage rate.

Imperfect Information

We return to equation (8.21) and determine the optimal monetary policy and wage indexation schemes in the situations where there is now imperfect information. The optimal policy rules are summarized in Table 8.1. The first row of that table deals with situation (ii) introduced in section 8.3 (under the heading "Availability of Information"), where private agents, but not the stabilization authority, observe the demand and productivity disturbances u_t, ε_t; the second row describes situation (iii) where neither the private agent nor the stabilization authority observes u_t, ε_t. The two columns in the table refer respectively to white noise disturbances and to disturbances that, having occurred, are then perceived as being permanent.

These optimal policies are determined as follows. Depending upon the disturbance, $e^*_{t+1,t}, e^*_{t,t-1}$ are calculated from (8.22) and substituted into (8.21). The policy parameters μ_i and τ are then chosen to minimize $\mathrm{var}(y_t - \tilde{y}_t)$.

Table 8.1
Optimal monetary policy and wage indexation with imperfect information

White noise	Perceived permanent shifts
Private agents observe u_t, ε_t	
μ_2 arbitrary	$\mu_1 = 1 + \alpha_2$
$\mu_3 = -\alpha_2$	μ_2, μ_3, μ_4 all arbitrary
$\mu_4 = -\alpha_2 + \mu_1$	τ arbitrary, but $\tau \neq 1$
$\dfrac{(1 + \alpha_2 - \mu_1)\phi}{1 + n\theta} = (1 - \tau)\left[\theta + \alpha_1\phi(1 - \theta) + \dfrac{\alpha_1 n(1 - \theta)\phi}{1 + n\theta}\right]$	
$\mu_1 \neq 1 + \alpha_2, \quad \tau \neq 1$	
imperfect stabilization	perfect stabilization
Private agents do not observe u_t, ε_t	
μ_2 arbitrary	(i) $\mu_1 = 1 + \alpha_2$
$\mu_3 = -\alpha_2$	μ_2, μ_3, μ_4 all arbitrary
$\mu_4 = -\alpha_2 + \mu_1$	τ arbitrary, but $\tau \neq 1$
$\dfrac{(1 + \alpha_2 - \mu_1)\phi}{1 + n\theta} = (1 - \tau)\left[1 + \dfrac{\alpha_1 n(1 - \theta)\phi}{1 + n\theta}\right]$	
$\mu_1 \neq 1 + \alpha_2, \quad \tau \neq 1$	(ii) μ_2 arbitrary
	$\mu_3 = -\alpha_2$
	$\mu_4 = \mu_1 + \mu_2$
	$\dfrac{(1 - \mu_1 - \mu_2)\phi}{1 + n\theta} = (1 - \tau)\left[1 + \dfrac{\alpha_1 n(1 - \theta)\phi}{1 + n\theta}\right]$
perfect stabilization	perfect stabilization

White Noise Disturbances

For white noise disturbances all expectations are zero, so from (8.23)

$$e^*_{t+1,t} = e^*_{t,t-1} = 0.$$

Thus, substituting into (8.21'),

$$
\begin{aligned}
y_t - \tilde{y}_t &= \frac{1}{\Delta}\left(\frac{1 - \theta}{\theta}\right)\Bigg\{ -(1 - \tau)E_t(z_t) \\
&\quad + (1 + \alpha_2 - \mu_1)\left[(1 - \tau)q_t + \frac{E_t(\varepsilon_t)}{1 + n\theta}\right]\Bigg\} \\
&= \frac{1}{\Delta}\left(\frac{1 - \theta}{\theta}\right)\Bigg\{ -(1 - \tau)(u_t + \alpha_1\varepsilon_t) \\
&\quad + \left[\frac{(1 + \alpha_2 - \mu_1) - (1 - \tau)\alpha_1(1 - \theta)n}{1 + n\theta}\right]E_t(\varepsilon_t) \\
&\quad + (1 - \tau)(\alpha_2 - \mu_1 + \mu_4)q_t + (1 - \tau)(\alpha_2 + \mu_3)\omega_t\Bigg\}. \quad (8.30)
\end{aligned}
$$

Observe that the solution is independent of the monetary policy parameter μ_2. This is because for white noise disturbances $e^*_{t+1,t} = 0$. It is evident from (8.30) that the values of the optimal policy parameters that minimize $\text{var}(y_t - \tilde{y}_t)$ can be obtained sequentially. First, the effects of the foreign variables q_t, ω_t can be neutralized by setting their respective coefficients in (8.30) to zero. Then the remaining variance due to the (unobserved) domestic variables can be minimized.

To stabilize for the foreign variables, set

$$\hat{\mu}_3 = -\alpha_2, \tag{8.31a}$$

$$\hat{\mu}_4 = -\alpha_2 + \hat{\mu}_1, \tag{8.31b}$$

thereby simplifying (8.30) to

$$y_t - \tilde{y}_t = \frac{1}{\Delta}\left(\frac{1-\theta}{\theta}\right)\left\{-(1-\tau)(u_t + \alpha_1\varepsilon_t)\right.$$

$$\left. + \left[\frac{(1+\alpha_2-\mu_1)-(1-\tau)\alpha_1(1-\theta)n}{1+n\theta}\right]E_t(\varepsilon_t)\right\}. \tag{8.30'}$$

The remaining choice is that of μ_1, τ, and this depends critically upon whether or not the productivity disturbance is observed.

Equation (8.30') brings out trade-offs between the degree of wage indexation τ, on the one hand, and the exchange rate regime, as reflected by the monetary policy parameter μ_1, on the other. But even more than that, the setting of one of these policies may completely destroy the effectiveness of the other. For example, suppose the domestic wage is fully indexed to the price level, that is, $\tau = 1$. In this case output is determined solely by supply conditions:

$$y_t - \tilde{y}_t = \left(\frac{1-\theta}{\theta}\right)\frac{1}{1+n\theta}E_t(\varepsilon_t),$$

thereby rendering monetary policy that operates through the demand side ineffective for further variance reduction. On the other hand, suppose the monetary authority sets $\mu_1 = (1+\alpha_2)$. This is a policy that accommodates the domestic money supply so as to exactly offset the change in the demand for money due to movements in the exchange rate. In this case (8.30') becomes

$$y_t - \tilde{y}_t = -\frac{1}{\alpha_1}\left[(u_t + \alpha_1\varepsilon_t) + \frac{\alpha_1(1-\theta)n}{1+n\theta}E_t(\varepsilon_t)\right].$$

Output becomes determined independently of price shocks, thereby rendering wage indexation ineffective for further stabilization.[4]

Observed Productivity Shock   Returning to (8.30′), if ε_t is observed, then $E_t(\varepsilon_t) = \varepsilon_t$, and as long as the two disturbances are uncorrelated, we may write

$$\text{var}(y_t - \tilde{y}_t) \equiv \sigma_y^2 = \left(\frac{1}{\Delta}\right)^2 \left(\frac{1 - \theta}{\theta}\right)^2 \left\{(1 - \tau)^2 \sigma_u^2 \right.$$

$$\left. + \left[\frac{(1 + \alpha_2 - \mu_1) - (1 - \tau)\alpha_1(1 + n)}{1 + n\theta}\right]^2 \sigma_\varepsilon^2 \right\}.$$

Despite the fact that there are two remaining policy parameters to be chosen, they each give rise to the same first-order optimality condition. Setting $\partial \sigma_y^2 / \partial \tau = \partial \sigma_y^2 / \partial \mu_1 = 0$, both lead to the optimality condition

$$\left(\frac{1 + \alpha_2 - \hat{\mu}_1}{1 + n\theta}\right)\varphi = (1 - \hat{\tau})\left[\theta + \alpha_1 \varphi(1 - \theta) + \frac{\alpha_1 n(1 - \theta)\varphi}{1 + n\theta}\right] \qquad (8.32)$$

where

$$\varphi \equiv \frac{\alpha_1 \sigma_\varepsilon^2}{\sigma_u^2 + \alpha_1^2 \sigma_\varepsilon^2}.$$

Equation (8.32) implies a trade-off between the degree of wage indexation and the extent to which monetary policy should respond to exchange rate movements. Either τ or μ_1 can be chosen arbitrarily, with the other being determined by this relationship. The extreme values $\tau = 1, \mu_1 = -(1 + \alpha_2)$ are ruled out for reasons just discussed. From (8.32), we see that $d\hat{\mu}_1/d\hat{\tau} > 0$, so that if the wage is more fully indexed to the price level, then the money supply should be expanded more (or contracted less) in response to a depreciation in the exchange rate.

Substituting (8.31a), (8.31b) into (8.14′) and using the PPP and UIP relationships, the optimal policies can be specified very simply by

$$m_t = (\hat{\mu}_1 - \alpha_2)p_t - \alpha_2 r_t \qquad (8.33a)$$

$$w_t = \hat{\tau}p_t \qquad (8.33b)$$

where $\hat{\tau}, \hat{\mu}_1$ are related by (8.32). Written in this way, both optimal policy rules have the convenience of enabling the domestic policymakers to monitor only domestic variables. In particular, one component of the optimal monetary rule requires accommodation to movements in the demand for money arising from changes in the domestic interest rate. It is also true that the optimum can be reached through monetary policy alone by setting $\hat{\tau} = 0$ and determining the corresponding value of the monetary policy parameter from (8.32).

Unobserved Productivity Shock   Turning now to the case where ε_t and therefore u_t are not observed by private agents, we have from (8.17b) that

$$E_t(\varepsilon_t) = \varphi(u_t + \alpha_1 \varepsilon_t), \tag{8.34}$$

in which case (8.30') becomes

$$y_t - \tilde{y}_t = \frac{1}{\Delta}\left(\frac{1 - \theta}{\theta}\right)\Bigg\{ -(1 - \tau) \\ + \left[\frac{(1 + \alpha_2 - \mu_1) - (1 - \tau)\alpha_1(1 - \theta)n}{1 + n\theta}\right]\varphi \Bigg\}(u_t + \alpha_1 \varepsilon_t). \tag{8.30''}$$

The optimal policy parameter, obtained by setting the coefficient of the composite disturbance $(u_t + \alpha_1 \varepsilon_t)$ to zero in (8.30''), now satisfies

$$\frac{(1 + \alpha_2 - \hat{\mu}_1)}{1 + n\theta}\varphi = (1 - \hat{\tau})\left[1 + \frac{\alpha_1(1 - \theta)n\varphi}{1 + n\theta}\right], \tag{8.35}$$

which again implies a positive trade-off between the monetary and indexation policy parameters. In this case, the slope is greater than before, implying that for a given degree of indexation, a greater monetary expansion (smaller monetary contraction) is required in response to a given depreciation of the exchange rate. Substituting (8.31a), (8.31b) into (8.14') and using the PPP and UIP conditions, the optimal policy rules are again given by (8.33a), (8.33b), except that the trade-off between μ_1 and $\hat{\tau}$ is now given by (8.35).

There is, however, one critical difference between these two cases. When private agents observe u_t and ε_t, the optimal stabilization rule, based on incomplete information, is unable to replicate the output of the frictionless economy. In effect, the inferior information available to the stabilization authority prevents it from being able to track perfectly the behavior of a private frictionless economy. There is, therefore, some residual positive variance to relative output fluctuations. By contrast, when these disturbances are not observed by private agents, the optimal rules, with u_t and ε_t satisfying (8.35), imply perfect stabilization. With equal (imperfect) information to that of the private sector, the stabilization authority is able to replicate exactly the behavior of a frictionless economy. The latter is precisely the result obtained by Aizenman and Frenkel (1985).

Perceived Permanent Disturbances

Suppose now that the disturbances occurring at each point of time t, although previously unanticipated, having occurred are now perceived as being permanent shifts. Thus, $q_{t,t-1}^* = q_{t-1}, \varepsilon_{t,t-1}^* = E_{t-1}(\varepsilon_{t-1})$, and $z_{t+j,t}^* = E_t(z_t)$ for all j and t. Thus exchange rate expectations are generated by

$$e^*_{t+1,t} = -\frac{E_t(z_t)}{1 - \mu_1 - \mu_2}; \qquad e^*_{t+1,t-1} = -\frac{E_{t-1}(z_{t-1})}{1 - \mu_1 - \mu_2} \qquad (8.36)$$

where $E_t(z_t)$ is given by (8.19′).

Substituting these expressions for expectations in (8.21′), the solution for $y_t - \tilde{y}_t$ is given by

$$y_t - \tilde{y}_t = (1 + \alpha_2 - \mu_1)\left[(1 - \tau)(q_t - q_{t-1}) + \frac{E_t(\varepsilon_t) - E_{t-1}(\varepsilon_{t-1})}{1 + n\theta}\right.$$

$$\left. - \frac{(1 - \tau)[E_t(z_t) - E_{t-1}(z_{t-1})]}{1 - \mu_1 - \mu_2}\right]. \qquad (8.37)$$

From (8.37) we can obtain the expressions for the optimal policies reported in the second column of Table 8.1.

In the case where private agents, but not the stabilization authority, observe u_t and ε_t, we see by inspection that output is stabilized perfectly at the frictionless level for all t, by setting $\mu_1 = (1 + \alpha_2)$. The optimal policy rules are therefore

$$m_t = (1 + \alpha_2)e_t + \mu_2 e^*_{t+1,t} + \mu_3 \omega_t + \mu_4 q_t \qquad (8.38a)$$

$$w_t = w^c_t + \tau(p_t - p^*_{t,t-1}) \qquad (8.38b)$$

where $\mu_1, \mu_2, \mu_3, \tau$ are all arbitrary, the only restriction being that $\tau \neq 1$.

To understand the economic reasoning underlying this result, consider the domestic money market. Combining equations (8.11), (8.12), and (8.1b′) yields

$$m_t = q_t + e_t + \alpha_1 y_t - \alpha_2[\omega_t + e^*_{t+1,t} - e_t] + u_t. \qquad (8.39)$$

If the domestic monetary authority intervenes in accordance with (8.38a), it follows from the first equation in (8.36) (and the assumption that u_t and ε_t are observed by the private agents) that

$$e^*_{t+1,t} = \frac{1}{\alpha_1 + \mu_2}\left[u_t + \frac{\alpha_1(1 + n)}{1 + n\theta}\varepsilon_t - (\alpha_2 + \mu_3)\omega_t + (1 - \mu_4)q_t\right]. \qquad (8.40)$$

Exchange rate expectations adjust in response to the stochastic disturbances $u_t, \varepsilon_t, \omega_t$, and q_t. The resulting adjustment in the domestic interest rate is precisely such as to eliminate the effects of the disturbances u_t, ω_t, and q_t from the excess demand function for nominal money balances. This can be seen by substituting (8.40) and (8.38a) into (8.39):

$$(1 + \alpha_2)e_t + \mu_3 \omega_t + \mu_4 q_t = q_t + e_t + \alpha_1 y_t$$

$$- \left[u_t + \frac{\alpha_1(1 + n)}{1 + n\theta}\varepsilon_t - (\alpha_2 + \mu_3)\omega_t + (1 - \mu_4)q_t\right] - \alpha_2(\omega_t - e_t) + u_t.$$

$$(8.41)$$

It is clear from this equation that whatever arbitrary values of μ_2, μ_3, and μ_4 are chosen, the expected exchange rate, given by the term in parentheses, simply adjusts to offset these stochastic effects. Upon simplification, (8.41) reduces to

$$y_t = \left(\frac{1+n}{1+n\theta}\right)\varepsilon_t = \tilde{y}_t, \tag{8.42}$$

thereby verifying that income is stabilized at its frictionless level.

It is interesting to observe that in contrast to the white noise disturbances discussed above, the stabilization authority, having incomplete information, can nevertheless replicate the equilibrium of a frictionless economy in response to this type of disturbance. It can dispense with wage indexation; and in fact, in light of the PPP and UIP conditions, the optimal monetary rule can be expressed in a number of equivalent ways, for example,

$$m_t = (1 + \alpha_2)e_t \quad m_t = (1 + \alpha_2)p_t \quad m_t = (1 + \alpha_2)r_t.$$

The most convenient form will presumably depend upon the availability and reliability of the necessary information.

The situation where the private agents do not observe u_t, ε_t, leads to *two* sets of optimal policy rules, both of which yield perfect stabilization at the frictionless output level for all t. Since (8.37) does not depend upon the observability of u_t, ε_t, one optimal solution is obviously $\mu_1 = (1 + \alpha_2)$, which again gives rise to (8.38a), (8.38b).

The term in parentheses in (8.37) can be written in terms of the differences $\Delta\omega_t, \Delta q_t, \Delta(u_t + \alpha_1\varepsilon_t)$. The second set of policy rules is obtained by setting the coefficients of these random variables to zero, thereby setting the right-hand side of (8.37) to zero. The resulting optimum is similar, but not identical to, that obtained previously. Specifically, $\hat{\mu}_3 = -\alpha_2$, $\hat{\mu}_4 = \hat{\mu}_1 + \hat{\mu}_2$, with $\hat{\mu}_1, \hat{\mu}_2, \hat{t}$ being arbitrary but subject to the constraint

$$\frac{(1 - \hat{\mu}_1 - \hat{\mu}_2)}{1 + n\theta}\varphi = (1 - \hat{t})\left[1 + \frac{\alpha_1(1-\theta)n\varphi}{1 + n\theta}\right].$$

If, further, we choose $\hat{\mu}_2 = -\alpha_2$, then this second set of policy rules reduces to (8.33a), (8.33b), and the trade-off between $\hat{\mu}_1, \hat{t}$, again is given by (8.35). This is identical to the optimal policy under white noise disturbances.

Uncertain Perceptions

Thus far, we have assumed that private agents are clear in their perceptions of whether the observed disturbances are permanent shifts or only transitory shocks. Of course, in time they may prove to be wrong, but our assumption has been that agents can form a subjective characterization of them. Suppose, instead, that agents are unable to decide whether a disturbance that has occurred represents a permanent shift or only a transitory shock. Assume that they formalize their uncertainty by assigning $\rho, 1 - \rho$, respectively, to these two outcomes. In the case where the private agents observe u_t, ε_t, the expected exchange rate is

$$e^*_{t+1,t} = -\frac{\rho z_t}{1 - \mu_1 - \mu_2},$$

and the analysis can be carried out by substituting this expression into (8.21). In this case it can be shown that if $\rho < 1$, perfect stabilization about the frictionless level of output is not possible. On the other hand, if private agents do not observe u_t, ε_t, we have seen that the rules (8.33a), (8.33b), together with (8.35), replicate the frictionless economy perfectly for both white noise and permanent shifts. This rule will therefore yield perfect stability regardless of the private agents' perceptions of the nature of the shocks (i.e., for all values of ρ).

8.7   The Barro-Gordon Model

In studying macroeconomic policymaking, most economists ignore the incentives of policymakers and the political constraints they may face. Having formulated some social objective function, the policymaker is assumed to proceed with the determination of policy, guided by the objectives which have been assumed. In discussing economic policymaking, the distinction has traditionally been drawn between *discretionary* policy, where the policymaker can vary his policy instruments as he wishes, and *rules*, which constrain the way policy is conducted. These rules may be of the type studied in this chapter, they may be based on past information, or they may be of other types.

A monetary authority following a discretionary policy always has the ability to generate unanticipated inflation, thereby generating short-run expansions in output by virtue of the Lucas supply function. In a world of rational expectations, agents learn these incentives and adjust their inflationary expectations, so that on average the equilibrium rate of inflation is increased. Monetary policy rules that rule out surprises will lead to a lower equilibrium rate of inflation. However, when rules are in place, the monetary authority has an incentive to renege on them in order to generate inflationary shocks and the benefits they yield, and this can threaten the viability of the equilibrium based on policy rules. This important idea was introduced and first developed by Barro and Gordon (1983a, 1983b) and will be outlined in this final section. Their exposition will be followed quite closely.

The policymaker is assumed to have an objective, which is to minimize the expected discounted costs associated with inflation. These costs shall be represented by

$$E \sum_{i=0}^{\infty} z_{t+i} \gamma_{it} \qquad (8.43a)$$

where

$$z_t = \frac{a}{2} \pi_t^2 - b_t(\pi_t - \pi_t^*) \qquad (8.43b)$$

and γ_{it} is a discount factor between time $t - i$ and time t; π_t, π_t^* are the actual and predicted rates of inflation for time t; and z_t denotes the short-run cost of inflation at time t. The latter consists of two parts. First, with output determined by the Lucas supply function, a positive unanticipated inflationary shock leads to an unanticipated short-run increase in output, thereby conferring a positive benefit on the agent. However, inflation itself incurs costs, which for simplicity are represented by the quadratic term, so that they increase with the rate of inflation. This is not intended to be a realistic model, but it suffices to illustrate the main point. The coefficients satisfy $a > 0, b_t > 0$, with the latter being stochastic and unknown to agents. The stabilization authority is assumed to conduct monetary policy in way that enables him to control the inflation rate directly each period. Stochastic shocks can be introduced into this aspect of the relationship without modifying the results.

Consider first *discretionary policy*, and assume that when choosing the current actual inflation rate π_t, the policymaker treats the expectations of the current and all future rates of inflation ($\pi_{t+i}^*, i > 1$) as given. Given the nature of the cost function, all future states are independent of current actions, so that (8.43a) can be minimized by minimizing the current costs z_t. Performing this calculation leads to the optimal rate of inflation under discretion $\hat{\pi}_t = \bar{b}/a$ where $\bar{b} = E_t(b)$. Agents, having rational expectations, form their predictions of inflation by solving the policymaker's optimization problem. They therefore predict the inflation rate to be as determined by the policymaker, namely, $\pi_t^* = \hat{\pi}_t = \bar{b}/a$. There are therefore no unanticipated shocks in equilibrium, and, substituting these expressions into (8.43b), the corresponding minimized costs are $\hat{z}_t = (1/2)(\bar{b}^2/a)$.

Now suppose that the policymaker follows a *policy rule* that commits him in advance to some chosen rate of inflation. By announcing the rule and relating it to variables that are observable and are known to the private agents, the policymaker can, in effect, control the private expected rate of inflation. Essentially he chooses both π_t and π_t^*, subject to $\pi_t = \pi_t^*$. Substituting this into (8.43a), there is no unanticipated inflation and inflation costs are minimized by setting $\tilde{\pi}_t = 0$, with the corresponding costs being $\tilde{z}_t = 0$.

Comparing the costs under the rule with those under discretion, we see that the latter exceed the former. The commitment in the rule prevents inflation from becoming excessive, thereby eliminating the costs associated with positive inflation rates. But does the policymaker have any incentive to renege on the commitment? The answer is yes.

To see this, suppose that private agents have initial inflationary expectations, formed from some prior rule, say equal to zero; that is, $\pi_o^* = 0$. If the policymaker takes this as given and chooses the inflation rate at time t to minimize z_t, the corresponding optimal inflation rate will be $\bar{z}_t = \bar{b}/a$, the same as it was with the discretionary policy. The expected cost of cheating in this way is now $-(1/2)(\bar{b}^2/a)$, which is less than the cost of sticking to the rule. Barro and Gordon define the temptation to renege as $E(\bar{z}_t - \tilde{z}_t) = (1/2)(\bar{b}^2/a) > 0$.

There is therefore a clear ranking. Discretionary policy yields the worst outcome, in that it leads to a perfectly anticipated excessive rate of inflation. The rule is better because it leads to no inflation. However reneging, when people anticipate the rule is still better. The benefits from the surprise more than outweigh the costs of the inflation.

As Barro and Gordon argue, the reneging outcome is feasible only in the short run. Such a rule is time inconsistent. People will not be fooled forever, the rule will cease to be credible, and the policymaker's reputation will be tarnished. In the latter part of their paper, Barro and Gordon (1983b) introduce mechanisms for enforcing rules so as to make them credible. These involve penalties that are imposed for deviating from the rule. Essentially the problem becomes a repeated game, in which the costs associated with the enforcement are weighed against the benefits of cheating. This idea of credible rules has been pursued further by other authors such as Backus and Driffill (1985a, 1985b). The issue of time inconsistency is an important one in the context of dynamic policy-making with forward-looking agents and is discussed at greater length in Chapter 11 in connection with the behavior of an intertemporally optimizing agent.

8.8 Conclusions

This chapter has pursued various issues concerning stabilization under rational expectations. Most of our attention has been devoted to analyzing wage indexation and monetary policy issues and, in particular, to examining their interdependence. For this purpose we have found the framework of a small open economy to be convenient, but the same issues arise with respect to a closed economy. In studying this interdependence we have presented a general treatment with respect to (i) the relative information available to private agents and to the stabilization authority; and (ii) the perceived nature of the disturbances impinging on the economy. Several conclusions are worth repeating:

If all agents have perfect information, then perfect stabilization can be achieved either through appropriate wage indexation or through a very simple monetary policy rule. However, most of the chapter has dealt with the condition of incomplete information. Where disturbances are unanticipated, we have drawn the distinction between those that are perceived as being transitory (white noise) and those that are perceived as being permanent shifts. In the case of the former, we find that the distortions due to the wage contract can be fully eliminated, thereby replicating the output of the frictionless economy, as long as private agents and the stabilization authority have the same (imperfect) information. On the other hand, for perceived permanent shifts, perfect stabilization is achieved whether or not private agents and the stabilization authority have identical information.

In deriving the various policy rules, the analysis emphasizes the policy redundancy issue. That is, some of the policy coefficients can be set arbitrarily, enabling the policy rules to be specified in many equivalent ways. The potential practical importance of the design of policy rules can be seen when one takes into account the relative scarcity and quality of different types of data that the policymaker may require. The final part of the chapter has discussed briefly the issues of rules versus discretionary policy in a rational expectations context, as introduced in the influential Barro-Gordon model.

Notes

1. See, e.g., Aizenman (1985) and Marston (1984).

2. This criterion is equivalent to minimizing the loss function in Aizenman and Frenkel (1985), which they motivate in terms of measuring the losses associated with the sum of consumers' and producers' surpluses.

3. The debate originated with Friedman (1953). Formal analysis of the relative stability properties of the two regimes was first carried out in the 1970s.

4. The implications of this trade-off between wage indexation and monetary policy are discussed in further detail by Turnovsky (1983).

III Intertemporal Optimization

9   The Representative Agent Model

9.1   Introduction

Both the traditional macro models discussed in Part I and the rational expectations models discussed in Part II have been criticized on the grounds that they are based on arbitrarily specified behavioral relationships. Critics have argued that a good macro model should be based on sound microeconomic foundations, and this has been taken to mean that the behavioral relationships should be derived from the intertemporal optimization of microeconomic agents. This has led to the representative agent model, which has become the dominant macroeconomic framework over the past decade or so. In fact, this approach is not new. The basic structure dates back to Ramsey's (1928) study of the optimal savings and economic growth rate, although the recent literature is much more focused on issues of macroeconomic policy.

Part III presents a progression of such models. The present chapter outlines the basic model and applies it to a number of issues. The following two chapters refine the model to include a more complete corporate sector and a more realistic tax structure, enabling us to present a more rigorous analysis of the macroeconomic consequences of tax policy. The representative agent framework has also been fruitfully applied to issues in international macroeconomics; these are surveyed in Chapter 12. Whereas the dynamic adjustment is a central component of the representative agent model, in most variants of the Ramsey model the equilibrium to which the economy converges either is stationary or grows at an exogenous rate, which is determined by such things as the rate of population growth or the rate of technological change. Macroeconomic policy typically has no impact on long-run growth. This is a direct consequence of the assumptions made with respect to the underlying production conditions in the economy. By contrast, the recent literature on endogenous growth introduces technological assumptions that permit macroeconomic policy instruments to influence the long-run equilibrium rate of growth. This matter is discussed in Chapter 13.

The representative agent framework is a rich one, and in this chapter we shall use it to illustrate a variety of issues. The basic model is a real one-good model, and it can be used to analyze the dynamic adjustment of the economy to a variety of policy changes and other shocks. In Sections 9.2–9.5 we shall focus on both permanent and temporary changes in government consumption expenditure. Our emphasis is on characterizing the general macrodynamic adjustments following such changes. We focus particularly on two aspects. The first is the intertemporal adjustment in the capital stock. Second, we analyze the consequences of government expenditure for economic welfare. The intertemporal optimizing framework is a natural one within which to address this issue, because the utility level of the representative agent provides a plausible criterion by which to assess the overall benefits of policy changes. Because of the gradual adjustment of the capital stock, the effects of government policy are spread over time. We therefore discuss the effects of these expenditure changes on the entire time path of instantaneous utility as well as on the overall accumulated level of welfare over the planning horizon of the agent. In the process it become clear how government expenditure involves an intertemporal trade-off in the benefits it provides.

The latter part of the chapter introduces various modifications to the basic model. The first of these considers the effects of government expenditure as a productive input rather than as a consumption good. This is becoming a topical issue and only recently has begun to receive analytical treatment by macroeconomists. The second modification is to introduce the term structure of interest rates, which, assuming financial market efficiency, can be easily introduced into this framework. The third extension is to introduce money into the basic framework and address the related issue of the optimal monetary growth rate, and a final modification is to introduce an exogeneously growing population.

9.2   The Framework and Macroeconomic Equilibrium

The main objective of this chapter is to set out and exposit the representative agent framework. Prices and money are inessential for this purpose; we therefore abstract from them, focusing on a real economy having a stationary population. Modifications to this basic model will be introduced during the latter parts of this chapter as well as in subsequent chapters. For present purposes, the household and production sectors may be consolidated, so that the private sector of the economy is modeled as a representative composite worker-entrepreneur. In the absence of distortionary taxes, this provides an adequate representation of the private sector. The decomposition of the private sector into households and firms becomes necessary in the more realistic case where the sectors are subject to differential distortionary taxes. This extension is taken up in Chapters 10 and 11.

Elements of the Model

The representative agent is assumed to have an infinite planning horizon, to face perfect capital markets, and to have perfect foresight. In this environment, he is postulated to choose his private rate of consumption, c, supply of labor, l, capital stock, k, and holdings of government bonds, b, (assumed to be short-term bonds) in order to maximize[1]

$$\int_0^\infty U(c, l, g)e^{-\beta t}\, dt \quad U_c > 0,\ U_{cc} < 0,\ U_l < 0,\ U_{ll} < 0,\ U_g > 0,\ U_{gg} < 0$$

$$(9.1a)$$

subject to the budget constraint

$$c + \dot{k} + \dot{b} = F(k, l) + rb - T \qquad (9.1b)$$

and initial conditions

$$b(0) = b_0, \qquad k(0) = k_0 \qquad (9.1c)$$

where:

g = real government consumption expenditure,

T = real lump-sum taxes, which in general may vary over time,

β = rate of consumer time preference, taken to be constant;

r = short (instantaneous) real interest rate.

The instantaneous utility function U is assumed to have the following properties. The representative agent is assumed to derive positive, but diminishing, marginal utility from the consumption of both private and government consumption goods. He also gets positive, but diminishing, marginal utility from leisure, implying that he derives positive and increasing marginal disutility from working. The utility function is further assumed to be strictly concave in its three arguments, private consumption, leisure, and government consumption expenditure. In addition, we postulate private consumption and leisure to be normal goods, meaning that they both increase with wealth. We do not, however, restrict the way in which government consumption expenditure impacts on the marginal utility of private consumption and the disutility of work effort, as measured by the partial derivatives U_{cg} and U_{1g}.

Output is produced by a neoclassical production function exhibiting positive, but diminishing, marginal physical productivity in the two factors of production, capital and labor; that is,

$$y = F(k, l); \qquad F_k > 0,\ F_{kk} < 0,\ F_l > 0,\ F_{ll} < 0.$$

For simplicity, capital is assumed not to depreciate; the introduction of capital that depreciates at a constant exponential rate is straightforward, but adds little. In addition, F is assumed to be linearly homogeneous in the private factors, capital and labor, implying that $F_{kk}F_{ll} - F_{kl}^2 = 0$; $F_{kl} > 0$.[2] All investment (or disinvestment, which is also assumed to be feasible) occurs at a continuous rate and does not incur adjustment costs.[3] These costs will be introduced in Chapter 11.

In determining his utility-maximizing decisions, the representative agent takes T, β, and r as given. To solve the formal optimization we construct the Lagrangean expression

$$H = U(c, l, g)e^{-\beta t} + \lambda e^{-\beta t}[F(k, l) + rb - T - c - \dot{k} - \dot{b}] \qquad (9.2)$$

where $\lambda(t)$ is the costate variable associated with the budget constraint (9.1b) and represents the marginal utility of wealth. Performing the optimization leads to the following first-order optimality conditions:

$$U_c(c, l, g) = \lambda, \qquad (9.3a)$$

$$U_l(c, l, g) = -\lambda F_l(k, l), \qquad (9.3b)$$

$$\lambda F_k(k, l) = -\dot{\lambda} + \lambda\beta, \qquad (9.3c)$$

$$\lambda r = -\dot{\lambda} + \lambda\beta. \qquad (9.3d)$$

The first two equations are straightforward static efficiency conditions. Equation (9.3a) asserts that for the consumer to be in equilibrium, the marginal utility of consumption must equal the marginal utility of wealth. Equation (9.3b) requires that the marginal utility of an additional unit of leisure must equal the marginal utility of the consumption forgone, priced at the opportunity cost of a unit of leisure, namely the real wage rate. The ratio of these two conditions is just a standard marginal rate of substitution relationship linking the ratio of marginal utilities to their relative price. The remaining two equations are dynamic efficiency conditions and will be discussed further in Section 9.2.

In addition, the following transversality conditions must be met:

$$\lim_{t \to \infty} \lambda k e^{-\beta t} = 0, \qquad (9.3e)$$

$$\lim_{t \to \infty} \lambda b e^{-\beta t} = 0, \qquad (9.3f)$$

thereby ruling out explosive equilibria. These equations assert that as long as the agent assigns some positive marginal value to the asset, the present discounted value of its stock at the end of the planning horizon must be reduced to zero. Otherwise, the agent would be wasting what would be a valuable asset. The significance of these latter two conditions in ensuring that the intertemporal budget constraints facing both households and the government are met will be discussed further in Section 9.3.

The other agent in the economy is the government. At any instant of time it makes expenditure decisions, taxation decisions, and financing decisions, which are subject to its flow constraint,

$$\dot{b} = g + rb - T. \tag{9.4}$$

This equation asserts that the government deficit, which consists of government expenditures plus interest payments on its outstanding debt, less tax receipts, must be financed by issuing additional debt. As noted, the government bonds are short-term bonds, the price of which, in terms of new output, is fixed at unity. In Section 9.7 we will briefly consider the implications of alternative forms of government debt, having differing terms to maturity. We will also be addressing, in Section 9.3, the issues of the sustainability of government debt policy.

Substituting equation (9.4) into the budget constraint faced by the representative agent (9.1b) leads to the following relationship:

$$F(k,l) = c + \dot{k} + g. \tag{9.5}$$

This equation describes short-term market clearing, namely that current output must either be consumed by the private sector, consumed by the government, or accumulated as additional capital stock. Implicit in this relationship is the assumption that any output can be converted costlessly into capital goods, an assumption that will be modified in Chapter 11. It is clear that the three constraints (9.1b), (9.4), and (9.5) are not independent; any two imply the third.

Short-Run Equilibrium

This completes the description of the economy, from which the macroeconomic equilibrium can be derived as follows. First, equations (9.2a) and (9.2b) can be solved for c and l in the form

$$c = c(\lambda, k, g), \tag{9.6a}$$

$$l = l(\lambda, k, g). \tag{9.6b}$$

The partial derivatives of private consumption demand and labor supply are found by differentiating the first-order conditions (9.3a) and (9.3b) with respect to λ, k, and g. They are given by the following expressions:

$$\frac{\partial c}{\partial \lambda} = \frac{(U_{ll} + \lambda F_{ll}) + U_{cl} F_l}{D} < 0 \qquad \frac{\partial l}{\partial \lambda} = \frac{-(U_{cc} F_l + U_{cl})}{D} > 0 \tag{9.7a}$$

$$\frac{\partial c}{\partial k} = \frac{U_{cl} \lambda F_{kl}}{D} \qquad \frac{\partial l}{\partial k} = \frac{-U_{cc} \lambda F_{kl}}{D} > 0 \tag{9.7b}$$

$$\frac{\partial c}{\partial g} = \frac{-U_{cg}(U_{ll} + \lambda F_{ll}) + U_{cl} U_{lg}}{D} \qquad \frac{\partial l}{\partial g} = \frac{U_{cl} U_{cg} - U_{cc} U_{lg}}{D} \tag{9.7c}$$

where $D \equiv U_{cc}(U_{ll} + \lambda F_{ll}) - U_{cl}^2 > 0$. The following explanation for these signs can be given. The signs of c_λ, l_λ follow from normality, namely that an increase in the marginal utility of wealth causes the agent to substitute work for consumption. An increase in the capital stock increases the marginal productivity of labor, raising the real wage rate and increasing the supply of labor. This will raise or lower consumption, according to whether the increase in labor supply raises or lowers the marginal utility of consumption. In practice it would seem reasonable to assume that the marginal utility of consumption increases with leisure, in which case $U_{cl} < 0$, but the reverse cannot be ruled out on a priori grounds. The partial effects of an increase in government expenditure depend more precisely upon how it interacts with the private decisions pertaining to utility and production.

Combining (9.3c) and (9.3d), we obtain the equality between the short-term interest rate and the marginal physical product of capital, which we can write as

$$r = F_k(k, l) = F_k(k, l(\lambda, k, g)). \tag{9.6c}$$

Thus with perfectly competitive financial markets, the short-run rate of interest equals the marginal physical product of capital.

Combining (9.6c) with either (9.3c) or (9.3d) yields the intertemporal arbitrage relationship

$$\beta - \frac{\dot{\lambda}}{\lambda} = r = F_k(k, l(\lambda, k, g)), \tag{9.6d}$$

which is one of the most fundamental relationships to appear in intertemporal macroeconomics. It asserts that in equilibrium the (equal) rates of return on the two assets in the economy must also equal the rate of return on consumption, given by the left-hand side of (9.6d).

To see this more intuitively, let us consider the options facing the agent at any instant of time t. If he takes a unit of output and allocates it to savings it will yield a rate of return per unit of time given by (9.6c). Suppose, on the other hand, that he chooses instead to consume it. The rate of return on taking this decision is given by

$$\frac{U_c(t)e^{-\beta t} - U_c(t + dt)e^{-\beta(t+dt)}}{U_c(t)e^{-\beta t}\,dt}.$$

Dividing the numerator and denominator by $e^{-\beta t}$, this expression simplifies to

$$\frac{U_c(t) - U_c(t + dt)e^{-\beta\,dt}}{U_c(t)\,dt}.$$

Noting that for small $dt, e^{-\beta\,dt} \cong 1 - \beta\,dt$, and $U_c(t + dt) \cong U_c(t) + \dot{U}_c(t)\,dt$, this expression can be approximated by the quantity

$$\frac{U_c(t) - [U_c(t) + \dot{U}_c(t)\,dt][1 - \beta\,dt]}{U_c(t)\,dt}.$$

Letting $dt \to 0$, this converges to $\beta - (\dot{U}_c/U_c)$, which is just the left-hand side of (9.6d) and shall be referred to as the rate of return on consumption. It will play a prominent role in the analysis of this and subsequent chapters.

Many intertemporal macro models assume that the supply of labor is fixed, in which case $U_c = U_c(c)$. Differentiating this expression with respect to $t, \dot{\lambda}/\lambda = U_{cc}\dot{c}/U_c$, in which case the intertemporal arbitrage condition (9.6d) can be expressed as

$$\frac{\dot{c}}{c} = -\frac{1}{\eta(c)}(r - \beta) \tag{9.8}$$

where $\eta(c) \equiv U_{cc}c/U_c < 0$ is the elasticity of the marginal utility of consumption with respect to consumption. The quantity η reflects the curvature of the utility function, and for the frequently used logarithmic function, $\eta = -1$. Equation (9.8) is known as the Keynes-Ramsey rule; it asserts that consumption will be increasing or decreasing over time according to whether the rate of interest is greater or less than the rate of time preference. In the former case, the agent is relatively patient and finds it optimal to reduce consumption in the short run, allowing it to increase over time.

The elasticity η plays prominent role in macroeconomic dynamics and has been used to measure two distinct characteristics. In a continuous-time deterministic context, such as the present, $-1/\eta$ can be shown to equal the instantaneous elasticity of substitution of consumption over time; see, for example, Blanchard and Fischer (1989, 40). At the same time $-\eta$ also measures the degree of relative risk aversion in a stochastic context; see Part IV. The constant elasticity utility function c^γ/γ has the property that both measures are characterized by the same parameter γ. This need not be the case, and a more general utility function that separates out these concepts is used by Obstfeld (1994).[4]

Dynamics

The dynamics of the economy are obtained by substituting the short-run solutions for c and l, presented in (9.6a) and (9.6b), into the product market clearing condition (9.5) and the arbitrage condition (9.6d), rewriting these relations as

$$\dot{k} = F[k, l(\lambda, k, g)] - c(\lambda, k, g) - g, \tag{9.9a}$$

$$\dot{\lambda} = \lambda[\beta - F_k(k, l(\lambda, k, g))]. \tag{9.9b}$$

Equations (9.9a), (9.9b) make up an autonomous dynamic system that jointly determines the intertemporal evolution of k and λ, and hence of the macroeconomy as a whole. The equilibrium must be supported by a sustainable government fiscal policy. But, provided that it is viable, the precise policy—say, the choice between lump-sum tax financing and debt financing—does not impact on the behavior of the economy.

The steady state of the economy, reached when $\dot{k} = \dot{\lambda} = 0$, is obtained from the equations

$$F[\tilde{k}, l(\tilde{\lambda}, \tilde{k}, g)] = c(\tilde{\lambda}, \tilde{k}, g) + g \tag{9.10a}$$

$$F_k[\tilde{k}, l(\tilde{\lambda}, \tilde{k}, g)] = \beta \tag{9.10b}$$

where $\tilde{k}, \tilde{\lambda}$ denote steady-state values. Equation (9.10a) describes the steady-state equilibrium in the product market when investment is zero, and equation (9.10b) states that in the long run the marginal physical product of capital is constrained to equal the constant rate of time preference. Together, the steady-state conditions (9.10) determine the steady-state values $\tilde{k}$ and $\tilde{\lambda}$ implied by a specified level of government consumption expenditure. Because of the homogeneity of F, (9.10b) determines the long-run capital-labor ratio.

Linearizing the system (9.9a), (9.9b) about the stationary equilibrium (9.10a), (9.10b), corresponding to given initial levels of g, the dynamics can be approximated by the following matrix equation in k and λ:

$$\begin{pmatrix} \dot{k} \\ \dot{\lambda} \end{pmatrix} = \begin{pmatrix} \omega_{11} & \omega_{12} \\ -\tilde{\lambda}\omega_{21} & -\tilde{\lambda}\omega_{22} \end{pmatrix} \begin{pmatrix} k - \tilde{k} \\ \lambda - \tilde{\lambda} \end{pmatrix} \tag{9.11}$$

where[5]

$$\omega_{11} \equiv F_k + F_l l_k - c_k > 0 \qquad \omega_{12} \equiv F_l l_\lambda - c_\lambda > 0$$

$$\omega_{21} \equiv F_{kk} + F_{kl} l_k < 0, \qquad \omega_{22} \equiv F_{kl} l_\lambda > 0.$$

Since $\Delta \equiv \omega_{11}\omega_{22} - \omega_{12}\omega_{21} > 0$, the eigenvalues of (9.11), μ_1, μ_2 can be shown to satisfy $\mu_1 < 0, \mu_2 > 0$ and to satisfy the additional properties $\mu_2 > |\mu_1|$, $\mu_2 + \mu_1 = \beta$.[6] The general form of the solution to (9.11) is given by

$$k = \tilde{k} + A_1 e^{\mu_1 t} + A_2 e^{\mu_2 t} \tag{9.12a}$$

$$\lambda = \tilde{\lambda} - \frac{\tilde{\lambda}\omega_{21}}{\tilde{\lambda}\omega_{22} + \mu_1} A_1 e^{\mu_1 t} - \frac{\tilde{\lambda}\omega_{21}}{\tilde{\lambda}\omega_{22} + \mu_2} A_2 e^{\mu_2 t}, \tag{9.12b}$$

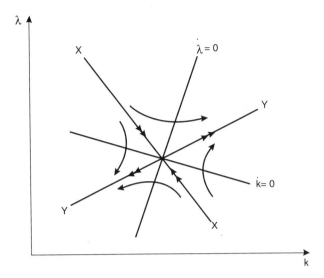

Figure 9.1
Phase diagram

and the equilibrium is therefore a saddlepoint, with the constants A_i being determined by the appropriate initial and terminal conditions on k and λ. The phase diagram summarizing the dynamics is illustrated in Figure 9.1. We shall assume that although the capital stock always evolves gradually, marginal utility may respond instantaneously to new information as it becomes available. The precise boundary conditions depend on the type of shock and its duration—on whether the shock is, for instance, permanent or temporary. Substituting the solutions (9.12a), (9.12b) into the transversality condition (9.3e), it can be readily shown that this condition will be met if and only if $A_2 = 0$. This implies a purely *stable* adjustment path, which, starting from the initial capital stock $k = k_0$, is described by

$$k = \tilde{k} + (k_0 + \tilde{k})e^{\mu_1 t} \tag{9.13a}$$

$$\lambda - \tilde{\lambda} = -\left(\frac{\tilde{\lambda}\omega_{21}}{\tilde{\lambda}\omega_{22} + \mu_1}\right)(k - \tilde{k}) = \left(\frac{\mu_1 - \omega_{11}}{\omega_{12}}\right)(k - \tilde{k}) \tag{9.13b}$$

and corresponds to the negatively sloped locus XX in Figure 9.1.[7] As long as no future shock is anticipated, the economy must lie on this stable locus in order for the transversality condition to hold. Likewise, the solution for which $A_1 = 0$ implies a purely *unstable* trajectory, given by

$$\lambda - \tilde{\lambda} = -\left(\frac{\tilde{\lambda}\omega_{21}}{\tilde{\lambda}\omega_{22} + \mu_2}\right)(k - \tilde{k}) = \left(\frac{\mu_2 - \omega_{11}}{\omega_{12}}\right)(k - \tilde{k}). \tag{9.13c}$$

This unstable locus, illustrated by $Y'Y'$ in Figure 9.1, has a slope that is positive although smaller in absolute value than that of the stable trajectory.[8]

9.3 Sustainability of Equilibrium

Before analyzing the dynamic adjustment of the macroeconomic equilibrium, it is important to determine whether or not it is economically sustainable. To do so, we need to analyze the government budget constraint (9.4).

To begin, we write this equation as the following explicit function of time:

$$\dot{b}(t) = r(t)b(t) + g(t) - T(t) \tag{9.14}$$

where the interest rate $r(t) = F_k(k, l(\lambda, k, g))$; see (9.6c). Starting from an initially given stock of government bonds $b(0) = b_0$, the solution to (9.14) is

$$b(t) = e^{\int_0^t r(s)ds}\left[b_0 + \int_0^t [g(\tau) - T(\tau)]e^{-\int_0^\tau r(s)ds}\,d\tau \right]. \tag{9.15}$$

In order to be sustainable, this solution for $b(t)$ must satisfy the consumer transversality condition (9.3f), and this will be so if and only if the limit, as $t \to \infty$, of the term in parenthesis in (9.15) is zero, that is,

$$b_0 + \int_0^\infty [g(\tau) - T(\tau)]e^{-\int_0^\tau r(s)ds}\,d\tau = 0. \tag{9.16}$$

This equation is precisely the *intertemporal government budget constraint* and requires that the initial stock of government bonds b_0, plus the present value of subsequent fiscal deficits $g(t) - T(t)$, discounted at the appropriate interest rate $r(s)$, must sum to zero. Provided that (9.16) is met, the stock of bonds will follow the stable adjustment path

$$b(t) = -\int_t^\infty [g(\tau) - T(\tau)]e^{-\int_t^\tau r(s)ds}\,d\tau. \tag{9.17}$$

It is clear that, starting from an initial nonnegative stock of bonds $b_0 \geq 0$, (9.16) cannot be met if the fiscal deficit $g(t) - T(t)$ is sustained at a positive level indefinitely. This point was made by McCallum (1984) in discussing the feasibility of bond financing. On the other hand, a fixed specified time path of government expenditures can be sustained by any combination of bond financing and lump-sum tax financing that satisfies the constraint

$$\int_0^\infty g(\tau)e^{-\int_0^\tau r(s)ds}\,d\tau = \int_0^\infty T(\tau)e^{-\int_0^\tau r(s)ds}\,d\tau - b_0. \qquad (9.18)$$

Clearly there are an infinite number of possible time paths for lump-sum taxes $T(t)$ that will enable (9.18) to be met. But at some point on each of them, the government must run a surplus in order to pay for previous deficits as well as the interest on its initial outstanding stock of government debt, b_0.

Alternative forms of fiscal policy are sustainable. For example, suppose the government maintains $g(t) - T(t) + r(t)b(t) \equiv \bar{d}$. This involves continuously adjusting $g(t)$ or $T(t)$ in order to accomodate the changing interest payments.[9] In this case the stock of bonds increases at the linear rate $b(t) = b_0 + \bar{d}t$, and the transverality condition (9.3f) is certainly met.

Equation (9.18) can also be viewed as a statement of Ricardian Equivalence. The macrodynamic equilibrium summarized in Section 9.2 depends upon the time path of government expenditure $g(t)$ but is independent of the time path of lump-sum taxes or the initial stock of government debt. It therefore follows that for a given time path of government spending, the real macroeconomic equilibrium is independent of whether the expenditure is financed through lump-sum taxation or by debt. This is because debt financing merely postpones taxes, and the timing of taxes does not affect the individual's lifetime budget constraint, on which these decisions are based. The private agent knows that if, having chosen a time path for expenditures, the government decides to reduce taxes today, thereby increasing its current deficit, it will have to raise taxes at some later date in order to meet its intertemporal budget constraint. Thus, for example, a decrease in taxes equal to dT_0, say, will require an increase equal to $dT_0 e^{\int_0^\tau r(s)ds}$ at time τ in the future in order for (9.18) to hold. In present value terms these are exactly offsetting, leaving the behavior of the private agent completely unaffected.

The Ricardian Equivalence proposition is a striking one and has generated a great deal of analysis, both theoretical and empirical, over the years; see Barro (1974, 1989), Bernheim (1987), and others. The conditions under which it holds are stringent, though they are satisfied in the present analysis. They include the following: (i) the economy consists of an infinitely lived representative agent; (ii) perfect capital markets exist; (iii) taxes are nondistortionary; (iv) future taxes are foreseen; (v) the time path of government purchases is given. It is well known that if any of these conditions ceases to hold, the indifference between debt and taxes no longer applies. For example, by impacting on incentives, the timing of distortionary taxes is important. The robustness of the proposition has been investigated at length and is discussed by Barro (1989).

The important aspect of the intertemporal budget constraint from the present point of view is that it emphasizes the *intertemporal constraints* on a feasible fiscal policy. This was not an aspect that was addressed in the earlier models, which were not based on intertemporal optimization. For the remainder of this chapter, we shall not concern ourselves with the financing side of the government's expenditures, aside from requiring it to be intertemporally feasible and achieved through the appropriate choice of lump-sum taxes.

It is also possible and instructive to view the intertemporal budget constraint from the viewpoint of the representative agent. To do this, we consider the flow budget constraint (9.1b). Applying Euler's theorem to the production function, we may write

$$F(k,l) = wl + rk, \tag{9.19}$$

which simply expresses the standard proposition that under constant returns to scale the value of output equals the value of income, where $w = F_l = $ real wage and $r = F_k = $ returns to capital. Substituting (9.19) into (9.1c) and defining real wealth $W \equiv k + b$, the agent's flow budget constraint becomes

$$\dot{W}(t) = r(t)W(t) + w(t)l(t) - C(t) - T(t). \tag{9.1b'}$$

Integrating this equation and applying the transversality conditions (9.3e), (9.3f) leads to the agent's intertemporal budget constraint

$$b_0 + k_0 + \int_0^\infty [w(\tau)l(\tau) - T(\tau)]e^{-\int_0^\tau r(s)ds}\, d\tau = \int_0^\infty c(\tau)e^{-\int_0^\tau r(s)ds}\, d\tau, \tag{9.20}$$

which is analogous to the government's intertemporal budget constraint (9.18). The initial stocks of assets $b_0 + k_0$ are his initial *nonhuman wealth*, and the integral of discounted future earnings from labor less taxes measures his *human wealth*. Thus, we observe that <u>the present discounted value of consumption is constrained by the sum of the agent's human and nonhuman wealth.</u>

In the case where utility is represented by an additively separable logarithmic utility function in consumption and labor, $[\eta(c) = -1]$, (9.8) can be solved to yield

$$c(\tau) = c_0 e^{\int_0^\tau r(s)ds - \beta\tau}.$$

Substituting this expression into the right-hand side of (9.20) yields

$$c_0 = \beta \left[b_0 + k_0 + \int_0^\infty [w(\tau)l(\tau) - T(\tau)]e^{-\int_0^\tau r(s)ds}\, d\tau \right]. \tag{9.21}$$

This relationship, which in fact holds at all points of time, asserts that for the logarithmic utility function, current consumption is proportional to the sum of nonhuman and human wealth, with the proportionality factor being the agent's rate of time preference. This equation makes clear from the viewpoint of the representative agent how it is the present discounted value of lump-sum taxes that is relevant to his consumption decision and how any changing in the timing of taxes, which leaves the present value of his tax liabilities unchanged, has no impact on his behavior.

9.4   Unanticipated Permanent Increase in Government Expenditure

To illustrate the behavior of the model, the next two sections are devoted to the analysis of an increase in government expenditure.

Steady-State Effects

Since the analysis is based on the assumption of perfect foresight, the transitional adjustment is determined in part by expectations of the steady state. It is therefore convenient to begin with a consideration of the long-run equilibrium effects of a change in government expenditure. In describing such a policy change it is important to spell out whether it is permanent or temporary, on the one hand, and anticipated or unanticipated, on the other. This section is devoted to the most commonly studied shock, namely an unanticipated permanent increase. The effects of such a change on $\tilde{k}$ and $\tilde{\lambda}$ are obtained by differentiating the steady-state system (9.10a) and (9.10b) with respect to g.

Performing this operation, the long-run effects on $\tilde{k}$ and $\tilde{\lambda}$ can be expressed in the form[10]

$$\frac{d\tilde{k}}{dg} = \frac{\omega_{22}}{\Delta} - \frac{U_c F_l^2 F_{kl}}{D\Delta} \frac{d}{dg}\left[\frac{U_c}{U_l}\right], \tag{9.22a}$$

$$\frac{d\tilde{\lambda}}{dg} = -\frac{\omega_{21}}{\Delta} + \frac{(\tilde{y}/\tilde{l})F_{kk}(U_{cl}U_{cg} - U_{cc}U_{lg})}{D\Delta} + \frac{F_{kk}(U_{ll}U_{cg} - U_{cl}U_{lg})}{D\Delta} \tag{9.22b}$$

where $D \equiv U_{cc}(U_{ll} + \tilde{\lambda}F_{ll}) - U_{cl}^2 > 0$. The expressions in equations (9.22) have been broken down into two sets of effects. The first, given by the first term on the right-hand side of each equation, represents what we shall refer to as the *resource withdrawal effect*, or *wealth effect*, of an increase in g. This reflects the fact that resources expropriated by the government are not available to the private sector. Secondly, the remaining terms represent the effect of an increase in g through its impact on the subjective evaluations of private consumption and work effort.

The resource withdrawal effect tends to raise both the long-run capital stock and the marginal utility of wealth. The intuition behind this result is that because government consumption expenditure is not directly productive and does not affect the marginal physical productivities of capital and labor, an increase in g, with its accompanying increase in taxes over time, leads to a fall in private wealth and consumption, and consequently to a less than proportional increase in output, $d\tilde{y}/dg < 1$. The marginal utility of wealth therefore rises, inducing agents to increase their supply of labor. During the transition to the new steady state, the increase in labor supply raises the marginal physical product of capital above its (unchanged) long-run equilibrium value, thereby encouraging capital accumulation until the capital-labor ratio is restored to its original fixed equilibrium level, implied by (9.10b).

The degree of capital accumulation is, however, also influenced by the effect that a long-run increase in government consumption expenditure has on the marginal rate of substitution between private consumption and work effort, U_c/U_l. As is evident from equation (9.22a), a rise in g that lowers the marginal rate of substitution will reinforce the wealth effect just described and thus provide an extra impetus to capital accumulation. This is due to the fact that a decline in the marginal rate of substitution encourages greater employment, and therefore capital accumulation, by increasing the amount of private consumption that a representative agent is willing to forgo to obtain a reduction in work effort. By contrast, if a rise in g raises the marginal rate of substitution—that is, if it lowers the amount of private consumption that the agent is willing to forgo to obtain a reduction in work effort—then greater employment is discouraged and the positive impact of the resource withdrawal effect on capital accumulation is lessened.

Several special cases, in which the expressions in (9.22a) and (9.22b) simplify, should be noted.

Additively Separable Utility Function

If, as is commonly assumed, the utility function is additively separable in c, l, on the one hand, and in g on the other (i.e., it is of the form $U(c, l) + V(g)$), there is no interaction between public consumption expenditure and private decisions, in which case these expressions reduce to just the resource withdrawal effect.

Multiplicatively Separable Utility Function

Second, the response of the capital stock continues to be given by the resource withdrawal effect if the utility function is multiplicatively separable in c, l, and in g (i.e., it is of the form $U(c, l)V(g)$); however, in this case the response of the marginal utility of wealth will now depend upon the interaction of government consumption expenditure with the private consumption and labor supply decisions.

Private and Public Goods Substitutes

An important special case familiar from the work of Barro (1981), (1989), Aschauer (1988), Christiano and Eichenbaum (1992), and others, treats preferences over consumption as preferences over a composite of private and government consumption expenditures; that is, $U(c, l, g) \equiv U(c + \alpha g, l)$, $0 < \alpha < 1$, where the parameter α measures the degree of substitutability between private and public consumption. Under this formulation, equations (9.22) reduce to

$$\frac{d\tilde{k}}{dg} = \frac{\omega_{22}(1 - \alpha)}{\Delta},$$

(9.23a)

$$\frac{d\tilde{\lambda}}{dg} = -\frac{\omega_{21}(1 - \alpha)}{\Delta}.$$

(9.23b)

These expressions consist simply of the resource withdrawal effect scaled by $(1 - \alpha)$. Clearly, the more closely public expenditure substitutes for private (i.e., the greater is α), the smaller is the decline in wealth and in the increase in its marginal utility. As a result, the long-run increase in work effort and thus in the capital stock is mitigated. In the limiting case where $\alpha = 1$, the agent views the public and private goods as perfect substitutes. Any increase in the former leads to a one-for-one reduction in the latter; there is complete "crowding out," and the increase in government expenditure has no effect on the accumulation of capital stock or growth. It merely leads to an instantaneous compensating switch in consumption, leaving everything else unchanged.

Using (9.22), one can readily derive the following expressions for the long-run effects of the fiscal expansion on employment, output, and consumption:

$$\frac{1}{\tilde{l}}\frac{d\tilde{l}}{dg} = \frac{1}{\tilde{y}}\frac{d\tilde{y}}{dg} = \frac{1}{\tilde{k}}\frac{d\tilde{k}}{dg},$$

(9.24a)

$$\frac{d\tilde{c}}{dg} = -\frac{F_{kk}}{D\Delta}\left\{(U_{ll} + F_l U_{cl}) - \left(\frac{\tilde{y}}{\tilde{l}}\right)U_c F_l^2 \frac{d}{dg}\left(\frac{U_c}{U_l}\right)\right\}.$$

(9.24b)

The proportionality in the long-run adjustment of capital, employment, and output is a consequence of the linear homogeneity of the production function, together with the fact that the equilibrium capital-labor ratio is independent of g. Like the capital stock, the response in private consumption reflects both the resource withdrawal effect and a substitution effect. The former is negative, reflecting the fact that additional government expenditure crowds out private consumption. The latter is negative, reinforcing the former if the increase in government expenditure lowers the marginal rate of substitution between consumption and work effort U_c/U_l.

Dynamic Adjustment

Figure 9.2 illustrates the transitional adjustment of k and λ following a permanent increase in government consumption expenditure. We will describe the case in which both $\tilde{k}$ and $\tilde{\lambda}$ rise in the steady state.[11] Let

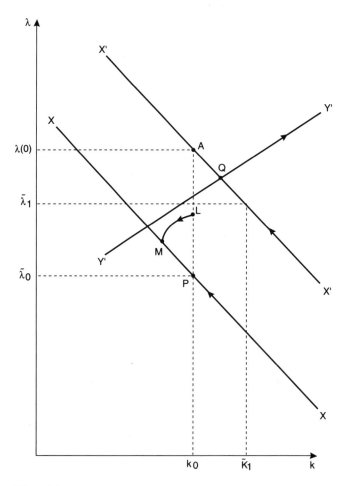

Figure 9.2
Increase in government consumption expenditure

the economy begin at point P, which represents initial equilibrium. The stable, XX, and unstable, YY, adjustment loci, described by equations (9.13b) and (9.13c) respectively, intersect at this point. (To avoid cluttering Figure 9.2, the unstable locus corresponding to the initial equilibrium is not drawn.) A permanent increase in g will increase the long-run capital stock $\tilde{k}$, and marginal utility of wealth, $\tilde{\lambda}$, and cause the economy to settle eventually at a point such as Q, lying to the northeast of the initial equilibrium. The corresponding movement in the stable and unstable adjustment paths are to $X'X'$ and $Y'Y'$, respectively. Since the capital stock is constrained to adjust continuously, the entire burden of the initial response to a permanent increase in g falls on the marginal utility of wealth, which jumps positively at $t = 0$. This movement in $\lambda(0)$ takes the economy immediately to point A on the new stable locus $X'X'$. The rise in $\lambda(0)$ reflects the fall in private wealth that the increase in government consumption expenditure brings about. In the short run, the higher marginal utility of wealth leads to a reduction in both consumption and leisure. The short-run increase in labor supply raises the marginal physical product of capital, thereby raising the interest rate.

At the same time, when the marginal physical product of capital is raised above its (unchanged) steady-state equilibrium level, the rate of return on consumption must rise in order for the arbitrage condition (9.3c) to be met, and this requires $\dot{\lambda} < 0$. In addition, the higher marginal utility generates additional positive savings equal to $(F_l l_\lambda - c_\lambda) d\lambda(0)$. This exceeds the additional government expenditure so that the economy begins to accumulate capital.[12] The declining marginal utility, accompanied by the accumulating capital stock along the transitional path, is represented by a movement along the path AQ on the stable path $X'X'$ to the new steady state at Q. These two effects together contribute to a declining marginal physical product, so that during the transition the short-term interest rate converges back to its long-run equilibrium.

A more formal analysis of the short-run responses can be obtained by analyzing the initial adjustments of the short-run equilibrium, as described in Section 9.2. For example, the short-run responses of consumption and employment can be determined by differentiating (9.6a), (9.6b), and are given by the following expressions:

$$\frac{dc(0)}{dg} = \frac{\partial c}{\partial \lambda} \frac{\partial \lambda(0)}{\partial g} + \frac{\partial c}{\partial g}, \tag{9.25a}$$

$$\frac{dl(0)}{dg} = \frac{\partial l}{\partial \lambda} \frac{\partial \lambda(0)}{\partial g} + \frac{\partial l}{\partial g}. \tag{9.25b}$$

These equations describe the two influences of the expansion in government expenditure that impact on the short-run response of consumption and employment. The first are the direct effects, given by the partial derivatives reported in (9.7c). In addition, the initial increase in the marginal utility of wealth leads to a substitution of labor for consumption given by the first terms on the right-hand side of these two equations. The formal expression for $\partial\lambda(0)/\partial g$ is obtained by differentiating (9.13b), namely,

$$\frac{\partial\lambda(0)}{\partial g} = \frac{d\tilde{\lambda}}{dg} + \left(\frac{\tilde{\lambda}\omega_{21}}{\tilde{\lambda}\omega_{22} + \mu_1}\right)\frac{d\tilde{k}}{dg} \tag{9.13b'}$$

where, in obtaining this expression, we are assuming that the capital stock remains fixed instantaneously. Combining (9.13b') with (9.23) and the expressions in (9.7) enables us to derive the short-run responses appearing in (9.25), and also their effects on the short-run level of output, the rate of capital accumulation, and so on. The present circumstance is sufficiently straightforward that such a formal analysis is not really necessary, though we will have occasion to pursue this approach further in Chapter 11.

We have seen the crucial role played by the labor supply in the dynamic adjustment of the economy. We now consider what would happen if employment were held fixed. The steady-state optimality condition (9.10b) now implies that the steady-state capital stock, $\tilde{k}$, (rather than the capital-labor ratio), is determined by the fixed rate of time preference, β, and is independent of g. It therefore follows from the dynamic solution (9.13a) that the capital stock and output remain constant at all points of time. *There are no transitional dynamics.* Instead, the economy moves instantaneously to its new steady state, in which g crowds out private consumption one for one.[13] In terms of Figure 9.2, the economy immediately jumps from P on XX to A on $X'X'$ and stays there. The unstable locus $Y'Y'$ consequently passes through point A rather than point Q.[14] The fall in private wealth is greater if employment is fixed, because the representative agent has no opportunity to offset through capital accumulation the impact of greater government expenditure.

Welfare Effects

Thus far, we have been describing the macroeconomic adjustments of the economy to a fiscal expansion. These operate in a variety of directions and are obviously important. But what is ultimately of overriding significance is the effect on economic welfare. To address this question, we must introduce some welfare criterion. One of the attractive aspects of the intertemporal optimizing framework we are currently employing is that the welfare of the representative agent serves as a natural criterion for this purpose. With all agents being assumed to be identical, the welfare implications for the individuals are then extrapolated to represent those of the aggregate economy. In this section, therefore, we shall consider the effects of fiscal policy from this standpoint. However, welfare (as measured by utility) changes over time, as the capital stock accumulates. Indeed, we shall see how an increase in government expenditure involves an intertemporal trade-off in welfare. We will therefore consider both the time path of the instantaneous utility level of the representative agent, as well as the overall accumulated welfare over his infinite planning horizon.

The instantaneous level of utility of the representative agent at time $t, Z(t)$, is specified to be

$$Z(t) = U(c(t), l(t), g) \tag{9.26}$$

with the overall level of utility over the agent's infinite planning horizon being the discounted value of (9.26), namely

$$W = \int_0^\infty U(c, l, g) e^{-\beta t}\, dt = \int_0^\infty Z(t) e^{-\beta t}\, dt. \tag{9.27}$$

We will analyze the effects of government expenditure on both $Z(t)$ and W when c and l satisfy the equilibrium paths described by (9.6a), (9.6b), and k and λ evolve in accordance with (9.13a), (9.13b).

We begin by differentiating $Z(t)$ with respect to g:

$$\frac{dZ(t)}{dg} = U_c \frac{dc(t)}{dg} + U_l \frac{dl(t)}{dg} + U_g. \tag{9.28}$$

Using the optimality condition for work effort, (9.3b), (9.28) becomes

$$\frac{dZ(t)}{dg} = U_c \left[\frac{dc(t)}{dg} - F_l \frac{dl(t)}{dg} \right] + U_g. \tag{9.29}$$

Next, differentiating the product market equilibrium condition (9.5) with respect to g yields

$$F_k \frac{dk(t)}{dg} + F_l \frac{dl(t)}{dg} = \frac{dc(t)}{dg} + \frac{d\dot{k}(t)}{dg} + 1, \tag{9.30}$$

enabling us to rewrite (9.30) as

$$\frac{dZ(t)}{dg} = U_g(c, l, g) - U_c(c, l, g) + U_c \left[F_k \frac{dk(t)}{dg} - \frac{d\dot{k}(t)}{dg} \right]. \tag{9.31}$$

Using equation (9.13a), describing the (linearized) equilibrium adjustment path followed by the capital stock, (9.31) can be linearly approximated by the expression[15]

$$\frac{dZ(t)}{dg} = U_g - U_c + U_c[F_k(1 - e^{\mu_1 t}) + \mu_1 e^{\mu_1 t}]\frac{d\tilde{k}}{dg}. \tag{9.31'}$$

Examination of (9.31) or (9.31') reveals that the effect of an increase in either form of government expenditure on the level of instantaneous welfare consists of two distinct components. The first consists of what we shall call the *direct crowding-out effect*. This reflects the fact that as the government increases its expenditures, it takes away resources from the private sector, thereby reducing private consumption one for one. This is measured by the difference between the marginal utility of public consumption and that of the forgone private consumption.[16]

The second component of the effect of g on $Z(t)$ consists of intertemporal influences that operate through the response of the capital stock, which we shall term the *intertemporal capital accumulation effect*. From (9.31) this effect is seen to depend upon how the government expenditure influences the rate of capital accumulation, and how, in turn, the resulting change in the accumulated capital stock impacts on output and therefore on private consumption. It is important to observe that these two influences have conflicting effects on the agent's instantaneous level of welfare. This is because, by taking away resources from current consumption, a given level of investment lowers instantaneous welfare, whereas accumulated capital raises output, thereby increasing consumption and welfare over time. The intertemporal trade-off can be demonstrated most easily by evaluating (9.31'), for the initial impacts, $Z(0)$, and the steady-state impacts, $\tilde{Z}$, of government expenditure. The resulting expressions are

$$\frac{dZ(0)}{dg} = U_g - U_c + U_c\mu_1\frac{d\tilde{k}}{dg}; \qquad \frac{d\tilde{Z}}{dg} = U_g - U_c + U_cF_k\frac{d\tilde{k}}{dg}. \tag{9.32}$$

Leaving aside the crowding-out terms, which scale the adjustment paths of welfare, equations (9.32) show that to the extent that government expenditure induces an instantaneous rise in investment, $d\dot{k}(0)/dg = -\mu_1 d\tilde{k}/dg$, and consequently a reduction in private consumption, its short-run effect is welfare deteriorating. Such a deterioration in welfare is, however, eventually reversed as the accumulation of capital over time raises output, which makes possible greater private consumption, and this is welfare improving in the long run. Indeed, provided government expenditure raises the long-run capital stock, the time derivative of (9.31') shows that these fiscal policies lead to continuous improvements in welfare as the economy moves toward its steady state.

A linear approximation to the overall level of welfare, represented by equation (9.27), can be obtained by observing that along the equilibrium path, $Z(t)$ can be approximated by

$$Z(t) = \tilde{Z} + (Z(0) - \tilde{Z})e^{\mu_1 t}. \tag{9.33}$$

Substitution of (9.33) into (9.27), and integrating, yields

$$W = \frac{\tilde{Z}}{\beta} + \frac{(Z(0) - \tilde{Z})}{\beta - \mu_1}. \tag{9.34}$$

The first term of (9.34) is the capitalized value of instantaneous welfare, $Z(t)$, evaluated at the steady state. It is the level of welfare that would result if the steady state were attained instantaneously. The remaining term reflects the adjustment to this, due to the fact that the steady state is reached only gradually along the transitional path.

Differentiating (9.34) with respect to g and using equations (9.32), we derive the following expression:

$$\frac{dW}{dg} = \frac{1}{\beta}\left[U_g - U_c\left(1 - F_k\frac{d\tilde{k}}{dg}\right)\right] - U_c\left(\frac{\mu_1 - F_k}{\mu_1 - \beta}\right)\frac{d\tilde{k}}{dg}. \tag{9.35}$$

Noting further that in the neighborhood of equilibrium $F_k = \beta$, equation (9.35) reduces to

$$\frac{dW}{dg} = \frac{1}{\beta}(U_g - U_c). \tag{9.36}$$

Thus the net effect of a permanent increase in g on total welfare is simply the crowding-out effect. Since this lasts indefinitely, it is just equal to the instantaneous effect, capitalized, at β. Most importantly, the influence of the path of $Z(t)$ on total welfare nets out to zero, with the capitalized gains to W stemming from the steady-state increase in the capital stock, $U_c d\tilde{k}/dg$, precisely offsetting the discounted losses from the consumption forgone along the transitional path.

It is important to stress that the essentially static relationship (9.36) represents the welfare effects both along the dynamic transitional path and in the new steady state. Indeed, the total negative effect of a permanent increase in government expenditure on private activity, $-U_c/\beta$, can be decomposed into $-U_c d\tilde{k}/dg$ and $-(U_c/\beta)(1 - \beta d\tilde{k}/dg)$, which represent, respectively, these two phases.

Setting equation (9.36) equal to zero enables us to find the conditions for which g is at its welfare-maximizing level. This is determined by

$$\frac{\partial U(c, l, g)}{\partial g} = \frac{\partial U(c, l, g)}{\partial c}. \tag{9.37}$$

In other words, the marginal utility of public consumption should be equated to the marginal utility of private consumption. The optimality condition (9.37) is precisely the same as that obtained previously in

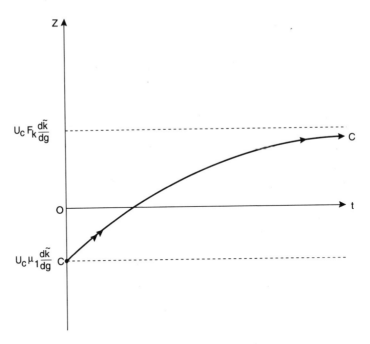

Figure 9.3
Time path for instantaneous utility permanent increase in government expenditure $U_c = U_g$

models that abstract from capital accumulation (see, e.g., Turnovsky and Brock 1980). But there is a crucial difference. The Turnovsky-Brock analysis abstracts from capital accumulation so that there are no transitional dynamics; the economy is always in steady-state equilibrium. By contrast, in the present analysis, the dynamics are gradual, and although optimal levels of government expenditure are determined by similar static conditions, they nevertheless incorporate the welfare along the transitional path.

The analysis of this section is summarized in Figure 9.3, which depicts the path for $Z(t)$ generated by a permanent increase in g. We illustrate the case in which g is set optimally so that the crowding-out effect is set to zero, so that the overall intertemporal welfare effect is normalized to zero.

9.5   Temporary Increase in Government Expenditure

Dynamic Adjustment

This section briefly discusses the dynamic adjustment to a temporary increase in government expenditure. Because the increase is temporary, in the long run the economy returns to its initial steady state, so that what is of interest is the nature of the transitional adjustment path. In analyzing such a temporary increase, care must be taken to specify its nature precisely. Specifically, we assume that at time 0, say, the government increases its expenditure, which it maintains at the higher level until time $T > 0$, say, when it is restored to its original level. We assume that the agents understand at the outset (time 0) that the change is only for the duration of the period $(0, T)$, so that at time T, when the expenditure is cut back, it has been fully anticipated, so that there is no surprise. The only new piece of information occurs at time 0, when the temporary increase is first put into effect, and this is the only time at which the shadow value of wealth undergoes a discrete jump. The fiscal expansion can thus be characterized as being a priori temporary. This is in contrast to a situation where what is initially considered to be a permanent increase at time 0 in fact turns out to be only temporary, when at time T, say, agents learn that government expenditure is being reduced to its initial level. This type of fiscal expansion can be characterized as being ex post temporary. There are two instances when new information is acquired, a time 0 and at time T, and each of these is associated with a jump in the shadow value of wealth, giving rise to a different transitional adjustment path.

The formal solutions underlying this analysis are presented in the Appendix to this chapter. These solutions are, however, derived under the assumption of fixed employment. This restriction has been imposed primarily in order obtain tractable expressions for the solutions of k and λ for temporary increases in g, which—because of the generality of the steady-state responses, equations (9.22), derived under endogenous employment—would otherwise be difficult to attain.

The dynamic adjustment path is illustrated in Figure 9.2. When the temporary increase in g commences, the stable and unstable loci shift to $X'X'$, $Y'Y'$, respectively. This system passes through point A, which denotes the steady state the economy would attain, and would attain instantaneously, under fixed employment, if the rise in g were permanent. The stable and unstable loci remain in this position for the duration of this fiscal expansion, at the end of which they revert to their original locations, XX, YY, intersecting once again at point P.

As in the case of a permanent increase in g, the adjustment begins with a positive jump in the marginal utility of wealth. However, because the economy discounts the effects of a temporary increase in g, the rise in $\lambda(0)$ falls short of its response in the permanent case. This leaves the economy at some point, such as L, between P and A in Figure 9.2. The height of the jump in $\lambda(0)$ increases with duration T of the temporary disturbance, reflecting the fact that the more prolonged is the increase in g the more closely its initial impact on the economy corresponds to that of a permanent increase. During the period that g is its higher level, the economy traverses the unstable path LM, reaches the original stable locus XX at point M, and from there, after g has been restored to its initial level, moves down XX to its steady-state equilibrium at point P.

For a temporary increase in g, the economy, in contrast to its response in the permanent case (with fixed employment), does not immediately reach its steady state, and thus its adjustment is characterized by transitional dynamics. The source of this distinction is the difference in the behavior of $\lambda(0)$ for the two cases. Since the increase in $\lambda(0)$ in the temporary case is less than its increase in the permanent case, the initial fall in private consumption is likewise less than its fall in the permanent case. Recalling that a permanent rise in g immediately crowds out an equal amount of private consumption, the fact that the initial decline in private consumption falls short of this in the temporary case implies that with the capital stock, and consequently output, given at $t = 0$, the initial response of the economy is disinvestment, $\dot{k}(0) < 0$. In other words, the agent, discounting the negative wealth effect of a temporary increase in g, but also lacking the opportunity to counteract it with greater work effort, enjoys a greater level of private consumption by decumulating capital. As long as g is at its higher level, the capital stock continues to decline. This raises its marginal physical product above its long-run value β and requires, consistent with the optimality condition (9.3c), that $\dot{\lambda} < 0$ during this period. The return of g to its original level reverses the prior decumulation of capital. Investment is immediately crowded in at $t = T$ and is followed by a rise in the capital stock. We illustrate this by the movement of the economy down the stable locus XX. Until $k = k_0$ at P, the marginal physical product of capital remains above β, and hence $\dot{\lambda} < 0$ for $t > T$.

Welfare Effects

As before, the agent's welfare is evaluated both along the transitional path and over the agent's infinite planning horizon, although the derivations of $Z(t)$ and W for temporary fiscal policies are relegated to the Appendix. In Figure 9.4, the path $RS-UV$ depicts the response of $Z(t)$ to a temporary rise in g, and is drawn under the assumption of fixed employment. In describing the evolution of $Z(t)$, we also assume, as we did previously in deriving Figure 9.3, that the fiscal policy authorities set g at its welfare-maximizing level. Notably, the same welfare-maximizing conditions apply for both temporary and permanent fiscal expansions, due to the fact (shown in the Appendix) that the effect on overall welfare of a

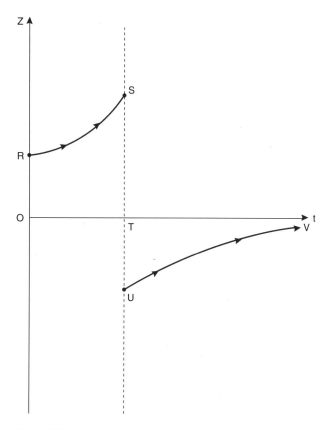

Figure 9.4
Time path for instantaneous utility (for fixed employment) temporary increase in government expenditure $U_c = U_g$

temporary increase in g is simply the crowding-out effect discounted over a finite, rather than an infinite, horizon.

As is evident from Figure 9.4, a temporary increase in g leads to an initial rise in $Z(0)$, to a point such as R. This result occurs because a temporary increase in g leads to disinvestment, which, as noted above, prevents private consumption from being crowded out one for one with the increase in g. This means that, with g set optimally, the welfare loss associated with the lower private consumption is exceeded by the welfare gains associated with greater g, and consequently that $Z(0)$ takes a positive jump. Further welfare gains, illustrated by the movement of $Z(t)$ along the locus RS, accrue to the agent while g remains temporarily at its higher level. Welfare continues to improve, due to the fact that the decumulation of capital that occurs during this period permits the agent to enjoy greater private consumption.

At time T, when government expenditure is restored to its original level, $Z(T)$ takes a discrete jump from a point such as S above its initial value, to a point such as U below its initial value. This is because government consumption expenditure generates direct welfare benefits for the household, so that its contraction at time T causes a fall in welfare—a fall, moreover, that takes $Z(T)$ below its initial level, due to the fact that private consumption at the close of the fiscal expansion is less than its initial value.[17] After g returns to its original level, the agent receives the welfare benefits that accrue from the subsequent rise in the capital stock and output. We depict this by the movement of $Z(t)$ along UV, the path that takes welfare back to its original steady-state level.

9.6   Government Expenditure as a Productive Input

Traditionally, macroeconomics has treated government expenditure as representing a demand shock. In the conventional Keynesian models this is done through an outward shift in the *IS* curve, without specifying what the nature of the public expenditure is. In the representative agent model, we have assumed that government expenditure is on a consumption good, which we have permitted to interact with the private consumption good in the utility of the agent. In practice, government expenditure is on a variety of goods, some of which are intended to enhance the productive capacity in the economy. Expenditures on such things as roads, bridges, education, and job training are of this type and can be broadly classified as expenditure on infrastructure. Recently, several economists have begun to recognize this and to incorporate this form of government expenditure into their macro models. See, for example, Aschauer (1988, 1989), Barro (1989), and Turnovsky and Fisher (1995). This section briefly describes such an extension to the model.

The modification this extension entails is to the production function, which we now write as

$$y = F(k, l, h) \tag{9.38}$$

where h now denotes government expenditure on infrastructure. We now assume that output exhibits positive, but diminishing, marginal physical product in all three factors, so that $F_k > 0$, $F_l > 0$, $F_h > 0$, $F_{kk} < 0$, $F_{ll} < 0$, $F_{hh} < 0$. In addition, it is assumed to be linearly homogeneous in the two private factors, so that $F_{kk}F_{ll} - F_{kl}^2 = 0$; $F_{kl} > 0$, as before. At this point, we do not impose restrictions on the cross partial derivatives F_{kh}, F_{lh}, so that, in principle, government expenditure on infrastructure can be either a complement to or a substitute for capital or labor in production. However, we should observe that the assumption of the homogeneity of the production function in the two private factors of production implies the constraint $F_h = F_{kh}k + F_{lh}l$, so that the assumption $F_h > 0$ implies that both $F_{kh} < 0$ and $F_{lh} < 0$ cannot hold simultaneously.

Differences in the specification of government expenditure on production can be found in the literature. For example, Aschauer (1988) does not restrict the sign of the marginal productivity of public inputs, with $F_h < 0$ referring to productivity-inhibiting government regulations. This contrasts with our focus on F_h as reflecting infrastructure, with its presumed positive effects on total output. Second, our assumption of linear homogeneity in the two private factors views infrastructure as providing economies of scale in production. An alternative assumption, discussed by Aschauer (1989), is that the production function is linearly homogeneous in all three factors of production. The choice between these two alternative specifications makes little difference, as long as one assumes $F_{kl} > 0$ in the alternative specification. One further point is that almost all of the existing literature formulates government productive expenditure as a flow, paralleling the traditional treatment of government consumption expenditure. An alternative, and arguably more realistic, formulation would be to specify it as a capital stock, which accumulates along with the private productive capital stock. This would introduce an additional dynamically adjusting state variable into the analysis, thereby increasing the dimensionality of the dynamics correspondingly.

The dynamic structure of this modified model as described in Section 9.2 remains unchanged from before. The difference is that the expenditure on infrastructure represents a supply shock, rather than a demand shock, as before. Detailed analysis of the dynamic adjustments in response to both temporary and permanent changes in infrastructure, as well as their effects on welfare, is provided by Turnovsky and Fisher (1995). To give some notion of the differences that arise, we shall focus on the steady-state responses of capital and the marginal utility of wealth. Parallel to (9.10), these are now determined by

$$F(\tilde{k}, l(\tilde{\lambda}, \tilde{k}, h), h) = c(\tilde{\lambda}, \tilde{k}, h) + h, \tag{9.39a}$$

$$F_k(\tilde{k}, l(\tilde{\lambda}, \tilde{k}, h), h) = \beta. \tag{9.39b}$$

In writing these equations, we have assumed that government consumption expenditure $g = 0$. These two equations highlight the differences in how the two types of government expenditure impact on the economy. From the product market condition (9.39a) one observes that h has both a demand effect (like g) and a supply effect, through its impact on production. One further important difference, apparent from (9.39b), is that the long-run capital-labor ratio does depend upon h. Thus, even if the labor supply is fixed, an increase in government expenditure on infrastructure will affect the long-run capital stock, and in so doing will generate a nondegenerate dynamic adjustment path.

Differentiating (9.39a), (9.39b) with respect to h, the following effects on the long-run capital stock and the marginal utility of wealth are obtained:

$$\frac{d\tilde{k}}{dh} = \frac{\omega_{22}(1 - F_h)}{\Delta} + \frac{\omega_{12}F_{kh}}{D\Delta} + \frac{\tilde{\lambda}F_{kl}F_{lh}}{D\Delta} \tag{9.40a}$$

$$\frac{d\tilde{\lambda}}{dh} = -\frac{\omega_{21}(1 - F_h)}{\Delta} - \frac{(F_k + \tilde{\lambda}l_\lambda F_{kl})F_{kh}}{\Delta} - \frac{(U_{cc}(\tilde{y}/\tilde{l}) + U_{cl})\tilde{\lambda}F_{kk}F_{lh}}{D\Delta}. \tag{9.40b}$$

Parallel to (9.22), these expressions consist of two effects. The first is the net withdrawal effect, which is analogous to that in (9.22), though it is now scaled by the factor $(1 - F_h)$. Second, the remaining terms reflect the impact of directly productive government expenditure on the marginal physical products of capital and labor.

An interesting feature of these expressions is that, to the extent that infrastructure contributes directly to the production of output (i.e., $F_h > 0$), it tends to have a contractionary effect on the long-run capital stock. This is because as long as expenditure on infrastructure contributes positively to output, it provides resource augmentation rather than resource withdrawal. By the argument presented in Section 9.4, it therefore generates a positive wealth effect, causing a decline in the marginal utility of wealth, thereby reducing the labor supply and the long-run stock of capital. Taking this into account, the factor $(1 - F_h)$, which measures the direct resource cost of a unit of infrastructure expenditure relative to its direct benefit, thus measures the *net* resource withdrawal effect. Comparing this with the corresponding expression in (9.22a), it is seen that this component is less expansionary than in the case of a rise in g. In fact, it will be contractionary if $F_h > 1$.

In the borderline case where the marginal physical product of infrastructure just equals its resource cost $F_h = 1$, the net resource withdrawal effect is zero. Infrastructure expenditure then affects $\tilde{k}$ and $\tilde{\lambda}$ only through its influence on the marginal products of capital and labor. This is an interesting case, because if infrastructure expenditure is complementary to the private factors of production, $F_{kh} > 0$, $F_{lh} > 0$, then work effort and capital accumulation will be encouraged, despite the fact that this influence also tends to raise private wealth and hence to lower $\tilde{\lambda}$. The fiscal expenditure multiplier is now greater than unity, $d\tilde{y}/dh > 1$. Thus, under these circumstances, an increase in h raises private wealth and crowds in private consumption in the long run. Indeed, the rise in private wealth also tends to encourage the consumption of the other private good, leisure. This provides an offsetting influence to the effect of $F_{lh} > 0$ and implies that the long-run response of employment to a rise in h is ambiguous. These effects, and other aspects of the model, including a detailed comparison with the effects of government consumption expenditure, are analyzed by Turnovsky and Fisher (1995).

9.7   Term Structure of Interest Rates

The government bonds we have introduced are short-term bonds, having a fixed price and being continually rolled over. The term structure of interest rates has long been of interest to macroeconomists, both as an empirical issue and a mechanism for the transmission of macroeconomic policy. Chapter 7 introduced the term structure into a simple *IS-LM* framework to illustrate the methods of saddlepoint analysis. It is straightforward to introduce a term structure into the present intertemporal optimizing framework.

We now introduce a second bond, which is taken to be a perpetuity (consol) paying a constant real coupon of unity. We shall denote the price of the bonds by P and its yield by R, so that $R = 1/P$. In the absence of risk and with efficient financial markets, the instantaneous rates of return on the short-term and long-term bonds must be equal, being related by

$$r = \frac{1 + \dot{P}}{P} = R - \frac{\dot{R}}{R}. \tag{9.41}$$

While this equation is being posited directly, it can in fact be readily derived from the optimality conditions when the representative agent holds both long and short bonds. The main point is that the short-run rate of return on the long bond consists of the rate of capital gain $\dot{P}/P$, in addition to the coupon $1/P$.

Combining (9.41) with (9.6c), the evolution of the long-term rate can be expressed in terms of k and λ, by the differential equation

$$\dot{R} = R[R - F_k(k, l(\lambda, k, g))]. \tag{9.42}$$

Solving (9.41) or, equivalently, (9.42), the long-term rate may be expressed in the form

$$R(t) = \frac{1}{\displaystyle\int_t^\infty e^{-\int_t^s r(t')dt'}\,ds} = \frac{1}{\displaystyle\int_t^\infty e^{-\int_t^s F_k(k,l(\lambda,k))dt'}\,ds}. \tag{9.43}$$

This relationship expresses the current long-term rate in terms of future (expected) short-term rates, which themselves are dependent upon the future time paths of k and λ. It is evident from (9.6d) and (9.42) that in long-run equilibirum, the short-term rate, the long-term rate, and the marginal physcial product of capital, all must converge to the (exogenously given) rate of time discount; that is, $\tilde{r} = \tilde{R} = \tilde{F}_k = \beta$. By defining

$$P(t,s) \equiv e^{-\int_t^s r(t')dt'} \tag{9.44}$$

to be the price at time t of a zero-coupon bond that matures at time s, the first equality in (9.43) may be written as

$$R(t) = \frac{1}{\displaystyle\int_t^\infty P(t,s)\,ds}, \tag{9.43'}$$

which can be readily transformed to[18]

$$R(t) = \frac{\displaystyle\int_t^\infty r(s)P(t,s)\,ds}{\displaystyle\int_t^\infty P(t,s)\,ds}. \tag{9.43''}$$

Equation (9.43″) expresses the current long rate $R(t)$ as a weighted average of the correctly forecast future short-term rates, though the weights themselves depend upon the short-term rates through the pricing of the zero-coupon bonds.[19]

We have now provided the additional structure necessary to analyze the effects of various shocks on the both the short-term and long-term interest rates. Linear approximations to the dynamic time paths can be obtained by linearizing (9.6c) and (9.42) about the respective steady-state equilibria:

$$r = \tilde{r} + \omega_{21}(k - \tilde{k}) + \omega_{22}(\lambda - \tilde{\lambda}) \tag{9.45a}$$

$$\dot{R} = \beta[(R - \tilde{R}) - \omega_{21}(k - \tilde{k}) - \omega_{22}(\lambda - \tilde{\lambda})] \tag{9.45b}$$

By substituting the appropriate solutions for k and λ into (9.45a), (9.45b), the solution for the short-term rate can be found directly, and the solution for the long-term rate can be determined by solving the resulting first-order differential equation. Fisher and Turnovsky (1992) use this approach to analyze the effects of various types of permanent, temporary,

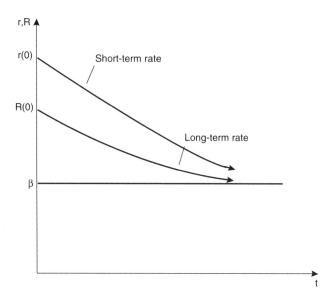

Figure 9.5
Time paths of interest rates following unanticipated permanent fiscal expansion

and expected future fiscal shocks on the term structure. This is a direct application of the methods discussed in Sections 9.4 and 9.5.

Figure 9.5 illustrates the responses of the short and long rates to the simplest shock, namely an unanticipated permanent increase in government expenditure. This is very straightforward. We have previously observed that a permanent expansion in government expenditure leads to an immediate increase in the short-term interest rate, which then declines continuously over time as it returns to its unchanged long-run equilibrium. With the long-term rate $R(t)$ being a discounted sum of uniformly declining future short-term rates, it must initially increase by some smaller amount than the initial increase in the short-term rate. And since this must be true at all points of time, the long rate must always lie below the short rates. With $R(t) < r(t)$, the long rate must also decline over time in order to generate the capital gains, which will compensate for its lower yield and thus ensure that the arbitrage condition (9.41) is satisfied.

The basic intertemporal macroeconomic equilibrium derived in Section 9.2 determines the time path for the short-term (instantaneous) interest rate. The long-term rate we have just introduced was not essential to the equilibrium, but is determined by it in accordance with the arbitrage condition (9.41). In fact, once the time path for the short-term interest rate is obtained, it is possible to derive the entire yield curve for bonds having arbitrary terms to maturity. This can be most conveniently done

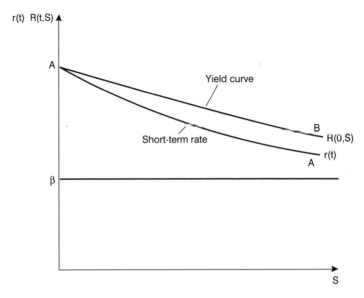

Figure 9.6
Response of yield curve to unanticipated permanent fiscal expansion

in the case where the bonds are zero-coupon discount bonds paying a unit of output at their maturity date.

Recalling the definition (9.44), the price of a discount bond at time t, maturing S periods in the future (at time $t + S$), is

$$P(t, t + S) \equiv e^{-\int_t^{t+S} r(t')dt'} \qquad \text{or} \qquad \ln(P(t, t + S)) = -\int_t^{t+S} r(t')\,dt'.$$

With the bond yielding no coupon, the instantaneous rate of return is just $(\partial/\partial t)\ln(P(t, t + S)) = r(t)$. The yield to maturity, $R(t, S)$, is therefore

$$R(t, S) = \frac{1}{S} \int_t^{t+S} r(t')\,dt' \tag{9.46}$$

where $R(t, 0) = r(t)$. The entire yield curve at time t is then described by $R(t, S)$, considered as a function of the term to maturity, S.

Equation (9.46) indicates that the interest rate on a discount bond in a perfect foresight model such as this is simply the average of the time path of the short-term rate taken over the term of the bond. Having derived the time paths for the short-term rate in response to various types of fiscal expansions, we can use (9.46) to determine the corresponding behavior of the yield curve over time. Explicit solutions for $R(t, S)$ can be obtained by substituting the solutions for $r(t)$ and integrating. However, this is not really necessary, because one can generally infer the shape of the yield curve for a particular shock by "smoothing" the time path of the short-term rate over the appropriate time horizon; see Fisher and Turnovsky (1992).

Figure 9.6 derives the response of the yield curve to the simplest case of an unanticipated permanent fiscal expansion. The line AA is the time path for the short-term rate and declines over time, as we have discussed. The locus AB is the yield curve $R(0, S)$, at the initial time $t = 0$, when the fiscal expansion first occurs. Since $R(0, 0) = r(0)$, it starts out at the point A. Also, since at each term S it is an average of the future declining short-term rates, $R(0, S)$ declines as the term to maturity increases, though at a slower rate than does $r(t)$. The yield curve therefore lies everywhere above $r(t)$. Over time, as $r(t)$ declines, the yield curve $R(t, S)$ shifts down. It is always downward sloping, although it flattens out as, over time, all rates converge to their common long-run equilibrium value β.

9.8   Money in the Utility Function

Several approaches can be found in the literature for introducing the role of money into the intertemporal optimizing framework. These are intended to capture, if only imperfectly, the three key roles of money in the economy: (i) its role as a store of wealth; (ii) its role as the medium of exchange; and (iii) its role as a unit of account. One of the important contributions of the overlapping generations model, which we are not discussing in this volume, was that it enabled money to be introduced in a fundamental way, as a means of transferring assets between generations. This was the significance of Samuelson's (1958) seminal contribution, and a simple two-period model is discussed by Blanchard and Fischer (1989).

Within the infinite horizon model two approaches have been adopted to incorporate the role of money. The first is to incorporate its role as a medium of exchange through the so-called cash-in-advance constraint, originally proposed by Clower (1967). The basic idea here is to formulate the role that money plays in carrying out transactions by the explicit introduction of a "transactions technology." One difficulty with this approach is that the introduction of the various constraints, embodying the role played by money in transactions, can very quickly become intractable. Accordingly, a shorthand alternative to this, originally due to Sidrauski (1967b) is to introduce money directly into the utility function. By facilitating transactions, money is assumed to yield a direct utility to the representative agent that is not associated with other assets such as bonds, which yield only an indirect utility through the income they generate and the consumption goods they enable the agent to purchase.

The introduction of money into the utility function has often been the subject of severe criticism by monetary economists, who have argued that one should model the process of transactions explicitly. Recently, however, this criticism appears to have been muted, at least in part because of an important paper by Feenstra (1986), who studied the relationship between the two approaches. He showed that under certain regularity conditions, the maximization problem with money, modeled by means of a cash-in-advance constraint, may be equivalent to a maximization problem with money in the utility function. Thus the procedure of introducing money directly into the utility function seems to be generally viewed as being an acceptable approximation. This is the approach we shall discuss in this section.

The role of money in the portfolio allocation decision cannot really be dealt with adequately until risk is introduced, as we shall do in Part IV. However, we may observe that, by assigning it direct utility, we are ensuring that even though as an asset money is dominated by others in terms of the return it yields, it still performs a positive economic role.

The Sidrauski Model

We now augment the model of Section 9.2 by introducing money. The representative agent is thus assumed to maximize the utility function

$$\int_0^\infty U(c, l, g, m)e^{-\beta t}\, dt, \tag{9.47a}$$

where $m \equiv M/P$ denotes real money balances, M denotes the nominal stock of money, and P denotes the price level. We assume that money balances yield positive marginal utility, though only up to some level m^*, say, which denotes some "satiation level." The idea is that although holding money yields utility, it also involves costs, such as security precautions, which eventually dominate when balances held are too high. All other variables are as defined before, and the utility function remains concave in all of its arguments.

The maximization is subject to the budget constraint, which it is convenient to express initially in nominal terms in the form:

$$Pc + P\dot{k} + \dot{M} + \dot{B} = PF(k, l) + iB + PT \tag{9.47b}$$

where B = nominal stock of government bonds, i = nominal interest rate. For simplicity we drop government expenditure on infrastructure and assume that the government bonds are short bonds, denominated in nominal terms. Differentiating the quantities $m \equiv M/P$, $b \equiv B/P$, with respect to time, the budget constraint can be transformed to real terms as follows:

$$c + \dot{k} + \dot{m} + \dot{b} = F(k,l) + rb - pm - T \tag{9.47b$'$}$$

where now $p \equiv \dot{P}/P =$ the rate of inflation, $r = i - p$ is the real rate of interest. By writing the equation in this way, we see that inflation acts like a tax on those assets (money and bonds) that are denominated in nominal terms, and the quantity pm is frequently referred to as being the "inflation tax" on real money balances. The initial conditions are now

$$k(0) = k_0, \qquad M(0) = M_0, \qquad B(0) = B_0. \tag{9.47c}$$

The initial real stocks of money and bonds are endogenously determined through an initial jump in the price level, associated with the attainment of the equilibrium.

Performing the optimization leads to the following equilibrium:

$$U_c(c, l, g, m) = \lambda \tag{9.48a}$$

$$U_l(c, l, g, m) = -\lambda F_l(k, l) \tag{9.48b}$$

$$\frac{U_m(c, l, g, m)}{\lambda} - p = r = F_k(k, l) \tag{9.48c}$$

$$\frac{\dot{\lambda}}{\lambda} = \beta - F_k(k, l). \tag{9.48d}$$

These conditions are analogous to (9.3a)–(9.3d); the only difference is that we now have an additional static optimality condition, (9.48c), relating the real return on money to that on income-earning assets. It asserts that the real rate of return on money, which equals the utility from the consumption of money services less its real return as an income-earning asset $(-p)$, must equal the real rate of return on bonds and capital. In the absence of direct utility benefits, money would be dominated by the other assets and would not be held in equilibrium. There are also now three transversality conditions, one for each of the assets, k, b, and m.

To complete the description of the system, we must specify product market equilibrium and make some assumption about government policy. The former remains specified by (9.5). With respect to government policy, the Sidrauski model assumes that the monetary policy is specified by the constant nominal monetary growth rule

$$\frac{\dot{M}}{M} = \phi,$$

implying that the real rate of monetary growth is

$$\dot{m} = m(\phi - p). \tag{9.48e}$$

Having specified monetary policy, we assume that the government's intertemporal budget constraint is met through a combination of debt policy and lump-sum taxes, the details of which, given Ricardian Equivalence, need not concern us.

Superneutrality of Money

Much of the analysis of the Sidrauski model has revolved around the question of whether or not real variables such as the capital stock and consumption are dependent upon the rate of monetary growth. If they are independent, then money is said to be *superneutral* and the equilibrium is essentially unchanged from the previous real model. Whether or not money is superneutral depends upon certain critical aspects of the model, and to address the issue further, it is convenient to write down the equilibrium structure.

The three static equilibrium conditions (9.48a)–(9.48c) may in general be solved for c, l, p in the form

$$c = c(\lambda, k, m; g) \tag{9.49a}$$

$$l = l(\lambda, k, m; g) \tag{9.49b}$$

$$p = p(\lambda, k, m; g). \tag{9.49c}$$

Next, substituting these solutions into the product market equilibrium condition (9.5), the dynamic efficiency equation, (9.48d), and the monetary growth equation, (9.48e), lead to

$$\dot{k} = F(k, l(\lambda, k, m; g)) - c(\lambda, k, m; g) - g \tag{9.50a}$$

$$\dot{\lambda} = \lambda[\beta - F_k(k, l(\lambda, k, m; g))] \tag{9.50b}$$

$$\dot{m} = m[\phi - p(\lambda, k, m; g)]. \tag{9.50c}$$

This is a third-order system, which in general has one stable and two unstable roots, so that the stable path is described by a first-order system. One difference from the real model is that, in general, the transverality conditions do not suffice to rule out all unstable paths, as was the case previously. We do not propose to discuss the dynamics in any detail. This is straightforward to do, and the interested reader is referred to Fischer (1979b) and Turnovsky (1987a), where this is carried out for variants of the model.

It is apparent that, in general, the rate of monetary growth ϕ will influence both the time path of capital and its steady-state equilibrium level. The original Sidrauski model assumed that the supply of labor is inelastic. This means that the optimality condition (9.48b) does not apply, so that labor is given exogenously rather than by (9.49b). This is one case in which money is superneutral with respect to the steady-state stock of capital and consumption. To see this, consider (9.50a) and (9.50b), which in steady state become

$$F(\tilde{k}) - \tilde{c} - g = 0 \tag{9.50a'}$$

$$F_k(\tilde{k}) = \beta. \tag{9.50b'}$$

The marginal product of capital condition (9.50b') determines the long-run capital stock, which with fixed labor determines output, and hence consumption; all are independent of the rate of monetary growth. However, with the labor supply fixed, the monetary growth rate will still have temporary effects on the rate of capital accumulation, as long as real money balances are not additively separable from consumption in utility; see Fischer (1979b).

Superneutrality, both during the transition and in the long run, occurs if the utility function is additively separable in consumption and labor decisions, on the one hand, and real money balances, on the other, that is, if utility is of the form $U(c, l, g) + W(m)$. In this case we can easily show $c = c(\lambda, k; g)$, $l = l(\lambda, k; g)$, and $p = p(m)$, and the dynamics of (9.50) become

$$\dot{k} = F(k, l(\lambda, k; g)) - c(\lambda, k; g) - g \tag{9.50a''}$$

$$\dot{\lambda} = \lambda[\beta - F_k(k, l(\lambda, k; g))] \tag{9.50b''}$$

$$\dot{m} = m[\phi - p(m)]. \tag{9.50c''}$$

The system essentially dichotomizes. The first two equations describe the real part of the system and are identical to (9.9a) and (9.9b) discussed previously. The behavior of real money balances is then given by (9.50c''). Because of the concavity of the utility function in real money balances, the eigenvalue describing the decoupled equation (9.50c'') is unstable (i.e., $p'(m) < 0$), and in order for the system to remain stable we require $p = \phi$. This is accomplished by an initial jump in the price level. Money plays no essential role under these conditions.

Under the weaker condition where the utility function is of the multiplicatively separable form $U(c, l, g)W(m)$, one can show that money is again superneutral in the long run, though not during the transition. We should also observe that, using the cash-in-advance approach, Stockman (1981) has shown the long-run capital stock to be inversely related to the rate of monetary growth. This is perfectly consistent with the superneutrality results we have been discussing. Indeed, the relationship between the two approaches considered by Feenstra (1986) demonstrated that the equivalent specification of money in the utility function generally implies *nonseparability* of money and consumption, when we have seen that money is nonsuperneutral.

Optimal Monetary Growth Rate

The question of the optimal monetary growth rate has been discussed at length in the literature from a variety of perspectives. Early authors such as Bailey (1956) and Friedman (1971) have analyzed the question from the viewpoint of the maximization of government revenue from the inflation tax and have shown how the optimal monetary growth rate depends upon the interest elasticity of the demand for money. Tobin (1968) focused on the consumption-maximizing monetary growth rate and showed that this involves driving the economy to the golden rule capital-labor ratio. Most important is the work that originated with Bailey (1956) and Friedman (1969), which examines the optimal growth of money within a utility-maximizing framework. The most significant proposition to emerge from this last approach is the so-called Friedman full liquidity rule, which concludes that the optimal rate of monetary growth is to contract the money supply at a rate equal to the rate of consumer time preference.

The present analysis is identified most closely with this last approach. In the case that the utility function is additively separable in real money balances, so that the monetary growth rate is superneutral, the time path of consumption and labor is independent of the monetary growth rate. The only impact of ϕ on welfare is through its impact on real money balances. The utility of real money balances can therefore be maximized independently, and this is achieved by driving m to the satiation level m^*, defined by $U_m(m^*) = 0$. As we noted above, in the additively separable case this is attained instantaneously through an initial jump in the price level. From (9.48c) we see that this implies setting the nominal interest rate to zero. If, further, the real part of the system is in steady-state equilibrium, (9.48d) implies $\phi + \beta = 0$, or, equivalently, that the monetary growth rate should be contracted a rate equal to the rate of time preference. This is precisely the Friedman rule.

When the assumption of the additively separable utility function is relaxed, the monetary growth rate does impact on consumption and employment and thus on the entire utility function. Turnovsky and Brock (1980) derived the optimal monetary growth rate in the case where labor is the only productive input and showed that in general the optimal monetary growth rate should be set in accordance with what they call a "distorted" Friedman rule, which takes into account the interaction between real money balances and the marginal rate of substitution between labor and consumption. They show that if $\partial(U_l/U_c)/\partial m < 0$, then m should be set below the satiation level m^*, so that $U_m > 0$ and $\phi > -\beta$. The marginal rate of substitution of labor for consumption will be increased; workers will be willing to supply more labor, output will increase, and the utility from consumption will rise correspondingly. The opposite is true if $\partial(U_l/U_c)/\partial m > 0$. In effect, the optimal monetary policy calls for balancing off the direct utility of money against its indirect effects, which result from its interaction with consumption and leisure. This type of analysis can be extended to the present framework, which includes capital, although the welfare analysis will involve an intertemporal dimension along the lines discussed in Section 9.4.[20]

9.9 Population Growth

Thus far, we have assumed that the population is fixed, although the supply of labor is elastic. This assumption will be maintained throughout the remainder of Part III. However, the original Ramsey model and much of the literature—in particular, the growth literature—that has evolved from it makes the assumption that the supply of labor grows inelastically over time. This section briefly discusses the consequences of that specification.

Population—N, say—which with full employment is also labor supply, is assumed to grow at a steady rate n, so that $\dot{N}/N = n$. Assuming there is no government, the basic intertemporal optimization problem, analogous to (9.1), is to maximize

$$\int_0^\infty U(c)e^{-\beta t}\,dt \qquad U_c > 0, \quad U_{cc} < 0 \tag{9.51a}$$

subject to the budget constraint

$$c + \dot{k} = f(k) - nk \qquad f'(k) > 0, \quad f''(k) < 0 \tag{9.51b}$$

and initial conditions

$$k(0) = k_0 \tag{9.51c}$$

where c is now per capita consumption and k denotes the capital-labor ratio. The dynamics of the model proceeds in per capita terms. Analytically, this is reflected in the term nk appearing in the accumulation equation, which describes the fact that part of the output produced at each instant of time must be devoted to equipping the growing labor force if the per capita stock of capital is to be maintained. This remains true in steady state, implying that steady-state output cannot all be consumed as it was in (9.10a). In effect, all rates of return are now net of population growth, which plays much the same role as the rate of inflation or the rate of depreciation on capital (which has been taken to be zero).

Two key concepts associated with this model are (i) the golden rule of capital accumulation and (ii) the modified golden rule. The first of these, described by the condition

$$f'(k) = n, \tag{9.52a}$$

is the condition that maximizes the steady-state consumption per capita. It was originally introduced by Phelps (1961). Under the assumptions that we have introduced on the production function, this equality cannot be satisfied for a finite value of the capital-labor ratio in the absence of positive growth.

The main welfare significance of the golden rule is that it defines a value of the capital-labor ratio beyond which it is not Pareto optimal to accumulate capital. That is, everyone could be made better off from the viewpoint of maximizing steady-state consumption by reducing the capital stock. This is because the capital stock has become so large that its marginal productivity is outweighed by the amount of output necessary to provide the growing population with the existing capital-labor ratio. Such an economy has overaccumulated capital and is said to be dynamically inefficient.

The modified golden rule is described by

$$f'(k) = \beta + n. \tag{9.52b}$$

This relationship asserts that the long-run capital-labor ratio—and hence the marginal physical product of capital, and the real interest rate—is determined by the sum of the rate of time preference plus the rate of population growth. This is the analogue to the steady-state condition (9.10b), to which it reduces, when the population is constant, and indeed it plays the same important role in the context of a growing population.

For an extensive discussion of these models, the reader is referred to Blanchard and Fischer (1989, chapter 2). However, we should point out that with a steadily growing population, the constancy of the long-run equilibrium capital-labor ratio implies that the long-run equilibrium growth rate of the economy is tied to the growth rate of labor. In most cases this is taken to be exogenous, or determined by long-term demographical or technological factors. It is clearly unlikely to be responsive to any of the conventional instruments of macroeconomic policy.

The basic Ramsey model with growing population has the same characteristics with respect to issues such as Ricardian Equivalence as does the stationary population model exposited in previous sections. Recently, Blanchard (1985) and Weil (1989) have developed alternative but not unrelated approaches aimed at breaking the neutrality of debt and lump-sum taxes. Blanchard does so by assuming that each agent faces a constant probability of death, independent of age, with the probability being described by an exponential distribution. This introduces a distinction between the discount rate of the private agent, who takes account of his probability of death, and the social rate of discount, which, because the economy is ongoing and the assets of the deceased are redistributed to the living, does not take this into account. In the Blanchard model, each agent dies with probability one, and it is therefore often referred to as a finite horizon model. Weil introduces infinitely lived families, which are introduced over time and are therefore overlapping. Both models offer very elegant analyses, although in order to achieve this, the authors are forced to introduce special assumptions regarding the form of the utility function.

9.10   The Representative Agent Model: Some Caveats

This chapter has presented an exposition of the basic representative agent model and used it to derive a dynamic macroeconomic equilibrium. To illustrate the behavior of the model, we have analyzed the effects of various kinds of government expenditure shocks, although the same analytical methods can be applied to other types of disturbances, and indeed will be in the chapters to follow. We have also introduced some simple extensions to the model, including the addition of a term structure of interest rates and the inclusion of money via the utility services it provides.

The representative agent framework has many desirable features and for this reason has become the standard tool for modern macroeconomic dynamics. Apart from its tractability, it possesses two particularly attractive attributes. First, it is based on rational behavior, embodying forward-looking agents, so that the full intertemporal dimensions of economic events, both inherited from the past and looking into the future, have an impact on the evolution of the economy. In particular, the intertemporal budget constraints confronting the agents in the economy are brought to the fore. Second, because it is based on utility maximization, it provides a natural framework for analyzing the welfare implications of macroeconomic policy shocks or other structural changes, which many would argue are of ultimate concern. But despite its almost uniform adoption as the standard macroeconomic paradigm, it is viewed much more critically by economic theorists; see for example, Kirman (1992).

The conventional assumption made in macroeconomic theory is that there are many identical agents, whose behavior is summarized by that of the "representative agent." Under certain conditions, such as homothetic utility functions and linearity, aggregation may well be possible and the representative agent may indeed be a reliable representation of the individuals (see, e.g., Lewbel 1989). But such an ideal situation is not generally the case, and Kirman has articulated the difficulties that may arise when those conditions are not met. For instance , he discusses a simple example where, even though the representative agent makes the same choices as the aggregate of choices of the individuals in the economy, the preferences of that agent may be opposite to those of the individuals he represents. In such a case, the representative agent model is a poor indicator for welfare analysis.

A second line of criticism revolves around the empirical evidence supporting the representative agent approach. Empirical studies are frequently based upon the estimation of stochastic Euler equations, derived as first-order optimality conditions, which are the stochastic analogues to the arbitrage relationships such as (9.6d). These conditions are frequently rejected by the data. As Kirman points out, this raises the question of what is being rejected. Is it the particular relationship that is being tested, or the representation of the economy by a single optimizing agent? He argues that one should be focusing on heterogeneous agents and that some of the paradoxes identified in the data may be the result of the special framework and might be resolved by extending the economy to different agents with different preferences. The same observation has been made by others (see, e.g., Summers 1991; Lippi 1988).

Do these criticisms mean that we should abandon the representative agent model? Kirman seems to suggest that we should, although that view seems extreme. There are several points in support of the representative agent model. First, it is important to have some tightly structured framework to serve as a benchmark in order to avoid, or at least reduce, the arbitrariness of the earlier macroeconomic models. For this purpose, the representative agent model is the best available at the present time, although the extent to which it succeeds in eliminating the arbitrariness associated with macroeconomic modeling should be kept in perspective. A good deal of arbitrariness still remains and is inevitable in any theorizing. The nature of the objective function, the range of decision variables, the specification of the constraints, the market structure—all are often taken for granted, yet all are typically subject to choice. Second, few could deny that by emphasizing the importance of intertemporal budget constraints the representative agent model has enhanced our understanding of intertemporal issues in macroeconomics. Furthermore, although simple examples can be constructed wherein the preferences of the aggregate might misrepresent those of diverse agents, it has not been established that this is a significant problem in the analysis of macroeconomic shocks.

Suppose, for example, that instead of one agent, we had introduced several heterogeneous agents, each having utility and production functions with the same qualitative properties as those we have assumed. Suppose also that the behavioral relationships for each agent were obtained by intertemporal optimization and all aggregate variables such as output, etc., were obtained by summing over the individuals. Unless the agents have very different characteristics, it seems reasonable to expect that each individual will respond to *aggregate* macroeconomic shocks hitting the general economy in more or less the same qualitative way, (though not necessarily identically), in which case the aggregate should behave in a qualitatively similar way as well. If the government increases national defense expenditure, say, raising taxes in general on all individuals, then it seems reasonable that if they are all governed by the same general behavioral characteristics, they will all respond in the same qualitative way, which will then be reflected in aggregate behavior. Simulation analysis by McKibbin (1991) using large econometric models based on intertemporal optimization of representative agents, supports this general view. He finds the differences in the aggregate response to macroeconomic disturbances to be rather small between the procedures of (i) having a single representative agent and (ii) aggregating over the responses of a number of individual agents from a disaggregated version of the model.

Any model employed as widely as the representative agent model begins to take on a life of its own and to be accepted almost as an axiom. It is therefore useful to remind ourselves periodically of its limitations. Despite the criticisms that have been made, we feel that the representative agent model provides a useful framework that offers a good deal of insight, and we shall continue to develop it further. It should be viewed as a step in the continuing development and understanding of macroeconomic theory, just as the models discussed in Parts I and II have been. Over time, models become superseded, and indeed the extension to heterogeneous agents seems like a promising avenue for future research.

Appendix

Solutions for the Capital Stock and the Marginal Utility of Wealth for Temporary Fiscal Shocks

As noted in the text, temporary shocks are analyzed under the simplifying assumption of fixed employment. In this case, the linearized dynamic system simplifies to

$$\begin{pmatrix} \dot{k} \\ \dot{\lambda} \end{pmatrix} = \begin{pmatrix} F_k & -1/U_{cc} \\ -\tilde{\lambda}F_{kk} & 0 \end{pmatrix} \begin{pmatrix} k - \tilde{k} \\ \lambda - \tilde{\lambda} \end{pmatrix}. \qquad (9.A.1)$$

We assume that the system starts at $t = 0$ in steady state with $\tilde{k} = k_0$, $\tilde{\lambda} = \tilde{\lambda}_0$. For temporary fiscal expansions, the solutions for k and λ are over two phases: (i) the initial phase of higher government expenditure; and (ii) and the subsequent phase in which government expenditure has returned to its original level. The shift in the steady state occurs at time T. The steady states corresponding to these two phases are $(\tilde{k}_1, \tilde{\lambda}_1)$ and $(k_0, \tilde{\lambda}_0)$, respectively. The general solution to (9.A.1) is

$0 \le t \le T$:

$$k = \tilde{k}_1 + A_1 e^{\mu_1 t} + A_2 e^{\mu_2 t} \qquad (9.A.2a)$$

$$\lambda = \tilde{\lambda}_1 + U_{cc}\mu_2 A_1 e^{\mu_1 t} + U_{cc}\mu_1 A_2 e^{\mu_2 t}. \qquad (9.A.2b)$$

$t \ge T$:

$$k = k_0 + A_1' e^{\mu_1 t} + A_2' e^{\mu_2 t} \qquad (9.A.3a)$$

$$\lambda = \tilde{\lambda}_0 + U_{cc}\mu_2 A_1' e^{\mu_1 t} + U_{cc}\mu_1 A_2' e^{\mu_2 t}. \qquad (9.A.3b)$$

where $\mu_1 < 0$, $\mu_2 > 0$ are the eigenvalues. There are four arbitrary constants, A_1, A_2, A_1', and A_2', to be determined. These are evaluated as follows:

i. In order for the transversality condition (9.3e) to be met, we require

$A_2' = 0.$

ii. We assume that the capital stock adjusts continuously from its initial given stock k_0, that is,

$k_0 = \tilde{k}_1 + A_1 + A_2.$

iii. The time paths for k and λ are assumed to be continuous for $t > 0$. In particular, at time $t = T$, the solutions for (9.A.2) and (9.A.3) must coincide, yielding two more equations for A_1, A_2, and A_1', which together with (i) and (ii) uniquely determine the solution.

We now use this method to determine the solutions for k and λ for temporary increases in g. As discussed in Section 9.3, $\tilde{k}_1 = k_0$ for a temporary increase in g. The solutions are as follows:

$0 \le t \le T$:

$$k = k_0 + \frac{e^{-\mu_2 T}[e^{\mu_2 t} - e^{\mu_1 t}](\tilde{\lambda}_1 - \tilde{\lambda}_0)}{U_{cc}(\mu_2 - \mu_1)} \qquad (9.A.4a)$$

$$\lambda = \tilde{\lambda}_1 + \frac{e^{-\mu_2 T}[\mu_1 e^{\mu_2 t} - \mu_2 e^{\mu_1 t}](\tilde{\lambda}_1 - \tilde{\lambda}_0)}{(\mu_2 - \mu_1)}. \tag{9.A.4b}$$

$t \geq T$:

$$k = k_0 + \frac{[e^{-\mu_1 T} - e^{-\mu_2 T}]e^{\mu_1 t}(\tilde{\lambda}_1 - \tilde{\lambda}_0)}{U_{cc}(\mu_2 - \mu_1)} \tag{9.A.5a}$$

$$\lambda = \tilde{\lambda}_0 + \frac{\mu_2[e^{-\mu_1 T} - e^{-\mu_2 T}]e^{\mu_1 t}(\tilde{\lambda}_1 - \tilde{\lambda}_0)}{(\mu_2 - \mu_1)}. \tag{9.A.5b}$$

Solutions for Welfare for Temporary Fiscal Shocks

For the fixed employment case, instantaneous welfare Z is given by

$$Z = U(c(\lambda, g), g). \tag{9.A.6}$$

To obtain expressions for Z for temporary increases in government consumption and infrastructure expenditure, we take a first-order approximation to (9.A.6):

$$Z \approx u(c(\tilde{\lambda}, g), g) + \frac{U_c(\lambda - \tilde{\lambda})}{U_{cc}}, \tag{9.A.7}$$

and substitute the solution $(\lambda - \tilde{\lambda})$ for the appropriate phase.

Using equations (9.A.4b) and (9.A.5b), we determine the following solutions for Z for a temporary increase in g_c:

$0 \leq t \leq T$:

$$Z = U(c(\tilde{\lambda}_1, \hat{g}), \hat{g}) + \frac{U_c[\mu_1 e^{\mu_2 t} - \mu_2 e^{\mu_1 t}](\tilde{\lambda}_1 - \tilde{\lambda}_0)}{U_{cc}}; \tag{9.A.8}$$

$t \geq T$:

$$Z = U(\tilde{\lambda}_0, g), g) + \frac{U_c[\mu_1 e^{-\mu_2 T} - \mu_2 e^{-\mu_1 T}]e^{\mu_1 t}(\tilde{\lambda}_1 - \tilde{\lambda}_0)}{U_{cc}(\mu_2 - \mu_1)}, \tag{9.A.9}$$

where $\hat{g}$ denotes the temporarily greater level of government consumption expenditure.

To evaluate the impact of temporary fiscal policies on overall welfare W, we take the discounted value of the two phases of Z over an infinite horizon:

$$W = \int_0^T Z(t)e^{-\beta t}\, dt + \int_T^\infty Z(t)e^{-\beta t}\, dt. \tag{9.A.10}$$

Substituting (9.A.8) and (9.A.9) into (9.A.10) yields the overall welfare generated by a temporary increase in g:

$$W = \frac{U(c(\tilde{\lambda}_1, \hat{g}), \hat{g})[1 - e^{-\beta T}]}{\beta} + \frac{U(c(\tilde{\lambda}_0, g), g)e^{-\beta T}}{\beta}. \tag{9.A.11}$$

Differentiating (9.A.11) with respect to $\hat{g}$ yields

$$\frac{dW}{dg} = -\frac{(U_g - U_c)[1 - e^{-\beta T}]}{\beta} \frac{dW}{dg_c} = \frac{-(U_g - U_c)[1 - e^{-\beta T}]}{\beta}, \tag{9.A.12}$$

from which we see that the condition for welfare maximization is identical to that of a permanent fiscal expansion.

Notes

1. We adopt the following notation. Partial derivatives are indicated by corresponding subscripts. Time derivatives are denoted by dots. To conserve notation, we write the first, second, and cross partials of the utility function U with respect to g as U_g, U_{gg}, U_{cg}, and U_{lg}. Similarly, we write the first, second, and cross partials of the production function F with respect to h as F_h, F_{hh}, F_{kh}, and F_{lh}.

2. Linear homogeneity in the private factors, k, l, implies the following relationships: $F_{kk}F_{ll} = F_{kl}^2$, $F_{kk}F_l - F_{kl}F_k = F_{kk}(y/l)$; and $F_{kl}F_l - F_{ll}F_k = F_{kl}(y/l)$.

3. We do, however, impose the constraint $k \geq 0$.

4. This involves the use of a recursive utility function, specified by a difference equation.

5. The signs of ω_{11}, ω_{12}, and ω_{22} follow directly from the signs of the partial derivatives of the expressions appearing in (9.7a), (9.7b). The sign of ω_{21} is determined by substituting l_k and evaluating.

6. These properties are obtained by studying the roots of the characteristic equation to (9.11), $\mu^2 + (\omega_{11} + \tilde{\lambda}\omega_{22})\mu - \tilde{\lambda}(\omega_{11}\omega_{22} - \omega_{12}\omega_{21}) = 0$.

7. Because μ_1 is an eigenvalue of (9.11), $-\tilde{\lambda}\omega_{21}/(\tilde{\lambda}\omega_{22} + \mu_1) = (\mu_1 - \omega_{11})/\omega_{12}$, which implies that $\tilde{\lambda}\omega_{22} + \mu_1 < 0$.

8. This follows from the fact that $(\mu_2 - \omega_{11}) - |\mu_1 - \omega_{11}| = (\mu_1 + \mu_2 - 2\omega_{11}) = \beta - 2\omega_{11} < 0$.

9. Tobin and Buiter (1976) analyze the effects of an increase in government expenditure specified as inclusive of interest payments. McCallum (1984) also discusses how this form of government expenditure is sustainable.

10. In evaluating the following steady-state expressions, we make use of the constant returns to scale properties of the production function described in note 2.

11. In other words, we assume that even if the increase in g raises the marginal rate of substitution between private consumption and work effort, this negative influence on long-run capital accumulation is dominated by the positive influence of the resource withdrawal effect of greater government expenditure.

12. This can be shown as follows in the case where the utility function is additively separable in government consumption expenditure. From (9.13b),

$$[F_l l_\lambda - c_\lambda] d\lambda(0) = \omega_{12}\left[d\tilde{\lambda} - \left(\frac{\mu_1 - \omega_{11}}{\omega_{12}}\right)d\tilde{k} \right].$$

Recalling (9.22), this expression equals

$$\frac{\omega_{12}}{\omega_{11}\omega_{22} - \omega_{12}\omega_{21}}\left[-\omega_{21} - \left(\frac{\mu_1 - \omega_{11}}{\omega_{12}}\right)\omega_{22} \right]dg = \left[1 - \frac{\mu_1\omega_{22}}{\omega_{11}\omega_{22} - \omega_{12}\omega_{21}} \right]dg > dg.$$

13. The fixed employment analogue to (9.22b) is given by

$$\frac{d\tilde{\lambda}}{dg} = -(U_{cc} - U_{cg}).$$

To guarantee that $d\tilde{\lambda}/dg > 0$, we assume that if $U_{cg} < 0$, then $|U_{cc}| > |U_{cg}|$.

14. Note that, because the stable and unstable loci for the fixed employment case possess the identical slope characteristics to their variable employment counterparts, Figure 9.1 can be used to trace out the dynamic effects of government expenditure under both fixed and variable employment; see the Appendix to this chapter for details.

15. These expressions are only approximations in that all derivatives are evaluated at steady state.

16. Because (9.31′) is an approximation, $(U_g - U_c)$ is a constant term, evaluated at the steady state. This is in contrast to the corresponding term in the exact expression (9.31), which varies as the economy adjusts toward its steady state.

17. Private consumption itself takes a discrete jump at time T, because it too depends directly on the level of g. However, we can show that the jump in private consumption, unlike that of instantaneous welfare, is ambiguous and equal to U_{cg}/U_{cc}. Thus the jump in private consumption is positive if $U_{cg} < 0$ and negative if $U_{cg} > 0$. (See also Djajic 1987 for this result.) Even if the jump in private consumption is positive, $c(T)$ is still less than its value prior to the increase in g. This guarantees that the jump in $Z(T)$ is negative.

18. The equivalence between (9.43′) and (9.43″) can be obtained by integration by parts and utilizes the pricing relationship (9.44).

19. Recall that capital can be adjusted costlessly. The same recursive relationship between the short and long rates applies if the accumulation of capital is subject to a convex cost of adjustment function, as will be introduced in Chapter 11. In this case, one can show that the short-term interest rate is now determined as a discounted sum of expected future marginal physical products of capital. But once the short rates have been determined in this way, the long-term rate is then a discounted sum of all expected future short-term rates.

20. The question of the optimal rate of monetary growth has continued to receive the attention of economists; see, e.g., Kimbrough (1986) and Abel (1987) for more recent discussions.

10 Equilibrium in a Decentralized Economy with Distortionary Taxes and Inflation

10.1 Introduction

Most macroeconomic models treat the corporate sector in an overly simplistic manner. This is true of most textbook models, which typically assume that all private investment is financed through borrowing. Authors such as Tobin (1969) and Mussa (1976) introduced very crude stock markets into their models, doing so by identifying one unit of equity with one unit of physical capital. But this is typically not how real-world stock markets operate. Physical capital on the one hand, and the financial claims to these physical assets on the other, are distinct entities, the relative prices of which are continually changing over time, thereby invalidating the one-to-one relationship frequently assumed.

This criticism also applies to the models developed thus far in this volume. In some circumstances, the distinction between capital and the corresponding financial claims on that capital is not of great significance. Under the assumptions of a riskless world, freely adjustable capital, and the absence of distortionary taxes, equity claims can essentially be identified with the underlying capital stock, and these are the assumptions that we have in fact adopted.

But in the real world, agents are subject to various forms of distortionary taxes. Households pay personal income taxes, whereas firms pay corporate income taxes. Once this is recognized, a tax wedge is driven between the firms who produce the output and the households who own them, and it becomes necessary to distinguish between productive capital on the one hand, and the financial claims on the other. One can no longer consolidate the private sector into the "representative consumer-entrepreneur," as we did in Chapter 9, but instead must decentralize the private sector of the economy.

Accordingly, the objective of this chapter is to introduce a more complete corporate sector into the representative agent framework developed in the previous chapter. The approach we shall adopt draws upon the general equilibrium framework developed by Brock (1974, 1975) and extended by Brock and Turnovsky (1981). This approach includes the following key features: (i) All demand and supply functions of households and firms are derived from maximizing behavior as in Chapter 9; (ii) in a decentralized economy, expectations become important, and these are determined under the assumption of perfect foresight; (iii) all markets are continually cleared. Under these assumptions all expectations will be "self-fulfilling," and for this reason an equilibrium characterized by (i), (ii), and (iii) has been termed a "perfect foresight equilibrium."

The early Brock analysis essentially abstracted from the government and corporate sectors, and it is these aspects—particularly the latter—that we wish to emphasize in the present discussion. More specifically, we shall assume that the government can finance its deficits either by issuing bonds or by creating money. Likewise, firms can finance their investment plans either by issuing debt, by issuing equities, or by using retained earnings. We consider a riskless world with perfect foresight, so that government bonds and both types of private securities are all assumed to be mutually perfect substitutes. We shall introduce corporate and personal taxes on various forms of income, and these will assume an important role in the determination of the resulting equilibrium conditions. In introducing these taxes, we shall specify tax rates so as to approximate what one might consider to be a "real-world" tax structure (see, e.g., Feldstein, Green, and Sheshinski 1979; Auerbach 1979a).

The question of the impact of various corporate and personal taxes on the real and financial decisions of the firm has been widely discussed in the literature (see, e.g., Stiglitz 1973, 1974; Feldstein, Green, and Sheshinski 1979; Auerbach 1979a; Summers 1981; Sinn 1987). These taxes impinge on the firm primarily through the cost of capital, and hence it is important to make sure that this is defined appropriately. The approach taken in this chapter is to derive the appropriate cost of capital facing firms, and hence determining their decisions, taking into account the optimizing decisions of households.

The basic idea is that, beginning with the budget constraint for firms, a differential equation determining the market value of the firm may be derived. This equation is then solved to determine the cost of capital for firms, expressed in terms of market yields. Using the optimality conditions for consumers, these market yields can be translated to consumers' rate of return on consumption and the various tax parameters. The resulting objective function for the firm separates into two parts. First, financial decisions are made to minimize the cost of capital; second, having determined the minimized cost of capital, real productive decisions may then be made. The implications of this approach turn out to be fully consistent with the standard treatments of taxes in the corporate finance literature; see, for example, Modigliani and Miller (1958) and Miller (1977). Except in special cases when the debt-to-equity ratio of firms turns out to be indeterminate, the optimal financial structure will be a corner solution, consisting either of all-debt financing or of all-equity financing.

One of the important insights to emerge from this more complete macroeconomic model is that in the presence of taxes, when firms are faced with a well-defined choice of how to finance their investment, the effect of government policy is highly dependent upon the financing mode chosen by firms. To take one example, in the presence of distortionary taxes monetary growth ceases to be superneutral. However, whether an increase in the monetary growth is expansionary or contractionary depends upon whether the firm finds it optimal to employ debt financing or equity financing. The reason is that the inflation rate resulting from this form of monetary policy impacts on the cost of debt capital on the one hand, and of equity capital on the other, in directly opposite ways. Thus the disaggregation we are about to undertake and the more complete specification of the corporate sector is extremely important in our analysis of macroeconomic policy.

The careful construction of this decentralized intertemporal optimizing macroeconomic model involves a substantial amount of detail. Accordingly, we should indicate that our objective in this section is primarily to develop the framework, rather than to analyze the dynamics extensively . A brief outline of the dynamic properties is presented in Section 10.9, but a more detailed treatment will be undertaken in Chapter 11.

10.2   The Macroeconomic Structure

We consider a decentralized economy that contains three basic sectors— households, firms, and the government—all of which are interrelated through their respective budget constraints. We shall consider these sectors in turn, in all cases expressing their behavioral constraints directly in real terms. In so doing, we shall denote demand and supplies by appropriate superscripts, although in equilibrium, when markets clear, these quantities coincide.

Household Sector

We assume that households can be aggregated into a single consolidated unit. The objective of this composite unit is to choose its consumption demand; its labor supply; and the rates at which it wishes to add to its real holdings of money balances, government bonds, corporate bonds, and equities; so as to maximize the intertemporal utility function

$$\int_0^\infty U(c, l^s, m^d, g)e^{-\beta t}\, dt \qquad U_c > 0, U_l < 0, U_g > 0 \tag{10.1a}$$

subject to the budget constraint

$$c + \dot{b}_g^d + \dot{m}^d + \dot{b}_p^d + s\dot{E}^d$$
$$= wl^s + r_g b_g^d + r_p b_p^d - p^*(b_g^d + b_p^d + m^d) + isE^d - T_h \tag{10.1b}$$

and initial conditions

$$M(0) = M_o, \quad B_g(0) = B_{go}, \quad B_p(0) = B_{po}, \quad E(0) = E_o \qquad (10.1c)$$

where:

c = real private consumption plans by households,

l^s = planned supply of labor by households,

m^d = M^d/P = demand for real money balances,

M = nominal stock of money,

P = nominal price of output,

g = real government expenditure, taken to be exogenous,

b_g^d = real demand for government bonds,

B_g = nominal stock of government bonds,

b_p^d = real demand for corporate bonds,

B_p = nominal stock of corporate bonds,

E = number of shares outstanding,

s = relative price of equities in terms of current output,

i = D/sE = dividend yield, taken to be parametrically given to the household sector,

D = real dividends,

sE^d = real demand for equities,

w = real wage rate,

r_g = nominal interest rate on government bonds,

r_p = nominal interest rate on corporate bonds,

p^* = anticipated instantaneous rate of inflation,

T_h = personal income tax paid in real terms, specified more fully below,

β = consumer's rate of time discount.

The utility function has the same properties as those assumed in Chapter 9, and the rationale presented there applies here as well. The introduction of real money balances in the utility function is justified by the transactions costs arguments discussed in Section 9.8. As before, we shall assume that for given values of c, l, g, the marginal utility of money satisfies $sgn(U_m) = sgn(m^* - m)$, so that m^* denotes the corresponding satiation level of real money balances, discussed in Chapter 9. For the real stock of money less than this level, the marginal utility of money is positive; for real stocks of money in excess of m^*, the holding costs outweigh the benefits and the net marginal utility of money becomes negative. Although most of our discussion will focus on the general utility function U, it is expositionally convenient at appropriate places below to assume that it is additively separable in m, enabling us to separate out the real part of the system from the monetary component.

The household sector's budget constraint expressed in (10.1b) is in *real* flow terms. At each instant of time the representative household is assumed to acquire resources from a variety of sources. Households supply labor to firms at a real wage w; they earn interest income on their holdings of government and corporate bonds; they experience instantaneous capital gains or losses on their holdings of financial assets denominated in nominal terms (money and bonds); they receive dividend payments at a rate on their holdings of equities. The dividend payout rate is taken to be parametrically given to households, but it is one of the financial decisions made by corporations. This income can be used in a variety of ways. Households may use it to purchase real consumption goods; to add to their holdings of money balances, government bonds, corporate bonds, and equities (the relative price of which in terms of real output is s); and to pay taxes to the government. It is important to observe that the decisions from this optimization procedure represent *planned* demands (or supply, in the case of labor). We have recorded this fact explicitly by the inclusion of the superscript $d(s)$. In making its decisions, the representative household takes all market-determined prices and rates of return as given. These will all ultimately be determined in the resulting macroeconomic equilibrium.

Corporate Sector

As noted previously, the corporate sector is "driven" by households in the sense that the optimizing decisions by the households determine the appropriate cost of capital facing the firms, which in turn governs their real and financial decisions. Thus, before the firm's optimization problem can be explicitly formulated and solved, it is necessary to solve the optimization problem for the household sector. At this stage we will simply report the financial and production constraints facing the firm and note the general form of the objective function we shall derive.

The constraints facing the firm are summarized as follows:

$$y^s = F(k^d, l^d) \tag{10.2a}$$

$$\Pi = y^s - wl^d \tag{10.2b}$$

$$\Pi = r_p b_p^s + D + RE + T_f \tag{10.2c}$$

$$\dot{k}^d = RE + s\dot{E}^s + \dot{b}_p^s + p^* b_p^s \tag{10.2d}$$

$$k(0) = k_o, \quad E(0) = E_o, \quad B_p(0) = B_o \tag{10.2e}$$

where:

l^d = real demand for labor by firms,

k^d = real demand for physical capital by firms,

y^s = supply of real output,

Π = real gross profit,

b_p^s = real supply of corporate bonds,

E^s = quantity of equities, issued by corporations,

RE = retained earnings, expressed in real terms,

T_f = corporate profit tax paid in real terms, specified more fully below,

and all other symbols are as defined above.

Equation (10.2a) describes the production function, which is assumed to have the usual neoclassical properties of positive but diminishing marginal productivities, and constant returns to scale, as assumed in Chapter 9. Equation (10.2b) is the conventional definition of gross profits in real terms as being gross revenue less payments to labor. Equation (10.2c) describes the allocation of gross profit. After paying corporate income taxes, this may be used to pay interest to bond holders, used to pay dividends to stockholders, or retained within the firm. Equation (10.2d) expresses the firm's financial constraint. Any additions to its capital stock must be financed in one of three ways: either out of retained earnings, by issuing equities, or by issuing additional debt. The final term in this equation, $p*b_p^s$, is the revenue on private bonds accruing to the firm by virtue of the fact that the bonds are denominated in nominal terms. It is precisely analogous to the inflation tax generated on financial wealth issued by the government, which is a source of real revenue for the government. Finally, equations (10.2e) specify initial conditions on the stocks of capital, the number of equities outstanding, and the nominal stock of corporate bonds.

We shall define the market value of the firm's securities outstanding at time t by

$$V(t) = b_p(t) + s(t)E(t) \tag{10.3}$$

(where we suppress superscripts) and shall assume that the firm's objective is to maximize the initial real market value of its securities $V(o)$. Given the constraints in (10.2a)–(10.2e) and the optimality conditions for households, we shall show in Section 10.5 that this objective leads to the following optimization for firms. Their problem is to choose production decisions (k^d, l^d) and financial decisions (b_p^s, E^s, i) to maximize the initial value of its outstanding securities. We shall demonstrate in Section 10.5 that this objective function can be expressed as

$$V(0) = \int_0^\infty \gamma(t) e^{-\int_0^t \theta^*(\tau)d\tau} dt \tag{10.4}$$

where

$\gamma(t)$ = real net cash flow,

$\theta^*(t)$ = instantaneous cost of capital at time t.

Thus (10.4) expresses the objective function of the firm in terms of the future (expected) discounted flow of real earnings. The precise forms of $\gamma(t)$ and $\theta^*(t)$ depend crucially upon the firm's chosen dividend policy. The specific case being assumed in the present analysis will be developed in Section 10.5. Alternative hypotheses will be considered in Chapter 11. The point to be emphasized at this juncture is that $\gamma(t)$ is a function of the real *production* variables; the *financial* variables are all embodied in the cost of capital $\theta^*(t)$. As a consequence of this, the two sets of decisions can be obtained in a convenient, sequential manner.

One technical point should be noted. In general, the interests of bondholders may conflict with those of stockholders, and if that is the case, maximizing the market value of all claims against the firm does not coincide with maximizing the market value of equity. As we will see in the equilibrium we obtain, the value-maximizing firm will specialize in either all-debt or all-equity financing, depending upon the tax structure. It will want to jump immediately to the optimal level of debt or equity at time 0. There are two natural ways around this. One is to impose exogenous bounds on the rate of change of debt or equity. Then the equilibrium would involve eliminating the undesired security at the most rapid rate. This introduces a lot of messy detail. The second is to allow these variables to undergo initial jumps. This latter method will be discussed further in Section 10.6.

The choice of the maximization of the market value of the firm as the objective function requires further comment. Auerbach (1979a) has developed a model in which this objective is inappropriate from the viewpoint of maximizing the welfare of existing stockholders. In fact, the appropriateness of the value maximization criterion depends upon the dividend policy adopted by the firm. In the Auerbach model, at the margin all equity-based investment is financed through retained earnings. By contrast, in the present model, dividend policy is assumed to follow a fixed payout rule, so that at the margin all equities come through new issues. Under the present assumption it can be shown that value maximization is indeed appropriate from the viewpoint of maximizing the welfare of existing stockholders.

The Government

The government is assumed to provide real goods and services g, which it finances out of real tax receipts, or by issuing some form of government debt. Its budget constraint is described in real terms by:[1]

$$\dot{m}^s + \dot{b}_g^s = g + r_g b_g^s - T_h - T_f - (m^s + b_g^s)p* \tag{10.5}$$

where the superscript s denotes the planned supply by the government. This equation defines the real deficit net of the inflation tax by the right-hand side of (10.5) and asserts that this is financed either by increasing the real money supply or by increasing the real stock of government bonds. The choice between these two alternatives, or any other specification of monetary or debt policy for that matter, represents a policy decision that we must specify in order to close the model.

Finally, we specify the tax functions T_h, T_f as follows:

$$T_h = \tau_y(wl^s + r_g b_g^d + r_p b_g^d + isE^d) + \tau_c(\dot{s} + sp*)E \tag{10.6a}$$

$$T_f = \tau_p(y^s - wl^d - r_p b_p^s) \qquad 0 \le \tau_y \le 1; 0 \le \tau_c \le 1; 0 \le \tau_c \le 1 \tag{10.6b}$$

where all tax structures are assumed to be linear. According to (10.6a), ordinary personal income—that is, income from wages, interest, and dividends—is taxed at the same flat rate τ_y. Nominal capital gains on equities are assumed to be taxed at the rate τ_c, which in general is not equal to τ_y.[2] In most economies, $\tau_c < \tau_y$, and indeed, in many, $\tau_c = 0$. For analytical convenience, the model assumes that capital gains are taxed on accrual. In practice they are taxed on realization. Thus, even if $\tau_c = \tau_y$— as is the case for certain tax brackets in the United States—because at any point of time only a fraction of capital gains are realized, the effective tax rate on capital gains $\tau_c < \tau_y$, further justifying this assumption.

Turning to corporate income taxes, gross profit is assumed to be taxed at the proportionate rate τ_p, with the interest payments to bond holders being fully deductible. In all cases, full loss offset provisions are assumed. We should point out that the full deductibility of interest payments assumed in (10.6b) raises an analytical issue that must be addressed. As will become apparent in due course, with full deductibility of interest costs, an equilibrium having a positive inflation rate, such as would occur with a positive monetary growth rate, implies that the long-run taxable corporate profits become negative (see note 8 to this chapter). Firms are, in effect, subsidized by the government indefinitely to issue debt. Not surprisingly, this encourages bond financing, but it is unrealistic because interest deductibility applies only against positive corporate profits. There are two ways around this problem. The first is simply to allow only partial deductibility of interest payments. The other is to allow full deductibility of interest payments, but to add some fixed specific factor that adds to production, but the costs of which are not deductible. With these comments in mind, we shall continue to assume full deductibility without any real loss of generality.

We have specified these tax functions as reasonable approximations to real-world tax structures. As we shall demonstrate below, this in general implies nonneutrality of the various tax rates. In order to restore neutrality it would be necessary to introduce appropriate tax deductions for the capital losses arising from inflation on the holdings of money and bonds as well as appropriate offset provisions for firms. Since such taxes are not in general characteristic of real-world tax structures, we do not incorporate them, although it would be straightforward to do so.

One further institutional aspect should be noted. The formulations in (10.6a) and (10.6b) assume that households do not receive any credit for taxes paid by corporations on that portion of corporate profit which is paid out as dividends. This is the so-called double taxation of dividends. Although this is characteristic of the U.S. tax law and that of some other, smaller economies, it is not the case in most European countries, where households typically receive partial, and in come cases total, credit for such taxes paid by corporations; see Sinn (1987) for a comprehensive description. Under this "European" tax structure, the household would receive a tax credit $z\tau_p D$, where z is the rate at which taxes paid by corporations on dividends are rebated to consumers.

10.3 Perfect Foresight Equilibrium

We shall consider a *perfect foresight equilibrium (PFE)* and define it as follows. First, consider the household sector's maximization problem defined by (10.1a)–(10.1c), with T_h defined by (10.6b). Carrying out this maximization yields a set of demand functions for consumption and the various securities, together with a labor supply function, in terms of p^*, w, r_b, r_g, etc., and other parameters that consumers take as given. Likewise, the corporate sector's optimization problem, defined by (10.2a)–(10.2e) and (10.4), with T_f defined in (10.6b), yields a set of demand functions for capital and labor and a set of supply functions for the various securities together with output. These are also functions of p^*, w, r_b, and so forth, which firms also treat as parametrically given. Third, the government policy decisions constrained by (10.5) generate supplies of money and government bonds and a demand for goods.

The perfect foresight equilibrium is defined as a situation in which the planned demands for output, labor, and the various securities in the economy all equal the corresponding real supplies, and in addition, all anticipated variables are correctly forecast. In this case $m^d = m^s$, and so forth; thus where no confusion can arise, we shall simply drop the superscript. The quantity m, for example, will denote the real money supply in a perfect foresight equilibrium. Henceforth we shall focus on these equilibrium quantities. We shall assume that an equilibrium always exists, although in fact it may not under all tax structures.

10.4   Determination of Optimality Conditions for Households

As noted, the household sector's optimization problem is to choose c, l, m, b_g, b_g, E, subject to its budget constraint (10.1b), with T_h defined by (10.6a), and subject to the initial conditions (10.1c). Substituting for T_h enables us to write the discounted Hamiltonian function:

$$H \equiv e^{-\beta t} U(c, l, m, g) + \lambda e^{-\beta t} \{(1 - \tau_y)(wl + r_g b_g + r_b b_p + isE)$$

$$- (b_g + b_p + m)p - \tau_c(\dot{s} + sp)E - c - \dot{b}_g - \dot{b}_p - \dot{m} - s\dot{E}\}.$$

Since we are dealing with a perfect foresight equilibrium, we have set $p^* = p$, the actual rate of inflation. Also, for notational convenience, all superscripts have been dropped.

We shall assume that $[c(t), m(t), l(t), b_g(t), b_p(t), E(t)] \geq 0$ for all t.[3] The Hamiltonian H is observed to be linear in the financial decision variables $b_g(t), b_p(t), E(t)$. In view of this, depending upon the precise tax structure assumed, some of these securities may or may not appear in strictly positive quantities in the equilibrium demands of the household sector. To allow for the possibility that some may turn out to be zero in equilibrium, it is necessary to solve the optimization by using Euler inequalities rather than in terms of the more familiar Euler equations.[4] These are simply analogues to the Kuhn-Tucker conditions in conventional nonlinear programming. Performing the optimization yields the following conditions:

$$U_c \leq \lambda \tag{10.7a}$$

$$c(U_c - \lambda) = 0 \tag{10.7b}$$

$$U_l \leq -\lambda w(1 - \tau_y) \tag{10.8a}$$

$$l(U_l + \lambda w(1 - \tau_y)) = 0 \tag{10.8b}$$

$$\frac{U_m}{\lambda} - p \leq \beta - \frac{\dot{\lambda}}{\lambda} \tag{10.9a}$$

$$m\left\{\frac{U_m}{\lambda} - (p + \beta) + \frac{\dot{\lambda}}{\lambda}\right\} = 0 \tag{10.9b}$$

$$r_i(1 - \tau_y) - p \le \beta - \frac{\dot{\lambda}}{\lambda} \qquad i = p, g \tag{10.10a}$$

$$b_p\left\{r_p(1 - \tau_y) - (p + \beta) + \frac{\dot{\lambda}}{\lambda}\right\} = 0 \tag{10.10b}$$

$$b_g\left\{r_g(1 - \tau_y) - (p + \beta) + \frac{\dot{\lambda}}{\lambda}\right\} = 0 \tag{10.10c}$$

$$i(1 - \tau_y) + \frac{\dot{s}}{s}(1 - \tau_c) - \tau_c p \le \beta - \frac{\dot{\lambda}}{\lambda} \tag{10.11a}$$

$$E\left\{i(1 - \tau_y) + \frac{\dot{s}}{s}(1 - \tau_c) - \tau_c p - \beta + \frac{\dot{\lambda}}{\lambda}\right\} = 0 \tag{10.11b}$$

where $\lambda > 0$ is the Lagrange multiplier associated with the household sector budget constraint and measures the marginal utility of wealth. In addition, the following transversality conditions must hold:

$$\lim_{t \to \infty} \lambda m e^{-\beta t} = \lim_{t \to \infty} \lambda b_g e^{-\beta t} = \lim_{t \to \infty} \lambda b_p e^{-\beta t} = \lim_{t \to \infty} \lambda s E e^{-\beta t} = 0.$$

Inequalities (10.7a), (10.8a), (10.9a), (10.10a), and (10.11a) are the Euler inequalities with respect to c, l, m, b_p and b_g (which are identical), and E, respectively. If any of these inequalities are met *strictly*, then the corresponding activity is set equal to zero. Conversely, if any of the activities is strictly positive in equilibrium, the corresponding constraint is satisfied with equality. These duality-type relationships are reflected in equations (10.7b), (10.8b), (10.9b), (10.10b), (10.10c), and (10.11b). They are most relevant in the case of those assets that enter the Hamiltonian function linearly and which are the reason for introducing them. The conditions assert that the real rate of return on any asset cannot exceed the rate of return on consumption, given by the right-hand side of (10.9a), for example. In the event that the rate of return on an asset is strictly less than that of consumption, then that asset is dominated and its equilibrium quantity is zero.

Throughout the analysis we shall assume that consumption, employment, and money are "essential," so that in equilibrium these quantities exist in strictly positive amounts, that is, $c > 0$, $l > 0$, $m > 0$. Equations (10.7a), (10.8a), and (10.9a) thus all hold with equality. This assumption is plausible on economic grounds and can be ensured by imposing appropriate curvature (Inada) conditions on the utility function of consumers. Introducing the above equalities, the optimality conditions (10.7)–(10.11) can be simplified and interpreted more readily. For this purpose, we shall let

$$\theta \equiv \beta - \frac{\dot{\lambda}}{\lambda} \tag{10.12}$$

denote the rate of return on consumption. The optimality conditions for consumers may thus be written as

$$\frac{U_l}{U_c} = -w(1 - \tau_y) \tag{10.13a}$$

$$\frac{U_m}{U_c} = p + \theta \tag{10.13b}$$

$$r_i(1 - \tau_y) - p \le \theta \qquad i = p, g \tag{10.13c}$$

$$b_i[r_i(1 - \tau_y) - p - \theta] = 0 \qquad i = p, g \tag{10.13c'}$$

$$i(1 - \tau_y) + \frac{\dot{s}}{s}(1 - \tau_c) - \tau_c p \le \theta \tag{10.13d}$$

$$E\left[i(1 - \tau_y) + \frac{\dot{s}}{s}(1 - \tau_c) - \tau_c p - \theta\right] = 0. \tag{10.13d'}$$

Equation (10.13a) asserts that the marginal rate of substitution between labor and consumption should equal the after-tax real wage, and (10.13b) states that the marginal rate of substitution between money and consumption is equal to the equilibrium nominal rate of return, which is given by $\theta + p$. The after-tax return on both types of bonds reflects the assumption that only the nominal component of the return is subject to tax. The after-tax rate of return on equities contains two components. The first is the return on dividends, which is taxed at the "ordinary income" rate, τ_y. The other is the after-tax rate of capital gain. The quantity $\tau_c p$ is an adjustment for the fact that the quantity $(\dot{s}/s)(1 - \tau_c)$ is the after-tax real capital gain, whereas the tax is being assumed to be levied on the *nominal* gain. These optimality conditions will now be used to derive an explicit objective function for the firm.

10.5 Determination of Optimality Conditions for Firms

To derive the objective function for firms, we begin by eliminating RE from the firms' financial constraint (10.2c), (10.2d) to yield

$$\Pi + s\dot{E} + \dot{b}_p + p\dot{b}_p = r_p b_p + D + T_f + \dot{k}$$

where, because we are dealing with PFE, the superscripts have been dropped. Adding $\dot{s}E$ to both sides of this equation and noting the definition of V, given in (10.3), and hence $\dot{V}$, we obtain

$$\dot{V} + \Pi = (r_p - p)b_p + D + T_f + \dot{k} + \dot{s}E. \tag{10.14}$$

We now define the firm's real cash flow $\gamma(t)$ to be

$$\gamma(t) \equiv (1 - \tau_p)\Pi - \dot{k} = (1 - \tau_p)[F(k,l) - wl] - \dot{k}. \tag{10.15}$$

That is, $\gamma(t)$ equals gross after-tax profit less the cost of additional capital purchased. Now using the definition of T_f together with (10.15), and recalling the definitional relationship $D/sE \equiv i$, equation (10.14) becomes

$$\dot{V} + \gamma = (r_p(1 - \tau_p) - p)b_p + isE + \dot{s}E. \tag{10.16}$$

We now define the firm's debt-to-equity ratio as follows:

$$\delta \equiv \frac{b_p}{sE}, \tag{10.17}$$

enabling us to write (10.16) in the form

$$\dot{V} + \gamma = \left\{ [r_p(1 - \tau_p) - p]\frac{\delta}{1 + \delta} + \left(i + \frac{\dot{s}}{s}\right)\frac{1}{1 + \delta} \right\} V. \tag{10.18}$$

Next, letting

$$\theta^*(\delta, i, r_p, \dot{s}/s) \equiv [r_p(1 - \tau_p) - p]\frac{\delta}{1 + \delta} + \left(i + \frac{\dot{s}}{s}\right)\frac{1}{1 + \delta},$$

(10.18) can be written more conveniently as

$$\dot{V}(t) + \gamma(t) = \theta^*(\delta, i, r_p, \dot{s}/s)V \tag{10.19}$$

where θ^* is in general a function of t, but is independent of V. Equation (10.19) can now be integrated to yield a general solution,

$$V(s) = e^{\int_0^s \theta^*(t)dt}\left(A - \int_0^s \gamma(t)e^{-\int_0^s \theta^*(\tau)d\tau}\,dt\right),$$

where A is an arbitrary constant. Suppose for the moment that $\theta^* > 0$ (an assumption that will be justified below and certainly holds in steady state), then in order for $V(s)$ to remain finite as $s \to \infty$, we require[5]

$$A = \int_0^\infty \gamma(t)e^{-\int_0^t \theta^*(\tau)d\tau}\,dt,$$

and hence the value of the firm at any arbitrary time s is

$$V(s) = e^{\int_0^s \theta^*(t)dt} \int_s^\infty \gamma(t)e^{-\int_0^t \theta^*(\tau)d\tau}\, dt.$$

The *initial* value of the firm, which we assume is what the firm seeks to maximize, is therefore

$$V(0) = \int_0^\infty \{(1-\tau_p)[F(k,l) - wl] - \dot{k}\}e^{-\int_0^t \theta^*(\tau)d\tau}\, dt \qquad (10.20)$$

where we have substituted for $\gamma(t)$. Thus we have derived the objective function (10.4) and shown that $V(0)$ is an appropriately discounted integral of the future net real cash flows.

The fact that $\gamma(t)$ depends only upon the real production variables (k,l), whereas the discount rate depends upon the financial variables $(\delta, i, r_p, \dot{s}/s)$, means that the firm's optimization can be conducted sequentially. First it chooses its financial decisions to minimize θ^*, and then, having determined the optimal θ^*, it chooses the optimal production decisions.

The critical factor in the firm's objective function is θ^*. Using the definitions of V and δ (see [10.3] and [10.17], respectively), it may be written as

$$\theta^* = [r_p(1-\tau_p) - p]\frac{b_p}{V} + \left(i + \frac{\dot{s}}{s}\right)\frac{sE}{V}. \qquad (10.21)$$

In other words, θ^* is simply the weighted average of the real costs of debt capital and equity capital to the firm, and hence will surely be positive. The real cost of debt capital is the after–corporate income tax nominal interest rate less the rate of inflation; the real cost of equity capital to firms is the dividend payout rate plus the real rate of capital gains on equity. Hence (10.21) is an expression that turns out to be familiar from basic corporate finance theory.

However, the expression for θ^* given in (10.21) is inappropriate from the viewpoint of determining the firm's financial decisions. The reason is that these decisions are themselves constrained by the preferences of households. These preferences, which are embodied in the optimality conditions (10.13c'), (10.13d'), impose constraints on the components of the financial rates of return. To obtain an appropriate expression for θ^*, we invoke the optimality conditions (10.13c'), (10.13d') for consumers to eliminate r_p and $\dot{s}E$:

$$r_p b_p = \frac{(\theta + p)}{(1-\tau_y)}b_p, \qquad (10.13c'')$$

$$\dot{s}E = \left(\frac{(\theta + \tau_c p)}{(1-\tau_c)} - \frac{(1-\tau_y)i}{(1-\tau_c)}\right)sE. \qquad (10.13d'')$$

Substituting these expressions into (10.21), we may express θ^* as

$$\theta^*(\delta, i) \equiv \theta + \frac{(\tau_y - \tau_p)(\theta + p)}{(1 - \tau_y)} \frac{\delta}{1 + \delta} + \frac{(\theta + p)\tau_c + i(\tau_y - \tau_c)}{(1 - \tau_c)} \frac{1}{1 + \delta}.$$

$$(10.21')$$

It becomes evident from this expression how the cost of capital θ^* provides the means whereby consumers "drive" the firms. From (10.21'), it is seen that the relevant cost of capital is equal to the consumer's rate of return on consumption θ, adjusted by the various corporate and personal income tax rates, the adjustments themselves being weighted by the shares of bonds and equities in the firm's financial structure. Equation (10.21') may also be written as a weighted average in the form

$$\delta^*(\delta, i) \equiv \left[\theta + \frac{(\tau_y - \tau_p)(\theta + p)}{(1 - \tau_y)} \right] \frac{\delta}{1 + \delta}$$

$$+ \left[\theta + \frac{(\theta + p)\tau_c + i(\tau_y - \tau_c)}{(1 - \tau_c)} \right] \frac{1}{1 + \delta},$$

$$(10.21'')$$

which is the form in which it shall be used.

The expressions (10.21') and (10.21'') are in terms of the firm's financial decision variables, together with other variables parametric to the firm, and are therefore in a form suitable for determining the firm's optimal financial policies. This is done by calculating the partial derivatives with respect to δ, i. It is straightforward to show

$$sgn\left(\frac{\partial \theta^*}{\partial i}\right) = sgn\left(\frac{\tau_y - \tau_c}{1 - \tau_c}\right),$$

$$(10.22a)$$

$$sgn\left(\frac{\partial \theta^*}{\partial \delta}\right) = sgn\left[\frac{(\tau_y - \tau_p)(\theta + p)}{1 - \tau_y} - \frac{(\theta + p)\tau_c + i(\tau_y - \tau_c)}{1 - \tau_c}\right].$$

$$(10.22b)$$

The optimal dividend policy and the optimal capital structure will therefore involve corner solutions. Note that in the absence of taxes, θ^* is independent of i. Dividend policy is therefore irrelevant, confirming the well-known Miller and Modigliani (1961) proposition.

In light of the fact that the capital gains in the analysis really reflect accruals, whereas tax rates in reality apply to realized capital gains, it seems reasonable to assume $\tau_c < \tau_y$, a restriction we in fact suggested at the outset. Thus, if the firm is to minimize its cost of capital, it should minimize the dividend payout ratio i. In the absence of any constraints this would involve the repurchase of shares, as long as D remained positive. In fact, such behavior is discouraged in the United States by Section 302 of the Internal Revenue Code. To model fully the legal restrictions included in this code would be extremely difficult, and we do not attempt to do so here. Rather, we shall simply argue that the firm minimizes its dividend payments by setting $i = \bar{i}$, where $\bar{i}$ is some legal minimum payout rate (possibly zero), which we take to be exogenously given. Thus, setting $i = \bar{i}$, the optimal financial mix (δ) is determined as follows:

If:$\quad\dfrac{(\tau_y - \tau_p)(\theta + p)}{1 - \tau_y} < \dfrac{(\theta + p)\tau_c + \bar{i}(\tau_y - \tau_c)}{1 - \tau_c},\quad$ set $\quad\delta = \infty,\qquad$ (10.23a)

that is, employ all-bond financing $(E = 0)$.

If$\quad\dfrac{(\tau_y - \tau_p)(\theta + p)}{1 - \tau_y} > \dfrac{(\theta + p)\tau_c + \bar{i}(\tau_y - \tau_c)}{1 - \tau_c},\quad$ set $\quad\delta = 0,\qquad$ (10.23b)

that is, employ all-equity financing $(b_p = 0)$.

Defining the average tax rate on income from equities, say τ_e, to be a weighted average of the tax rates on income from dividend and from capital gains:

$$\tau_e = \frac{\bar{i}\tau_y + (\dot{s}/s + p)\tau_c}{\bar{i} + \dot{s}/s + p},$$

and using the optimality condition (10.13d'), the criterion for determining the optimal financial mix (δ) can be rewritten as follows:[6]

$$(1 - \tau_y) > (1 - \tau_p)(1 - \tau_e)\qquad \text{set}\quad \delta = \infty \qquad\qquad (10.24a)$$

$$(1 - \tau_y) < (1 - \tau_p)(1 - \tau_e)\qquad \text{set}\quad \delta = 0. \qquad\qquad (10.24b)$$

By writing it in this way, we see that our criterion is identical to that of Miller (1977).[7] In effect, (10.24a) asserts that if the net after-tax income exceeds the net after-tax income from equity, where the latter is taxed twice, first as corporate profit and then as personal income to stockholders, no investors will wish to hold equities, and the firm must engage in all-bond financing. The opposite applies if the inequality is reversed as in (10.24b). A simple, sufficient condition for (10.24a) to hold, not uncharacteristic of some real-world tax structures, is that the corporate profit tax rate τ_p exceed the personal income tax rate on ordinary income τ_y. No such simple condition for (10.24b) to hold exists. It simply requires τ_y to exceed τ_p by an amount that suffices to take account of the double taxation of income from equity. Clearly, the tax structure considered here, which is not uncharacteristic of the United States, favors bond financing and likely explains at least in part the massive corporate debt that exists there. Granting a tax credit to households for the corporate tax already paid on the dividends they receive would clearly make equity financing more attractive.

If $(1 - \tau_y) = (1 - \tau_p)(1 - \tau_e)$, the optimal debt-to-equity ratio is indeterminate. One special case of this arises if all tax rates are zero, when the conditions (10.23) simply reduce to a statement of the famous Modigliani and Miller (1958) theorem, namely that in the absence of taxes the firm's financial decision is irrelevant. Our results are also consistent with Miller's (1977) extension of this proposition, again in the case of a single agent. He shows that the value of the firm in equilibrium will be independent of the amount of debt in its capital structure, provided the marginal rate of tax payable by stockholders on income from shares is sufficiently far below the marginal rate of tax on personal income. This result immediately follows from the equality $(1 - \tau_y) = (1 - \tau_p)(1 - \tau_e)$. Thus, although our conclusions for the firm's financial policy turn out to be familiar from corporate finance theory, we believe that the derivation we have given for the cost of capital, in terms of the underlying optimality condition for consumers, has the merit in that it makes explicit the role played by consumers in determining the optimality conditions for value-maximizing firms.

Thus using (10.23), the firm's minimum cost of capital may be expressed as

$$\theta^*_{min} = \theta + \min \left[\frac{(\tau_y - \tau_p)(\theta + p)}{1 - \tau_y}, \frac{(\theta + p)\tau_c + \bar{i}(\tau_y - \tau_c)}{1 - \tau_c} \right]. \tag{10.25}$$

With all-bond financing, this reduces to

$$\theta^*_{min} = \frac{\theta(1 - \tau_p) + (\tau_y - \tau_p)p}{1 - \tau_y} = r_p(1 - \tau_p) - p, \tag{10.25'}$$

whereas with all-equity financing it becomes

$$\theta^*_{min} = \frac{\theta + \tau_c p + \bar{i}(\tau_y - \tau_c)}{1 - \tau_c} = \bar{i} + \frac{\dot{s}}{s}. \tag{10.25''}$$

In deriving the second equalities in these two equations, use has been made of (10.13c'') and (10.13d''). We should emphasize that the expression for the cost of equity financing depends upon our chosen assumption regarding dividend policy. In the presence of differential taxes on dividend income and capital gains, alternative assumptions lead to alternative costs of equity financing; some alternatives will be discussed in Chapter 11.

We are now finally in a position to state and solve the real part of the firm's optimization problem. Having chosen i, δ to minimize the cost of capital and thus determined θ^*_{min}, the firm must next choose k, l, to maximize

$$V(0) = \int_0^\infty \{(1 - \tau_p)[F(k, l) - wl] - \dot{k}\} e^{-\int_0^t \theta_{\min}^*(\tau)d\tau} \, dt \tag{10.26}$$

subject to the initial condition $k(0) = k_0$. The optimality conditions to this production decision are

$$(1 - \tau_p)F_k(k, l) = \theta_{\min}^*, \tag{10.27a}$$

$$F_l(k, l) = w. \tag{10.27b}$$

That is, the after-tax marginal physical product of capital should be equated to the minimized cost of capital, and the marginal physical product of labor should be equated to the real wage.

Moreover, substituting (10.27a), (10.27b) back into (10.26), we are able to use the transversality condition for the above optimization problem,

$$\lim_{t \to \infty} k(t)e^{-\int_0^t \theta^*(s)ds} = 0,$$

to establish the identity between the value of the firm's capital stock and the value of the financial claims, namely

$$V(t) = b_p(t) + s(t)E(t) = k(t). \tag{10.28}$$

This transversality condition requires that the capitalized value of the state variables be zero in the limit, which in effect rules out the possibility of the values of the claims becoming divorced from the underlying sources of earnings.

The result is obtained as follows. For ease of notation we shall denote $\theta_{\min}^*$ by θ^*. From the solution for $V(s)$ and the expression for $\gamma(t)$, we may write

$$V(t) = \lim_{t \to \infty} \left\{ e^{\int_0^t \theta^*(\tau)d\tau} \int_t^T \{(1 - \tau_p)[F(k, l) - wl] - \dot{k}\} e^{-\int_0^t \theta^*(\tau)d\tau} \, ds \right\}.$$

Using the linear homogeneity of the production function and the optimality conditions (10.27a), (10.27b), this expression may be simplified to yield

$$V(t) = \lim_{T \to \infty} \left\{ e^{\int_0^t \theta^*(\tau)d\tau} \int_t^T [\theta^* k - \dot{k}] e^{-\int_0^t \theta^*(\tau)d\tau} \, ds \right\}.$$

Now integrating by parts and canceling, we obtain

$$V(t) = k(t) - e^{\int_0^t \theta^*(\tau)d\tau} \lim_{T \to \infty} (e^{-\int_0^T \theta^*(\tau)d\tau} k(T)).$$

But the limit of the second term is zero, by the necessity of the transversality condition at infinity. Hence we conclude that $V(t) = k(t)$.

In effect, this relationship asserts that the Tobin $q = 1$. As Hayashi (1982) has demonstrated, the average q can be defined by the ratio $q(t) = V(t)/k(t)$. The fact that with this definition $q = 1$ is a consequence of the assumption that capital can be installed without adjustment costs. In Chapter 11, where convex adjustment costs are introduced, q will in general be found to evolve over time in such a way as to reflect the changing market value of the firm.

10.6   Equilibrium Structure and Dynamics of the System

The optimality conditions for the households and firms, together with the government budget constraint, can now be combined to describe the perfect foresight equilibrium of the decentralized economy and to determine its dynamic evolution.

Combining the optimality conditions in (10.13), (10.27), we may write

$$U_c(c, l, m, g) = \lambda \tag{10.29a}$$

$$\frac{U_l(c, l, m, g)}{U_c(c, l, m, g)} = -F_l(k, l)(1 - \tau_y) \tag{10.29b}$$

$$\frac{U_m(c, l, m, g)}{U_c(c, l, m, g)} = \theta + p \tag{10.29c}$$

$$(1 - \tau_p)F_k(k, l) = \theta^*_{\min} \tag{10.29d}$$

$$\theta^*_{\min} = \theta + \min\left[\frac{(\tau_y - \tau_p)(\theta + p)}{1 - \tau_y}, \frac{(\theta + p)\tau_c + i(\tau_y - \tau_c)}{1 - \tau_c}\right] \tag{10.29e}$$

$$\dot{k} = F(k, l) - c - g \tag{10.30a}$$

$$\dot{\lambda} = \lambda(\beta - \theta) \tag{10.30b}$$

$$\dot{m} + \dot{b}_g = g + \theta b_g - \tau_y F - mp + [\theta - (1 - \tau_y)F_k]k. \tag{10.30c}$$

Equations (10.29a)–(10.29e) repeat (10.7a), (10.13a), (10.13b), (10.27a), and (10.25), with (10.27b) substituted into (10.13a). These five equations may be used to obtain the short-run solutions for the five variables consumption c, employment l, the rate of inflation p, the rate of return on consumption θ, and the minimized cost of capital $\theta^*_{\min}$, in terms of the dynamically evolving variables, the marginal utility of wealth λ, the capital stock k, the real stock of money m, and the real stock of government bonds b_g. The dynamics governing these latter variables are expressed in equations (10.30a)–(10.30c). The first of these describes the rate of capital accumulation required to maintain product market equilibrium, and (10.30b) is a restatement of (10.12).

The final equation is the government budget constraint. The derivation of this equation involves several steps. Essentially it is obtained by first substituting the tax functions (10.6a), (10.6b) into (10.5), then using the optimality conditions for consumers (10.13c′), (10.13d′), the optimality conditions for firms (10.27a), (10.27b), together with the linear homogeneity of the production function and the identity between the value of the firm's capital and the financial claims (10.28), to simplify the resulting expression for the real deficit. The end product of this process is (10.30c). The following interpretation to the terms in this equation may be given. The first two terms on the right-hand side denote real government expenditures and the real interest payments owed on the outstanding government debt, the net of tax real interest rate on which is equal to the rate of return on consumption θ. The third term is the tax collected on personal income. Because income generated by the economy is ultimately accrued by households, it is taxed at the personal rate τ_y. The final term is a complex one. Because $(1 - \tau_p)F_k(k, l) = \theta^*_{\min}$, it reflects the differential tax rates between firms and households. Also, to the extent that firms employ equity financing, it reflects the fact that income from shares is taxed twice, first as profit, when it is taxed at the corporate profit rate τ_p, then as personal income when it is included in y and taxed at the rate τ_y. To the extent that these sources of revenue and finance do not balance, the resulting deficit must be financed either by issuing real bonds or by increasing real money balances.

As part of the specification of the dynamics of the system, something must be said about government financial policy. There are various policies that are traditionally chosen in dynamic models of this kind, some of which were discussed in Chapter 2. These policies included pegging the real stock of money, pegging the real stock of bonds, pegging the rate of nominal monetary growth, and so forth. Once such a policy is chosen, the dynamics are fully determined.

To complete the description of the system, we must consider the initial conditions, $k(0), E(0), m(0), b_p(0)$, and $b_g(0)$. The first two of these are exogenously given, by $k(0) = k_0$, $E(0) = E_0$. In the case of money and bonds, the initial nominal stocks are assumed to be given, with the initial real stocks being endogenously determined by an initial jump in the price level. The size of this jump and therefore the initial values for $m(0), b_p(0)$, and $b_g(0)$ are obtained from the transversality conditions.

Before concluding the present discussion, we should also explain how the equilibrium stocks of bonds and equities and their respective rates of return are determined. In the case where firms find it optimal to engage in all-bond financing, the constraint (10.28) implies that $b_p = k^8$. Note that with the nominal stock of bonds given, a jump may occur at time zero, through the price level, so that $k_0 = b_p(0) = B_{p0}/P(0)$). The nominal rate of interest can then be determined by inserting the known values into the consumer optimality condition (10.13c), which holds as an equality. Obviously this implies that the rate of interest on private and public bonds must be equal, that is $r_p = r_g$. Similarly, with all-equity financing, the price of equities can be obtained by substituting known values into (10.13d) and integrating. Again, an initial jump in $s(0)$ will be required to ensure that (10.28), which now becomes $k = sE$, is met. With both the value of equities and their price determined, the quantity of shares outstanding can be inferred.[9] In this case, the rate of interest on government bonds will again be given by (10.13c), with their after-tax rate of return now equaling that on equities, but exceeding that on corporate bonds.

10.7   Steady State

The steady state of the system is attained when

$$\dot{k} = \dot{\lambda} = \dot{m} = \dot{b}_g = 0. \tag{10.31}$$

The fact that the steady state requires $\dot{k} = \dot{\lambda} = \dot{m} = 0$ is readily apparent from (10.29) and (10.30a)–(10.30c). The requirement that $\dot{b}_g = 0$ is less immediate, because b_g is determined residually from the government budget constraint. Nevertheless, the need for bond accumulation to cease in steady state can be established by integrating the government budget constraint and imposing the transversality condition for consumers:

$$\lim_{t \to \infty} U_c(t)b_g(t)e^{-\beta t} = 0$$

The argument may be sketched as follows. First, integrate (10.12) to yield

$$U_c(t) = U_c(0)e^{\beta t - \int_0^t \theta(\tau)d\tau}.$$

Next, integrate the government budget constraint (10.30c) to obtain

$$b_g(t) = e^{\int_0^t \theta(s)ds}\left\{ C + \int_0^t x(s)e^{-\int_0^s \theta(\tau)d\tau}\,ds \right\}$$

where $x(s) \equiv g - \tau_y F - mp + [\theta - (1 - \tau_y)F_k]k - \dot{m}$ and is independent of b_g, and C is an arbitrary constant. Inserting these solutions for $U_c(t)$, $b_g(t)$ and taking the limit, we require (assuming $U_c(0)$ to be finite)

$$C = -\int_0^\infty x(s)e^{-\int_0^s \theta(\tau)d\tau}\,ds,$$

so that the implied time path for real government bonds is

$$b_g(t) = -e^{\int_0^t \theta(s)ds} \int_t^\infty x(s)e^{-\int_0^s \theta(\tau)d\tau} \, ds,$$

which converges to (10.32d), below, in steady state.

The implied endogenous initial value $b_g(0)$ is not necessarily equal to $B_{go}/P(0)$, even after allowing for the initial jump in the price level. There are three possible resolutions to this problem, which we view as a technical detail. The first is that the monetary authorities undertake an initial open-market exchange of money for bonds in order to ensure that the solution for $b_g(t)$ is consistent with the consumer's transversality condition. The second is that the government make any necessary adjustments through an appropriate choice of lump-sum taxes.[10] The third is that the government bonds be long bonds having an endogenous nominal price, which does the necessary adjusting.

From (10.31), together with (10.29a), and (10.29b), we obtain $F(k, l) = c + g$ and $\theta = \beta$. Accordingly, the long-run equilibrium of the system can be reduced to the following four equations:

$$\frac{U_l[F(k, l) - g, l, m, g]}{U_c[F(k, l) - g, l, m, g]} = -F_l(k, l)(1 - \tau_y) \tag{10.32a}$$

$$\frac{U_m[F(k, l) - g, l, m, g]}{U_c[F(k, l) - g, l, m, g]} = \beta + p \tag{10.32b}$$

$$(1 - \tau_p)F_k(k, l) = \beta + \min\left[\frac{(\tau_y - \tau_p)(\beta + p)}{1 - \tau_y}, \frac{(\beta + p)\tau_c + i(\tau_y - \tau_c)}{1 - \tau_c}\right] \tag{10.32c}$$

$$g + \beta b_g + \tau_y F - mp + [\beta - (1 - \tau_y)F_k]k = 0 \tag{10.32d}$$

The first three equations involve the four variables k, l, m, and p. Thus, if for given exogenous values of g and the tax rates, one specifies an independent government financial policy in terms of the real stock of money or the inflation rate, then these three equations, together with the policy specification, will determine the four variables k, l, m, and p. Inserting these stationary values into the steady-state government budget constraint determines the required real stock of bonds to maintain the budget in balance. On the other hand, if the policy is specified in terms of the real stock of government bonds, then, for given g and tax rates, the four equations determine the equilibrium values of k, l, m, and p.

It is of interest to note that in general, the systems summarized by (10.32a)–(10.32d) are interdependent: real production decisions and financial decisions are jointly determined. *Money is neither neutral nor superneutral.* This is in part a consequence of the fact that only the nominal component of the real interest rate is being taxed, and of the tax deductibility provisions assumed. It is also in part a consequence of the interdependence between real money balances m on the one hand, and consumption and labor, on the other, in the consumer's utility function. Under certain conditions, however, the system dichotomizes into two recursive subsystems. The first determines the real decisions k, l, and c, while the second determines the financial variables m and p, conditional on these initially chosen real variables. Finally, the equilibrium rates of return on the financial securities can be obtained by substituting from (10.32a)–(10.32d) into the appropriate arbitrage conditions for consumers, (10.13c′), (10.13d′).

10.8   Characterization of Alternative Steady States

In order to discuss the steady state of the system in further detail, it is necessary to introduce some form of government financial policy. We shall restrict most of our attention to the familiar case where the monetary authorities maintain the constant rate of nominal monetary growth:

$$\frac{\dot{M}}{M} = \phi. \tag{10.33}$$

The real money supply $m \equiv M/P$ therefore evolves in accordance with

$$\dot{m} = m(\phi - p), \tag{10.33′}$$

so that in steady state we have

$$p = \phi.$$

It is evident from previous sections that the steady state will be dependent upon the capital structure employed by firms. This is determined by the inequality condition (10.23) and the corresponding minimized cost of capital. Thus for the government monetary policy specified by (10.33), the following steady states may be characterized.

All-Bond Financing by Firms

In the case of all-bond financing, inequality (10.23a) holds and the steady state reduces to the following:

$$\frac{U_l[F(k, l) - g, l, m, g]}{U_c[F(k, l) - g, l, m, g]} = -F_l(k, l)(1 - \tau_y) \tag{10.34a}$$

$$\frac{U_m[F(k,l) - g, l, m, g]}{U_c[F(k,l) - g, l, m, g]} = \beta + \phi \tag{10.34b}$$

$$(1 - \tau_p)F_k(k,l) = \frac{\beta(1 - \tau_p) + (\tau_y - \tau_p)\phi}{1 - \tau_y} \tag{10.34c}$$

$$g + \beta b_g - \tau_y F - m\phi + [\beta - (1 - \tau_y)F_k]k = 0. \tag{10.34d}$$

Thus the steady state attained when the government fixes an exogenous monetary growth rate and where firms engage in all-bond financing can be obtained in the following recursive manner. First, given the parameters $\beta, \phi, \tau_y, \tau_p$, (10.34c) yields the marginal physical product of capital. With the linear homogeneity of the production function, this establishes the equilibrium capital-labor ratio, which in turn determines the equilibrium real wage $F_l(k,l)$. Once we have determined k/l, the two marginal rate of substitution conditions (10.34a), (10.34b) together determine the employment of labor l, and the real stock of money balances m. With k/l and l now fixed, the real stock of capital k is known, and the level of output y immediately follows from the production function. The government budget then determines the real stock of government bonds necessary to maintain the budget.

Being a perfect foresight equilibrium, equations (10.34a–10.34d) have important implications for the debate concerning the effectiveness of fully anticipated government policies, which accompanied the development of rational expectations. It is seen from these equations that the real productive decisions, k, l, are in general dependent upon the rate of growth of the nominal money supply, as well as upon both the corporate and personal income tax rates. Also, to the extent that public and private goods are viewed as imperfect substitutes by households, so that c and g enter as separate arguments in the utility function, an expansion in real government expenditure will have real effects insofar as output and employment are concerned. In the polar case that public and private goods are perfect substitutes, so that c and g enter additively in U, it is easily seen that an increase in government expenditure will cease to have any effect on the real part of the system. It will simply "crowd out" an equal quantity of private consumption. These properties also applied in the real model of Chapter 9. In general, then, these results confirm the view put forward by Fair (1978) in his critique of rational expectations models asserting that in a fully rational expectations model, generated from underlying optimizing behavior, anticipated government policies are indeed able to have real effects.

The presence of distortionary taxes in general renders money to be *nonsuperneutral*. In order for real activity to be independent of the monetary growth rate, the following two conditions must hold:

(i)   the corporate and personal income tax rates must be equal;

(ii)   the utility function must be separable in real money balances, so that the marginal rate of substitution U_l/U_c is independent of m.

We shall restrict the present analysis of the comparative static properties of (10.34) to the effects of taxes and the monetary growth on the capital-labor ratio. Both tax policy and monetary policy have been discussed extensively over the years and have generated a substantial literature. An extensive discussion of the effects of changes in the tax rates is presented in Chapter 11. Some further discussion of the impact of monetary growth in this model is presented in Section 10.9, and a more detailed analysis is provided by Turnovsky (1987a). The key observation is that these effects operate through the cost of capital, which therefore provides the critical channel through which these forms of government policy impinge on the economy. Also, when these results are compared to those we shall derive in the next subsection, where the firm employs all-equity financing, we see very clearly how the effects of government policy depend crucially upon the equilibrium financial structure employed by firms, and the need to derive macroequilibria from underlying optimizing behavior is emphasized once again.

From (10.34c) we can easily derive the following:

$$\frac{\partial(k/l)}{\partial \phi} = \frac{(\tau_y - \tau_p)}{f''(1 - \tau_p)(1 - \tau_y)} \tag{10.35a}$$

$$\frac{\partial(k/l)}{\partial \tau_y} = \frac{(\beta + \phi)}{f''(1 - \tau_y)} < 0 \tag{10.35b}$$

$$\frac{\partial(k/l)}{\partial \tau_p} = -\frac{\phi}{f''(1 - \tau_p)^2} > 0 \tag{10.35c}$$

where $lf(k/l) = F(k,l)$, so that $f'(k/l) = F_k(k,l)$. To understand these results it is useful to recall the expression for the nominal rate of interest (10.13c''), which in steady state is $r_p = (\beta + \phi)/(1 - \tau_y)$. An increase in the rate of nominal monetary growth raises the nominal before-tax interest rate by $1/(1 - \tau_y)$. The effect on the after-tax real rate of interest to firms, which with all-bond financing is their effective cost of capital, is thus equal to $[(1 - \tau_p)/(1 - \tau_y) - 1]$, so that the overall effect, and therefore the effect on the capital-labor ratio, depends upon $(\tau_p - \tau_y)$. In order for bond financing to be optimal, (10.23a) imposes a lower bound on this quantity. Thus, for example, if the rate of taxation on capital gains and the required minimum rate of dividend payments are both zero, then $\tau_p > \tau_y$ and the capital-labor ratio will rise. Although this is the more likely scenario, the reverse cannot be ruled out. An increase in the personal income tax rate τ_y raises the nominal interest rate and hence the after-tax interest rate to firms, thereby inducing them to lower their capital-labor ratio. On the other hand, an increase in the corporate tax rate τ_p has no effect on the nominal interest rate. It therefore leads to a reduction in the after-tax real interest rate for firms, inducing them to increase their capital-labor ratio. Given the effects summarized in (10.35), the implications for the other endogenous variables can be obtained by taking the appropriate differentials of (10.34). This will be pursued in the case of taxes in Chapter 11.

All-Equity Financing by Firms

With all-equity financing, (10.23b) applies and the steady state now becomes

$$\frac{U_l[F(k,l) - g, l, m, g]}{U_c[F(k,l) - g, l, m, g]} = -F_l(k,l)(1 - \tau_y) \tag{10.36a}$$

$$\frac{U_m[F(k,l) - g, l, m, g]}{U_c[F(k,l) - g, l, m, g]} = \beta + \phi \tag{10.36b}$$

$$(1 - \tau_p)F_k(k,l) = \frac{\beta + \tau_c\phi + \bar{i}(\tau_y - \tau_c)}{1 - \tau_c} \tag{10.36c}$$

$$g + \beta b_g - \tau_y F - m\phi + [\beta - (1 - \tau_y)F_k]k = 0. \tag{10.36d}$$

The steady state is obtained in much the same way as it was for bond financing in the previous subsection. The only difference is in the cost of capital determining the capital-labor ratio, which is now given by (10.36c). The government policy parameters $\phi, \tau_y, \tau_p, \tau_c$, all have real effects, as before. In this case, superneutrality with respect to the monetary growth rate will obtain if and only if (i) $\tau_c = 0$, and (ii) the utility function is separable in m. Finally, the previous comments made with respect to the "crowding-out" effects of an increase in government expenditure continue to hold.

The effects of change in the monetary growth rate and the various tax rates on the capital-labor ratio are obtained from (10.36c) and have the following general chacteristics:

$$\frac{\partial(k/l)}{\partial\phi} = \frac{\tau_c}{f''(1 - \tau_p)(1 - \tau_c)} < 0 \tag{10.37a}$$

$$\frac{\partial(k/l)}{\partial\tau_y} = \frac{\bar{i}}{f''(1 - \tau_p)(1 - \tau_c)} < 0 \tag{10.37b}$$

$$\frac{\partial(k/l)}{\partial\tau_p} = \frac{f'}{f''(1-\tau_p)} < 0 \tag{10.37c}$$

$$\frac{\partial(k/l)}{\partial\tau_c} = \frac{(\beta+\phi) - \bar{i}(1-\tau_y)}{f''(1-\tau_p)(1-\tau_c)^2}. \tag{10.37d}$$

It will be observed that the effects of a change in the corporate profit tax rate, and probably the monetary growth rate, are *opposite* to what would obtain under bond financing. The reason for these results can be understood by considering the expressions for the equilibrium rate of capital gains, which, from (10.13d″), is

$$\frac{\dot{s}}{s} = \frac{\beta + \tau_c\phi - \bar{i}(1-\tau_y)}{1-\tau_c}.$$

Thus an increase in either the rate of monetary growth ϕ, or the rate of personal income tax rate τ_y, will raise the equilibrium rate of capital gains on equities and hence the equilibrium rate of equity costs $(\bar{i} + \dot{s}/s)$, inducing firms to reduce their capital-labor ratio. By contrast, an increase in the corporate profit tax rate τ_p leaves equity costs unchanged. The after-tax marginal physical product of capital must remain fixed, so that as τ_p increases, the capital-labor ratio must fall. The effect of an increase in the rate of capital gains tax τ_c depends upon $sgn[\bar{i}(1-\tau_y) - (\beta+\phi)]$. This term can be shown to be inversely related to the *nominal* rate of capital gain, upon which τ_c is levied.[11] Thus an increase in the rate of capital gains tax will reduce the capital-labor ratio, as long as such gains are positive, and increase the ratio otherwise, when it is offsetting losses.

10.9 Dynamic Response to Monetary Expansion

Some of the important earlier work analyzing the effects of inflation (monetary growth) on real after-tax asset returns, was by Feldstein (1976, 1980), and Feldstein, Green, and Sheshinski (1978). In the latter, more general analysis, the authors show that if one abstracts from the induced changes in the debt-to-equity ratio and assumes that the rate of depreciation is zero (the assumption being made here), then the effects of an increase in the inflation rate upon the steady-state net yield on bonds equals $dp = (\tau_p - \tau_y)/(1 - \tau_p)$, whereas that on equities is $-\tau_c$. In our analysis, on the other hand, we find that under both modes of corporate financing, these two rates of return equal β in steady state and are therefore independent of the inflation rate. The difference in the result stems from the fact that the Feldstein, Green, and Sheshinski result abstracts from changes in the capital-labor ratio and is therefore associated with a much shorter time horizon. In fact it corresponds to our short-run value of θ. With the capital-labor ratio, and therefore $\theta^*_{\min}$, fixed in the short run (or at least independent of the inflation rate), it follows from (10.29e) that under bond financing $d\theta/dp = (\tau_p - \tau_y)/(1 - \tau_p)$, whereas with equity financing $d\theta/dp = -\tau_c$, precisely the result obtained by Feldstein, Green, and Sheshinski.

As we have noted previously, Turnovsky (1987a) presents a detailed analytical treatment of the effects of an increase in the monetary growth rate using this model. His analysis is based on the assumption that the utility function is additively separable in m, so that in the absence of distortionary taxes, money will be superneutral. In order to see the role of corporate financing in the presence of tax incentives, when superneutrality breaks down, we shall briefly discuss the dynamic structure he obtains.

First, we solve equations (10.29a)–(10.29e) for $c, l, p,$ and θ in the form

$$c = c(\lambda, k) \tag{10.38a}$$

$$l = l(\lambda, k) \tag{10.38b}$$

$$p = p(\lambda, k, m) \tag{10.38c}$$

$$\theta = \theta(\lambda, k, m) \tag{10.38d}$$

where for notational simplicity g and the relevant tax rates are suppressed from the functions. The fact that c and l are independent of m is a consequence of the assumed additive separability of the utility function. The forms of the solutions of p and θ depend upon the mode of financing adopted by corporations, and details of the signs of these expressions are provided by Turnovsky.

The next step is to substitute these expressions into the product market equilibrium condition (10.30a), the arbitrage condition (10.30b), and the real monetary growth relationship (10.33'), yielding an autonomous dynamic system analogous to (9.50a)–(9.50c). Linearizing this system, about steady-state equilibrium, enables the dynamics to be approximated by

$$\begin{bmatrix} \dot{k} \\ \dot{\lambda} \\ \dot{m} \end{bmatrix} = \begin{bmatrix} F_k + F_l l_k - c_k & F_l l_\lambda - c_\lambda & 0 \\ -\tilde{\lambda}\theta_k & -\tilde{\lambda}\theta_\lambda & -\tilde{\lambda}\theta_m \\ -\tilde{m}p_k & -\tilde{m}p_\lambda & -\tilde{m}p_m \end{bmatrix} \begin{bmatrix} k - \tilde{k} \\ \lambda - \tilde{\lambda} \\ m - \tilde{m} \end{bmatrix} \tag{10.39}$$

where tildes denote steady-state equilibrium values determined in Section 10.7. The corporate finance decisions influence the dynamics through the effects on the inflation rate and on the rate of return on consumption θ.

It can be shown that under mild restrictions (though different in the two forms of corporate finance), the dynamics described by (10.39) includes one negative (stable) root and two positive (unstable) roots.[12] The stable adjustment paths for k, λ, and m are of the form

$$k(t) = \tilde{k} + (k_0 - \tilde{k})e^{\lambda_1 t} \tag{10.40a}$$

$$\lambda(t) = \tilde{\lambda} + (\lambda(0) - \tilde{\lambda})e^{\lambda_1 t} \tag{10.40b}$$

$$m(t) = \tilde{m} + (m(0) - \tilde{m})e^{\lambda_1 t} \tag{10.40c}$$

where $\lambda_1 < 0$ denotes the stable eigenvalue and depends upon the mode of corporate finance. We assume that capital evolves continuously from its given initial stock k_o, and that the initial values of $\lambda(0), m(0)$, are determined endogenously. The initial jump in the marginal utility $\lambda(0)$ reflects the wealth effects of any change in policy. With the nominal supply of money being determined by the monetary growth rule (10.33), the initial nominal stock is predetermined, so that the initial real stock is determined by an appropriate initial jump in the price level.

Under the assumption of a separable utility function, everything is driven by the response of the long-run capital-labor ratio. Thus, assuming that $\tau_p > \tau_y$, under bond financing, an increase in the monetary growth rate raises the long-run capital-labor ratio, having a generally expansionary effect on the economy, which is reflected in its transitional path. By contrast, under equity financing, an increase in the monetary growth rate reduces the long-run capital-labor ratio, thereby having a generally contractionary effect on the economy, which is reflected in the transitional path applicable in that case as well.

One interesting feature of the dynamics is that in both cases, the immediate effect on the capital-labor ratio is in the opposite direction to its long-run adjustment. The following explanation for this may be given. In the case that firms employ bond financing, so that the long-run effect of the increase in the monetary growth rate is expansionary, agents are aware that their income will rise, and along with it, their taxes. They feel that these higher taxes will lead to a reduction in wealth, thereby raising their marginal utility of wealth and inducing them to increase their labor supply. With the capital stock fixed in the short run, this immediately lowers the capital-labor ratio, although the latter rises over time as capital is accumulated at a faster rate than labor. The argument is reversed when firms employ equity financing, when the long-run effect of a higher monetary growth rate is generally contractionary. In this case agents anticipate a reduction in their taxes, leading to an increase in their wealth. This causes a short-run reduction in the marginal utility of wealth, leading to a reduction in the labor supply and a rise in the short-run capital-labor ratio, which then declines over time. Further discussion of these adjustments is provided by Turnovsky (1987a).

10.10   Interior Debt-to-Equity Ratio

The model developed in this chapter leads to corner solutions for the debt-to-equity ratio. Depending upon the personal and corporate tax rates, the optimal financial structure involves either all-debt financing, all-equity financing, or a knife-edge case in between, where the firm is indifferent between the two forms of financing and the debt-equity ratio is indeterminate. The model is incapable of yielding a well-defined interior solution for the debt-to-equity ratio.

This problem is an old one in corporate finance and is not new to this model. It is the cornerstone of the seminal Modigliani and Miller theorem and the literature it generated. It reflects the fact that all agents face perfect markets and that tax rates are linear. In practice, firms do engage in a mixture of debt and equity financing. The development of a model that yields an interior debt-equity ratio has occupied the attention of corporate finance theorists for a generation now, and no particularly satisfactory solution has been achieved.

A recent paper by Osterberg (1989) derives a determinate debt-to-equity ratio in the Brock-Turnovsky model by introducing agency costs on debt. It is represented by a cost $a(\delta)b_p$ in equation (10.2c), describing the allocation of profits, which is now modified to

$$\Pi = r_p b_p + D + RE + T_f + a(\delta)b_p \tag{10.2c$'$}$$

and where the superscript s is omitted. This cost is assumed not to reduce output by utilizing productive resources. Rather it is an agency cost associated with contractual restrictions intended to control the conflict between bondholders and equity holders. As discussed by Osterberg, the cost can be thought of as reflecting restrictions on debt issue found in bond covenants. Smith and Warner (1979) indicate how the existence of bond covenants can be viewed as a method of controlling the conflict between bondholders and stockholders. In the absence of such restrictions, stockholders would issue more debt and incur greater agency costs. Barnea, Haugen, and Senbet (1985) argue that, as the face value of debt increases, it may be in the interest of stockholders to shift to riskier investment projects. If bond holders anticipate that such a shift would decrease the total value of the firm, they would demand higher interest rates. We thus assume that the bond covenants are negotiated to restrict the level of debt for a given value of equity, implying that the cost of issuing b

units of debt increases with the debt-equity ratio. Specifically, Osterberg assumes the function a to be convex, that is, $a(0) > 0$, $a'(\delta) > 0$, $a''(\delta) > 0$.

With the addition of the agency cost of debt, the cost of capital (10.21') is now modified to[13]

$$\theta^*(\delta, i) \equiv \theta + \left(a(\delta) + \frac{(\tau_y - \tau_p)(\theta + p)}{(1 + \tau_y)} \right) \frac{\delta}{1 + \delta}$$

$$+ \left(\frac{(\theta + p)\tau_c + i(\tau_y - \tau_c)}{1(-\tau_c)} \right) \frac{1}{1 + \delta} \tag{10.40}$$

where the debt component is modified by the inclusion of the per unit agency cost $a(\delta)$. It is clear that, with this function being convex, (10.40) has a well-defined minimum. This is obtained by differentiating (10.40) with respect to δ and setting the resulting expression to zero:

$$\left(a(\delta) + \frac{(\tau_y - \tau_p)(\theta + p)}{(1 - \tau_y)} \right) \frac{1}{1 + \delta} + a'(\delta)\delta$$

$$- \left(\frac{(\theta + p)\tau_c + i(\tau_y - \tau_c)}{(1 - \tau_c)} \right) \frac{1}{1 + \delta} = 0. \tag{10.41}$$

In economic terms, this equation determines the optimal debt-equity ratio to be where the marginal cost of debt capital inclusive of agency costs equals the (given) marginal cost of equity capital.

Any policy change thus has now two effects that must be taken into account in assessing its macroeconomic consequences. First, it will have effects on the costs of debt and equity capital discussed previously. Second, it will now induce firms to change their debt-equity mix. The effect on the overall cost of capital, and therefore on the equilibrium capital-labor ratio, will be the result of these two responses. We shall focus on the steady-state effects, when $\theta = \beta$ and $p = \mu$.

Differentiating (10.41), the following responses of the steady-state debt-equity ratio can be derived:

$$\frac{\partial \delta}{\partial \phi} = \frac{1}{(1 + \delta)[2a' + a''\delta]} \left[\frac{\tau_c}{1 - \tau_c} - \frac{(\tau_y - \tau_p)}{(1 - \tau_y)} \right] \tag{10.42a}$$

$$\frac{\partial \delta}{\partial \tau_y} = \frac{1}{(1 + \delta)[2a' + a''\delta]} \left[\frac{i}{1 - \tau_c} - (\beta + \phi)\frac{(1 - \tau_p)}{(1 - \tau_y)^2} \right] \tag{10.42a}$$

$$\frac{\partial \delta}{\partial \tau_p} = \frac{1}{(1 + \delta)[2a' + a''\delta]} \left[\frac{\beta + \phi}{1 - \tau_y} \right] > 0 \tag{10.42c}$$

$$\frac{\partial \delta}{\partial \tau_c} = \frac{1}{(1 + \delta)[2a' + a''\delta]} \left[\frac{(\beta + \phi) - i(1 - \tau_y)}{(1 - \tau_c)^2} \right] \tag{10.42d}$$

Substituting (10.41) into (10.40) (at steady state), we find that the minimized overall cost of capital is given by the expression

$$\theta^*_{\min} = \beta - a'(\hat{\delta})\hat{\delta}^2 + \frac{(\beta + \phi)\tau_c + \bar{i}(\tau_y - \tau_c)}{1 - \tau_c} \tag{10.43}$$

where $\hat{\delta}$ is the optimal debt-equity ratio determined by (10.41). The effects on the overall cost of capital are obtained by differentiating (10.43) and combining with (10.42).

A higher monetary growth tends to lower the cost of debt capital (provided $\tau_y < \tau_p$) and raise the cost of equity capital, so that both of these effects will tend to induce a switch toward debt financing. Whether this results in an overall decline in the cost of capital depends upon whether the switch toward the cheaper debt dominates the more expensive equity capital, as well as the relative importance of the two types of assets in the firm's financial structure. A higher personal income tax rate raises the cost of both debt and equity capital. Whether this induces a switch toward bonds or toward equitie depends upon which is less adversely affected. Almost certainly, the overall cost of capital will rise, although this is not necessarily the case. Paradoxically, it is possible for a higher personal income tax rate to actually lower the overall cost of capital. This possibility exists if the initial cost of equity capital is sufficiently higher than debt and the switch toward the latter is sufficiently strong. By contrast, a corporate income tax rate induces a switch to debt, the cost of which is reduced while that of equity rises. This implies an unambiguous reduction in the overall cost of capital.

10.11   A Final Comment

This chapter has extended the intertemporal optimizing model to include a more complete corporate sector. Most of our attention has been devoted to developing the macroeconomic framework, and we have discussed its steady-state structure in detail for only one particular form of monetary policy. Other forms of policy can be analyzed using this approach. The most important general conclusion to emerge from this enriched model is that a more complete corporate sector must be integrated into a macroeconomic framework if the effects of macroeconomic policy-making are to be fully understood. The examples we have just been discussing illustrate that point very clearly. An increase in the monetary growth rate is likely to have one set of effects if firms finance with bonds, the opposite effects if they finance with equities, and to be even less clear if they adjust their financial mix. But the model developed in the present chapter is hardly the final word, and subsequent chapters are devoted to further developments.

Notes

1. This formulation of the government budget constraint parallels the treatment of the two private sectors' budget constraints by assuming that government decisions are based on the anticipated rate of inflation. This is somewhat in contrast to the usual specification, which typically replaces p^* in (10.5) with p, the actual rate of inflation. Since we are dealing with a perfect foresight equilibrium (defined below) where $p^* = p$, these two formulations are identical for our purposes.

2. Let S denote the nominal price of equities, so that $s = S/P$. The real value of the nominal value being taxed is $\dot{S}/P = \dot{s} + ps$.

3. The assumption that financial variables are nonnegative rules out short selling.

4. The use of Euler inequalities is discussed in further detail in the appendix to Brock and Turnovsky (1981).

5. Note that we are assuming that $\lim_{s \to \infty} \int_0^s \theta^* \, dt = \infty$.

6. The derivation of (10.24) from (10.23) is rather complicated. The key step involves substituting for $\dot{s}/s$ from (10.13d′) into the definition of τ_e.

7. This is true for the case of a single agent. See Miller (1977) and also Miller and Scholes (1978) for the multiple agent case.

8. Real taxable income, with full deductibility of interest costs, is defined by $\Pi = y - wl - rb_p$. Under all-bond financing and contant returns to scale, this implies $\Pi = (F_k - r)k$. Using the optimality conditions (10.29d), (10.29e), and (10.13c′), this reduces to $\Pi = -pk/(1 - \tau_y) < 0$, implying that taxable income is negative in the presence of positive inflation. One way around this is to assume a production function of the form $y = F(k, l) + h$, where h describes an inelastically supplied specific factor, such as a patent, which adds to production but whose costs are not deductible. Taxable profits become nonnegative provided $h > pk/(1 - \tau_y)$.

9. We should note that because θ and p appear in the cost of capital expression (10.29e), switching in the financial mode may occur during the transition to steady state. To incorporate this will require us to permit jumps in bonds and equities, in order to satisfy the inequality condition (10.23).

10. See the discussion of sustainability of equilibrium provided in Section 9.3. The constant $C = b_{g0}$, in which case $C = -\int_0^\infty x(s)e^{-\int_0^s \theta(\tau)d\tau} ds$, is just a statement of the intertemporal government budget constraint.

11. Steady-state nominal capital gains are given by $\dot{s}/s + \phi$.

12. For simplicity, assume that the utility function is additively separable in real money balances, being of the form $U(c, l, g) + V(m)$. The following mild restrictions suffice to ensure that a single stable root to the dynamic system (10.39) obtains. For bond financing by firms, $mV''/V' < -(\tau_y - \tau_p)/(1 - \tau_p)$; for equity financing by firms, $mV''/V' < -\tau_c$.

13. Osterberg's (1989) model actually employs somewhat different assumptions from those of Brock and Turnovsky (1981): (i) Investment is assumed to be subject to convex costs of adjustment; (ii) labor is fixed; (iii) the government issues no money or bonds; (iv) the only distortionary tax is τ_p, with the government budget being continually balanced through lump-sum taxes.

11 A Dynamic Analysis of Taxes

11.1 Introduction

This chapter extends the perfect foresight equilibrium framework developed in Chapter 10 to analyze the macroeconomic effects of tax policy in greater detail. As in the previous chapter, three taxes are considered, namely, a personal income tax, a corporate income tax, and a capital gains tax. The chapter has two broad purposes. The first is to carry out a *positive* analysis, which examines the dynamic adjustment of the economy to exogenous changes in the various tax rates. Both permanent and temporary tax changes are analyzed. The second is to address *normative* issues pertaining to tax policy, and in this respect two aspects, which have received attention in the literature, are considered. The first is the determination of the optimal taxation of capital and the discussion of a proposition due to Chamley (1986) that characterizes the dynamic adjustment path corresponding to the optimal rate of taxation. The second is the issue of "time inconsistency," which has been discussed extensively in conjunction with the issue of the optimal taxation of capital; see, for example, Kydland and Prescott (1977, 1980), Fischer (1980), Turnovsky and Brock (1980).

The past two decades have seen a growing literature analyzing the dynamic effects of changes in taxes. Early work on this topic was based on the neoclassical growth model (see, e.g., Feldstein 1974a, 1974b; Grierson 1975; Boadway 1979; Auerbach 1979b; Atkinson and Stiglitz 1980, lecture 8; Bernheim 1981). More recent work, however, has been conducted within the context of the intertemporal optimizing representative agent model, such as that developed in Chapters 9 and 10 (see, e.g., Brock and Turnovsky 1981; Turnovsky 1982, 1990; Judd 1985, 1987a, 1987b; Auerbach and Kotlikoff 1987; Frenkel and Razin 1987; Sinn 1987). Proponents of this approach find it to be attractive in that, being based on optimizing behavior, it provides a natural framework for studying rational responses to tax changes. One issue that arises in this framework is the intertemporal viability of a specified policy change. That is, any tax change undertaken at some instant of time will in general require compensating action at some later date, in order to maintain consistency with the intertemporal government budget constraint. This aspect, which we noted in Chapter 9, has been emphasized in particular by Frenkel and Razin (1987), using primarily a two-period horizon, as well as by Judd (1985, 1987a, 1987b).

As we discussed in Chapter 10, the key way in which taxes impact on the economy is through the cost of capital facing firms. This chapter builds on the previous one and the existing literature in several ways, in particular by developing a more comprehensive treatment of the dynamics. This was not dealt with in the discussion of taxes presented in Chapter 10, where the analysis was restricted to steady-state adjustments. Judd (1985, 1987a) does consider the dynamics, but his analysis is based on fixed employment, which for some purposes is restrictive. A more extensive discussion of the dynamics is provided by Turnovsky (1990), upon which the first part of this chapter draws.

In discussing the dynamics, the present analysis emphasizes aspects not previously addressed, but which nevertheless are important in studying the dynamic impact of tax policy. The first is the role of dividend policy adopted by firms. Chapter 10 was based on the assumption that dividend policy was specified in terms of a fixed dividend yield rule. Although this is reasonable, it is also special. Authors such as Auerbach (1979a, 1979b) and Poterba and Summers (1985) have stressed the importance of dividend policy on the cost of capital facing firms, although they do not address the corresponding macrodynamic implications. Auerbach considers the impact of dividend policy on the steady-state valuation of shares and the capital stock. The Poterba and Summers analysis is restricted to the behavior of the firm and is intended to serve as a basis for their empirical tests of alternative hypotheses regarding dividend behavior.

A second important component of the present model is the introduction of a convex cost-of-adjustment function constraining the rate of investment. This has a long history in economics, although its introduction into macroeconomics is relatively recent. Micro analyses of investment behavior based on this approach date back to the seminal work of Eisner and Strotz (1963), Lucas (1967), Gould (1968), and Treadway (1969). The implications of this cost of adjustment approach for macroeconomics, and in particular its link to the Tobin-q were first developed by Summers (1981) and Hayashi (1982) and were further explored within more specific macroeconomic models by Abel (1982) and Abel and Blanchard (1983). One area where the convex cost of adjustment function has played a central role is in the development of international models based on intertemporal optimization. Indeed, as we will see in Chapter 12, as long as the investment good is tradable, the convex cost of adjustment is necessary in order for there to be nontrivial dynamics. In the absence of such costs, by importing from abroad, a small open economy can adjust its capital stock instantaneously to any shock, and the dynamics degenerates.

The third issue we shall emphasize is the contrast between the short-run and the long-run effects of tax changes. In this respect, the results are often quite striking. For example, in general, an increase in any of the three tax rates will lead to an immediate reduction in employment, which, with the capital stock being predetermined, *raises* the capital-labor ratio in the short run. Over time, however, as the higher tax impacts on the cost of capital, the capital stock is reduced, ultimately *lowering* the capital-labor ratio in the new steady state. Since the capital-labor ratio is a critical element determining the distribution of income, this has an important bearing on the relative burdens of the tax borne by capital and labor over time. This question is pursued in Section 11.8.

11.2   The Framework

The structure of the economy parallels that developed in Chapter 10, consisting of households, firms, and the government. Although we choose to enrich the model in some dimensions in order to highlight the new aspects, we simplify it in others. Specifically, we shall abstract from money and thus focus on a real economy.[1] Also, in order to focus on the dividend aspect of the firm's financial decisions, we shall abstract from corporate bonds. Both these simplifications are made for expository purposes and can be relaxed in a straightforward manner.

Household Sector

The representative consumer chooses his level of consumption, supply of labor, and the rates at which he wishes to accumulate his holdings of government bonds and equities issued by firms, so as to maximize the following intertemporal utility function[2]

$$\int_0^\infty U(c, l)e^{-\beta t}\, dt \qquad U_c > 0,\, U_l < 0; \qquad U_{cc} < 0,\, U_{ll} < 0,\, U_{cl} < 0 \quad (11.1a)$$

subject to the budget constraint

$$\dot{b} + s\dot{E} + c = (1 - \tau_y)[wl + rb + D] - \tau_c \dot{s}E + R \qquad (11.1b)$$

and initial conditions

$$b(0) = b_o; \qquad E(0) = E_o \qquad (11.1c)$$

where all terms remain as defined in Chapter 10, with the following changes: r now refers to the real interest rate on government bonds, and R is the lump-sum tax rebate to consumers. The utility function is assumed to be concave in c and l. In addition, we assume that the marginal utility of consumption increases with leisure, and for simplicity we assume that government expenditure has no direct impact on the welfare of private agents.

Following the procedure of Chapter 10, the consumer optimality conditions are

$$U_c(c, l) = \lambda \tag{11.2a}$$

$$U_l(c, l) = -w(1 - \tau_y)\lambda \tag{11.2b}$$

$$r(1 - \tau_y) = \theta \tag{11.2c}$$

$$(1 - \tau_y)\frac{D}{sE} + (1 - \tau_c)\frac{\dot{s}}{s} = \theta \tag{11.2d}$$

$$\theta = \beta - \frac{\dot{\lambda}}{\lambda} \tag{11.2e}$$

where, as before, λ is the marginal utility of wealth, and θ is the rate of return on consumption. These equations are analogous to (10.13) and require little further comment. We assume that bonds and equities exist in strictly positive quantities in equilibrium so that their respective after-tax rates of return equal the rate of return on consumption. With the model being in purely real terms, (11.2d) defines the after-tax rate of return on equities to be the after-tax rate of return on dividends plus the after-tax rate of return on the (real) capital gains, whereas before, capital gains were assumed to be taxed on accrual. The optimality conditions for the consumers are completed with the addition of the transversality conditions

$$\lim_{t \to \infty} \lambda b e^{-\beta t} = \lim_{t \to \infty} \lambda E e^{-\beta t} = 0. \tag{11.2f}$$

Firms

Firms employ labor and capital to produce output in accordance with a neoclassical production function having the usual properties of positive but diminishing marginal physical product and constant returns to scale. We assume that firms finance their capital expenditures out of retained earnings or by issuing new equities.

Gross profit Π is defined by

$$\Pi = F(k, l) - wl \tag{11.3a}$$

where k is the stock of capital and the production function $F(\cdot, \cdot)$ has the usual neoclassical properties. Corporate profit is taxed at the rate τ_p, and the remainder is either paid out as dividends to stockholders or retained as earnings (RE) to finance further investment:

$$(1 - \tau_p)\Pi = D + RE. \tag{11.3b}$$

A critical new feature of the model is the assumption that investment involves installation costs. Expenditure on a given increase in capital $\dot{k} = I$ involves adjustment costs specified by the function

$$I + \psi(I, k) = \left(\frac{I}{k} + \psi\left(\frac{I}{k}, 1 \right) \right) k \equiv H\left(\frac{I}{k} \right) k \qquad \psi \geq 0 \qquad (11.3c)$$

where the addition of I units of capital requires the use of $\psi(I, k)$ units of output. The function $\psi(I, k)$ is specified to be a nonnegative, linearly homogeneous, convex function of the rate of investment and the capital stock. The convexity of the cost-of-adjustment component implies $H' \geq 0$; $H'' > 0$. The homogeneity property of the installation cost function ensures that the market value of the capital stock is invariant with respect to changes in the scale of the economy.[3] By choice of units we may set

$$\psi(0, k) = 0; \qquad \psi_I(0, k) = 0; \quad \text{i.e.,} \quad H(0) = 0; \qquad H'(0) = 1,$$

so that adjustment costs are minimized at a zero level of investment.

The cost of adjustment function has played a prominent role in recent macrodynamic models, and many variants of its specification can be found in the literature. It therefore merits further comment. First, the assumption of nonnegativity implies that disinvestment at the rate $I < 0$ involves positive dismantling costs also represented by ψ. Second, the homogeneity assumption is made largely for convenience, and much of the literature, including the early contributions by Eisner and Strotz (1963), Lucas (1967), and Gould (1968), assumes that ψ is a convex function of I alone. In many cases, little is lost by introducing this simpler assumption. Third, in models that include the depreciation of existing capital (taken to be zero here), the question arises of whether ψ should be specified to be a function of gross or net investment.[4] Both specifications can be found in the literature, and the latter is closer to the treatment here.[5] Further discussion of the cost of adjustment function is provided by Hayashi (1982).

At the same time, we should point out that the cost of adjustment approach is not without its critics. For example, Kydland and Prescott (1982) argue that when an adjustment cost function having plausible values of the adjustment cost parameter (at least for the absolute rather than the proportionate form of the cost function) is introduced into a small macro model, the implied covariance properties of that model are grossly at variance with the U.S. data over the postwar period. Thus the approach should be accepted with some caution insofar as its empirical relevance is concerned.

Noting (11.3c), the financing constraint facing firms is given by

$$RE + s\dot{E} = H\left(\frac{I}{k}\right)k, \tag{11.3d}$$

and eliminating RE between (11.3b) and (11.3d) yields

$$D = (1 - \tau_p)\Pi - H\left(\frac{I}{k}\right)k + s\dot{E}. \tag{11.4}$$

Now define the value of outstanding equities to be

$$V = sE, \tag{11.5}$$

differentiate this equation with respect to t, and combine with the consumer optimality condition (11.2d) and (11.4). This leads to the following differential equation in V:

$$\dot{V} = \frac{\theta}{1 - \tau_c} V - \left[(1 - \tau_p)\Pi - H\left(\frac{I}{k}\right)k\right] + \left(\frac{\tau_y - \tau_c}{1 - \tau_c}\right)D. \tag{11.6}$$

This equation is the analogue to (10.18), though it displays the interdependence between dividend policy and taxes much more prominently. As long as $\tau_y \neq \tau_c$, dividend policy is important in determining the value of the firm. In this equation, the coefficient of V is the rate at which firms discount their after-corporate-profit cash flow. If the dividend payout rate is related to V, the value of equity, then it will affect this discount rate and therefore the cost of capital faced by the firm. If, on the other hand, it is specified in terms of the flow of earnings, then it has no effect on the cost of capital, but instead impacts on the flows being accumulated.

We remarked in Chapter 10 that as long as $\tau_y > \tau_c$, as is being assumed here, it is not optimal for firms to pay dividends. Despite this, firms do in fact pay dividends, and payments generally are fairly stable.[6] In view of this, we shall consider three rules governing dividend policy:

I. $D/V = \bar{i}$

II. $D = (1 - \tau_p)\Pi$

III. $RE = H\left(\frac{I}{k}\right)k; \qquad D = (1 - \tau_p)\Pi - H\left(\frac{I}{k}\right)k$

Rule I is the policy assumed in Chapter 10, where firms offer a fixed dividend yield to stockholders on their equity. In the light of the nonoptimality of dividend payments, firms will set $\bar{i}$ to some acceptable minimum level. This rule therefore represents a form of constrained optimal dividend policy. The overall optimal policy of paying no dividends is obtained by setting $\bar{i} = 0$. Rules II and III are polar extremes of meeting the financial constraint (11.3d). The former implies that the marginal source of financing consists solely of new equities. Rule III implies that the marginal source of financing is through retained earnings, with dividends being determined residually (see, e.g., Summers 1981).[7] The problem with this latter rule is that it implies more volatile behavior on the part of dividends than in practice is observed. At the same time, the reason for focusing on polar extremes as in the case of I and II is to highlight the differences between the alternative marginal sources of finance available to the firm.

Substituting these rules into (11.6) leads to the corresponding differential equations determining the evolution of V:

$$\dot{V} = \left[\frac{\theta}{1 - \tau_c} + \frac{\bar{i}(\tau_y - \tau_c)}{1 - \tau_c} \right] V - \left[(1 - \tau_p)\Pi - H\left(\frac{I}{k}\right)k \right] \tag{11.7a}$$

$$\dot{V} = \frac{\theta}{1 - \tau_c} V - \left[\frac{(1 - \tau_p)(1 - \tau_y)}{1 - \tau_c}\Pi - H\left(\frac{I}{k}\right)k \right] \tag{11.7b}$$

$$\dot{V} = \frac{\theta}{1 - \tau_c} V - \left(\frac{1 - \tau_y}{1 - \tau_c} \right) \left[(1 - \tau_p)\Pi - H\left(\frac{I}{k}\right)k \right]. \tag{11.7c}$$

While these rules share many similarities, as we shall see below they also imply important differences.[8] For example, we shall see that with all investment financed out of retained earnings, the rate of personal income tax τ_y has no effect on the long-run capital-labor ratio. If, further, employment is always fixed, then the long-run stock of capital itself is independent of τ_y, and this implies that there is no dynamic adjustment to this tax. By contrast, if all profits are paid out as dividends, so that investment is financed by issuing new equities, it is the rate of capital gains tax τ_c that becomes irrelevant. Indeed, we shall show it has no effect in either the long run or the short run, irrespective of whether employment is fixed or not. Finally, we shall show that while Rule III is known to lead to the long-run undervaluation of equities (which depends upon τ_y, τ_c), for the other two rules, the long-run value of equities equals that of the underlying physical capital stock.[9]

Whatever dividend rule is assumed, the firm's objective is to choose I, l, and k, to maximize the initial value of equity $V(0)$. Writing the typical equation of (11.7) in the form

$$\dot{V} = \theta^* V - \gamma(k, l, I)$$

where θ^* represents the required rate of return on capital, and integrating this equation, the firm's optimization problem can be expressed

$$\max_{k,l,I} V(0) = \int_0^\infty \gamma(k,l,I)e^{-\int_0^t \theta^*(\tau)d\tau} \tag{11.8a}$$

subject to

$$\dot{k} = I \tag{11.8b}$$

and the given initial capital stock

$$k(0) = k_0. \tag{11.8c}$$

This is analogous to the problem as specified in Chapter 10, though the firm's range of financial decisions are now more restricted.

Focusing on the fixed dividend payout Rule I, the optimality conditions can be expressed as

$$F_l(k,l) = w \tag{11.9a}$$

$$H'\left(\frac{I}{k}\right) = q \tag{11.9b}$$

$$\frac{(1-\tau_p)F_k(k,l)}{q} + \frac{\dot{q}}{q} + \frac{qI - Hk}{qk} = \theta^* \tag{11.9c}$$

where, in this case,

$$\theta^* \equiv \frac{\theta}{1-\tau_c} + \frac{\bar{i}(\tau_y - \tau_c)}{1-\tau_c}, \tag{11.9d}$$

and q is the costate variable associated with the accumulation equation (11.8b). Equation (11.9a) is the familiar marginal product of labor condition, while equation (11.9b) equates the marginal cost of investment to the shadow price q. This equation may be solved for I/k in the form

$$I = \phi(q)k \qquad \phi'(q) > 0,$$

which is essentially a Tobin-q theory of investment. The higher the shadow value of capital, the faster is the optimal rate of capital accumulation. Equation (11.9c) is an arbitrage condition linking the rate of return on a unit of capital to the cost of capital. The latter, given by the right-hand side of this equation, is precisely the expression for the cost of equity financing (in the absence of inflation), given by (10.25″). The rate of return on a unit of capital, given by the left-hand side, consists of several components. First, there is the physical after-tax return on the underlying capital per unit of capital, valued at its shadow price, and given by the first expression. Second, there is the rate of change in the value of capital. Third, there is the return arising from the difference in the valuation of the new capital qI created and the value of the resources it utilizes Hk, again normalized by the value of capital. Seen another way, this third component reflects the fact that an additional source of benefits of a higher k is to reduce the installation costs (which depend upon I/k) associated with new investment. In the absence of adjustment costs, $q \equiv 1$, and (11.9c) simplifies to the familiar expression $(1 - \tau_p)F_k = \theta^*$.

For the all profit payout Rule II, the optimality conditions (11.9a), (11.9b) again obtain. The third equation is now modified to the following:

$$\frac{(1 - \tau_y)(1 - \tau_p)F_k(k,l)}{q(1 - \tau_c)} + \frac{\dot{q}}{q} + \frac{qI - Hk}{qk} = \theta^*, \tag{11.9c'}$$

whereas (11.9d) becomes

$$\theta^* \equiv \frac{\theta}{1 - \tau_c}. \tag{11.9d'}$$

There are two differences from Rule 1. As long as $\tau_y > \tau_c$, the cost of capital is now cheaper than before, and with all income earned by the firm being paid out at as dividends and therefore taxed at the higher rate, the net after-tax flow of income from capital, reflected by the first term in (11.9c'), is thus reduced from before.

In the case where all investment is financed out of retained earnings, the marginal condition determining investment (11.9b) is amended to

$$\left(\frac{1 - \tau_y}{1 - \tau_c}\right) H'\left(\frac{I}{k}\right) = q. \tag{11.9b'}$$

It is cheaper to finance new investment using retained earnings than by issuing new equitites. This is because the capital gains generated by the retained earnings are taxed at a lower rate than would be the corresponding dividends if these earning were instead paid out and new equitites used to finance the investment. In addition, (11.9c) now becomes

$$\left(\frac{1 - \tau_y}{1 - \tau_c}\right)\left[\frac{(1 - \tau_p)F_k(k,1)}{q} + \frac{\dot{q}}{q} + \frac{qI - Hk}{qk}\right] = \theta^* \tag{11.9c''}$$

where θ^* is also given by (11.9d').

At this point it is desirable to clarify our use of terminology. The quantity θ^* represents the required rate of return on capital *after* corporate income tax but *before* personal income taxes. For convenience we refer to this as the cost of capital. We should note, however, that the cost of capital is sometimes defined as being the value of the marginal physical product of capital, which satisfies an optimality condition such as (11.9c). In the absence of adjustment costs (and therefore in steady-state equilibrium) these two definitions differ by only the corporate tax factor $(1 - \tau_p)$. However, in the presence of adjustment costs, which prevent the marginal physical product of capital from being set at its optimum instantaneously, these two measures differ in more substantive ways; this should be kept in mind in the subsequent discussion.

Substituting the optimality conditions (11.9a) and (11.9b) into (11.6) yields the time path for the optimized value of equities $\hat{V}$. Focusing on Rule I and using the linear homogeneity of the production function, we have

$$\dot{\hat{V}} = \theta^* \hat{V} - (1 - \tau_p) F_k(k, l)k + H[\phi(q)]k. \tag{11.10}$$

We can now establish that along such an optimized path $\hat{V} = qk$. To do this, let

$$v \equiv \frac{\hat{V}}{qk}$$

so that

$$\frac{\dot{v}}{v} = \frac{\dot{\hat{V}}}{\hat{V}} - \frac{\dot{q}}{q} - \frac{\dot{k}}{k}.$$

Substituting for (11.10), (11.9c), (I/k), and (11.8b) into this equation leads to the differential equation

$$\dot{v} = \left[\frac{(1 - \tau_p)F_k - H}{q} \right] (v - 1).$$

It is clear that, in general, the only stable solution to this equation, one that ties the value of equities to the underlying capital stock, is $v = 1$; that is, $\hat{V} = qk$. Hence, we have established the links

$$q = \frac{\hat{V}}{k} = \frac{sE}{k} \tag{11.11}$$

so that q measures the ratio of the current value of equities to the underlying stock of capital. It is essentially the price of equities, and henceforth we shall refer to it as being the value of the stock market (see also Hayashi 1982).

The Government

The final agent in the economy is the government, which operates in accordance with its flow budget constraint,

$$\dot{b} = g + rb - \tau_y[wl + rb + D] - \tau_c \dot{s}E - \tau_p \Pi + R, \tag{11.12}$$

where g denotes real government expenditure, which is assumed to remain constant over time. This relationship is straightforward and requires no further comment. We shall assume that whenever the government changes a tax rate, it adjusts the time path of debt and/or lump-sum rebates R in order to satisfy its intertemporal budget constraint. The specifics of how this is done are unimportant, and as long as this is undertaken, (11.12) need be considered no further.

11.3   Macroeconomic Equilibrium

The macroeconomic equilibrium is obtained by combining the optimality conditions for households and firms, together with the market-clearing conditions, and insofar as it is relevant, the government budget constraint. Since the general characteristics are the same for all dividend policies, we shall focus on the fixed dividend yield policy (Rule I) and comment on the others only with respect to aspects where they differ in significant ways.

The macroeconomic equilibrium includes the three static conditions:

$$U_c(c,l) = \lambda, \tag{11.13a}$$

$$U_l(c,l) = -F_l(k,l)(1 - \tau_y)\lambda, \tag{11.13b}$$

$$I = \phi(q)k. \tag{11.13c}$$

The first two equations are identical to (10.29a) and (10.29b), and (11.13c) is the Tobin q investment function, as noted. The first two equations may be solved for consumption and employment:

$$c = c(\lambda, k, \tau_y) \qquad c_\lambda < 0, c_k < 0, c_{\tau_y} > 0 \tag{11.14a}$$

$$l = l(\lambda, k, \tau_y) \qquad l_\lambda > 0, l_k > 0, l_{\tau_y} < 0 \tag{11.14b}$$

having the partial derivatives as indicated. Intuitively, an increase in the marginal utility of wealth leads to more saving and less consumption, as well as a greater willingness to work. An increase in the capital stock tends to raise the real wage, causing consumers to substitute labor for consumption. Finally, the partial effect of an increase in the personal income tax is to lower the after-tax wage rate, causing consumers to substitute away from labor to more consumption. However, we must emphasize that this is only a partial effect, since τ_y (and indeed the entire future time path of all tax rates) will also impact on the marginal utility λ, having further effects on both these variables; see Section 11.7.

Equations (11.13c), (11.14a), and (11.14b) express $I, c,$ and l in terms of $k, q,$ and λ, the dynamics of which are described by

$$\dot{k} = \phi(q)k, \tag{11.15a}$$

$$\dot{q} = \theta^*q - (1 - \tau_p)F_k[k, l(\lambda, k, \tau_y)] - \phi(q)q + H[\phi(q)], \tag{11.15b}$$

$$\dot{\lambda} = \lambda(\beta - \theta), \tag{11.15c}$$

where for Rule I, θ^* is defined by (11.9d). Note that this equilibrium dynamic system depends upon the rate of return on consumption θ. This too needs to be determined, and to do so we consider the product market equilibrium condition expressed in the form

$$F[k, l(\lambda, k, \tau_y)] = c(\lambda, k, \tau_y) + H[\phi(q)]k + g. \tag{11.16}$$

This equation asserts that, in equilibrium, output must be allocated either to consumption, to government expenditure, or to capital formation, where the latter involves adjustment costs reflected in the function H. Differentiating this equation with respect to t yields

$$[F_k + F_l l_k - c_k - H[\phi(q)]]\dot{k} + [F_l l_\lambda - c_\lambda]\dot{\lambda} = H'\phi'(q)k\dot{q}, \tag{11.16'}$$

and substituting for $\dot{k}, \dot{q},$ and $\dot{\lambda}$ from (11.15a)–(11.15c), noting (11.9b), leads to

$$\left[\frac{k\phi'q^2}{1 - \tau_c} + (F_l l_\lambda - c_\lambda)\lambda\right]\theta$$
$$= [F_k + F_l l_k - c_k - H[\phi(q)]]\phi(q)k + (F_l l_\lambda - c_\lambda)\lambda\beta$$
$$- k\phi'(q)q\left[\frac{q\dot{i}(\tau_y - \tau_c)}{(1 - \tau_c)} - (1 - \tau_p)F_k + H[\phi(q)] - q\phi(q)\right], \tag{11.17}$$

which may be solved in the form

$$\theta = \theta(\lambda, k, q, \tau_y, \tau_c, \tau_p). \tag{11.18}$$

The partial derivatives of this function are important for our subsequent analysis of the dynamics and will be noted at the appropriate place below.

Finally, the equilibrium government budget constraint is obtained by substituting the optimality conditions into (11.12). As noted, the dynamics of bond accumulation do not affect the dynamics of the system as described by (11.15a)–(11.15c). All we require is that, through a combination of lump-sum rebates and bond accumulation, the government's intertemporal budget constraint be met.

11.4   Steady-State Effects

Because of the forward-looking characteristic of the economy, the transitional dynamics are determined to an important degree by the expectations of the long-run steady state. The long-run effects of various tax changes essentially drive the short-term dynamics, and it is therefore convenient to begin with the former. Again, we shall focus primarily on policy Rule I, commenting only on differences in the other cases.

The steady state of the system (11.15) is reached when $\dot{k} = \dot{q} = \dot{\lambda} = 0$. With no depreciation of capital, steady-state investment $I = 0$, implying that $\tilde{q} = 1$, (where tildes denote steady state), so that in the long run the value of equity equals that of the underlying stock of capital. The rate of return on consumption θ equals the consumer rate of time discount β. The steady-state solutions for $\tilde{k}, \tilde{l}$, and $\tilde{c}$ are obtained from the following:

$$U_c(\tilde{c}, \tilde{l}) + F_l(\tilde{k}, \tilde{l})(1 - \tau_y)U_l(\tilde{c}, \tilde{l}) = 0, \tag{11.19a}$$

$$(1 - \tau_p)F_k(\tilde{k}, \tilde{l}) = \frac{\beta}{1 - \tau_c} + \frac{\tilde{i}(\tau_y - \tau_c)}{1 - \tau_c}, \tag{11.19b}$$

$$F(\tilde{k}, \tilde{l}) = \tilde{c} + g. \tag{11.19c}$$

The analogy between (11.19) and (10.36) should be clear. As in Chapter 10, the long-run equilibrium is obtained recursively. The right-hand side of (11.19b) specifies the long-run required rate of return on capital, which in equilibrium is equated to the after-tax marginal physical product of capital.[10] Given the linear homogeneity of the production function, this establishes the capital-labor ratio, which in turn determines the real wage rate. Having determined $\tilde{k}/\tilde{l}$, the marginal rate of substitution condition (11.19a) and the product market equilibrium condition (11.19c) jointly determine the equilibrium level of employment and consumption. With $\tilde{k}/\tilde{l}$ and $\tilde{l}$ determined, the real stock of capital is now fixed, and the level of output follows from the production function.

It is apparent from this equilibrium that the two tax rates τ_p, τ_c both operate entirely through their effects on the required rate of return on capital and hence on the equilibrium capital-labor ratio. In addition to having a similar effect, the personal income tax rate τ_y has a further impact on the supply of labor through the consumption-leisure trade-off.

The expressions for the long-run responses to changes in the various tax rates are reported in Table 11.1. The qualitative responses for the three dividend policies are summarized in Table 11.2. These will be discussed in turn.

Increase in Personal Income Tax Rate

An increase in the personal income tax rate raises both the long-run interest rate and the long-run required rate of return on capital, thereby reducing the capital-labor ratio. This reduces the before-tax real wage, causing the after-tax real wage to fall by an even greater amount. The

Table 11.1
Long-run effects of various tax increases

$$d\tilde{\theta}^* = \frac{\bar{i}}{1 - \tau_c} d\tau_y + \frac{[\beta - \bar{i}(1 - \tau_y)]}{(1 - \tau_c)^2} d\tau_c \qquad \text{Dividend Rule I}$$

$$d\tilde{\theta}^* = \frac{\beta}{(1 - \tau_c)^2} d\tau_c \qquad \text{Dividend Rules II, III}$$

$$d(\tilde{k}/l) = \frac{1}{(1 - \tau_p)F_{kk}} \left\{ \frac{\bar{i}}{1 - \tau_c} d\tau_y + \frac{[\beta - \bar{i}(1 - \tau_y)]}{(1 - \tau_c)^2} d\tau_c + F_k d\tau_p \right\} \qquad \text{Dividend Rule I}$$

$$d(\tilde{k}/l) = \frac{F_k}{F_{kk}} \left\{ \frac{d\tau_y}{1 - \tau_y} + \frac{d\tau_p}{1 - \tau_p} \right\} \qquad \text{Dividend Rule II}$$

$$d(\tilde{k}/l) = \frac{F_k}{F_{kk}} \left\{ \frac{d\tau_p}{1 - \tau_p} + \frac{d\tau_c}{1 - \tau_c} \right\} \qquad \text{Dividend Rule III}$$

$$d\tilde{l} = \left\{ lf'[U_{lc} + F_l(1 - \tau_y)U_{cc}] - (1 - \tau_y)U_c(k/l)f'' \right\} \frac{d(k/\tilde{l})}{D} - F_l \frac{U_c}{D} d\tau_y$$

$$d\tilde{c} = -\left\{ lf'[U_{ll} + F_l(1 - \tau_y)U_{cl}] + f(1 - \tau_y)U_c f'' \right\} \frac{d(k/\tilde{l})}{D} - fF_l \frac{U_c}{D} d\tau_y$$

$$d\tilde{y} = -\left\{ lf'[U_{ll} + F_l(1 - \tau_y)U_{cl}] + f(1 - \tau_y)U_c(k/l)f'' \right\} \frac{d(k/\tilde{l})}{D} - fF_l \frac{U_c}{D} d\tau_y$$

$$d\tilde{k} = -\left\{ lF_l[U_{lc} + F_l(1 - \tau_y)U_{cc}] + [U_{ll} + F_l(1 - \tau_y)U_{cl}]l + (k/l)^2(1 - \tau_y)U_c f'' \right\} \frac{d(k/\tilde{l})}{D} - (k/l)F_l \frac{U_c}{D} d\tau_y$$

$$d\tilde{\lambda} = -\left\{ lf'(U_{cc}U_{ll} - U_{cl}^2) + (1 - \tau_y)(k/l)U_c f''[U_{cl} + U_{cc}f] \right\} \frac{d(k/\tilde{l})}{D} - F_l \frac{U_c}{D} [U_{cc}f + U_{cl}] d\tau_y$$

where

$$f \equiv F(k, l)/l; \qquad D \equiv -f[F_l(1 - \tau_y)U_{cc} + U_{lc}] - [U_{ll} + F_l(1 - \tau_y)U_{cl}] > 0$$

Table 11.2
Long-run qualitative effects of tax increases

	Dividend Rule I $D/V = \bar{i}$			Dividend Rule II $D = (1 - \tau_p)\pi$			Dividend Rule III $RE = H(I/k)k$		
					Increase in				
	τ_y	τ_p	τ_c	τ_y	τ_p	τ_c	τ_y	τ_p	τ_c
Cost of capital $\tilde{\theta}^*$	+	0	+	0	0	+	0	0	+
Interest rate $\tilde{r}$	+	0	0	+	0	0	+	0	0
Capital-labor ratio $\tilde{k}/l$	−	−	−	−	−	0	0	−	−
After-tax wage rate	−	−	−	−	−	0	−	−	−
Marginal utility of wealth $\tilde{\lambda}$	+	+	+	+	+	+	+	+	+
Stock value $\tilde{q}$	0	0	0	0	0	0	−	0	+
Capital stock $\tilde{k}$	−	−	−	−	−	0	−	−	−
Consumption $\tilde{c}$	−	−	−	−	−	0	−	−	−
Employment $\tilde{l}$	?	?	?	?	?	0	−	?	?
Output $\tilde{y}$	−	−	−	−	−	0	−	−	−

Note: for Rule I: $\tilde{\theta}^* = \beta/(1 - \tau_c) + \bar{i}(\tau_y - \tau_c)/(1 - \tau_c)$.
        for Rules II and III: $\tilde{\theta}^* = \beta/(1 - \tau_c)$.

increase in τ_y leads to two effects on both consumption and employment. The fall in the capital-labor ratio stemming from the higher cost of capital leads to a fall in consumption. In addition, consumption is reduced further by the fall in the after-tax real wage that results directly from the rise in τ_y. By contrast, the fall in the capital-labor ratio has an ambiguous effect on equilibrium employment. On the one hand, the resulting fall in the real wage decreases the supply of labor, while at the same time inducing firms to employ additional labor. In addition, the increase in τ_y, by lowering the after-tax real wage, has a further contractionary effect on labor supply. But, irrespective of the response of $\tilde{l}$, the decrease in the capital-labor ratio is sufficient to ensure that both the stock of capital and output fall.

In order to analyze the dynamics of employment and consumption, we need to know the response of the long-run marginal utility of wealth $\tilde{\lambda}$. This is given by

$$d\tilde{\lambda} = U_{cc}\,d\tilde{c} + U_{cl}\,d\tilde{l}.$$

The fall in the steady-state consumption raises the marginal utility of consumption and therefore the equilibrium marginal utility of wealth, while the effects due to employment are unclear. Nevertheless, by direct evaluation of the expressions in Table 11.2, we can show that the consumption effect dominates, so that overall, an increase in τ_y leads to a long-run increase in the marginal utility of wealth. More intuitively, the higher distortionary tax rate lowers the wealth of the agent, thereby raising its marginal utility.

Increase in Corporate Profit Tax Rate

The effects of an increase in the corporate profit tax rate are straightforward. Both the interest rate and the required rate of return on capital remain unchanged. In order for the after-tax marginal physical product of capital to remain fixed, the capital-labor ratio must fall. The subsequent responses are analogous to those stemming from the fall in the capital-labor ratio resulting from the increase in τ_y.

Increase in Capital Gains Tax Rate

All responses depend upon the quantity $\beta - \bar{i}(1 - \tau_y)$, with the exception of the interest rate, which remains unchanged. From (11.2d) we see that, in steady-state equilibrium, $\beta - \bar{i}(1 - \tau_y) = (\dot{s}/s)(1 - \tau_c)$, which is the after-tax rate of capital gains on equities earned by households. Taking this to be positive, the required rate of return on capital (i.e., the right-hand side of [11.19b]) increases with τ_c, and the responses are the same as those stemming from an increase in τ_p.

The effects of the tax increase under the other two forms of dividend policy are shown in columns 2 and 3 of Table 11.2. The following differences are worth noting:

i. When all profits are paid out, the capital gains tax has no effect. This can easily be seen from the optimality conditions (11.9c') and (11.9d'), which in steady state become

$$(1 - \tau_y)(1 - \tau_p)F_k(\tilde{k}, \tilde{l}) = \beta.$$

The long-run capital-labor ratio is therefore independent of τ_c, and so, therefore, are all other effects; see also Sinn (1987).

ii. When all investment is financed by retained earnings, the equilibrium marginal product of capital condition becomes

$$(1 - \tau_c)(1 - \tau_p)F_k(\tilde{k}, \tilde{l}) = \beta,$$

so that the equilibrium capital-labor ratio is independent of τ_y; see also Auerbach (1979b), Summers (1981), and Sinn (1987). Furthermore, if labor is assumed to be fixed, the long-run stock of capital itself, and therefore consumption, is also independent of τ_y. On the other hand, with endogenous employment, the substitution effect between consumption and labor still exists, and both fall. This result also holds in the overall optimal case where no dividends are paid out. It is also worth noting that the statements being made in (i) and (ii) depend in part upon the assumption that the consumer rate of time preference β remains fixed.

iii. Also, when all investment is financed out of retained earnings, the equilibrium value of equities is

$$\tilde{q} = \left(\frac{1 - \tau_y}{1 - \tau_c} \right),$$

which, with $\tau_y > \tau_c$, is less than unity. This result follows directly from (11.9b') and the fact that, by choice of units, $H'(0) = 1$. The long-run value of equity is therefore less than that of the underlying capital stock; it is increasing with the capital gains tax but declining with the personal income tax rate. This result is a familiar one from the literature (see, e.g., Auerbach 1979a, 1979b; Summers 1981; Poterba and Summers 1985; and Sinn 1987). The following simple intuitive explanation for this result may be given. Firms invest until owners are indifferent at the margin between having an additional unit of profit paid out as dividends and having the returns reinvested within the firm. In the former case, for every unit of dividend income received, the shareholder receives $(1 - \tau_y)$ of after-tax income. In the latter case, the firm retains the output and purchases a new unit of capital. Its share value will appreciate by q, yielding $(1 - \tau_c)q$ units of after-tax income. In order for the shareholder to be indifferent between these two sources of income, the equilibrium value of q must satisfy $\tilde{q} = (1 - \tau_y)/(1 - \tau_c)$.

11.5 Transitional Dynamics

We now turn to the more interesting aspect, namely the transitional adjustment of the economy to the various tax disturbances. We begin by linearizing the dynamic equations (11.15a)–(11.15c) about the steady-state equilibrium, enabling the dynamics to be expressed in the linearized form

$$
\begin{bmatrix} \dot{k} \\ \dot{q} \\ \dot{\lambda} \end{bmatrix}
=
\begin{bmatrix}
0 & \overset{(+)}{\phi'(k)} & 0 \\
\theta_k^* - (1-\tau_p)[\overset{(+)}{F_{kk}+F_{kl}l_k}] & \theta^* + \overset{(+)}{\theta_q^*} & \theta_\lambda^* - (1-\overset{(-)}{\tau_p})F_{kl}l_\lambda \\
-\tilde{\lambda}\overset{(-)}{\theta_k} & -\tilde{\lambda}\overset{(-)}{\theta_q} & -\tilde{\lambda}\overset{(-)}{\theta_\lambda}
\end{bmatrix}
\begin{bmatrix} k - \tilde{k} \\ q - \tilde{q} \\ \lambda - \tilde{\lambda} \end{bmatrix}
$$

(11.20)

where all terms and partial derivatives appearing in the matrix are evaluated at steady state. By direct evaluation, the elements can be shown to have the signs indicated.

The partial derivatives of θ are obtained by taking the differentials of (11.16) evaluated at steady state. (Away from steady state they are much more complicated). Intuitively, an increase in capital lowers the marginal physical product of capital, reducing the interest rate and the rate of return on consumption ($\theta_k < 0$). An increase in λ increases employment, thereby raising the marginal physical product of capital, the interest rate, and the rate of return on consumption ($\theta_\lambda > 0$). An increase in q raises investment, and in order to generate a higher rate of savings, the interest rate and the rate of return on consumption must rise ($\theta_q > 0$).

The eigenvalues of the linearized system (11.20), μ_1, μ_2, μ_3, have the properties $\mu_1 < 0$, $\mu_2 > 0$, $\mu_3 = 0$, the zero value stemming from the fact that the dynamics are linked by the product market equilibrium condition (11.16'). Of the dynamic variables, the capital stock is constrained to move continuously at all times, whereas the marginal utility of wealth and the stock price may both jump instantaneously in response to new information.

We shall consider stable adjustment paths beginning from an initial given capital stock k_0 and satisfying the consumer transversality conditions. The solutions for $k, q,$ and λ along such paths are given by

$$k = \tilde{k} + (k_0 - \tilde{k})e^{\mu_1 t} \tag{11.21a}$$

$$q - \tilde{q} = \frac{\mu_1}{\phi' k}(k - \tilde{k}) \tag{11.21b}$$

$$\lambda - \tilde{\lambda} = \frac{(a_{31} + (a_{32}/a_{12})\mu_1)}{\mu_1 - a_{33}}(k - \tilde{k}) \tag{11.21c}$$

where the terms a_{ij} can be identified as being the appropriate elements of the matrix appearing in (11.20). Note that (11.21b) describes a linear relationship between q and k that is negatively sloped. Equation (11.21c) is also linear and negative, although the latter fact is a little less obvious.[11]

Equations (11.13a)–(11.13c), (11.19a)–(11.19c), and (11.21a)–(11.21c) describe the dynamics of the economy. Starting from an initial capital stock k_0, (11.21b) and (11.21c) determine the initial stock price and the marginal utility of wealth, respectively. Equations (11.13a)–(11.13c) then determine the initial levels of investment, employment, and consumption. With the long-run steady state being determined by (11.19a)–(11.19c) and with $\tilde{q} = 1$, equations (11.21a)–(11.21c) determine the evolution of capital, the stock price, and the marginal utility of wealth, consistent with the ultimate attainment of steady state. Again, we should point out that in order for such an equilibrium to be sustainable, we require that the government adjust its debt and lump-sum financing to ensure that its intertemporal budget constraint is met.

11.6 The Dynamics of Policy Shocks

In Section 11.7 we will analyze the dynamic effects of changes in the three tax rates. We will do so by means of two sets of phase diagrams. The first, in $\lambda - k$ space, describes the employment-consumption dynamics; the second, in q-k space, describes the investment and stock market effects. All policy shocks are offset by lump-sum taxes, so that only the distortionary effects are being analyzed.

As long as no future shock is anticipated, the system must lie on a stable locus. Thus the initial adjustment in the marginal utility $\lambda(0)$ following some unanticipated permanent shock must satisfy (see [11.21c])

$$d\lambda(0) = d\tilde{\lambda} - \frac{[a_{31} + (a_{32}/a_{12})\mu_1]}{\mu_1 - a_{33}}d\tilde{k}. \tag{11.22}$$

This equation relates the instantaneous jump in $\lambda(0)$ to the respective steady-state changes in $\tilde{\lambda}, \tilde{k}$ and embodies the forward-looking behavior of the system.

In general, the steady-state market-clearing condition may be written as

$$F(\tilde{k}, (\tilde{l}, \tilde{k}, \tau_y)] - c(\tilde{\lambda}, \tilde{k}, \tau_y) - g = 0,$$

which, taking differentials, yields

$$\omega_{11} \, d\tilde{k} + \omega_{12} \, d\tilde{\lambda} + \omega_{13} \, d\tau_y = 0 \tag{11.23}$$

where

$$\omega_{11} \equiv F_k + F_l l_k - c_k > 0; \qquad \omega_{12} \equiv F_l l_\lambda - c_\lambda > 0;$$

$$\omega_{13} \equiv F_l l_{\tau_y} - c_{\tau_y} < 0.$$

Combining (11.22) and (11.23) implies

$$d\lambda(0) = -\left[\frac{a_{31} + (a_{32}/a_{12})\mu_1}{\mu_1 - a_{33}} + \frac{\omega_{11}}{\omega_{12}}\right] d\tilde{k} - \left[\frac{\omega_{13}}{\omega_{12}}\right] d\tau_y, \tag{11.24}$$

which expresses the initial jump in $\lambda(0)$ resulting from an unanticipated permanent policy change in terms of two components: (i) the response of the equilibrium capital stock; (ii) in the case of τ_y, a shift resulting from the effects on the consumption-leisure trade-off. By using the fact that μ_1 is an eigenvalue of (11.21) one can establish (tediously) that the coefficient of $d\tilde{k}$ in (11.24) is positive, and $-\omega_{13}/\omega_{12}$ is also obviously positive.[12]

The initial jump is in turn transmitted via equations (11.14a) and (11.14b) to initial changes in consumption and employment. But in addition to these, the complete short-run adjustment incorporates any direct impact that a change in policy may have on these variables (the implementation effect of Chapter 6). For example, the complete short-run response in employment to a change in the personal income tax rate is

$$\frac{dl(0)}{d\tau_y} = \frac{\partial l(0)}{\partial \lambda} \frac{d\lambda(0)}{d\tau_y} + \frac{\partial l}{\partial \tau_y} \tag{11.25}$$

Analogous relationships hold for other variables.

The response of the value of the stock market and investment is simpler to establish. From (11.21b) we have

$$dq(0) = d\tilde{q} - \frac{\mu_1}{\phi' k} d\tilde{k}.$$

For dividend payout Rules I and II, $d\tilde{q} = 0$, so that the short-run response of the stock market follows the long-run response of the capital stock. When all investment is financed from retained earnings, the short-run response in q is a little more complex, although it too can be shown to follow $\tilde{k}$.

11.7 Short-Run Effects of Increases in Tax Rates

Personal Income Tax Rate

As noted in Table 11.2, a permanent increase in the personal income tax rate leads to a decrease in the steady-state stock of capital $\tilde{k}$, accompanied by an increase in the steady-state marginal utility of wealth $\tilde{\lambda}$. From (11.24), the initial response of the marginal utility of wealth $d\lambda(0)$ is ambiguous. On the one hand, the decrease in $\tilde{k}$ implies a transitional decumulation of capital. There is an initial fall in investment, lowering aggregate demand. In order to maintain product market equilibrium with the capital stock fixed instantaneously, employment must fall or consumption must rise, and this is brought about by a decrease in $\lambda(0)$; see (11.16). We call this the *intertemporal decumulation effect*. On the other hand, the higher tax rate, by reducing the wage rate, causes a substitution from work to consumption, thereby generating an excess demand for output, which, in order to maintain product market equilibrium, is offset in the short run by an increase in $\lambda(0)$. We call this the *direct wage effect*. The overall response depends upon which dominates. Figure 11.1A illustrates the case where the intertemporal decumulation effect dominates. Figure 11.1B illustrates the dynamics in $q - k$, and in both cases the response to both a permanent and a temporary tax increase are considered.

Permanent Tax Increase

Suppose that the economy is initially in steady state at the point P on the stable arm XX and that there is a permanent increase in τ_y. The equilibrium shifts to the point Q, with a lower capital stock, coupled with an increase in $\tilde{\lambda}$. With the intertemporal accumulation effect being dominant, $\lambda(0)$ drops, so that the stable locus shifts down to $X'X'$. The marginal utility of wealth jumps from P to A on the new stable locus $X'X'$, which is then followed continuously to the new steady-state equilibrium Q.

Turning to Figure 11.1B, starting from the initial equilibrium at L, on the stable locus ZZ, q drops immediately to H on $Z'Z'$, investment declines, and q and k follow this locus to the new steady state. For dividend Rules I or II, where the steady-state $\tilde{q}$ is independent of τ_y, the new equilibrium will be at M. If all investment is financed out of retained

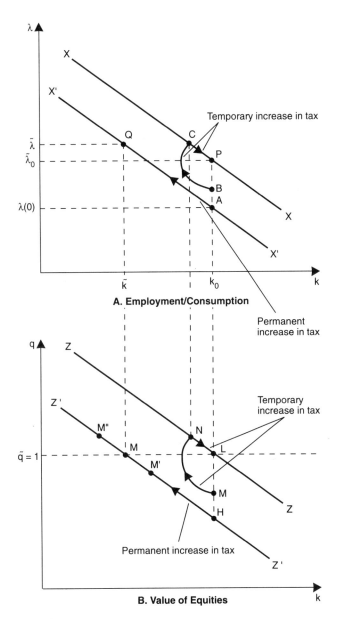

Figure 11.1
Transitional dynamics: intertemporal decumulation effect dominant

earnings, when $\tilde{q}$ is reduced permanently, it will be at a point such as M' (with Q also being adjusted correspondingly).

The case where the direct wage effect dominates is illustrated in Figure 11.2. The difference here is that the locus XX is shifted up to $X'X'$, so that the initial jump in marginal utility is up, rather than down. This turns out to have relatively little bearing on the behavior of the system.

The short-run effects of an increase in τ_y on the key economic variables are summarized in Table 11.3. They consist of the direct effects as well as the indirect effects generated by the induced jumps in $\lambda(0), q(0)$. Consider, first, employment. The direct effect of the higher personal income tax is to reduce the labor supply and hence employment. In addition, as noted in (11.25), there is the indirect effect brought about by the initial jump in $\lambda(0)$. Irrespective of whether $\lambda(0)$ rises or falls, we can show that the direct effect always dominates, so that in the short run, employment is reduced. With the stock of capital fixed in the short run, the capital-labor ratio initially rises; the before-tax wage therefore rises, though the after-tax wage may either rise or fall. The fall in employment leads to an immediate decline in output. The fall in the stock price leads to an initial decline in investment.

The response of the short-run rate of return on consumption (the after-tax interest rate) is critical and depends upon several factors, that is,

$$\frac{d\theta(0)}{d\tau_y} = \frac{\partial\theta}{\partial\lambda}\frac{d\lambda(0)}{d\tau_y} + \frac{\partial\theta}{\partial q}\frac{dq(0)}{d\tau_y} + \frac{\partial\theta}{\partial\tau_y}.$$

First, the direct effect, $\partial\theta/\partial\tau_y$, is negative. This is because, by reducing employment, the higher tax rate lowers the initial marginal physical product of capital, leading to downward pressure on the interest rate. Second, the initial fall in the stock price also has a negative effect, as noted earlier. Third, the effect due to $\lambda(0)$ depends upon whether it rises or falls. Even if $\lambda(0)$ rises, however, we can establish that its impact is dominated by the direct effect, so that overall, the higher personal income tax rate lowers the after-tax rate of interest in the short run. This discourages savings and stimulates current consumption. The before-tax interest rate, r, by contrast, may either rise or fall.

These responses persist with only one minor difference across the three dividend policies. The only difference occurs in the response of the cost of capital θ^*. For Rules II and III this falls, whereas for Rule I, the fall in this component is offset by a rise of $\bar{i}/(1 - \tau_c)$. But the striking feature is the contrast between the short run and the long run. With k being predetermined, the initial contraction in employment raises the capital-labor ratio. Over time, the decumulation of capital leads to an eventual decline

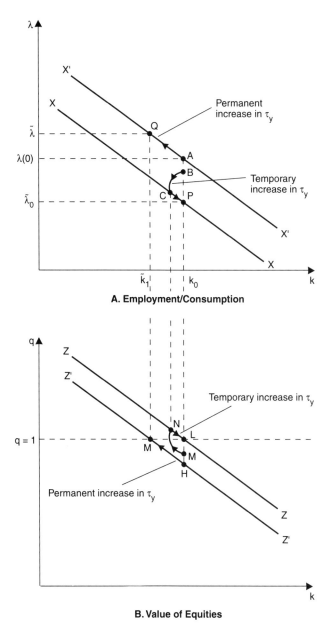

Figure 11.2
Transitional dynamics: direct wage effect dominant

Table 11.3
Short-run qualitative effects of tax increases

	Dividend Rule I $D/V = \dot{i}$			Dividend Rule II $D = (1 - \tau_p)\pi$			Dividend Rule III $RE = H(I/k)k$		
					Increase in				
	τ_y	τ_p	τ_c	τ_y	τ_p	τ_c	τ_y	τ_p	τ_c
Cost of capital θ^*	?	−	?	−	−	+	−	−	?
Interest rate r	?	−	−	?	−	0	?	−	−
Rate of return on consumption θ	−	−	−	−	−	0	−	−	−
Capital-labor ratio k/l	+	+	+	+	+	0	+	+	+
After-tax wage rate	?	+	+	?	+	0	?	+	+
Marginal utility of wealth λ	?	−	−	?	−	0	?	−	−
Stock value q	−	−	−	−	−	0	−	−	−
Rate of investment I	−	−	−	−	−	0	−	−	−
Consumption c	+	+	+	+	+	0	+	+	+
Employment l	−	−	−	−	−	0	−	−	−
Output y	−	−	−	−	−	0	−	−	−

Note: for Rule I: $\tilde{\theta}^* = \beta/(1 - \tau_c) + \dot{i}(\tau_y - \tau_c)/(1 - \tau_c)$.
for Rules II and III: $\tilde{\theta}^* = \beta/(1 - \tau_c)$.

in the capital-labor ratio. The increase in consumption is also only temporary; in the long run it declines as part of the overall contraction in the economy.

Temporary Tax Increase

We now consider a temporary tax increase. Specifically, assume that at time 0, the tax rate is increased, but also that it is expected to be restored at its original level at time T.[13] The steady-state equilibrium remains at P on XX. The stable arm will shift temporarily to $X'X'$ for the duration of the tax increase. Focusing on the case where the intertemporal decumulation effect dominates, the behavior of the system is as follows. As soon as the tax increase is put into effect, $\lambda(0)$ drops instantaneously to B in Figure 11.1A. The qualitative responses of the other key macro variables are as in Table 11.3, although with the initial smaller drop in the marginal utility of wealth, the responses are qualitatively smaller than those for a permanent increase. Subsequent to the initial tax increase, λ and k follow the path BC until time T when the tax increase is discontinued. At that time, the point C on the original stable locus is reached, and this path is then followed back to the original equilibrium P. The initial period of capital decumulation is followed by a period of accumulation, which actually begins before the point C is reached. The corresponding behavior of the stock market is illustrated in Figure 11.1B. During the transition, following its initial fall, the stock market overshoots its long-run equilibrium level. The knowledge that the tax is only temporary and that firms will eventually wish to restore their declining capital stock to its original level will drive up q in the interim, in order to create the incentive for the subsequent investment to take place.

Finally, we comment briefly on the case where all investment is financed out of retained earnings, but labor is fixed in supply. As already observed, this implies that the steady-state stock of capital $\tilde{k}$ remains fixed, and as a consequence a permanent increase in τ_y leads to no short-run dynamics. All that happens is that the stock price falls appropriately once and for all, and everything else remains unchanged. In terms of Figure 11.1B, the system will simply jump instantaneously from L to H. A temporary increase in τ_y, however, will lead to transitional dynamics, similar to those illustrated in the figure.

Corporate Income Tax Rate

The effects of an increase in τ_p are simpler than those we have just been discussing. This is because of the fact that the initial response of $\lambda(0)$, given by (11.24), now depends only upon $d\tilde{k}$, so that the fall in the steady-state stock of capital resulting from the higher corporate profit tax leads to an unambiguous reduction in the initial marginal utility of wealth. The dynamics of the economy can again be illustrated in Figure 11.1, with the stable paths XX, ZZ being shifted down to $X'X'$ and $Z'Z'$, respectively, for the duration of the tax increase.

The impact effects of the higher corporate profit tax rate are reported in Table 11.3 and are qualitatively the same across dividend policies. This is because the influence of dividend policy on the value of the firm depends little upon τ_p.[14] The responses are, for the most part, the same as those resulting from the higher personal income tax rate, and the reasoning is virtually identical.[15] The main difference worth noting is that now both the before- (personal income) tax and after-tax interest rate must fall in the short run (the latter being the source of the short-run stimulus in consumption). The contrast between the short-run and long-run responses also continues to hold, for essentially the same reasons as before.

Capital Gains Tax Rate

The response of the economy to an increase in the capital gains tax rate is more sensitive to dividend policy. In the case of the fixed dividend yield policy, Rule I, the effects are qualitatively almost identical to those obtained for τ_p. An increase in τ_c raises the long-run cost of capital, lowering the long-run capital stock, thereby reducing both $\lambda(0)$ and $q(0)$, giving rise to short-run dynamics in much the same way as in Figure 11.1. The same is true when all investment is financed out of retained earnings, the only difference being that after an initial fall, the stock market will eventually rise to a higher level than where it began (the point M'', say). In these two cases, the dynamics can be explained in essentially the same way as before.

By contrast, when all profit is paid out, an increase in the capital gains tax has no effect either in the short run or in the long run. This follows from the fact that in this case, the steady-state required rate of return on capital, and therefore the stock of capital, is independent of τ_c; see Section 11.4.[16] As a consequence there is no effect on either $\lambda(0)$ or $q(0)$, and so consumption, employment, and investment all remain unchanged. There are no dynamics. The reason why the capital gains tax has no effect is that, in contrast to the other two forms of dividend policy, there are no capital gains being earned in the neighborhood of the steady state being considered. To see this, recall the consumer arbitrage condition (11.2d), which for this form of dividend policy may be written as

$$(1 - \tau_c)\frac{\dot{s}}{s} = \theta - (1 - \tau_y)(1 - \tau_p)F_k.$$

Since in the neighborhood of steady-state equilibrium for this policy, $\theta = \beta = (1 - \tau_y)(1 - \tau_p)F_k$, it follows that in the neighborhood of steady state, $\dot{s} = 0$, and so obviously τ_c does not matter.

11.8 Tax Incidence

A central topic in the analysis of taxation concerns the incidence of the tax. This issue arises because of fact that the agent upon whom the tax is levied is not necessarily the person who ultimately pays the tax. There are many dimensions to this question, depending upon how one wishes to distinguish between different groups in the economy; for example, consumers versus producers, rich versus poor, old versus young, domestic residents versus foreigners, and so on; see Atkinson and Stiglitz (1980, chapter 6). An important distinction, and probably the most widely analyzed, at least in the theoretical literature, is the functional distribution between income going to labor and that going to capital. The present framework is convenient to address this aspect, emphasizing the time dimension involved.

Even focusing on the impact of taxes on labor and capital, there is no unique measure of tax incidence. Several can be found in the literature, and we shall consider just two. Also, in order to focus more sharply, we shall cut through the corporate structure and postulate directly a tax on wage income, τ_w, say, and a tax on capital, τ_k. One measure of incidence, proposed by Feldstein (1974a), is

$$\frac{dW^*}{dW^* + d\Pi^*} \equiv \frac{ld[(1 - \tau_w)F_l]}{ld[(1 - \tau_w)F_l] + kd[(1 - \tau_k)F_k]}. \tag{11.26}$$

This quantity measures the incidence of a tax as the ratio of the loss of net labor income to the loss of total income. The measure is net in that it subtracts out quantity changes, such as a withdrawal of labor supply, because these losses are offset by gains elsewhere (increased leisure in the case of labor). Evaluating the differential in (11.26) we may write

$$\frac{dW^*}{dW^* + d\Pi^*}$$

$$= \frac{-[(1 - \tau_w)f''\kappa\,d\kappa + (f - \kappa f')\,d\tau_w]}{-[(1 - \tau_w)f''\kappa\,d\kappa + (f - \kappa f')\,d\tau_w] + \kappa[(1 - \tau_k)f''\,d\kappa - f'\,d\tau_k]} \tag{11.27}$$

where, for convenience,[17]

$$\kappa \equiv \frac{k}{l}; \qquad f(\kappa) \equiv \frac{F(k, l)}{l}.$$

Equation (11.27) provides an expression for assessing the short-run and long-run effects of the alternative tax changes on the relative net incomes of the two factors of production.

Consider, first, an increase in the tax on labor income. In the short run, when capital is fixed, this raises the capital-labor ratio κ, thereby lowering the net income of capital Π^*. Although the higher capital-labor ratio raises the before-tax wage rate, this is offset by a higher tax on labor income, so that W^* may either rise or fall in the short run, depending upon the response of the labor supply and its effect on the wage rate. In the long run, the capital-labor ratio adjusts to equate $(1 - \tau_k)f' = \beta$. Net profit is therefore independent of the higher tax on labor income, and consequently $d\Pi^* = 0$. The unchanged long-run capital-labor ratio also implies that the before-tax wage rate remains unchanged, so that the after-tax wage income is reduced by the higher tax on labor income. Therefore $dW^* < 0$, and in the long run the full burden of the higher wage tax is borne by labor income.

An increase in the tax on capital also initially raises the capital-labor ratio. Thus both the before-tax and after-tax income earned by capital are reduced in the short run. The higher short-run capital-labor ratio also raises the short-run real wage. Thus, initially, $dW^* > 0$, $d\Pi^* < 0$. In the long run, when the after-tax marginal physical product of capital is equated to the rate of time preference, $d\Pi^* = 0$, and there is no burden on capital. The higher long-run tax on capital reduces the long-run capital-labor ratio and therefore net income to labor. Thus, again $dW^* < 0$, and labor bears the full long-run burden of the tax on capital.

An alternative measure of tax incidence, which Feldstein (1974a) argues is convenient in a growing economy, is the after-tax wage-rental ratio

$$\zeta \equiv \frac{[f(\kappa) - \kappa f'(\kappa)](1 - \tau_w)}{f'(\kappa)(1 - \tau_k)}. \tag{11.28}$$

Taking differentials of this expression leads to

$$d\zeta = \frac{-(1 - \tau_w)(1 - \tau_k)ff'' \, d\kappa + (f - \kappa f')f'[(1 - \tau_w) \, d\tau_k - (1 - \tau_k) \, d\tau_w]}{[(1 - \tau_k)f']^2}. \tag{11.29}$$

In the short run, an increase in the tax on labor has an ambiguous effect on the after-tax wage-rental ratio. The increase in the capital-labor ratio tends to raise it, but this is offset by the higher tax. In the long run, the capital-labor ratio is unchanged, and ζ declines unambiguously. By contrast, an increase in the tax on capital, by also initially raising the capital-labor ratio while reducing the net profit earned by capital, initially raises the after-tax wage to rental ratio. However, over time the decline in the capital-labor ratio more than offsets the effect on the net profit to capital, and the long-run after-tax wage to rental ratio declines.

Other measures of tax incidence are possible, and a more complete analysis of the costs and benefits of the higher tax would have to take into account the distribution of the revenues and how they affect the relevant agents. It would take us too far afield to pursue these issues further, but they certainly could be addressed within the present framework. The main point is that the relative burdens of taxation may shift dramatically between the factors over time. Because capital is adjusted only gradually over time, it is forced to accept a disproportionate burden of the taxes in the short run, although the burden is shifted back to labor as the capital supply adjusts over time.

11.9   Optimal Taxation

The theory of optimal taxation is one of the central issues in public finance. The characterization of the time path of optimal taxes in an intertemporal macroeconomic framework was addressed in two important papers by Chamley (1985, 1986), although he used a simpler version of the representative agent model than that developed in this chapter. Specifically, as in Section 11.8, Chamley abstracted from the corporate structure and focused on the taxation of capital and labor directly. Secondly, he abstracted from adjustment costs, allowing new output to be freely converted to additional capital. Our exposition will follow Chamley in both these respects, and we will only sketch the arguments, rather than presenting all the details.

With this simplified structure, the firm and the household can be aggregated as in Chapter 9. The representative agent's problem is now to maximize the concave utility function

$$\int_0^\infty U(c, l)e^{-\beta t}\, dt \tag{11.1a}$$

subject to the accumulation equation, now expressed as

$$\dot{k} + \dot{b} = r(1 - \tau_k)(k + b) + w(1 - \tau_w)l - c \tag{11.1b'}$$

and initial conditions $k(0) = k_0$; $b(0) = b_0$. The optimality conditions are

$$U_c(c, l) = \lambda \tag{11.2a}$$

$$U_l(c, l) = -w(1 - \tau_w)\lambda \tag{11.2b'}$$

$$\dot{\lambda} = \lambda[\beta - (1 - \tau_k)r] \tag{11.2e'}$$

where in short-run equilibrium and in the absence of adjustment costs

$$w = F_l; \qquad r = F_k. \tag{11.9'}$$

The interpretation of this equilibrium is familiar and requires no further discussion. As before, (11.2a) and (11.2b) can be solved in the form

$$c = c(\lambda, w(1 - \tau_w)), \tag{11.14a'}$$

$$l = l(\lambda, w(1 - \tau_w)). \tag{11.14b'}$$

Using (11.14a') and (11.14b'), we may substitute for c and l into the utility function U to generate the indirect utility function

$$U[c(\lambda, w(1 - \tau_w)), l(\lambda, w(1 - \tau_w))] \equiv V[\lambda, w(1 - \tau_w)],$$

which expresses the optimized level of the representative agent's utility in terms of the marginal utility and the after-tax real wage rate.

The policymaker's optimal tax problem is assumed to be to maximize the welfare of the representative agent, subject to (i) the economy-wide resource constraint, (ii) the government's budget constraint, and (iii) the representative agent's optimality conditions. Formally, this is described by the following problem:

maximize $\quad \displaystyle\int_0^\infty V(\lambda, w(1 - \tau_w)e^{-\beta t}\,dt$ $\qquad$ (11.30)

subject to

$$\dot{k} = F(k, l) - c - g, \qquad (11.31a)$$

$$\dot{b} = g + r(1 - \tau_k)b - \tau_k rk - \tau_w wl, \qquad (11.31b)$$

together with (11.2e′) and (11.9′). The following Lagrangean expression can be constructed:

$$H \equiv e^{-\beta t} V[\lambda, w(1 - \tau_w)] + \eta_1 e^{-\beta t}[F(k, l) - c - g - \dot{k}]$$
$$+ \eta_2 e^{\beta t}[g + r(1 - \tau_k)b - \tau_k rk - \tau_w wl - \dot{b}]$$
$$+ \eta_3 e^{-\beta t}[(\beta - r(1 - \tau_k))\lambda - \dot{\lambda}] + ve^{-\beta t}r(1 - \tau_k) \qquad (11.32)$$

where η_i are the costate variables associated with the accompanying dynamic constraints. The quantity $v \geq 0$ is a multiplier associated with the nonnegativity constraint $r(1 - \tau_k) \geq 0$; if $v > 0$, then the constraint is binding.

The optimality conditions for this policy problem include:

$$\eta_1 F_k - \eta_2 \tau_k r = -\dot{\eta}_1 + \beta\eta_1 \qquad (11.33a)$$

$$\eta_2 r(1 - \tau_k) = -\dot{\eta}_2 + \beta\eta_2 \qquad (11.33b)$$

$$\frac{\partial V}{\partial \lambda} + \eta_1(F_\lambda l_\lambda - c_\lambda) - \eta_2 \tau_w wl_\lambda = -\dot{\eta}_3 + \eta_3(1 - \tau_k)r \qquad (11.33c)$$

$$-\frac{\partial V}{\partial \tau_w} - \eta_1(F_l l_{\tau_w} - c_{\tau_w}) + \eta_2 \tau_w l_{\tau_w} = 0 \qquad (11.33d)$$

$$-(b + k)\eta_2 + \lambda\eta_3 - v = 0. \qquad (11.33e)$$

The first three equations are the dynamic efficiency conditions with respect to k, b, and λ, respectively; the last two equations are the optimality conditions with respect to the two tax rates τ_w, τ_k. In addition, the dynamic constraints (11.31a), (11.31b), (11.2e′) must continue to hold.

At time zero, the initial value of the consumer's marginal utility λ is unconstrained, so that the associated costate variable at that time $\eta_3(0) = 0$. The multiplier η_2 represents the marginal social value of public debt. It is also equal to the marginal value of replacing lump-sum taxation by distortionary taxation, that is, the marginal excess burden of taxation. Atkinson and Stern (1974) show how in a second-best context such as this, this variable is negative. Equation (11.33e) then implies that $v(0) > 0$, so that the constraint $r(1 - \tau_k) \geq 0$ is initially binding. Thus, at the first instant, capital should be taxed at its maximal feasible rate $\tau_k = 1$.

The next step is to take the time derivative of (11.33e). As an example, Chamley considers the case where the utility function is of the specific form

$$U(c, l) \equiv \frac{1}{1 - \sigma} c^{1-\sigma} + L(1 - l)$$

and shows that v satisfies a differential equation of the form

$$\dot{v} = \beta v + \frac{c}{\sigma} Z \tag{11.34}$$

where

$$Z \equiv \lambda - \eta_1 + \sigma \eta_2.$$

He further establishes that the time derivative of Z is equal to

$$\dot{Z} = Z(\beta - r(1 - \tau_k)) + (\eta_1 - \eta_2)\tau_k. \tag{11.35}$$

During an interval of time where the constraint $r(1 - \tau_k) \geq 0$ is not binding, then $v \equiv 0$. From (11.34), this implies $Z \equiv 0$. We have already noted that $\eta_2 < 0$. It is further true that η_1 measures the marginal social value of a unit of capital and in general is positive. Thus the condition $Z \equiv 0$ in (11.35) implies $\tau_k = 0$, so that when the constraint is not binding, capital should not be taxed.

It is clear that the constraint $r(1 - \tau_k) \geq 0$ cannot be binding forever, since otherwise the marginal utility of consumption would grow indefinitely; see (11.2e'). Chamley then establishes that the constraint is nonbinding for $t > T$.

He thus obtains two regimes for the tax rate on capital. Capital should be taxed either at its maximal rate or not at all. As Lucas (1990) argues, there are two conflicting principles at work, both stemming from Ramsey's (1927) early work on optimal taxation. The first of these is that factors in inelastic supply should be taxed at confiscatory rates. The second principle is that goods that appear symmetrically in consumer preferences should be taxed at the same rate; that is, taxes should be spread evenly over similar goods. As Lucas notes, in the capital context this implies that taxes should be spread evenly over consumption at different dates. Since capital taxation applied to new investment involves taxing later consumption at heavier rates than early consumption, the taxation of capital is not good. In the short run, capital is fixed in supply (being inherited from the past) and the first principle dominates, implying that capital should be taxed at the maximal rate. Over time, the second principle takes over, and in the long run the tax on capital should eventually be eliminated.

Chamley's analysis characterizes the entire dynamic path for the optimal tax rate, at least in a specific example. In fact, the result that, in steady state, capital should be untaxed can be obtained by comparing the steady-state equilibrium in the present economy with what it would be in the centrally planned economy where the policymaker controls quantities directly and is able to attain a first-best solution. Focusing on (11.2e′), we see that in steady state it implies

$$(1 - \tau_k)F_k = \beta.$$

Comparing this to the corresponding condition for the centrally planned economy, equation (9.10b),

$$F_k = \beta,$$

we immediately infer that the decentalized equilibrium will converge to the first-best optimum if and only if $\tau_k = 0$ in the new steady state.

11.10   Time Inconsistency

One further issue remains to be addressed. This concerns the dynamic consistency (or inconsistency) of the optimal tax policy. In terms of the Chamley model, we have made the assumption that the policymaker chooses his optimal path at the initial time zero and is fully and credibly committed to it over time. Part of the optimization involves setting the initial shadow value of the marginal utility of wealth $\eta_3(0) = 0$. Starting out from $\eta_3(0) = 0$, equation (11.33c) determines a differential equation describing the evolution of $\eta_3(t)$ over time, ultimately taking it to its new steady-state value, which, according to (11.33e), will be negative. Consider some time τ during the transition at which $\eta_3(\tau) < 0$. At this time, if the policymaker were to reoptimize, he would wish to set $\eta_3(\tau) = 0$, just as he chose to do initially. Thus the new optimal path, starting from time τ, would be different from the original optimal path, chosen at time 0. The optimal tax on capital is therefore said to be *time inconsistent*.

Beginning with an important paper by Kydland and Prescott (1977), the issue of time inconsistency of optimal policy-making has attracted a great deal of attention in models of intertemporal optimization with forward-looking agents. In general, an economic policy is said to be time inconsistent when a future policy decision that forms part of an optimal plan formulated at some initial date is no longer optimal when considered at some later date, even though no relevant information has changed in the meantime. These issues are particularly pertinent with respect to the optimal taxation of capital, and it is in that context that much of the discussion has taken place. Intuitively, the reason for the time inconsistency of the optimal tax on capital is that capital is fixed in the short run and variable in the long run. Over time, one wants to tax it differently.

The basic issues can be conveniently laid out using an example due to Fischer (1980), based on the contributions of Kydland and Prescott (1977, 1980), and we shall follow his exposition closely. The problem is formulated in terms of a two-period discrete-time model. The agent starts period 1 with an initial endowment of capital k_1. He consumes c_1, c_2 in the two periods and works only during the second period, with the quantity of work being denoted by l_2. The utility of the representative agent is described by the logarithmic function

$$U = \ln c_1 + \delta[\ln c_2 + \alpha \ln(\bar{l} - l_2) + \gamma \ln g_2] \qquad \alpha > 0, \gamma > 0 \qquad (11.36)$$

where $0 < \delta < 1$ is the discount factor, $\bar{l}$ denotes the fixed labor supply in period 2, and g_2 is the government expenditure in period 2, the only period in which the government is assumed to spend. The production function in each period is of the linear form, with the marginal product of labor being the constant a and the marginal physical product of capital equal to a constant b. The technological constraints facing the economy during the two periods are thus

$$c_1 + k_2 = (1 + b)k_1 \equiv Rk_1, \qquad (11.37a)$$

$$c_2 + g_2 = al_2 + Rk_2. \qquad (11.37b)$$

First-Best Optimum

Fischer begins by first solving the central planner's problem, that is, determining the equilibrium that would be chosen by a government setting quantities directly to maximize the welfare of the representative agent (11.36), subject to the economy-wide resource constraints (11.37). In this case the decision variables are c_1, c_2, l_2, k_2, g_2, leading to the first-best optimum

$$c_1 = \frac{a\bar{l}/R + Rk_1}{1 + \delta(1 + \alpha + \gamma)} \qquad (11.38a)$$

$$c_2 = \delta R c_1 \qquad (11.38b)$$

$$\bar{l} - l_2 = \alpha c_2/a \qquad (11.38c)$$

$$g_2 = \gamma c_2 \qquad (11.38d)$$

with k_2 determined residually from the first-period resource constraint (11.37a). This central planner's solution is time consistent. Given the choice of c_1 implied by the optimality condition (11.38a), and hence k_2, the government will still choose the solutions for c_2, l_2, g_2, implied by (11.38b)–(11.38d), when period two arrives. This solution is the best possible, given the resource constraints facing the economy.

Optimal Tax

Consider now a decentralized economy in which the government finances its expenditures by imposing taxes. The representative agent will now choose c_1, c_2, l_2, k_2 to optimize his utility function (11.36) subject to his budget constraints, which now reflect the future tax rate and are given by

$$c_1 + k_2 = Rk_1, \tag{11.37a}$$

$$c_2 = a(1 - \tau_2)l_2 + R_2 k_2, \tag{11.37b'}$$

where τ_2 is the tax rate on labor income and R_2 is the after-tax rate of return on capital. In making his decisions, the private agent treats τ_2, R_2, and g_2 as parametrically given. Carrying out the optimization for given expected values of these policy variables leads to the following solutions for c_1, c_2, l_2, k_2:

$$c_1 = \frac{a\bar{l}(1 - \tau_2^e)/R_2^e + Rk_1}{1 + \delta(1 + \alpha)} \tag{11.39a}$$

$$c_2 = \delta R_2^e c_1 \tag{11.39b}$$

$$\bar{l} - l_2 = \alpha c_2 / a(1 - \tau_2^e) \tag{11.39c}$$

where the superscript e denotes the expected value of the variable, and the corresponding solution for k_2 follows residually from (11.37a). The fact that these solutions are independent of g_2^e is a function of the additive separability of the logarithmic utility function.

The government's optimal policy problem is now to choose the tax rates R_2, τ_2 and its expenditure g_2 to maximize the welfare of the private agent (11.36), subject to the private agent's responses as described by solutions in (11.39a)–(11.39c) and the government budget constraint

$$(R - R_2)k_2 + \tau_2 a l_2 = g_2. \tag{11.40}$$

In order to make its decisions, the government needs to know private expectations, R_2^e, τ_2^e. We shall consider a rational expectations equilibrium in which agents correctly predict the government's behavior, that is, $R_2^e = R_2$, $\tau_2^e = \tau_2$. Carrying out the optimization under these conditions,

Fischer obtains the following optimality conditions determining the two tax rates:

$$a\bar{l}(1 - R/R_2)((1 - \tau_2)/\alpha\delta R_2) + \tau_2 Rk_1/(1 - \tau_2) = 0 \qquad (11.41a)$$

$$[R^2 k_1 \delta(1 + \alpha) + a\bar{l}(1 + \delta)] - \delta RR_2 k_1[1 + \alpha/(1 - \tau_2) + \gamma]$$
$$= a\bar{l}(1 - \tau_2)[R/R_2 + (1 + \gamma)\delta]. \qquad (11.41b)$$

In principle these two equations can be solved to yield the optimal tax rate on labor income τ_2^* and the after-tax rate of return on capital R_2^*, although in practice the equations are two complex to obtain closed-form solutions. Optimizing with respect to g_2 again leads to

$$g_2 = \gamma c_2, \qquad (11.39d)$$

so that it is optimal for the government to equate the marginal utility of government spending to that of private spending. Since the government can use only distortionary proportional taxation, then given rational expectations, the optimal tax rates $\tau_2^*, R - R_2^*$ are both believed and carried out. Such a solution is often referred to the solution with commitment.

Time Inconsistency of Optimal Tax Rates

However, these optimal tax rates are not time consistent. This is because in period 2 it is no longer optimal for the government to use the optimal tax rates $\tau_2^*, R - R_2^*$ derived in the first period. This arises because when it comes to the second period, the private sector takes the capital stock k_2 as given, having been determined in period 1 by that period's consumption decision; see (11.37a). Thus in period 2 the private agent chooses c_2, l_2 to maximize the static utility function

$$U = \ln c_2 + \alpha \ln(\bar{l} - l_2) + \gamma \ln g_2, \qquad (11.42)$$

subject to the one-period budget constraint

$$c_2 = (1 - \tau_2)al_2 + R_2 k_2, \qquad (11.43)$$

again taking τ_2, R_2, g_2 as given. The optimality conditions are now

$$c_2 = \frac{a\bar{l}(1 - \tau_2) + R_2 k_2}{1 + \alpha}, \qquad (11.44a)$$

$$\bar{l} - l_2 = \alpha c_2/a(1 - \tau_2). \qquad (11.44b)$$

The government now maximizes the same static utility function of the private agent, subject to (11.44a), (11.44b), and its budget constraint, which remains specified by (11.40). The resulting optimality conditions are

$$\tau_2 = 0, \tag{11.45a}$$

$$R_2 = \frac{R(1 + \alpha) - \gamma a\bar{l}/k_2}{1 + \alpha + \gamma}. \tag{11.45b}$$

Clearly, this solution does not coincide with solution with commitment (11.41a), (11.41b). With the capital stock fixed, the tax on capital is now nondistortionary. Accordingly, the government should raise its entire revenue by taxing capital, leaving labor untaxed and thereby avoiding the adverse effects of reducing the equilibrium supply of labor. As Fischer notes, this equilibrium is identical to what would obtain in a centrally planned economy in which k_2 is taken as fixed.

The time inconsistency of the optimal policy arises because the government has no nondistortionary taxes available. If, on the other hand, a lump-sum tax were available in the second period, the policymaker could simply announce in period 1 that a lump-sum tax equal to g_2, as implied by (11.39d), will be levied in the second period. The resulting rational expectations equilibrium will then replicate the first-best allocation of the centrally planned economy. Alternatively, if the government could levy taxes in the first period, that might provide it with another instrument for achieving the first-best optimum.

A Time-Consistent Solution

A time-consistent solution can be obtained by applying the Principle of Optimality of dynamic programming. This involves solving backward from period 2. Taking k_2 as given, both the representative agent and the government optimize during the second period, yielding precisely the solution in (11.42)–(11.45), in which there is a zero tax on labor and a positive tax on capital. Now go back to period 1. The private agent optimizes with respect to first-period consumption and savings, taking the government's future tax rates and spending plans as given.

To consider this further, the second period's optimized utility of the private agent can be calculated by substituting (11.44a), (11.44b) into (11.42) for given values of τ_2, R_2, and g_2. The resulting level of second period utility is

$$\hat{U}_2 = (1 + \alpha)\ln[a\bar{l}(1 - \tau_2) + R_2 k_2]$$

$$- (1 + \alpha)\ln(1 + \alpha) + \alpha\ln(\alpha/a(1 - \tau_2)) + \gamma\ln g_2. \tag{11.46}$$

In period 1, the agent maximizes,

$$U_1 = \ln c_1 + \delta \hat{U}_2, \tag{11.47}$$

taking τ_2, R_2, and g_2 as given. The decision variables are c_1 and k_2, which are now chosen to maximize (11.47), subject to the first-period budget constraint (11.37), again yielding the first-period consumption function (11.39a).

This consumption function depends upon the agent's expectations of government policy, and in the rational expectations equilibrium, where actual and expected tax rates coincide, actual consumption in period one is obtained by replacing the expected tax rates in (11.39a) with the corresponding actual rates, namely $c_1 = [1 + \delta(1 + \alpha)]^{-1}[a\bar{l}/R_2 + Rk_1]$. To solve for the equilibrium k_2, we combine this solution for c_1 with the optimal tax rule (11.45b) and the budget constraint (11.37). This leads to a quadratic equation for R_2. Once this equation is solved, the consistent optimal tax allocation can be calculated. Because τ_2 is being constrained to zero, the welfare associated with this solution is less than that of the time-inconsistent solution, which in turn is less than the welfare level of the first best optimum.

Further Developments

The two-period example of Fischer illustrates the problem of time inconsistency in its simplest form. However, the phenomenon is not restricted to taxation on capital. Chamley (1985) addressed the time consistency of the wage tax and found that it too was time inconsistent, arguing that this is a consequence of the endogeneity of factor prices and the fact that the factor price frontier is downward sloping. As discussed in Chapter 8, Barro and Gordon (1983a, 1983b) developed models in which monetary policy may be time inconsistent, and government debt policy is another potential area of time inconsistency; see Chari (1988). In addition, further cases of time inconsistency may arise where the government does not feel bound by the previous government or does not act with the interests of the representative agent in mind.

The issue of time inconsistency has presented a challenge to the theory of optimal policy-making, and it generated a lot of research during the 1980s. One solution is simply to focus on the commitment solution and assume that the government is able to bind all future governments to the decision it has made. However, governments typically lack this ability. Thus, the private agent, knowing that the present government is unable to bind future governments by the decision it makes, and knowing that future governments will have an incentive to renege, may not find the present government's decions to be credible. However, a government that continually breaks promises will lose its reputation, thereby incurring costs, and the question of how the private agents respond in these circumstances becomes important. Reputational equilibria have been analyzed by several authors; see, for example, Lucas and Stokey (1983), Persson, Persson, and Svensson (1987). Much of this literature was developed in the analysis of monetary policy within the context of an expectations-augmented Phillips curve and focused on the relative merits of policy rules versus policy discretion; see, for example, Kydland and Prescott (1977), Backus and Driffill (1985a, 1985b) Barro and Gordon (1983a, 1983b). A review of the relevant arguments is provided by Blanchard and Fischer (1989, chapter 11).

Other authors have extended the dynamic programming solution discussed in the two-period example of Fischer. One problem with extending this to an infinite horizon is that the backward induction may not capture all of the solutions; see Chari and Kehoe (1990), Stokey (1991).

Chari and Kehoe propose what they define to be a *sustainable equilibrium*, characterized as follows. Consider a government policy plan starting at some initial time 0 proceeding over an infinite horizon, together with the corresponding set of decision rules by private agents (consumers). An equilibrium is sustainable if (i) the continuation of the decision rule solves the consumer's problem at the first stage for every history, at time $t - 1$, say, and the continuation of this allocation rule solves the consumer's problem at the second stage for every history, one period later, at time t; and (ii) given the decision rule by the private sector, the continuation of the government plan solves the government's problem for every history at time $t - 1$. As Chari and Kehoe discuss, this is an equilibrium in which private agents behave competitively while the government behaves strategically. They characterize their equilibrium by adapting some results from repeated game theory due to Abreu (1988). The approach by Stokey (1991) is analogous. She characterizes a credible policy to be one where the government has no incentive to change its strategy and also characterizes a credible outcome equilibrium using results from game theory. These contributions are right at the frontier of current research and suggest an important role to be played by modern game theory in modeling the interaction between the private and public sectors.

Notes

1. By abstracting from money, our analysis fails to capture the distortions arising from the interaction of inflation and taxes, though for present purposes little is lost by doing so.

2. In previous chapters we have included government in the utility function. Since the present analysis teats government expenditure as fixed, its exclusion from U involves no loss.

3. See Hayashi (1982). In his discussion he draws the distinction between the average q and the marginal q and shows how the relationship between them depends upon the linear homogeneity of the installation cost function.

4. Because we abstract from physical depreciation, we are not able to consider issues pertaining to the tax treatment of depreciation.

5. Abel and Blanchard (1983, 677).

6. Early influential work by Lintner (1956) lent empirical support to the view that firms gradually adjust dividend payments in order to eventually pay out a desired fraction of after-tax profit to stockholders. For a comprehensive discussion explaining dividend behavior in the presence of taxes, see Poterba and Summers (1985).

7. Summers (1981) and Auerbach (1979b) also consider models that include corporate bonds but in which no new equities are issued. Since bonds do not play a critical role, Rule III is essentially equivalent to these models.

8. For key discussions of cost of capital and taxes, see King (1977) and Auerbach (1979a, 1979b).

9. The dividend rule suggested by Lintner, where firms choose to pay out a fixed fraction of after-tax profit $D = \alpha(1 - \tau_p)\Pi$, leads to the following differential equation in V:

$$\dot{V} = \frac{\theta}{1 - \tau_c} V - \left[(1 - \tau_p) \left[1 - \alpha \frac{(\tau_y - \tau_c)}{1 - \tau_c} \right] \Pi - H\left(\frac{I}{k}\right) k \right].$$

The polar case, where $\alpha = 0$ and all profits are retained, is identical to Rule I, with $\bar{i} = 0$. The other polar case, $\alpha = 1$, is Rule II.

10. What is usually referred to as the cost of capital is just the right-hand side of (11.19b) divided by $(1 - \tau_p)$.

11. The numerator of (11.21c) is readily seen to be positive. Noting that $\mu_1 < 0$ is the negative root of the characteristic equation, one can determine further that $\mu_1 < a_{33}$, implying that the whole expression is negative.

12. This can be established by noting the definitions of the elements a_{ij} and the partial derivatives appearing in (11.20), and manipulating the characteristic equation.

13. The case where it is known at the outset that the tax cut will be only temporary is to be contrasted with a situation in which the tax cut is initially expected to be permanent but at time T, say, is learned to be only temporary. In this latter case, the response of the system can be determined by treating both disturbances at times 0 and T as being perceived as permanent at those respective times.

14. The partial effect $\partial\theta/\partial\tau_p < 0$. This is because an increase in τ_p lowers the after-tax marginal physical product of capital, thereby lowering the interest rate.

15. The only difference is in the response of θ^*. This arises primarily because of the fact that one effect of increasing τ_c is to raise θ^* by an amount $[\theta - \bar{i}(1 - \tau_y)] d\tau_c/(1 - \tau_c)^2$, and this offsets the decline due to the lower θ.

16. Also in this case a temporary increase in τ_c will have no effect.

17. Writing $F(k, l) = lf(k/l)$, we have the well-known relationships

$$F_k = f', \qquad F_l = f - (k/l)f'; \qquad \frac{F_{kk}k}{l} = \frac{F_{ll}l}{k} = -F_{kl} = f''\frac{k}{l^2}.$$

12 The Representative Agent Model in the International Economy

12.1 Introduction and Overview

Paralleling the developments in the macroeconomic modeling of the closed economy, the models used in international macroeconomics have undergone a similar evolution. The static Mundell-Fleming model of the 1960s was the counterpart to the old *IS-LM* model, and the typical 1970s model emphasized the dynamic interaction between exchange rates, prices, and asset accumulation, very much in the spirit of the model developed in Part I. Likewise, the stochastic models of the period 1975–1985 were predominantly based on rational expectations and were extensions to the Sargent and Wallace type models that dominated that period and were reviewed in Part II. In fact, the argument that exchange rate expectations be rational is probably much more compelling than the corresponding assumption for price expectations. Beginning in the early 1980s, international macroeconomic models came to be routinely based on intertemporal optimization, and just as in the closed economy, that too has become the dominant paradigm.

This chapter extends the representative agent model we have been discussing to an open economy and overviews the vast literature that has evolved over the past decade or so. In so doing, we wish to emphasize some of the additional features that the international economy introduces. In particular, three should be highlighted. First, most international macroeconomic models are based on the assumption of perfect capital markets. This assumption, together with the assumption that the representative agent's rate of time preference is constant, implies that the agent's equilibrium marginal utility of wealth remains constant over time. This is shown to have important consequences for the dynamic adjustment paths followed by such an economy. Second, if the investment good is tradable, then the convex cost of adjustment function, introduced in Chapter 11, is necessary in order for well-defined dynamics to exist. Third, the international trading of capital imposes an intertemporal budget constraint on the economy in its transactions with the rest of the world, and this must be met if the equilibrium is to be intertemporally viable.

Section 12.2 begins with what would seem to be a natural extension of a simple, but standard, monetary model of the 1970s. It consists of a single good produced by a single factor of production, labor, and two assets, domestic money and traded bonds. The main point we make here is that in this simple model the dynamics degenerates unless some form of sluggishness is introduced into the evolution of the economy. There are various ways in which this may be accomplished. Some of these are discussed, including (i) the introduction of a variable rate of time preference; (ii) the introduction of imperfections in the bond market; and (iii) a growing population of infinitely lived households.

But the most important source of sluggishness introduced in the recent intertemporal optimizing models of the international economy is the accumulation of physical capital, which in general is assumed to take place subject to convex costs of adjustment. Such a model is set out in detail in Section 12.3, which constitutes the core of this chapter. We illustrate the model by analyzing the dynamic adjustment to increases in government expenditure on both domestic and imported goods. Other types of shocks, such as the transmission of tax changes, productivity shocks, and others, have been extensively analyzed, as noted in the appropriate sections below.

Section 12.4 indicates some of the directions in which the type of model exposited in Section 12.3 has been extended. These include (i) relaxing the assumption of perfect financial capital markets to allow for an upward supply curve for debt; (ii) introducing two or more production sectors; and (iii) multicountry models. Our objective here is modest: it is simply to point out some of the issues involved. The extension to two countries opens up a whole range of issues relating to strategic behavior, the formation of unions between countries, and so forth, which are at the forefront of research in international macroeconomics. These aspects are not discussed at all, although they seem to be directions in which the representative agent model, in its application to the open economy, is headed.

12.2   Basic Monetary Model

We begin with a monetary model of a small open economy operating in a world of ongoing inflation. The model has the same basic structure as in the previous two chapters, consisting of consumers, firms, and the government. Perfect foresight is also assumed to hold.

Structure of Economy

The environment we consider is characteristic of those assumed in the standard monetary models of the 1970s (see, e.g., Dornbusch and Fischer 1980). The domestic economy produces a single traded good, the foreign price of which is given in the world market. In the absence of any impediments to trade, purchasing power parity (PPP) is assumed to hold, which, expressed in percentage change terms, is described by

$$p = q + e \tag{12.1a}$$

where

p = rate of inflation of the good in domestic currency,

q = rate of inflation of the good in terms of foreign currency, assumed to be given to the small economy,

e = rate of exchange depreciation of domestic currency.

This equation asserts that under free trade the rate of inflation in the domestic economy must equal the exogenously given world rate of inflation, plus the rate of depreciation of the domestic currency.

We assume that domestic residents may hold two assets. The first is domestic money, which is not held by foreigners. Second, we assume that there is a traded world bond, with uncovered interest parity (UIP) holding at all times:

$$i = i^* + \varepsilon \tag{12.1b}$$

where

i = domestic nominal interest rate,

i^* = foreign nominal interest rate, assumed to be exogenously given,

ε = expected rate of exchange depreciation, which, assuming perfect foresight, is equal to the actual rate of exchange depreciation, e.

For the present, we abstract from physical capital.

The assumptions we have made of PPP and UIP are standard benchmarks in the international macroeconomic literature. We do not pretend that they are good assumptions, empirically. They are not. They do, however, serve as a starting point, from which the analysis can be extended.

The representative consumer is assumed to choose his level of consumption, labor supply, real money balances, and his holdings of the traded bond, by solving the now familiar intertemporal optimization problem:

$$\text{Maximize} \quad \int_0^\infty U(c, l, m, g) e^{-\beta t}\, dt \qquad U_c > 0, U_l < 0 \tag{12.2a}$$

subject to the budget constraint, expressed in real terms as

$$c + \dot{m} + \dot{b} = wl + \Pi + (i^* - q)b - (q + e)m - T, \tag{12.2b}$$

and initial conditions

$$m(0) = \frac{M_0}{P(0)} \quad b(0) = \frac{E(0)B_0}{P(0)} = \frac{B_0}{Q_0}, \tag{12.2c}$$

where:

c = real consumption;

g = real government expenditure;

m = real money balances, M = nominal money balances;

b = real stock of traded bonds, B = nominal stock of traded bonds;

l = supply of labor;

w = real wage rate;

Π = real profit, paid out to consumers;

β = rate of time preference, taken to be constant;

P = domestic price level;

Q = foreign price level;

E = nominal exchange rate;

T = real lump-sum taxes.

The utility function has the conventional concavity properties, and the budget constraint is standard as well. The only point requiring comment is that, given the assumptions of PPP and UIP, the real rates of return on holding bonds and money are $(i - q)$ and $-p = -(q + e)$, respectively.

Taking all prices and rates of return as parametric, the optimality conditions for the agent are described by

$$U_c(c, l, m, g) = \lambda \tag{12.3a}$$

$$U_l(c, l, m, g) = -w\lambda \tag{12.3b}$$

$$U_m(c, l, m, g) = (i^* + e)\lambda \tag{12.3c}$$

$$\dot{\lambda} = \lambda[\beta - (i^* - q)] \tag{12.3d}$$

together with the transversality conditions

$$\lim_{t \to \infty} \lambda m e^{-\beta t} = \lim_{t \to \infty} \lambda b e^{-\beta t} = 0 \tag{12.3e}$$

where λ, the Lagrange multiplier associated with the accumulation equation (12.2b), is the shadow value of wealth.

Equations (12.3a)–(12.3c) are familiar and need no further comment. Equation (12.3d), rewritten as

$$\beta - \frac{\dot{\lambda}}{\lambda} = i^* - q, \tag{12.3d$'$}$$

is just the Keynes-Ramsey rule, describing the optimal intertemporal allocation of consumption. This relationship differs in one important respect from the corresponding condition in the closed economy. With the rate of time preference β and the real interest rate $i^* - q$ both being exogenously given constants from the standpoint of the small open economy, in order for (12.3d') to imply a nondegenerate steady-state value for the marginal utility λ, we require $\beta = i^* - q$. That is, the rate of time preference must equal the given world real interest rate. But this further implies that $\dot{\lambda} = 0$, for all t, so that the marginal utility of wealth is constant over all time, that is, $\lambda = \bar{\lambda}$. As we will discuss in Section 12.3, this has important consequences for the dynamics.

The assumption that the rate of time preference in the small economy equals the given world rate of interest is standard in virtually all of this literature of a small open economy, based on intertemporal optimization. Although it is a strong assumption and has been the source of much criticism of the representative agent model as applied to the small open economy, it is what is required if an interior equilibrium is to be attained, when β and $i^* - q$ are both constant. One justification is that a small open economy, facing a perfect world capital market, must constrain its rate of time preference by the investment opportunities available to it, which are ultimately determined by the exogenously given rate of return in the world capital market. For if that were not the case, the domestic agent would end up either in infinite debt or in infinite credit to the rest of the world, and that would not represent a viable interior equilibrium. The economy would cease to be a small open economy.

How acceptable this assumption is depends in part upon the specific shock one is analyzing. For demand and productivity shocks, that typically leave β and $i^* - q$ both unchanged, it is adequate. However, it would be unsatisfactory if one wished to analyze changes in either β or i^*, which would break the assumed equality between them. In this case, one alternative has been to allow the rate of time preferences to be variable. This approach was first adopted by Obstfeld (1981), who does so by endogenizing the consumer rate of time preference through the introduction of Uzawa (1968) preferences, although this too is subject to criticisms, as we shall note.

In the absence of physical capital, the firm's optimization problem is simple. It is to hire labor so as to maximize real profit

$$\Pi = F(l) - wl \qquad F' > 0, F'' < 0 \tag{12.4}$$

where the production function $F(l)$ has the property of positive but diminishing marginal physical product of labor. The optimality condition is, as usual,

$$F'(l) = w. \tag{12.5}$$

The final agent, the government, operates in accordance with its flow budget constraint:

$$\dot{m} + \dot{a} = g + (i^* - q)a - (q + e)m - T \tag{12.6}$$

where a = stock of traded bonds issued by the domestic government. In addition, government policy must be specified. As an example, we shall assume that the government allows the domestic nominal money supply to grow at the fixed rate ϕ and continually balances its budget with lump-sum taxes. These policies are specified by

$$\dot{m} = (\phi - q - e)m, \tag{12.7a}$$

$$T = g + (i^* - q)\bar{a} - \phi m \tag{12.7b}$$

where the bar denotes the fact that a remains fixed over time. Note that summing the constraints (12.2b), (12.4), and (12.6) leads to

$$\dot{n} = F(l) - c - g + (i^* - q)n \tag{12.8}$$

where $n \equiv b - a$ is the net stock of traded bonds (i.e., the net credit) of the domestic economy. This equation simply confirms that the balance of payments on current account equals the balance of trade (output less domestic absorption) plus the real interest earned on foreign bond holdings. There is nothing to rule out $n < 0$, in which case the country is a debtor nation rather than a creditor.

Macroeconomic Equilibrium

Combining the optimality conditions (12.3a)–(12.3d), (12.5), together with the accumulation equation (12.6), policy specifications (12.7a), (12.7b), and the current account relationship (12.8), the macroeconomic equilibrium is described by the following set of relationships:

$$U_c(c, l, m, g) = \bar{\lambda} \tag{12.9a}$$

$$U_l(c, l, m, g) = -F'(l)\bar{\lambda} \tag{12.9b}$$

$$U_m(c, l, m, g) = (i^* + e)\bar{\lambda} \tag{12.9c}$$

$$\dot{m} = (\phi - q - e)m \tag{12.9d}$$

$$\dot{n} = F(l) - c - g + (i^* - q)n \tag{12.9e}$$

$$T = g + (i^* - q)\bar{a} - \phi m \tag{12.9f}$$

together with the transversality conditions.

Unfortunately, the dynamics of this macroeconomic equilibrium degenerate. This can be seen most clearly by considering the case where the utility function is additively separable in m, though it extends to the general case as well. With the shadow value of wealth remaining constant over time, the marginal conditions (12.9a), (12.9b) imply that both c and l must remain constant over time. Extreme consumption smoothing is optimal. Next, (12.9c) can be solved for the rate of exchange depreciation as a function $e = e(m)$, with $e'(m) < 0$. Substituting this into (12.9d) yields the following differential equation in m:

$$\dot{m} = (\phi - q - e(m))m.$$

This is an unstable equation and implies a finite steady-state stock of real money balances if and only if[1]

$$\phi = q + e(m), \tag{12.10}$$

which implies that both m and e remain constant over time. With c and l being constant, the equation (12.9e), describing the accumulation of bonds, can easily be solved. It can be verified that the economy's intertemporal budget constraint will be met if and only if

$$F(l) - c - g + (i^* - q)n_0 = 0 \tag{12.11}$$

where n_o is the initial stock of bonds held by the economy. No accumulation of bonds in fact occurs. The economy is always in steady state. Equations (12.9a)–(12.9c), (12.10), and (12.11) determine these stationary solutions for c, l, e, m, and $\bar{\lambda}$. Once these are known, (12.9f) determines the lump-sum taxes necessary to maintain the government budget balance.

Despite the rigor with which the underlying equilibrium is derived, it is not very interesting. Basically what happens is that any shock to the system generates an instantaneous jump in the nominal exchange rate E, causing the real money balances to jump, such that (12.10) holds. The fundamental problem is that there is no sluggishness in the system. Nothing prevents it from fully adjusting to any shock instantaneously. Sluggish adjustment can be introduced in various ways. One key way is through the accumulation of physical capital, and this will be discussed at length in Section 12.3. Within the context of as simple a model as this, sluggishness can be conveniently introduced by modifying the assumptions relating to time preference and capital mobility. These are briefly discussed in the following.

Sluggish Adjustment in Basic Monetary Model

The key feature of the model giving rise to the degeneracy of the dynamics is the condition

$$\beta = i^* - q. \tag{12.12}$$

The earliest monetary models restored nondegenerate dynamics to this model by in effect modifying this relationship. Obstfeld (1981) does so by endogenizing the consumer rate of time preference β, through the introduction of Uzawa (1968) preferences, postulating for his chosen specification of the utility function

$$B(t) = \int_0^t \beta(s)\,ds, \qquad \beta(s) = \beta[U(c(s), m(s))].$$

The instantaneous rate of time preference is thus a function of the level of utility at time t. The marginal utility of wealth is no longer constant over time, and the condition

$$\beta[U(c, m)] = i^* - q$$

now holds only in steady-state equilibrium. In effect, the exogenously given world real interest rate $i^* - q$ now determines the equilibrium level of instantaneous utility, which will equilibrate the domestic rate of time preference to the world real interest rate. By assuming that the function β is positive and satisfies

$$\beta'(U) > 0, \qquad \beta''(U) > 0, \qquad \beta(U) - U\beta'(U) > 0$$

one can show that the dynamics of λ and m will have a saddlepoint property, thereby giving rise to nondegenerate dynamics. The problem with this approach is that the rationale for the restrictions on the function β are not particularly compelling and have also been subject to criticism. In particular, the requirement that the rate of time discount β must increase with the level of utility, and therefore with consumption, is not particularly appealing. It implies that as agents become richer and increase their consumption levels, their preference for current consumption over future consumption increases, whereas intuitively one would expect the opposite to be more likely.

Turnovsky (1985) adopts a somewhat different approach. He introduces nontraded bonds, which are imperfect substitutes for traded bonds. He does so by introducing quadratic costs on holding foreign bonds. This is meant to capture, in a certainty-equivalent framework, the imperfect substitutability between domestic and foreign bonds. In a stochastic model, such as the one we shall develop in Part IV, the cost parameter would be a function of the degree of exchange risk and the degree of risk aversion of the domestic investors. This procedure also gives rise to a saddlepoint property, but it suffers from two drawbacks. First, although it does generate a perfectly plausible demand function for foreign bonds, dependent upon the uncovered interest differential, the fact is that this formulation represents a shortcut. It is clearly preferable to model imperfect capital mobility (or imperfect substitutability) within an explicit stochastic framework, something we undertake in Part IV. Second, dynamic responses to shocks may or may not degenerate, depending upon the shocks and on the precise formulation of the costs associated with holding foreign bonds. In fact, this procedure tends to highlight the arbitrariness that remains even when the model is grounded in intertemporal optimization.

Alternatively, nondegenerate dynamics can be restored by introducing the uncertain lifetime assumption of Blanchard (1985), or by assuming a growing population of overlapping infinitely lived households as in Weil (1989). In either case, for specific forms of the utility function—for example, if it is logarithmic—an aggregate consumption function of the form

$$\dot{c} = (i^* - q - \beta)c - \xi(m + b) \tag{12.12'}$$

is obtained. In effect, this equation replaces the condition (12.12) and is a source of sluggishness, which may give rise to saddlepoint behavior.[2]

12.3   Real Model of Capital Accumulation

The recent literature based on optimizing models of small open economies has introduced capital accumulation, and the models have generally been real. This section is devoted to such a model, which we illustrate by analyzing various types of government expenditure shocks. While this type of shock serves as a useful vehicle for displaying the model, the framework is very adaptable, and essentially the same structure can be applied to the analysis of other disturbances.

The model we shall analyze consumes two goods, one of which is produced domestically and the other of which is imported from abroad. We characterize the economy as being a "semi-small" open economy, meaning that, although it is small in the international asset market and in the price of its import good, it is able to influence the price of its export good. Investment behavior is generated by a Tobin-q function, along the lines discussed in Chapter 11.[3]

Using this framework, we analyze the effects of changes in government expenditure on both the domestically produced good and the imported good on a number of key macroeconomic variables. These include the rate of capital accumulation, employment, output, the current account deficit, the real interest rate, and the real exchange rate. The model is sufficiently tractable to enable us to characterize in detail the dynamic adjustment of the economy and to highlight the critical role played by the accumulating capital stock in this process. In particular, the evolution of the current account is seen to mirror that of capital.

For both forms of government expenditure, two types of changes are analyzed, namely, an *unanticipated permanent* and an *unanticipated temporary* expansion. A striking feature of the latter is that a temporary fiscal (or other) shock has a permanent effect on the economy. The reason for this is that, as we will demonstrate below, the steady state corresponding to some sustained policy depends in part upon the initial conditions of the economy prevailing at the time that policy is introduced. The adjustment that occurs during some temporary policy change will have an important bearing on the initial conditions in existence at the time the temporary policy is permanently revoked.

The fact that the steady state may depend upon initial conditions in models with infinitely lived, maximizing agents, having a constant rate of time discount, and facing perfect capital markets (assumptions being made here), has been discussed by Giavazzi and Wyplosz (1984). However, its significance for the implications of temporary shocks was not immediately apparent, although it has been recently investigated in a number of papers by Sen and Turnovsky (1989a, 1989b, 1990). Yet this is an important issue, especially in light of the recent interest pertaining to hysteresis and the random walk behavior of real variables such as output and employment. The present model provides a plausible framework for generating this type of behavior, at least in a small open economy.

In characterizing the dynamic adjustment paths generated by these fiscal disturbances, the analysis identifies several channels through which they are transmitted to the rest of the economy. First, there is the usual direct impact effect. This is simply the channel whereby a fiscal expansion on the domestic good impinges directly on the domestic output market, whereas a fiscal expansion on the imported good impinges directly on the trade balance. Second, a fiscal expansion induces a short-run change in the price of capital (the Tobin q), which in turn determines the transitional adjustment in the capital stock over time. The model is forward looking, and as a consequence of this, the short-run adjustment depends upon the long-run response of the capital stock. As we will show below, this in turn depends upon the form of fiscal expansion. Although government expenditure on the domestic good is unambiguously expansionary, government expenditure on the imported good is not. Third, a fiscal expansion generates a wealth effect, just as it did in the model of Chapter 9. However, in contrast to the closed economy, with access to a perfect world capital market this effect remains constant over time. Moreover, because the economy accumulates wealth while a temporary policy is in effect, thereby determining the initial conditions in existence when the policy ceases, this wealth effect provides the channel whereby the temporary policy has a permanent effect. It is the essential source of the hysteresis generated by the model.

The Macroeconomic Framework

For present purposes, the household and production sectors may be consolidated. The representative agent accumulates capital (k) for rental at its competitively determined rental rate and supplies labor (l) at its competitive wage. The agent is specialized in the production of a single commodity, using the stock of capital and labor, by means of a neoclassical production function $F(k, l)$. Expenditure on any given increase in the capital stock is an increasing function of the rate of capital accumulation. That is, there are increasing costs of investment associated with investment (I), which for simplicity we represent by the convex function $C(I)$; $C'(I) > 0$; $C''(I) > 0$. By choice of units, we assume

$$C(0) = 0; \qquad C'(0) = 1,$$

so that the total cost of zero investment is zero and the marginal cost of the initial installation is unity.

Domestic output is used in part for investment, in part as a domestic private consumption good (x), and in part as a domestic government good (g_x), with the rest being exported. Thus domestic investment is a tradable good. In addition to consuming part of the domestically produced output, the private agent also consumes another good (y), which is imported from abroad. The domestic government similarly imports the quantity (g_y) of this latter good. Even though the price of the import good is taken as given, the economy is large enough in the production of the domestic good to affect its relative price and therefore the nation's terms of trade.

The representative agent can also accumulate net foreign bonds (b) that pay an exogenously given world interest rate (i^*). Equation (12.13a) describes the agent's instantaneous budget constraint, expressed in terms of units of foreign output:

$$\dot{b} = \frac{1}{\sigma}[F(k, l) - C(I) - x - \sigma y + \sigma i^* b - T] \tag{12.13a}$$

where σ = relative price of the foreign good in terms of the domestic good (the real exchange rate), and T = lump-sum taxes. In addition, the rate of capital accumulation and investment are related by the constraint

$$\dot{k} = I \tag{12.13b}$$

where for simplicity we continue to abstract from the depreciation of capital.

The agent's decisions are to choose his consumption levels for x and y, labor supply l, the rate of investment I, and the rates of asset accumulation $\dot{k}, \dot{b}$ to maximize:

$$\int_0^\infty [U(x, y) + V(l) + W(g_x, g_y)]e^{-\beta t}\, dt \qquad U_x > 0,\ U_y > 0,\ V' < 0,$$

$$W_{g_x} > 0,\ W_{g_y} > 0. \qquad (12.13c)$$

The optimization is subject to the constraints (12.13a), (12.13b), and the given initial stocks $k(0) = k_0, b(0) = b_0$. For simplicity, the instantaneous utility function is assumed to be additively separable in the private consumption goods, x and y, labor l, and the public expenditures g_x and g_y. We also assume that the utility function is concave and that the two private goods are Edgeworth complementary, meaning that $U_{xy} > 0$.

The discounted Lagrangean for this optimization is expressed by

$$H \equiv e^{-\beta t}[U(x, y) + V(l) + W(g_x, g_y)]$$

$$+ \frac{\lambda}{\sigma}e^{-\beta t}[F(k, l) - C(I) - x - \sigma y + \sigma i^* b - T - \dot{b}] + q^* e^{-\beta t}[I - \dot{k}]$$

$$(12.14)$$

where λ is the shadow value of wealth in the form of internationally traded bonds, and q^* is the shadow value of the agent's capital stock. Exposition of the model is simplified by using the shadow value of wealth as numeraire. Consequently, $q \equiv \sigma q^*/\lambda$ is defined to be the market price of capital in terms of the (unitary) price of foreign bonds.

The optimality conditions to this problem with respect to x, y, l, and I are, respectively,

$$U_x(x, y) = \frac{\lambda}{\sigma} \qquad\qquad\qquad (12.15a)$$

$$U_y(x, y) = \lambda \qquad\qquad\qquad (12.15b)$$

$$V'(l) = -\frac{\lambda}{\sigma}F_l(k, l) \qquad\qquad\qquad (12.15c)$$

$$C'(I) = q. \qquad\qquad\qquad (12.15d)$$

The first three equations are familiar, and (12.15d) equates the marginal cost of investment to the market price of capital. With a nonhomogeneous cost of adjustment function the Tobin-q determines the absolute level of investment.

In addition, the shadow value of wealth and the market value of capital evolve in accordance with

$$\dot{\lambda} = \lambda(\beta - i^*), \tag{12.15e}$$

$$\dot{q} = \left(i^* + \frac{\dot{\sigma}}{\sigma}\right)q - F_k(k, l). \tag{12.15f}$$

Since both β and i^* are fixed, the ultimate attainment of a steady state is possible if and only $\beta = i^*$, and henceforth we shall assume this to be the case. As noted before, this implies that λ remains constant at its steady-state value $\bar{\lambda}$ to be determined below. Given the assumption of interest rate parity, the domestic interest rate $i(t)$ is related to the world interest rate by

$$i(t) = i^* + \frac{\dot{\sigma}}{\sigma}. \tag{12.16}$$

Equation (12.15f) is therefore an arbitrage condition equating the rate of return on capital $(F_k + \dot{q})/q$ to the domestic interest rate $i(t)$.

Finally, in order to ensure that the private agent satisfies his intertemporal budget constraint, the transversality conditions must hold:

$$\lim_{t \to \infty} \lambda b e^{-i^*t} = \lim_{t \to \infty} q k e^{-i^*t} = 0. \tag{12.15g}$$

Turning to the domestic government, its flow constraint, expressed in terms of the foreign good, is described by the equation

$$\dot{a} = \frac{1}{\sigma}[g_x + \sigma g_y + \sigma i^* a - T] \tag{12.17}$$

where a is the stock of (traded) bonds issued by the domestic government. This equation is perfectly straightforward and requires no further comment.

Subtracting (12.17) from (12.13a) yields the national budget constraint

$$\dot{n} = \frac{1}{\sigma}[F(k, l) - (x + g_x) - \sigma(y + g_y) - C(I) + \sigma i^* n] \tag{12.18}$$

where $n \equiv b - a =$ stock of net credit of the domestic economy. That is, the rate of accumulation of traded bonds by the domestic economy equals the balance of payments on current accounts, which in turn equals the balance of trade plus the net interest earned on the traded bonds. To rule out the possibility that the country can run up infinite debt or credit with the rest of the world, we impose the following intertemporal budget constraint:

$$\lim_{t \to \infty} ne^{-i^*t} = 0. \tag{12.19a}$$

This relationship, together with the transversality condition (12.15g), imposes a corresponding intertemporal budget constraint on the domestic government:

$$\lim_{t \to \infty} ae^{-i^*t} = 0. \tag{12.19b}$$

The complete macroeconomic equilibrium can now be described as follows. First, there are the static optimality conditions (12.15a)–(12.15d), with $\lambda = \bar{\lambda}$, together with the domestic output market clearing condition

$$F(k, l) = x + Z(\sigma) + C(I) + g_x \tag{12.20}$$

where $Z(\cdot)$ is the amount of the domestic good exported, with $Z'(\cdot) > 0$; that is, the quantity of exports increases as the domestic exchange rate depreciates (i.e., as σ increases). Second, there are the dynamic equations (12.13b), (12.15f), (12.17), and (12.18), together with the transversality conditions (12.15g), (12.19a), and (12.19b).

The five static equations may be solved for x, y, l, I, and σ in terms of $\bar{\lambda}, k, q$, and g_x as follows:

$$x = x(\bar{\lambda}, k, q, g_x) \qquad x_{\bar{\lambda}} < 0, x_k > 0, x_q < 0, x_{g_x} < 0 \tag{12.21a}$$

$$y = y(\bar{\lambda}, k, q, g_x) \qquad y_{\bar{\lambda}} < 0, y_k > 0, y_q < 0, y_{g_x} < 0 \tag{12.21b}$$

$$l = l(\bar{\lambda}, k, q, g_x) \qquad l_{\bar{\lambda}} \gtrless 0, l_k \gtrless 0, l_q > 0, l_{g_x} > 0 \tag{12.21c}$$

$$\sigma = \sigma(\bar{\lambda}, k, q, g_x) \qquad \sigma_{\bar{\lambda}} > 0, \sigma_k > 0, \sigma_q < 0, \sigma_{g_x} < 0 \tag{12.21d}$$

$$I = I(q) \qquad I' > 0. \tag{12.21e}$$

The explicit expressions for the partial derivatives can be obtained by the usual methods, and the following intuitive explanation can be given.

i. An increase in the marginal utility of wealth induces domestic consumers to reduce consumption of both goods and to increase their savings and labor supply. Because the economy is large in the market for the domestic good, this reduction in the demand for that good causes its relative price to fall, that is, σ rises, thereby stimulating exports. The overall effect on the demand for domestic output depends upon whether this exceeds the reduction in x. If it does, then domestic output and (given k) employment both rise, if not, both fall.

ii. An increase in the stock of capital raises output and the real wage. The higher domestic output stimulates the consumption of x, though by a lesser amount, and the relative price σ rises. Because the two private goods are Edgeworth complementary ($U_{xy} > 0$), the increase in the consumption of the domestic good increases the demand for the imported good as well. Whereas the rise in the real wage rate tends to decrease V', thereby stimulating employment, the rise in σ has the opposite effect; the net effect on employment depends upon which influence dominates.

iii. An increase in q stimulates investment. This increases the demand for the domestic good and its relative price rises; that is, σ falls. This in turn raises the marginal utility of the domestic good, implying that the consumption of x must fall, and with $U_{xy} > 0$, y falls as well. On balance, the increase in investment exceeds the fall in demand stemming from the reduction in x and lower exports, so that domestic output and employment rise.

iv. An increase in government expenditure on domestic output raises the demand for that good, thereby raising its relative price (lowering σ). Employment and domestic output are therefore stimulated. However, the increased output, together with the reduced exports stemming from the fall in σ, is smaller than the increase in demand generated by the additional government expenditure, so that x must fall in order for domestic goods market equilibrium to prevail. With $U_{xy} > 0$, the reduced demand for the domestic good spills over to the import good.

All this describes only the partial effects of a short-run change in government expenditure g_x. In addition, such an expenditure generates jumps in the marginal utility of wealth and the shadow value of capital, thereby inducing further responses. The complete short-run responses consist of a combination of these effects and will be discussed below. Finally, we may note that given the additive separability of the utility function in private and public goods, the short-run equilibrium does not depend directly upon g_y. However, as we will see presently, government expenditure on the imported good has an indirect effect through its impact on $\bar{\lambda}$ and q.

The evolution of the system is determined by substituting the short-run equilibrium into the dynamic equations and ensuring that the transversality conditions are met. It is readily apparent that in fact the dynamics can be determined sequentially. Equations (12.13b) and (12.13f) can be reduced to a pair of autonomous differential equations in the capital stock k and its shadow value q, and these constitute the core of the dynamics. This can be achieved by first differentiating (12.21d) with respect to t:

$$\dot{\sigma} = \sigma_k \dot{k} + \sigma_q \dot{q}, \tag{12.21d'}$$

which describes the rate of change of the real exchange rate in terms of the rate of accumulation of capital and its shadow value, and then substituting this equation, together with (12.21c) and (12.21d), into (12.13b) and (12.15f).

Next, (12.18) equates the accumulation of foreign assets by the economy to its current account surplus. Using the domestic goods market-clearing condition (12.20), this may be expressed equivalently in terms of exports minus imports plus the interest service account:

$$\dot{n} = \frac{1}{\sigma}[Z(\sigma) - \sigma(y + g_y) + \sigma i^* n]. \tag{12.18d'}$$

This equation may in turn be reduced to an autonomous differential equation in n, after substituting the solutions for q and k. The same applies to the government budget constraint (12.17).

Equilibrium Dynamics

Carrying out the procedure outlined above, (12.15f) and (12.13b) may be reduced to the following pair of linearized equations around steady state:[4]

$$\begin{pmatrix} \dot{k} \\ \dot{q} \end{pmatrix} = \begin{pmatrix} 0 & 1/C'' \\ -\rho[F_{kk} + F_{kl}l_k] & i^* \end{pmatrix} \begin{pmatrix} k - \tilde{k} \\ q - \tilde{q} \end{pmatrix} \tag{12.22}$$

where

$$\rho \equiv \frac{\tilde{\sigma}}{(\tilde{\sigma} - \tilde{q}\sigma_q)} > 0$$

and the tilde denotes steady-state values.

The determinant of the coefficient matrix in (12.22) can be shown to be negative, and therefore the long-run equilibrium is a saddlepoint with eigenvalues $\mu_1 < 0$, $\mu_2 > 0$. Although the capital stock always evolves continuously, the shadow price of capital q may jump instantaneously in response to new information. Along the stable locus, therefore, k and q follow the paths

$$k = \tilde{k} + (k_0 - \tilde{k})e^{\mu_1 t}, \tag{12.23a}$$

$$q = \tilde{q} + \mu_1 C''(k - \tilde{k}). \tag{12.23b}$$

It is evident from (12.22) that the convexity of the adjustment cost function is an important component of the dynamics. In the absence of such costs, q adjusts instantaneously to its steady-state equilibrium value $\tilde{q}$ (shown below to equal unity). Capital adjusts immediately to its steady-state level, with no new investment; see (12.15d) and (12.15f). This instantaneous adjustment is possible because the small economy facing a perfect world capital market and no adjustment costs can purchase as much capital as it desires from the world market. It is not constrained by its own productive capacities, as was the case for the closed economy.

To complete the discussion of the dynamics, we must consider the two budget constraints, namely, the domestic government budget constraint (12.17) and the national budget constraint (12.18). First, solving the former and invoking the intertemporal condition (12.19b) leads to the intertemporal government budget constraint

$$a_0 + \int_0^\infty \left[\left(\frac{g_x}{\sigma} \right) + g_y - \left(\frac{T}{\sigma} \right) \right] e^{-i^* t} \, dt = 0 \tag{12.24}$$

where a_0 is the initial stock of bonds issued by the domestic government. This equation is standard. If the domestic government has an initial stock of debt outstanding, then it cannot run a deficit in each period. At some point it must run a surplus to pay off the interest on the debt. With lump-sum tax financing, the time path for $T(t)$ must be chosen to satisfy (12.24) in order for the government to be intertemporally solvent; we shall assume this to be the case.

The national budget constraint (12.18′), together with (12.19a), can be similarly solved to yield the intertemporal national budget constraint,

$$n_0 + \int_0^\infty \left[\frac{Z(\sigma)}{\sigma} - (y + g_y) \right] e^{-i^* t} \, dt = 0, \tag{12.25}$$

where n_o is the initial stock of foreign bonds held by the domestic economy. If the country starts out as a net creditor to the rest of the world, it cannot run a trade surplus indefinitely; at some point it must run a trade deficit in order for (12.25) to be met.

However, (12.25) differs in a fundamental way from (12.24): in that given the time path for government purchases of imports g_y, there is nothing the government can directly choose to ensure that (12.25) is satisfied. The relative price σ and the quantity of private imports y are all determined by market forces. In fact, this intertemporal constraint imposes an additional constraint on the evolution of the economy, determining the stable adjustment of the current account.

To see this, we consider (12.18d′) in the form

$$\dot{n} = \frac{Z[\sigma(\bar{\lambda}, k, q, g_x)]}{\sigma(\bar{\lambda}, k, q, g_x)} - [y(\bar{\lambda}, k, q, g_x) + g_y] + i^* n. \tag{12.26}$$

Linearizing this equation around steady state yields

$$\dot{n} = \frac{1}{\tilde{\sigma}}[(\delta\sigma_k - \sigma y_k)(k - \tilde{k}) + (\delta\sigma_q - \sigma y_q)(q - \tilde{q})] + i^*(n - \tilde{n})$$

where $\delta \equiv Z' - Z/\sigma$. Using (12.23a), (12.23b), this equation may be written as

$$\dot{n} = \Omega(k_0 - \tilde{k})e^{\mu_1 t} + i^*(n - \tilde{n}) \tag{12.27}$$

where

$$\Omega \equiv \frac{1}{\tilde{\sigma}}[\delta(\sigma_k + \sigma_q \mu_1 C'') - \sigma(y_k + y_q \mu_1 C'')].$$

Assuming that the economy starts out with an initial stock of traded bonds $n(0) = n_0$, the solution to (12.27) is

$$n(t) = \tilde{n} + \frac{\Omega}{\mu_1 - i^*}(k_0 - \tilde{k})e^{\mu_1 t} + \left[n_0 - \tilde{n} - \frac{\Omega}{\mu_1 - i^*}(k_0 - \tilde{k})\right]e^{i^* t}.$$

Invoking the transversality condition (12.19a) implies

$$n_0 = \tilde{n} + \frac{\Omega}{\mu_1 - i^*}(k_0 - \tilde{k}), \tag{12.28}$$

so that the solution for $n(t)$ consistent with long-run solvency is

$$n(t) = \tilde{n} + \frac{\Omega}{\mu_1 - i^*}(k_0 - \tilde{k})e^{\mu_1 t}. \tag{12.29}$$

Equation (12.28) is a linear approximation to the general national intertemporal budget constraint (12.25), and (12.29) describes the relationship that must exist between the accumulation of capital and the accumulation of traded bonds during the transition if this condition is to be met. Of particular significance is the sign of this relationship. The definition of Ω given in (12.27) emphasizes that capital exercises two channels of influence on the current account. First, an increase in k raises the relative price σ, both directly and also through the accompanying fall in q, as seen in (12.23b). What this does to the trade balance depends upon δ. From the above definition of δ, $\delta > 0$ if and only if the relative price elasticity of the foreign demand for exports exceeds unity. At the same time, the increase in k increases imports both directly and again indirectly through the fall in q, and this reduces the trade balance. Although either case is possible, we shall assume that the relative price effect dominates, so that $\Omega > 0$.

Steady State

The steady state of the economy is obtained when $\dot{k} = \dot{q} = \dot{n} = 0$ and is given by the following set of relationships:

$$U_x(\tilde{x}, \tilde{y}) = \frac{\overline{\lambda}}{\tilde{\sigma}} \tag{12.30a}$$

$$U_y(\tilde{x}, \tilde{y}) = \overline{\lambda} \tag{12.30b}$$

$$V'(\tilde{l}) = -F_l(\tilde{k}, \tilde{l})\frac{\overline{\lambda}}{\tilde{\sigma}} \tag{12.30c}$$

$$\tilde{q} = 1 \tag{12.30d}$$

$$F_k(\tilde{k}, \tilde{l}) = i^* \tag{12.30e}$$

$$F(\tilde{k}, \tilde{l}) = \tilde{x} + Z(\tilde{\sigma}) + g_x \tag{12.30f}$$

$$Z(\tilde{\sigma}) + \tilde{\sigma}i^*\tilde{n} = \tilde{y} + g_y \tag{12.30g}$$

$$n_0 = \tilde{n} + \frac{\Omega}{\mu_1 - i^*}(k_0 - \tilde{k}). \tag{12.30h}$$

These equations jointly determine the steady-state equilibrium solutions for $\tilde{x}, \tilde{y}, \tilde{k}, \tilde{l}, \tilde{q}, \tilde{\sigma}, \tilde{n}, \overline{\lambda}$.

Several aspects of this steady state merit comment. First, the steady-state value of q is unity, consistent with the Tobin-q theory of investment and the discussion in Chapter 11. Second, the steady-state marginal physical product of capital is equated to the exogenously given foreign interest rate, thereby determining the domestic capital-labor ratio in precisely the same ways as it was determined by the rate of time discount in Chapters 9–11. Third, (12.30g) implies that in steady-state equilibrium, the current account balance must be zero. Export earnings plus net interest earnings on traded bonds must just finance net imports. Equation (12.30h) describes the equilibrium relationship between the accumulation of capital over time and the accumulation of traded bonds consistent with the nation's intertemporal budget constraint. It is through this relationship that the steady state depends upon the initial stocks of assets k_0, n_0, as a result of which *temporary* policy (or other) shocks have *permanent* effects. Finally, we should recall that this steady state is sustainable only as long as the government maintains a feasible debt and taxing policy consistent with (12.24).

Long-Run Effects of Fiscal Expansions

The long-run effects of fiscal expansions, taking the form of increases in government expenditure on domestic goods and on imported goods

Table 12.1
Long-run effects of increase in government expenditure

A. Domestic good g_x

1. Capital-labor ratio:
$$\frac{d(\tilde{k}/l)}{dg_x} = 0$$

2. Capital, employment, and output:
$$\frac{1}{k}\frac{d\tilde{k}}{dg_x} = \frac{1}{l}\frac{d\tilde{l}}{dg_x} = \frac{1}{z}\frac{d\tilde{z}}{dg_x} = \frac{F_l}{\sigma l D}[\delta\Delta - \bar{\lambda}U_{xx}] > 0$$

3. Relative price (real exchange rate):
$$\frac{d\tilde{\sigma}}{dg_x} = \frac{1}{D}\left\{V''[U_{xy} - \sigma U_{xx}] - \frac{\Delta\psi F_l}{\sigma}\right\} \gtreqless 0$$

4. Consumption of domestic good:
$$\frac{d\tilde{x}}{dg_x} = \frac{1}{D}\left\{\frac{V''\delta}{\sigma}[\sigma U_{xy} - U_{yy}] + \frac{\bar{\lambda}}{\sigma}\left[V'' + U_{xy}\frac{\psi F_l}{\sigma}\right]\right\} < 0$$

5. Consumption of imported good:
$$\frac{d\tilde{y}}{dg_x} = \frac{1}{D}\left\{\frac{V''\delta}{\sigma}[U_{xy} - \sigma U_{xx}] - \frac{\bar{\lambda}}{\sigma^2}U_{xx}\psi F_l\right\} < 0$$

6. Marginal utility:
$$\frac{d\bar{\lambda}}{dg_x} = \frac{1}{D}\left[U_{xy}V''\frac{\bar{\lambda}}{\sigma} - \Delta\left(\delta V'' + \psi F_l\frac{\bar{\lambda}}{\sigma^2}\right)\right] \gtreqless 0$$

7. Net foreign assets:
$$\frac{d\tilde{n}}{dg_x} = -\frac{\Omega}{i^* - \mu_1}\left(\frac{d\tilde{k}}{dg_x}\right) < 0$$

where
$$\psi \equiv -\frac{\sigma i^*\Omega}{i^* - \mu_1}\left(\frac{\tilde{k}}{\tilde{l}}\right) < 0; \quad \delta \equiv Z' - Z/\sigma > 0; \quad \Delta \equiv U_{xx}U_{yy} - U_{xy}^2 > 0$$
$$D \equiv -V''[U_{xy}Z' + (\bar{\lambda}/\sigma) - Z'U_{xx}\sigma] - V''\delta[U_{xy} - (1/\sigma)U_{yy}]$$
$$\quad - F_l\psi U_{xy}(\bar{\lambda}/\sigma^2) - F_l(F/l)U_{xx}(\bar{\lambda}/\sigma) + \Delta(F_l/\sigma)[(F_l\delta/l) + \psi Z'] > 0$$

B. Import good g_y

1. Capital-labor ratio:
$$\frac{d(\tilde{k}/l)}{dg_y} = 0$$

2. Capital, employment, and output:
$$\frac{1}{k}\frac{d\tilde{k}}{dg_y} = \frac{1}{l}\frac{d\tilde{l}}{dg_y} = \frac{1}{z}\frac{d\tilde{z}}{dg_y} = \frac{F_l}{\sigma l D}[Z'\Delta - \bar{\lambda}U_{xy}] \gtreqless 0$$

3. Relative price (real exchange rate):
$$\frac{d\tilde{\sigma}}{dg_y} = \frac{1}{D}\left\{V''[U_{yy} - \sigma U_{xy}] + \frac{\Delta F F_l}{\sigma}\right\} \gtreqless 0$$

4. Consumption of domestic good:
$$\frac{d\tilde{x}}{dg_y} = \frac{1}{D}\left\{V''Z'[[\sigma U_{xy} - U_{yy}] - \frac{\bar{\lambda}}{\sigma}U_{xy}\frac{F F_l}{l}\right\} < 0$$

Table 12.1 (cont.)

---

5. Consumption of imported good:

$$\frac{d\tilde{y}}{dg_y} = \frac{1}{D}\left\{V''Z'[U_{xy} - \sigma U_{xx}] + \frac{\bar{\lambda}}{\sigma}\left[V'' + \frac{\bar{\lambda}}{\sigma}U_{xx}\frac{FF_l}{\sigma}\right]\right\} < 0$$

6. Marginal utility:

$$\frac{d\bar{\lambda}}{dg_y} = \frac{1}{D}\left[U_{yy}V''\frac{\bar{\lambda}}{\sigma} + \Delta\left(\frac{\bar{\lambda}}{\sigma}\frac{FF_l}{l} - V''Z'\sigma\right)\right] > 0$$

7. Net foreign assets:

$$\frac{d\tilde{n}}{dg_y} = -\frac{\Omega}{i^* - \mu_1}\left(\frac{d\tilde{k}}{dg_x}\right) \gtreqless 0$$

---

respectively, are reported in parts A and B of Table 12.1 and shall be discussed in turn.

Increase in Government Expenditure on Domestic Good

First, because the world interest rate i^* remains fixed, the marginal physical product condition (12.30e) implies that the long-run capital-labor ratio is constant, independent of either g_x or g_y. Capital and labor therefore change in the same proportions, so that the marginal physical product of labor and hence the real wage rate also remain constant. The increase in taxes necessary to finance an increase in g_x raises the long-run marginal utility of wealth (measured in terms of domestic goods and equal to $\bar{\lambda}/\sigma$), inducing more labor supply, raising the productivity of capital, and thereby generating an expansion in capital and in output, much as it does in the closed economy. However, in contrast to the closed economy, the stimulus to demand generated by government expenditure may or may not exceed the addition to output, and the relative price σ of the import good may either rise or fall. At the same time, the increase in the steady-state stock of capital leads to a decline in the steady-state stock of traded bonds held by the domestic economy. The higher taxes, coupled with the reduction in net interest earnings by the economy, means a reduction in real disposable income, a consequence of which is that the private consumptions of the two goods, $\tilde{x}$ and $\tilde{y}$, both decline. The fact that the marginal utility, measured in terms of domestic goods, rises, while the relative price σ may either rise or fall, means that the response of the marginal utility as measured in terms of the foreign good $\bar{\lambda}$ can also respond in either way, although it too will certainly be increased if the utility function is additively separable in the two goods.

Looking at (12.30g), we see that a fiscal expansion on the domestic good raises the equilibrium trade balance when measured in terms of the foreign good $(= -i^*\tilde{n})$. It will do so even more strongly, in terms of the domestic good, as long as the domestic economy is a net creditor nation $(\tilde{n} > 0)$. However, for a debtor country, the trade balance in terms of the domestic good may fall if the relative price effect is sufficiently strong.

Increase in Government Expenditure on Import Good

The long-run effects on domestic activity, as measured by employment, capital, and output, may now be either all expansionary or all contractionary. What is going on is the following. The increase in government expenditure on the import good raises its relative price, thereby stimulating the demand for the domestic good, and this is expansionary. But at the same time, the increase in lump-sum taxes necessary to finance the additional expenditure reduces disposable income, reducing private expenditure on the domestic good (without any corresponding increase in public expenditure on that good), and this is contractionary. The net impact on domestic activity depends upon which effect dominates. In addition, the reduction in disposable income lowers the private consumption of the import good as well. The response of the marginal utility $\bar{\lambda}$ is an unambiguous increase. This is because the higher tax raises the marginal utility measured in terms of the domestic good; and the increase in the relative price σ raises it further, when measured in terms of the foreign good.

The response of the equilibrium stock of bonds $\tilde{n}$ depends upon whether the long-run effect of this form of fiscal policy is expansionary or contractionary. What happens to the trade balance as measured in terms of the foreign good depends upon what happens to $\tilde{n}$. In the expansionary case it will rise, whereas in the contractionary case it will fall. In terms of the domestic good, the relative price effect must also be taken into account.

Transitional Dynamics

As discussed previously, the dynamics of k and q are described by a saddlepoint in k-q space. The stable arm XX, illustrated in Figure 12.1A, is given by

$$q = 1 + \mu_1 C''(k - \tilde{k}) \tag{12.31a}$$

and is negatively sloped. The unstable arm (not illustrated) is described by

$$q = 1 + \mu_2 C''(k - \tilde{k}) \tag{12.31b}$$

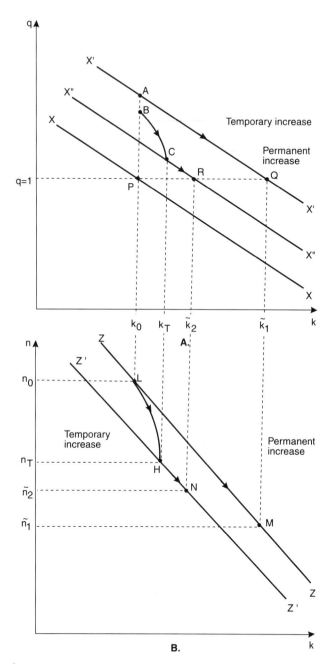

Figure 12.1
Increase in government expenditure on export good

and is positively sloped. The two types of fiscal expenditure shall be considered in turn.

Permanent Increase in Government Expenditure on Domestic Good

As long as no future change is anticipated, the economy must lie on the stable locus XX. The initial jump in $q(0)$ following an unanticipated permanent increase in g_x is

$$\frac{dq(0)}{dg_x} = -\mu_1 C'' \frac{d\tilde{k}}{dg_x} > 0. \tag{12.32}$$

The long-run increase in the capital stock thus gives rise to a short-run increase in the shadow price $q(0)$.

The dynamics following an unanticipated permanent increase in g_x are illustrated in Figure 12.1A and Figure 12.1B. Part A of the figure describes the adjustment in q and k, while part B describes the evolution of the stock of traded bonds. Suppose that the economy starts in steady-state equilibrium at the point P on the stable arm XX and that there is a permanent increase in g_x. The new steady state is at the point Q, with a higher equilibrium stock of capital $\tilde{k}$, and an unchanged shadow value of capital $\tilde{q} = 1$. In the short run, q jumps from P to A on the new stable locus $X'X'$. From (12.15d), it is seen that the increase in q has an immediate expansionary effect on investment and that capital begins to accumulate.

The initial responses of other key variables include

$$\frac{dl(0)}{dg_x} = \frac{\partial l}{\partial g_x} + \frac{\partial l}{\partial \bar{\lambda}} \frac{\partial \bar{\lambda}}{\partial g_x} + \frac{\partial l}{\partial q} \frac{\partial q(0)}{\partial g_x} > 0, \tag{12.33a}$$

$$\frac{d\sigma(0)}{dg_x} = \frac{\partial \sigma}{\partial g_x} + \frac{\partial \sigma}{\partial \bar{\lambda}} \frac{\partial \bar{\lambda}}{\partial g_x} + \frac{\partial \sigma}{\partial q} \frac{\partial q(0)}{\partial g_x} < 0, \tag{12.33b}$$

$$\frac{dx(0)}{dg_x} = \frac{\partial x}{\partial g_x} + \frac{\partial x}{\partial \bar{\lambda}} \frac{\partial \bar{\lambda}}{\partial g_x} + \frac{\partial x}{\partial q} \frac{\partial q(0)}{\partial g_x} < 0, \tag{12.33c}$$

$$\frac{dy(0)}{dg_x} = \frac{\partial y}{\partial g_x} + \frac{\partial y}{\partial \bar{\lambda}} \frac{\partial \bar{\lambda}}{\partial g_x} + \frac{\partial y}{\partial q} \frac{\partial q(0)}{\partial g_x} < 0, \tag{12.33d}$$

which consist of two channels of influence. First, there are the direct effects or "implementation" effects, consisting of the partial derivatives such as $\partial l/\partial g_x$. Second, there are the indirect effects, or "news" effects, which operate through induced jumps in $\bar{\lambda}$ and q.

Despite the fact that the various effects may or may not work in the same direction (and in fact the effects through $\bar{\lambda}$ are ambiguous), we are able to establish that, overall, a permanent increase in g_x will have the same qualitative effect on employment and consumption in the short run as it will have in the steady state. Namely, it will raise employment while reducing the consumptions of the two goods. In addition, it will lower the relative price σ. How the magnitudes of these short-run responses compare with those of the long-run adjustments depends upon whether the short-run effects resulting from the rise in the shadow price of investment $q(o)$ dominate the long-run effects stemming from the eventual increase in the capital stock.

From (12.21d′) and the fact that upon reaching the point A in Figure 12.1A on the new stable locus $\dot{q} < 0, \dot{k} > 0$, we infer that in the short run and during the subsequent transition, $\dot{\sigma} > 0$, that is, the relative price of the import good must be increasing. This means that the short-run fall in the relative price overshoots its long-run response. At the same time, the fact that $\dot{\sigma} > 0$ means that the fiscal expansion raises the domestic interest rate above the fixed real-world rate, during the transition.

Differentiating (12.21a), (12.21b) analogously with respect to t, one can show, using a similar argument, that during the transition $\dot{x} > 0, \dot{y} > 0$, so that these consumptions also overreact in the short run. In both cases, the shadow price of investment effect dominates. In the case of employment, however, we are unable to determine the relative sizes of the short-run and long-run adjustments.

As in the closed economy, the endogeneity of labor is critical to these adjustments. To see this, consider the steady-state relationships (12.30) and assume instead that employment is fixed, so that the optimality condition (12.30c) is no longer applicable. The marginal productivity condition (12.30f) now implies that the equilibrium stock of capital (rather than the capital-labor ratio) is determined exogenously by i^* and is independent of g_x. It therefore follows from (12.23a), (12.23b) that the capital stock and the shadow price of investment remain constant at all points of time. Output is therefore unchanged. There are no dynamics, and all that happens is that the fiscal expansion leads to a once-and-for-all decline in the relative price σ and in the private consumptions x and y.[5]

Part B of Figure 12.1 illustrates the relationship between n and k, which combining, (12.23a) and (12.29), is

$$n(t) - \tilde{n} = \frac{\Omega}{\mu_1 - i^*}(k(t) - \tilde{k}).$$

This is a negatively sloped line, denoted by ZZ. Since $d\tilde{n}/dg_x = (\Omega/(\mu_1 - i^*))(d\tilde{k}/dg_x)$, this line remains fixed. The movement along A to Q in Figure 12.1A corresponds to a movement along LM in Figure 12.1B. From this figure, we see that an increase in government expenditure on the domestic good leads to an immediate decumulation of foreign bonds. This is brought about by the fact that the increase in g_x leads to an immediate reduction in the relative price σ, which with $\Omega > 0$ creates an immediate current account deficit. With the stock of traded bonds being predetermined, the trade balance, measured in terms of the foreign good, also falls, and with the fall in σ, the trade balance in terms of the domestic good falls even more. Over time, the rate of decline of the stock of foreign bonds is reduced. This occurs through the rising relative price σ, which causes the trade deficit to decline over time.

Temporary Increase in Government Expenditure on Domestic Good

Consider now a temporary increase in g_x. Specifically, suppose that at time 0 the government increases its expenditure on the domestic good, but is expected to restore its expenditure to the original level at time T. The transitional adjustment is now as follows. As soon as the increase in g_x occurs, the stable arm XX will shift up instantaneously (and temporarily) to $X'X'$ while the shadow price q increases to the point B, which lies below $X'X'$, at which point the initial rate of capital accumulation is moderated. The same is true of employment. As is the case for a permanent expansion, the increase in (iq) is less than the increase in the marginal physical product of capital that results from the additional employment, so that q begins to fall; see (12.15f). Moreover, the accumulation of capital is accompanied by a decumulation of traded bonds. Hence, immediately following the initial jump, q and k follow the path BC in Figure 12.1A, while k and n follow the corresponding path LH in Figure 12.1B. At time T, when the level of government expenditure is restored to its original level, the stock of capital and traded bonds will have reached a point such as H in Figure 12.1B. The accumulated stocks of these assets, denoted by k_T and n_T, will now serve as initial conditions for the dynamics beyond T, when g_x reverts permanently to its original level. As noted in Section 12.3, they will, therefore, in part determine the new steady-state equilibrium. With no information being received at time T (because the temporary nature of the fiscal expansion was announced at the outset) and no further jumps, the stable locus relevant for subsequent adjustments in q and k beyond time T is the locus $X''X''$, parallel to XX, which passes through the point $k = k_T$. Likewise, the relevant locus linking the accumulation of capital and traded bonds is now $Z'Z'$.

After time T, q and k follow the stable locus CR in Figure 12.1A to the new steady-state equilibrium at R, while, correspondingly, k and n follow the locus HN in Figure 12.1B to the new equilibrium point N. One can establish formally that $X''X''$ lies above the original locus XX, while $Z'Z'$ lies below ZZ, as indicated in the figure. In the new steady state, the shadow value q reverts to 1, but with a higher stock of capital and a lower stock of traded bonds than initially. The striking feature of the adjustment is that the *temporary* increase in government expenditure leads to a *permanent* increase in the stock of capital, accompanied by a lower stock of traded bonds. This is because, during the transitional adjustment period, during which the fiscal expansion is in effect, the accumulation of capital and bonds will influence subsequent initial conditions that in turn affect the subsequent steady state.

As the figures are drawn, C lies above R and H lies above N, respectively. The complete adjustment paths BCR and LHN are therefore monotonic. We are unable to rule out the possibility of C lying below R and H lying above N, in which case the accumulation of capital and decumulation of bonds would be reversed at some point during the transition. In any event, the temporary increase in the relative price of domestic goods generates an initial current account deficit, which continues as long as capital is being accumulated.

To understand the intuition behind this result further, it is useful to define the quantity[6]

$$V(t) \equiv n(t) + \frac{\Omega}{\mu_1 - i^*} k(t),$$

which represents a linear approximation to the present value of total resources available to the economy—national wealth, say—starting from the stock of assets $[k(t), n(t)]$ at time t. Using this notion, $V(0)$ is the national wealth starting from the initial endowment at time 0. From (12.29), the equation $V(t) = V_0$ describes the comovement of n and k along the stable adjustment path. It corresponds to a movement along the locus ZZ in Figure 12.1B and represents how the initial endowment constrains the final equilibrium.

Similarly, $V_T \equiv n_T + (\Omega/\mu_1 - i^*)k_T$ serves as the initial value of wealth conditioning the movement for the period after time T, when the temporary fiscal expansion ceases. The economy will converge to its original level after the removal of a temporary policy if and only if $V_T \neq V_0$, which is therefore a necessary and sufficient condition for a temporary shock to have only a permanent effect. In general, however, $V_T \neq V_0$ following a temporary shock, and this is the case here. This is because during the period $(0, T)$ while the temporary shock is in effect, the economy will follow an unstable path, taking it off the locus ZZ at time T. It will revert to a new stable path only after time T, when the temporary shock has been permanently removed. Typically, the wealth effects generated while a policy is temporarily in effect will permanently change the present value of resources available to the economy after the shock is removed.

This will cause the capital stock to return to some point other than where it initially began, thereby giving rise to a permanent effect.

Government Expenditure on Import Good

The initial response of $q(0)$ to a fiscal expansion taking the form of an increase in government expenditure on the import good g_x is given by

$$\frac{dq(0)}{dg_y} = -\mu_1 C'' \frac{d\tilde{k}}{dg_y} \gtreqless 0 \qquad (12.34)$$

and depends upon whether the long-run effect on the capital stock is expansionary or contractionary. In the former case, the dynamics are essentially as illustrated in Figure 12.1. There is an initial stimulus to investment, leading to a long-run accumulation of capital and decumulation of traded bonds. In the latter case, the adjustment paths are as depicted as in Figure 12.2. The fiscal expansion now generates an initial drop in the shadow price $q(0)$, leading to a long-run decline in the capital stock, accompanied by an accumulation of traded bonds.

The initial responses of l, σ, x and y are given by

$$\frac{dx(0)}{dg_y} = \frac{\partial x}{\partial \bar{\lambda}} + \frac{\partial x}{\partial q} \frac{\partial q(0)}{\partial g_y}; \qquad x = l, \sigma, x, y. \qquad (12.35)$$

In contrast to the fiscal expansion on the domestic good, there is no direct effect; government expenditure on the import good operates entirely through $\bar{\lambda}$ and q. This is a consequence of the assumption of additive separability of utility in private and public consumption.

By a parallel argument to that given above, we can show that the short-run response of the relative price overadjusts in the direction of the long-run response. In the case that the long-run effect of the expenditure increase is expansionary, the initial fall in $\sigma(0)$ exceeds the corresponding long-run reduction in $\tilde{\sigma}$. On the other hand, if the long-run effect of g_y is contractionary, σ overincreases in the short run. In this case, the fact that $\dot{\sigma} < 0$ over time as the capital stock falls and the shadow price of investment increases means that the domestic interest lies below the world rate during the transition. The overresponse of x and y also occurs when g_y is expansionary. But in the contractionary case this is not necessarily so. In this case both consumptions may actually increase on impact, though they will thereafter fall continuously to their lower long-run equilibrium levels. Finally, the short-run employment effect is unclear. This is due in part to the fact that one effect of the higher g_y is to raise the marginal utility $\bar{\lambda}$, the effects of which on employment are ambiguous.

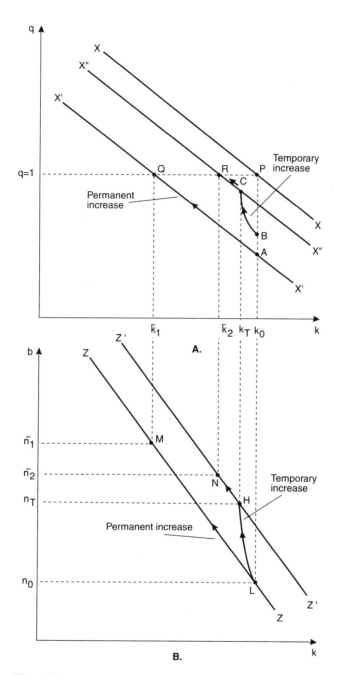

Figure 12.2
Increase in government expenditure on import good: contractionary case

The relationship between rate of accumulation of traded bonds (the current account) and the accumulation of capital is analogous to that already given, as is the analysis of temporary expenditure increases. This is illustrated in Figure 12.2 and should be self-explanatory.

Some Applications

The model we have presented in the foregoing section is a generic model of a single-sector, "semi-small" open economy accumulating capital and facing perfect capital markets. It has become something of a workhorse and has been applied to a number of types of real shocks. This subsection is devoted to a brief review of some of these applications. First, it is straightforward to carry out the kind of welfare analysis developed in Chapter 9, where the effects of the fiscal expansion on the intertemporal utility of the representative agent are evaluated; see Turnovsky and Sen (1991), Buiter and Kletzer (1991). Other authors to use this type of model to examine government expenditure shocks include Frenkel and Razin (1987), Buiter (1987), Brock (1988), and Obstfeld (1989).

International economists have long been interested in the economic impacts of tariffs. This issue has traditionally been studied within the context of the static trade model, although recently several authors have analyzed it using the type of framework developed in this chapter. Relevant references include Edwards (1987), Sen and Turnovsky (1989a), Engel and Kletzer (1990), Gavin (1991). Related to this is the literature on relative price shocks or terms of trade shocks. This originated with the Laursen-Metzler proposition and has been analyzed within the intertemporal macroeconomic framework by authors such as Svensson and Razin (1983), Persson and Svensson (1985), Matsuyama (1988), and Sen and Turnovsky (1989b). Productivity shocks have been analyzed by Murphy (1986) and by Matsuyama (1987). Finally, capital income tax issues are receiving a good deal of attention, and authors such as Nielsen and Sorensen (1991) should be mentioned.

12.4   Some Extensions

The models discussed in the previous sections have three characteristics: (i) they are based on perfect markets; (ii) they are aggregate (single-sector) models; (iii) they are small economies that take the rest of the world as given. Current research in progress is directed at relaxing these and other assumptions. In this section, we briefly discuss some of that work.

Upward-Sloping Supply Schedule for Debt

Most of the literature is restricted to small open economies and assumes that such economies face perfect capital markets for debt and are free to borrow or lend as much as desired at the given world rate of interest. As we have seen, in this case the dynamic adjustment has a simple recursive structure. On the one hand, the dynamic adjustment within the economy is driven by the accumulation of capital and does not depend directly upon the stock of foreign asset holdings (or debt). On the other hand, the current account and the stock of foreign assets itself mirror the stable adjustment of the capital stock.

Although for many countries the assumption of perfect capital markets may not be unacceptable, for others, particularly developing countries, the assumption of a perfectly elastic supply of debt is clearly unrealistic. Experience with external borrowing in such economies has shown that debt repayments are not always made on time and are sometimes made with difficulty. International capital markets are likely to react to their perception of a country's ability to repay, with lenders requiring risk premiums on the rate at which they are willing to lend to such nations.

Bhandari, Haque, and Turnovsky (1990) incorporate this idea into a macrodynamic model, such as that developed in Section 12.3, by assuming that the small economy faces an upward-sloping schedule for debt, which embodies the risk premium associated with lending to the sovereign borrower. This is formalized by postulating

$$i(z) = i^* + \omega(z) \tag{12.36}$$

where i^* is the interest prevailing nationally and $\omega(z)$ is the country-specific risk premium, which varies with the stock of debt, z say, held by the country. Carrying out the intertemporal optimization, as in Section 12.3, one can show that if the representative agent treats the country-specific risk premium as given, the shadow value of wealth λ now evolves in accordance with

$$\dot{\lambda} = \lambda[\beta - i(z)]. \tag{12.37}$$

With the domestic interest rate now being a function of debt, z, λ is no longer constant over time. Indeed (12.37) now determines the long-run equilibrium stock of debt (possibly measured relative to output) as being the level that will equate the domestic interest rate to the given rate of time preference. With this formulation, the recursive dynamic structure associated with a perfectly elastic supply of debt breaks down. This is because the marginal cost of capital facing firms, and therefore determining their investment decisions, is dependent upon the outstanding stock of national debt. Conditions in the international capital market therefore become important in determining the growth of capital in the domestic economy. Bhandari, Haque, and Turnovsky show analytically how this causes the dynamics involving (i) the stock of capital k; (ii) the marginal utility of wealth λ; (iii) the shadow value of wealth q; and (iv) the stock of national debt z (or credit $n = -z$) all to become interdependent. Formal analytical solutions become harder to derive, although not impossible. The system involves two "jump" variables λ and q, and two "sluggish" variables k and n. Under reasonable conditions one can show that the dynamics include two stable and two unstable roots, giving rise to a saddlepoint. The stable dynamics in response to a permanent shock are no longer linear, although one can characterize the asymptotic adjustment path using the dominant eigenvalue method of Calvo (1987). Bhandari, Haque, and Turnovsky were able to conduct a fairly explicit analysis of the dynamic adjustment of the system in response to a variety of conventional disturbances. It is felt that this offers a promising formulation to address a number of pertinent issues pertaining to policy-making in developing economies, such as questions relating to the taxation of capital and trade liberalization.

Sectoral Models

The dependent economy model of Salter (1959) and Swan (1960) has played an important role in international macroeconomics. By distinguishing between traded and nontraded goods, it provides a convenient framework for analyzing the behavior of the real exchange rate, both in a static and a dynamic context. Recently, several authors have begun to incorporate capital formation into this framework (see, e.g., Razin 1984; Murphy 1986; van Wincoop 1993; Brock 1988, 1993; Obstfeld 1989; Engel and Kletzer 1989; Turnovsky 1991; Brock and Turnovsky 1994). Many of these papers address the types of traditional macroeconomic issues considered in the standard one-sector model. But other issues pertaining to sector-specific responses are also studied. Most notably, issues pertaining to the "Dutch disease" problem have been fruitfully addressed within this framework (see, e.g., van Wincoop 1993).

Once the distinction between traded and nontraded goods is introduced, how investment is to be classified becomes important. At an intuitive level, investment can reasonably fall into either category. Capital goods taking the form of infrastructure and construction are presumably nontraded; investment in the form of machinery or inventories, obviously, are potentially tradable. Different treatments of investment, reflecting these different possibilities, can be found in the literature. For example, Obstfeld (1989), while allowing for capital to be instantaneously movable between sectors, assumes that only the traded good is used for investment. He therefore allows the capital stock to be instantaneously augmented at any point in time by an exchange of traded financial assets for capital. Brock (1988) also treats capital as being traded, although the investment process involves convex costs of adjustment, thereby constraining the rate of investment at any point of time to remain finite. By contrast, other authors such as Murphy (1986), Brock (1993), Turnovsky (1991), and van Wincoop (1993) treat investment as being nontraded.

The nature of investment is important for the dynamics. If the investment good is traded, then, in the absence of any installation costs, it is easily shown that the adjustment of the capital stock occurs instantaneously. Convex costs of adjustment are necessary in order for nondegenerate dynamics to obtain, just as was the case for the aggregate model of Section 12.3 (which, it will be recalled, was based on the assumption that capital is tradable).

By contrast, if the capital accumulation is in the form of the nontraded good, then, even in the absence of adjustment costs associated with investment, nondegenerate dynamics are obtained. The rate of investment remains finite due to the fact that the supply of traded goods is subject to increasing marginal costs. In other words, these increasing marginal costs play the same role as do adjustment costs in the traded case. The dynamics are shown to involve a saddlepoint structure in terms of (i) the aggregate capital stock and (ii) the relative price of the nontraded good; that is, the real exchange rate. The nature of the dynamics turns out to depend critically upon the relative intensities of the two sectors in the nontraded capital. If the traded sector is more capital intensive, the complete adjustment of the real exchange rate to any unanticipated permanent shock occurs immediately. The subsequent accumulation or decumulation of capital in response to such a shock takes place with no concurrent change in the real exchange rate. By contrast, if the nontraded sector is the more capital intensive, then the transitional adjustment in the capital stock is accompanied by further, continuous changes in the real exchange rate.

A recent paper by Brock and Turnovsky (1994) introduces both traded and nontraded capital simultaneously into this model. The authors show, rather unexpectedly, that the properties of the saddlepath just discussed continue to depend upon the relative intensities of the two sectors in the nontraded capital good. The relative intensities of the two sectors in the traded capital good are essentially irrelevant insofar as the basic dynamic structure is concerned. They are relevant, however, in determining the evolution of the current account balance.

Two-Country Models

Most of the literature applying the representative agent model to the international economy deals with small open economies, which may take the behavior in the rest of the world as given. But there is a growing recognition of the interdependence of the world economy and of the need to extend the framework to two (or more) economies. Needless to say, such a task is analytically difficult, in effect doubling the dimensions of the dynamics. But some interesting work is being done, and progress is being made. Probably the most comprehensive treatment of two-country models is provided by Frenkel and Razin (1987) and Frenkel, Razin, and Sadka (1991). Both studies deal primarily with fiscal shocks, the latter focusing more on the transmission of various forms of taxes. However, their analysis abstracts from physical capital accumulation, and by making appropriate assumptions they are able, in effect, to collapse much of their analysis to a two-period framework, consisting of the present and the future. The closest two-country analogues to the type of model developed in Section 12.3 include that of Devereux and Shi (1991), who analyze the determination of debt and its accumulation over time, and those of Turnovsky and Bianconi (1992), Christensen and Nielsen (1992), and Bianconi (1995), who analyze the transmission of tax shocks in a two-country world. We also note that stochastic versions of this type of representative agent model are widely used in the two-country real business cycle analysis of productivity and fiscal shocks; see, for example, Baxter and Crucini (1991), Baxter and King (1993).

One emerging issue in the development of the two-country model is the international harmonization of taxes. With perfectly integrated financial markets, arbitrage conditions—as reflected by the appropriate optimality conditions—are shown to impose constraints on the tax rates on capital income that may be set by the two countries. Different principles of tax collection may or may not be consistent with these constraints; see, for example, Sinn (1990) and Frenkel, Razin, and Sadka (1991). In the increasingly interdependent world economy this issue promises to present an interesting research agenda.

Notes

1. This condition is stronger than the transversality condition on money contained in (12.3e). That is, it is sufficient, but not necessary, for that condition to hold.

2. One further possible way to generate dynamics in this model is through the introduction of nominal price or wage rigidities; see, e.g., van de Klundert and van der Ploeg (1988) for an example of such an analysis. Another is to confront the agent with an upward-sloping supply schedule for debt. This approach is discussed further in Section 12.4.

3. This approach to investment is also adopted by Buiter (1987). His analysis of the small-small economy is based on numerical simulations. The present model is investigated entirely analytically. For other applications of the cost of adjustment approach to investment to the analysis of alternative macro disturbances in open economies, see, e.g., Matsuyama (1987), Brock (1988), and Sen and Turnovsky (1989a, 1989b).

4. Note that the (2-2) element i^* in the matrix (12.22) is obtained as follows. In general, following the procedure outline it is equal to $\rho[i^* + (\sigma_k/C''\sigma) - F_{kl}l_q]$. Evaluating the derivatives σ_k, l_q, and noting the steady-state conditions given in (12.30), this expression evaluated at steady state reduces to i^*.

5. Actually, it is the assumption of endogeneity of employment in conjunction with infinitely lived agents that is critical. This is because this gives rise to short-run dynamics that are driven by long-run changes in the capital stock alone; see equations (12.21), (12.23). This may be compared to Buiter's (1987) model, for example, where employment is fixed but consumers have finite lives. In this case, the long-run capital stock is also independent of everything other than the foreign interest rate, and is therefore independent of domestic fiscal policy. However, in contrast to the present analysis, temporary changes in the capital stock may still occur. This is due to the fact that the short-run dynamics are also driven by long-run changes in other forms of financial wealth, which may be generated by changes in domestic fiscal policy.

6. The formal solution procedure for analyzing the dynamics of temporary shocks is provided by Sen and Turnovsky (1990). Although the solution presented there is in response to a temporary investment tax credit, the method outlined is generic.

13 An Introduction to Endogenous Growth Models

13.1 Introduction

Economic growth is probably the issue of primary concern to economic policymakers. Economic growth statistics are the most widely publicized measures of economic performance and are always discussed with much interest. Unfortunately, the intertemporal models we have been considering so far in Part III are not well suited to addressing issues pertaining to growth. This is because, for the most part, they are ultimately stationary. That is, although they emphasize the central activities of economic growth—namely, savings and investment—this process of asset accumulation is only a transitional one, in that ultimately the capital stock, and the associated productive capacity of the economy, will approach some new stationary level. Long-run growth in this model is incorporated by the introduction of a growing population coupled with a more efficient labor force, and this, of course, was the source of long-run growth in the standard neoclassical growth model of Solow (1956) and Swan (1956). An implication of this view of the world is that long-run growth is ultimately tied to demographic factors such as the growth rate of population, the structure of the labor force, and the productivity of the labor force (technological change), all of which were typically taken to be exogenous. Consequently, the only policies that might contribute to long-run growth were policies that would increase the growth of population, and manpower training programs aimed at increasing the efficiency of the labor force. From the present standpoint, macroeconomic policy had nothing to say about long-run growth performance.

This is clearly an unsatisfactory state of affairs. It is hard to imagine that sustained macroeconomic policies will not ultimately be reflected in economic growth in some way or other. Despite the elegance of the neoclassical growth model, which was a central topic of research activity in economic dynamics through the decade of the 1960s, the model was essentially dropped from the research agenda in the 1970s when the focus shifted to more short-term macroeconomic issues related to inflation and unemployment trade-offs.[1]

Since the mid-1980s, there has been a resurgence of interest in economic growth theory with the development of the so-called *endogenous growth models*. This research activity has been motivated by several concerns, including an attempt to explain aspects of the data not discussed by the neoclassical model; the need for a more satisfactory explanation of international differences in economic growth rates; and the pursuit of a larger role for the instruments of macroeconomic policy in explaining the growth process. The term *endogenous* refers to the fact that these models are able to explain the long-run growth rate as an endogenous equilibrium outcome, reflecting the structural characteristics of the economy, such as technology and preferences, as well as the instruments of macroeconomic policy. They do not require exogenous elements such as a growing population in order to generate an ongoing growth process. These models differ in a fundamental way from the neoclassical growth model: they assume the absence of diminishing returns in the accumulation of produced resources.

As a matter of historical record, explanation of growth as an endogenous process is not new; in fact, it dates back to Harrod (1948). In his famous book Harrod defines the "warranted" growth rate to be the product of the savings rate and the output-capital ratio, both of which are structural parameters of the economy, controllable by government policy. His analysis shows that the warranted growth rate, as so defined, ensures the equilibrium equality between savings and investment. In fact, the equilibrium growth rate we shall derive in the course of this chapter is essentially of the Harrod type, the only difference being that consumption (or savings) behavior is derived as part of an intertemporal optimization instead of being posited directly.

The objective of this chapter is limited. It is not intended to present a detailed discussion of the new growth theory. That is a very far-reaching topic, and comprehensive treatments are available elsewhere; see, for example, Grossman and Helpman (1991) and Barro and Sala-i-Martin (1995). Rather, the purpose is much narrower: to present a series of dynamic models, derived from intertemporal optimization, all of which have the properties of generating endogenous growth, which is sensitive to the conventional instruments of fiscal policy, such as tax rates and government expenditure. In this respect we view it as a continuation of the models we have been developing in chapters 9–12, although with the important difference that the structural characteristics it contains permit it to exhibit an internally generated ongoing equilibrium rate of economic growth. The present analysis is also intended to serve as a transition to the stochastic models to be developed in Part IV, which for reasons of analytical tractability are also linear and also have a stochastic endogenous growth structure.

Three models will be presented in the present chapter. The first is a simple model involving production externalities of the type pioneered by Romer (1986, 1989). The second is a simple linear model in which output is determined by the capital stock alone, of the type analyzed by Barro (1990), Rebelo (1991), and King and Rebelo (1990). Most of our attention will be devoted to this model, which turns out to be analytically very tractable and thus serves as a convenient vehicle for presenting an integrated analysis of fiscal policy that includes the interaction between debt, tax, and government expenditure instruments. Third, we will discuss a model, originally due to Lucas (1988) and further developed by Rebelo (1991) and Mulligan and Sala-i-Martin (1993), that disaggregates capital into nonhuman and human capital. This leads to a two-sector production technology, which, unlike the second model, has transitional dynamics, but which nevertheless also has long-run endogenous growth characteristics.

13.2   Externalities and Ongoing Growth

We begin with the following simple model, due to Romer (1986, 1989). The key modification to the previous model is in the technology, which is represented as follows. There are a large number of firms, N, say, in the economy, and the supply of labor is fixed inelastically at one worker per firm. We denote the capital stock (per worker) held by firm j to be k_j so that the aggregate stock of capital in the economy, K, is

$$K = \sum_{j=1}^{N} k_j.$$

The aggregate capital stock in the economy is taken to represent the stock of knowledge in the economy and generates an externality with respect to the production possibilities for firm j. This is captured in the firm's production function $f(k_j, K)$. Romer rationalizes this formulation by arguing that if new physical capital and new knowledge are produced in fixed proportions, then K not only measures the aggregate capital stock but is also an index of knowledge available to the firm. However, because each firm is small relative to the aggregate, in choosing k_j it takes the aggregate capital stock K as given.

The optimization problem facing the representative agent is to choose his consumption path and the rate of capital accumulation in order to

$$\text{maximize} \quad \int_0^\infty U(c)e^{-\beta t}\, dt \tag{13.1a}$$

subject to

$$\dot{k} = (1 - \tau)f(k, K) - c + T \tag{13.1b}$$

where the subscript j parameterizing the firm is dropped, τ denotes the rate of income tax, and T denotes lump-sum transfers to the consumer. We assume that income tax revenues are rebated to the consumer, in accordance with

$$T(t) = \tau f(k, K), \tag{13.1c}$$

so that the government runs a continuously balanced budget.

We define the usual Lagrangean expression

$$H \equiv U(c)e^{-\beta t} + \lambda e^{-\beta t}[(1 - \tau)f(k, K) - c + T - \dot{k}],$$

the first-order conditions to which are as follows:

$$U_c(c) = \lambda, \tag{13.2a}$$

$$\lambda(1 - \tau)f_k(k, K) = -\dot{\lambda} + \beta\lambda, \tag{13.2b}$$

together with the transversality condition

$$\lim_{t \to \infty} \lambda k e^{-\beta t} = 0. \tag{13.2c}$$

In order to characterize the solution more explicitly, Romer introduces specific functional forms, taking the utility function to be of the logarithmic form $U(c) = \ln c$ and the production function to be Cobb-Douglas $F(k, K) = k^\varepsilon K^\eta$. Assuming further that all firms are identical so that $K = Nk$, the production function is represented by $F(k, K) = k^{\varepsilon+\eta}N^\eta$. Substituting the appropriate derivatives of these functions into the optimality conditions (13.2a) and (13.2b) yields

$$\frac{1}{c} = \lambda, \tag{13.3a}$$

$$\frac{\dot{\lambda}}{\lambda} = \beta - \varepsilon(1 - \tau)N^\eta k^{\varepsilon+\eta-1}. \tag{13.3b}$$

Furthermore, substituting (13.3a), together with the production function and the balanced budget condition (13.1c), into the consumer accumulation equation (13.1b) leads to

$$\dot{k} = N^\eta k^{\varepsilon+\eta} - \frac{1}{\lambda}. \tag{13.3c}$$

The dynamics depend critically upon whether $\varepsilon + \eta \gtrless 1$. If $\varepsilon + \eta < 1$, the dynamics are essentially as in the representative agent model discussed in Chapter 9. The stationary point defined where the shadow value satisfies $\dot{\lambda} = 0$ implies that the right-hand side of (13.3b) equals zero and is equivalent to $f_k(k, K) = \beta$. This is the analogue to (9.10b). By writing the production function in the form $k^\varepsilon l^{1-\varepsilon}(Nk)^\eta$, Romer shows that increasing returns are in themselves insufficient to generate ongoing growth. In addition, the private marginal product of capital $f_k(k, K)$ must not fall too rapidly with k.

The dynamics change dramatically when $\varepsilon + \eta = 1$. In that case (13.3b) reduces to

$$\frac{\dot{\lambda}}{\lambda} = \beta - \varepsilon(1 - \tau)N^\eta \equiv -a. \tag{13.3b'}$$

This case can be solved explicitly and, if $a > 0$, leads to sustained growth. To see this, solve (13.3b') to yield $\lambda(t) = \lambda(0)e^{-at}$. Substituting into the accumulation equation (13.3c) leads to

$$\dot{k} = N^\eta k - \frac{1}{\lambda(0)}e^{at}, \tag{13.3c'}$$

the solution to which, starting from an initial given stock of capital k_0, is

$$k(t) = \frac{1}{\lambda(0)[N^\eta - a]}e^{at} + \left(k_0 - \frac{1}{\lambda(0)[N^\eta - a]}\right)e^{N^\eta t}. \tag{13.5}$$

Substituting this expression, together with the expression for $\lambda(t)$, into the transversality condition (13.2c), we find that in order for this to be met we require

$$\lambda(0) = \frac{1}{k_0[N^\eta - a]} > 0.$$

Thus the second term in (13.5) must be zero, and we conclude that the equilibrium is one of steady growth in which

$$\frac{\dot{k}}{k} = -\frac{\dot{\lambda}}{\lambda} = \frac{\dot{c}}{c} = \varepsilon(1 - \tau)N^\eta - \beta. \tag{13.6a}$$

This steady state of growth depends positively upon the productivity of capital ε, and negatively upon the rate of time preference β and the tax rate τ, and thus depends upon the structure of the economy, including the tax rate. To complete the description of the equilibrium in this case, we may also observe that the consumption-capital labor ratio is

$$\frac{c}{k} = \beta + [1 - \varepsilon(1 - \tau)]N^\eta. \tag{13.6b}$$

If $\varepsilon + \eta > 1$, the same general principles will apply. The equilibrium will be one of accelerating growth; however, a closed-form solution will in general be more difficult to obtain.

13.3 Integrated Fiscal Policy and Endogenous Growth

From the viewpoint of macroeconomic policy, the most interesting aspect of (13.6) is that the equilibrium growth rate depends upon the tax rate. Fiscal policy thus clearly has an impact on the long-run equilibrium growth rate. In order to explore this aspect in greater depth, we focus on the second model mentioned at the beginning, in which output is determined as a simple linear function of the capital stock alone. From the above discussion, this is equivalent to setting $\varepsilon + \eta = 1$ in the Romer model with the Cobb-Douglas technology.

As a policy matter, the general question of tax policy, savings, and growth is important. Consider, for example, the recent U.S. experience, which has been characterized by a low growth rate and a low savings rate. During the decade of the 1980s the annual growth rate of real GNP averaged around 2.6 percent while during the same period the personal savings rate averaged around 6.5 percent.[2] Both these figures are lower than the corresponding figures of earlier decades and are below those of other leading economies, most notably Japan's.[3] It is also the case that in the United States, as in most other countries, the main source of government revenue is the income tax, a consequence of which is that savings are taxed along with consumption. From time to time in the course of policy debates, the suggestion has been made that tax incentives should be used to stimulate savings and growth. In the course of this discussion, it has been argued that the income tax should be replaced, either in part or in total, by a consumption tax, thereby partially, or totally, exempting savings from taxation. This view is discussed, for example, in the 1993 United States *Economic Report of the President.*[4]

The proposition that direct taxation should be based on consumption rather than on income is not new. Early proponents of such a tax included Fisher (1937) and Kaldor (1955). Early debates centered around the traditional efficiency and equity arguments have been reviewed by Atkinson and Stiglitz (1980). The efficiency argument is based on the distortion associated with the taxation of savings. Taxing income in its entirety distorts the consumption-savings decision. By contrast, although a consumption tax eliminates this distortion, it introduces a distortion into the work-leisure choice. Equity arguments have expressed the view that it is fairer to tax people on what they consume rather than on what they produce. However, overall there is no clear presumption for one tax over another.

The linear endogenous growth model provides a very tractable framework within which to examine these issues, and that is the focus our discussion will present. The issue of the effect of fiscal policy on growth has been considered within this general type of framework by a number of authors; see Barro (1990), Jones and Manuelli (1990), Rebelo (1991), King and Rebelo (1990), and Jones, Manuelli, and Rossi (1993), among others. These authors have shown how different fiscal policies may account for differential long-run growth rates. Barro (1990) focuses on the effects of government spending, dealing primarily with the case of expenditure on infrastructure, which impacts directly on the productivity of capital. The income tax rate is set so as to finance the chosen level of expenditure. Rebelo (1991) discusses in detail the effects of taxation on the equilibrium growth rate. His analysis is based on the assumption that the revenues finance the provision of public goods, which, however, have no impact on the decisions of private agents in the economy. The levels of these nondistortionary government expenditures grow endogenously with the tax revenues generated. Hartman (1992) considers both income and consumption taxes in a stochastic linear model of endogenous growth.

The separability of the effects of taxation, on the one hand, and government expenditure, on the other, is standard in public economics and is clearly a useful pedagogic device. But in practice the revenue and expenditure decisions are interdependent, and this interdependence is important, particularly in the determination of an overall optimal fiscal policy. How taxes should be set depends in general upon how the revenue is spent and on the impact this expenditure is perceived by private agents to have on their economic decisionmaking and environment. We will see how results in the literature are sensitive to the assumptions being made regarding the specification of fiscal policy.

Sections 13.4 and 13.5 focus on deriving such an overall optimal integrated fiscal policy. Specifically, the government is one that issues debt and taxes both income and consumption, using the revenues so generated to finance public expenditures that directly affect the decisions of the private agents in the economy. Two types of public expenditure are considered. The first is expenditure on a public consumption good that interacts directly with the private consumption good in the welfare of private agents in the economy. The second is expenditure on a productive input, which impacts on the productivity of private capital in the economy and which we shall refer to as infrastructure. We shall consider cases where the public good being supplied is arbitrarily fixed, as well as cases where it is optimally determined along with the mode of financing.

The economy we consider is one experiencing ongoing growth in which total government expenditure increases in proportion to the aggregate stock of capital in the economy. An important feature of the analysis is the extent to which the private agent perceives the public services he receives as increasing with the growth in the economy, and in particular with the growth in his own capital stock. To a large degree that depends upon the nature of the public good being provided.

The general approach we adopt is to consider the first-best optimum equilibrium attainable by a central planner and then to consider the extent to which this may be replicated by appropriate debt and tax policies in a decentralized economy. In general, except in a special polar case, the first-best optimum cannot be attained by means of an income tax alone. However, it can be achieved if either government debt and/or a consumption tax is appropriately set as well. One of our main results is to show that in the absence of a consumption tax, the first-best optimum will involve the government being a net *lender*, rather than a net *debtor*, to the private sector. Because this is a rather implausible (although not infeasible) equilibrium, our analysis suggests an important role for a consumption tax as a component of an overall first-best fiscal policy.

13.4   A Linear Endogenous Growth Model

This section derives the optimal fiscal policy in the case where the government expenditure is in the form of a consumption good that interacts with a private good in the utility function of the representative agent. Our approach to determining the optimal fiscal package is to derive the first-best optimum of the central planner and then to obtain the tax structure that will enable this first-best optimum to be replicated.

As the Romer model discussed in Section 13.2 indicated, an equilibrium with ongoing steady growth at a constant rate will result only if the underlying economic structure is of the appropriately specified form. The reduced-form dynamic system must be linearly homogeneous in the variables that are being accumulated. In the case of a single accumulated factor of production, to be discussed in the present section, all quantitites must be linearly proportional to the index of growth in the economy, in this case the capital stock. This imposes restrictions on the underlying utility function, the production function, and the specification of government policy.

First Best Optimum

Consider a representative agent who consumes and derives utility from both private consumption goods, C, and government consumption goods, G, over an infinite planning horizon. A tractable utility function that is consistent with an equilibrium having a constant endogenous growth rate is the intertemporal isoelastic utility function:

$$Z \equiv \int_0^\infty \frac{1}{\gamma}(CG^\rho)^\gamma e^{-\beta t}\,dt \qquad \rho > 0 \quad -\infty < \gamma < 1/(1+\rho) \quad \rho\gamma < 1$$

$$(13.7a)$$

where ρ measures the impact of public consumption on the welfare, Z, of the private agent. We assume that both private and public consumption yield positive marginal utility, so that $\rho > 0$. For the isoelastic utility function, we can interpret the parameter ρ as representing the marginal rate of substitution between public and private goods, expressed in percentage terms. The exponent γ is related to the intertemporal elasticity of substitution, s, say, by $s = 1/(1 - \gamma)$, with the logarithmic utility function being equivalent to setting $\gamma = 0$.[5] The additional constraints on the coefficients in (13.7a) are implied by the assumption we shall make that the utility function is concave in C and G.

In due course, we shall determine the optimal tax and debt structure to maximize (13.7a). In determining this, we shall show that two critical elements are: (i) the parameter ρ and the potential externality this generates for the agent; and (ii) the extent to which the private agent internalizes the externality generated by government consumption expenditure. Our strategy in discussing the optimal debt-tax policy is to determine the extent to which it is able to replicate the first-best optimum achievable by a central planner having direct control over the resources in the economy.

Output Y in the economy is determined by the capital stock K, using a simple linear technology $Y = \alpha K, a > 0$, with the economy-wide resource contraint being

$$\dot{K}(t) = \alpha K(t) - C(t) - G(t) \tag{13.7b}$$

where dot denotes the time derivative. As usual, equation (13.7b) simply asserts that the rate of capital accumulation in the economy is the excess of current production over private and government consumption.

Initially, we consider the case where the government acts as a central planner and chooses C, G, and K directly to maximize (13.7a), subject to the resource constraint (13.7b). In order to sustain an equilibrium with steady growth, government expenditure cannot be fixed at some exogenous level, as it has been previously, but rather must be linked to the scale of the economy in some way. This can be achieved most conveniently by assuming that the government sets its expenditure as a fixed fraction of output:

$$g = \frac{G}{\alpha K}, \qquad 0 < g < 1. \tag{13.7c}$$

In an environment of growth this is a reasonable assumption. As economies have grown, government expenditure has grown with them (often at a faster rate), and (13.7c) is a specific formulation of that fact. We shall focus on two cases: (i) the case where g is set arbitrarily and (ii) the case where g is set optimally, along with C and K.

g Set Arbitrarily

In the case where g is set arbitrarily, the central planner's problem is to choose C and K to maximize (13.7a), subject to (13.7b), an initial capital stock K_o, and the given government share of output g. To solve this problem, we write the Lagrangean expression

$$\frac{1}{\gamma}C^{\gamma}(\alpha g K)^{\rho\gamma}e^{-\beta t} + \lambda e^{-\beta t}[\alpha(1-g)K - C - \dot{K}].$$ (13.8)

For arbitary g, the optimal choices of C and K satisfy

$$C^{\gamma-1}(\alpha g K)^{\rho\gamma} = \lambda,$$ (13.9a)

$$\alpha\rho C^{\gamma}(\alpha g K)^{\rho\gamma-1}g + \lambda\alpha(1-g) = -\dot{\lambda} + \lambda\beta.$$ (13.9b)

The solution proceeds by trial and error, by postulating a solution of the form $C = \mu K$, where μ is a constant to be determined. Differentiating (13.9a) with respect to t yields

$$\frac{\dot{\lambda}}{\lambda} = [\gamma(1+\rho) - 1]\frac{\dot{K}}{K};$$ (13.10a)

(13.9a) and (13.9b) can be combined and written as

$$\frac{\dot{\lambda}}{\lambda} = \beta - \alpha(1-g) - \rho\mu \qquad \text{or} \qquad \beta - \frac{\dot{\lambda}}{\lambda} = \alpha(1-g) + \rho\mu.$$ (13.10b)

This equation is just the familiar Keynes-Ramsey optimal consumption rule, asserting that the rate of return on private consumption, given by the left-hand side of the second equation, must equal the rate of return on capital. Now the return on capital has two components. The first is the usual net return $\alpha(1-g)$ as an asset. But, in addition, capital yields a utility return resulting from the fact that an increase in the capital stock raises the consumption benefits to the agent from government expenditure. This component is described by the term $\rho\mu$.

Dividing (13.7b) by K, the aggregate resource constraint becomes

$$\frac{\dot{K}}{K} = \alpha(1-g) - \mu.$$ (13.10c)

Combining equations (13.10a)–(13.10c) leads to the following explicit solutions for the optimal growth path:

$$\frac{C}{K} \equiv \hat{\mu} = \frac{\beta - \gamma\alpha(1-g)(1+\rho)}{(1+\rho)(1-\gamma)},$$ (13.11a)

$$\frac{\dot{K}}{K} \equiv \hat{\phi} = \frac{\alpha(1-g)(1+\rho) - \beta}{(1+\rho)(1-\gamma)} = \alpha(1-g) - \hat{\mu}.$$ (13.11b)

These two expressions specify the ratio of consumption to capital and the rate of growth of capital (and therefore consumption) along the optimal path, in terms of all exogenous parameters, including the arbitrarily given ratio of government expenditure, g. At this point the relationship of (13.11b) to the Harrod "warranted" growth rate should be noted. Noting that $Y = \alpha K$ and the definition of g, the right-hand side of (13.11b) can be written as $(Y/K)(1 - G/Y - C/Y)$. With the government expenditure essentially serving as a tax, the expression $(1 - G/Y - C/Y)$ is essentially the private savings rate. Thus (13.11b) asserts that the equilibrium rate of growth of capital equals the product of the savings rate and the output-capital ratio, precisely as in Harrod (1948). The difference—and it is significant—is that the savings rate is endogenously determined through intertemporal optimization, rather than being assumed exogenously.

These two equilibrium conditions merit further comment. First, consider the benchmark case, where the utility function is logarithmic ($\gamma = 0$) and government expenditure yields no externalities ($\rho = 0$). In this case, $\hat{\mu} = \beta$ and $\hat{\phi} = \alpha(1 - g) - \beta$. That is, the consumption-capital ratio equals the rate of time preference, and the equilibrium growth rate equals the difference between the net rate of return and the rate of time preference. These results are standard.

In the more general case where $\gamma \neq 0$, the effects of an increase in government expenditure on the consumption-capital ratio depend upon whether $\gamma \gtrless 0$. This effect characterizes many of the growth models we will consider, including the linear stochastic models to be developed in Part IV. It reflects the fact that in this case an increase in g (which acts like a tax insofar as the resources available to the private agent for expenditure on the private good C are concerned) has both a *negative income* effect and a *positive substitution* effect. The former is simply $-\alpha dg$ and measures the resources taken from the private sector by the government. The latter, measured by $\alpha dg/(1 - \gamma)$, reflects the fact that the increase in g reduces the return on capital, thereby inducing a switch to more consumption. The net effect on the equilibrium consumption-capital ratio, given by the sum, is $\alpha \gamma dg/(1 - \gamma)$, and the two effects are precisely offsetting in the case of the logarthmic utility function.

By contrast, we see from (13.11b) that an increase in the ratio of government consumption expenditure is growth-reducing. Even though an increase in government expenditure may reduce private consumption (if $\gamma < 0$), this effect is more than offset by the direct claim on the fixed (per unit of capital) rate of output by the increase in G, causing a net crowding out of investment and reduced real growth.

In addition, the equilibrium requires that the following transversality condition be met:

$$\lim_{t \to \infty} \lambda K e^{-\beta t} = 0. \tag{13.11c}$$

Substituting (13.10b) and (13.11b) into this equation we obtain

$$\lim_{t \to \infty} \lambda K e^{-\beta t} = \lim_{t \to \infty} \lambda(0) K_0 e^{-(1+\rho)\hat\mu t} = 0.$$

Using (13.11a) and (13.11b), this implies the following constraint on the equilibrium growth rate in the economy:

$$\beta - \gamma(1 + \rho)\hat\phi > 0; \equiv \hat\mu > 0; \quad \text{i.e.,} \quad \beta - \gamma\alpha(1 - g)(1 + \rho) > 0. \tag{13.11d}$$

This condition is automatically satisfied for $\gamma \le 0$ (thereby including the logarithmic utility function), but otherwise it imposes a constraint on the admissible share of government expenditure. In any event, the condition that $C/K > 0$ for a viable solution is a weak one, which any reasonable economy must surely satisfy.

g Set Optimally

Suppose now that the government chooses g optimally, in conjunction with C, K. It is straightforward to show the optimal choice of g leads to the additional optimality condition, $\partial U/\partial G = \partial U/\partial C$, equating the marginal utility for the two goods C, G. For the isoelastic utility function being assumed, this implies

$$G = \rho C, \quad \text{or, equivalently,} \quad g = \frac{\rho}{\alpha}\frac{C}{K}. \tag{13.12}$$

That is, the ratio of government to private consumption expenditure should equal ρ, their relative elasticities in the utility function. Substituting the additional optimality condition (13.12) into (13.11a), (13.11b) leads to the following overall first best optimum:

$$\frac{C}{K} \equiv \tilde\mu = \frac{\beta - \gamma\alpha(1 + \rho)}{(1 + \rho)[1 - \gamma(1 + \rho)]} \tag{13.13a}$$

$$\alpha\tilde{g} \equiv \frac{G}{K} = \rho\frac{C}{K} \equiv \rho\tilde\mu = \left(\frac{\rho}{1 + \rho}\right)\frac{[\beta - \gamma\alpha(1 + \rho)]}{[1 - \gamma(1 + \rho)]} \tag{13.13b}$$

$$\frac{\dot{K}}{K} \equiv \tilde\phi = \frac{\alpha - \beta}{1 - \gamma(1 + \rho)}. \tag{13.13c}$$

In this case, the corresponding transversality condition is

$$\beta > \gamma\alpha(1 + \rho), \tag{13.13d}$$

which is a condition involving the underlying taste and technology parameters of the economy.

The main point of the optimality conditions (13.11) and (13.13) is to serve as benchmarks against which the equilibrium in the decentralized economy can be compared. In making this comparison, our primary focus is on economic welfare, as measured by the intertemporal utility function (13.7a). Substituting for (13.7c), (13.11a) into (13.7a), and using (13.11b), we can show that, starting from an initially given stock of capital K_o, the maximized welfare corresponding to an arbitrarily set ratio of government expenditure g is

$$
\hat{Z} = \int_0^\infty \frac{1}{\gamma}(CG^\rho)^\gamma e^{-\beta t}\, dt = \int_0^\infty \frac{1}{\gamma}\hat{\mu}^\gamma(\alpha g)^{\rho\gamma} K_0^{\gamma(1+\rho)} e^{[\gamma(1+\rho)\hat{\phi}-\beta]t}\, dt
$$

$$
= \frac{\hat{\mu}^\gamma(\alpha g)^{\rho\gamma} K_0^{(1+\rho)\gamma}}{\gamma[\beta - \gamma(1+\rho)\hat{\phi}]} \tag{13.11e}
$$

where $\hat{\mu}, \hat{\phi}$ are given by (13.11a), (13.11b), respectively. It can be verified by recalling (13.11b), that the transversality condition (13.11d) ensures that the term $\beta - \gamma(1+\rho)\hat{\phi}$ appearing in the denominator of (13.11e) is positive, so that the maximized welfare $\hat{Z}$ is well defined. In the case that g is set optimally, the corresponding expression for maximized welfare is analogous to this expression with $\tilde{\mu}, \tilde{g}, \tilde{\phi}$, given by (13.13a)–(13.13c), replacing $\hat{\mu}, g, \hat{\phi}$, respectively. With welfare being maximized at $g = \tilde{g}$, it follows that

$$
sgn\left(\frac{\partial \hat{Z}}{\partial g}\right) = sgn(\tilde{g} - g),
$$

a fact that can also be verified directly from (13.11e). Thus we infer that increasing the growth rate by reducing government expenditure is not necessarily welfare improving. It will be so only if initially g is above its optimum.[6]

Equilibrium in a Decentralized Economy

We now turn to the representative agent operating in a market economy. For convenience, we normalize the size of the population to be unity. The agent purchases consumption out of the income generated by his holdings of physical capital and government bonds. For convenience, the government bonds are assumed to be perpetuities, paying a coupon equal to a unit of output. The value of these bonds, B, expressed in terms of output as numeraire, is $B = pb$, where b is the number of bonds and p is their price in terms of the numeraire. The reason for choosing this type of bond is simply to permit the equilibrium to be one having constant portfolio shares, which can be attained instantaneously through an initial jump in the price p. Otherwise, if the bonds were fixed-price bonds, the equilibrium would involve transitional dynamics as the portfolio shares adjust gradually from those determined by the initially given stocks of assets, K_0, b_0.

The objective of the agent is to maximize his constant elasticity utility function (13.7a), subject to a wealth accumulation equation, which may be expressed in terms of the numeraire by

$$\dot{K} + \dot{B} = \alpha(1 - \tau)K + r(1 - \tau)B - (1 + \omega)C \tag{13.14}$$

where r denotes the before-tax real rate of return on government bonds and is defined by $r = (1 + \dot{p})/p$, and wealth is defined by $W = K + B$. The agent is subject to two types of taxation. Both sources of income are taxed at the constant rate τ, and consumption is taxed at the rate ω.

To determine the optimal consumption and portfolio decisions of the representative agent, it is crucial to know the nature of the public good and the relation, if any, the agent may perceive it to have to his growing level of income (capital). While we maintain the assumption that the government sets its aggregate expenditure share $g = G/\alpha K$, so that the actual level of G increases linearly with K over time, it may or may not be perceived in this way by the agent in performing his optimization. That depends in part upon the nature of the public good being provided. We shall specify the representative agent's perception of government expenditure, $G^p(t)$, by

$$G^p(t) = g\alpha\overline{K}^{1-\delta}K(t)^\delta = g\alpha(K(t)/\overline{K})^\delta\overline{K} \qquad 0 \le \delta \le 1. \tag{13.15}$$

The exponent δ parameterizes the extent to which the agent perceives the level of public expenditure he receives as being tied to his growing personal capital stock, whereas $\overline{K}$ denotes some index of the capital stock perceived as being exogenous by the agent. For example, $\overline{K}$ may be the economy-wide capital stock, which although perceived by the agent to be unrelated to his own decisions, in equilibrium grows at the same rate as K.

The specification of (13.15) is important and merits further discussion. The two polar values of $\delta = 0, 1$ represent extreme types of public goods. If $\delta = 1$, the agent perceives the level of public consumption expenditures he receives as being directly proportional to his growing capital stock (and hence to his income). Public goods such as fire protection and city services, which tend to be proportional to property and presumably to income, may be thought of as being of this type. In the other polar case, $\delta = 0$, the agent perceives the level of government expenditures he receives as being independent of his current income level. Nonrival public goods such as national defense can be put into this category.

The second equality in (13.15) suggests an alternative interpretation in terms of "congestion" effects. Suppose the aggregate stock of the public good is $g\overline{K}$. The term $(K(t)/\overline{K})^\delta$ represents a scaling down of the aggregate public good available to the individual, due to congestion. The absence of any congestion is represented by $\delta = 0$, in which case the public good is fully available to the representative agent. The other polar case, $\delta = 1$, corresponds to complete congestion, that is, a situation where the amount of the public good available to the agent is strictly proportional to his individual capital stock and its implied contribution to the aggregate. As we will see, in this case the agent, in effect, sees the world through the eyes of the central planner and solves the same problem.

Thus we can either view (13.15) as characterizing an intermediate case where the public good has a mixture of the attributes we have been describing, or, alternatively, we can view (13.15) simply as a convenient way of parameterizing the two extreme cases, $\delta = 0, 1$. From this standpoint, the formulation is a convenient way of parameterizing the contrast between the representative agent and the central planner.

We should add that setting $\rho = 0$ describes the situation, often assumed in the optimal tax literature, in which the government expenditure represents a pure drain on resources and provides no benefit to the economy. But, in contrast to the frequent interpretation of the exclusion of government expenditure from the objective function as yielding positive utility that is additively separable from that yielded by private consumption, such an assumption is not possible here. The reason is that with g growing with the capital stock, decisions made with respect to the latter do, in general, impact on the amount of benefits yielded by the publicly provided good. The only case where such an interpretation would be valid is if the agent perceives no link between his capital stock and the government services he obtains—that is if and only if $\delta = 0$ in (13.15). However, the case where the utility function is of the additively separable form

$$\int_0^\infty \frac{1}{\gamma}[C^\gamma + b(G^p)^\gamma]e^{-\beta t}\,dt$$

can also be readily analyzed.

The agent's formal optimization problem is to choose $C, K,$ and B to maximize:

$$\int_0^\infty \frac{1}{\gamma}(CG^p(t)^\rho)^\gamma e^{-\beta t}\,dt, \tag{13.7a$'$}$$

subject to his wealth accumulation equation (13.14) and his perception of government expenditure as set out in (13.15). In deriving the equilibrium, we assume that the consumption-capital ratio $C/K \equiv \mu$ is constant, just as it was for the centralized problem, and that the equilibrium portolio share of capital, $K/W \equiv n$, is constant. As we will see, the equilibrium we obtain does indeed have these properties, thereby validating this assumption.

The optimality conditions for this problem are now

$$C^{\gamma-1}(g\alpha\overline{K}^{1-\delta}K^{\delta})^{\rho\gamma} = \lambda(1 + \omega) \tag{13.16a}$$

$$\rho\delta C^{\gamma}(g\alpha\overline{K}^{1-\delta}K^{\delta})^{\rho\gamma}K^{-1} + \lambda\alpha(1 - \tau) = -\dot{\lambda} + \lambda\beta \tag{13.16b}$$

$$\lambda r(1 - \tau) = -\dot{\lambda} + \lambda\beta. \tag{13.16c}$$

Combining the optimality conditions with respect to the two assets, we find that

$$r(1 - \tau) = \alpha(1 - \tau) + \rho\delta\mu(1 + \omega). \tag{13.17}$$

This equation is just the arbitrage condition equating the after-tax rates of return on the two assets. If $\rho = 0$ or $\delta = 0$, then (13.17) reduces to the usual equality of net rates of return, which must hold under certainty. However, to the extent that $\rho, \delta \neq 0$, the rate of return on capital has two components. In addition to the after-tax rate of return, it yields a utility return resulting from the fact that an increase in the capital stock raises the consumption benefits to the agent from government expenditure.[7]

Subtracting the private resource constraint (13.14) from the aggregate economy-wide resource constraint (13.7b) yields the government budget constraint

$$\dot{B} = g\alpha K + r(1 - \tau)B - \tau\alpha K - \omega C. \tag{13.18}$$

Given the tax rates τ, ω, and the proportion of government expenditure, g, this equation determines the evolution of bonds. Next, differentiating (13.16a) with respect to t and noting that in equilibrium $\dot{K}/K = \dot{\overline{K}}/\overline{K}$ yields

$$\frac{\dot{\lambda}}{\lambda} = [\gamma(1 + \rho) - 1]\frac{\dot{K}}{K}. \tag{13.19}$$

Combining the three accumulation equations (13.7b), (13.14), and (13.18), utilizing the optimality condition (13.17), and (13.19), and noting the constancy of $C/W, K/W$, the decentralized equilibrium can be summarized by the following relationships:

$$\frac{C}{K} = \overline{\mu} = \frac{\alpha(1 - g)[1 - \gamma(1 + \rho)] + \beta - \alpha(1 - \tau)}{1 - \gamma(1 + \rho) + \rho\delta(1 + \omega)} \tag{13.20a}$$

$$\frac{\dot{K}}{K} = \frac{\dot{B}}{B} = \frac{\dot{W}}{W} = \overline{\phi} = \frac{\alpha(1 - g)\rho\delta(1 + \omega) + \alpha(1 - \tau) - \beta}{1 - \gamma(1 + \rho) + \rho\delta(1 + \omega)} \tag{13.20b}$$

$$\bar{n} = \frac{\alpha(g - \tau) + \bar{\mu}[1 + \rho\delta(1 + \omega)]}{\bar{\mu}(1 + \omega)(1 + \rho\delta)}. \tag{13.20c}$$

In addition, the following transversality conditions must hold:

$$\lim_{t \to \infty} \lambda K e^{-\beta t} = \lim_{t \to \infty} \lambda B e^{-\beta t} = 0 \tag{13.20d}$$

where the shadow value of wealth λ now grows in accordance with (13.19). Using this expression together with (13.20b) to evaluate (13.20d), the transversality conditions now reduce to the following constraint on the equilibrium growth rate in the economy:

$$\bar{\phi} < \frac{\beta}{\gamma(1 + \rho)}. \tag{13.21}$$

Furthermore, substituting from (13.20b) for $\bar{\phi}$, this constraint can in turn be expressed in terms of the underlying policy and structural parameters of the economy.

As written, these three equations determine the decentralized equilibrium values for the consumption-capital ratio $\bar{\mu}$, the equilibrium real growth rate $\bar{\phi}$, and the equilibrium portfolio share of capital to wealth $\bar{n}$, all in terms of the given tax rate τ, ω; the share of government expenditure g; and the taste and technology parameters.[8] Denoting government debt policy by $\chi \equiv B/K$, equation (13.20c) can be viewed as determining the endogenous adjustment in government debt. Alternatively, it is possible for the government to set its debt policy χ exogenously, in which case one of the two tax rates, τ or ω, must accomodate accordingly.

Before proceeding further, it is instructive to demonstrate that the transversality condition (13.20d) ensures that the intertemporal government budget constraint is met. Starting from an initial stock of government bonds B_0, the accumulation equation (13.18) implies that at time t the stock of government bonds outstanding is

$$B(t) = e^{r(1-\tau)t}\left[B_0 + \int_0^t [\alpha(g - \tau) - \omega\bar{\mu}]K(s)e^{-r(1-\tau)s}\,ds\right]. \tag{13.22}$$

Next, combining (13.19) with (13.20b) yields

$$\lambda(t) = \lambda(0)e^{[\gamma(1+\rho)-1]\bar{\phi}t}$$

Substituting these expressions into the second transversality condition appearing in (13.20d) leads to

$$\lambda(t)B(t)e^{-\beta t}$$

$$= e^{[r(1-\tau)+\gamma(1+\rho)\bar{\phi}-\bar{\phi}-\beta]t}\left[B_0 + \int_0^t [\alpha(g - \tau) - \omega\bar{\mu}]K(s)e^{-r(1-\tau)s}\,ds\right].$$

Using (13.17) and the definitions of $\bar{\mu}$ and $\bar{\phi}$, the expression outside the parenthesis involving the exponential reduces to one, so that the transversality condition (13.20d) implies

$$B_0 + \int_0^\infty [\alpha(g - \tau) - \omega\bar{\mu}]K(s)e^{-r(1-\tau)s}\,ds = 0. \tag{13.23}$$

Equation (13.23) is precisely the intertemporal government budget constraint, requiring that the present value of government expenditures, less tax receipts, plus initial debt, must sum to zero. With $\alpha, g, \tau, \omega, \bar{\mu}$ all being constants, and capital accumulating at a constant growth rate $\bar{\phi}$, (13.23) can be readily evaluated. Utilizing the relationship (13.17), together with (13.20a), (13.20b), this reduces to

$$B_0 + \frac{\alpha(g - \tau) - \omega\bar{\mu}}{\beta - \gamma(1 + \rho)\bar{\phi}}K_0 = 0 \tag{13.23'}$$

where the transversality condition (13.21) implies $\beta > \gamma(1 + \rho)\bar{\phi}$ and ensures that the integral in (13.23) is well defined. We observe from this last expression that, assuming that the initial stock in the economy is positive ($K_0 > 0$) and that the government begins with a positive stock of outstanding debt ($B_0 > 0$), then the steady growth path will be intertemporally viable if and only if $\alpha g < \alpha\tau + \omega\bar{\mu}$—that is, if and only the government maintains a continuous budget surplus. Alternatively, if the government maintains a balanced budget or, as is more commonly the case, a current deficit, then the only way for the intertemporal budget constraint to be met is for the government to be a net creditor to the private sector. The implications of this will be considered further in connection with our discussion of optimal debt structure.

Fiscal Policy and Growth

It is straightforward to analyze the effects of various exogenous shocks to this equilibrium. Because we are particularly interested in the impact of fiscal policy on the equilibrium growth rate of the economy, we will focus on the following two aspects.

Increase in Government Expenditure

The effect of a debt-financed increase in the rate of government expenditure on the equilibrium growth rate is given by

$$\frac{\partial \bar{\phi}}{\partial g} = -\frac{\alpha\rho\delta(1 + \omega)}{D} \leq 0 \tag{13.24a}$$

where, for notational convenience,

$$D \equiv 1 - \gamma(1 + \rho) + \rho\delta(1 + \omega) > 0.$$

To understand the response of the growth rate described in (13.24a), we begin with the case, originally considered by Eaton (1981), where government consumption expenditure yields no direct utility ($\rho = 0$). In this case, like Eaton, we find that a debt-financed increase in the proportion of output going to government expenditure has no effect on the growth rate. It simply crowds out an equal amount of private consumption, leaving the rate of capital accumulation unaffected. As compared to the case of the central planner discussed in equation (13.11b), an increase in g now has two (offsetting) effects on the growth rate. The first is the direct negative effect, discussed previously in that case. But in addition, with the increased expenditure now being financed by the issuing of more debt, the price of bonds is reduced. This leads to a decline in financial wealth, thereby reducing private consumption, doing so by an amount equal to the increase in government expenditure. In short, private consumption is fully crowded out, leaving the net rate of capital accumulation (i.e., the growth rate) unchanged.

In contrast with this result, (13.24a) implies that as long as (i) $\rho > 0$, so that government expenditure yields positive marginal utility; and (ii) $\delta > 0$, so that the representative private agent perceives the level of public expenditure he receives to increase (at least partially) with his growing stock of capital, the agent will tend to reduce the amount by which he cuts back on consumption, thereby leading to an overall reduction in the growth rate.

The fact that an increase in government expenditure reduces the growth rate in a situation where the benefits of government expenditure are perceived to increase with the capital stock may appear surprising. Intuitively, one might have expected such a situation to encourage the accumulation of capital, thereby enhancing the benefits from the increased government expenditure. The reason for this seemingly counterintuitive result can be seen most readily by focusing on the logarithmic case ($\gamma = 0$), and setting the consumption tax to zero ($\omega = 0$). In the case of "useless" government expenditure ($\rho = 0$), the consumption-capital ratio is $\beta - \alpha(g - \tau)$, and the corresponding growth rate is $\alpha(1 - \tau) - \beta$. By contrast, in the economy described here, with perceived growth-related welfare-augmenting government expenditure ($\rho, \delta > 0$), the equilibrium is one with a *lower* consumption-capital ratio, $[\beta - \alpha(g - \tau)]/[1 + \rho\delta]$, together with a *higher* growth rate, $[\alpha(1 - g)\rho\delta + \alpha(1 - \tau) - \beta]/[1 + \rho\delta]$. This is indeed as one would expect. With the level of private consumption reduced in the present economy, its marginal utility is higher, and agents are accordingly less willing to cut their private consumption expenditure at the margin. Consequently, any increase agents in government expenditure leads to a partial crowding out of both private consumption and investment, the latter implying a lower growth rate. The larger is δ the more the response resembles that of the centrally planned economy (see [13.11b]). Viewed from this standpoint, the contrast with the Eaton result regarding the effect of government expenditure on growth ceases to be surprising.

Switch from a Tax on Capital Income to a Consumption Tax

It is of particular interest to consider the impact of a switch from a tax on capital income to a tax on consumption on the equilibrium rate of growth. More specifically, consider a government that is committed to financing a given level of expenditure g and decides to substitute a higher consumption tax for a reduced income tax and reduced debt financing. The effect on the the equilibrium growth rate is given by the following expression:

$$\frac{\partial \bar{\phi}}{\partial \omega} = \frac{1}{1 - \gamma(1 + \rho) + \rho \delta (1 + \omega)} \left(-\alpha \frac{\partial \tau}{\partial \omega} + \rho \delta \bar{\mu} \right) \geq 0. \tag{13.24b}$$

Equation (13.24b) indicates that an increase in the consumption tax will impact positively on the growth rate in two ways. First, to the extent that the government holds debt constant and the higher consumption tax enables its fixed expenditures to be financed with a lower income tax, the effect is growth enhancing. If, on the other hand, the government simply substitutes the consumption tax for debt, with no adjustment in the income tax, this effect vanishes. But in addition there is a second effect, which operates through the private sector's perception of government expenditure. To the extent that private agents perceive the level of expenditure to increase with their capital stock ($\delta > 0$), they will have an incentive to reduce current consumption, increase savings, and accumulate capital, thereby enhancing the benefits they receive from government expenditure in the future. This response is also growth enhancing, but it too will vanish if the private agents do not perceive any relationship between their own capital stock and the aggregate benefits from government expenditure.

The fact that the increase in the consumption tax ω tends to *increase* the growth rate would appear to contradict the result obtained by Rebelo (1991) suggesting that the growth rate is independent of the consumption tax. However, the differences in effects are due to differences in the assumptions that are being made with respect to the expenditure of the revenue generated by the consumption tax and how that expenditure affects the welfare of private agents. If instead of assuming that g remains fixed, as in (13.24b), we were to assume that τ remains fixed, with the additional revenues being spent, as assumed by Rebelo; and if in addition we set $\rho = 0$, also assumed by Rebelo, then (13.24b) reduces to $\partial \bar{\phi}/\partial \omega = 0$, thereby easily reconciling the two sets of results. This comparison serves to emphasize just how important it is to spell out precisely the assumptions under which a particular fiscal experiment is being conducted.

Optimal Debt and Tax Structure

The key question to be addressed is the extent to which, through appropriate tax policy, the decentralized economy is able to attain the first-best optimum described by (13.11a), (13.11b). Equating the right-hand sides of (13.11a), (13.20a)—or, equivalently, (13.11b), (13.20b)—yields the following relationship:

$$\frac{\alpha(1 - g)}{(1 - \gamma)} - \frac{\beta}{(1 + \rho)(1 - \gamma)} = \frac{\alpha(1 - g)\rho\delta(1 + \omega) + \alpha(1 - \tau) - \beta}{1 - \gamma(1 + \rho) + \rho\delta(1 + \omega)}. \qquad (13.25)$$

Equation (13.25) provides a trade-off between the tax on capital income τ and the consumption tax ω, which, given the fixed exogenous proportion of government expenditure g, will enable the decentralized economy to replicate both the consumption-capital ratio and the real growth rate of the centrally planned economy. In general, there are an infinite number of tax configurations that enable the attainment of the first-best optimum, each associated with a different equilibrium level of government debt.

In the case that $\delta = 0$ and $\gamma = 0$, (13.25) yields the following unique solution for the tax on capital:

$$\hat{\tau} = g - \frac{\rho}{1 + \rho}\frac{\beta}{\alpha}, \qquad (13.25')$$

implying that the consumption tax may now be set arbitrarily. Accordingly, (13.20c), taken in conjunction with (13.25'), implies the following trade-off between the arbitrarily set consumption tax and debt structure:

$$\bar{n} = \frac{1}{(1 + \omega)} + \frac{\beta\rho}{\bar{\mu}(1 + \rho)}. \qquad (13.20c')$$

The more revenue raised by the government through a consumption tax, the less debt it needs to float.

In fact, the consumption tax plays an important role in facilitating the attainment of the first-best equilibrium. In the case where there is no consumption tax ($\omega = 0$), the corresponding equilibrium portfolio share of capital $\bar{n} > 1$, implying a *negative* stock of government debt; that is, the government is a net creditor to the private sector. This can be seen immediately from (13.20c') for the case $\delta = 0$. However, it also obtains more generally as well. For example, setting $\omega = 0$ and $\gamma = 0$ in (13.25) and (13.20c), we find that

$$\bar{n} = 1 + \frac{\rho\beta(1 - \delta)}{\bar{\mu}(1 + \rho)(1 + \rho\delta)} \geq 1. \tag{13.20c''}$$

As long as $0 \leq \delta < 1$, the proposition that the equilibrium stock of government debt is negative continues to hold. This important result can be summarized as follows:

Proposition 1   In the absence of a consumption tax, the decentralized economy can replicate the first best optimum of the centrally planned economy if and only if the government is a net creditor to the private sector. The government can render the stock of government debt to be nonnegative in such an equilibrium by imposing a positive tax on consumption.

To gain some intuitive understanding of this proposition, it is useful to focus first on the polar case $\delta = 1$, in which the representative agent correctly perceives the growth of government expenditure when making decisions, in effect perceiving the economy through the eyes of the central planner. Setting $\delta = 1, \omega = 0$ in (13.25), we see that the first-best optimum is attained by setting $\tau = g$. This full financing of government expenditures by an income tax rate in effect operates like a user fee, internalizing the effects of an individual's choices on his level of public services. Individuals are essentially paying for the services they receive, so that the equilibrium is Pareto optimal. With the government budget being balanced, there is no role for debt, as can be seen from (13.20c), which implies $\bar{n} = 1$.

Suppose now that $\delta < 1$, so that the private agent underpredicts the rate of growth of government expenditures and therefore the future benefits they will provide. If the capital income tax rate is maintained at the self-financing rate $\tau = g$, the consumption-capital ratio increases, raising it above the first-best optimum of the central planner. Private agents consume too much and accumulate capital too slowly. To restore the consumption-capital ratio and growth rate to their respective Pareto optimal levels, the income tax on capital, τ, would need to be lowered, implying $g > \tau$ and thus a continuous current fiscal deficit. This can be seen from the intertemporal government budget constraint (13.23), which with $\omega = 0$ becomes

$$B_0 + \alpha \int_0^\infty (g - \tau)K(t)e^{-r(1-\tau)t}\, dt = 0. \tag{13.23''}$$

With $g > \tau$ everywhere, the intertemporal constraint will be met if and only if $B_0 < 0$, which, with B growing at the constant rate $\bar{\phi}$, implies that $B < 0$ at all points of time. In effect, the government finances its continuous deficit using the interest income it earns by being a net lender to the public. At the same time, we should note that a steady state in which $B < 0$ amounts to the implicit introduction of an initial lump-sum tax. This is because in order to place the public into debt at the initial time $t = 0$, it is necessary to capture the public's resources via a lump-sum tax at that initial instant.

As a final observation, we should point out that because the economy is always on its steady-state growth path, the optimal tax structure is time consistent. At any point of time the fiscal authority is assumed to choose a set of constant tax rates. If it were to reoptimize at some later point of time, there would be nothing to induce it to deviate from its initial set of decisions.

Optimal Capital Income and Consumption Taxes

The previous analysis has made it clear that debt plays no welfare-enhancing role in this economy.[9] Accordingly, we shall henceforth drop government bonds, enabling us to focus more directly on the two forms of taxation. Imposing the constraint $\bar{n} = 1$ in (13.20c), the equation reduces to

$$\alpha\tau + \omega\mu = \alpha g. \tag{13.20c'''}$$

This equation asserts that in the absence of government debt, the government must maintain a continuously balanced budget: the revenues raised by taxing capital and taxing consumption must just finance its consumption expenditures. The growth rate and the consumption-capital ratio in the decentralized equilibrium continue to be given by (13.20a), (13.20b), although now, given g, one of the tax rates, τ, ω must be chosen to meet the budget constraint (13.20c''').

Equations (13.25) and (13.20c''') jointly determine the solutions for the two tax rates that (i) will enable the first best optimum to be attained, and (ii) are consistent with the government budget constraint. To keep calculations simple we shall continue to restrict ourselves to the logarithmic case. For an arbitrarily given fraction of government expenditure g, the resulting expressions are

$$\bar{\omega} = \frac{\rho(1 - \delta)}{1 + \rho\delta}, \tag{13.26a}$$

$$\bar{\tau} = g - \frac{\rho\beta(1 - \delta)}{\alpha(1 + \rho)(1 + \rho\delta)}. \tag{13.26b}$$

In general, optimal tax policy calls for financing expenditure g partially by a tax on capital and partially by a consumption tax. The optimal taxes themselves depend upon (i) the production coefficient a; (ii) taste parameter, ρ; and (iii) government expenditure g, its perception δ, and how it impacts on utility β. In particular, the higher the utility associated with the public good, the greater the relative size of the consumption tax. In addition, equations (13.20c‴) and (13.26b) together imply that the total amount of revenue raised by the consumption tax, $\omega\mu$, is independent of g. Thus, even if the government chooses (nonoptimally) to let $g \rightarrow 0$, the optimal fiscal policy is to subsidize the income from capital by means of a tax on consumption.[10] Discounting the benefits of capital accumulation and the growing externalities associated with government expenditure, the agent overconsumes and underinvests. Subsidizing the returns to capital and taxing consumption correct for this distortion. Equation (13.26b) also implies that any incremental increase in government expenditure should be fully financed by an increase in the tax on capital, that is, $d\tau = dg > 0$.

In certain special cases a single tax will suffice to yield the optimum. A tax on capital alone will be optimal in either of two polar cases: (i) $\delta = 1$, when, as we have seen, the representative agent in effect behaves like a central planner, in which case the income tax fully internalizes the effects of the expenditure benefits; or (ii) $\rho = 0$, when the government expenditure does not impact on the marginal utility of consumption and therefore generates no externalities. At the other extreme, it will be optimal to finance, by means of a consumption tax alone if and only if the government sets

$$g = \rho\beta(1 - \delta)/\alpha(1 + \rho)(1 + \rho\delta).$$

At this point it is useful to compare the present optimal tax on capital with the Chamley (1986) result discussed in Section 11.9, which requires that asymptotically the optimal tax on capital converge to zero. The Chamley analysis did not consider any externalities from government expenditure. Setting $\rho = 0$ we still find that the optimal policy is to set the tax on capital equal to the share of output claimed by the government ($\bar{\tau} = g$). The difference is that when government expenditure is specified as a fraction of output, its level is not exogenous but instead is proportional to the size of the growing capital stock. The decision by the private sector to accumulate capital stock leads to an increase in the supply of public goods in the future. If the private sector treats government spending as independent of its investment decision (when in fact it is not), a tax on capital is necessary to internalize the externality and thereby correct the distortion. Thus, in general, the Chamley rule of not taxing capital in the long run will be nonoptimal, although in specific examples to be given below, it may form part of an overall optimal fiscal policy.

In the case that the government expenditure is set optimally in accordance with (13.13b), the corresponding optimal consumption and income tax rates become

$$\bar{\omega} = \frac{\rho(1 - \delta)}{1 + \rho\delta} \tag{13.27a}$$

$$\bar{\tau} = \frac{\rho\beta\delta}{\alpha(1 + \rho\delta)} \tag{13.27b}$$

Apart from the limiting case where $\rho = 0$—when $\tilde{g} = 0$, implying both $\bar{\omega} = \bar{\tau} = 0$—a zero consumption tax will be optimal in the case where $\delta = 1$. On the other hand, if $\delta = 0$, then the optimal consumption tax $\bar{\omega} = \rho$, the exponent of public consumption in utility. That is, the optimally set government expenditure should now be fully financed by a consumption tax, in which case the Chamley rule of a zero tax on capital reemerges as being optimal.

An alternative perspective on the role of the consumption tax in achieving the optimum can be obtained by comparing the private and social returns to capital in the presence of government consumption expenditure. As we have seen in (13.17), the former is

$$\alpha(1 - \tau) + \rho\delta\bar{\mu}(1 + \omega),$$

whereas the social return to capital is

$$\alpha(1 - g) + \rho\hat{\mu}.$$

Both returns include their impact on utility; the essential difference revolves around how this is perceived by the government and the private agents. In the absence of any impact of government consumption on private utility (i.e., if $\rho = 0$) then these two rates of return are equalized and the externality internalized by fully taxing the benefits, $\tau = g$, which is also self-financing, and thus setting $\omega = 0$. Furthermore, if $\rho > 0$ and $\delta = 1$, so that the private agent views the world as would the central planner, $\hat{\mu} = \bar{\mu}$, and again the rates of return will be equalized by setting $\tau = g$ and $\omega = 0$. However, if $d < 1$, the private agent underestimates the social returns to investment and overconsumes. This can be corrected for by imposing a strictly positive tax on consumption.

13.5   Productive Government Expenditure

We now turn to the case where the government expenditure enhances productivity in the economy by raising the marginal physical product of capital in accordance with

$$Y = \alpha\left(\frac{H}{K}\right)K \qquad \alpha' > 0; \alpha'' < 0 \tag{13.28}$$

where H denotes the level of this type of government expenditure. We shall identify such productive expenditure as being expenditure on infrastructure and as having the property of positive but diminishing marginal physical product. The structure of this section mirrors that of the previous one, so that our treatment can be more brief.[11] As in the previous case, debt plays no welfare-enhancing role; we shall therefore focus solely on taxation.[12]

First-Best Optimum

Abstracting from government consumption, the first-best central planning problem is to maximize

$$\int_0^\infty \frac{1}{\gamma} C^\gamma e^{-\beta t}\, dt \tag{13.29a}$$

subject to

$$\dot{K}(t) = \alpha\left(\frac{H(t)}{K(t)}\right)K(t) - C(t) - H(t). \tag{13.29b}$$

As before, we assume that the government ties its expenditure to the capital stock:

$$h = \frac{H}{K} \qquad 0 > h > \alpha,$$

so that the actual level of government expenditure grows with the economy. Again, we distinguish the cases where h is set arbitrarily and where h is set optimally along with C and K.

h Set Arbitrarily

In the case that h is set arbitrarily, the central planner's problem is to choose C and K to maximize (13.29a), subject to (13.29b) and given h. The following equilibrium paths for consumption and capital are obtained:

$$\frac{C}{K} \equiv \hat{\mu} = \frac{\beta - \gamma(\alpha(h) - h)}{1 - \gamma}, \tag{13.30a}$$

$$\frac{\dot{K}}{K} \equiv \hat{\phi} = \frac{\alpha(h) - h - \beta}{1 - \gamma}. \tag{13.30b}$$

h Set Optimally

In the case that h is set optimally, in conjunction with C and K, the following additional optimality condition obtains:[13]

$$\alpha'(h) = 1. \tag{13.30c}$$

That is, the optimal ratio of infrastructure to capital, $\tilde{h}$, say, is attained where the marginal benefits to productivity just match the unit resource costs of the additional government expenditure. In this case, the equilibrium paths for consumption and capital accumulation continue to be given by (13.30a), (13.30b), where $\tilde{h}$ is determined by the optimality condition (13.30c).

Differentiating (13.30b) with respect to h, we see that the effect of an increase in government expenditure on infrastructure on the equilibrium growth rate is

$$\frac{\partial \hat{\phi}}{\partial h} = \frac{\alpha'(h) - 1}{1 - \gamma}, \tag{13.31}$$

implying that the equilibrium growth rate is maximized at the optimal infrastructure-capital ratio. This is in constrast to the relationship between growth and welfare that applies in the case of government consumption expenditure.

Equilibrium in a Decentralized Economy

A critical feature of the decentralized economy is the representative agent's perception of the impact of the infrastructure expenditure on the marginal product of his capital. Analogous to (13.15), we shall assume

$$H^p(t) = h\overline{K}^{1-\sigma}K(t)^\sigma = h(K(t)/\overline{K})^{1-\sigma}\overline{K} \qquad 0 \le \sigma \le 1. \tag{13.32}$$

The exponent σ parameterizes the extent to which the agent perceives the services he receives from infrastructure as growing with his capital stock. If $\sigma = 0$, he expects H to be independent of his own decisions, so that H/K is perceived to decline with his growing capital stock; if $\sigma = 1$, he expects H to grow proportionately with K, so that H/K remains constant $(= h)$. As before, (13.32) can also be interpreted in terms of a congestion function.

In the absence of government debt, we express the optimization of the agent to be to maximize (13.29a), subject to the accumulation equation

$$\dot{K} = \alpha\left(h\left(\frac{K}{\overline{K}}\right)^{\sigma-1}\right)(1-\tau)K - (1+\omega)C. \qquad (13.29b')$$

The corresponding equilibrium time paths are now[14]

$$\frac{C}{K} = \bar{\mu} = \frac{(\alpha-h)(1-\gamma) - (1-\tau)[\alpha - (1-\sigma)\alpha'h] + \beta}{1-\gamma}, \qquad (13.33a)$$

$$\frac{\dot{K}}{K} \equiv \bar{\phi} = \frac{(1-\tau)[\alpha - (1-\sigma)\sigma'h] - \beta}{1-\gamma}. \qquad (13.33b)$$

In addition, the two tax rates must satisfy the government budget constraint

$$\alpha\tau + \omega\mu = h. \qquad (13.33c)$$

Thus equations (13.33a), (13.33b), and (13.33c) jointly determine the equilibrium growth rate, the consumption-capital ratio, and one of the two tax rates.

From these equilibrium relationships, the following responses of the equilibrium growth rate can be obtained:

i. An increase in government expenditure on infrastructure that is financed by means of a consumption tax will be growth-enhancing. The same holds true if the expenditure is debt-financed.

ii. An increase in government expenditure on infrastructure that is financed by means of a tax on capital may either raise or lower the growth rate. The positive effects of higher productivity are offset by the negative effects of the reduced after-tax return to capital.

iii. A switch in the financing of a given level of infrastructure expenditure from a tax on capital to a tax on consumption will be growth-enhancing.

Optimal Tax Structure

Equating the right-hand sides of (13.30a) and (13.33a), or, equivalently, of (13.30b) and (13.33b),

$$\hat{t} = \frac{h[1 - (1-\sigma)\alpha']}{\alpha - (1-\sigma)\alpha'h}. \qquad (13.34a)$$

This expression provides the tax on capital income that will replicate the consumption-capital ratio and equilibrium growth rates of the Pareto-optimal equilibrium. In order to finance its expenditures, the government must, in conjunction with $\hat{\tau}$, set a corresponding consumption tax $\hat{\omega}$:

$$\hat{\omega} = \frac{(1 - \gamma)(1 - \sigma)\alpha'h(\alpha - \alpha'h)}{[\beta - \gamma(\alpha - h)][\alpha - (1 - \sigma)\alpha'h]}. \tag{13.34b}$$

In the case that h is set optimally, these expressions are modified to

$$\hat{\tau} = \frac{\tilde{h}\sigma}{\alpha - (1 - \sigma)\tilde{h}}, \tag{13.34a'}$$

$$\hat{\omega} = \frac{(1 - \gamma)(1 - \sigma)\tilde{h}(\alpha - \tilde{h})}{[\beta - \gamma(\alpha - \tilde{h})][\alpha - (1 - \sigma)\tilde{h}]}. \tag{13.34b'}$$

As in the case of government consumption expenditure, a tax on capital income alone will be optimal if $\sigma = 1$, the case where the representative agent in effect behaves like a central planner. It will also be optimal if $\alpha' = 0$, in which case government expenditure ceases to have any impact on the productivity of capital. Financing fully by the use of a consumption tax will be optimal if and only if $\alpha'(h) = 1/(1 - \sigma)$, which implies a value for h that is, in general, less than the optimum $\tilde{h}$. In the case that h is set optimally, a zero tax on capital will be optimal if and only if $\sigma = 0$, and again the Chamley result applies.

13.6 Two-Sector Model

The models we have been discussing in the previous two sections have the property that the equilibrium steady-state growth path is reached instantaneously. This is very convenient from an analytical viewpoint because it makes the welfare analysis extremely tractable. Furthermore, because the equilibrium does not involve any transitional dynamics, problems such as time consistency of the optimal policy do not arise. The problem is stationary, so if at any point of time the policymaker wishes to reoptimize, he will choose the same steady-state growth path.

But this simplification comes at a price. Output is proportional to the capital stock, and labor is absent from the analysis. In a seminal paper, Lucas (1988) extended this type of growth model by introducing labor through human capital, embodied in the labor force. The general idea of the model is that at each point of time there is an existing stock of non-human and human capital in existence. Part of the stock of each type of capital is allocated to the production of new output, part of which is consumed, the rest of which is accumulated as nonhuman capital. The remainder of each of the two types of capital stock is allocated to the production of additional human capital.

Lucas presents a simplified version of this model, in which the production of human capital depends linearly upon only human capital, with all nonhuman capital being allocated to the production of new goods. There is therefore only one capital allocation decision to be made. Our exposition will simplify the discussion further, by abstracting from the externalities—analogous to those of the Romer model—considered in the Lucas analysis.

The basic model can be set out as follows. The agent's problem is to choose (i) his rate of consumption C; (ii) his rate of accumulation of non-human capital K, (iii) his rate of accumulation of human capital E (education); and (iv) the allocation of the fraction $u(t)$ of his human capital to the production of new output, to maximize his intertemporal utility function. The formal optimization problem is

$$\text{maximize} \quad \int_0^\infty \frac{1}{\gamma} C^\gamma e^{-\beta t} \, dt \tag{13.35a}$$

subject to the two accumulation equations

$$\dot{K} = AK^\varepsilon (uE)^{1-\varepsilon} - C, \tag{13.35b}$$

$$\dot{E} = v(1 - u)E. \tag{13.35c}$$

The following observations about this formulation should be noted. Again the utility function is of the constant elasticity form, and the production of goods is Cobb-Douglas in the two forms of capital. Both production processes are constant returns to scale in the two factors being accumulated, and that is what permits the equilibrium to be one of endogenous growth. The allocation of human capital must lie in the range $0 \le u \le 1$, so that v actually represents the maximum rate of growth of human capital.

We write the Lagrangean for this problem as

$$\frac{1}{\gamma} C^\gamma e^{-\beta t} + \lambda_1 e^{-\beta t} [AK^\varepsilon (uE)^{1-\varepsilon} - C - \dot{K}] + \lambda_2 e^{-\beta t} [v(1 - u)E - \dot{E}]. \tag{13.36}$$

The optimality conditions with respect to C, K, E, and the allocation u are as follows:

$$C^{\gamma-1} = \lambda_1 \tag{13.37a}$$

$$\varepsilon \lambda_1 AK^{\varepsilon-1}(uE)^{1-\varepsilon} = -\dot{\lambda}_1 + \lambda_1 \beta \tag{13.37b}$$

$$(1-\varepsilon)\lambda_1 AK^\varepsilon (uE)^{-\varepsilon} u + \lambda_2 v(1-u) = -\dot{\lambda}_2 + \lambda_2 \beta \tag{13.37c}$$

$$(1-\varepsilon)\lambda_1 AK^\varepsilon (uE)^{-\varepsilon} = \lambda_2 v \tag{13.37d}$$

where λ_1, λ_2 are the shadow values of nonhuman and human capital respectively.

Lucas derives a balanced-growth solution using the following procedure. First, combining equations (13.37c) and (13.37d), the shadow value of human wealth changes at the constant rate

$$\frac{\dot{\lambda_2}}{\lambda_2} = \beta - v. \tag{13.38a}$$

Next, look for a solution in which consumption C, nonhuman wealth K, and human wealth E all grow at the constant rates

$$\frac{\dot{C}}{C} = c; \qquad \frac{\dot{K}}{K} = k; \qquad \frac{\dot{E}}{E} = e, \tag{13.38b}$$

and the sectoral allocation of human capital u is constant. It then follows from (13.37a) that the shadow value of nonhuman capital declines at the rate

$$\frac{\dot{\lambda_1}}{\lambda_1} = -(1 - \gamma)c. \tag{13.38c}$$

Using (13.38c), equation (13.37b) can be written as

$$\varepsilon A \left(\frac{K}{uE}\right)^{\varepsilon-1} = (1 - \gamma)c + \beta. \tag{13.37b'}$$

Differentiating this equation with respect to time, with the right-hand side constant, we see that the two types of capital must grow at the same rate, namely $k = e$. The ratio (K/uE) therefore remains constant over time.

Now consider the accumulation equations. First, dividing (13.35b) by K implies

$$k = A \left(\frac{K}{uE}\right)^{\varepsilon-1} - \frac{C}{K}.$$

With k and the ratio (K/uE) both being constant over time, it follows that (C/K) must remain constant over time, implying that consumption must grow at the same rate as the two capital goods; that is, $c = k = e$. Dividing (13.37b) by E yields the following expression for the common growth rate:

$$c = k = e = v(1 - u). \tag{13.39}$$

Finally, differentiating (13.37d) we find that the shadow values of the two types of capital must change at the same rate:

$$\frac{\dot{\lambda}_2}{\lambda_2} = \frac{\dot{\lambda}_1}{\lambda_1}. \tag{13.40}$$

Combining (13.38a), (13.38c), (13.39), and (13.40) implies the following solution for the equilibrium allocation of human capital $\hat{u}$ and the corresponding equilibrium growth rates $\hat{c} = \hat{k} = \hat{e}$:

$$\hat{u} = \frac{\beta - \gamma v}{v(1 - \gamma)}, \tag{13.41a}$$

$$\hat{c} = \hat{k} = \hat{e} = \frac{v - \beta}{1 - \gamma}. \tag{13.41b}$$

Note too that in order for the equilibrium allocation of human capital to be viable, that is, in order for $0 < \hat{u} < 1$, we require that

$$v > \beta > \gamma v,$$

implying that the equilibrium is one with a strictly positive growth rate.

This balanced-growth solution abstracts from the transitional dynamics. In general, a complete characterization of the dynamics is difficult. But the fact that such a balanced growth path is not reached immediately can be seen as follows.

Define $K_1 \equiv K/uE$ to be the ratio of nonhuman to human capital in the goods market. Differentiate (13.37d) with respect to t:

$$\frac{\dot{\lambda}_1}{\lambda_1} + \varepsilon \frac{\dot{K}_1}{K_1} = \frac{\dot{\lambda}_2}{\lambda_2} = \beta - v. \tag{13.42}$$

Next, combine this with (13.37b), rewritten as

$$\frac{\dot{\lambda}_1}{\lambda_1} = \beta - \varepsilon A K_1^{\varepsilon - 1}, \tag{13.43}$$

and substitute into (13.42). This leads to the following differential equation in the nonhuman to human capital ratio in the goods market:

$$\dot{K}_1 = -\left(\frac{v}{\varepsilon}\right) K_1 + A K_1^{\varepsilon}. \tag{13.44}$$

This is a standard Bernoulli equation, the solution to which, starting out from $K_1 = K_{1,0}$, is

$$K_1(t)^{1-\varepsilon} = \left(K_{1,0}^{1-\varepsilon} - A\frac{\varepsilon}{v} \right) e^{-v[(1-\varepsilon)/\varepsilon]t} + A\frac{\varepsilon}{v}. \tag{13.45}$$

This converges to $\hat{K}_1^{1-\varepsilon} = A(\varepsilon/v)$, which is the stationary solution to the above balanced-growth solution, obtained by combining (13.37b') with (13.41b).

Rebelo (1991) discusses the balanced-growth solution for the more general technology where both capital goods are used in the production of both goods and human capital. He also discusses tax policy in that context, as do Lucas (1990) and Pecorino (1993). A recent paper by Mulligan and Sala-i-Martin (1993) gives a detailed characterization of the transitional paths; the interested reader who wishes to pursue this topic further should consult these papers.

13.7   Conclusions

This chapter has presented a selective exposition of endogenous growth models. In discussing these models, our focus has been primarily on their use as a vehicle for developing an integrated fiscal policy. Two main aspects have been emphasized: (i) the role of a consumption tax in enhancing economic growth and welfare; and (ii) the relationship between government expenditure and growth. We shall conclude by focusing on the implications of our analysis for these two sets of issues.

In general, our analysis suggests a potentially important role for a consumption tax as part of an overall optimal fiscal package. As long as government expenditure exercises impacts a direct impact on the decisions of private agents—whether on their consumption decisions or their production decisions—the government will almost certainly need to choose *two* fiscal instruments to bring about the first best optimum. One instrument is required to correct the distortion, which, except in polar cases, is generated by the government intervention. The other is to ensure that the government expenditure is financed. In addition to an income tax, in our analysis this can be accomplished either by an appropriate choice of debt, by a consumption tax, or by some combination of the two. In the absence of any consumption tax, however, the equilibrium involves the government being a net lender, rather than a net debtor, to the public.

Ruling out this situation assigns an important role to a consumption tax as part of an optimal fiscal policy. We have considered the trade-offs between the optimal income and consumption taxes and have shown how these depend upon technology and taste parameters, as well as upon the form of the government expenditure and how it is perceived by private agents in the economy. In general, the optimal tax structure will be one where expenditure is partially financed by the two taxes, although in certain polar cases it will be optimal to finance expenditure entirely by either one tax or the other.

Two further aspects of our results should be emphasized. First, our specific results concerning the optimal taxation of capital depend upon the fact that the government expenditure rule is assumed to tie the growing level of government expenditure to current output. Although this is a very natural specification of government expenditure policy in an environment of ongoing growth, it is not the only one. The optimal configuration of taxes will be substantially different if, instead, the government links its expenditure to, say, the level of private consumption, maintaining a fixed ratio of G/C, a policy that is equally capable of sustaining a steady growth path. Second, we should acknowledge that although we have chosen to focus on the consumption tax, the distortion between the private and social returns to capital that are generated by public expenditure can be corrected by other forms of taxation. One obvious example of this is a credit to investment.[15] Like the consumption tax, such a credit changes the relative price of consumption and investment.

The question of the relationship between government expenditure and growth has been the subject of a substantial amount of empirical literature. Overall, our analysis is consistent with the existing evidence. Although Kormendi and Meguire (1985) found no significant relationship between the growth of GDP and government consumption expenditure, other authors, such as Landau (1983), Barth and Bradley (1987), Grier and Tullock (1989), and Barro (1991), found negative relationships. The theoretical relationship between government consumption expenditure and growth, reported in (13.24a) is perfectly consistent with these empirical results. Although we argue that the relationship is likely to be a negative one, the theoretical analysis is also perfectly consistent with no relationship, as will be the case if either $\rho = 0$, or $\delta = 0$. There is less evidence on the effects of government productive investment on growth. Barro (1991) obtains a generally positive although small relationship. Our analysis is also consistent with this evidence, especially if the level of productive government expenditure is near the optimum.

Notes

1. For an excellent comprehensive exposition of traditional growth theory, see Burmeister and Dobell (1970).

2. These figures are obtained from the 1993 U.S. *Economic Report of the President*; see tables B-2, B-24 of that work.

3. The corresponding figures for Japan are typically reported as a personal savings rate of around 16 percent and a real growth rate of around 5 percent.

4. See the section (pp. 268–272) discussing the U.S. Treasury proposal for a consumption tax.

5. Strictly speaking, the logarithmic utility function emerges as

$$\lim_{\gamma \to 0} \{[(CG^\beta)^\gamma - 1]/\gamma\}.$$

This function differs from (15.7a) by the subtraction of the term -1 in the numerator, and the two forms of utility function have identical implications.

6. This type of result is also obtained by Chamley (1992), who identifies certain simple revenue neutral tax reforms that, though they improve the growth rate, also lower welfare.

7. Note that with r determined from (13.17), the time path for the price of bonds, p, is determined by solving the differential equation $r = (1 + \dot{p})/p$. In the present case where r is constant, the stable solution is simply $r = 1/p$.

8. Notice that (13.20a) expresses equilibrium consumption in terms of the consumption-capital ratio. Much of the literature expresses consumption in terms of its ratio to wealth. The consumption-wealth ratio is simply $\bar{\mu}\bar{n}$ and is immediately obtained as the product of (13.20a) and (13.20c).

9. Saint-Paul (1992) obtains a similar kind of result using the well-known Blanchard (1985) continuous-time overlapping generations model.

10. As a technical point, g must be strictly bounded away from zero, for otherwise the utility function would collapse to zero everywhere.

11. The case of productive government expenditure is discussed in detail by Barro (1990).

12. Proposition 1, pertaining to the negative equilibrium stock of debt in the absence of a consumption tax, continues to hold.

13. This condition characterizing the first best optimal degree of productive government expenditure is not new; see Barro (1990). Hartman (1992) derives an analogous condition in a stochastic context.

14. In deriving the macroeconomic equilibrium, the perceived ratio H^p/K, which appears in the optimality condition of the representative agent, is replaced by the actual ratio H/K.

15. The use of an investment subsidy to correct for the discrepancy between the private and social returns to capital is discussed by Saint-Paul (1992).

IV Continuous-Time Stochastic Models

14 Continuous-Time Stochastic Optimization

14.1 Introduction

All of the models based on intertemporal optimization and developed in Part III assume complete certainty so that agents are endowed with perfect foresight. The two chapters of Part IV extend the model to introduce uncertainty. The present chapter outlines the techniques and applies them to a closed economy, and Chapter 15 analyzes the behavior of an open economy under stochastic conditions. We choose to formulate and solve the problem using continuous-time intertemporal optimizing methods, rather than the more familiar discrete-time approach. Our main reason for this choice is that although such problems are tractable only under restrictive conditions, when these conditions are met the solutions they yield are highly transparent and provide substantial insight into the characteristics of the equilibrium.

The present chapter is rather far-reaching and is structured in the following way. Section 14.2 introduces the necessary results from continuous-time stochastic calculus. The key observation here is that under reasonable assumptions, variances are of the first order of magnitude in time and therefore interact with the first moments (the means) in the dynamic evolution of the system. Section 14.3 then sets out a stochastic version of the basic representative agent model initially discussed in Chapter 9. This is developed under general conditions and emphasizes, as we did before, the role of the intertemporal government budget constraint as part of the equilibrium. One important issue that arises concerns the question of the robustness of Ricardian Equivalence under risk. This question has received some attention in the literature; see, for example, Chan (1983), Barsky, Mankiw, and Zeldes (1986), Kimball and Mankiw (1989), and Barro (1989). Essentially, our analysis will show that although Ricardian Equivalence holds with respect to the deterministic component of lump-sum tax changes, it will not hold with respect to individual-specific risk.

The general model typically cannot be solved to yield closed-form solutions. Accordingly, the next two sections focus on specific examples for which tractable solutions can be obtained. In Section 14.4, two examples in which all stochastic disturbances are additive are considered. The first is based on the quadratic utility function; the second assumes that the utility function exhibits constant absolute risk aversion.

The most important and most widely applied model using these continuous-time methods is developed in Section 14.5. This is the stochastic analogue to the linear endogenous growth model developed in Chapter 13. The additional assumption necessary to sustain such an equilibrium is that all stochastic disturbances are proportional to the current state of the economy, as represented by the capital stock or wealth. This is not an unreasonable assumption; in fact, the idea of the magnitude of stochastic shocks being linked to the size of the economy is much more plausible than the alternative where they are taken to be purely additive. Assuming a constant relative risk-averse utility function, this leads to an equilibrium having ongoing stochastic growth in which means and variances of relevant endogenous variables are jointly and consistently determined. Such an equilibrium, which we term a *mean-variance equilibrium,* is analogous to that familiar from finance theory, the elements of which may thereby be incorporated into a complete macroeconomic framework in a more satisfactory way.

It is also useful to think of what is being done here from the perspective of the rational expectations methodology, which we discussed in Part II. There the objective was the development of an internally consistent, stochastic system to examine the economy, under the assumption that the underlying relationships depend only upon the *means* (first moments) of the relevant variables and not on any higher moments. That approach might therefore be termed as providing a *certainty equivalent* macroeconomic framework. By contrast, the objective here is to develop a model that is internally consistent in both the means *and* the variances, thereby enabling us to address important trade-offs that, in general, exist between the *level* of macroeconomic performance and the associated *risk.* We view this as an important step forward in the construction of a comprehensive macroeconomic model.

One characteristic of the equilibrium we shall derive in Section 14.5 is that portfolio shares remain constant over time. Given the stationarity of the structure of the model and that it yields a recurring ongoing equilibrium, this is not an unreasonable property for it to have. But although the derivation of such a consistent equilibrium is tractable, it involves a certain amount of detail. Again, the analogy here with the rational expectations methodology is useful. The general strategy we adopt for determining the macroeconomic equilibrium is to posit specific forms for the stochastic processes facing the agents in the economy and then to determine restrictions on these processes that make them consistent with optimizing behavior and market clearance. This procedure will be recognized as an application of the method of undetermined coefficients, which was introduced in Chapter 3 as one of the standard procedures for solving linear rational expectations equilibria.

Once the closed-form equilibrium in Section 14.5 is derived, it is then used to address analogous issues, now in an environment entailing risk, to those discussed in Chapter 13 under certainty. Thus we analyze the determinants of growth and how they respond to changes in tax rates, levied on both the deterministic and stochastic components of income, as well as to changes in the mean and associated variance of government expenditure. Equilibrium asset pricing relationships, familiar from finance theory, can now be introduced, and we are able to explain the risk premia in terms of the exogenous sources of risk impacting on the economy. Welfare and optimal tax issues are addressed, and again, parallel results to those obtained in Chapter 13 under certainty are derived.

The last three sections are more general, serving in part to place the earlier discussion in a broader context. Section 14.6 indicates some direct extensions to the model of Section 14.5, and Section 14.7 seeks to place the present discussion in the context of the literature. Finally, Section 14.8 relates the discussion to some of the influential work being done, using a not dissimilar framework, in the real business cycle literature.

14.2 Some Basic Results from Continuous-Time Stochastic Calculus

Recognizing that the methods of continuous-time stochastic calculus are not widely known to economists, this section presents a brief summary of the main results to be used in Chapters 14 and 15. More detailed but still nontechnical treatments accessible to economists are provided by Chow (1979), Malliaris and Brock (1982), and more recently Dixit and Pindyck (1994). For our purposes, Chow provides a compact review of the relevant techniques, and to some extent we shall draw upon his exposition.

Linear Stochastic Differential Equations

The starting point is a system of linear stochastic difference equations, expressed over the period t to $t + h$:

$$y(t + h) - y(t) = [A(t)y(t) + B(t)]h + v(t + h) - v(t) \qquad (14.1)$$

where h is arbitrary and not necessarily an integer. We assume that the stochastic residual term $v(t + h) - v(t)$ has the following properties: (i) it is a Markov process, meaning that its probability distribution is independent of anything prior to time t; (ii) it has mean zero and is independently distributed over time. We shall consider the continuous limit of this system as the time interval h approaches zero. In the absence of the residual, one could derive this limit by dividing through by h, letting $h \to 0$, and obtain the usual system of deterministic ordinary differential equations. However, this process is complicated by the presence of the stochastic term, which must be considered further.

In the case of a unit time interval $h = 1$, we have the usual system of first-order linear stochastic difference equations and let us assume that the covariance matrix of the residuals is Σ. Suppose we divide the unit period $(t, t + 1)$ into n segments of length $h = 1/n$ units each. By the assumption that each successive increment $v(t + h) - v(t)$ is statistically independent and identically distributed, the covariance matrix Σ of their sum equals n times the covariance matrix of each increment, implying

$$\mathrm{cov}[v(t + h) - v(t)] = h\Sigma = (1/n)\Sigma \tag{14.2}$$

Thus the variance-covariance matrix increases linearly with h. If one assumes further that the successive increments are normally distributed, the process is called a *Wiener process* or *Brownian motion*. This is the assumption upon which almost all of continuous-time stochastic calculus is based, and it is the assumption that we shall invoke. As will become apparent in the course of this chapter, a great advantage of this formulation is that variances are introduced into the dynamics in a most natural way.

The key observation about (14.2) is that the covariance matrix of the increment $v(t + h) - v(t)$ is proportional to the time interval h, implying that the standard deviation of each component of the vector $v(t + h) - v(t)$ is proportional to $\sqrt{h}$. This is an important property because it means that terms involving squares of elements of $v(t + h) - v(t)$ are of order h and not h^2. In other words, the variances are of the first order and do not vanish as the time interval $h \to 0$. This is what makes the methods of continuous-time stochastic calculus so attractive: the means and variances are interdependent. As $h \to 0$, we denote h by dt, rewriting (14.1) as

$$dy = [A(t)y + B(t)]\, dt + dv \tag{14.3}$$

where $E(dv) = 0$ and $\mathrm{cov}(dv) = \Sigma(t)\, dt$. Thus (14.3) is a system of linear stochastic differential equations. The covariance matrix Σ may or may not be a function of t. That depends upon how the stochastic disturbances impact on the system. Since dv is of order $\sqrt{dt}$, the derivative dv/dt does not exist, and we must write the stochastic differential equation as in (14.3). It is a fundamental property of the Wiener process that while it is continuous everywhere, it is differential nowhere. On the other hand, because $E(dv) = 0, E(dy)/dt = A(t)y + B(t)$ and is well defined.

In the case that $A(t)$ is constant, by a formal argument one can show that the solution to (14.3), starting from y_0 at time t_0 is

$$y(t) = e^{A(t-t_0)}y_0 + \int_{t_0}^{t} e^{A(t-s)}[B(s)\, ds + dv(s)]; \tag{14.4}$$

such an integral is called a *stochastic integral* (see, e.g., Arnold 1974). Economists are often interested in forward-looking solutions. With independent increments, and provided appropriate convergence conditions are met, the forward-looking solution to (14.3) is just

$$y(t) = e^{A(t-t_0)}E_t \int_t^\infty e^{-A(s-t)}B(s)\,ds.$$ (14.5)

Itô's Lemma

The fact that the variances are of order dt means that we have to be careful in taking differentials of stochastic functions. We essentially have to take second-order expansions of the relevant Taylor series, in order to be sure that we have retained all the appropriate first-order terms. This is the central aspect to Itô's rule for stochastic differentiation.

Suppose dy is generated by the nonlinear system of stochastic differential equations

$$dy = f(y,t)\,dt + dv$$

$$\quad = f(y,t)\,dt + S(y,t)\,dz$$ (14.6)

where f and the variance-covariance of $dv \equiv \Sigma(y,t)\,dt$ may be functions of y. If z is a Wiener process with the variance-covariance matrix of the increment dz being $R\,dt$, we can write $dv = S(y,t)\,dz$, where $SRS' = \Sigma$, and here the prime denotes the vector transpose.

In the course of solving continuous-time stochastic optimization problems we are required to study functions of stochastic processes. Let $G(y,t)$ be a function that is twice differentiable in y and continuously differentiable in t. We seek to derive its stochastic differential. To do so, expand:

$$dG = G(y(t+dt), t+dt) - G(y(t),t)$$

$$\quad = \frac{\partial G}{\partial t}dt + \left(\frac{\partial G}{\partial y}\right)' dy + \frac{1}{2}(dy)' \frac{\partial^2 G}{\partial y\,\partial y'}dy + o(dt),$$ (14.7)

where $o(dt)$ denotes terms of order smaller than dt. Denoting the matrix of second partial derivatives of G with respect to y by G_{yy}, and substituting (14.6) for $dy, (dy)'$ while noting that dv is of order $\sqrt{dt}$, we show that to $o(dt)$

$$(dy)'G_{yy}\,dy = (dv)'G_{yy}\,dv + o(dt) = tr(G_{yy}\,dv(dv)') + o(dt)$$ (14.8)

where tr denotes the trace of the matrix. Substituting (14.6) and (14.8) into (14.7) leads to

$$dG = \left[\frac{\partial G}{\partial t} + \left(\frac{\partial G}{\partial y}\right)'f\right]dt + \frac{1}{2}tr(G_{yy}\,dv(dv)') + \left(\frac{\partial G}{\partial y}\right)'dv + o(dt).$$

Since $E[dv(dv)'] = \Sigma \, dt$, we can write the stochastic differential dG as

$$dG = \left[\frac{\partial G}{\partial t} + \left(\frac{\partial G}{\partial y} \right)' f + \frac{1}{2} tr(G_{yy}\Sigma) \right] dt + \left(\frac{\partial G}{\partial y} \right)' dv. \tag{14.9}$$

The coefficient of dt is thus $E(dG)$, and $var(dG) = (\partial G/\partial y)'\Sigma(\partial G/\partial y)\, dt$. In our applications we will be dealing with scalar systems, in which (14.9) becomes

$$dG = \left[\frac{\partial G}{\partial t} + \frac{\partial G}{\partial y}f + \frac{1}{2}G_{yy}\sigma_v^2 \right] dt + \frac{\partial G}{\partial y}dv \tag{14.9'}$$

where in the scalar case $E(dv)^2 = \sigma_v^2 \, dt$.

Differential Generator

An important operator that emerges as part of the optimization of a stochastic system is the differential generator of a function $G(y, t)$. This measures the expected rate of change over time dt of the function $G(y, t)$, resulting from the evolution of the underlying stochastic process $y(t)$. Formally, it is defined as

$$L_y[G(y, t)] \equiv \lim_{dt \to 0} E_t \left[\frac{dG}{dt} \right]. \tag{14.10}$$

From (14.9) this is given by the expression

$$L_y[G(y, t)] \equiv \frac{\partial G}{\partial t} + \left(\frac{\partial G}{\partial y} \right)' f + \frac{1}{2}tr(G_{yy}\Sigma). \tag{14.11}$$

Stochastic Control and the Stochastic Bellman Equation

The stochastic optimal control problems we shall consider are of the following generic form:

maximize: $$V(y(0), 0) = E_0 \int_0^\infty U(y(s), x(s), s)\, ds, \tag{14.12a}$$

subject to

$$dy(t) = Q[y(t), x(t)] + T[y(t), x(t)]\, dv, \tag{14.12b}$$

where $y(t)$ is a vector of state variables and $x(t)$ is a vector of control variables. Define

$$V(y(t), t) = \max_{x(s)} E_t \int_t^\infty U(y(s), x(s), s)\, ds \tag{14.13}$$

to be the optimized value of (14.12a) starting from time t. Splitting up the integral appearing in (14.13), we have

$$V(y(t), t) = \max_{x(s)} E_t \int_t^\infty U(y(s), x(s), s) \, ds$$

$$= \max_{x(s)} E_t \int_t^{t+\Delta t} U(y, x, s) \, ds + \max_{x(s)} E_{t+\Delta t} \int_{t+\Delta t}^\infty U(y, x, s) \, ds$$

$$= \max_{x(s)} E_t \left\{ \int_t^{t+\Delta t} U(y, x, s) \, ds + V[y(t + \Delta t), t + \Delta t] \right\}$$

$$= \max_{x(s)} \left\{ U(y(t), x(t), t)\Delta t + E_t[V(y(t + h), t + h)] \right\},$$

implying that

$$V(y(t), t) = \max_{x(s)} \left\{ U(y(t), x(t), t)\Delta t + V(y(t), t) + E_t \, dV \right\}, \tag{14.14}$$

where $E_t \, dV$ is as defined in (14.9). Subtracting $V(y(t), t)$ from both sides of (14.14), dividing by Δt, denoted in the limit by dt, and recognizing the definition of the differential generator given in (14.10), the optimality condition (14.14) can be written as

$$0 = \max_{x(s)} \left\{ U(y(t), x(t), t) + L_y[V(y(t), t)] \right\}. \tag{14.15}$$

This is the stochastic Bellman equation, which the optimum has to satisfy. In deriving this condition, the control variables $x(t)$ are taken to be optimally chosen in accordance with their corresponding first-order optimality conditions. As we will see in the applications to be developed below, this equation introduces a partial differential equation, which the value function is required to satisfy.

In all of our examples, the utility function will assume a constant rate of time discount and will therefore be of the form $Ue^{-\beta t}$. In this case, it is possible to rewrite the Bellman equation (14.15) in a more intuitive and familiar form. For a time-separable utility function, the corresponding value function will also be of an analogous form, $V(y)e^{-\beta t}$, say. Now recall the definition of the differential generator function given in (14.10) and (14.11). In particular, observe that the expectation defined in $L_y[V(y(t), t)]$ also takes into account the effect on the value due to the expected change in t, as measured by the term $\partial V/\partial t$. For the constant discount function, this is just $-\beta V(y)e^{-\beta t}$. Subtracting this term out from $L_y[V(y(t), t)]$, moving it to the left-hand side of (14.15), and dividing by $e^{-\beta t}$, the Bellman equation can be written in the equivalent form

$$\beta V(t) = \max_{x} \left\{ U(y(t), x(t)) + E_t' \left[\frac{dV}{dt} \right] \right\} \tag{14.15'}$$

where the expectation operator E_t' takes account of the fact that we have netted out the term $-\beta V(y)e^{-\beta t}$.

This form of the Bellman function is written in familiar asset pricing terms. The left-hand side describes the required return on holding an asset, where the agent discounts at his rate of time preference. The right-hand side consists of the payout (in terms of utility) from holding the asset, plus its expected rate of capital gain or loss over the next instant of time, with the maximization ensuring that current decisions are made optimally. This equation is just a stochastic version of the standard arbitrage conditions encountered throughout Part III.

14.3   A Basic Stochastic Intertemporal Model

The Framework

We shall now apply these methods to a stochastic version of the representative agent model discussed in Chapter 9. We consider a real economy in which the household and production sectors are consolidated.[1] The representative agent consumes output over the period $(t, t + dt)$ at the nonstochastic rate $C(t) dt$. His objective is to maximize the expected value of lifetime utility as measured by the concave utility function

$$E_0 \int_0^\infty U(C)e^{-\beta t} dt \quad U'(C) > 0; \qquad U''(C) < 0, \tag{14.16a}$$

subject to the stochastic accumulation equation

$$dB + dK = dY + iB\, dt - C\, dt - dT, \tag{14.16b}$$

where

$B(t)$ = stock of real government bonds held at time t,

$K(t)$ = stock of capital at time t,

dY = flow of output over the instant $(t, t + dt)$,

dT = rate of taxes paid over the instant $(t, t + dt)$,

i = real rate of interest on bonds at time t.

The initial stocks of bonds and capital are given by B_o and K_o respectively. For the present, we assume that government bonds are fixed-price bonds paying a nonstochastic interest rate $i(t)$ over the time interval $(t, t + dt)$. Later in this chapter, when we wish to permit the economy to attain instantaneously a steady growth having constant portfolio shares, we will amend the bonds to be perpetuities, allowing their price to make the adjustment necessary to ensure that the economy is always on its steady-state growth path.

Output is assumed to be generated from capital by the stochastic process

$$dY(t) = F(K)\,dt + H(K)\,dy; \qquad F'(K) > 0, \qquad F''(K) < 0. \qquad (14.17a)$$

This equation has the following economic interpretation. It asserts that the accumulated flow of output over the period $(t, t + dt)$, given by the left-hand side of this equation, consists of two components. First, there is the deterministic component, described by the first term on the right-hand side, with $F(K)$ now representing the *mean rate* of output per unit of time. In addition, there is a stochastic component, reflecting the various random influences that impact on production. The stochastic term dy shall be referred to generically as a productivity shock and assumed to be a temporally independent, normally distributed, stochastic process having zero mean and variance $\sigma_y^2\, dt$. The specification in (14.17a) allows for the possibility that the overall size of the stochastic disturbance in output may vary with the size of the existing capital stock, and hence with the size of current output.

The two most common assumptions are that $H(K)$ is constant, in which case the stochastic disturbance is independent of the stock of capital and in which case the shocks are purely *additive*; or that $H(K) = hK$, say, in which case the disturbance is proportional to the capital stock (or output) and in which case it is often described as being *multiplicative*. The assumptions one makes with respect to the form of the stochastic disturbance term are crucial for obtaining tractable closed-form solutions to the optimization problem.

Taxes follow the stochastic process

$$dT(t) = T(t)\,dt + dv \qquad (14.17b)$$

where $T(t)\,dt$ is the known mean level of taxes to be paid over the instant of time $(t, t + dt)$, and dv is a stochastic component, assumed to be temporally independent, and normally distributed with zero mean and variance $\sigma_v^2\, dt$. Equation (14.17b) thus specifies taxes to be lump sum but stochastic, with the mean assumed to be a known function of time.

The assumption that the individual perceives the tax shock dv as being intertemporally independent at each instant of time is not as innocuous as may appear. As will be seen later (see equation [14.31]), the intertemporal government budget constraint imposes an overall intertemporal constraint on the aggregate tax shocks in the economy. If the individual agent is aware of this, and if, in addition, his share of the aggregate tax shock is constant over time, then from the government budget constraint he can infer the corresponding intertemporal constraint on his individual tax shocks (see Chan 1983; Aschauer 1988). The procedure being adopted here of ignoring such an intertemporal constraint at the individual level can be justified if one makes the plausible assumption that the individual agent is uncertain about his individual share of the aggregate tax burden. In that case he will be unable to distinguish between (i) a stochastic rise in the aggregate tax rate, which will be offset at some later date in accordance with the intertemporal government budget constant; and (ii) a stochastic shift in his personal share of the tax burden.[2]

We shall denote the total stock of bonds plus capital held by the representative agent by

$$W \equiv B + K, \tag{14.18a}$$

with the corresponding portfolio shares being

$$n \equiv \frac{K}{W} \quad 1 - n \equiv \frac{B}{W}. \tag{14.18b}$$

Thus substituting (14.17a), (14.17b), (14.18a), and (14.18b) into (14.16b), the agent's optimization problem can be stated as being to choose C and n to

$$\text{maximize} \quad E_0 \int_0^\infty U(C) e^{-\beta t} \, dt \tag{14.19a}$$

subject to

$$dW = [F(nW) + i(1 - n)W - C - T(t)] \, dt + H(nW) \, dy - dv \tag{14.19b}$$

and $n(0) = n_0$; $W(0) = W_0$.

To solve the problem, we introduce the value function

$$V(W, t) = X(W, t) e^{-\beta t}.$$

To facilitate notation, we denote the stochastic components of the rate of wealth accumulation by

$$dw \equiv H(K) \, dy - dv = H(nW) \, dy - dv,$$

so that

$$\sigma_w^2 = H^2 \sigma_y^2 - 2H \sigma_{yv} + \sigma_v^2. \tag{14.20}$$

To solve the problem, we use the methods outlined in Section 14.2. Specifically, consider

$$U(C)e^{-\beta t} + L_y[V(W, t)]$$

$$\equiv U(C)e^{-\beta t} - \beta X(W, t)e^{-\beta t} + \frac{\partial X}{\partial t}e^{-\beta t}$$

$$+ [F(nW) + i(1 - n)W - C - T]X_W(W, t)e^{-\beta t}$$

$$+ \frac{1}{2}\sigma_w^2(nW)X_{WW}(W, t)e^{-\beta t}. \tag{14.21}$$

To maximize (14.19a), we set the derivatives of (14.21) with respect to C and n to zero, yielding

$$U'(C) = X_W, \tag{14.22a}$$

$$[F'(nW) - i]X_W + H'[H\sigma_y^2 - \sigma_{yv}]X_{WW} = 0, \tag{14.22b}$$

and, in addition, the stochastic Bellman equation must be satisfied:

$$\max_{C,n} \left\{ U(C) - \beta X(W) + \frac{\partial X}{\partial t} + [F(nW) + i(1 - n)W - C - T]X_W(W) \right.$$

$$\left. + \frac{1}{2}\sigma_w^2(nW)X_{WW}(W) \right\} = 0. \tag{14.22c}$$

Equation (14.22a) is the usual first-order optimality condition, equating the marginal utility of consumption to X_W, the marginal utility of wealth. From the viewpoint of the representative agent, (14.22b) determines his optimal portfolio share in terms of the differential rate of return on bonds i, which is nonstochastic, and the risk-adjusted rate of return on physical capital.

From the definition of the value function $X(W, t)$, it is clear that the partial derivatives X_W, X_{WW} are functions of the form

$$X_W = X_W(W, t); \qquad X_{WW} = X_{WW}(W, t), \tag{14.23a}$$

which, together with the optimality condition (14.22a), imply

$$C = C(W, t). \tag{14.23b}$$

Our objective is to simplify the optimality conditions. To do so, first take the stochastic differential of (14.23a). By Itô's lemma this is given by the expression

$$dX_W = X_{WW}\,dW + X_{Wt}\,dt + \tfrac{1}{2}X_{WWW}\sigma_w^2\,dt. \tag{14.24}$$

Next, take the partial derivative of the Bellman equation (14.22c) with respect to W, to obtain[3]

$$U'C_W - \beta X_W + X_{Wt} + [F'(n + n_W W) + i(1 - n - n_W W) - C_W]X_W$$

$$+ [F + i(1 - n)W - C - T]X_{WW} + \tfrac{1}{2}\sigma_w^2 X_{WWW}$$

$$+ H'(n + n_W W)[H\sigma_y^2 - \sigma_{yv}]X_{WW} = 0.$$

Using the optimality conditions (14.22a), (14.22b), this last equation reduces to

$$(i - \beta)X_W + X_{Wt} + [F + i(1 - n)W - C - T]X_{WW} + \tfrac{1}{2}\sigma_w^2 X_{WWW} = 0.$$

Finally, substituting this equation into (14.24), and noting the accumulation equation (14.16b) and the definition of W given in (14.18a), we find that the marginal utility of wealth X_W evolves in accordance with the stochastic differential equation

$$dX_W = (\beta - i)X_W \, dt + X_{WW} \, dw. \tag{14.25}$$

Using the optimality condition (14.22a), equation (14.25) may be written as

$$\frac{dU'(C)}{U'(C)} = (\beta - i) \, dt + \frac{U''(C)C_W}{U''(C)} \, dw. \tag{14.25'}$$

This equation will be recognized as a stochastic version of the Keynes-Ramsey optimal consumption rule discussed in Chapter 9. Taking expected values of this equation leads to

$$\frac{E[dU'(C)/dt]}{U'(C)} = (\beta - i), \tag{14.25''}$$

which in turn is the continuous-time version of the Euler equation used as the basis for recent empirical estimation of the consumption function; see, for example, Hall (1978, 1989).

To complete the characterization of the macroeconomic equilibrium, we need to combine the equilibrium decisions of the representative agent with the corresponding market-clearing conditions. First, equating the optimal portfolio share implicit in (14.22b) with the actual existing portfolio share n, this equation may be expressed as

$$i = F'(K) + H'(K)\sigma_{yw}\frac{X_{WW}}{X_W} \tag{14.22b'}$$

where

$$\text{cov}(dy, dw) = \sigma_{yw} \, dt = (H\sigma_y^2 - \sigma_{yv}) \, dt.$$

At the macroeconomic level, this condition relates the equilibrium interest rate $i(t)$ to the risk-adjusted marginal physical product of capital. If the agent is risk averse ($X_{WW} < 0$) and if the rate of wealth accumulation is positively correlated with output shocks ($\sigma_{yw} > 0$), then the rate of interest will be less than the marginal physical product of capital. In effect, the agent will require a risk premium in order to be willing to hold the equilibrium stock of capital. We should note that although i is a non-stochastic function of K, over time it does change stochastically as K itself responds to the random influences impacting on the economy.

The final component of the system is the product market equilibrium condition, which may be conveniently expressed as

$$dK = dY - C\, dt - dG \tag{14.26}$$

where government expenditure is postulated to follow the stochastic process

$$dG = G(t)\, dt + M(K)\, dz. \tag{14.27}$$

The stochastic component dz is an intertemporally independent, normally distributed, random variable with zero mean and variance $\sigma_z^2\, dt$. The overall disturbance in government expenditure may vary with the level of capital stock, and hence with the rate of output. As expressed, (14.26) describes the rate of capital accumulation in the economy over the instant $(t, t + dt)$ as being the residual element out of the stochastic output produced over that instant, after the nonstochastic private consumption and stochastic government consumption claims on output have been met.

The model has introduced three stochastic elements: dy, dv, and dz. These may or may not be mutually correlated. If, for example, the government maintains a continuously balanced budget so that $dT = dG$, then (14.17b) and (14.27) imply $dv = M(K)\, dz$, and this will have to be taken into account in determining the equilibrium.

Macroeconomic Equilibrium

Combining the previous elements, the macroeconomic equilibrium can be summarized by the set of relationships

$$U'(C) = X_W \tag{14.28a}$$

$$i = F'(K) + H'(K)\sigma_{yw}\frac{X_{WW}}{X_W} \tag{14.28b}$$

$$dX_W = (\beta - i)X_W\, dt + X_{WW}\, dw \tag{14.28c}$$

$$dK = [F(K) - C - G]\, dt + H(K)\, dy - M(K)\, dz. \tag{14.28d}$$

together with the stochastic Bellman equation (14.22c). The solutions for C and i obtained from (14.28a) and (14.28b) can be substituted into (14.28c) and (14.28d), leading to a pair of stochastic differential equations in X_W and K. However, in general, (14.28c) includes the term X_{WW}, so that the solution to this pair of equations involves solving the Bellman equation, which typically is intractable. But nevertheless the following observations can be made.

i. In the absence of risk ($dy = dw = dz = 0$), the macroeconomic equilibrium described by (14.28a)–(14.28d) reduces to

$$U'(C) = X_W \tag{14.28a}$$

$$i = F'(K) \tag{14.28b'}$$

$$\frac{dX_W}{dt} = (\beta - i)X_W \tag{14.28c'}$$

$$\frac{dK}{dt} = F(K) - C - G. \tag{14.28d'}$$

This is the equilibrium of the conventional representative agent model developed in Chapter 9, with two minor differences. The first is that in the previous discussion labor was endogenous. The second is a notational difference, namely that the shadow value of wealth, previously denoted by λ, is now represented by X_W, the marginal impact of wealth on the value function. Solving (14.28a) for C in terms of the marginal utility of wealth and substituting the resulting expression into (14.28d'), and substituting (14.28b') into (14.28c'), yields a pair of ordinary equations in K and X_W that are identical to (9.9a) and (9.9b) and can be solved by the usual methods. Because of the forward-looking behavior of X_W, this pair of equation depends upon the entire (expected) future time path of government expenditure. However, it is clear from these equations that they are independent of the stock of bonds and the time path of lump-sum taxes. This of course is just a manifestation of the familiar Ricardian Equivalence property of this model.

ii. The value function $X(W, t)$ reflects the degree of risk aversion of the representative agent. In the event that the agent is risk neutral, $X_{WW} = 0$ and the macroeconomic equilibrium reduces to (14.28a), (14.28b'), (14.28c'), together with (14.28d). While this now reduces to a pair of stochastic differential equations, the equilibrium time paths for X_W, K, and C all remain independent of either the deterministic or the stochastic component of taxes. Ricardian Equivalence continues to hold.

iii. More generally, if the representative agent is not risk neutral, so that $X_{WW} \neq 0$, the time path of the equilibrium remains independent of the mean component of lump-sum taxes $T(t)$. It is also independent of specific realizations of the stochastic component dv. However, through σ_w^2, it generally depends upon the variance of the probability distribution governing dv, together with its covariance with the shocks in output. To see this, we need to consider the solution to the stochastic Bellman equation.

Fiscal Policy and Macroeconomic Equilibrium with Non-Risk-Neutral Agents

For convenience, we shall henceforth assume that the deterministic component of the production function is of the simple linear form

$$F(K) = \alpha K,$$

which, for the single factor of production being considered, is just constant returns to scale.

As we emphasized in Chapter 9, an important part of the equilibrium involves the intertemporal government budget constraint. To derive this, we begin with the instantaneous flow government budget constraint,

$$dB(t) = iB\,dt + G(t)\,dt + H(t)\,dz - T(t)\,dt - dv, \tag{14.29}$$

where for notational convenience we write $H(K(t)) \equiv H(t)$. Starting from a given initial stock of government debt B_0, the stock of accumulated government debt at time t is

$$B(t) = e^{\int_0^t i(t')dt'}\left\{ B_0 + \int_0^t e^{-\int_0^s i(t')dt'}[(G(s) - T(s))\,ds + db(s)] \right\} \tag{14.30}$$

where for notational convenience we let

$$db \equiv H\,dz - dv.$$

Intertemporal viability of the government requires

$$\lim_{t \to \infty} B(t)e^{-\int_0^t i(t')dt'} = 0,$$

which together with (14.30) implies

$$B_0 + \int_0^\infty e^{-\int_0^s i(t')dt'}[(G(s) - T(s))\,ds + db(s)] = 0. \tag{14.31}$$

This equation describes the intertemporal government budget constraint starting from an initial stock of government debt B_0. It requires that the present value of tax revenues (including both the deterministic and stochastic components) just equal the present value of government expenditures (including both the deterministic and stochastic components), together with the initial stock of outstanding debt. Equation (14.31) imposes an intertemporal constraint on aggregate tax shocks, as noted earlier. This can be seen most clearly in, say, a two-period horizon. If for some reason tax revenues were unexpectedly low in period one, they will need to be correspondingly high in period two in order to meet the budget constraint over the two periods. In the event that the representative agent's share of aggregate taxes is fixed over time, then using this constraint he can infer a corresponding constraint with respect to his own individual shock in taxes. Under this condition, it is clear that uncertainty in tax policy per se has no effect on consumption or the rest of the macroeconomic equilibrium. Only uncertainty in taxes, reflecting aggregate intertemporal uncertainty in government expenditures, would be relevant. One simple example of this would arise if the government maintained a continuously balanced budget, in which case $dv = H\,dz$.

Substituting equation (14.31) into (14.30), the latter may be written as

$$B(t) + e^{\int_0^t i(t')\,dt'} \int_t^\infty e^{-\int_0^s i(t')\,dt'}[(G(s) - T(s))\,ds + db(s)] = 0, \qquad (14.31')$$

which is analogous to (14.31), starting at the point of time t. Taking the expected value of (14.31') at time t, and noting that db is white noise, yields

$$B(t) + e^{\int_0^t i(t')\,dt'} E_t \int_t^\infty e^{-\int_0^s i(t')\,dt'}[G(s) - T(s)]\,ds = 0. \qquad (14.32)$$

This equation expresses the intertemporal consistency between expected revenues and expenditures.

As with most differential equations, the solution of the Bellman equation is by trial and error. We propose a value function of the form

$$X(W, t) \equiv X(Z) \qquad (14.33a)$$

where

$$Z(t) \equiv K(t) + B(t) - e^{\int_0^t i(t')\,dt} E_t \int_t^\infty e^{-\int_0^s i(t')\,dt} T(s)\,ds. \qquad (14.33b)$$

The motivation for this choice comes from the discussion of Ricardian Equivalence in Chapter 9 and the fact that the term defined by $Z(t)$ measures (discounted) human and nonhuman wealth (in the absence of labor income); see (9.20). Differentiating $X(W, t)$ partially with respect to t, W yields

$$\frac{\partial X}{\partial t} = X'(Z)[-i(t)(K + B - Z) + T(t)],$$

$$X_W = X'(Z) \quad X_{WW} = Z''(Z).$$

Thus the first-order condition for consumption

$$U'(C) = X_W = X'(Z)$$

can be solved in the form

$$C = C(Z).$$

Substituting these expressions for $\partial X/\partial t, X_W, X_{WW}$, and C into the Bellman equation (14.22c) leads to

$$U[C(Z)] - \beta X(Z) + [(\alpha - i)K + iZ - C(Z)]X'(Z) + \tfrac{1}{2}\sigma_w^2 X''(Z) = 0 \tag{14.34a}$$

where, now,

$$i = \alpha + H'(K)\sigma_{yw}\frac{X''(Z)}{X'(Z)}. \tag{14.34b}$$

Together equations (14.34a) and (14.34b) give a second-order differential equation in $X(Z)$, which can in principle be solved once the utility function U is specified. Having determined $X(Z)$, we can then derive consumption and the evolution of marginal utility and capital. Explicit examples will be presented in later sections.

The key observation to be made is that everything is driven by Z, as defined in (14.33b). Combining this definition of Z with (14.32), we find

$$Z(t) = K(t) - e^{\int_0^t i(t')dt'} E_t \int_t^\infty e^{-\int_0^s i(t')dt'} G(s)\, ds, \tag{14.35}$$

which is seen to be independent of the time path of the deterministic component of taxes $T(s)$ and the existing stock of bonds at time t.

The macroeconomic equilibrium thus depends upon the expected discounted present value of government expenditure and is independent of the time profile of the expected financing of this expenditure. Ricardian Equivalence therefore can be said to hold with respect to the mean. Thus the equilibrium is invariant with respect to a current tax cut of dT_0, which is to be financed by an expected tax increase of $dT(\tau) = e^{\int_0^t i(t')dt'} dT_0$ at some future time τ. From the characterization of the macroeconomic equilibrium given in (14.28), it can also be seen that it is independent of any specific exogenous realization of the tax rate dv. However, because the Bellman equation given in (14.34a) now depends upon σ_w^2, equilibrium does depend upon the variance of the tax rate σ_v^2, as well as its covariance with real shocks σ_{yv}; see (14.20).

The important point is that Ricardian Equivalence with respect to the variance breaks down because the individual is subject to an individual-specific tax risk. The same kind of phenomenon is responsible for the breakdown of Ricardian Equivalence in recent papers by Barsky, Mankiw, and Zeldes (1986) and Kimball and Mankiw (1989). In these papers the idiosyncratic tax risk is generated by uncertain future incomes on which future taxes are to be levied. In the present example, it is generated by the exogenous stochastic component of current lump-sum taxes.

Further insight can be obtained by considering special cases, to which we now turn.

14.4 Two Examples

In this section all stochastic disturbances are assumed to be additive, so that

$$H(K) = 1; \qquad M(K) = 1.$$

We continue to assume that production is specified by the linear technology $F(K) = \alpha K$, so that the equilibrium interest rate $i = \alpha$ is fixed over time.[4] Under these conditions

$$Z(t) \equiv K(t) + B(t) - e^{\alpha t}E_t \int_t^\infty e^{-\alpha s}T(s)\,ds = K - e^{\alpha t}E_t \int_t^\infty e^{-\alpha s}G(s)\,ds,$$

$$(14.36)$$

and the Bellman equation simplifies to

$$U[C(Z)] - \beta X(Z) + [\alpha Z - C(Z)]X'(Z) + \tfrac{1}{2}\sigma_w^2 X''(Z) = 0. \qquad (14.34a')$$

Quadratic Utility Function

As a first example, assume that the utility function is quadratic:

$$U(C) = C - \tfrac{1}{2}bC^2. \qquad (14.37)$$

To solve the Bellman equation, postulate a value function of the analogous form

$$X(Z) = x_0 + x_1 Z - \tfrac{1}{2}x_2 Z^2. \qquad (14.38)$$

where the coefficients x_0, x_1, x_2 are obtained by the method of undetermined coefficients. Applying (14.37) and (14.38) to the consumer optimality condition (14.28a) yields

$$C = \frac{1}{b}[(1 - x_1) + x_2 Z].$$

Next, substitute this expression for C, along with (14.37), (14.38), and its derivatives, into the Bellman equation (14.34a'). This leads to a quadratic equation in Z. In order for this to hold for all values of Z, the coefficients of Z^2, Z, and the constant in this equation must each be zero. This leads to the following values for the coefficients:

$$x_0 = \frac{1}{2b\beta}\left(\frac{\beta - \alpha}{\alpha}\right)^2 - \frac{b}{2\beta}(2\alpha - \beta)\sigma_w^2; \quad x_1 = \frac{2\alpha - \beta}{\alpha}; \quad x_2 = b(2\alpha - \beta),$$

so that

$$X(Z) = \frac{1}{2b\beta}\left(\frac{\beta - \alpha}{\alpha}\right)^2 - \frac{b}{2\beta}(2\alpha - \beta)\sigma_w^2 + \left(\frac{2\alpha - \beta}{\alpha}\right)Z - \frac{b}{2}(2\alpha - \beta)Z^2,$$

$$\tag{14.39a}$$

$$C = \frac{\beta - \alpha}{\alpha b} + (2\alpha - \beta)Z, \tag{14.39b}$$

where Z is as defined in (14.36). To remain economically plausible, the quadratic utility function requires that we assume $2\alpha > \beta$. Substituting the solution for (14.39b), together with (14.36), into the product market clearing condition (14.28d), the rate of growth of capital in the economy, dK, is generated by

$$dK = (\beta - \alpha)K - G - \frac{\beta - \alpha}{\alpha b} + (2\alpha - \beta)e^{\alpha t}E_t \int_t^\infty G(s)e^{-\alpha s}\, ds + dy - dz,$$

$$\tag{14.39c}$$

which, provided the mean rate of government expenditure G is expected to remain constant over time, reduces to

$$dK = \left(\frac{\beta - \alpha}{\alpha}\right)\left[\alpha K - G - \frac{1}{b}\right]dt + dy - dz. \tag{14.39c'}$$

The solution to this last equation is

$$K(t) = e^{(\beta - \alpha)t}\left[K_0 - \left(\frac{G}{\alpha} + \frac{1}{\alpha b}\right)(1 - e^{-(\beta - \alpha)t})\right] + \int_0^t e^{-(\beta - \alpha)s}[dy(s) - dz(s)],$$

$$\tag{14.40}$$

which satisfies the transversality condition

$$\lim_{t \to \infty} E[K(t)e^{-\alpha t}] = 0$$

as long as $2\alpha > \beta$, as is being assumed. Observe that this solution is consistent with a positive stochastic growth provided $2\alpha > \beta > \alpha$.

These solutions for C and K are independent of the timing of taxes and therefore illustrate how Ricardian Equivalence holds with respect to the deterministic component of lump-sum taxes. But in contrast to the general result noted in Section 14.3, C and K are also independent of the variance of the rate of wealth accumulation and therefore of the variance of the tax rate. Accordingly, the economy exhibits certainty-equivalent behavior. This characteristic is a consequence of two assumptions underlying the present example—the quadratic utility function and additive stochastic disturbances—and simply confirms the well-known certainty equivalence principles that have been shown to exist under these conditions by Simon (1956) and Theil (1958).

The value function also enables us to assess the effects of policy and other disturbances on welfare. Starting from the given initial point Z_o, the value function

$$X(Z_0) = \frac{1}{2b\beta}\left(\frac{\beta - \alpha}{\alpha}\right)^2 - \frac{b}{2\beta}(2\alpha - \beta)\sigma_w^2 + \left(\frac{2\alpha - \beta}{\alpha}\right)Z_0 - \frac{b}{2}(2\alpha - \beta)Z_0^2$$

$$(14.41)$$

measures the level of intertemporal welfare of the representative agent when the optimal path is followed. It is apparent from (14.41) (recalling the assumption that $2\alpha > \beta$) that an increase in the variance of wealth accumulation has an adverse effect on welfare. This is because a higher variance in σ_w^2 generates greater uncertainty with respect to future consumption, thereby lowering the welfare of a risk-averse agent.

Constant Absolute Risk Aversion

As a second example, assume that the representative agent has constant absolute risk aversion, with utility being specified by[5]

$$U(C) = -\frac{1}{\eta}e^{-\eta C}; \quad \eta > 0. \tag{14.42}$$

Postulating a value function of the form

$$X(Z) = -\frac{\omega_1}{\omega_2}e^{-\eta Z} \tag{14.43}$$

(where ω_1 and ω_2 are to be determined), the optimality condition for consumption implies

$$C = -\frac{\ln \omega_1}{\eta} + \frac{\omega_2}{\eta}Z.$$

Substituting for C, X, X', X'' into the Bellman equation (14.34a') and solving for the coefficients ω_1 and ω_2, we find that the value function is

$$X(Z) = -\frac{1}{\alpha\eta} e^{1 - \beta/\alpha + \alpha\eta^2\sigma_w^2/2 - \alpha\eta Z}. \tag{14.44a}$$

The corresponding solution for consumption is

$$C = \frac{\beta - \alpha}{\alpha\eta} - \frac{1}{2}\alpha\eta\sigma_w^2 + \alpha Z \tag{14.44b}$$

where Z remains as defined in (14.36).

Substituting for (14.44b) into (14.28d), the rate of growth satisfies

$$dK = \left[\alpha e^{\alpha t} E_t \int_t^\infty G(s) e^{-\alpha s} ds - G + \frac{\alpha - \beta}{\alpha\eta} + \frac{1}{2}\alpha\eta\sigma_w^2 \right] + dt + dy - dz, \tag{14.44c}$$

which, if G is constant over time, simplifies to

$$dK = \left[\frac{\alpha - \beta}{\alpha\eta} + \frac{1}{2}\alpha\eta\sigma_w^2 \right] dt + dy - dz. \tag{14.44c'}$$

Thus capital evolves in accordance with a simple diffusion process, the solution to which,

$$K(t) = K_0 + \left[\frac{\alpha - \beta}{\alpha\eta} + \frac{1}{2}\alpha\eta\sigma_w^2 \right] t + \int_0^t (dy - dz), \tag{14.45}$$

clearly meets the transversality condition.

Again, this example illustrates how the macroeconomic equilibrium is invariant with respect to the timing of the mean tax rate and independent of any specific tax shock dv. But in contrast to the quadratic case, and consistent with the general result discussed in Section 14.3, consumption varies inversely with the variance of wealth accumulation σ_w^2, which in turn may depend upon the variance of tax policy. Intuitively, a higher degree of risk associated with the accumulation of wealth induces more saving, less consumption, and therefore more output devoted to the accumulation of capital, leading to more growth.[6] The reduction in consumption through the term $-1/2\alpha\eta\sigma_w^2$ more than offsets the present value of the increase in consumption resulting from the higher growth rate of capital, and on balance the overall level of welfare declines. This can be seen by observing that $X(Z)$, given in (14.44a), is a decreasing function of σ_w^2.

Another difference from the quadratic case is in the impact of government expenditure on the growth rate. With a quadratic utility function, an expansion in government expenditure has an adverse effect on the growth rate. In the present example it has no effect. The positive effect on growth through the reduction in private consumption it generates is exactly offset by the direct negative effects resulting from the greater claim by the government on the economy's resources.

14.5   Proportional Disturbances and Stochastic Growth

We now consider in some detail the case where the stochastic disturbances in output are assumed to be proportional to the mean level of output:

$$dY = \alpha K(dt + dy), \tag{14.46}$$

$$dG = g\alpha K\, dt + \alpha K\, dz, \tag{14.47}$$

where in (14.47), the deterministic component of government expenditure policy is also expressed in terms of a fraction of mean output. These two equations are stochastic analogues to the specification of production and government expenditure in the endogenous growth model developed in Chapter 13, and with an appropriate utility function they will lead to a stochastic endogenous growth equilibrium. Such a model was first discussed by Eaton (1981) and is a very convenient vehicle for analyzing the impact of distortionary taxes under stochastic conditions.

As in Chapter 13, the tractability of the analysis is enhanced by assuming that the government bonds are perpetuities paying a fixed coupon of one unit of output over the period dt. The price of these bonds, expressed in terms of output, is P, so that $B = Pb$ (where b now denotes the quantity of bonds outstanding). However, the price of these bonds now becomes stochastic, reflecting the random influences in the economy.

The stochastic real rate of return on bonds, dR_B, is postulated to be of the form

$$dR_B = r_B dt + du_B \tag{14.48a}$$

where r_B and du_B will be determined endogenously in the macroeconomic equilibrium to be derived. As will become apparent, the equilibrium will determine only the *value* of the outstanding bonds, rather than their specific price. Accordingly, the nature of the process generating their price is unimportant and will reflect the characteristics of the bonds. Turning to the other asset, capital, with output determined from capital by (14.46a), and in the absence of adjustment costs to capital, the stochastic real rate of return on capital is

$$dR_K = \frac{dY}{K} = \alpha\,dt + \alpha\,dy \equiv r_K\,dt + du_K \tag{14.48b}$$

and is given by the technology.

Because the after-tax rate of return on government bonds will adjust to whatever market level is necessary for bonds to be held in equilibrium, only the tax on capital has any real impact on the equilibrium. Thus we may assume, without any loss of generality, that taxes are levied on only the income from physical capital, namely,

$$dT = \tau r_K K\,dt + \tau' K\,du_K = \tau\alpha K\,dt + \tau'\alpha K\,dy. \tag{14.49}$$

Allowing the tax rate τ on the deterministic component of income to differ from τ', the tax rate on the stochastic component reflects the possibility that the tax code might include offset provisions, having the effect of taxing the two components of income differently. We shall see below the extent to which the potential existence of these differential tax rates is significant from a welfare point of view.

Determination of Equilibrium

With proportional disturbances, it is convenient to represent the preferences of the representative agent by the constant elasticity utility function used in Chapter 13. Thus, the stochastic optimization problem of the representative consumer is expressed as being to choose the consumption-wealth ratio, C/W, and the portfolio shares, n_B, n_K, to[7]

$$\text{maximize} \quad E_0 \int_0^\infty (1/\gamma)C(t)^\gamma e^{-\beta t}\,dt \tag{14.50a}$$

subject to

$$\frac{dW}{W} = \left(n_B r_B + n_K(1-\tau)r_K - \frac{C}{W}\right)dt + dw, \tag{14.50b}$$

$$n_B + n_K = 1. \tag{14.50c}$$

It is notationally convenient to introduce the portfolio shares of capital and bonds symmetrically as n_K, n_B, respectively, and to denote the stochastic component of dW/W by

$$dw \equiv n_B\,du_B + n_K(1-\tau')\,du_K. \tag{14.50d}$$

In performing the optimization, the representative agent takes the rates of returns of the assets and the relevant variances and covariances as given, although these will all ultimately be determined in the macroeconomic equilibrium.

The details to the solution to this problem are presented in the Appendix to this chapter, where it is shown that the first-order optimality conditions can be written in the form

$$\frac{C}{W} = \frac{\beta - \rho\gamma - \frac{1}{2}\gamma(\gamma - 1)\sigma_w^2}{1 - \gamma} \tag{14.51a}$$

$$\left(r_B - \frac{\eta}{\delta\gamma W^\gamma}\right) dt = (1 - \gamma)\,\text{cov}(dw, du_B) \tag{14.51b}$$

$$\left(r_K(1 - \tau) - \frac{\eta}{\delta\gamma W^\gamma}\right) dt = (1 - \gamma)\,\text{cov}(dw, (1 - \tau')\,du_K) \tag{14.51c}$$

where η is the Lagrange multiplier associated with the normalized wealth constraint (14.50c), δ is a constant determined from the stochastic Bellman equation (see [14.66]), and

$$\rho \equiv n_B r_B + n_K(1 - \tau)r_K, \tag{14.51d}$$

$$\sigma_w^2 \equiv \frac{E(dw)^2}{dt} = n_B^2\sigma_B^2 + n_K(1 - \tau')^2\sigma_K^2 + 2n_B n_K(1 - \tau')\sigma_{BK}.$$

The form of the consumption-wealth ratio in (14.51a) is the stochastic analogue to that derived in Chapter 13 under deterministic conditions (see, e.g., [13.11a]). For the logarithmic utility function, $\gamma = 0$, and (14.51a) reduces to the familiar relationship $C/W = \beta$. If $\gamma \neq 0$, an increase in the expected net of tax return ρ will raise the consumption-wealth ratio if $\gamma < 0$ and lower it otherwise. As noted in Chapter 13, this is because an increase in expected income can be broken down into a positive income effect, $d\rho$, inducing more consumption, and a negative substitution effect, $-d\rho/(1 - \gamma)$, encouraging a switch away from consumption, with the net effect on the consumption-wealth ratio being $-\gamma\,d\rho/(1 - \gamma)$. An increase in the variance of wealth σ_w^2 can be decomposed in an analogous (but opposite) way.[8] As long as the agent is risk averse $(1 > \gamma)$, a higher variance is equivalent to a reduction in income and therefore leads to a reduction in the consumption-wealth ratio. At the same time, the higher variance raises the risk associated with savings, thereby inducing more consumption. These two effects are exactly offsetting in the case of the logarithmic function, and also for the risk-neutral agent, when they are both separately equal to zero.

Equations (14.51b) and (14.51c) are asset pricing relationships, familiar from finance theory, with the term $\eta/\delta\gamma W^\gamma$ representing the real rate of return on the asset whose return is uncorrelated with dw. In the absence of risk, (14.51b), (14.51c) imply equality of after-tax real rates of return. Otherwise, the covariance expressions on the right-hand side of these equations determine the risk premium associated with the two assets. We will return to this later when we discuss the overall equilibrium and determine the equilibrium beta coefficients, which summarize the risk. Solving (14.51b) and (14.51c), in conjunction with the normalized wealth constraint (14.50c), one can determine the agent's portfolio demands n_B, n_K, (together with the Lagrange multiplier, η).

Equations (14.47) and (14.49) describe government expenditure policy and tax policy, both of which are proportional to current output. In the absence of any lump-sum taxation, these are linked by the government budget constraint,

$$d(Pb) = (Pb)\,dR_B + dG - dT, \tag{14.52}$$

which, dividing both sides by W and combining with (14.47) and (14.49), can be written in the form

$$\frac{d(Pb)}{Pb} = \left[r_B + \alpha\frac{n_K}{n_B}(g - \tau)\right]dt + du_B + \alpha\frac{n_K}{n_B}(dz - \tau'\,dy). \tag{14.52'}$$

As before, the model is completed by assuming product market equilibrium, (14.26), which, dividing by K, can be expressed as

$$\frac{dK}{K} = \left[\alpha(1 - g) - \frac{C}{n_K W}\right]dt + \alpha(dy - dz) \equiv \psi\,dt + \alpha(dy - dz). \tag{14.53}$$

This equation will ultimately determine the equilibrium stochastic growth rate of the economy.

Macroeconomic Equilibrium

In equilibrium, the economy determines the rates of consumption and savings, the value and rates of return on all assets, the economy's investment and growth rate, and the risk characteristics of each asset. The exogenous variables include the government policy parameters: government expenditure (g); tax rates (τ, τ'); and the preference and technology parameters, γ, ρ, and α. The exogenous stochastic processes consist of government expenditure (dz) and productivity shocks (dy), which, for convenience only, are taken to be mutually uncorrelated.[9] The remaining stochastic disturbances—real rate of return on bonds, du_B, and real wealth, dw—are both endogenous and will be determined. Remaining key endogenous variables include the following: the consumption-wealth ratio, the mean growth rate in the economy, the expected real returns on the two assets (r_B, r_K), and the corresponding portfolio shares (n_B, n_K). At each moment of time, b and K are predetermined from the previous instant.

Our objective is to reduce the components of Section 14.5 to a simple set of core relationships that jointly determine the deterministic and stochastic components of the macroeconomic equilibrium. From the relationships in (14.51) it is reasonable to posit that if assets have the same stochastic characteristics through time, they will generate the same allocation of portfolio holdings, as well as the same consumption-wealth ratio. Our strategy, therefore, is to look for an equilibrium in which portfolio shares, n_i, and C/W ratio are nonstochastic functions of the underlying parameters of the model and to show that the restrictions thus implied are in fact consistent with this assumption. As in all rational expectations equilibria, this procedure need not rule out other equilibria, in which these constancy properties do not prevail. But if such an equilibrium can be found, it is certainly a legitimate one, and one that by virtue of its simplicity is of real economic significance.

Determination of Stochastic Components

The intertemporal constancy of portfolio shares implies

$$\frac{dW}{W} = \frac{dK}{K} = \frac{d(pB)}{pB} \tag{14.54}$$

so that all real assets grow at a common stochastic rate. To solve for the equilibrium, we first consider the stochastic components of the wealth accumulation equation (14.50b), the government budget constraint (14.52′), and the product market clearing condition (14.53). These equations, together with the definitions (14.48b) and (14.50c), and the proportionality relationship (14.54), imply

$$dw = n_B du_B + n_K(1 - \tau')\alpha \, dy = du_B + \alpha \frac{n_K}{n_B}(dz - \tau' \, dy) = \alpha(dy - dz), \tag{14.55}$$

only two of which are independent. The following solutions for dw and du_B are obtained:

$$dw = \alpha(dy - dz), \tag{14.56a}$$

$$du_B = \frac{\alpha}{n_B}[(n_B + n_K\tau') \, dy - dz]. \tag{14.56b}$$

These two expressions enable us to compute all the necessary variances and covariances. In particular, we note the following expressions, which appear in the consumer optimality conditions (14.51):

$$\sigma_w^2 = \alpha^2(\sigma_y^2 + \sigma_z^2) \tag{14.57a}$$

$$\text{cov}(dw, du_B) = \frac{\alpha^2}{n_B}[(n_B + n_K\tau')\sigma_y^2 + \sigma_z^2] \tag{14.57b}$$

$$\text{cov}(dw, (1 - \tau')du_K) = \alpha^2(1 - \tau')\sigma_y^2. \tag{14.57c}$$

Note that (14.57b) is not a complete solution because it involves the equilibrium portfolio shares n_i, which are yet to be determined.

Equilibrium System

We may now collect the equations of the complete model. First, combining (14.57a), (14.57b) with the consumer optimality condition (14.51b), (14.51c) implies the following expression for r_B:

$$r_B = \alpha(1 - \tau) + \frac{1 - \gamma}{n_B}\alpha^2[\tau'\sigma_y^2 + \sigma_z^2]. \tag{14.58a}$$

The second term on the right-hand side of this equation represents the differential risk premium on bonds over capital and will be considered further below. Next, equating the deterministic components of the rate of growth of government bonds from the government budget constraint (14.52′) and the rate of growth of capital from the product market equilibrium condition (14.53), (in accordance with [14.54]) leads to

$$\psi = \alpha\frac{n_K}{n_B}(g - \tau) + r_B. \tag{14.58b}$$

Equations (14.58a) and (14.58b), together with the consumption-wealth ratio (14.51a) (after substituting for ρ, σ_w^2), the deterministic component of the market-clearing condition (14.53), and the portfolio adding up condition (14.50c), form a complete system determining the equilibrium values of

i. the consumption-wealth ratio C/W;

ii. the portfolio shares n_B, n_K;

iii. the real rate of return on government bonds r_B;

iv. the equilibrium growth rate ψ.

Substituting further for the portfolio shares n_B, n_K into (14.56) we can derive the reduced-form solution for the stochastic component of the price of bonds. In addition, the definitions of n_B, n_K add two additional relationships:

$$W(0) = \frac{K_0}{K}; \qquad P(0)b_0 = \frac{n_B}{n_K}K_0, \tag{14.58c}$$

which express initial wealth $W(0)$, and market value of bonds, $P(0)b_0$ in terms of the endogenously determined portfolio shares and the predetermined stock of capital. This is an appropriate point at which to observe that the equilibrium described is indeed one in which portfolio shares and the consumption-wealth ratio are constant, thereby validating the assumption made at the outset.

The fact that the equilibrium determines only the market value of bonds implies that it is invariant with respect to the particular type of bond offered. The specific characteristics of the bond, such as the nature of its coupon and its maturity, are therefore unimportant. This is because what is relevant to consumers is the real rate of return the bond offers, and this is ultimately determined by the after-tax rate of return on the productive asset, capital, in accordance with the relationship (14.58a). Given the type and quantity of the bond, its price adjusts as required to support this equilibrium. The implications of bond pricing are discussed further by Grinols and Turnovsky (1994) in a monetary version of this model and need not be pursued further here.

Equilibrium Solutions

To obtain closed-form solutions for the key variables, it is useful to observe that (14.50b), (14.51d), and (14.53) together imply the equilibrium relationship

$$\psi = \rho - \frac{C}{W}. \tag{14.59}$$

This equation is just the equality between the real rate of growth of assets, given by the left-hand side of (14.59), and the growth of savings. Using this equation, the following solutions for the consumption-wealth ratio C/W, the real growth rate ψ, and the portfolio share of capital n_K obtain:[10]

$$\frac{C}{W} = \frac{1}{1-\gamma}\left(\beta - \gamma\alpha(1-\tau) + \frac{1}{2}\gamma(\gamma-1)\alpha^2((2\tau'-1)\sigma_y^2 + \sigma_z^2)\right) \tag{14.60a}$$

$$\psi = \alpha(1-\tau) - \frac{C}{W} + \alpha^2(1-\gamma)(\tau'\sigma_y^2 + \sigma_z^2) \tag{14.60b}$$

$$n_K = \frac{C/W}{\alpha(\tau-g) + (C/W) - \alpha^2(1-\gamma)(\tau'\sigma_y^2 + \sigma_z^2)}. \tag{14.60c}$$

Equation (14.60a) is obtained by substituting (14.51d), together with (14.58a), into (14.51a); equation (14.60b) is obtained by substituting (14.51d) and (14.58a) into (14.59); and (14.60c) combines (14.60b) with

(14.53). The portfolio share of the other asset, government bonds, is determined residually from the stock constraint (14.50c), which then determines their equilibrium rate of return from (14.58a).[11] This last characteristic implies that the equilibrium would be independent of any tax on government bonds. If a tax were imposed on interest income, all that would happen would be that the before-tax real return on government bonds would adjust so as to produce the after-tax return required to ensure that the equilibrium relationship (14.58a) was met.

The equilibrium as determined by (14.60) must also satisfy certain feasibility conditions. The first of these is the transversality condition, which for the constant elasticity utility function is

$$\lim_{t \to \infty} E[W^\gamma e^{-\beta t}] = 0. \tag{14.61}$$

Using (14.53) and (14.54), this condition can be shown to reduce to the condition $C/W > 0$, as originally shown by Merton (1969). To see this, these two equations together enable us to express the accumulation of wealth by the equation

$$dW = \psi W \, dt + W \, dw, \tag{14.54'}$$

the solution to which, starting from initial wealth $W(0)$ at time 0, is (see, e.g., Arnold 1974)

$$W(t) = W(0)e^{(\psi - (1/2)\sigma_w^2)t} + w(t) - w(0).$$

The transversality condition (14.61) will be met if and only if

$$\gamma(\psi - (1/2)\sigma_w^2) - \beta < 0.$$

Combining (14.51a) with (14.59), this condition is equivalent to $C/W > 0$, as asserted.

With the equilibrium being one of balanced real growth, in which all real assets grow at the same stochastic rate, (14.61) also implies that the intertemporal government budget constraint is met. Using (14.60a), the condition (14.61) implies the following constraint on the tax rates on capital τ, τ' and on other parameters:

$$\beta - \gamma\alpha(1 - \tau) + \tfrac{1}{2}\gamma(\gamma - 1)\alpha^2[(2\tau' - 1)\sigma_y^2 + \sigma_z^2] > 0. \tag{14.61'}$$

This condition is automatically met for the logarithmic utility function ($\gamma = 0$). In other cases, this condition may impose restrictions in order for the tax rate to remain feasible.

Second, with nonnegative stocks of capital, the equilibrium portfolio share of capital $n_K \geq 0$. Thus, in addition to (14.61), the denominator of (14.60c) must be positive. If private agents are permitted to borrow from the government, then no restriction on n_B is imposed. However, if such borrowing is ruled out, the additional restriction $n_K \leq 1$ must be met.

Determinants of Equilibrium Growth Rate

The equilibrium is one of stochastic endogenous growth, and of particular interest is to determine its response to policy and structural changes in the economy.

Growth and Taxes

An examination of the equilibrium relationships (14.60) reveals that taxes on capital income impact on the equilibrium through the linear combination

$$T \equiv \tau - \alpha(1 - \gamma)\sigma_y^2\tau',$$

from which we see that raising the tax rate τ' on the *stochastic* component of capital income has the opposite effect to raising the tax rate τ on the *deterministic* component of income. On the one hand, an increase in τ reduces the after-tax return to capital, thereby inducing a reduction in the holdings of capital, and reducing the equilibrium growth rate. By contrast, an increase in τ' reduces the variances and associated risk on the return to capital, inducing investors to hold a higher fraction of their portfolios in capital, thereby increasing the growth rate. The qualitative effect of a uniform increase in the tax on capital $d\tau = d\tau'$ thus depends upon $1 - \alpha(1 - \gamma)\sigma_y^2$. It follows that the qualitative effects of a uniform tax increase applied under certainty continue to hold under uncertainty if and only if $1 > \alpha(1 - \gamma)\sigma_y^2$. However, if this inequality is reversed, the stochastic effect prevails, and a tax increase in this circumstance will reverse those effects that would obtain under certainty.

The proposition that under uncertainty a tax on corporate capital income may increase economic performance has also been discussed by Gordon (1985). He argues that by taxing capital income, the government absorbs a certain fraction of both the expected return and its associated risk, and in his analysis these two effects are largely offsetting. Further implications of changing tax rates will be presented in Section 14.5 in connection with our discussion of optimal tax policy.

Growth and Government Expenditure

The equilibrium growth rate ψ is independent of the mean proportion of government expenditure g, just as it was for the deterministic economy discussed in Chapter 13 under the present assumption that government expenditure does not impact on private utility. Although an increase in g

reduces the growth rate directly (see [14.53]), this effect is exactly offset by the fact that it also increases the portfolio share of capital n_K, thereby increasing the consumption-capital ratio and maintaining the overall rate of growth; see also Eaton (1981).

By contrast, the growth rate increases with the *variance* of government expenditure. This is because an increase in σ_z^2 increases the relative risk on government bonds, inducing agents to switch to holding more capital, thereby increasing the growth rate.

Growth and Productivity Risk

From a consideration of (14.60) it is apparent that productivity risk impacts on the equilibrium in almost the same way as does the variance of government expenditure. We can in fact show that

$$\frac{\partial \psi}{\partial \sigma_y^2} = \alpha^2(\tau' - \gamma/2). \tag{14.62}$$

As long as $\tau' > 0$, an increase in the variance of the productivity shocks raises the risk premium on government bonds, inducing a portfolio switch toward capital, thereby increasing the growth rate directly by an amount $\alpha^2(1 - \gamma)\tau'$. At the same time, this raises both ρ and σ_w^2 in the consumption function (14.51a) by the respective amounts $\alpha^2(1 - \gamma)\tau'$ and α^2. The net effect of these increases on the consumption-wealth ratio, reflecting both the income and substitution effects, is $-\gamma\alpha^2(\tau' - 1/2)$ and depends upon the degree of risk aversion of the agent, with the overall effect on the growth rate being given by (14.62).

Equilibrium Asset Pricing

One of the attractive features of the stochastic model is that it enables us to integrate the macroeconomic equilibrium with corporate finance theory. An initial attempt to do this was undertaken in Chapter 10, but clearly a more satisfactory treatment requires risk, and the present framework is well suited to this purpose. Recall the consumer equilibrium asset pricing relationships (14.51b) and (14.51c). As noted in our discussion of the consumer equilibrium, $\eta/\delta\gamma W^\gamma$ represents the real return on the asset whose return is uncorrelated with dw. Substituting for $r_K = \alpha$ in (14.51c) and using (14.57c), we find[12]

$$\frac{\eta}{\delta\gamma W^\gamma} = \alpha(1 - \tau) - (1 - \gamma)\alpha^2(1 - \tau')\sigma_y^2 > 0.$$

If we define the market portfolio to be $Q = n_B W + n_K W$, the net expected real return on this portfolio is $r_Q = r_B n_B + r_K(1 - \tau)n_K$, which, using (14.58a), implies

$$r_Q = \alpha(1 - \tau) + (1 - \gamma)\alpha^2[\tau'\sigma_y^2 + \sigma_z^2],$$

so that

$$r_Q - \frac{\eta}{\delta\gamma W^\gamma} = (1 - \gamma)\alpha^2[\sigma_y^2 + \sigma_z^2]. \tag{14.63}$$

Thus, we may express the equilibrium pricing relationships (14.51b) and (14.51c) in the familiar capital asset pricing form

$$r_i - \frac{\eta}{\delta\gamma W^\gamma} = \beta_i\left[r_Q - \frac{\eta}{\delta\gamma W^\gamma}\right], \tag{14.64}$$

where the net excess return on asset i ($i = B, K$) is proportional to the excess return on the market portfolio, with the proportionality constant β_i—the asset's beta coefficient—being defined as

$$\beta_B = \frac{\text{cov}(dw, du_B)}{\text{var}(dw)} = \frac{(n_B + n_K\tau')\sigma_y^2 + \sigma_z^2}{n_B(\sigma_y^2 + \sigma_z^2)} > 1, \tag{14.65a}$$

$$\beta_K = \frac{\text{cov}(dw, du_K)}{\text{var}(dw)} = \frac{(1 - \tau')\sigma_y^2}{(\sigma_y^2 + \sigma_z^2)} < 1. \tag{14.65b}$$

Comparing these equations we see that in this model bonds are riskier than capital, confirming their greater risk premium as noted in (14.58a). The fact that taxing the stochastic component of capital income is stabilizing is seen directly from the beta coefficient of capital, which is a declining function of τ'. The relative riskiness of the two assets contrasts with the short bonds considered in Section 14.3, where, in general, the interest rate is less than the marginal physical product of capital; see (14.22b′). The difference is that in the present analysis the bonds are perpetutities, having a stochastic price P, which embodies the risks of the system. This is in contrast to capital, which is denominated in terms of the numeraire good, new output, and therefore is less risky when measured in these terms.

Welfare and Optimal Capital Tax

As we have discussed in previous chapters (particularly Chapters 11 and 13), an important topic that has attracted much attention is the effect of a capital tax on economic welfare, and in particular the optimal tax on capital from a welfare point of view. The discussions in the previous chapters have been carried out in the absence of risk. It is straightforward to analyze these issues in the present framework, although to do so requires the introduction of a welfare criterion. For this purpose, we consider the welfare of the representative agent, as specified by the intertemporal utility function (14.50a), evaluated along the optimal path. By definition, this equals the value function used to solve the intertemporal optimization problem.

As shown in the Appendix, for the constant elasticity utility function the optimized level of utility starting from an initial stock of wealth $W(0)$ is given by

$$X(W(0)) = \delta W(0)^\gamma \qquad \text{where} \quad \delta \equiv \frac{1}{\gamma}\left(\frac{\hat{C}}{W}\right)^{\gamma-1} \tag{14.66}$$

and $\hat{C}/W$ is the equilibrium value given in (14.60a). However, $W(0)$ is itself endogenously determined, and, using the relationship (14.58c), the welfare criterion (14.66) can be expressed in terms of the initially given capital stock, as

$$X(K_0) = \frac{1}{\gamma} n_K^{-\gamma}\left(\frac{C}{W}\right)^{\gamma-1} K_0^\gamma \tag{14.67}$$

where $C/W, n_K$ are obtained from (14.60a) and (14.60c). Assuming that these solutions are positive implies $\gamma X(K_0) > 0$, as well.

Taking the differential of (14.67) yields

$$\frac{dX}{X} = -\gamma\frac{dn_K}{n_K} + (\gamma - 1)\frac{d(C/W)}{C/W}. \tag{14.68}$$

We see that the effect of any policy change on welfare can be assessed in terms of its impact on (i) the consumption-wealth ratio, C/W; and (ii) the portfolio share of capital, n_K. The expression for $X(K_0)$ becomes more intuitive in the case of the logarithmic utility function $(\gamma \to 0)$ when (14.67) can be shown to reduce to

$$X(K_0) = \frac{1}{\beta}\ln\beta + \frac{\psi}{\beta^2} - \frac{1}{2\beta^2}\alpha^2(\sigma_y^2 + \sigma_z^2) - \frac{1}{\beta}\ln n_K + \frac{1}{\beta}\ln K_0. \tag{14.67'}$$

This expression indicates the channels whereby policy exerts its impact on welfare. First, to the extent that the policy stimulates growth, ψ, it increases future consumption possibilities and is welfare-improving. Second, to the extent that it increases the variance along the growth, σ_w^2, it is welfare-deteriorating. Third, to the extent that it leads to an instantaneous increase in the portfolio share n_K, it generates an initial drop in the price of bonds, $P(0)$, causing a welfare-deteriorating decline in wealth. Optimal welfare policy involves trading off these effects. If one were to abstract from this last effect, then the fact that a tax on the mean income reduces growth while having no effect on the variance would imply that the optimal tax $\hat{\tau} = 0$. Likewise, the fact that τ' is growth-enhancing would imply that it would be optimal to tax the stochastic component of capital income fully, that is, $\hat{t}' = 1$. However, the initial jump in $P(0)$ induced by such a policy cannot be ignored, and, in fact, once it is taken into account, the optimal tax policy is an interior one.

As we have already observed, the effects if a change in the tax on capital impact on the equilibrium through the linear combination $T \equiv \tau - \alpha(1 - \gamma)\sigma_y^2\tau'$. Differentiating the expressions in (14.60), we find

$$\frac{d(C/W)}{dT} = \frac{\alpha\gamma}{1 - \gamma}; \qquad sgn\left(\frac{d(C/W)}{dT}\right) = sgn(\gamma); \tag{14.69a}$$

$$\frac{d\psi}{dT} = -\frac{\alpha}{1 - \gamma} < 0; \tag{14.69b}$$

$$\frac{1}{n_K}\frac{dn_K}{dT} = \frac{\alpha}{(1 - \gamma)(C/W)}(\gamma - n_K); \tag{14.69c}$$

and using (14.69a) and (14.69c) in (14.68), the net effect on welfare is

$$\frac{dX}{dT} = \frac{\alpha(\gamma X)}{(1 - \gamma)(C/W)}(n_K - 1). \tag{14.69d}$$

We have already commented that an increase in T will lower the growth rate, whereas for by now familiar reasons, the effect on the consumption-wealth ratio depends upon γ, which reflects the net impact of the income and substitution effects of the higher tax rate. As a benchmark case, it is useful to focus on the logarithmic utility function, $\gamma = 0$, when C/W is independent of the tax rate. An increase in T, by lowering the return to capital, will cause agents to switch away from capital toward bonds. The net effect on welfare in this case depends upon $n_K - 1 \equiv -n_B$. On the one hand, the decrease in growth caused by the higher tax rate reduces the expected future income flow, thereby reducing welfare by the amount $-\alpha^2/\beta$. At the same time, the reduction in n_K reduces the negative wealth effect resulting from the price rise (measured by $-(1/\beta)d\ln n_K/dT = \alpha n_K/\beta^2$), and this is welfare-improving. The same argument applies when $\gamma \neq 0$.

As long as the private sector cannot borrow from the government—that is, as long as we require $n_B \geq 0$—it is clear that the optimal tax policy is to eliminate government bonds, setting $n_B = 0$. This result is identical to that obtained in Chapter 13 under certainty (see equation [13.20c″]) and is achieved by driving the equilibrium price of government bonds to zero. In that chapter it was shown that if government expenditure does not impact on the utility of the private agent—the assumption being made here—then the optimal fraction of government debt in the agent's portfolio is zero, just as we have found here. The previous result thus extends to the present stochastic context.

To determine the optimal tax itself, set $n_K = 1$ in (14.60c). This leads to the relationship

$$T \equiv \tau - \alpha(1 - \gamma)\sigma_y^2\tau' = g + \alpha(1 - \gamma)\sigma_z^2. \tag{14.70}$$

This expression is a risk-adjusted version of equation (13.26b), with the modification that the latter allowed for some interaction of government expenditure in utility. In the absence of risk, (14.70) reduces to $\tau = g$, so that the tax on capital should just equal the share of output claimed by the government. In the presence of risk, this relationship is modified.

Further understanding of this relationship is obtained by considering the government budget constraint, when the government ceases to issue additional debt. Focusing on the deterministic component of (14.52′), this leads to

$$\alpha n_K g + r_B n_B = \alpha n_K \tau. \tag{14.71}$$

This equation asserts that the tax revenues on capital must suffice to finance total government expenditures plus the interest owing on its outstanding debt. Now let $n_K \to 1, n_B \to 0$, as the optimal tax policy requires. In the absence of risk, (14.71) reduces to $\tau = g$, as in Chapter 13.

As long as the economy starts with a strictly positive stock of government bonds, the share n_B is reduced to zero, by driving the price of bonds to zero. Thus, in the present stochastic environment, as this occurs, the risk premium on these bonds implied by (14.58a) tends to infinity, so that in the presence of risk, these bonds, though negligible as a fraction of wealth in the limit, actually generate nonzero interest income:

$$\lim_{n_B \to 0} r_B n_B = (1 - \gamma)\alpha^2[\tau'\sigma_y^2 + \sigma_z^2]. \tag{14.72}$$

Substituting (14.72) into (14.71) thus yields (14.70). A further observation is that any combination of τ and τ' satisfying the linear constraint (14.70) will succeed in reaching the optimum. Thus the flexibility of being able to tax the deterministic and stochastic components of capital income at differential rates has no welfare benefits. The same can be achieved by taxing both components uniformly.

But this optimal equilibrium can hold only as a limit. If, instead, the economy sets the actual quantity of bonds to zero, thereby attaining the equilibrium $n_B = 0$ exactly, then the government's budget would need to balance at all times, that is, $dG = dT$ in (14.52). Equating the deterministic and stochastic components in this case implies $\tau = g, dz = \tau' dy$. In order for this to be sustainable, the government can no longer set its stochastic expenditures independently, but instead must adjust them in response to the stochastic component of tax receipts. Another possibility may be to introduce a state-dependent tax rate.

14.6 Some Extensions

The model we have discussed at length Section 14.5 is a convenient one for addressing risk in a stochastic growth environment. The model is a simplified one, focusing on just two assets in the portfolio. It lends itself to a number of obvious extensions, and here we focus briefly on three.

Introduction of Money

The portfolio model developed in Chapter 10, to which the last model can be viewed as a stochastic analogue, also included money. In fact, it is straightforward to add money to this model, and this has been carried out by Grinols and Turnovsky (1992). In their analysis, money yields direct utility, along with consumption, and is represented in the utility function

$$\int_0^\infty \frac{1}{\gamma} \left(C^\theta \left(\frac{M}{P} \right)^{1-\theta} \right)^\gamma e^{-\beta t} \, dt \qquad 0 \le \theta \le 1$$

where M/P represents real money balances. They introduce money through a nominal stochastic monetary growth rule:

$$\frac{dM}{M} = \phi \, dt + dx,$$

where ϕ is the mean monetary growth rate and dx is its stochastic component, having the usual properties and a variance $\sigma_x^2 \, dt$.

This modification to the model can be solved along the lines of Section 14.5 and leads to several results that are worth noting:

i. Monetary policy is found to be superneutral in both its first and second moments. That is, the real part of the equilibrium, the consumption-wealth ratio, the rate of growth, and the equilibrium share of capital, are all independent of both the mean rate of nominal monetary growth μ and its variance σ_x^2. Thus the superneutrality of money associated with the Sidrauski (1967b) model extends to this stochastic economy.[13] Also as in the Sidrauski model, monetary growth does affect welfare through the equilibrium real money balances. There is an optimal rate of monetary growth, which is to reduce the stock of bonds to its lowest feasible level, presumably $n_B = 0$, thereby maximizing the utility gained from real money balances. However, for the present constant elasticity utility function, the optimal rate of monetary growth is obtained as a corner solution rather than as an interior optimum that corresponds to the satiation level of real money balances.

ii. The optimal tax policy is no longer to drive bonds to zero, but rather is now characterized by $n_K = \theta(1 + \gamma n_M)$, where n_M is the portfolio share of money. This relationship reduces to the optimum derived in Section 14.5, when money is absent or yields no utility.

iii. There is a jointly optimal tax-monetary policy obtained by combining (i) and (ii) and characterized by

$$n_M = \frac{1 - \theta}{1 + \theta\gamma} \geq 0 \qquad n_B = 0 \qquad n_K = \frac{\theta(1 + \gamma)}{1 + \theta\gamma} \geq 0,$$

in which both money, which yields direct utility, and capital are held in strictly positive quantitites in equilibrium.

Adjustment Costs in Investment

The model we have been considering has treated investment as costless. It is possible to impose adjustment costs on investment along the lines of Chapter 11. In order to retain tractability, we must do this in a specific way so as to retain the proportionality of the equilibrium. Benavie, Grinols, and Turnovsky (1992) consider adjustment costs that are proportional to the rate of investment, just as they were in Chapter 11. This leads to an equilibrium having an equilibrium Tobin-q, which is responsive to the parameters (particularly the variances) characterizing the stochastic environment. They then use the model to analyze the question of the optimal tax on capital. The main conclusion they establish is that in the presence of adjustment costs and uncertainty, it is no longer optimal to eliminate bonds from the equilibrium, as was the case in Section 14.5.

Utility-Enhancing and Productive Government Expenditure

Our analysis in this chapter has assumed that government expenditure is "useless" and represents a pure drain on the economy. It is possible to introduce beneficial government expenditure, along the lines done in Chapter 13. If government consumption expenditure appears in the utility function of the representative agent multiplicatively with private consumption and with a constant elasticity, then the results will essentially be "risk adjusted" versions of those presented in Chapter 13. The same applies if government expenditure is productive and its impact on the marginal physical product of capital is proportional to the existing capital stock.

14.7   Some Previous Applications of Continuous-Time Stochastic Methods to Economics

We have presented in some detail various types of tractable continuous-time stochastic intertemporal optimizing models. At this point it is useful to review briefly some of the previous applications of this approach to economics. It would be fair to say that these have been sporadic. This is in part a reflection of the fact that they involve a certain amount of technical apparatus, not very familiar to economists, and in part a consequence of the fact that they are often intractable. However, it is our view that when they are tractable, continuous-time methods yield transparent solutions that significantly facilitate our understanding of the particular issue to which they are being applied.

As a historical matter, continuous-time stochastic optimization methods have been more readily adopted by finance theorists than by economists. Most economists would agree that the application of such methods, particularly to finance but also to economics, was pioneered by Robert Merton. A collection of his seminal contributions has been brought together in his book Merton (1990), which also contains an extensive bibliography. A review of many of the examples in both finance and economics is provided by Malliaris and Brock (1982). Among the earliest applications to finance, the contributions by Black and Scholes (1973) to the option pricing model and by Merton (1973) to the capital asset pricing model should be mentioned; see also Cox, Ingersoll, and Ross (1985a). Important applications to the term structure of interest rates were first presented by Vasicek (1977) and more recently by Cox, Ingersoll, and Ross (1985b). In the portfolio area, the key contributions are due to Merton (1969, 1971, 1973), and more recently to Adler and Dumas (1983) and Stulz (1981, 1983, 1984, 1987), for the international economy.

The first applications of continuous-time stochastic methods to investment theory include the contributions by Pindyck (1982) and Abel (1983), and a comprehensive treatment of investment theory using these methods is provided by Dixit and Pindyck (1994). The early applications to economic growth theory include the contributions by Bourguignon (1974), Merton (1975), and Bismut (1975). The model we have presented in Section 3 is very much in this tradition. The applications to macroeconomics are relatively sparse, although they are increasing. Tax policy was first analyzed in a stochastic endogenous growth model, such as that developed in Section 14.5, by Eaton (1981), and was further pursued by Corsetti (1991). Monetary policy was first studied by Gertler and Grinols

(1982), who were interested in studying the effects of monetary uncertainty on investment, and later by Stulz (1986), who analyzed its effects on the interest rate. More complete macroeconomic general equilibrium models, directed at analyzing integrated debt, tax, and monetary policies, have been developed more recently by Grinols and Turnovsky (1992, 1993) and by Turnovsky (1993). Recent general equilibrium applications to international economics include Grinols and Turnovsky (1994), Obstfeld (1994), among others. This last topic will be addressed in greater detail in Chapter 15.

14.8 Real Business Cycle Model

One of the powerful modern schools of macroeconomics is the so-called theory of real business cycles (RBC). In many respects, the type of model we have developed is similar to those employed in the RBC literature, which are typically based on the intertemporal optimization of risk-averse agents in a stochastic environment. Our analysis differs from the RBC approach in two respects. The first (but less important) difference is that we have chosen to use continuous time, whereas the RBC models are typically formulated in discrete time.

The second and substantial difference is in the focus. After developing our model, we have carried out what one might call a *structural* comparative static analysis of the equilibrium. That is, our concern has been with examining issues such as the effects of policy changes and structural changes, including increases in risk as measured by variances, on the equilibrium behavior of the economy, focusing on aspects such as the growth rate, consumption, welfare, and so on. By contrast, the RBC literature is concerned with studying the short-run comovements of certain key variables. In doing this it is particularly interested in seeing how well the model is able to mimic the pattern of variances and covariances characteristic of the real-world economies. This is often then used as a test of the model. This analysis typically makes intensive use of numerical methods, using numerical calibration methods to make the comparison.

As a starting point, Hansen (1985) has presented a small table summarizing stylized facts pertaining to the stochastic structure of the U.S. economy; this table has served as a benchmark for the calibration analysis of real business cycle theorists; see also Backus, Kehoe and Kydland (1992), Baxter and Crucini (1991, 1993), and Danthine and Donaldson (1993). The comparisons include the following:

$$\sigma_I = 8.60 > \sigma_Y = 1.76 > \sigma_C = 1.29 > \sigma_K = 0.63,$$

$$\rho_{IY} = 0.92 > \rho_{CY} = 0.85 > \rho_{KY} = 0.04,$$

where σ_i is the standard deviation of variable i in percentage form, where $i = I$ (investment), Y (output), C (consumption), and K (capital). The terms ρ_{ij} refer to corresponding correlations.[14] Thus, the stylized data suggest that investment is substantially more volatile than output, while consumption is less so, and the capital stock much less so still. Output is most highly correlated with investment, less so but still substantially with consumption, and only slightly with the capital stock. This pattern is generally confirmed for other countries, although the conformity is more robust for investment than for consumption, because for several economies the variability of consumption exceeds that of output; see Danthine and Donaldson (1993).

The question is the extent to which a particular model is able to replicate this pattern of stochastic characteristics. To consider this, we consider the model with multiplicative shocks discussed in Section 14.5. One characteristic of this model is that, in equilibrium, all real quantitites grow at the same stochastic rate, as determined by (14.54). Denoting the stochastic components by $\sim$, we have the following:

$$\frac{d\tilde{C}}{C} = \frac{d\tilde{W}}{W} = \frac{d\tilde{K}}{K} = \alpha(dy - dz) \tag{14.73a}$$

$$\frac{d\tilde{Y}}{E(Y)} = dy, \tag{14.73b}$$

implying the following variances and covariances:

$$\sigma_C^2 = \sigma_K^2 = \alpha^2(\sigma_y^2 + \sigma_z^2); \qquad \sigma_Y^2 = \sigma_y^2; \qquad \sigma_{CY} = \sigma_{KY} = \alpha\sigma_Y^2 \tag{14.74}$$

From the solutions for the stochastic components in (14.73), we infer that a stochastic increase in output will be accompanied by a stochastic increase in consumption and in the accumulation of capital, consistent with the data. It is also the case that a positive shock to government consumption expenditure will lead to a reduction in private consumption expenditure, a pattern that also tends to be supported by the data.

Although this model performs reasonably well in terms of the *signs* of comovements, it does poorly in matching up the relative magnitudes of the moments as summarized by the stylized data. One of the immediate and obvious consequences of having an equilibrium in which portfolio shares remain constant is that most real quantities move closely with one another, so it is almost inevitable that such a simple model will fail miserably to replicate the real-world pattern of variances and covariances, which embodies millions of independent shocks. Thus this model finds that consumption and capital stocks both move together with perfect correlation, and furthermore have equal proportionate variances. In addition, with no adjustment costs, the model would imply that investment also moves at the same proportionate rate. Moreover, taking as rough magnitudes $\sigma_y^2 \approx \sigma_z^2, \alpha = 0.1$, we find $\sigma_c = 0.141\sigma_Y$, which is far below the relative magnitudes contained in the stylized facts summarized above. When one repeats this kind of exercise for the model based on constant absolute risk aversion, these kinds of comparisons perform somewhat better, but still not particularly well.

This model does not fare well in terms of the RBC criterion of replicating the relevant moments, but we do not view this as particularly discouraging. Our objective was a different one, namely to understand policy and to yield insights into policy-making in a stochastic intertemporal environment. In this respect, we have found the simple model to be quite helpful.

The failure of simple models like the one just discussed to replicate the stochastic characteristics of real-world economies is common, and hardly unexpected. In fact, the opposite result would be surprising. One response is to introduce additional shocks into the model, thereby weakening the stochastic relationships between the variables. A difficulty with this approach is that although one adjustment to the model may succeed in doing a better job of matching up one set of correlations, in the process it may worsen the ability of the model to replicate other statistics. Also, why focus on the second moment? Why not the third, or higher moments? Still, the real business cycle model has introduced an interesting methodology that presents serious challenges for the construction of stochastic intertemporal models.

Appendix: Derivation of Consumer Optimality Conditions (14.51)

The representative consumer's stochastic optimization problem is to choose consumption and portfolio shares to

$$\max \quad E \int_0^\infty \frac{1}{\gamma} C^\gamma e^{-\beta t} \, dt \qquad -\infty < \gamma < 1, \tag{14.A.1a}$$

subject to the stochastic wealth accumulation equation

$$\frac{dW}{W} = \left(\rho - \frac{C}{W} \right) dt + dw, \tag{14.A.1b}$$

where for notational convenience

$$\rho \equiv n_B r_B + n_K (1 - \tau) r_K,$$

$$dw \equiv n_B \, du_B + n_K (1 - \tau') \, du_K,$$

$$\sigma_w^2 \equiv n_B^2 \sigma_B^2 + n_K^2 (1 - \tau')^2 \sigma_K^2 + 2 n_B n_K (1 - \tau') \sigma_{BK}.$$

We define the differential generator of the value function $V(W, t)$ by

$$L_W[V(W,t)] \equiv \frac{\partial V}{\partial t} + \left(\beta - \frac{C}{W}\right)W\frac{\partial V}{\partial W} + \frac{1}{2}\sigma_w^2 W^2 \frac{\partial^2 V}{\partial W^2}. \qquad (14.A.2)$$

Given the exponential time discounting, V can be assumed to be of the time-separable form

$$V(W,t) = e^{-\beta t}X(W).$$

The formal optimization problem is now to choose C, n_B, n_K, to maximize the Lagrangean expression

$$e^{-\beta t}\frac{1}{\gamma}C^\gamma + L_W[e^{-\beta t}X(W)] + e^{-\beta t}\eta[1 - n_B - n_K]. \qquad (14.A.3)$$

Taking partial derivatives of this expression, and canceling $e^{-\beta t}$, yields

$$C^{\gamma-1} = X_W \qquad (14.A.4a)$$

$$(r_B X_W W - \eta)\,dt + \operatorname{cov}(dw, du_B)X_{WW}W^2 = 0 \qquad (14.A.4b)$$

$$((1 - \tau)r_K X_W W - \eta)\,dt + \operatorname{cov}(dw, (1 - \tau')\,du_K)X_{WW}W^2 = 0 \qquad (14.A.4c)$$

$$n_B + n_K = 1. \qquad (14.A.4d)$$

These equations determine the optimal values for $C/W, n_B, n_K, \eta$, as functions of X_W, X_{WW}. In addition, the value function must satisfy the Bellman equation

$$\max_{C, n_B, n_K}\left\{\frac{1}{\gamma}C^\gamma e^{-\rho t} + L_W[e^{-\rho t}X(W)]\right\} = 0. \qquad (14.A.5)$$

This involves substituting for the optimized values obtained from (14.A.4) and solving the resulting differential equation for $X(W)$, namely,

$$\frac{1}{\gamma}\hat{C}^\gamma - \beta X(W) + \left(\hat{\rho} - \left(\frac{\hat{C}}{W}\right)\right)WX_W + \frac{1}{2}\hat{\sigma}_w^2 W^2 X_{WW} = 0 \qquad (14.A.6)$$

where $\hat{\ }$ denotes optimized value.

To solve the Bellman equation we postulate a solution of the form

$$X(W) = \delta W^\gamma \qquad (14.A.7)$$

where the coefficient δ is to be detemined. This equation immediately implies

$$X_W = \delta\gamma W^{\gamma-1}; \qquad X_{WW} = \delta\gamma(\gamma - 1)W^{\gamma-2}. \qquad (14.A.8)$$

Substituting for these derivatives into (14.A.4) yields

$$\frac{C}{W} = (\delta\gamma)^{1/(\gamma-1)} \tag{14.A.9a}$$

$$(r_B(\delta\gamma)W^\gamma - \eta)\,dt + (\delta\gamma)(\gamma-1)\operatorname{cov}(dw, du_B)W^\gamma = 0 \tag{14.A.9b}$$

$$((1-\tau)r_K(\delta\gamma)W^\gamma - \eta)\,dt + (\delta\gamma)(\gamma-1)\operatorname{cov}(dw, (1-\tau')\,du_K)W^\gamma = 0. \tag{14.A.9c}$$

Substituting for C into the Bellman equation leads to

$$\frac{1}{\gamma}(\delta\gamma)^{\gamma/(\gamma-1)} - \beta\delta + [\hat{\rho} - (\delta\gamma)^{1/(\gamma-1)}]\delta\gamma + \tfrac{1}{2}\hat{\sigma}_w^2(\gamma-1)\delta\gamma = 0,$$

implying

$$(\delta\gamma)^{1/(\gamma-1)} = \frac{\beta - \hat{\rho}\gamma - \tfrac{1}{2}\gamma(\gamma-1)\hat{\sigma}_w^2}{1-\gamma}.$$

Combining this with (14.A.9a) leads to

$$\frac{C}{W} = \frac{\beta - \hat{\rho}\gamma - \tfrac{1}{2}\gamma(\gamma-1)\hat{\sigma}_w^2}{1-\gamma}, \tag{14.A.10a}$$

which is the expression for C/W presented in equation (14.51a). Furthermore, dividing (14.A.9b), (14.A.9c) by $(\delta\gamma)W^\gamma$ leads to

$$\left(r_B - \frac{\eta}{\delta\gamma W^\gamma}\right)dt = (1-\gamma)\operatorname{cov}(dw, du_B), \tag{14.A.10b}$$

$$\left(r_K(1-\tau) - \frac{\eta}{\delta\gamma W^\gamma}\right)dt = (1-\gamma)\operatorname{cov}(dw, (1-\tau')\,du_K), \tag{14.A.10c}$$

which are equations (14.51b) and (14.51c) of the text.

The solution for the value function is obtained by substituting the expression for δ implied by (14.A.9a) into (14.A.6). This leads to the expression

$$\delta = \frac{1}{\gamma}\left(\frac{\hat{C}}{W}\right)^{\gamma-1}, \tag{14.A.11}$$

which is expression (14.66) of the text.

Notes

1. In the first part of Section 14.3, all quantities, and in particular stochastic disturbances, should be interpreted as pertaining to the individual. Later, when aggregate behavior is being described, they should be reinterpreted appropriately. The intended interpretation should be clear from the context.

2. The analysis also assumes away any market for the insurance of tax risk.

3. In taking this partial derivative, i is perceived as being independent of W, consistent with the assumption used to derive the optimality conditions.

4. See (14.28b). In this case, because the real interest rate is fixed over time, it is obviously independent of debt and tax policy. If shocks are proportional to capital, as in the examples of Section 14.5, then it can be shown that $i(t)$ will be independent of the deterministic component of taxes but dependent upon the variance.

5. This utility function is considered by Kimball and Mankiw (1989) in their analysis of income tax uncertainty and consumption.

6. The finding that consumption falls with uncertainty in wealth is similar to that obtained by Chan (1983) in a two-period model with nonincreasing absolute risk aversion.

7. For simplicity we assume that consumers do not assign direct utility to government expenditure. For present purposes, this assumption is inessential and can be relaxed along the lines of Chapter 13.

8. For early discussions of the effect of uncertainty on consumption for this type of utility function, see Levhari and Srinivasan (1969) and Sandmo (1970), who showed how the effects of risk could be decomposed into income and substitution effects.

9. It is straightforward to allow dy and dz to have some assigned pattern of correlations.

10. It may appear from the equilibrium that a stochastic shock in output dy has no effect on consumption. This is not so. In fact, a random shock in output will stimulate consumption through the accumulation of real wealth. By increasing the rate of return on capital it increases the proportionate change in real wealth, which, given the constancy of the consumption-wealth ratio, implies a proportionate increase in consumption; see also (14.74), where short-run covariances are discussed.

11. This equilibrium depends upon the assumption that the stochastic processes are uncorrelated and that the deficit is bond-financed. Changing these assumptions will change the equilibrium covariance structure.

12. Observe that if initially $\tau = \tau'$, then $1 > \alpha(1 - \gamma)\sigma_y^2$, implying that a uniform increase in both tax rates, $d\tau = d\tau' > 0$, always has a contractionary effect on growth.

13. The assumption that bonds are long bonds, as in the present analysis, is important for this result. Grinols and Turnovsky (1994) analyze a model in which bonds are short bonds, as in Section 14.3. In order to generate an equilibrium having constant portfolio shares, debt policy must be severely restricted; namely, the ratio of bonds to money must be held constant. Under this form of debt policy, monetary policy ceases to be superneutral. Such a moel is developed in Chapter 15 for a small open economy.

14. These comparisons are taken from Danthine and Donaldson (1993, table 1). Backus, Kehoe, and Kydland (1992) and Baxter and Crucini (1991) report slightly different benchmark statistics.

15 A Stochastic Intertemporal Model of a Small Open Economy

15.1 Introduction

This final chapter extends the stochastic growth model developed in Section 14.5 to a small open economy. The model developed here can also be viewed as a stochastic version of the model of international capital accumulation developed in Chapter 12, although the costs of adjustment associated with investment in that analysis are not introduced. As in Chapter 14, the objective is to develop a stochastic macroeconomic general equilibrium system in which both the means and the variances of the endogenous variables are simultaneously determined.

Among the variables to be determined, the endogenous process describing the exchange rate is particularly relevant, and the equilibrium will determine both its deterministic and its stochastic components. This approach builds on work of the early 1980s, in which asset demands were determined and in which exchange rate dynamics, returns on traded and domestic bonds, and stochastic movements in prices were all specified as exogenous Brownian motion processes.[1] This chapter also describes the relationship between the investor's choices in the same way, although we endogenize the stochastic processes describing the domestic price level, the exchange rate, and the real rates of return on assets. International finance has provided a fruitful area for the application of continuous-time stochastic methods, and the important contributions of Stulz (1981, 1984, 1986, 1987) and of Adler and Dumas (1983) should be mentioned in this regard. The primary focus in these papers is on the establishment of equilibrium portfolio relationships, the determination of asset demands, and the equilibrating pricing of assets. By contrast, the goal of the present chapter is to embed these considerations into a more complete macroeconomic framework and to investigate the effects of macroeconomic policy shocks (and other changes) on this stochastic equilibrium (see also Grinols and Turnovsky 1994).

This type of mean-variance optimization framework has formed the basis for much important empirical work pertaining to interest rate parity relationships and the determination of exchange rate risk premia; see, for example, Frankel (1986), Giovannini and Jorion (1987), Hodrick and Srivastava (1986), and Lewis (1988), among others. By incorporating this financial subsector into a general equilibrium macroeconomic context, the present model provides a convenient vehicle for analyzing the determinants of the foreign exchange risk premium within a general equilibrium setting and for examining its responsiveness to the exogenous risks impinging on the economy.

In contrast to the model of Chapter 14, money is introduced and plays an important role. After developing the model, we use it to address a number of issues that have been studied in the international macroeconomic literature. First, we analyze the effects of both domestic monetary and fiscal policy on the domestic economy, contrasting the effects of changes in the levels of these instruments with the effects of changes in their associated risks.

Second, we analyze the effects of changes in the foreign inflation rate, and in its associated variance, on the domestic economy. The extent to which flexible exchange rates insulate an economy against foreign price shocks was discussed at some length in the 1970s following the worldwide move toward flexible exchange rates. These analyses were based on the portfolio balance models of the time. The present stochastic model is a useful vehicle for revisiting the issue, and, as it turns out, for confirming some of the previous propositions.

Substantial attention is devoted to analyzing the determinants of the equilibrium growth rate of the economy. This is determined by a stochastic differential equation, and both its deterministic and its stochastic components are investigated. The short-run covariation between the stochastic shocks to growth and other key macroeconomic variables are discussed, along the lines of the real business cycle literature. The effects of increased risk, arising from policy as well as from exogenous sources, on both the mean growth rate and its variance are also considered. As a final application, we use the model to analyze the relationship between export instability and the rate of growth, a relationship that has undergone substantial empirical investigation. The model is able to shed some light on the wide range of empirical results that have been obtained.

It is important to emphasize that the implications of this type of mean-variance equilibrium model, in which risks are endogenously determined, can sometimes overturn those derived from more conventional models where the endogeneity of some aspects of the structure is ignored. To give one result, simple ad hoc stochastic models, in which the structural parameters are assumed to be independent of the stochastic structure, typically predict that an increase in the variance of the foreign price shocks will increase the variance of the nominal exchange rate. In the present model, the reverse may turn out to be true. An increase in the variance of foreign price shocks may bring about a sufficient readjustment of the equilibrium portfolio so as to mitigate the effects of foreign price shocks on the exchange rate, thereby reducing the variance of the latter. In effect, the structural changes induced by the change—the key element of the Lucas Critique—are the dominant influence.

15.2   The Analytical Framework

The model we consider is that of a small open economy, in that the economy is a price taker in all its international trading activities. In contrast to the previous chapter, the economy is a monetary one. We begin by describing the stochastic environment, financial assets, and choices of consumers and the government.

Prices and Asset Returns

The domestic representative agent chooses at each instant of time the consumption of a single traded good and the allocation of his wealth between four assets. The assets include domestic money, M, and domestic government bonds, B, both of which are denominated in terms of domestic currency and are assumed to be internationally nontraded; tradable foreign bonds, B^*, which are denominated in terms of foreign currency; and equity claims on capital, denominated in terms of domestic output and also assumed to be internationally traded. The reason for assuming that domestic bonds are nontraded is the following. If, instead, they were internationally traded, then because the domestic economy is small, the risk parity conditions between the foreign and domestic bonds would become exogenously determined by risk conditions and preferences in the rest of world. Rather than impose such a condition arbitrarily or attempt to model the economy of the rest of the world, we assume that domestic bonds are nontraded, thereby determining the risk parity condition between the two assets endogenously in the market of the small open economy.

There are three prices in the model: P, the domestic price of the traded good; Q, the foreign price level of the traded good; and E, the nominal exchange rate, measured in terms of domestic currency per unit of foreign currency. With this convention an increase in E corresponds to a depreciation of the domestic currency. Q is assumed to be exogenous; P and E are to be endogenously determined. These prices evolve in accordance with the Brownian motion processes

$$\frac{dP}{P} = \pi \, dt + dp \tag{15.1a}$$

$$\frac{dQ}{Q} = \eta \, dt + dq \tag{15.1b}$$

$$\frac{dE}{E} = \varepsilon \, dt + de \tag{15.1c}$$

where π, η, ε are the respective expected instantaneous rates of change. The terms dp, dq, and de are temporally independent, normally distributed random variables with zero means and instantaneous variances $\sigma_p^2 \, dt, \sigma_q^2 \, dt, \sigma_e^2 \, dt$. Assuming free trade and a single traded good, the price level in the domestic economy must be related to that in the rest of the world by the purchasing power parity (PPP) relationship

$$P = QE. \tag{15.2}$$

Taking the stochastic derivative of this relationship implies

$$\frac{dP}{P} = \frac{dQ}{Q} + \frac{dE}{E} + \frac{dQ}{Q}\frac{dE}{E}. \tag{15.3}$$

Substituting for (15.1a)–(15.1c) into this relationship and retaining terms to order dt implies

$$\pi = \eta + \varepsilon + \sigma_{qe} \tag{15.4a}$$

$$dp = dq + de \tag{15.4b}$$

where $\sigma_{qe} \, dt$ is the instantaneous covariance between dq and de.

Equation (15.4a) portrays an important difference from the conventional specification of inflation in a small open economy under conditions of PPP. Under these conditions it is standard to assert that the domestic inflation rate is the sum of the world inflation rate plus the rate of exchange depreciation of the domestic currency; see Chapter 12. In a stochastic world, such as that being studied here, account also must be taken of the covariance between the world inflation rate and the domestic exchange rate. As we will see in due course, the latter term tends to be negative, in which case the conventional PPP relationship would overstate the rate of domestic inflation. Equation (15.4b) describes the stochastic component of the PPP relationship. A positive random shock in the foreign price level or a stochastic depreciation of the domestic currency leads to a proportionate stochastic increase in the domestic price level.

Domestic and foreign bonds are assumed to be short bonds, paying nonstochastic nominal interest rates i and i^*, respectively, over the period dt. Using the Itô calculus, we find the real rates of return to domestic residents on their holdings of money, the domestic bond, and the foreign bond to be, respectively,

$$dR_M = r_M \, dt - dp; \qquad r_M \equiv -\pi + \sigma_p^2, \tag{15.5a}$$

$$dR_B = r_B \, dt - dp; \qquad r_B \equiv i - \pi + \sigma_p^2, \tag{15.5b}$$

$$dR_F = r_F \, dt - dq; \qquad r_F \equiv i^* - \eta + \sigma_q^2. \tag{15.5c}$$

Again, it will be observed that these rates of return differ from the corresponding standard deterministic quantities by two terms: first the stochastic component, and second the variances. Consider the rate of return on money. In general, this is defined by the quantity

$$dR_M \equiv \frac{d(1/P)}{(1/P)}.$$

Taking the second-order differential of the right-hand side of this expression yields

$$dR_M \cong -\left(\frac{dP}{P}\right) + \left(\frac{dP}{P}\right)^2.$$

Under deterministic conditions, the second term is negligible, so that this expression is simply $-dP/P$, which, per unit of time, is simply $-\pi$. Under stochastic conditions, however, $(dP/P)^2 = \sigma_p^2\, dt$, in which case we obtain

$$dR_M \equiv [-\pi + \sigma_p^2]\, dt - dp,$$

which is (15.5a). The important point to observe is that because of the convexity of $1/P$ in P, the variance of the stochastic component of P contributes positively to the expected rate of return. The same procedures can be used to derive the returns on the bonds; the only point to note is the plausible assumption that the nominal interest rate over the period $(t, t + dt)$ is nonstochastic.

The production technology remains similar to that of Chapter 14. The flow of domestic output dY is produced from capital K by means of the stochastic constant returns technology

$$dY = \alpha K(dt + dy), \tag{15.6}$$

where α is the (constant) marginal physical product of capital and dy is a temporally independent, normally distributed stochastic process with mean zero and variance $\sigma_y^2\, dt$. The equity investment available to the agent is thus the real investment opportunity represented by this technology. Hence, in the absence of adjustment costs to investment, the real rate of return on capital (equity) is

$$dR_K = \frac{dY}{K} = r_K\, dt + dk \equiv \alpha\, dt + \alpha\, dy. \tag{15.5d}$$

Consumer Optimization

The representative consumer's asset holdings are subject to the wealth constraint

$$W \equiv \frac{M}{P} + \frac{B}{P} + \frac{EB^*}{P} + K \tag{15.7}$$

where W denotes real wealth. In addition, he is assumed to consume output over the period $(t, t + dt)$ at the nonstochastic rate $C(t)\,dt$ generated by these asset holdings.

The objective of the representative agent is to select his rate of consumption and his portfolio of assets to maximize the expected value of lifetime utility,

$$E_o \int_0^\infty \frac{1}{\gamma}\left(C(t)^\theta\left(\frac{M(t)}{P(t)}\right)^{1-\theta}\right)^\gamma e^{-\beta t}\,dt \qquad 0 \le \theta \le 1; \; -\infty \le \gamma \le 1, \tag{15.8a}$$

subject to the wealth constraint (15.7) and the stochastic wealth accumulation equation, expressed in real terms as

$$dW = W[n_M\,dR_M + n_B\,dR_B + n_K\,dR_K + n_F\,dR_F] - C(t)\,dt - dT \tag{15.8b}$$

where

$$n_M \equiv \frac{M/P}{W} = \text{share of protfolio held in money,}$$

$$n_B \equiv \frac{B/P}{W} = \text{share of portfolio held in domestic government bonds,}$$

$$n_K \equiv \frac{K}{W} = \text{share of portfolio held in terms of capital,}$$

$$n_F \equiv \frac{EB^*/P}{W} = \frac{B^*/Q}{W} = \text{share of portfolio held in foreign bonds,}$$

$$dT \qquad = \text{taxes paid to the domestic government.}$$

The consumer's objective function reflects utility from the holding of real money balances, as well as from current consumption. As in Section 14.5, the specification of the constant elasticity utility function is convenient, with the choice of θ measuring the relative importance of money. The comments we made in Section 9.8 with regard to introducing money into the utility function apply here as well and should be kept in mind in interpreting the present analysis. We should also note that government expenditure yields no utility, although this too can be introduced along the lines of Chapter 13.

In the present analysis, taxes will be endogenously determined to satisfy the government budget constraint, specified in equation (15.12), and will therefore include a stochastic component reflecting the changing need for taxes. Because in a growing economy taxes and other real variables grow with the size of the economy, measured here by real wealth, we relate total taxes to wealth according to

$$dT = \tau W \, dt + W \, dv \tag{15.9}$$

where dv is a temporally independent, normally distributed random variable with zero mean and variance $\sigma_v^2 \, dt$. As we will see below, the parameters τ, dv must be set to ensure that the government's budget constraint is met. It will also become evident presently that, in a steadily growing economy, the tax rate on the deterministic component of total wealth τ is nondistortionary; it operates essentially as a lump-sum tax. This is not true, however, of the stochastic component, which will have real effects through the portfolio decision.

Substituting for n_i into (15.7), for n_M into (15.8a), for (15.5a)–(15.5d) and (15.9) into (15.8b), the stochastic optimization problem can be expressed as being to choose the consumption-wealth ratio C/W, and the portfolio shares n_i to maximize (15.8a) subject to

$$\frac{dW}{W} = \left[n_M r_M + n_B r_B + n_K r_K + n_F r_F - \frac{C}{W} - \tau \right] dt + dw, \tag{15.10a}$$

$$n_M + n_B + n_K + n_F = 1, \tag{15.10b}$$

where for convenience, we denote the stochastic component of dW/W by

$$dw \equiv -(n_M + n_B) \, dp + n_K \alpha \, dy + n_F \, dq - dv. \tag{15.10c}$$

In performing this optimization, the representative agent takes the real rates of return, the tax rate τ, and the relevant first and second moments of all stochastic processes (including those involving dv) as given. However, these will all ultimately be determined in the stochastic equilibrium to be derived.

The details of the optimization parallel those of the previous chapter, particularly Section 14.5, and can be solved by following an identical procedure to that presented in the Appendix to Chapter 14. The resulting optimality conditions can be expressed as

Consumption: $$\frac{C}{W} = \frac{\theta}{1 - \gamma\theta} \left(\beta - \rho\gamma - \frac{1}{2}\gamma(\gamma - 1)\sigma_w^2 \right) \tag{15.11a}$$

Money balances: $$n_M = \left(\frac{1 - \theta}{\theta} \right) \frac{(C/W)}{i} \tag{15.11b}$$

Equities and bonds: $(r_K - r_B) \, dt = (1 - \gamma) \operatorname{cov}(dw, \alpha \, dy + dp)$ (15.11c)

$(r_F - r_B) \, dt = (1 - \gamma) \operatorname{cov}(dw, -dq + dp)$ (15.11d)

where

$$\rho \equiv n_M r_M + n_B r_B + n_K r_K + n_F r_F,$$

$$\sigma_w^2 = \lim_{dt \to o} E \frac{(dw)^2}{dt} = (n_M + n_B)^2 \sigma_p^2 + n_K^2 \alpha^2 \sigma_y^2 + n_F^2 \sigma_q^2 + \sigma_v^2$$

$$- 2(n_M + n_B) n_K \alpha \sigma_{py} - 2(n_M + n_B) n_F \sigma_{pq} + 2(n_M + n_B) \sigma_{pv}$$

$$+ 2 n_K n_F \alpha \sigma_{yq} - 2 n_K \alpha \sigma_{yv} - 2 n_F \sigma_{qv}.$$

The form of consumption-wealth ratio is analogous to that derived in Chapter 14, so that the comments we made previously continue to apply. The only change is in the parameter θ, which represents the relative importance of consumption in utility. Equation (15.11b) determines the demand for real money balances. Because domestic bonds and money belong to the same risk class, (15.11b) is in effect the equality between the real rate of return on domestic money and the real rate of return on bonds, the former including its utility return, measured by $((1 - \theta)/\theta)((C/W)/n_M)$. To see this, we may observe that the optimality condition determining the demand for money, analogous to (15.11c), (15.11d), is

$$\left(r_M + \left(\frac{1 - \theta}{\theta} \right) \left(\frac{C/W}{n_M} \right) - r_B \right) dt = (1 - \gamma) \operatorname{cov}(dw, dp - dp) = 0. \quad (15.11b')$$

Noting from (15.5a), (15.5b) that $r_B - r_M = i$, this equation immediately implies (15.11b). The implied demand for money obtained from this latter equation can be written as

$$\frac{M}{P} = \left(\frac{1 - \theta}{\theta} \right) \frac{C}{i},$$

which can be seen to be an interest-elastic cash-in-advance constraint.

Equations (15.11c) and (15.11d) describe the differential real rates of return on the assets, in terms of their respective risk differentials, as measured by the covariance with the overall market return. These relationships are analogous to (14.51b), (14.51c) (or more exactly their difference). Observe that if the investor is risk neutral (i.e., $\gamma \to 1$), all expected real rates of return would have to be equal. Solving equations (15.11b)–(15.11d), in conjunction with the normalized wealth constraint (15.10b), one can determine the agent's portfolio demands n_M, n_B, n_K, n_F.

Government Policy

Government policy is characterized by the choice of government expenditures, the printing of money and bonds, and the collection of taxes, all of which must be specified subject to the government budget constraint. This is expressed in real terms as

$$d\left(\frac{M}{P}\right) + d\left(\frac{B}{P}\right) = dG + \left(\frac{M}{P}\right) dR_M + \left(\frac{B}{P}\right) dR_B - dT \qquad (15.12)$$

where dG denotes the stochastic rate of real government expenditure. Like the analogous equation for the representative agent (15.8b), this can be derived from the basic nominal budget constraint, as in Merton (1971).

Government expenditure policy is specified by the process

$$dG = g\alpha K \, dt + \alpha K \, dz \qquad (15.13a)$$

where dz is an intertemporally independent, normally distributed random variable with zero mean and variance $\sigma_z^2 \, dt$. As in Section 14.5, government expenditure is specified to be a stochastic share of output. Although, on average, government spending is a fraction g of the economy's mean output, the stochastic term reflects the possibility that policymakers may not be able to set government expenditures with certainty. For example, program needs may not be foreknown exactly, because real resources required to meet a policy objective are known only imperfectly.

Having introduced money, we must introduce monetary policy, which we specify by the stochastic growth rule

$$\frac{dM}{M} = \phi \, dt + dx \qquad (15.13b)$$

where ϕ is the mean monetary growth rate and dx is an independently distributed random variable with zero mean and variance $\sigma_x^2 \, dt$. This equation reflects how monetary policy is chosen and encompasses a potentially rich set of policies. To be concrete, we shall assume that the monetary authority sets the growth rate, ϕ, directly. The stochastic component dx may reflect exogenous failures to meet this target. Alternatively, it may reflect stochastic adjustments in the money supply as the authorities respond to stochastic movements in intermediate targets, such as the exchange rate or the interest rate.

Debt policy is formulated in terms of maintaining a chosen ratio of domestic government (nontraded) bonds to money,

$$\frac{B}{M} = \lambda, \qquad (15.13c)$$

where λ is a policy parameter set by the government. This specification can be thought of as being a stochastic version of a balanced growth equilibrium assumption that has a well-established tradition in the monetary growth literature; see, for example, Foley and Sidrauski (1971). In the present international context, the choice of λ also reflects sterilization policy.

There are several aspects, both practical and empirical, motivating the specification of debt policy by (15.13c). As we commented in Section 14.6, if we assume as we did in Chapter 14 (i) that debt is determined residually so as to finance the government budget constraint, and (ii) that government bonds are long bonds (perpetuities), then monetary policy turns out to be superneutral. If we want to assign a more central role to monetary policy, one or both of these assumptions must be modified. Suppose we were to continue to adopt what might seem the most natural assumption, namely that government bonds are determined residually by the need to finance the government budget. We would then find that the ratio of money to short government bonds would evolve stochastically over time as bonds were issued as necessary to meet the stochastic borrowing requirements of the government. This would mean that it would be impossible to have an equilibrium in which portfolio shares remain constant over time, as we assumed previously. On the contrary, they would have to change stochastically through time, and this leads to a substantial complication in the derivation of the portfolio equilibrium. In effect, it becomes impossible to represent the stochastic dynamics in terms of only one state variable, wealth, as we have been doing. Instead, we would need to include a second state variable, such as the stochastic ratio of bonds to money. This converts the optimization into a two-state variable problem, which in general becomes much more difficult, and frequently intractable to solve.

Although the assumption that deficits are bond-financed is the prevalent one in the analytical modeling of macroeconomic equilibria, it is not clear that it is necessarily the appropriate description of actual debt policy. In fact, historically, there have been substantial swings in U.S. debt policy, and the specification (15.13c) provides a reasonable characterization of debt policy over substantial periods of time. For example, over the period 1967–1985, the ratio of publicly held debt to M3 in the United States averaged 0.24 with a standard deviation of only 0.055, while the ratio of maturities less than one year to M3 averaged 0.11 with a standard deviation of only 0.018. In this case, the constancy of bonds to money in the long run is also dictated by the fact that assuming differential growth rates for B and M would imply that the asset with the smaller growth rate would ultimately become vanishingly small in the portfolio of the representative investor. In any event, when the ratio of bonds to money is held fixed, it is more appropriate to refer to the common growth rate of money and bonds (ϕ) and its stochastic component (dx) as being a more general characterization of *government finance* policy, rather than a pure monetary policy. It is also the reason why the superneutrality of money no longer obtains in this case.

Given the policy specification (15.13a)–(15.13c), both the mean and the stochastic components of taxes, dT, must be set to meet the government budget constraint (15.12). The treatment of taxes as the residual budget item is a consequence of the restrictions imposed on the specification of debt policy.

Product Market Equilibrium and Balance of Payments

Net exports of the physical commodity are determined as being the excess of domestic production over domestic uses, $dY - dC - dK - dG$. Balance of payments equilibrium in turn requires the transfer of new foreign bonds (in excess of interest on earlier issues) to finance the net exports of the domestic country. This is expressed in real terms by the relationship

$$d\left(\frac{B^*}{Q}\right) = [dY - dC - dK - dG] + \left(\frac{B^*}{Q}\right)dR_F \tag{15.14}$$

and is the stochastic analogue to equations (12.8) and (12.18). Rearranging (15.14) and using equations (15.5c), (15.6), and (15.13a) leads to the following equation describing the real rate of accumulation of traded assets in the economy:

$$d\left(\frac{B^*}{Q}\right) + dK = \left[\alpha K(1 - g) - C + \left(\frac{B^*}{Q}\right)(i^* - \eta + \sigma_q^2)\right]dt$$

$$+ \alpha K(dy - dz) - \left(\frac{B^*}{Q}\right)dq. \tag{15.15}$$

15.3 Macroeconomic Equilibrium

The elements described in the previous section can now be combined to yield the overall equilibrium of the small open economy. Our solution procedures will parallel those of Section 14.5, although with stochastic prices and additional assets the equilibrium is more complicated to derive. The exogenous factors include (i) the specification of monetary policy ϕ, (ii) the mean rate of government expenditure g, (iii) debt policy λ, (iv) the mean foreign inflation rate η, and (v) the preference and technology parameters γ, β, α. There are three exogenous stochastic processes impinging on the economy. These include government expenditure shocks dz, productivity shocks dy, and foreign inflation shocks dq. These are assumed to be mutually uncorrelated. Other shocks could be included, but this set is characteristic of the more important exogenous stochastic influences on a small open economy. The stochastic rate of return on equities is defined in (15.5d), while the stochastic component of taxes dv and real wealth dw are determined endogenously. At least two of the three purely monetary shocks, dx, dp, and de, are endogenous, depending upon the specification of government financial policy. We shall assume that the monetary growth rate is targeted independently, in which case dx is exogenous, and dp and de reflect the endogenous stochastic adjustments in the exchange rate and price level. However, if instead government finance policy were to target the exchange rate, say, then dx would also adjust endogenously in response to the stochastic movements in the latter. From the solutions for the stochastic components, the endogenous variances and covariances can be determined and the overall mean-variance macroeconomic equilibrium obtained.

The Price Level

The optimality conditions imply that if assets have the same stochastic characteristics through time (i.e., the means and variance-covariance matrix of asset returns are stationary), they will lead to the same allocation of portfolio holdings. Such a recurring equilibrium will be characterized by constant portfolio shares through time. We shall therefore look for an equilibrium in which portfolio shares have this property, and verify that the equilibrium is consistent with this assumption.

Assuming constant portfolio shares implies that $(M/P)/(K + B^*/Q) = n_M/(n_K + n_F)$ is constant over time. The price level can then be written as

$$P = \left(\frac{n_K + n_F}{n_M}\right)\left(\frac{M}{B^*/Q + K}\right). \tag{15.16}$$

Taking the stochastic differential of (15.16) (noting that portfolio shares are constant through time) leads to

$$\frac{dP}{P} \equiv \pi\, dt + dp$$

$$= \frac{dM}{M} - \frac{d[(B^*/Q) + K]}{(B^*/Q) + K} - \left(\frac{dM}{M}\right)\left(\frac{d[(B^*/Q) + K]}{(B^*/Q) + K}\right)$$

$$+ \left(\frac{d[(B^*/Q) + K]}{(B^*/Q) + K}\right)^2. \tag{15.17}$$

Using (15.13b) and (15.15), and noting that the variances are of order dt, the right-hand side of this equation can be expressed as

$$\left\{ \phi - \left(\omega \left[\alpha(1-g) - \frac{1}{n_K}\frac{C}{W} \right] + (1-\omega)[i^* - \eta + \sigma_q^2] \right) + \alpha^2\omega^2(\sigma_y^2 + \sigma_z^2) \right.$$

$$\left. + (1-\omega)^2\sigma_q^2 - \alpha\omega(\sigma_{xy} - \sigma_{xz}) + (1-\omega)\sigma_{xq} \right\} dt$$

$$+ dx - \alpha\omega(dy - dz) + (1-\omega)dq$$

where for notational convenience we define $\omega \equiv n_K/(n_K + n_F)$ to be the share of capital in the traded portion of the consumer's portfolio. Equating the deterministic and stochastic components of (15.17) implies

$$\pi = \phi - \left(\omega \left[\alpha(1-g) - \frac{1}{n_K}\frac{C}{W} \right] + (1-\omega)[i^* - \eta + \sigma_q^2] \right)$$

$$+ \alpha^2\omega^2(\sigma_y^2 + \sigma_z^2) + (1-\omega)^2\sigma_q^2 - \alpha\omega(\sigma_{xy} - \sigma_{xz})$$

$$+ (1-\omega)\sigma_{xq} \tag{15.18a}$$

$$dp = dx - \alpha\omega(dy - dz) + (1-\omega)dq. \tag{15.18b}$$

Equation (15.18a) specifies the expected rate of domestic inflation that is consistent with maintaining unchanging portfolio balance. It varies positively with the expected rate of monetary growth and inversely with the expected rate of growth of traded assets. In addition, it increases with the variance of the growth of traded assets (through the last term on the right-hand side of [15.17]) and decreases with the covariance of the monetary growth rate and the growth of traded assets. The second equation determines the endogenous stochastic component of the domestic inflation rate in terms of the stochastic components of financial asset growth, the fiscal and productivity shocks, and the foreign inflation rate. The share of domestic capital in the traded portion of the portfolio ω is an important determinant of how these shocks affect domestic inflation. For example, the influence of foreign price disturbances increases with the share of foreign bonds in the portfolio of traded assets.

Determination of Tax Adjustments

To determine the tax adjustments, recall the government budget constraint (15.12). Dividing both sides by W, we may rewrite this equation as

$$n_M \frac{d(M/P)}{M/P} + n_B \frac{d(B/P)}{B/P} = \frac{dG - dT}{W} + n_M dR_M + n_B dR_B. \tag{15.12'}$$

Substituting for government expenditure policy, (15.13a), monetary policy, (15.13b), debt policy, (15.13c), tax collection, (15.9), and the price
evolution, (15.1a), into (15.12′), while noting the stochastic derivatives of
$d(M/P), d(B/P)$, this equation becomes

$$(n_M + n_B)(\phi - \pi - \sigma_{xp} + \sigma_p^2)\,dt + (n_M + n_B)(dx - dp)$$

$$= [\alpha n_K g - \tau + n_M(-\pi + \sigma_p^2) + n_B(i - \pi + \sigma_p^2)]\,dt - (n_M + n_B)\,dp. \tag{15.12″}$$

Equating the deterministic and stochastic parts of this equation leads to
the two relationships

$$\tau = \alpha n_K g - (n_M + n_B)\phi + n_B i + (n_M + n_B)\sigma_{xp}, \tag{15.19a}$$

$$dv = \alpha n_K\,dz - (n_M + n_B)\,dx. \tag{15.19b}$$

These equations determine the endogenous adjustments in the mean and
stochastic components of taxes necessary to finance the government budget. Observe that whereas τ need be set only once to maintain equilibrium, dv must adjust continuously to offset the stochastic shocks in monetary and fiscal policy as they occur. Equation (15.19a) asserts that an
increase in government expenditure will ceteris paribus require a higher
mean tax rate, as will higher interest payments. However, a higher monetary growth rate will generate higher inflation tax revenues, permitting
a reduction in the mean rate of tax. A positive covariance between the
monetary growth rate and the price level reduces the growth rates of the
real stocks of money and bonds and thus requires a higher tax rate to
finance the government's expenditures. Equation (15.19b) has an analogous interpretation with respect to the stochastic components.

Summary of Stochastic Adjustments

The stochastic adjustments in the economy include (i) the PPP relationship, (15.4b); (ii) the definition of the stochastic component of wealth,
(15.10c); (iii) the stochastic adjustment in the domestic price level, (15.18b);
and (iv) the stochastic adjustment in taxes, (15.19b). Combining (ii) and
(iv) leads to the following expression for the stochastic adjustment in real
wealth dw:

$$dw = \alpha\omega(dy - dz) - (1 - \omega)\,dq, \tag{15.20a}$$

and the remaining stochastic expressions can be summarized as

$$dp = dx - \alpha\omega(dy - dz) + (1 - \omega)\,dq \tag{15.20b}$$

$$de = dx - \alpha\omega(dy - dz) - \omega\,dq \tag{15.20c}$$

$$dv = \alpha n_K\,dz - (n_M + n_B)\,dx. \tag{15.20d}$$

These four independent equations determine the stochastic adjustments in the four quantities dw, dp, de, and dv. Observe that these are functions of the portfolio shares, which have yet to be determined.

Core Equilibrium Relationships

Using equations (15.20a)–(15.20d), together with (15.5d), one can calculate the endogenous variances and covariances that appear in the optimality conditions (15.11a), (15.11c), and (15.11d), and elsewhere. The calculations are straightforward, and here record we the key expressions only:

$$\sigma_w^2 = \alpha^2 \omega^2 (\sigma_y^2 + \sigma_z^2) + (1 - \omega)^2 \sigma_q^2 \tag{15.21a}$$

$$\text{cov}(dw, \alpha \, dy + dp)$$

$$= [\alpha^2 \omega (1 - \omega)\sigma_y^2 - \alpha^2 \omega^2 \sigma_z^2 - (1 - \omega)^2 \sigma_q^2] \, dt \tag{15.21b}$$

$$\text{cov}(dw, -dq + dp) = [-\alpha^2 \omega^2 (\sigma_y^2 + \sigma_z^2) + \omega(1 - \omega)\sigma_q^2] \, dt. \tag{15.21c}$$

The variance of the domestic real wealth is essentially a weighted average of the domestic and foreign sources of variances, the weights being the squares of the relative portfolio shares of the two traded assets.

Substituting (15.21b) into (15.11c), the latter may be written as

$$r_K - r_B = (1 - \gamma)[\alpha^2 \omega (1 - \omega)\sigma_y^2 - \alpha^2 \omega^2 \sigma_z^2 - (1 - \omega)^2 \sigma_q^2]. \tag{15.22a}$$

This equation expresses the differential expected rate of return between domestic bonds and domestic capital. The right-hand side of (15.22a) thus represents the real risk premium on domestic capital over domestic bonds, with risk being "priced" at $(1 - \gamma)$. As long as $0 < \omega < 1$, this differential may be either positive or negative.

The fact that there may be a positive risk premium on bonds over capital may appear to contradict studies that suggest that the real return on equities substantially exceeds that on bonds (see, e.g., Mehra and Prescott 1985). The apparent inconsistency can be reconciled by noting that the definition of r_B includes the equilibrium variance of the inflation rate σ_p^2. If one were to ignore this term and define the expected real rate of return on bonds by the more conventional (but incorrect) expression $r_B' = i - \pi$, then (15.22a) would imply the relationship

$$r_K - r_B' = \sigma_x^2 + \alpha^2 \omega \sigma_y^2. \tag{15.22a'}$$

In general, r_K will exceed r_B' and may do so by substantial margins if the variances σ_x^2, σ_y^2 are sufficiently large. Substituting for r_K and r_B into (15.22a), this relationship may be expressed in the equivalent form

$$\alpha - (i - \pi) = (1 - \gamma)[\alpha^2 \omega(1 - \omega)\sigma_y^2 - \alpha^2 \omega^2 \sigma_z^2 - \omega(1 - \omega)^2 \sigma_q^2] + \sigma_p^2.$$
$$(15.23a)$$

Likewise, substituting (15.21c) into (15.11d) yields

$$r_F - r_B = (1 - \gamma)[-\alpha^2 \omega^2 (\sigma_y^2 + \sigma_z^2) + \omega(1 - \omega)\sigma_q^2], \qquad (15.22b)$$

expressing the differential between the expected real rate of return on domestic and traded bonds. The right-hand side is the real risk premium on foreign bonds. Substituting for r_B and r_F from (15.5b) and (15.5c), this can be written as

$$(i^* - \eta) - (i - \pi) = (1 - \gamma)[-\alpha^2 \omega^2 (\sigma_y^2 + \sigma_z^2) + \omega(1 - \omega)\sigma_q^2] + \sigma_p^2 - \sigma_q^2.$$
$$(15.23b)$$

Next, subtracting (15.23b) from (15.21a) yields the following solution for ω:

$$\omega = \frac{\alpha - (i^* - \eta + \sigma_q^2)}{(1 - \gamma)(\alpha^2 \sigma_y^2 + \sigma_q^2)} + \frac{\sigma_q^2}{\alpha^2 \sigma_y^2 + \sigma_q^2} \qquad (15.24)$$

Equation (15.24) expresses the relative share of capital in the traded portion of the representative agent's portfolio. It is seen to be *independent* of monetary policy. It thus obtains, whether the authority is targeting the monetary growth rate—as is being assumed here—is trageting the exchange rate, or is following some other form of monetary policy. As written, the determinants of the optimal portfolio share have been decomposed into two components. The first involves the differential real rate of return on capital and traded bonds and represents the *speculative* behavior on the part of the representative agent. The second involves the relative variances of the two assets and thus represents the *hedging* behavior on the part of the agent.

Having determined ω, we can now summarize the remainder of the equilibrium by the following sets of relationships.

Consumption, Growth, and Portfolio Shares

With portfolio shares remaining constant over time, all real components of wealth must grow at the same stochastic rate, that is,

$$\frac{d(M/P)}{M/P} = \frac{d(B/P)}{B/P} = \frac{d(B^*/Q)}{B^*/Q} = \frac{dK}{K} = \frac{dW}{W} \equiv \psi\, dt + dw. \qquad (15.25)$$

Taking expectations of the accumulation equation (15.15), using (15.25) and the definition of ω, the mean real rate of growth is given by the expression

$$\psi = \omega\left(\alpha(1 - g) - \frac{1}{n_K}\frac{C}{W}\right) + (1 - \omega)(i^* - \eta + \sigma_q^2). \tag{15.26a}$$

The expected growth rate is thus seen to be a weighted average of the domestic sources of growth, that is, net domestic output less the amount used for private and public consumption, and the growth attributable to interest earnings from abroad, the weights being the relative portfolio shares, ω and $(1 - \omega)$, respectively.

Next, substituting for σ_w^2 into the consumer optimality condition (15.11a), the equilibrium consumption-wealth ratio is

$$\frac{C}{W} = \frac{\theta}{1 - \gamma\theta}\left(\beta - \rho\gamma - \frac{1}{2}\gamma(\gamma - 1)[\alpha^2\omega^2(\sigma_y^2 + \sigma_z^2) + (1 - \omega)^2\sigma_q^2]\right) \tag{15.26b}$$

where by combining (15.10a), (15.25) with the definition of return ρ, defined in (15.11), the latter can be expressed as

$$\rho = \psi + \frac{C}{W}. \tag{15.26c}$$

The real part of the equilibrium is completed by recalling (15.11b),

$$n_M = \left(\frac{1 - \theta}{\theta}\right)\frac{(C/W)}{i}, \tag{15.26d}$$

and the normalized wealth constraint (15.10b), which, recalling (15.13c), can be written as

$$(1 + \lambda)n_M + \frac{n_K}{\omega} = 1. \tag{15.26e}$$

Having determined the partial portfolio share ω, equations (15.26a)–(15.26e) can be viewed as determining the equilibrium solutions for the consumption-wealth ratio C/W, the total net rate of return ρ, the mean growth rate ψ, and the portfolio shares of money and capital n_M, n_K, in terms of the domestic nominal interest rate i; debt policy λ, and other exogenous real parameters such as the exogenous real sources of risk, $\sigma_y^2, \sigma_z^2, \sigma_q^2$; preference parameters θ, β; the technology parameter α; and the target share of government expenditure g.

The remaining portfolio shares n_F and n_B are obtained by combining ω with n_K, and from the debt policy specification (15.13c), respectively. Furthermore, having obtained this "core" set of relationships, and with r_F, r_K being exogenously given from (15.5c) and (15.5d) respectively, the real rates of return on domestic bonds and on money can be obtained from (15.22a) and (15.11b'), respectively.

Nominal Quantities

Once the real part of the equilibrium is determined, the nominal quantities can be derived from the following relationships:

$$\pi = \eta + \varepsilon - \omega \sigma_q^2 \tag{15.27a}$$

$$i = i^* + \varepsilon - \sigma_x^2 - \gamma \alpha^2 \omega^2 (\sigma_y^2 + \sigma_z^2) + \gamma \omega (1 - \omega) \sigma_q^2 \tag{15.27b}$$

$$\pi = \phi - \psi(i, \lambda, g, \sigma_y^2, \sigma_z^2, \sigma_q^2) + \sigma_w^2. \tag{15.27c}$$

Equation (15.27a) is the "risk-adjusted" PPP equation (15.4a). Assuming that the agent holds a positive stock of capital, the sum of the world inflation rate plus the expected rate of exchange depreciation overstates the expected rate of domestic inflation. Equation (15.27b) is a "risk-adjusted" statement of nominal interest parity. This equation is obtained by substituting (15.27a) into (15.23b) and simplifying. It is clear that, in general, uncovered nominal interest parity, $i = i^* + \varepsilon$, does not hold, which is hardly surprising. More surprising is that, in the absence of domestic monetary risk ($\sigma_x^2 = 0$) and if the utility function is logarithmic ($\gamma = 0$), uncovered interest parity does obtain, even when agents are risk-averse, as they are assumed to be here. The fact that uncovered interest parity may hold even for risk-averse agents has been emphasized recently by Engel (1992), and our analysis provides a simple confirmation of that result. The third equation, (15.27c), describes the rate of inflation necessary to maintain portfolio balance (15.18a). It asserts that for portfolio balance to be maintained, the risk-adjusted rate of real monetary growth must equal the real equilibrium growth rate in the economy. Given the specification of monetary policy, these three equations jointly determine the equilibrium solutions for (i) the domestic rate of inflation π, (ii) the rate of exchange depreciation ε, and (iii) the domestic nominal interest rate i. In particular, the stochastic process generating the equilibrium exchange rate can be expressed as

$$\frac{dE}{E} = \tilde{e} \, dt + dx - \tilde{\omega}[\alpha(dy - dz) + dq],$$

where $\tilde{\omega}$ is determined from (15.24) and $\tilde{\varepsilon}$ is the equilibrium obtained from (15.27a)–(15.27c).

Determination of Initial Exchange Rate and Initial Wealth

The attainment of a new equilibrium is associated with a one-time discrete jump in the initial exchange rate $E(0)$. This is necessary to maintain portfolio balance in stock terms. From the definition of portfolio shares, we obtain

$$E(0) = \left(\frac{n_K + n_F}{n_M + n_B}\right)\left(\frac{M_0 + B_0}{Q_0 K_0 + B_0^*}\right) = \frac{n_K}{\omega(1 + \lambda)n_M}\left(\frac{M_0 + B_0}{Q_0 K_0 + B_0^*}\right) \quad (15.28a)$$

where M_0, B_0, K_0, B_0^* are the given initial stocks of assets, and Q_0 is the initial foreign price level. The corresponding endogenously determined initial value of wealth $W(0)$ is

$$W(0) = \frac{K_0 + (B_0^*/Q_0)}{n_K + n_F} = (K_0 + (B_0^*/Q_0))\left(\frac{\omega}{n_K}\right). \quad (15.28b)$$

Economic viability of this equilibrium requires that $E(0) > 0$. Assuming that positive stocks of money, domestic bonds, and capital are always held, this condition will be met if and only if $0 < n_K/\omega \equiv n_K + n_F < 1$; that is, if the share of traded assets in the agent's portfolio is positive. It is possible, however, for $\omega > 1$. If this is the case, $n_F < 0$, and the country is a net debtor rather than a creditor (as we will tend to assume).

Equilibrium also requires that the transversality condition

$\lim_{t \to \infty} E[W^\gamma e^{-\beta t}] = 0$ be met. This is again equivalent to $C/W > 0$ and is thus automatically satisfied for the logarithmic utility function. It also ensures that all relevant intertemporal budget constraints are met. Finally, we may observe that the equilibrium satisfies the assumption of constant portfolio shares and the C/W ratio.

15.4   Equilibrium Properties

We are now in a position to analyze the properties of the equilibrium. To do so, it is convenient to understand the structure of the equilibrium in more detail. First, the solution for the *real* quantities, determined by the system (15.26), are of the form

$$\frac{C}{W} = \frac{C}{W}(i, i^* - \eta, \lambda, g, \sigma_y^2, \sigma_z^2, \sigma_q^2) \quad (15.29a)$$

$$\psi = \psi(i, i^* - \eta, \lambda, g, \sigma_y^2, \sigma_z^2, \sigma_q^2) \quad (15.29b)$$

$$n_K = n_K(i, i^* - \eta, \lambda, g, \sigma_y^2, \sigma_z^2, \sigma_q^2) \quad (15.29c)$$

$$n_M = n_M(i, i^* - \eta, \lambda, g, \sigma_y^2, \sigma_z^2, \sigma_q^2). \quad (15.29d)$$

In the case of the logarithmic utility function, which serves as a useful benchmark, these solutions simplify to the following:

$$\frac{C}{W} = \theta\beta \quad (15.29a')$$

$$\psi = \omega\left[\alpha(1-g) - \frac{i\theta\beta}{i-(1-\theta)(1+\lambda)\beta}\right] + (1-\omega)[i^* - \eta + \sigma_q^2]$$

$$\equiv \psi(i, i^* - \eta, \lambda, g, \sigma_y^2, \sigma_q^2) \tag{15.29b'}$$

$$n_K = 1 - \frac{(1-\theta)(1+\lambda)\beta}{i} \equiv n_K(i, \lambda) \tag{15.29c'}$$

$$n_M = \frac{(1-\theta)\beta}{i} \equiv n_M(i). \tag{15.29d'}$$

In either case, these are only partial solutions, in that they involve the equilibrium domestic nominal interest rate i, which has yet to be determined.

The *nominal* variables may be conveniently solved as follows. Equation (15.23a) may be combined with (15.27c) to yield the following expression for the equilibrium nominal interest rate:

$$i = \alpha + \phi - \psi(i, i^* - \eta, \lambda, g, \sigma_y^2, \sigma_z^2, \sigma_q^2) - \sigma_x^2$$

$$+ (1-\gamma)(\sigma_w^2 - \alpha^2\omega\sigma_y^2) \tag{15.30}$$

where the solution for σ_w^2 is obtained by combining (15.21a) and (15.24). This equation, together with the expression for the growth rate contained in (15.29b), provides a complete reduced-form solution for the domestic nominal interest rate of the form

$$i = \psi(\phi, i^* - \eta, \lambda, g, \sigma_x^2, \sigma_y^2, \sigma_z^2, \sigma_q^2). \tag{15.31}$$

Once i is thus determined, the rest of the real equilibrium, summarized in (15.30), follows. Furthermore, given i, the expected rate of exchange depreciation ε and the domestic equilibrium rate of inflation π follow from (15.27b) and (15.27c), respectively.

The key point to observe is that *monetary* policy, as reflected in the mean rate of monetary growth ϕ and its variance σ_x^2, impacts on the real part of the system only through the domestic nominal interest rate i. Monetary policy may be characterized as being partially superneutral. Any form of nominal monetary policy that delivers the same domestic nominal interest rate will, given the bond-to-money ratio λ, yield the same equilibrium level of real activity in the domestic economy. The fact that nominal monetary policy is now able to have some real effects is due to the form of debt policy and to the fact that any nominal monetary growth is accompanied by a corresponding growth of government debt, in order for the money-debt ratio to remain constant. Debt policy, as reflected by a change in λ, will also have an independent effect on the real equilibrium.

Changing the Domestic Interest Rate

To understand the transmission of policy further, it is necessary to consider the impact of changes in the domestic nominal interest rate (which may result from a change in policy) on the equilibrium consumption-wealth ratio, growth rate, and portfolio shares. Differentiating the equilibrium set of relationships (15.26), the following expressions can be derived:

$$\frac{\partial (C/W)/(C/W)}{\partial i/i} = -\frac{(1 + \lambda)n_M \gamma \theta \omega}{n_K^2/\omega - \gamma \theta \omega} \tag{15.32a}$$

$$\frac{\partial \psi}{\partial i} = \frac{(1 + \lambda)n_M \omega (C/W)}{i[n_K^2/\omega - \gamma \theta \omega]} > 0 \tag{15.32b}$$

$$\frac{\partial n_K/n_K}{\partial i/i} = -\frac{(1 + \lambda)n_M(n_K - \gamma \theta \omega)}{n_K^2/\omega - \gamma \theta \omega}$$

$$= (1 + \lambda)n_M \left(1 + \frac{(1 + \lambda)n_M n_K}{n_K^2/\omega - \gamma \theta \omega} \right) > 0 \tag{15.32c}$$

$$\frac{\partial n_M/n_M}{\partial i/i} = -\frac{(n_K/\omega)(n_K - \gamma \theta \omega)}{n_K^2/\omega - \gamma \theta \omega}$$

$$= -\left(\frac{n_K}{\omega} \right)\left(1 + \frac{(1 + \lambda)n_M n_K}{n_K^2/\omega - \gamma \theta \omega} \right) < 0 \tag{15.32d}$$

where we assume that $n_K^2/\omega > \gamma \theta \omega$, a condition that is clearly met for the logarithmic utility function. From (15.27c) and (15.5b) we see that $dr_B/di = 1 - d\pi/di = 1 + d\psi/di > 0$, so that the equilibrium real and nominal interest rates move together.

The effects reported in (15.32) are seen to depend upon the elasticity of the utility function γ. In the case of the logarithmic utility function, the consumption-wealth ratio remains unchanged. The higher interest rate reduces the demand for money and therefore domestic bonds (which are tied to money via debt policy λ), while the shares of foreign bonds and equities are correspondingly increased. The ratio of consumption to capital is thus reduced. With output being proportional to the capital stock, the consumption-output ratio declines as well, thereby increasing the equilibrium real growth rate ψ.

In the more general case, where the elasticity $\gamma \neq 0$, these effects are compounded by the impact of the increase in i on the consumption-wealth ratio. In general, an increase in i will increase ρ, giving rise to the usual income and substitution effects in consumption. The latter will dominate if $\gamma > 0$, thereby reducing the consumption-wealth ratio. In this case, the decline in C/W will reduce the equilibrium share of money and domestic bonds even further. If the income effect prevails, the rise in the C/W ratio will tend to offset, although only partially, the direct effect of the increase in i, and the portfolio shares of money and domestic bonds will still decline. The portfolio shares of traded bonds and capital rise correspondingly, as does the equilibrium growth rate.

Domestic Policy and Policy Risk

We now analyze the effects of domestic monetary and government expenditure policies, and their associated risks, on the equilibrium.

Domestic Monetary Policy

We have already observed that monetary growth influences the real equilibrium only through the domestic nominal interest rate. Differentiating (15.30) with respect to the mean and variance of the monetary growth rate, while noting (15.27b), (15.27c), we find

$$\frac{\partial i}{\partial \phi} = \frac{\partial \pi}{\partial \phi} = \frac{\partial \varepsilon}{\partial \phi} = \frac{1}{1 + \partial \psi / \partial i} > 0 \tag{15.33a}$$

$$\frac{\partial i}{\partial \sigma_x^2} = -\frac{1}{1 + \partial \psi / \partial i} < 0; \qquad \frac{\partial \pi}{\partial \sigma_x^2} = \frac{\partial \varepsilon}{\partial \sigma_x^2} = \frac{\partial \psi / \partial i}{1 + \partial \psi / \partial i} > 0 \tag{15.33b}$$

A one-percentage-point increase in the rate of monetary growth will lead to equiproportionate increases in the domestic nominal interest rate, the rate of inflation, and the expected rate of exchange depreciation—although, in all cases these increases will be of a lesser amount than the monetary expansion itself. This is because the higher nominal interest rate also stimulates growth in the economy, thereby reducing the pressure on the nominal quantities.

By contrast, an increase in domestic monetary uncertainty will reduce the domestic nominal interest rate, thereby reducing the equilibrium growth rate. The following intuitive explanation for this effect may be given. A higher variance in the monetary growth rate increases the variance in the domestic price level, which ceteris paribus will raise the real rate of return on bonds (see [15.5b]). However, with the rate of return on domestic capital and the real risk premium on domestic bonds both unchanged by the increased variance of this nominal quantity, r_B must be restored to its original level in order for the equilibrium asset pricing condition (15.22a) to continue to hold. This equilibration is accomplished by a combination of a higher domestic inflation rate and a lower domestic nominal interest rate.

Domestic Fiscal Policy

Fiscal policy impacts on the real equilibrium both through the domestic interest rate and directly. Differentiating (15.30) with respect to g and noting (15.27b), (15.27c), we obtain

$$\frac{\partial i}{\partial g} = \frac{\partial \pi}{\partial g} = \frac{\partial \varepsilon}{\partial g} = -\frac{\partial \psi / \partial g}{1 + \partial \psi / \partial i} > 0, \tag{15.34a}$$

$$\frac{d\psi}{dg} = \frac{\partial \psi}{\partial g} + \frac{\partial \psi}{\partial i} \frac{\partial i}{\partial g} = -\frac{\partial \pi}{\partial g} < 0. \tag{15.34b}$$

The immediate effect of an increase in the share of government expenditure g is to leave less output available for investment, thereby reducing the growth rate; that is, $\partial \psi / \partial g < 0$. With the nominal growth of the money supply fixed at ϕ, the rate of inflation must increase in order to reduce the real monetary growth correspondingly and thereby maintain portfolio balance in accordance with (15.27c). The higher domestic inflation rate will in turn increase the rate of exchange depreciation and raise the domestic nominal interest rate. The latter, in turn, will tend to stimulate the real growth rate, partly but not completely offsetting the initial reduction in the growth rate.

In discussing the effect of a higher variance in domestic fiscal policy, we shall restrict our attention to the case of the logarithmic utility function, when it has only an indirect effect on growth, through the nominal interest rate. Differentiating the equilibrium, we obtain

$$\frac{\partial i}{\partial \sigma_z^2} = \frac{\partial \pi}{\partial \sigma_z^2} = \frac{\partial \varepsilon}{\partial \sigma_z^2} = \frac{\alpha^2 \omega^2}{1 + \partial \psi / \partial i} > 0, \tag{15.35a}$$

$$\frac{d\psi}{d\sigma_z^2} = \frac{\partial \psi}{\partial i} \frac{\partial i}{\partial \sigma_z^2} = \frac{(\partial \psi / \partial i) \alpha^2 \omega^2}{1 + \partial \psi / \partial i} > 0. \tag{15.35b}$$

Intuitively, the partial effect of an increase in σ_z^2 is to raise σ_p^2, thereby raising the real return on domestic bonds. It also raises the risk premium on these assets relative to both domestic capital and foreign bonds. In order for equilibrium to be maintained in the asset market, the rate of return on domestic bonds must rise, forcing up the domestic interest rate. The higher interest rate raises the rate of exchange depreciation, thereby increasing the domestic inflation rate but also inducing a higher equilibrium growth rate. In the case of the more general utility function, these effects would also need to take into account the impact of the higher fiscal risk on the consumption-wealth ratio and its resulting impact on the equilibrium growth rate.

It is important to recall from (15.28a) that any of these policy changes (or other policy shocks) will be associated with a concurrent one-time discrete jump in the level of the exchange rate $E(0)$. Consider an increase in the monetary growth rate. By raising the nominal interest rate it lowers the portfolio share of money and raises the share of domestic capital, thereby increasing the ratio (n_K/n_M). Given that M_0, B_0, K_0, B_0^*, and Q_0 are predetermined, this requires a one-time depreciation of the exchange rate in order for portfolio balance to be maintained. Thereafter, the nominal exchange rate evolves continuously in accordance with the equilibrium stochastic process. Furthermore, the initial depreciation of the exchange rate has an adverse effect on the initial level of wealth $W(0)$. An increase in the variance of the monetary growth rate has the exact opposite effect. By lowering i it lowers the ratio (n_K/n_M), inducing a discrete appreciation of the exchange rate, the effect of which is to increase the initial level of wealth.

This, however, should not be interpreted as meaning that an increase in monetary risk is necessarily welfare-improving. Other consequences of the increased risk must be taken into account. Using a closed economy version of this model, Turnovsky (1993) has shown that optimal (welfare-maximizing) monetary policy can be characterized in terms of an optimal target nominal interest rate. To the extent that increasing the variance of the monetary growth rate may move the interest rate closer to its target, a higher variance will be welfare-improving. However, Turnovsky also argues that manipulating the variance of the monetary growth rate may be of limited effect in attaining this target, and that setting the mean growth rate is a more appropriate way of operating.

Foreign Inflation and Inflation Risk

Early discussions of flexible exchange rates focused on the extent to which such a regime insulates the domestic economy against foreign price disturbances.[2] Using a portfolio balance model, Turnovsky (1977) showed that a necessary and sufficient condition for a flexible exchange rate regime to provide perfect insulation against changes in the foreign inflation rate is that the rest of the world be "Fisherian," in the sense that the foreign nominal interest rate fully adjusts to changes in the foreign inflation rate, that is, $di^*/d\eta = 1$. If this condition holds, then $d\varepsilon/d\eta = -1$, and the higher inflation rate leads to an equivalent decrease in the rate of exchange depreciation of the domestic currency, thereby fully insulating the domestic economy from the foreign inflationary shock. This same condition was later shown to provide perfect insulation in a deterministic intertemporal utility maximizing model; see Turnovsky (1985).

Examining the solution for the real part of the system summarized by (15.29), it follows that the Fisherian condition $di^*/d\eta = 1$ is also a necessary and sufficient condition to ensure perfect insulation against changes in the foreign mean inflation rate in the present stochastic setting. If this condition is met, then the increase in η is matched by an equal reduction in the rate of exchange depreciation ε, leaving the domestic inflation rate and interest rate unchanged.

By contrast, an increase in the variance of the foreign inflation rate σ_q^2 will generate real effects on the domestic economy. In general, holding i^* and η fixed, an increase in σ_q^2 will increase the rate of return on foreign bonds. This leads to adjustments in the representative agent's portfolio, leading to real effects in the economy.

15.5   Foreign Exchange Risk Premium

An important concept in international finance is the foreign exchange risk premium. The present stochastic general equilibrium model offers a convenient vehicle for examining its determinants. Although the literature frequently distinguishes between real and nominal measures, we shall focus primarily on the former, which we consider to be of greater relevance. Adapting a measure used by Engel (1992) and others, we shall define the real risk premium over the period (t, T) by[3]

$$\Omega(t, T) \equiv 1 - \frac{F(t, T)}{\Phi(t, T)}$$

where

$$\Phi(t, T) = \frac{E_t[E(T)/P(T)]}{E_t[1/P(T)]}. \tag{15.36}$$

E_t is the conditional expectation formed at time t, and $F(t, T)$ is the forward exchange rate at time t, for the future time T. If agents are risk neutral and markets efficient, then $\Phi(t, T) = F(t, T)$, and the foreign exchange risk premium $\Omega(t, T) = 0$. As defined, a positive real risk premium on the foreign exchange risk implies an expected value of the real exchange rate in excess of the forward rate so that $\Omega > 0$.

We shall derive the expression for $\Omega(t, T)$ under the assumption that _covered interest parity_ (CIP) prevails. This condition, which is much less restrictive and receives much more empirical support than does uncovered interest parity, requires that the real rate of return on an investment in a foreign bond, with the exchange risk covered by a corresponding position in the forward exchange market, must equal the rate of return on the domestic bond. Formally, this equality is described by the relationship

$$\frac{F(t, T)}{E(t)} \exp[i^*(T - t)] = \exp[i(T - t)]. \tag{15.37}$$

To determine $E_t[E(T)/P(T)]$, we consider the stochastic process followed by the real exchange rate $E(t)/P(t)$. Taking the stochastic differential of this quantity, we obtain

$$\frac{d(E(t)/P(t))}{E(t)/P(t)} = \frac{dE(t)}{E(t)} - \frac{dP(t)}{P(t)} - \left(\frac{dE(t)}{E(t)}\right)\left(\frac{dP(t)}{P(t)}\right) + \left(\frac{dP(t)}{P(t)}\right)^2.$$

Substituting the stochastic processes for $P(t)$ and $E(t)$ from (15.1a), (15.1c), and retaining terms to the order dt implies

$$\frac{d(E(t)/P(t))}{E(t)/P(t)} = [\varepsilon - \pi - \sigma_{ep} + \sigma_p^2] dt + de - dp.$$

The expected value of this expression is

$$\frac{E\{d(E(t)/P(t))\}}{E(t)/P(t)} = [\varepsilon - \pi - \sigma_{ep} + \sigma_p^2] dt,$$

which may be solved to yield

$$E_t[E(T)/P(T)] = [E(t)/P(t)] \exp[(\varepsilon - \pi - \sigma_{ep} + \sigma_p^2)(T - t)]. \tag{15.38a}$$

Similarly,

$$E_t[1/P(T)] = [1/P(t)] \exp[(-\pi + \sigma_p^2)(T - t)], \tag{15.38b}$$

and, substituting (15.38a), (15.38b) into (15.36) and dividing leads to the expression

$$\Phi(t, T) = E(t) \exp[(\varepsilon - \sigma_{ep})(T - t)]. \tag{15.39}$$

Substituting for $F(t, T)$ from (15.37) and $\Phi(t, T)$ from (15.39) into $\Omega(t, T)$ implies

$$\Omega(t, T) = 1 - \exp[(i - i^* - \varepsilon + \sigma_{ep})(T - t)].$$

Using (15.27b), and computing σ_{ep} from (15.20b), (15.20c), we obtain

$$\Omega(t, T) = 1 - \exp[(1 - \gamma)(\alpha^2 \omega^2(\sigma_y^2 + \sigma_z^2) - \omega(1 - \omega)\sigma_q^2)(T - t)]$$

$$= 1 - \exp[(r_B - r_F)(T - t)]. \tag{15.40}$$

Thus, under conditions of CIP, the real risk premium as measured by $\Omega(t, T)$ is an increasing function of the differential expected real return on foreign and domestic bonds.

Equation (15.40) expresses the real foreign exchange risk premium in terms of exogenous sources of risk, and it can be seen to be either positive or negative, depending upon the relative magnitudes of the domestic and foreign sources of risk. It is immediately apparent that an increase in either of the domestic sources of risk, σ_y^2, σ_z^2, lowers the risk premium on foreign bonds, as one would expect. The risk premium on foreign bonds declines with the expected rate of foreign inflation if $1 > \omega > 1/2$, that is, if the domestic economy holds more traded capital than traded bonds. Because, from (15.24), ω is a function of $i^* - \eta$, it is independent of any change in η that is accompanied by an equal change in the foreign interest rate. An increase in foreign price risk σ_q^2 directly raises the risk premium on foreign bonds. It also induces a shift in the traded portion of investors' portfolios in their favor, thereby serving to reduce the equilibrium risk premium. The net effect depends upon ω, and under the reasonable condition $1 > \omega > 1/2$, the risk premium will rise.

Analogously, one can show that the more frequently studied, but less relevant, nominal risk premium is given by

$$\Omega^N(t, T) = 1 - \exp[-\sigma_x^2(T - t)]. \tag{15.40'}$$

Comparing this expression with (15.40) we see that the nominal risk premium depends upon the variance of the nominal stochastic shock, whereas the real risk premium depends upon the variances of the real disturbances.

Under what conditions is the real risk premium zero? One simple condition in which this will be so is if $\alpha = i^* - \eta + \gamma\sigma_q^2$, in which case the speculative and hedging components in (15.24) are precisely offsetting, so that $\omega = 0$ and the domestic investors hold no equities. In this case, the equilibrium stochastic processes describing the real returns on the income-earning assets can be readily shown to be

$$dR_B = (i^* - \eta + \sigma_q^2)\,dt - (dx + dq) \tag{15.41a}$$

$$dR_K = (i^* - \eta + \gamma\sigma_q^2)\,dt + \alpha\,dy \tag{15.41b}$$

$$dR_F = (i^* - \eta + \sigma_q^2)\,dt - dq. \tag{15.41c}$$

Note that although domestic and foreign bonds have the same expected real rates of return, their stochastic components are not identical. However, the two assets are perfect substitutes, because their market risks (i.e., their systematic risks as measured by their respective beta coefficients), β_B and β_F, are the same. To see this, recall that in general the market risk for asset i having a stochastic component in its rate of return du_i is defined as $\beta_i = \text{cov}(dw, du_i)/\text{var}(dw)$, where in the present context dw is given by (15.20a). Assuming $\omega = 0$, we see that $\sigma_w^2 = \sigma_q^2$, implying that

$\beta_B = \beta_F = 1$. Capital has a lower expected return, and $\beta_K = 0$. But the lower risk is insufficient to compensate for the lower return, and the asset is not held in the equilibrium portfolio of domestic investors.

An alternative condition yielding a zero foreign exchange risk premium is

$$\omega^* = \frac{\alpha - (i^* - \eta + \sigma_q^2)}{(1 - \gamma)(\alpha^2 \sigma_y^2 + \sigma_q^2)} + \frac{\sigma_q^2}{\alpha^2 \sigma_y^2 + \sigma_q^2} = \frac{\sigma_q^2}{\alpha^2(\sigma_y^2 + \sigma_z^2) + \sigma_q^2}. \qquad (15.42)$$

In this case, the equilibrium stochastic processes characterizing the rates of return are

$$dR_B = (i^* - \eta + \sigma_q^2)\,dt - [dx - \alpha\omega^*(dy - dz) + (1 - \omega^*)\,dq], \qquad (15.41a')$$

$$dR_K = \alpha\,dt + \alpha\,dy, \qquad (15.41b')$$

and (15.41c). Again the two bonds are perfect substitutes, having equal rates of return and equal beta coefficients: $\beta_B = \beta_F = 1$. The expected rate of return on capital is lower, but given the risk on capital, as measured by $\beta_K = \alpha^2 \omega^* \sigma_y^2 / \sigma_w^2$, is now sufficient to induce domestic investors to hold this asset. The difference between the returns on capital and on bonds is accounted for by the presence of fiscal risk. If $\sigma_z^2 = 0$, (15.42) becomes $\alpha = i^* - \eta + \sigma_q^2$ and all three assets have identical expected returns and beta coefficients equal to unity.

To understand further these conditions for zero foreign exchange risk premium, it is useful to consider the optimality condition (15.11d), in conjunction with (15.4b), and to observe that the foreign exchange risk premium will be zero if and only if $\text{cov}(dw, de) = 0$, that is, if and only if domestic wealth is uncorrelated with the nominal exchange rate. Recalling the solutions for dw and de reported in (15.20a) and (15.20c), we see that if $\omega = 0$, stochastic movements in domestic wealth depend only upon foreign price shocks, and those of the exchange rate depend only upon domestic monetary shocks. By assumption, these two stochastic processes are uncorrelated. By contrast, when $\omega = 0$, stochastic movements in dy generate a negative correlation between de and dw, whereas foreign price shocks generate a positive correlation. However, if the condition (15.42) is met, these two effects are exactly offsetting, thereby again ensuring that de and dw remain uncorrelated.

The issue of when the foreign exchange risk premium is zero has received some attention in the recent international finance literature. Domowitz and Hakkio (1985) and Hodrick and Srivastava (1986) consider models in which the risk premium is zero and where there is no government spending, expenditure shares are constant, and monetary and real shocks are independent. Engel (1992) reports a zero risk premium for a model in which spending shares are constant, the share of output devoted to government is constant, and monetary shocks are independent of endowment shocks, in the absence of production. Explicit comparisons between these models is not easy, because they are based on different assumptions. For example, in the present model, because dz is not proportional to dy, government expenditure cannot be a constant share of output. The role of foreign price shocks is also important here, but is excluded from some of the other models.

15.6   Risk and the Equilibrium Growth Rate

Constancy of equilibrium portfolio shares implies that the equilibrium rates of growth of all real assets are equal. Recalling (15.25) and (15.26a), this common stochastic rate of growth is

$$\frac{dK}{K} = \left\{ \omega \left(\alpha(1 - g) - \frac{1}{n_K} \frac{C}{W} \right) + (1 - \omega)(i^* - \eta + \sigma_q^2) \right\} dt$$
$$+ [\alpha\omega(dy - dz) - (1 - \omega)\, dq]. \tag{15.43}$$

As noted, the mean growth rate comprises two components. The first, $\omega[\alpha(1 - g) - (1/n_K)(C/W)]$, is associated with the growth of domestic output; the second, $(1 - \omega)[i^* - \eta + \sigma_q^2]$, is the growth generated by foreign income earnings. In general, the equilibrium we are considering is one in which capital is steadily accumulating or decumulating, though at a sufficiently slow rate to be sustainable in the sense of being consistent with the intertemporal budget constraint facing the economy.

This section discusses four aspects of the equilibrium growth rate in further detail. These include (i) short-run stochastic components of growth, (ii) further comments on the determinants of the mean growth rate, (iii) variance of the growth rate, (iv) the relationship between export instability and growth.

Short-Run Stochastic Behavior of Growth

We discussed in Section 14.8 how the recent business cycle literature focuses on the covariation of contemporaneous stochastic movements of various key macroeconomic variables. Although that literature was originally formulated in terms of a closed economy, it has increasingly focused on international correlations and covariances. Among the variables that have received particular attention are those pertaining to growth and the accumulation of assets; we shall restrict our observations to these aspects.

Consider the stochastic component of the real growth rate: $dw = \alpha\omega(dy - dz) - (1 - \omega)\,dq$. It is evident that this responds positively to productivity shocks and negatively to fiscal shocks. Its response to foreign price shocks is also negative as long as the nation is a creditor, but is positive otherwise. These stochastic responses are summarized by the covariance expressions

$$\text{cov}(dw, dy) = \alpha\omega\sigma_y^2; \quad \text{cov}(dw, dz) = -\alpha\omega\sigma_z^2; \quad \text{cov}(dw, dq) = \alpha(1 - \omega)\sigma_q^2.$$
$$(15.44)$$

The magnitudes of these responses depend upon the relative proportion of traded bonds in the economy's portfolio of traded assets. The smaller the fraction of traded bonds (i.e. the closer ω is to 1), the more sensitive are the fluctuations in growth to the domestic shocks and the less sensitive they are to the foreign shocks. The fact that government expenditure is negatively correlated with growth (investment) is consistent with results from the real business literature investigating this aspect.

One issue that has received a good deal of attention is the correlation between domestic savings and investment. This phenomenon was originally investigated empirically by Feldstein and Horioka (1980), who argued that the high correlation they obtained between the savings-to-GDP ratio and the investment-to-GDP ratio was inconsistent with the assumption of perfect capital markets. An immediate consequence of the fixed portfolio shares equilibrium is that the real growth rate of capital dK/K and the real savings rate dW/W are perfectly correlated, at least in the present model. This is more or less consistent with the empirical findings of Feldstein and Horioka, and it provides an example of how, in an environment of ongoing growth, their results are in fact compatible with a high degree of capital mobility.

The relationship between the current account and the rate of domestic investment has been investigated analytically by Stockman and Svensson (1987) and empirically by Glick and Rogoff (1995), who found an almost unambiguous negative relationship between these two variables. The precise definition is of some importance, and the choice is not an unambiguous one. One natural definition is the quantity dB^*/Q, which nets out the capital gains or losses associated with changes in the foreign price level. From (15.14), the stochastic component of this expression, denoted by $d\tilde{N}$, is given by

$$d\tilde{N} = (1 - \omega)K[\alpha(dy - dz) + dq].$$

Taking this in conjunction with the stochastic component of (15.43) (and denoting the stochastic component of dK by $d\tilde{K}$) implies

$$\text{cov}(d\tilde{N}, d\tilde{K}) = (1 - \omega)K^2[\alpha\omega(\sigma_y^2 + \sigma_z^2) - (1 - \omega)\sigma_q^2]. \tag{15.45}$$

To the extent that the sources of stochastic disturbances are of domestic origin, the current account surplus and the rate of capital accumulation will be positively correlated if the country is a creditor nation, and will be negatively correlated otherwise. The two quantities will be unambiguously negatively correlated if the shocks are in the form of foreign price disturbances.

Finally, considering (15.20c) in conjunction with (15.43), we find that the covariance between the nominal exchange rate and the rate of growth is

$$\text{cov}(de, dw) = -\alpha^2 \omega^2 (\sigma_y^2 + \sigma_z^2) + \omega(1 - \omega)\sigma_z^2 \qquad (15.46)$$

Thus an appreciation of the domestic currency resulting from either an increase in domestic output or a decline in government expenditure will be accompanied by a higher growth rate. If the source of the appreciation is a foreign price increase, then whether this is accompanied by a lower or a higher growth rate depends upon whether the country is a net creditor or a net debtor. Recalling (15.22b), we see that

$$sgn\{\text{cov}(de, dw)\} = sgn(r_F - r_B).$$

That is, the covariance between the nominal exchange rate and the growth rate is positive if and only if the real foreign exchange rate premium is positive.

Mean Growth Rate

We have already considered this to some extent in the course of discussing the impact of domestic monetary and fiscal policy on the macroeconomic equilibrium. In Section 15.4 we showed that an increase in the mean monetary growth rate raises the real growth rate, whereas an increase in its variance has an adverse effect. Fiscal policy tends to have the opposite effect. An increase in the target share of output claimed by the government lowers the growth rate, while an increase in its variance will be growth-enhancing, at least for the logarithmic utility function. The key channel by which these influences operate is through the nominal interest rate, a consequence of the specified form of debt policy.

The effects of an increase in the variance of the productivity shock σ_y^2, or of the foreign price shock σ_q^2, are more complicated to determine because each has a portfolio adjustment effect as well as an impact through the nominal interest rate and consumption. Higher production risk will induce a shift away from capital toward traded bonds; that is, ω will decline. Whether this is in itself growth-enhancing depends upon whether or not this portfolio switch is toward the higher-yielding asset. Moreover, although the higher productivity variance will impact on the share of output claimed by consumption, through the nominal interest rate, the net impact is not an unambiguous one. Many of the same comments apply to the effects of a higher variance in foreign prices, σ_q^2. In fact, the impact of an increase in σ_q^2 on the portfolio adjustment is even less clear. This is because it raises both the mean return on the foreign asset and its associated risk, with the net effect on the portfolio depending upon both its preexisting composition and the agent's degree of risk aversion.

Variance of the Equilibrium Growth Rate

The variance of the equilibrium growth rate is given by the expression (15.21a)

$$\sigma_w^2 = \alpha^2 \omega^2 (\sigma_y^2 + \sigma_z^2) + (1 - \omega)^2 \sigma_q^2.$$

The behavior of this expression is of interest, not only in its own right but also insofar as it impacts on the equilibrium consumption-wealth ratio and the equilibrium growth rate itself. With the portfolio share being independent of both σ_x^2 and σ_z^2, it is immediate that the variance of the growth path (i) is independent of the variance of the monetary growth rate; and (ii) increases directly with the variance of fiscal policy. The latter effect has an adverse impact on the welfare of a risk-averse agent and offsets any welfare gains resulting from any higher mean growth rate it may generate.

Increases in the remaining variances σ_y^2, σ_q^2 involve two effects. First, for given portfolio shares $\omega, (1 - \omega)$ they will both directly increase the variance of the growth rate. Second, an increase in either will involve a portfolio adjustment. To see the net effects most clearly, we focus on the logarithmic utility function, and obtain

$$\frac{d\sigma_w^2}{d\sigma_y^2} = \frac{\alpha^2 \omega}{\alpha^2 \sigma_y^2 + \sigma_q^2} [-\alpha^2 \omega(\sigma_y^2 + 2\sigma_z^2) + (2 - \omega)\sigma_q^2], \qquad (15.47a)$$

$$\frac{d\sigma_w^2}{d\sigma_q^2} = \frac{1}{\alpha^2 \sigma_y^2 + \sigma_q^2} [\alpha^2 (1 - 2\omega - \omega^2)\sigma_y^2 - 2\alpha^2 \omega^2 \sigma_z^2 + (1 - \omega^2)\sigma_q^2]. \qquad (15.47b)$$

The interesting aspect of these expressions is that an increase in either of these variances may quite plausibly reduce the variance of the growth path. Paradoxically, increased exogenous risk may be stabilizing. This occurs if the portfolio adjustment in favor of the more stable asset more than offsets the direct destabilizing effect of the increased exogenous risk. In the case of the productivity shock, for example, this arises if $\sigma_q^2 = 0$, when traded bonds become a riskless asset.

Export Instability and Growth

A widely discussed issue among development economists concerns the effects of export instability on investment and growth. Several authors have studied correlations between measures of export instability and growth, with a variety of conflicting results. For example, Kenen and Voidodas (1972) find the investment-GNP ratio to be negatively correlated with export instability. By contrast, Yotopoulos and Nugent (1976) find a positive correlation. Other studies, focusing on the growth of GNP and export instability, also obtain conflicting results. Voidodas (1974) and Ozler and Harrigan (1988) find a negative correlation between instability and growth rates of GNP. By contrast, Yotopoulos and Nugent (1976) obtain a positive correlation, and Kenen and Voidodas find no correlation. The type of model we have been discussing is able to reconcile these findings.

To eliminate problems of dimensionality, we normalize net exports, $dX = dY - dC - dK - dG$, by the growing stock of capital. Also, for expositional simplicity, we shall assume a logarithmic utility function, so that[4]

$$\frac{dX}{K} = (1 - \omega)\left[\alpha(1 - g) - \frac{\theta\beta}{n_K} - (i^* - \eta + \sigma_q^2)\right]dt$$

$$+ (1 - \omega)[\alpha(dy - dz) + dq]. \tag{15.48a}$$

The variance of this measure of net exports is therefore

$$E\left(\frac{dX}{K}\right)^2 = (1 - \omega)^2[\alpha^2(\sigma_y^2 + \sigma_z^2) + \sigma_q^2]dt, \tag{15.48b}$$

and the issue of the effect of export instability on growth thus centers around the relationship between (15.48a) and the deterministic component of the growth rate in (15.43). In the present framework, export instability is endogenous and will reflect the exogenous sources of risk, σ_z^2, σ_y^2, and σ_q^2. We therefore consider each in turn.

An increase in fiscal instability σ_z^2 has no effect on ω and will therefore raise export instability by the amount $(1 - \omega)^2\alpha^2$. With ω unchanged and a logarithmic utility function, its only effect on the mean growth rate is through the portfolio share n_K. An increase in the fiscal variance has been shown to raise the nominal interest rate, which, from (15.32c), will raise n_K. The consumption-capital ratio therefore falls, so that expected growth will therefore rise. Export instability arising from domestic fiscal variability will therefore be *positively* correlated with growth.

An increase in domestic production instability is more complicated. It will raise export instability on two counts. In addition to having a direct effect, analogous to the fiscal variability just discussed, it will also cause the previously considered portfolio shift toward bonds ($1 - \omega$ increases), and this will introduce additional instability into exports. To see what happens to the mean growth rate, consider the simplest case, where $\sigma_z^2 = \sigma_q^2 = g = 0$, when for the logarithmic utility function, the deterministic component of (15.43) reduces to

$$\frac{[\alpha - (i^* - \eta)]^2}{\alpha \sigma_y^2} - \frac{\theta \beta}{n_K + n_F}.$$

It is immediate that an increase in σ_y^2, by inducing a shift away from capital, will reduce the first component. Under these same assumptions, it will also lower ε, and hence i, thereby lowering $n_K + n_F$, raising consumption, and lowering growth further. In this case, higher export instability resulting from higher variability in domestic production will therefore be *negatively* correlated with growth; see also Brock (1991). If $g > 0$ and the other sources of risk are present, the results become ambiguous.

Finally, an increase in σ_q^2, although generally similar to σ_y^2, is less clearcut. It will raise export instability, both directly and by lowering ω. The latter will tend to reduce growth, but this is offset by a positive effect, resulting from the higher real rate of return on foreign securities. Thus export instability, resulting from variability in the foreign inflation rate, may be either positively or negatively correlated with growth.

In summary, the model is consistent with all patterns of correlation between export instability and growth. The critical element is the origin of the shocks impinging on the economy.

15.7   Some Further Extensions

The previous three sections have applied the model to various issues in international macroeconomics and finance. We conclude by touching upon two further issues to which it is relevant and could be applied.

Welfare Analysis

This aspect was discussed in Chapter 14 in conjunction with the analysis of optimal tax policy. The same kind of analysis can be pursued with the present model, although the implications will be somewhat different because of the different specification of debt policy. In Section 14.5 we showed how the criterion function could be expressed in terms of the initial capital stock; see (14.67). By an identical analysis, one can show that the optimized level of utility is of the form

$$X(W(0)) = \frac{\theta}{\gamma} n_M^{\gamma(1-\theta)} (C/W)^{\theta\gamma-1} W(0)^\gamma$$

where $W(0)$ is given by (15.28b) The important point is that monetary policy impacts on welfare through the consumption-wealth ratio C/W and the portfolio shares n_K, n_F, and n_M, in each case doing so through the nominal interest rate i. Thus optimal monetary policy is equivalent to choosing the optimal target nominal interest rate, and, in general, there are an infinite number of ways that this may be accomplished. The choice involves the following trade-offs. A higher nominal interest rate leads to more growth and more future consumption, which is welfare-improving. At the same time it reduces real money balances and generates a larger initial reduction of wealth, and these effects are welfare-deteriorating. Turnovsky (1993) discusses the optimal choice of interest rate in the context of a closed economy, but the same ideas can be developed in the present model as well. With debt policy fixed parametrically by the choice of λ, this will influence the choice of the optimal interest rate target. One can choose an optimal debt policy in conjunction with the interest rate, and, not surprisingly, it is to set $\lambda = 0$. In this case, the corresponding tax rate, which is being set residually here, is essentially the same as the optimal tax rate derived in Chapters 13 and 14.

International Tax Issues

A second issue for which the present model is extremely important concerns the analysis of taxation in an international context. This is an issue that is beginning to attract significant attention among public finance economists; see, for example, Frenkel, Razin, and Sadka (1991). Most of the literature is based on complete certainty, and the arbitrage conditions that characterize efficient capital markets severely constrain the choice of taxation. The introduction of risk adds flexibility, as well as realism, to the analysis.

The issue can be seen as follows. Consider the present model in the absence of uncertainty. In order for there to be an interior equilibrium, the rate of return on domestic capital would have to equal the exogenously given rate of return on world capital; that is, $\alpha = i^* - \eta$. In the present analysis, that is not the case. As equation (15.24) makes clear, agents will adjust their portfolios so as to equate the risk-adjusted rates of return, given their attitudes to risk taking.

The same applies in the presence of taxes. Suppose that the agent is taxed at the rate τ_k on his holdings of capital and at the rate τ_f on his foreign bond holdings. In a riskless world an interior equilibrium will imply $\alpha(1 - \tau_k) = (i^* - \eta)(1 - \tau_f)$. With the before-tax rates of return being fixed, it is clear that the authority cannot set the two tax rates independently if an interior equilibrium is to be always maintained.

In a world economy it is even more complicated. Now consider another agent facing similar investment opportunities under perfect world capital markets but domiciled in another tax jurisdiction, typically another country. Suppose he is taxed at the corresponding rates τ_k^*, τ_f^*. His arbitrage opportunities will require $\alpha(1 - \tau_k^*) = (i^* - \eta)(1 - \tau_f^*)$ for an interior solution to prevail. These two sets of arbitrage conditions together thus imply the following stringent constraint involving the four tax rates in order for an interior equilibrium in the world capital markets to obtain:

$$[(1 - \tau_k)/(1 - \tau_k^*)] = [(1 - \tau_f)/(1 - \tau_f^*)].$$

A significant literature has developed analyzing the international viability of alternative tax regimes, most notably the residence-based principle and the source-based principle; see, for example, Giovannini (1990), Sinn (1990), and Frenkel, Razin, and Sadka (1991).

However, as Slemrod (1988) has suggested, the stringent arbitrage conditions characterizing the viability of alternative taxation regimes are essentially an artifact of the absence of risk and of the corner solutions this yields with respect to portfolio decisions. This can be seen immediately from (15.24), which in the presence of capital income taxes (and assuming that these tax revenues are rebated) is modified to:

$$\omega = \frac{\alpha(1 - \tau_k) - (i^* - \eta + \sigma_q^2)(1 - \tau_f)}{(1 - \gamma)(\alpha^2(1 - \tau_k)\sigma_y^2 + (1 - \tau_f)\sigma_q^2)} + \frac{(1 - \tau_f)\sigma_q^2}{\alpha^2(1 - \tau_k)\sigma_y^2 + (1 - \tau_f)\sigma_q^2}.$$

An analogous condition can be derived for the foreign-based agent, and again there are no constraints on how the tax rates may be set. Each agent will choose his individual portfolio in response to the risks, his own degree of risk aversion, and the tax rates he faces. Equilibrium in the world capital markets will be brought about through adjustments in the before-tax yields on the traded world assets to ensure that all capital is willingly held.

This completes our overview of the methods of macroeconomic dynamics, at least from the perspective of this book. Much has changed over the past two decades. That is how it should be, and hopefully this process will continue. At this time, the methods of stochastic calculus that we have been expositing in the last two chapters present a promising avenue for future research. Although they have been around for a considerable period of time, they have never been widely applied in economics. We have merely tried to introduce the methods and to illustrate their applicability to a limited range of issues, using examples for which closed-form solutions are easy to obtain. As we have tried to emphasize, the structures of the problems for which this is possible are limited. Inevitably, as these methods are applied to increasingly complex and realistic situations, numerical solutions will become necessary. But, with increased computing capabilities, richer and more relevant models will surely become solvable and help provide insight into better macroeconomic policy-making. That is the ultimate objective.

Notes

1. Branson and Henderson (1985) review the literature and discuss asset demands in a three-asset partial equilibrium stochastic model.

2. This issue was discussed at some length in the 1970s using the portfolio balance framework; see, e.g., Floyd (1978), Laidler (1977), Turnovsky (1977). In this discussion, the distinction was drawn between once-and-for-all increases in the foreign price level and increases in the steady foreign rate of inflation. Our discussion considers only the latter.

3. See also Stockman (1978), Frankel (1979), and Sibert (1989) for discussion of the risk premium.

4. Equation (15.48a) can be derived as follows. Dividing (15.14) by K, net exports can be written as

$$\frac{dX}{K} = \frac{(B^*/Q)}{K}\left[\frac{d(B^*/Q)}{B^*/Q} - dR_F\right] = \frac{(1-\omega)}{\omega}\left[\frac{d(B^*/Q)}{B^*/Q} - dR_F\right].$$

Now combining (15.25), (15.26a), and the definition of dR_F from (15.5c), and recalling that for the logarithmic utility function, $C/W = \theta\beta$, immediately leads to the expression in the text.

References

Abel, A. B. 1982. "Dynamic Effects of Permanent and Temporary Tax Policies in a q Model of Investment." *Journal of Monetary Economics* 9:353–373.

Abel, A. B. 1983. "Optimal Investment under Uncertainty." *American Economic Review* 73:228–233.

Abel, A. B. 1985. "A Stochastic Model of Investment, Marginal q and the Marginal Value of the Firm." *International Economic Review* 26:305–322.

Abel, A. B. 1987. "Optimal Monetary Growth." *Journal of Monetary Economics* 19:437–450.

Abel, A., and O. J. Blanchard. 1983. "An Intertemporal Model of Saving and Investment." *Econometrica* 51:675–692.

Abreu, D. 1988. "On the Theory of Infinitely Repeated Games with Discounting." *Econometrica* 56:383–396.

Adler, M., and B. Dumas. 1983. "International Portfolio Choice and Corporation Finance: A Synthesis." *Journal of Finance* 38:925–984.

Aizenman, J. 1985. "Wage Flexibility and Openness." *Quarterly Journal of Economics* 100:539–550.

Aizenman, J., and J. A. Frenkel. 1985. "Optimal Wage Indexation, Foreign Exchange Market Intervention, and Monetary Policy." *American Economic Review* 75:402–423.

Aizenman, J., and J. A. Frenkel. 1986. "Supply Shocks, Wage Indexation and Monetary Accomodation." *Journal of Money, Credit, and Banking* 18:304–322.

Ando, A. K., and F. Modigliani. 1963. "The 'Life-Cycle' Hypothesis of Saving: Aggregate Implications and Tests." *American Economic Review* 53:55–84.

Arnold, L. 1974. *Stochastic Differential Equations: Theory and Applications*. New York: Wiley.

Aschauer, D. A. 1988. "The Equilibrium Approach to Fiscal Policy." *Journal of Money, Credit, and Banking* 20:41–62.

Aschauer, D. A. 1989. "Is Public Expenditure Productive?" *Journal of Monetary Economics* 23:177–200.

Atkinson, A. B., and N. H. Stern. 1974. "Pigou, Taxation, and Public Goods." *Review of Economic Studies* 41:119–128.

Atkinson, A. B., and J. E. Stiglitz. 1980. *Lectures on Public Economics* Maidenhead, U.K.: McGraw-Hill.

Auerbach, A. J. 1979a. "Wealth Maximization and the Cost of Capital." *Quarterly Journal of Economics* 93:433–446.

Auerbach, A. J. 1979b. "Share Valuation and Corporate Equity Policy." *Journal of Public Economics* 11:295–305.

Auerbach, A. J., and L. Kotlikoff. 1987. *Dynamic Fiscal Policy*. Cambridge, U.K.: Cambridge University Press.

Azariadis, C. 1981. "Self-Fulfilling Prophecies." *Journal of Economic Theory* 25:380–396.

Azariadis, C. 1993. *Intertemporal Macroeconomics*. Oxford: Basil Blackwell.

Backus, D., and J. Driffill. 1985a. "Inflation and Reputation." *American Economic Review* 75:530–538.

Backus, D., and J. Driffill. 1985b. "Rational Expectations and Policy Credibility following a Change in Regime." *Review of Economic Studies* 52:211–222.

Backus, D. K., P. J. Kehoe, and F. E. Kydland. 1992. "International Real Business Cycles." *Journal of Political Economy* 100:745–775.

Bailey, M. J. 1956. "The Welfare Cost of Inflationary Finance." *Journal of Political Economy* 64:83–110.

Barnea, A., R. Haugen, and L. Senbet. 1985. *Agency Problems and Financial Contracting*. Edgewood-Cliffs, N.J.: Prentice-Hall.

Barro, R. J. 1974. "Are Government Bonds Net Wealth?" *Journal of Political Economy* 82:1095–1117.

Barro, R. J. 1976. "Rational Expectations and the Role of Monetary Policy." *Journal of Monetary Economics* 2:1–32.

Barro, R. J. 1981. "Output Effects of Government Purchases." *Journal of Political Economy* 89:1086–1121.

Barro, R. J. 1989. "The Neoclassical Approach to Fiscal Policy," in *Modern Business Cycle Theory*, R. J. Barro, ed. Cambridge, MA: Harvard University Press.

Barro, R. J. 1990. "Government Spending in a Simple Model of Endogenous Growth." *Journal of Political Economy* 98:S103–S125.

Barro, R. J. 1991. "Economic Growth in a Cross Section of Countries." *Quarterly Journal of Economics* 106:407–443.

Barro, R. J., and D. B. Gordon. 1983a. "Rules, Discretion and Reputation in a Model of Monetary Policy." *Journal of Monetary Economics* 12:101–121.

Barro, R. J., and D. B. Gordon. 1983b. "A Positive Theory of Monetary Policy in a Natural Rate Model." *Journal of Political Economy* 91:589–610.

Barro, R. J., and X. Sala-i-Martin. 1995. *Economic Growth*, New York: McGraw-Hill Inc.

Barsky, R. B., N. G. Mankiw, and S. P. Zeldes. 1986. "Ricardian Consumers with Keynesian Propensities." *American Economic Review* 76:676–691.

Barth, J. R., and M. D. Bradley. 1987. "The Impact of Government Spending on Economic Activity," working paper, George Washington University.

Baxter, M., and M. J. Crucini. 1991. "Business Cycles and the Asset Structure of Foreign Trade," working paper, University of Rochester.

Baxter, M., and M. J. Crucini. 1993. "Explaining Saving-Investment Correlations." *American Economic Review* 83:416–436.

Baxter, M., and R. G. King. 1993. "Fiscal Policy in General Equilibrium." *American Economic Review* 83:315–334.

Benavie, A. E. Grinols, and S. J. Turnovsky. 1992. "Adjustment Costs and Investment in a Stochastic Equilibrium Macro Model," working paper, University of Washington.

Benhabib, J. 1992. *Cycles and Chaos in Economic Equilibrium.* Princeton, N.J.: Princeton University Press.

Bernheim, B. D. 1981. "A Note on Dynamic Tax Incidence." *Quarterly Journal of Economics* 96:705–723.

Bernheim, B. D. 1987. "Ricardian Equivalence: Theory and Evidence." *NBER Macroeconomics Annual* 2:263–304.

Bhandari, J. S., ed. 1985. *Exchange Rate Management under Uncertainty.* Cambridge, MA: MIT Press.

Bhandari, J. S. N. Haque, and S. J. Turnovsky. 1990. "Growth, External Debt, and Sovereign Risk in a Small Open Economy." *IMF Staff Papers* 37:388–417.

Bianconi, M. 1995. "Fiscal Policy in a Simple Two-Country Dynamic Model." *Journal of Economic Dynamics and Control* 19:395–419.

Bismut, J. M. 1975. "Growth and Intertemporal Allocation of Risks." *Journal of Economic Theory* 10:239–257.

Black, F. 1974. "Uniqueness of the Price Level in Monetary Growth Models with Rational Expectations." *Journal of Economic Theory* 7:53–65.

Black, F., and M. Scholes. 1973. "The Pricing of Options and Corporate Liabilities." *Journal of Political Economy.* 81:637–654.

Blanchard, O. J. 1981. "Output, the Stock Market, and Interest Rates." *American Economic Review* 71:132–143.

Blanchard, O. J. 1985. "Debt, Deficits, and Finite Horizons." *Journal of Political Economy* 93:223–247.

Blanchard, O. J., and S. Fischer. 1989. *Lectures on Macroeconomics.* Cambridge, MA: MIT Press.

Blanchard, O. J., and C. M. Kahn. 1980. "The Solution of Linear Difference Models under Rational Expectations." *Econometrica* 48:1305–1311.

Blinder, A. S., and S. Fischer. 1981. "Inventories, Rational Expectations and the Business Cycle." *Journal of Monetary Economics* 8:277–304.

Blinder, A. S., and R. M. Solow. 1973. "Does Fiscal Policy Matter?" *Journal of Public Economics* 2:319–337.

Boadway, R. 1979. "Long-Run Tax Incidence: A Comparative Dynamic Approach." *Review of Economic Studies* 46:505–511.

Bourguignon, F. 1974. "A Particular Class of Continuous-Time Stochastic Growth Models." *Journal of Economic Theory* 9:141–158.

Branson, W. H., and D. W. Henderson. 1985. "The Specification and Influence of Asset Markets," in *Handbook in International Economics*, R. W. Jones and P. B. Kenen, eds. Amsterdam: North-Holland.

Branson, W. H., and A. Klevorick. 1969. "Money Illusion and the Aggregate Consumption Function." *American Economic Review* 59:832–849.

Bray, M., and N. E. Savin. 1986. "Rational Expectations Equilibria, Learning, and Model Specification." *Econometrica* 54:1129–1160.

Brock, P. L. 1988. "Investment, the Current Account and the Relative Price of Nontraded Goods in a Small Open Economy." *Journal of International Economics* 24:235–253.

Brock, P. L. 1991. "Export Instability and the Economic Performance of Developing Countries." *Journal of Economic Dynamics and Control* 15:129–147.

Brock, P. L. 1993. "International Transfers, the Relative Price of Nontraded Goods and the Current Account," working paper, University of Washington.

Brock, P. L., and S. J. Turnovsky. 1994. "The Dependent Economy Model with Both Traded and Nontraded Capital Goods." *Review of International Economics* 2:306–325.

Brock, W. A. 1974. "Money and Growth: The Case of Long-Run Perfect Foresight." *International Economic Review* 15:750–777.

Brock, W. A. 1975. "A Simple Perfect Foresight Monetary Model." *Journal of Monetary Economics* 1:133–150.

Brock, W. A. 1977. "A Note on Hyperinflationary Equilibria in Long-Run Perfect Foresight Monetary Models: A Correction," manuscript, University of Chicago.

Brock, W. A., and S. J. Turnovsky. 1981. "The Analysis of Macroeconomic Policies in Perfect Foresight Equilibrium." *International Economic Review* 22:179–209.

Buiter, W. H. 1984. "Saddlepoint Problems in Continuous Time Rational Expectations Models: A General Method and Some Macroeconomic Examples." *Econometrica* 52:665–680.

Buiter, W. H. 1987. "Fiscal Policy in Open Interdependent Economies," in *Economic Policy in Theory and in Practice*, A. Razin and E. Sadka, eds. New York: St. Martins Press.

Buiter, W. H., and K. Kletzer. 1991. "The Welfare Economics of Cooperative and Non-cooperative Fiscal Policy." *Journal of Economic Dynamics and Control* 15:215–244.

Burmeister, E., and A. R. Dobell. 1970. *Mathematical Theories of Economic Growth*. New York: Macmillan.

Burmeister, E. R. P. Flood, and S. J. Turnovsky. 1981. "Dynamic Macroeconomic Stability with or without Equilibrium in Money and Labour Markets." *Economica* 28:251–265.

Cagan, P. 1956. "The Monetary Dynamics of Hyperinflation," in *Studies in the Quantity Theory of Money*, M. Friedman, ed. Chicago: University of Chicago Press.

Calvo, G. A. 1977. "The Stability of Models of Money and Perfect Foresight: A Comment." *Econometrica* 45:1737–1739.

Calvo, G. A. 1987. "Real Exchange Rate Dynamics with Nominal Parities: Structural Change and Overshooting." *Journal of International Economics* 22:141–155.

Canzoneri, M. B. 1982. "Exchange Rate Intervention Policy in a Multiple Country World." *Journal of International Economics* 13:267–289.

Canzoneri, M. B., D. W. Henderson, and K. S. Rogoff. 1983. "The Information Content of the Interest Rate and Optimal Monetary Policy." *Quarterly Journal of Economics* 98:545–565.

Chamley, C. 1985. "Efficient Taxation in a Stylized Model of Intertemporal General Equilibrium." *International Economic Review* 26:451–468.

Chamley, C. 1986. "Optimal Taxation of Capital Income in General Equilibrium with Infinite Lives." *Econometrica* 54:607–622.

Chamley, C. 1992. "The Welfare Cost of Taxation and Endogenous Growth," IED discussion paper, Boston University.

Chan, L. K. C. 1983. "Uncertainty and the Neutrality of Government Financing Policy." *Journal of Monetary Economics* 11:435–445.

Chari, V. V. 1988. "Time Consistency and Optimal Policy Design." *Federal Reserve Bank of Minneapolis Quarterly Review* 12:17–31.

Chari, V. V., L. J. Christiano, and P. J. Kehoe. 1991. "Optimal Fiscal and Monetary Policy: Some Recent Results." *Journal of Money, Credit, and Banking* 23:519–539.

Chari, V. V., and P. J. Kehoe. 1979. "Sustainable Plans." *Journal of Political Economy* 98:783–802.

Chow, G. C. 1979. "Optimum Control of Stochastic Differential Equation Systems." *Journal of Economic Dynamics and Control* 1:143–175.

Christ, C. F. 1967. "A Short-Run Aggregate-Demand Model of the Interdependence and Effects of Monetary and Fiscal Policies with Keynesian and Classical Interest Elasticities." *American Economic Review, Proceedings* 57:434–443.

Christ, C. F. 1968. "A Simple Macroeconomic Model with a Government Budget Constraint." *Journal of Political Economy* 76:53–67.

Christensen, T. A., and S. B. Nielsen. 1992. "International Repercussions of Capital Income Taxation in Large Economies: The Source versus Residence Principle." manuscript, Copenhagen Business School.

Christiano, L. J., and M. Eichenbaum. 1992. "Current Real Business-Cycle Theories and Aggregate Labor-Market Fluctuations." *American Economic Review* 82:430–450.

Clark, S. J. 1985. "The Effects of Government Expenditure on the Term Structure of Interest Rates." *Journal of Money, Credit, and Banking* 17:397–400.

Clower, R. W. 1967. "A Reconsideration of the Microeconomic Foundations of Monetary Theory." *Western Economic Journal* 6:1–8.

Corsetti, G. 1991. "Fiscal Policy and Endogenous Growth: A Mean-Variance Approach," working paper, Yale University.

Cox, J. C., J. E. Ingersoll, and S. A. Ross. 1985a. "An Intertemporal General Equilibrium Model of Asset Prices." *Econometrica* 53:363–384.

Cox, J. C., J. E. Ingersoll, and S. A. Ross. 1985b. "A Theory of the Term Structure of Interest Rates." *Econometrica* 53:385–408.

Danthine, J. P., and J. B. Donaldson. 1993. "Methodological and Empirical Issues in Real Business Cycle Theory." *European Economic Review* 37:1–35.

Darby, M. R. 1984. "Some Pleasant Monetarist Arithmetic." *Federal Reserve Bank of Minneapolis Quarterly Review* 8:15–20.

Devereux, M. B., and S. Shi. 1991. "Capital Accumulation and the Current Account in a Two-Country Model." *Journal of International Economics* 30:1–25.

Dixit, A. K., and R. S. Pindyck. 1994. *Investment under Uncertainty*. Princeton, N.J.: Princeton University Press.

Djajic, S. 1987. "Government Spending and the Optimal Rates of Consumption and Capital Accumulation." *Canadian Journal of Economics* 20:544–554.

Domowitz, I., and C. Hakkio. 1985. "Conditional Variance and the Risk Premium in the Foreign Exchange Market." *Journal of International Economics* 19:47–66.

Dornbusch, R. 1976a. "Expectations and Exchange Rate Dynamics." *Journal of Political Economy* 84:1161–1176.

Dornbusch, R. 1976b. "Comments on Brunner and Meltzer," in *Monetarism*, J. Stein, ed. Amsterdam: North-Holland.

Dornbusch, R., and S. Fischer. 1980. "Exchange Rate and the Current Account." *American Economic Review* 170:960–971.

Dornbusch, R., and J. A. Frenkel. 1973. "Inflation and Growth: Alternative Approaches." *Journal of Money, Credit, and Banking* 5:141–156.

Duesenberry, J. S. 1948. *Income, Saving, and the Theory of Consumer Behavior.* Cambridge, MA: Harvard University Press.

Eaton, J. 1981. "Fiscal Policy, Inflation, and the Accumulation of Risky Capital." *Review of Economic Studies* 48:435–445.

Edwards, S. 1987. "Tariffs, Terms of Trade, and the Real Exchange Rate in an Intertemporal Optimizing Model of the Current Account." Working Paper No. 2175, National Bureau of Economic Research.

Eisner, R., and R. H. Strotz. 1963. "Determinants of Business Investment." in *Commission on Money and Credit: Impacts of Monetary Policy.* Englewood Cliffs, N.J.: Prentice-Hall.

Engel, C. 1992. "On the Foreign Exchange Risk Premium in a General Equilibrium Model." *Journal of International Economics* 32:305–319.

Engel, C., and K. Kletzer. 1989. "Saving and Investment in an Open Economy with Non-traded Goods." *International Economic Review* 30:735–752.

Engel, C., and K. Kletzer. 1990. "Tariffs and Saving in a Model with New Generations." *Journal of International Economics* 28:71–91.

Evans, G. W. 1985. "Expectational Stability and the Multiple Equilibria Problem in Linear Rational Expectations Models." *Quarterly Journal of Economics* 100:1217–1233.

Evans, G. W. 1986. "Selection Criteria for Models with Non-Uniqueness." *Journal of Monetary Economics* 18:147–157.

Evans, G. W., and S. Honkapohja. 1986. "A Complete Characterization of ARMA Solutions to Linear Rational Expectations Models." *Review of Economic Studies* 53:227–239.

Evans, G. W., and S. Honkapohja. 1992. "Adaptive Learning and Expectational Stability: An Introduction," manuscript.

Fair, R. 1978. "A Criticism of One Class of Macroeconomic Models with Rational Expectations." *Journal of Money, Credit, and Banking* 10:411–417.

Farmer, R. E. A. 1993. *The Macroeconomics of Self-Fulfilling Prophecies.* Cambridge, MA: MIT Press.

Feenstra, R. 1986. "Functional Equivalence between Liquidity Costs and the Utility of Money." *Journal of Monetary Economics* 17:271–291.

Feldstein, M. S. 1974a. "Tax Incidence in a Growing Economy with Variable Factor Supply." *Quarterly Journal of Economics* 88:551–573.

Feldstein, M. S. 1974b. "Incidence of a Capital Income Tax in a Growing Economy with Variable Savings Rate." *Review of Economic Studies* 41:505–513.

Feldstein, M. S. 1976. "Inflation, Income Taxes, and the Rate of Interest: A Theoretical Analysis." *American Economic Review* 66:809–820.

Feldstein, M. S. 1980. "Inflation, Tax Rules, and the Stock Market." *Journal of Monetary Economics* 6:309–331.

Feldstein, M. S., J. Green, and E. Sheshinski. 1978. "Inflation and Taxes in a Growing Economy with Debt and Equity Finance." *Journal of Political Economy* 86:S53–S70.

Feldstein, M. S., J. Green, and E. Sheshinski. 1979. "Corporate Financial Policy and Taxation in a Growing Economy." *Quarterly Journal of Economics* 93:412–432.

Feldstein, M. S., and C. Horioka. 1980. "Domestic Saving and International Capital Flows." *Economic Journal* 90:314–329.

Fischer, S. 1977a. "Long Term Contracts, Rational Expectations., and the Optimum Money Supply Rule." *Journal of Political Economy* 85:191–205.

Fischer, S. 1977b. "Wage Indexation and Macroeconomic Stability," in *Stabilization of the Domestic and International Economy*, K. Brunner and A. H. Meltzer, eds. Carnegie-Rochester Conference Series on Public Policy. Amsterdam: North-Holland, vol. 5, 107–148.

Fischer, S. 1979a. "Anticipations and the Nonneutrality of Money." *Journal of Political Economy* 87:225–252.

Fischer, S. 1979b. "Capital Accumulation on the Transition Path in a Monetary Optimizing Model." *Econometrica* 47:1433–1439.

Fischer, S. 1980. "Dynamic Inconsistency, Cooperation, and the Benevolent Dissembling Government." *Journal of Economic Dynamics and Control* 2:93–107.

Fisher, I. 1937. "Income in Theory and Income Tax in Practice." *Econometrica* 5:1–55.

Fisher, W. H., and S. J. Turnovsky. 1992. "Fiscal Policy and the Term Structure of Interest Rates: An Intertemporal Optimizing Analysis." *Journal of Money, Credit, and Banking* 24: 1–26.

Flood, R. P., and N. P. Marion. 1982. "The Transmission of Disturbances under Alternative Exchange Rate Regimes with Optimal Indexing." *Quarterly Journal of Economics* 97: 43–66.

Floyd, J. E. 1978. "The Asset Market Theory of the Exchange Rate: A Comment." *Scandinavian Journal of Economics* 80:100–103.

Foley, D. K., and M. Sidrauski. 1971. *Monetary and Fiscal Policy in a Growing Economy*. New York: MacMillan.

Frankel, J. A. 1979. "The Diversifiability of Exchange Risk." *Journal of International Economics* 9:379–393.

Frankel, J. A. 1986. "The Implications of Mean-Variance Optimization for Four Questions in International Macroeconomics." *Journal of International Money and Finance* 5:S53–S75

Frenkel, J. A., and A. Razin. 1987. *Fiscal Policies and the World Economy*. Cambridge, MA: MIT Press.

Frenkel, J. A., A. Razin, and E. Sadka. 1991. *International Taxation in an Integrated World*. Cambridge, MA: MIT Press.

Friedman, B. M. 1979. "Optimal Expectations and the Extreme Information Assumptions of 'Rational Expectations' Models." *Journal of Monetary Economics* 5:23–41.

Friedman, M. 1953. "The Case for Flexible Exchange Rates," in *Essays in Positive Economics*, M. Friedman, ed. Chicago: University of Chicago Press.

Friedman, M. 1957. *A Theory of the Consumption Function*. Princeton, N.J.: Princeton University Press.

Friedman, M. 1968. "The Role of Monetary Policy." *American Economic Review* 58:1–17.

Friedman, M. 1969. "The Optimum Supply of Money," in *The Optimum Supply of Money and Other Essays*, M. Friedman, ed. Chicago: Aldine.

Friedman, M. 1971. "The Revenue from Inflation." *Journal of Political Economy* 79:846–856.

Frydman, R., and E. S. Phelps, eds. 1983. *Individual Forecasting and Aggregate Outcomes*. Cambridge, U.K.: Cambridge University Press.

Gavin, M. 1991. "Tariffs and the Current Account: On the Macroeconomics of Commercial Policy." *Journal of Economic Dynamics and Control,* 15:27–52.

Gertler, M., and E. Grinols. 1982. "Monetary Randomness and Investment." *Journal of Monetary Economics* 10:239–258.

Giavazzi, F., and C. Wyplosz. 1984. "The Real Exchange Rate, the Current Account, and the Speed of Adjustment," in *Exchange Rate Theory and Practice*, J. Bilson and R. Marston, eds. Chicago: University of Chicago Press.

Giovannini, A. 1990. "International Capital Mobility and Capital Income Taxation: Theory and Policy." *European Economic Review* 34:480–488.

Giovannini, A., and P. Jorion. 1987. "Interest Rates and Risk Premia in the Stock Market and in the Foreign Exchange Market." *Journal of International Money and Finance* 6:107–123.

Glick, R., and K. Rogoff. 1995. "Global versus Country-Specific Productivity Shocks and the Current Account," *Journal of Monetary Economics* 35:159–192.

Goodwin, R. M. 1951. "The Nonlinear Accelerator and the Persistence of Business Cycles." *Econometrica* 19:225–239.

Gordon, R. H. 1985. "Taxation of Corporate Capital Income: Tax Revenues Versus Tax Distortions." *Quarterly Journal of Economics* 100:1–27.

Gould, J. P. 1968. "Adjustment Costs in the Theory of Investment of the Firm." *Review of Economic Studies* 35:47–56.

Grandmont, J. M. 1985. "On Endogenous Competitive Business Cycles." *Econonetrica* 53:995–1046.

Gray, J. A. 1976. "Wage Indexation: A Macroeconomic Approach." *Journal of Monetary Economics* 2:221–235.

Gray, M. R., and S. J. Turnovsky. 1979a. "Expectational Consistency, Informational Lags, and the Formulation of Expectations in Continuous Time Models." *Econometrica* 47:1457–1474.

Gray, M. R., and S. J. Turnovsky. 1979b. "The Stability of Exchange Rate Dynamics under Perfect Myopic Foresight." *International Economic Review* 20:643–660.

Grier, K. B., and G. Tullock. 1989. "An Empirical Analysis of Cross-National Economic Growth, 1950–1980. *Journal of Monetary Economics* 24:259–276.

Grierson, R. E. 1975. "The Incidence of Profits Taxes in a Neoclassical Growth Model." *Journal of Public Economics* 4:75–85.

Grinols, E., and S. J. Turnovsky. 1992. "Risk, Optimal Tax, and Monetary Policies in a Growing Economy," working paper, Universities of Illinois and Washington.

Grinols, E., and S. J. Turnovsky. 1993. "Risk, the Financial Market, and Macroeconomic Equilibrium." *Journal of Economic Dynamics and Control* 17:1–36.

Grinols, E. L., and S. J. Turnovsky. 1994. "Exchange Rate Determination and Asset Prices in a Stochastic Small Open Economy." *Journal of International Economics* 36:75–97.

Grossman, G. M., and E. Helpman. 1991. *Innovation and Growth in the Global Economy.* Cambridge, MA: MIT Press.

Hall, R. E. 1978. "Stochastic Implications of the Life-Cycle Permanent Income Hypothesis: Theory and Evidence." *Journal of Political Economy* 86:971–987.

Hall, R. E. 1989. "Consumption," in *Modern Business Cycle Theory*, R. J. Barro, ed. Cambridge, MA: Harvard University Press.

Hansen, G. D. 1985. "Indivisible Labor and the Business Cycle." *Journal of Monetary Economics* 16:309–327.

Harrod, R. F. 1948. *Towards a Dynamic Economics.* London: Macmillan.

Hartman, R. C. 1992. "Optimal Income and Consumption Taxes in a Simple Stochastic Endogenous Growth Model," working paper, University of Washington.

Hayashi, F. 1982. "Tobin's Marginal q, Average q: A Neoclassical Interpretation." *Econometrica* 50:213–224.

Hicks, J. R. 1950. *A Contribution to the Theory of the Trade Cycle.* Oxford: Oxford University Press.

Hodrick, R. J., and S. Srivastava. 1986. "The Covariation of Risk Premiums and Expected Future Spot Exchange Rates." *Journal of International Money and Finance* 5:5–21.

Infante, E. F., and J. L. Stein. 1976. "Does Fiscal Policy Matter?" *Journal of Monetary Economics* 2:473–500.

Jones, L. E., and R. Manuelli. 1990. "A Convex Model of Equilibrium Growth: Theory and Policy Implications." *Journal of Political Economy* 98:1008–1038.

Jones, L. E., R. E. Manuelli, and P. E. Rossi. 1993. "Optimal Taxation in Models of Endogenous Growth." *Journal of Political Economy* 101:485–517.

Jorgenson, D. W. 1963. "Capital Theory and Investment Behavior." *American Economic Review, Proceedings* 53:247–259.

Jorgenson, D. W. 1965. "Anticipations and Investment Behavior," in *The Brookings Quarterly Econometric Model of the United States,* J. S. Duesenberry, G. Fromm, L. R. Klein, and E. Kuh, eds. Chicago: Rand McNally.

Judd, K. L. 1985. "Short-Run Analysis of Fiscal Policy in a Perfect-Foresight Model." *Journal of Political Economy* 93:298–319.

Judd, K. L. 1987a. "The Welfare Cost of Factor Taxation in a Perfect-Foresight Model." *Journal of Political Economy* 95:675–709.

Judd, K. L. 1987b. "Debt and Distortionary Taxation in a Simple Perfect-Foresight Model." *Journal of Political Economy* 20:51–72.

Kaldor, N. 1955. *An Expenditure Tax.* London: Allen and Unwin.

Kalecki, M. 1935. "A Macrodynamic Theory of Business Cycles." *Econometrica* 3:327–344.

Karni, E. 1983. "On Optimal Wage Indexation." *Journal of Political Economy* 91:282–292.

Kehoe, T. J., and D. K. Levine. 1985. "Comparative Statics and Perfect Foresight in Infinite Horizon Models." *Econometrica* 53:433–453.

Kenen, P. B., and C. S. Voidodas. 1972. "Export Instability and Economic Growth." *Kyklos* 25:791–804.

Kimball, M. S., and N. G. Mankiw. 1989. "Precautionary Saving and the Timing of Taxes." *Journal of Political Economy* 97:863–879.

Kimbrough, K. P. 1984. "Aggregate Information and the Role of Monetary Policy in an Open Economy." *Journal of Political Economy* 92:268–285.

Kimbrough, K. P. 1986. "The Optimum Quantity of Money Rule in the Theory of Public Finance." *Journal of Monetary Economics* 18:277–284.

King, M. 1977. *Public Policy and the Corporation.* London: Chapman and Hall.

King, R. G., and S. Rebelo. 1990. "Public Policy and Economic Growth: Developing Neoclassical Implications." *Journal of Political Economy* 98:S126–S150.

Kingston, G. H. 1982. "The Semi-Log Portfolio Balance Schedule Is Tenuous." *Journal of Monetary Economics* 9:389–399.

Kirman, A. P. 1992. "Whom or What Does the Representative Individual Represent?" *Journal of Economic Perspectives* 6:117–136.

Klundert, T. van de, and F. van der Ploeg. 1989. "Wage Rigidity and Capital Mobility in an Optimizing Model of a Small Open Economy." *De Economist* 137:47–75.

Kormendi, R. C., and P. G. Meguire. 1985. "Macroeconomic Determinants of Growth: Cross Country Evidence." *Journal of Monetary Economics* 16:141–163.

Kydland, F. E., and E. C. Prescott. 1977. "Rules Rather than Discretion: The Inconsistency of Optimal Plans." *Journal of Political Economy* 85:473–491.

Kydland, F. E., and E. C. Prescott. 1980. "Dynamic Optimal Taxation, Rational Expectations, and Optimal Control." *Journal of Economic Dynamics and Control* 2:79–91.

Kydland, F., and E. C. Prescott. 1982. "Time to Build and Aggregate Fluctuations." *Econometrica* 50:1345–1370.

Laidler, D. E. W. 1977. "Expectations and the Behaviour of Prices and Output under Flexible Exchange Rates." *Economica* 44:327–336.

Landau, D. L. 1983. "Government Expenditure and Economic Growth: A Cross-Country Study." *Southern Economic Journal* 49:783–792.

Levhari, D., and D. Patinkin. 1968. "The Role of Money in a Simple Growth Model." *American Economic Review* 58:713–754.

Levhari, D., and T. N. Srinivasan. 1969. "Optimal Savings under Uncertainty." *Review of Economic Studies* 36:153–163.

Lewbel, A. 1989. "Exact Aggregation and a Representative Consumer." *Quarterly Journal of Economics* 104:622–633.

Lewis, K. K. 1988. "Inflation Risk and Asset Market Disturbances: The Mean-Variance Model Revisited." *Journal of International Money and Finance* 7:273–288.

Lintner, J. 1956. "Distribution of Incomes of Corporations among Dividends, Retained Earnings, and Taxes." *American Economic Review* 46:97–113.

Lippi, M. 1988. "On the Dynamic Shape of Aggregate Error Correction Models." *Journal of Economic Dynamics and Control* 12:561–585.

Long, J., and C. Plosser. 1983. "Real Business Cycles." *Journal of Political Economy* 91:39–69.

Lucas, R. E. 1967. "Adjustment Costs and the Theory of Supply." *Journal of Political Economy* 75:321–334.

Lucas, R. E. 1972. "Expectations and the Neutrality of Money." *Journal of Economic Theory* 4:103–124.

Lucas, R. E. 1973. "Some International Evidence on Output-Inflation Tradeoffs." *American Economic Review* 68:326–334.

Lucas, R. E. 1975. "An Equilibrium Model of the Business Cycle." *Journal of Political Economy* 83:1113–1144.

Lucas, R. E. 1976. "Econometric Policy Evaluation: A Critique," in *The Phillips Curve and Labor Markets*, K. Brunner and A. H. Meltzer, eds. Carnegie-Rochester Conference Series on Public Policy. Amsterdam: North-Holland. Vol. 1, 19–46.

Lucas, R. E. 1988. "On the Mechanics of Economic Development." *Journal of Monetary Economics* 22:3–42.

Lucas, R. E. 1990. "Supply-Side Economics: An Analytical Review." *Oxford Economic Papers* 42:293–316.

Lucas, R. E., and N. L. Stokey. 1983. "Optimal Fiscal and Monetary Policy in an Economy without Capital." *Journal of Monetary Economics* 12:55–94.

Malliaris, A. G., and W. A. Brock. 1982. *Stochastic Methods in Economics and Finance.* Amsterdam: North-Holland.

Marcet, A., and T. J. Sargent. 1989a. "Convergence of Least Squares Learning in Environments with Hidden State Variables and Private Information." *Journal of Political Economy* 97:1306–1322.

Marcet, A., and T. J. Sargent. 1989b. "Convergence of Least Squares Learning Mechanisms in Self-Referential Linear Stochastic Models." *Journal of Economic Theory* 48:337–368.

Marston, R. C. 1982. "Wages, Relative Prices and the Choice between Fixed and Flexible Exchange Rates." *Canadian Journal of Economics* 15:87–103.

Marston, R. C. 1984. "Real Wages and the Terms of Trade: Alternative Indexation Rules for an Open Economy." *Journal of Money, Credit, and Banking* 16:285–301.

Marston, R. C., and S. J. Turnovsky. 1985. "Imported Materials Prices, Wage Policy and Macroeconomic Stabilization." *Canadian Journal of Economics* 18:273–284.

Matsuyama, K. 1987. "Current Account Dynamics in a Finite Horizon Model." *Journal of International Economics* 23:299–313.

Matsuyama, K. 1988. "Terms of Trade, Factor Intensities, and the Current Account in a Life-Cycle Model." *Review of Economic Studies* 55:247–262.

McCafferty, S. A., and R. Driskill. 1980. "Problems of Existence and Uniqueness in Nonlinear Rational Expectations Models." *Econometrica* 48:1313–1317.

McCallum, B. T. 1980. "Rational Expectations and Macroeconomic Stabilization Policy." *Journal of Money, Credit, and Banking* 12:714–746.

McCallum, B. T. 1981a. "Monetarist Principles and the Money Stock Growth Rule." *American Economic Review, Papers and Proceedings* 71:134–138.

McCallum, B. T. 1981b. "Price Level Determinacy with an Interest Rate Policy Rule and Rational Expectations." *Journal of Monetary Economics* 8:319–329.

McCallum, B. T. 1983. "On Non-Uniqueness in Rational Expectations Models: An Attempt at Perspective." *Journal of Monetary Economics* 11:139–168.

McCallum, B. T. 1984. "Are Bond-Financed Deficits Inflationary? A Ricardian Analysis." *Journal of Political Economy* 92:123–135.

McCallum, B. T., and J. K. Whitaker. 1979. "The Effectiveness of Fiscal Feedback Rules and Automatic Stabilizers under Rational Expectations." *Journal of Monetary Economics* 5:181–186.

McCandless, G. T., and N. Wallace. 1993. *Introduction to Dynamic Macroeconomic Theory.* Cambridge, MA: Harvard University Press.

McKibbin, W. 1991. "A Multi-Sector Growth Model of the World Economy Focussing on the Linkages between OECD and Non-OECD Economies," prepared for International Economic Conditions and Prospects Section, the World Bank.

Mehra, R., and E. C. Prescott. 1985. "The Equity Premium: A Puzzle." *Journal of Monetary Economics* 15:145–161.

Merton, R. C. 1969. "Lifetime Portfolio Selection under Uncertainty: The Continuous-Time Case." *Review of Economics and Statistics* 51:247–257.

Merton, R. C. 1971. "Optimum Consumption Rules in a Continuous-Time Model." *Journal of Economic Theory* 3:373–413.

Merton, R. C. 1973. "An Intertemporal Capital Asset Pricing Model." *Econometrica* 41:867–887.

Merton, R. C. 1975. "An Asymptotic Theory of Growth under Uncertainty." *Review of Economic Studies* 42:375–393.

Merton, R. C. 1990. *Continuous-Time Finance.* Oxford: Blackwell.

Metzler, L. A. 1941. "The Nature and Stability of Inventory Cycles." *Review of Economics and Statistics* 23:113–129.

Miller, M. H. 1977. "Debt and Taxes." *Journal of Finance* 32:261–275.

Miller, M. H., and F. Modigliani. 1961. "Dividend Policy, Growth, and the Valuation of Shares." *Journal of Business* 34:411–432.

Miller, M. H., and M. S. Scholes. "Dividends and Taxes." *Journal of Financial Economics* 6:333–364.

Miller, P., and T. J. Sargent. 1984. "Some Monetarist Arithmetic: A Reply." *Federal Reserve Bank of Minneapolis Quarterly Review* 8:21–26.

Mills, E. S. 1962. *Price, Output, and Inventory Policy.* New York: Wiley.

Modigliani, F., and M. H. Miller. 1958. "The Cost of Capital, Corporation Finance and the Theory of Investment." *American Economic Review* 48:261–297.

Mulligan, C. B., and X. Sala-i-Martin. 1993. "Transitional Dynamics in Two-Sector Models of Endogenous Growth." *Quarterly Journal of Economics* 108:739–773.

Murphy, R. G. 1986. "Productivity Shocks, Nontraded Goods and Optimal Capital Accumulation." *European Economic Review* 30:1081–1095.

Mussa, M. 1976. *A Study in Macroeconomics.* Amsterdam: North-Holland.

Muth, J. F. 1961. "Rational Expectations and the Theory of Price Movements." *Econometrica* 29:315–335.

Nerlove, M. 1958. "Adaptive Expectations and Cobweb Phenomena." *Quarterly Journal of Economics* 73:227–240.

Nguyen, D. T., and S. J. Turnovsky. 1979. "Monetary and Fiscal Policies in an Inflationary Economy: A Simulation Approach." *Journal of Money, Credit, and Banking* 11:259–283.

Nielsen, S. B., and P. B. Sørensen. 1991. "Capital Income Taxation in a Growing Open Economy." *European Economic Review* 34:179–197.

Obstfeld, M. 1981. "Macroeconomic Policy, Exchange Rate Dynamics and Optimal Asset Accumulation." *Journal of Political Economy* 89:1142–1161.

Obstfeld, M. 1989. "Fiscal Deficits and Relative Prices in a Growing World Economy." *Journal of Monetary Economics* 23:461–484.

Obstfeld, M. 1994. "Risk-Taking, Global Diversification, and Growth," *American Economic Review* 84:1310–1329.

Osterberg, W. P. 1989. "Tobin's *q*, Investment, and the Endogenous Adjustment of Financial Structure." *Journal of Public Economics* 40:293–318.

Ott , D. J., and A. Ott. 1965. "Budget Balance and Equilibrium Income." *Journal of Finance* 20:71–77.

Ozler, S., and J. Harrigan. 1988. "Export Instability and Growth." Working Paper No. 486, UCLA.

Parkin, J. M. 1978. "A Comparison of Alternative Techniques of Monetary Control under Rational Expectations." *The Manchester School* 46:252–287.

Patinkin, D. 1965. *Money, Interest, and Prices*, 2nd ed. New York: Harper and Row.

Pecorino, P. 1993. "Tax Structure and Growth in a Model with Human Capital." *Journal of Public Economics* 52:251–271.

Persson, M., Persson, T., and L. E. O. Svensson. 1987. "Time Consistency of Monetary and Fiscal Policy." *Econometrica* 55:1249–1273.

Persson, T., and L. E. O. Svensson. 1985. "Current Account Dynamics and the Terms of Trade: Harberger-Laursen-Metzler Two Generations Later." *Journal of Political Economy.* 93:43–65.

Pesaran, M. H. 1987. *The Limits to Rational Expectations*. Oxford: Blackell.

Phelps, E. S. 1961. "The Golden Rule of Accumulation: A Fable for Growthmen." *American Economic Review* 51:638–643.

Pindyck, R. S. 1982. "Adjustment Costs, Demand Uncertainty, and the Behavior of the Firm." *American Economic Review* 72:415–427.

Poole, W. 1970. "Optimal Choice of Monetary Policy Instruments in a Simple Stochastic Macro Model." *Quarterly Journal of Economics* 84:197–216.

Poterba, J., and L. Summers. 1985. "The Economic Effects of Dividend Taxation," in *Recent Advances in Corporate Finance*, E. I. Altman and M. G. Subrahmanyan, eds. Homewood, IL: Irwin.

Ramsey, F. P. 1927. "A Contribution to the Theory of Taxation." *Economic Journal* 37:47–61.

Ramsey, F. P. 1928. "A Mathematical Theory of Saving." *Economic Journal* 38:543–559.

Razin, A. 1984. "Capital Movements, Intersectoral Resource Shifts and the Trade Balance." *European Economic Review* 26:135–152.

Rebelo, S. 1991. "Long-Run Policy Analysis and Long-Run Growth." *Journal of Political Economy* 99:500–521.

Romer, P. M. 1986."Increasing Returns and Long-Run Growth." *Journal of Political Economy* 94:1002–1037.

Romer, P. M. 1989. "Capital Accumulation in the Theory of Long-Run Growth," in *Modern Business Cycle Theory*, R. J. Barro, ed. Cambridge, MA: Harvard University Press.

Saint-Paul, G. 1992. "Fiscal Policy in an Endogenous Growth Model." *Quarterly Journal of Economics* 107:1243–1259.

Salter, W. 1959. "Internal and External Balance: The Role of Price and Expenditure Effects." *Economic Record* 35:226–238.

Samuelson, P. A. 1939. "Interaction between the Muliplier Analysis and the Principle of Acceleration." *Review of Economics and Statistics* 21:75–78.

Samuelson, P. A. 1947. *The Foundations of Economic Analysis*. Cambridge, MA: Harvard University Press.

Samuelson, P. A. 1958. "An Exact Consumption Loan Model of Interest with or without the Social Contrivance of Money." *Journal of Political Economy* 66:1002–1011.

Sandmo, A. 1970. "The Effect of Uncertainty on Savings Decisions." *Review of Economic Studies* 37:353–360.

Sargent, T. J. 1973. "Rational Expectations, the Real Rate of Interest, and the Natural Rate of Unemployment." *Brookings Papers on Economic Activity* 2:429–472.

Sargent, T. J. 1977. "The Demand for Money during Hyperinflations under Rational Expectations: I." *International Economic Review* 18:59–82.

Sargent, T. J. 1987. *Dynamic Macroeconomic Theory* Cambridge, MA: Harvard University Press.

Sargent, T. J., and N. Wallace. 1973a. "Rational Expectations and the Dynamics of Hyperinflation." *International Economic Review* 14:328–350.

Sargent, T. J., and N. Wallace. 1973b. "The Stability of Models of Money and Growth with Perfect Foresight." *Econometrica* 41:1043–1048.

Sargent, T. J., and N. Wallace. 1975. "Rational Expectations, the Optimal Monetary Instrument, and the Optimal Money Supply." *Journal of Political Economy* 83:241–254.

Sargent, T. J., and N. Wallace. 1976. "Rational Expectations and the Theory of Economic Policy." *Journal of Monetary Economics* 2:169–183.

Sargent, T. J., and N. Wallace. 1981. "Some Unpleasant Monetarist Arithmetic." *Federal Reserve Bank of Minneapolis Quarterly Review* 5:1–17.

Scarth, W. M. 1976. "A Note on the 'Crowding Out' of Private Expenditures by Bond-Financed Increases in Government Spending." *Journal of Public Economics* 5:385–387.

Scarth, W. M. 1980. "Rational Expectations and the Instability of Bond-Financing." *Economics Letters* 6:321–327.

Scarth, W. M. 1985. "A Note on Non-Uniqueness in Rational Expectations Models." *Journal of Monetary Economics* 15:247–254.

Sen, P., and S. J. Turnovsky. 1989a. "Deterioration of the Terms of Trade and Capital Accumulation: A Re-examination of the Laursen-Metzler Effect." *Journal of International Economics* 26:227–250.

Sen, P., and S. J. Turnovsky. 1989b. "Tariffs, Capital Accumulation and the Current Account in a Small Open Economy." *International Economic Review* 30:811–831.

Sen, P., and S. J. Turnovsky. 1990. "Investment Tax Credit in an Open Economy." *Journal of Public Economics* 42:277–309.

Sibert, A. 1989. "The Risk Premium in the Foreign Exchange Market." *Journal of Money, Credit, and Banking* 21:49–65.

Sidrauski, M. 1967a. "Inflation and Economic Growth." *Journal of Political Economy* 75:796–810.

Sidrauski, M. 1967b. "Rational Choice and Patterns of Growth in a Monetary Economy." *American Economic Review* 57:534–544.

Simon, H. A. 1956. "Dynamic Programming under Uncertainty with a Quadratic Criterion Function." *Econometrica* 24:74–81.

Sinn, H. W. 1987. *Capital Income Taxation and Resource Allocation.* Amsterdam: North-Holland.

Sinn, H. W. 1990. "Tax Harmonization and Tax Competition in Europe." *European Economic Review* 34:489–504.

Slemrod, J. 1988. "Effects of Taxation with International Capital Mobility," in *Uneasy Compromise: Problems of a Hybrid Income-Consumption Tax*, H. Aaron, H. Galper, and J. A. Pechman, eds. Washington, D.C.: Brookings Institution.

Smith, C. W., and J. B. Warner. 1979. "On Financial Contracting: An Analysis of Bond Covenants." *Journal of Financial Economics* 7:117–161.

Solow, R. M. 1956. "A Contribution to the Theory of Economic Growth." *Quarterly Journal of Economics* 70:65–94.

Stemp, P. J., and S. J. Turnovsky. 1984. "Equilibrium, Stability, and Deficit Financing in a Simple Nonlinear Monetary Model under Perfect Foresight." *Journal of Macroeconomics* 6:377–397.

Stiglitz, J. E. 1973. "Taxation, Corporate Financial Policy, and the Cost of Capital." *Journal of Public Economics* 2:1–34.

Stiglitz, J. E. 1974. "On the Irrelevance of Corporate Financial Policy." *American Economic Review* 64:851–866.

Stockman, A. C. 1978. "Risk, Information, and Forward Exchange Rates," in *The Economics of Exchange Rates*, J. A. Frenkel and H. G. Johnson, eds. Reading, MA: Addison-Wesley.

Stockman, A. C. 1981. "Anticipated Inflation and the Capital Stock in a Cash-in-Advance Economy." *Journal of Monetary Economics* 8:357–393.

Stockman, A. C., and L. Svensson. 1987. "Capital Flows, Investment, and Exchange Rates." *Journal of Monetary Economics* 19:171–201.

Stokey, N. L. 1991. "Credible Public Policy." *Journal of Economic Dynamics and Control* 15:627–656.

Stulz, R. 1981. "A Model of International Asset Pricing." *Journal of Financial Economics* 9:383–406.

Stulz, R. 1983. "The Demand for Foreign Bonds." *Journal of International Economics* 15:225–238.

Stulz, R. 1984. "Currency Preferences, Purchasing Power Risks, and the Determination of Exchange Rates in an Optimizing Model." *Journal of Money, Credit, and Banking* 16:302–316.

Stulz, R. 1986. "Interest Rates and Monetary Policy Uncertainty." *Journal of Monetary Economics* 17:331–347.

Stulz, R. 1987. "An Equilibrium Model of Exchange Rate Determination and Asset Pricing with Nontraded Goods and Imperfect Information." *Journal of Political Economy* 95:1024–1040.

Summers, L. H. 1981. "Taxation and Corporate Investment: A q-Theory Approach." *Brookings Papers on Economic Activity* 1:67–127.

Summers, L. H. 1991. "The Scientific Illusion in Empirical Macroeconomics." *Scandinavian Journal of Economics* 93:129–148.

Svensson, L. E. O., and A. Razin. 1983. "The Terms of Trade and the Current Account: the Harberger-Laursen-Metzler Effect." *Journal of Political Economy* 91:97–125.

Swan, T. W. 1956. "Economic Growth and Capital Accumulation." *Economic Record* 32:334–361.

Swan, T. W. 1960. "Economic Control in a Dependent Economy." *Economic Record* 36:51–66.

Taylor, J. B. 1977. "Conditions for Unique Solutions in Stochastic Macroeconomic Models with Rational Expectations." *Econometrica* 45:1377–1385.

Taylor, J. B. 1979. "Staggered Wage Setting in a Macroeconomic Model." *American Economic Review, Papers and Proceedings* 69:108–113.

Taylor, J. B. 1980. "Aggregate Dynamics and Staggered Contracts." *Journal of Political Economy* 88:1–23.

Theil, H. 1958. *Economic Forecasts and Policy*. Amsterdam: North-Holland.

Tinbergen, J. 1968. *On the Theory of Economic Policy*. Amsterdam: North-Holland.

Tobin, J. 1968. "Notes on Optimal Monetary Growth." *Journal of Political Economy* 76:833–859.

Tobin, J. 1969. "A General Equilibrium Approach to Monetary Theory." *Journal of Money, Credit, and Banking* 1:15–29.

Tobin, J. 1970. "Money and Income: Post Hoc Ergo Propter Hoc?" *Quarterly Journal of Economics* 84:301–317.

Tobin, J. 1975. "Keynesian Models of Recesssion and Depression." *American Economic Review, Papers and Proceedings* 65:195–202.

Tobin, J., and W. H. Buiter. 1976. "Long-Run Effects of Fiscal and Monetary Policy on Aggregate Demand." in *Monetarism*, J. L. Stein, ed. Amsterdam: North-Holland, 273–309.

Treadway, A. B. 1969. "On Rational Entrepreneurial Behaviour and the Demand for Investment." *Review of Economic Studies* 36:227–239.

Turnovsky, S. J. 1969. "A Bayesian Approach to the Theory of Expectations." *Journal of Economic Theory* 1:220–227.

Turnovsky, S. J. 1977. *Macroeconomic Analysis and Stabilization Policy*. Cambridge, U.K.: Cambridge University Press.

Turnovsky, S. J. 1980. "The Choice of Monetary Instruments under Alternative Forms of Price Expectations." *The Manchester School* 48:39–63.

Turnovsky, S. J. 1982. "The Incidence of Taxes: A Dynamic Macroeconomic Analysis." *Journal of Public Economics* 18:161–194.

Turnovsky, S. J. 1983. "Wage Indexation and Exchange Market Intervention in a Small Open Economy." *Canadian Journal of Economics* 16:574–592.

Turnovsky, S. J. 1985. "Domestic and Foreign Disturbances in an Optimizing Model of Exchange Rate Determination." *Journal of International Money and Finance* 4:151–171.

Turnovsky, S. J. 1987a. "Monetary Growth, Inflation, and Economic Activity in a Dynamic Macro Model." *International Economic Review* 28:707–730.

Turnovsky, S. J. 1987b. "Optimal Monetary Policy and Wage Indexation under Alternative Disturbances and Information Structures." *Journal of Money, Credit, and Banking* 19:157–180.

Turnovsky, S. J. 1990. "The Effects of Taxes and Dividend Policy on Capital Accumulation and Macroeconomic Behavior." *Journal of Economic Dynamics and Control* 14:491–521.

Turnovsky, S. J. 1991. "Tariffs and Sectoral Adjustments in an Open Economy." *Journal of Economic Dynamics and Control* 15:53–89.

Turnovsky, S. J. 1993. "Macroeconomic Policies, Growth, and Welfare in a Stochastic Economy." *International Economic Review* 35:953–981.

Turnovsky, S. J., and M. Bianconi. 1992. "The International Transmission of Tax Policies in a Dynamic World Economy." *Review of International Economics* 1:49–72.

Turnovsky, S. J., and W. A. Brock. 1980. "Time Consistency and Optimal Government Policies in Perfect Foresight Equilibrium." *Journal of Public Economics* 13:183–212.

Turnovsky, S. J., and E. Burmeister. 1977. "Perfect Foresight, Expectational Consistency and Macroeconomic Equilibrium." *Journal of Political Economy* 85:379–393.

Turnovsky, S. J., and W. H. Fisher. 1995. "The Composition of Government Expenditure and its Consequences for Macroeconomic Performance." *Journal of Economic Dynamics and Control* 19:747–786.

Turnovsky, S. J., and M. H. Miller. 1984. "The Effects of Government Expenditure on the Term Structure of Interest Rates." *Journal of Money, Credit, and Banking* 16:16–33.

Turnovsky, S. J., and P. Sen. 1991. "Fiscal Policy, Capital Accumulation, and Debt in an Open Economy." *Oxford Economic Papers* 43:1–24.

Uzawa, H. 1968. "Time Preference, the Consumption Function and Optimum Asset Holdings," in *Value, Capital and Growth: Papers in Honour of Sir John Hicks*, J. N. Wolfe, ed. Chicago: Aldine.

Vasicek, O. 1977. "An Equilibrium Characterization of the Term Structure." *Journal of Financial Economics* 5:177–188.

Voidodas, C. S. 1974. "The Effect of Foreign Exchange Instability on Growth." *Review of Economics and Statistics* 56:410–412.

von Weizsäcker, C. C. 1965. "Existence of Optimal Programs of Accumulation for an Infinite Time Horizon." *Review of Economic Studies* 32:85–104.

Weber, W. E. 1970. "The Effect of Interest Rates on Aggregate Consumption." *American Economic Review* 60:591–600.

Weber, W. E. 1975. "Interest Rate, Inflation, and Consumer Expenditures." *American Economic Review* 65:843–858.

Weil, P. 1989. "Overlapping Families of Infinitely-Lived Agents." *Journal of Public Economics* 38:183–198.

Weiss, L. 1980. "The Role for Active Monetary Policy in a Rational Expectations Model." *Journal of Political Economy* 88:221–233.

Wincoop, E. van 1993. "Structural Adjustment and the Construction Sector." *European Economic Review* 17:177–201.

Woglom, G. 1979. "Rational Expectations and Monetary Policy in a Simple Macroeconomic Model." *Quarterly Journal of Economics* 83:91–105.

Yotopoulos, P. A., and J. B. Nugent. 1976. *Economics of Development: Empirical Investigations.* New York: Harper and Row.

Name Index

Subject Index

Aggregate demand, 30–31
Aggregate supply, 31–33
Arbitrage condition, 238–239, 263, 367, 436
Assets
  asset accumulation, 34–35, 38, 235, 237, 283, 317, 357, 363–365, 399, 451, 478
  asset demand, 25–27
  asset pricing, 452, 459–460, 475
  beta coefficients, 460, 499
  expected growth rate of traded assets, 485
  rate of return on, 285, 291–292, 475, 477, 480, 484
  real growth rate of, 456, 501
  stationarity of the covariance matrix of asset returns, 484

Balance of payments, 360, 367, 483
Barro-Gordon model, 227–229
Blanchard-Kahn model, 130–132, 172, 198
Blanchard model, 273, 363
Blinder-Solow model, 148–159, 198
Bonds
  as component of real wealth, 22
  differential rate of return on, 439
  in dynamic portfolio balance, 21–22
  non-traded, 362, 475
Brownian motion (Wiener process), 432–434
Bubbles
  in Cagan model, 80–81
  in models with learning, 83–85
Business cycles
  and economic growth, 1
  Long-Plosser model, 115
  persistence of shocks, 112–116
  productivity shocks, 210–227, 437
  real business cycle models, 4–5, 467–469
  stylized facts, 467–469

Cagan model
  and bubbles, 80–81
  in discrete time, 76
  dynamics of, 72–76
  and forward-looking behavior, 69–76
  and hyperinflation, 66–69
  monetary expansion in, 73–76
  nonuniqueness of solutions due to policy, 121–123
  with sluggish wages, 141–148
  stability condition, 68
Calibration, 115–116, 467
Capital-consumption ratio, 400–401, 411, 459, 493
Capital-labor ratio, 240, 246, 272, 304–309, 327, 341–342
Certainty equivalence, 448
Chamley model, 342–346
Clower (cash-in-advance) constraint, 265
Constancy of portfolio shares, 430, 437, 484
Consumption
  the consumption function, 19–21, 440

crowding-out effect on, 247, 252, 304, 306
  as a function of current vs. permanent income, 20
  as a function of the interest rate, 21
  rate of return on, 238–239, 291–292, 308, 318
Consumption-output ratio, 493
Consumption-wealth ratio, 451–452, 454–456, 461–462, 479–480, 489, 493
Continuous-time versus discrete-time modeling, 61, 429
Corporate finance
  additions to the stock of capital, 286
  cost of capital, 287, 294–299, 311–312
  debt-to-equity ratio, 293, 297, 307, 310–312
  dividend policy, 287, 295–297, 320–324
  double taxation of dividends, 289, 296
  equity vs. bond financing, 287, 296–297, 303–307, 309
  interests of bondholders vs. interests of stockholders, 287
  market value of firm's securities, 286
  value of firm, 293–294, 297–298, 320
Covered interest parity, 497
Current account, 360, 371, 380–381, 387

Debt, upward-sloping supply curve of, 385–386
Debt policy, 288, 397, 399, 407–408, 411–413, 481, 492
Decentralized economy, 283–289, 403–408
Differential generator, 434–435
Dornbusch overshooting model, 159–164
Dynamics of second-order system of differential equations, 164–170
Dynamic programming, 4, 350, 352
Dynamic systems
  backward-looking dynamics, 1–3, 16, 67–68, 172
  the correspondence principle, 128
  disequilibrium dynamics, 65
  forward-looking dynamics, 2, 69–71
  intrinsic dynamics, 1
  "jump" variables, 2, 69, 130
  "sluggish" variables, 2, 69, 130
  transitional dynamics, 239–243, 299–301, 331–332, 370, 376, 378
  transversality condition, 70, 123, 188–189

Economic growth
  and business cycles, 1
  endogenous growth models, 391–393
  and export instability, 505
  and fiscal policy, 408–411
  neoclassical growth theory, 3, 391–392
  and risk, 501–506
  stochastic endogenous growth, 458–459
  warranted growth rate, 392
Efficient markets, 59, 148, 497